8th March 1990

To Dear Miriam
With best wishes and
Love
From Lazar + Fay.

An Illustrated History of
South Africa

The publishers acknowledge gratefully the generous contribution by the Gencor Group which facilitated the publication of this book in its present form

An Illustrated History of South Africa

General Editor: Trewhella Cameron
Advisory Editor: S B Spies

Southern Book Publishers
Johannesburg

Human & Rousseau
Cape Town and Pretoria

Many persons and organizations have been extremely helpful in the preparation of this book. Although it is not possible to mention each by name, particular thanks are extended to the following:

Hans Fransen of the University of Natal, Pietermaritzburg, for information on art and architecture. Henry Bredekamp of the University of the Western Cape for providing details of certain maps. T I Steenkamp and C van Zyl for their interest and co-operation.

A special debt of gratitude is owed to the staff of the Africana Museum, the Transvaal and Central Archives Depots, the Cape Archives Depot, the Natal Archives Depot, the Director of the William Fehr Collection, the South African Library, the Library of Parliament, the National Cultural History and Open-air Museum, the Institute for the Study of Contemporary History, the South African Museum of Military History, the Local History Museum, Durban, the Cory Library, Grahamstown, the 1820 Settlers Museum, and the following newspapers: *The Star*, *Rand Daily Mail*, *Die Burger*, *Cape Times* and *The Argus*.

   Private individuals who supplied information so willingly are thanked, as are the Human Sciences Research Council and the editorial and production staff of Jonathan Ball and Human & Rousseau.

   Every effort has been made to trace the owners of copyright for the quotations and illustrations used in this book. We apologise for any inadvertent oversight.

Chapters 3 (pp. 29-30), 8 (pp. 101-105), 10, 11, 13, 18 and 19 translated from Afrikaans by Alan Hendry

ISBN 1 86812 190 9

Copyright © 1986 by the respective contributors
1st impression 1986
2nd impression 1987
3rd impression 1988

Published jointly by Southern Book Publishers (Pty) Ltd,
P O Box 548, Bergvlei, Johannesburg
and Human & Rousseau (Pty) Ltd,
State House, 3-9 Rose Street, Cape Town
Atrium Building, 60 Glenwood Road, Pretoria
Illustration research and captions by Trewhella Cameron
Maps by the Institute for Cartographical Analysis, University of Stellenbosch
Typography and cover design by Etienne van Duyker
Typeset in 9½ on 11 pt Plantin by McManus Bros, Cape Town
Lithographic reproduction by McManus Bros, Cape Town
Printed and bound by National Book Printers, Goodwood

Contents

LIST OF MAPS

Foreword

This general illustrated history, which spans a period of millions of years, tells the story of man in South Africa, and aims at giving the reader a clear understanding of historical processes and structures.

It is the first authoritative, yet popular, illustrated history to be published simultaneously in English and Afrikaans, and is written by a panel of professional historians. The contributors are all leading academics or specialists in their own fields, and they have endeavoured to produce a book which is not heavy or academic in tone. The text includes many lively descriptions, enlightening biographical sketches, and dramatic or humorous accounts, and is aimed at the interested, intelligent, general reader.

The illustrations have been chosen to provide visual extensions of the narrative, and the captions are intended to place them in perspective. Some prominence has been given to cartoons, which feature as reflections of public opinion or of a particular point of view regarding a contemporary issue.

Suggested reading lists at the end of each chapter indicate further sources of information on relevant themes. Selected general books, as well as some important biographical and autobiographical works, are brought to the reader's attention at the back of the book.

No uniform approach or theoretical framework has been imposed on contributors. They are aware of changing philosophies and new attitudes in South African historiography, and have tried to include as many different authoritative points of view, and to depict as many aspects of South African society as possible. Political and constitutional developments, economic, social, cultural and intellectual issues all receive attention, while special emphasis is placed on the influence of society on the environment and *vice versa*.

The book follows a loose chronological design, but since such a long period is covered, it is clearly impossible to allocate equal numbers of words to equal units of time. 'Era' and 'in depth' approaches have been followed, in that aspects of South African history are dealt with broadly and an overview is provided, while detailed examinations of particular incidents, groups, individuals and problems are also presented. The book invites readers to examine the inner mechanics of South African society through the eyes of prominent historians, who reach certain conclusions about our past (and present).

It has been difficult to avoid traditional chronological divisions, particularly in the modern period, but a conscious attempt has been made to present and analyse, wherever possible, the motives, actions and reactions of all members of South African society. A number of myths of South African history are exposed, giving different insights into a most complex society.

This is 'An Illustrated History of South Africa'. Other histories emphasize other facets and highlight other scenes. Interpretations of the past do not remain static, and perspectives change. This book represents the views on South Africa's past of a number of honestly-motivated historians in the mid-1980s.

THE EDITORS

Skull of the Taung child, the first of
Africa's 'missing links' to be discovered.
Its human-like features were revealed to
the world by Professor Raymond A Dart
in 1925. In the background is the
Catalogue of the Department of Anatomy
of the University of the Witwatersrand
showing the entry for the Taung skull.
(Photo: Margo Crabtree, by courtesy of
the American Association for the
Advancement of Science)

Part I

The Prehistory and Early History of Man in Southern Africa

When did the history of South Africa begin? Was it in 1652, when Jan van Riebeeck landed at the Cape? Or in 1488, when Bartolomeu Dias rounded the southern tip of Africa? Possibly between AD 200 and 300, when Bantu-speaking peoples established the first Iron Age communities in the Transvaal and Natal? Should the historian go even further back to approximately 1000 BC, when hunter-gatherer communities inhabited southern Africa?

In Part I of this history a case is made for starting the history of South Africa three million years ago. In a multi-disciplinary approach, embracing geological, palaeo-anthropological, archaeological and historical findings, the development of man in Africa is traced from the advent of the *Hominidae* (or family of man) in Africa over five million years ago, to the birth of the lineage of the genus *Homo*, which emerged about 2,3 million years ago when the hominid lineage split, and which transcended the divide between 'animal hominids' and 'human hominids'. This remarkable line of hominids is traced from *Homo habilis*, through *Homo erectus*, to the emergence of early and late representatives of *Homo sapiens*, the living hominid species.

Thereafter, the San, Khoikhoi and black communities of the Stone and Iron Ages are examined. The closeness of the relationship between the various indigenous groups is explained, and their way of life and interaction with one another are depicted as they were prior to the period of European colonization.

The excavations at Sterkfontein, with Swartkrans hill in the background. Michaka Makgothokgo (left), Simon Sekowe (middle) and Alun R Hughes (right) stand on the heavily consolidated cave earth or breccia which contains the fossilized remains of ape-men, baboons, antelopes and many other vertebrates.

Chapter 1

The Dawn of the Human Family in Africa

P V Tobias

Scholars of human origins are virtually unanimous today that the family of man arose in Africa. The revelation of this concept and the harvesting of corroborative evidence have been seminal contributions of twentieth century science. Indeed the discovery in 1924 of the first crucial fossil evidence – the Taung skull from South Africa – has been included some sixty years later by a prominent American journal as one of twenty scientific discoveries of the twentieth century which changed our lives.

Why Africa?

The question is often asked: Why was Africa the probable cradle of mankind? The very nature of this query implies a belief that, because this occurred in Africa, it *had* to happen in Africa. This view cannot be substantiated and all we can hope to understand, therefore, is *how* this came about. What set of circumstances prevailed on the African continent at the relevant time so as to favour the emergence and subsequent evolution of the family of man or hominids?

The first set of factors is geographical. Africa comprises almost a quarter of the earth's habitable land surface, and close to three quarters of the continent's 30 million square kilometres lie between the Tropics of Cancer and Capricorn. This immense warm area was the crucible within which there developed one of the world's great regional faunas, the Ethiopian Faunal Region, as part of which, according to palaeontologists, the hominids arose. Molecular and fossil evidence strongly suggests that this happened late in the Miocene or at the beginning of the Pliocene epoch, somewhere between five and seven million years (Myr) ago. Man's family was therefore a product of the tropics and sub-

tropics and to this day his bodily functions bespeak a heat-adapted organism.

Africa's links with Eurasia are of particular importance since, from time to time, great faunal interchanges between Africa and Asia took place. About 5-6 Myr ago the Mediterranean basin largely dried up, an event geologists call the Messinian 'crisis'. During this period many ancient Asiatic animals seem to have entered Africa for the first time, including the elephant family, numbers of antelope families, hyaenas and sabre-toothed cats.

Against this faunistic background it seems that the Hominidae appeared in Africa although there is no evidence that they were one of the groups that walked dry-footed from Asia to Africa. On the contrary, all available evidence suggests that the hominids arose *in* Africa by genetic changes from pre-existing higher primates. Appropriate predecessor groups must have lived on the African continent before that time; relevant gene mutations must have occurred in some populations; the environment – both physical and biotic (plants and other animals) – must have been just right for the survival and prospering of the newly risen hominids. The role of the old Asiatic animals entering Africa and the extent of the challenge posed by an increasingly arid African continent remain to be elucidated, but clearly these factors were part of the backdrop, the threat and the stimulus to the strange new two-legged beasts which, within several millions of years, were to conquer the earth.

The Taung child

In February 1925 the world was surprised at an announcement made by Professor Raymond A Dart, then newly appointed Professor of Anat-

Phillip V Tobias has been Professor of Anatomy at the University of the Witwatersrand since 1959. His researches have been in human biology (of the living peoples of Africa), genetics, human development and palaeo-anthropology. He has worked on fossil hominids from South, East and North Africa, Asia and Europe, has run an excavation at Sterkfontein since 1966 and has published more than a dozen books and over 600 articles. He is a leading authority on hominid evolution. (Photo: Peter M Faugust)

Mr Alun R Hughes stands in the sinkhole in the Sterkfontein formation where he discovered, in August 1976, the first example of a skull of *Homo habilis* to be found in South Africa. The plaque above his head marks the discovery site and in his hands he holds the specimen in question, as reconstructed by R J Clarke.

Africa's great apes

The fauna of Africa includes many different orders of mammals, of which the primate order is one. This order comprises two subdivisions, the *Prosimians,* ie the lemurs, lorises and tarsiers, and the *Anthropoids,* ie the marmosets, monkeys and baboons, gibbons, great apes and humans. Of all the non-human primates to be found today in Africa, the most highly developed are the various forms of chimpanzees and gorillas. These, along with the orang-utan of Asia, are known as the great apes.

Biologically, the great apes are more closely related to the human species than is any other living group. This is true of their bodily structure, biochemical composition, chromosomes and some aspects of their behaviour. The African great ape resembles man more closely than does the Asian one, *Pongo,* or the orang-utan. Thus the chimpanzee and gorilla are man's closest living relatives.

omy at the infant medical school of the University of the Witwatersrand in Johannesburg. He reported that, in November 1924, the skull of a fossil child had been found at the Buxton Limeworks close to the Tswana village of Taung ('the place of Tau, the Lion'), about 80 kilometres north of Kimberley, and today part of Bophuthatswana.

In his account of the skull, Dart drew attention to the small canine teeth, which were like those of hominids and quite unlike those of apes. The base of the cranium showed that the head must have been fairly well balanced on what must have been a virtually upright spine, in contrast with the position in apes, where the head hangs forward from an obliquely postured spine. Hence Dart detected signs of two important hallmarks of hominids, namely canine reduction and upright posture. However, it was the features of the brain that Dart found most arresting.

The Taung skull was accompanied by a beautifully preserved endocranial cast. This results when the brain-case or calvaria becomes filled with sand after death. If this sand is consolidated, for instance by lime, the resulting endo-

cranial cast faithfully reflects the size and form of the interior of the calvaria, as well as the features of the brain surface which have become imprinted on the inside of the brain-case during life. The surface of the Taung endocranial cast reflected a wealth of convolutional and vascular detail. The first eye-opening feature was that in overall size the cast was scarcely bigger than that of a chimpanzee and of about the size of the brain of a gorilla. Its volumetric capacity was no greater than one-third of the capacity of the modern human brain. On the other hand Dart detected markings on the endocast which he interpreted as indicating hominid rather than ape affinities.

It seemed to him that he had in his hands a heavily fossilized skull whose small brain size was ape-like, but whose other anatomical features were close to those of the family of man. Such a combination of traits was unprecedented. Dart was convinced that the Taung skull did not belong to the family of apes (the Pongidae) and so he assigned the specimen to a new genus and species which he named *Australopithecus africanus* (southern ape of Africa). Initially he did not place this species among the

Dr Robert Broom, FRS (1866-1951) was one of Dart's first supporters. Twelve years after the Taung skull came to light, he discovered the first adult skull of an *Australopithecus* at Sterkfontein. He is shown here immediately after the discovery of the beautifully preserved cranium of 'Mrs Ples', or Sterkfontein hominid 5. (Photo: Transvaal Museum)

Professor Raymond A Dart holding the Taung skull. The photograph was taken only a few days after the 32-year-old professor announced the discovery of this specimen of what he called *Australopithecus* on 3 February 1925. He claimed that it represented a species of ape with so many human-like features that it should be regarded as an intermediate form of primate between the apes and humanity. (Photo: Barlow Rand)

hominids as he believed that it represented a new family, intermediate between the two well-known higher primate families, the Pongidae and the Hominidae. Much later, after careful studies had been made on other specimens of similar aspect from the Transvaal, it came to be accepted that *Australopithecus* belonged to the hominids, and that Dart had in fact found a very early member of the family of man.

The location of the find in southern Africa was unexpected, for the world had focused its search for man's origin on Asia. Now Dart reminded his fellow scientists of the long-forgotten prophecy made by Darwin – 'It is somewhat more probable that our early progenitors lived on the African continent than elsewhere'. Indeed Dart went so far as to claim that *Australopithecus* had confirmed Darwin's prediction.

If the geographical location of the skull was disturbing, its morphology was positively startling, since it was the first of the small-brained hominids to be discovered. Man's disproportionately large brain has long been accepted as one of his most striking hallmarks. In weight and volume the brain of modern man is about three times the size of the brain of the gorilla, yet his body weight is much less than that of the gorilla. Anatomists and anthropologists had grown accustomed to the idea that man is a higher primate with an exceptionally enlarged brain. It was therefore a shock to find that, despite the presence of many hominid features, the skull's estimated cranial capacity testified to a brain

size no bigger than that of the apes. The presence of milk teeth and erupting first permanent molars indicated that when it died the Taung child was between three and five years of age (judging by modern ape and human standards), so it was reasonable to expect that its brain and brain-case would have grown further had it lived to adulthood. However, even when the Taung brain size was brought up to its estimated adult value, it remained no bigger than those of the modern apes.

Reaction to Dart's discovery

Dart's claim that the Taung creature was not simply an aberrant chimpanzee, as some of his detractors asserted, led to intense argument among scientists, argument which raged for over twenty-five years. The controversy revolved around two points: should the small brain be considered so important as to deny hominid status to *Australopithecus*, despite its other hominid-like features, or should its status be based on most of its anatomical characters – which were hominid – even though the hominid trend toward disproportionate brain enlargement was not evident?

The issue was not resolved until many new southern African fossils had been found and until detailed studies had been made of them and of numbers of skeletons and brains of modern apes and men. Eventually it was recognized

---

Charles Darwin's 1871 prediction

Charles Darwin

In one of Charles Darwin's major works, *The Descent of Man*, published in 1871, he pointed out that 'In every great region of the world, the living mammals are closely related to the evolved species of the same region'. He went on to make a remarkable prediction:

'It is therefore probable that Africa was formerly inhabited by extinct apes closely allied to the gorilla and chimpanzee. . . [the fossil remains of such extinct apes had not been found by then, although they have come to light in the twentieth century] . . . and, as these two species are now man's nearest allies, it is somewhat more probable that our early progenitors lived on the African continent than elsewhere.'

Since no fossil evidence for the presence in Africa of man's early progenitors was known at the time, Darwin added, 'But it is useless to speculate on the subject.'

Over half a century later, in 1924, the rocks of southern Africa were to yield the first evidence that confirmed Darwin's prophecy. In the intervening years, spectacular finds of fossil hominids were made in Java (now part of Indonesia) and China, and it was thought that man had originated in Asia. For a long time Darwin's old prediction was forgotten.

that, as Dart had believed, the Taung child differed from the apes in far too many respects to be classified as just another ape, and that he resembled later forms of man, of the genus *Homo*, in so many traits that his claim to be a member of the hominids was irresistible.

Dart forced palaeo-anthropologists to realize that there *had* once been small-brained members of the family of man, represented in the known fossil annals by the remains of *Australopithecus*. The discovery of the Taung skull and Dart's recognition of its evolutionary status thus constituted one of the most significant and revolutionary advances in man's quest to seek and understand his origins.

The discoveries at Sterkfontein

One of the factors that delayed acceptance of Dart's claims was that the Taung skull belonged to a child, whose characteristics would have developed only during and after adolescence. From a mere child one could not be quite sure of the features of the adult, nor of the population. It was another twelve years before the first adult specimen came to light, and this was obtained by Dr Robert Broom at Sterkfontein near Krugersdorp in the southern Transvaal in 1936.

'Mrs Ples', or Sterkfontein hominid 5, one of the most perfectly preserved crania of *Australopithecus africanus*, found by R Broom and J T Robinson in April 1947. The cranium is quite undistorted; only the teeth are missing.

Broom was a Scottish medical man and palaeontologist who had worked in Australia before coming to South Africa. He discovered numerous fossils of mammal-like reptiles in the Karoo, and threw much light on the origins of mammals from reptilian ancestors. He was one of Dart's few well-informed supporters, and he was determined to substantiate Dart's 1925 claim by finding an adult australopithecine. He was one of the first to assign the species represented by the Taung child to the Hominidae, and in 1933 he also published a prescient restoration of what he expected the adult *Australopithecus* had looked like. Within eight days of his arriving at Sterkfontein on 9 August 1936, there fell into his hands the first adult *Australopithecus*, which bore a strong resemblance to his restoration.

The 1936 finds of Sterkfontein ape-men confirmed for the adult the morphological trends Dart had detected in the child. The particular stratum (layer) of the Sterkfontein cave deposit proved rich in fossils and by the outbreak of World War II in 1939 Broom had recovered some nineteen specimens of *Australopithecus*, including crania, jaw-bones, teeth and post-cranial bones. T C Partridge later designated this stratum Member 4 of the Sterkfontein Formation.

His study of these fossils convinced Broom that the Sterkfontein ape-man was different in some respects from that of Taung, and he assigned the Sterkfontein hominid to a separate genus and species which he called *Plesianthropus transvaalensis*. Later, most scholars came to accept that the Sterkfontein hominid was in fact of the same species as that of the Taung child, but belonged to a different subspecies, which was called *Australopithecus africanus transvaalensis*.

After World War II Broom resumed work at Sterkfontein at the instance of General J C Smuts, then Prime Minister. In this second phase, between 1947 and 1949, Broom, assisted by J T Robinson, found many new specimens, including the splendid cranium of 'Mrs Ples' (Sterkfontein hominid 5) in 1947. They then transferred activities to the Swartkrans cave close by. A third phase of excavation occurred from 1956 to 1958, under J T Robinson and C K Brain.

The fourth and longest phase in the excavation of Sterkfontein began in 1966 when P V Tobias and A R Hughes, of the University of the Witwatersrand, embarked on a large-scale excavation of the site, seeking evidence for dating, stratigraphy, hominid remains and their ecology. This long-term project had produced about 350 new hominid specimens by the mid-1980s. Most of them were of *Australopithecus africanus* from Member 4, but some belonged to an early species of *Homo* (*Homo habilis*) and were associated with stone implements in Member 5. (The deposit in the cave was divided by Partridge into six members.)

One of the robust, crested ape-man crania from Swartkrans. This specimen represents a species called *Australopithecus robustus,* which appears to have become specialized on to a side branch, away from the main line of human evolution. (Photo: D C Panagos)

The animal bones in Member 4 most closely resembled those from East Africa which were dated to about 2,5-2,75 million years before the present. This seemed the most probable date for the Sterkfontein *Australopithecus,* though there was still much argument about the date of the apparently younger deposits at Taung.

Kromdraai and Swartkrans

In June 1938 a schoolboy named Gert Terblanche found the first specimen of a bigger-toothed kind of ape-man at Kromdraai, some 9,6 km north of Krugersdorp. The Kromdraai caves are situated about 1,6 km east-north-east of Sterkfontein. The hominid remains found there were recognized by Broom as belonging to a patently different kind of ape-man from the one found at Sterkfontein. It had a small brain-case, but was more heavily boned and muscled, and its cheek teeth (premolars and molars) were larger. Broom called the new ape-man *Paranthropus robustus,* though it is generally known today as *Australopithecus robustus.* The evidence of the associated animal bones from Kromdraai showed that it was of younger (ie more recent) geological age than Sterkfontein. Additional specimens of *A. robustus* found at Kromdraai between 1941 and 1980 supported the view that *A. robustus* showed specialized features, which disqualified it from the direct line of human ancestry.

In 1948 Broom and Robinson found abundant remains of an even bigger-toothed austra-

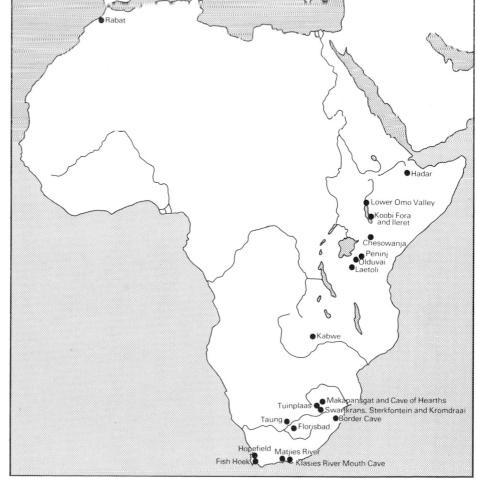

African sites of early hominid discoveries

15

Basal layers of sandy travertine, or banded limestone, very low in the Makapansgat sequence of strata. (Photo: J T Robinson)

of the derivative branches, though still legitimately hominid, had not been ancestral to later men of the genus *Homo*. Thus, at the hands of Broom, Africa had yielded another revolutionary yet contentious concept to palaeo-anthropologists. For many years afterwards some scholars would try to place all archaic African hominids on a single lineage leading to modern man. For most investigators, however, the fossils of Kromdraai and Swartkrans (later reinforced by East African fossils known as *A. boisei*) provided unequivocal evidence that the earlier hominids had split, during their development, into at least two distinct lineages.

Makapansgat

A fifth South African site bearing australopithecine remains is Makapansgat, some 320 km north of Johannesburg and 23 km from Potgietersrus. In September 1947 the first of a series of australopithecine specimens was discovered there by James Kitching of the Bernard Price Institute for Palaeontological Research, his brothers Ben and Schepers, and A R Hughes. The Makapansgat hominids were similar to those of Sterkfontein, though some anatomical differences suggested that the Makapansgat population was slightly more primitive in form. Dart originally allocated them to a different species of *Australopithecus*, *A. prometheus*, but J T Robinson subsequently 'lumped' them into the species *A. africanus*, along with those of Taung and Sterkfontein, and proposed to sort them into two subspecies, *A. africanus africanus* – Taung, and *A. africanus transvaalensis* – Sterkfontein and Makapansgat.

T C Partridge identified five members in the stratigraphy of the Makapansgat Formation. All of the hominid specimens except one come from Member 3, the faunal content of which is more ancient than that of Sterkfontein. Both faunal evidence and palaeomagnetic results indicate an age of 3 million years for Makapansgat Member 3. Thus far these are the oldest hominids found in South Africa.

Summation on South African contributions

By the middle of the twentieth century South Africa had yielded five sites, from each of which had come fossils attributed to a new early genus, *Australopithecus*, and it was becoming accepted that this genus, though it represented creatures with brains no bigger in absolute size than those of modern anthropoid apes, should be classified within the Hominidae. Until mid-century, the australopithecine phase of evolving humanity appeared to be an essentially South African phenomenon. There were a few claims that some fossil hominids of China and Java were related to *Australopithecus*, but there was no convincing

lopithecine at Swartkrans, about 1,6 km northwest of Sterkfontein. From that one cave deposit at Swartkrans more early hominid specimens have been extracted than have come from any other single site in the world, save Sterkfontein. Most Swartkrans hominids possessed even bigger cheek teeth than those of Kromdraai, combined with small front teeth. They also had small brains and skeletal adjustments to the upright stance and bipedal gait, sharing these two sets of characteristics with all other members of the genus *Australopithecus*.

While it was not difficult to see *A. africanus* of Sterkfontein as a possible ancestor of *Homo*, *A. robustus* of Kromdraai and Swartkrans showed too many of what palaeontologists call specialized or derived (or apomorphic) characters to have been on the lineage of *Homo*. These specialized traits pointed away from the main pathway of hominization. Moreover, the faunal evidence indicated that the two Transvaal caves bearing robust ape-men were of more recent geological age than Sterkfontein and Makapansgat, bearing the more slenderly built *A. africanus*. Yet, on anatomical criteria, *A. robustus* was justifiably regarded as a hominid species, no less than was *A. africanus:* both species comprised small-brained bipeds with modest to small canine teeth.

Thus the Kromdraai discovery of 1938 yielded the earliest evidence that not all ancient African hominids should be seen as ancestral to the later hominids leading to *Homo sapiens*. It appeared that along the line of hominid development there had been a major branching of the lineage and that the ancient hominids had diversified into more than one kind. This concept was common in the palaeontology of other animals, yet in anthropological studies it had until that time seldom been recognized that this had happened to the hominids as well, nor that some

evidence that any Asian fossils actually belonged to that genus. Then, in the third quarter of the century, East African discoveries revealed the presence there of a variety of ancient hominids, some earlier than any found in South Africa.

The East African contribution

Since 1955 numerous early hominids have emerged from East African sites extending along the Great Rift Valley from Tanzania in the south to Ethiopia in the north. In contrast with the South African sites, which are sealed deposits in dolomitic limestone caves or fissures, the East African sites are for the most part on and in lacustrine and riverine sediments, often of considerable surface area.

Early gracile australopithecine fossils from East Africa

While the Transvaal robust species was shown to have a counterpart in East Africa, signs of the gracile form, *A. africanus*, were not discovered there until the late 1960s. Certain isolated teeth recovered from the earlier members of the Omo

P V Tobias and American students excavating in the baboon-rich layer called Member 4 of the Makapansgat Formation, in 1973. (Photo: Educational Expeditions International)

Dr Mary Leakey standing at the edge of the great Olduvai Gorge in northern Tanzania. In this gorge, she and the late Dr L S B Leakey, their sons and other colleagues discovered thousands of Pleistocene fossils, including four species of hominids, along with great quantities of stone tools, often still lying where dropped on prehistoric living floors. (Photo: P V Tobias)

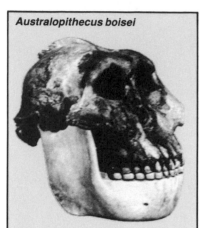
Dr Robert Broom had shown that there had been a robust kind of *Australopithecus* in South Africa, and it was not unreasonable to expect that similar ape-men might be found in East Africa. Nothing, however, could have prepared anthropologists for the extravagantly large-toothed and powerfully muscled specimen which Mary Leakey found in the Olduvai Gorge, northern Tanzania, in July 1959. It was a still more robust cranium than that of Swartkrans. Louis Leakey recognized the Olduvai specimen as representing another kind of australopithecine which at first he called *Zinjanthropus boisei* (*Zinj* being the old name for East Africa and Charles Boise having financed the Leakeys' reseaches). Later a detailed study of the cranium by P V Tobias led him to place the East African form in the genus *Australopithecus*, as a separate species, *A. boisei*, whose closest resemblance lay with *A. robustus* of the Transvaal.

Lower jaws of *A. boisei* were found at Peninj, close to Lake Natron in northern Tanzania, and at Omo at the northern end of Lake Turkana (formerly Lake Rudolf). Further crania of the same kind were discovered at Ileret and Koobi Fora, east of Lake Turkana, by Richard Leakey from 1968 onwards, and at Chesowanja near Lake Baringo in Kenya in 1970. This East African fossil 'population' showed that the diversity of the small-brained, bipedal hominids had been more striking even than the Transvaal fossil finds had demonstrated. Moreover, both *A. robustus* and *A. boisei* were relatively late, most examples being dated between 2 and 1 million years before the present.

Dr Ronald J Clarke holds his reconstruction of *Homo habilis* of Sterkfontein. The specimen provided the first evidence that this species had been present also in South Africa. (Photo: A R Hughes)

formation in southern Ethiopia suggested that a gracile form had been present in East Africa too.

Then, from 1973 onwards, came a series of spectacular discoveries from Hadar in the Afar Depression of north-eastern Ethiopia. These finds, by D C Johanson and his collaborators, included skulls, jaw-bones and teeth, limb-bones and a large proportion of a single individual's skeleton (nicknamed 'Lucy'). Bones of yet older gracile hominids were discovered in Laetoli in Tanzania by Mary Leakey. The Hadar finds represented a population very similar to *A. africanus transvaalensis*. They were regarded by some as members, along with the Laetoli specimens, of a new species for which the name *A. afarensis* (after the Afar of Ethiopia) was proposed, while others considered that the fossils belonged to the species *A. africanus*, though possibly to an earlier, different geographical variant or subspecies. The Laetoli hominids were dated to about 3,7 million years, and those of Hadar to 3,2-2,9 million years. Thus the Hadar fossils overlap the dating of Makapansgat Member 3, namely 3,0 million years.

Summation on *Australopithecus*

Between 1924 and 1984 tropical and sub-tropical Africa yielded hundreds of fossils of upright-walking, small-brained creatures with reduced canines and other man-like traits, belonging to the family Hominidae and to the extinct genus *Australopithecus*. The morphology of *Australopithecus* in a number of respects bridged the ana-

tomical gap between man of the genus *Homo* and the living great apes of Africa. It thus fulfilled the requirements of the nineteenth century concept of a 'missing link' and corroborated Charles Darwin's 1871 prediction.

What of the behavioural characteristics of *Australopithecus?* The search for early hominids had been paralleled by a quest for signs of 'fossilized behaviour', in the form of implements of stone and bone and other archaeological archives. Raymond Dart believed that *A. africanus* had plied an *osteodontokeratic* ('bone, tooth and horn') culture, but C K Brain showed later that the distinctive features of the Makapansgat bone hoards, which formed the main basis of Dart's claims, were probably to be explained as

the results of carnivore activities, with lesser contributions by porcupines, hyaenas and other animals, and perhaps minimal participation by hominids in the aggregating and breaking of the bones.

Thus, although *Australopithecus* went upright and enjoyed manual freedom, there were few indications of a material culture, or at least a culture which employed imperishable materials. Studies of the behavioural operations of the modern great apes have shown that they are capable of several implemental activities, using perishable materials such as sticks, leaves and bark. It is probable, therefore, that similar activities of *Australopithecus* were executed largely in perishable materials which left no trace in the archaeological record.

The appearance of the genus *Homo*

Another major surprise from Africa was the revelation that hominids having every anatomical justification to be included in the genus *Homo* had lived there as late as the early Pliocene, from about 2,3 million years ago. These early specimens of *Homo* were more hominized than *A. africanus* but not as advanced as *H. erectus* which had been known previously from Java, China, North Africa and possibly Europe. In 1964 Louis Leakey, P V Tobias and J R Napier gave the name of *H. habilis* ('handyman') to these specimens, a name suggested to them by R A Dart.

Specimens of African early *Homo*, comprising mandibles and other bones, were first discovered by R Broom and T J Robinson in 1949 at Swartkrans. In 1957 and 1958 teeth and jaw fragments were found along with stone tools in Member 5 at Sterkfontein. P V Tobias suggested in 1965 that these belonged to early *Homo*, like *Homo habilis* which had been found at Olduvai Gorge in 1959 and 1960. The Olduvai hominid remains revealed that, contemporary with *A. boisei*, there had lived 1,9-1,6 million years ago another hominid with narrower teeth (especially the premolars and first molar) than *A. africanus*, but with a cranial capacity close to 50 per cent greater than the average for *A. africanus*. More specimens found in Olduvai in 1963 and 1968 enabled Mary Leakey to establish that there were close links between the presence of this hominid and that of stone tools of the Oldowan culture. In 1976 the claim that Member 5 of Sterkfontein contained *H. habilis* was confirmed when A R Hughes revealed, on the fortieth anniversary of Broom's first visit to Sterkfontein, a major part of a cranium with close resemblances to the Olduvai *H. habilis*. R J Clarke's reconstruction of this cranium in

1984 strongly confirmed its *H. habilis* features.

In its bodily structure *H. habilis* was nearer to modern man than was *A. africanus*. It marked the birth of the lineage of the genus *Homo*, which emerged about 2,3 million years ago, when the hominid lineage split. Many investigators agree that, while one or more derivatives of that split comprised the robust australopithecines, another major derivative was *H. habilis*. *A. africanus* (including *A. afarensis*) is thought by many to be the most likely common ancestor of these derivative lineages. *H. habilis* persisted into the Lower Pleistocene, the most recent specimens being dated to about 1,6 million years before the present. Then it gave way to what was almost certainly its descendant species, the bigger-brained, distinctive *H. erectus* (described in Chapter 2). Throughout its span on earth, *H. habilis* was a contemporary in Africa of one or other of the robust australopithecine species. In both South and East Africa, therefore, at least two different kinds of hominids held their own, side by side, perhaps for as many as 1,3 million years.

Behaviourally and culturally, *H. habilis* marked a crucial phase in hominization, its brain having taken a major step forward in absolute size and perhaps in quality. Its cultural achievements included the working of hard, imperishable materials, the making of a suite of varied kinds of stone implements, and at Olduvai, about 1,9 million years ago, the construction of a stone wall, presumably to form a shelter. It has even been suggested that, since Broca's and Wernicke's speech areas bulge on its endocranial casts, *H. habilis* might have possessed rudimentary articulate speech.

From *Australopithecus* to *H. habilis*, evolving humanity had seemingly crossed another hurdle: in effect it had transcended the divide between 'animal hominids' and 'human hominids'.

Suggested Reading List

C K Brain (1981) *The Hunters or the Hunted*, Chicago and London

R A Dart with Dennis Craig (1959) *Adventures with the Missing Link*, New York

G Findlay (1972) *Dr. Robert Broom F.R.S., Palaeontologist and Physician*, Cape Town

R E Leakey (1981) *The Making of Mankind*, London

J Reader (1981) *Missing Links – The Hunt for Earliest Man*, London

P V Tobias (1984) *Dart, Taung and the 'Missing Link'*, Johannesburg

P V Tobias (ed) (1985) *Hominid Evolution – Past, Present and Future*, New York

Chapter 2

The Last Million Years in Southern Africa

P V Tobias

> ***Homo erectus* in North and East Africa**
>
> Although the presence of *H. erectus* in Africa was not recognized until the second half of the twentieth century, the earliest discovery of a specimen later appreciated as having resemblances to *H. erectus* was made in 1933 in North Africa. From a consolidated dune just south of Rabat in Morocco, quarrymen blasted out what originally might well have been a complete fossil skull. All that was saved, however, were parts of the upper and lower jaws and fragments of the skull-vault. Years later, when better preserved remains attributable to *H. erectus* came to light in Morocco and Algeria, re-examination of the Rabat specimens led to their being ascribed to the same species.
>
> In East Africa fossils attributable to nine or ten *H. erectus* individuals were recovered by Louis and Mary Leakey at Olduvai Gorge in northern Tanzania. Most of them are associated with an Acheulian stone industry and are, in the main, older than 700 000 years BP, ie from the Lower Pleistocene age. The remains of over twenty individuals were recovered from Richard Leakey's famous Koobi Fora site in northern Kenya. The oldest are about 1,5 Myr BP in age, thus making the East African *H. erectus* populations older than those of northwest Africa. The oldest of them may well be of greater antiquity than the oldest specimens from Java. Hence, fairly early in the Lower Pleistocene, and not long after the last known occurrence of *H. habilis, H. erectus* appears in the African fossil record.

The African fossil archives indicate that about a million years ago the last of the robust australopithecines vanished from the geological record. From about 2,3 million years until approximately 1 million years ago, at least two distinct kinds of hominid, *Homo* and *Australopithecus*, lived in Africa at the same time. In the latter part of the Pliocene epoch and the earlier part of the Lower Pleistocene, *H. habilis* and *A. robustus* coexisted in the Transvaal, whilst *H. habilis* and *A. boisei* were East African contemporaries. Later in the lower Pleistocene, *H. erectus* existed side by side with *A. robustus* in southern Africa and with *A. boisei* in East Africa.

Parts of the hominid world become extinct

Then, about a million years ago, the world's last small-brained hominids, the australopithecines, became extinct. Various scenarios leading to this occurrence may be envisaged. Food supplies might have diminished as a result of the African environment having deteriorated, and the two hominid species may have had to compete for a common or related food base. Ultimately, the hominid with the more advanced survival strategy and the more versatile tool-kit, namely *Homo erectus*, seems to have prevailed, while the robust australopithecines died out.

In a second scenario, the advancement of the culture of *H. erectus* might have threatened the survival of *A. robustus* and *A. boisei*. For example, if *H. erectus* had learned to capture, control and maintain naturally caused fire, as recent evidence from Chesowanja in Kenya seems to indicate, he might have possessed a critical edge over late *Australopithecus*. This crucial item of cultural advancement might have hastened the extinction of the small-brained survivors.

Thirdly, if the survival strategy of *H. erectus* did increase dramatically at any stage, for example by improved methods for warding off predators or obtaining food, this might have led to an increase in population, which in turn might have constituted a serious menace to the australopithecines.

Changes in the physical environment, therefore, in cultural effectiveness, in demography, or varying combinations of such factors might have led to the disappearance of *A. robustus* and *A. boisei*. Whatever the cause or causes, from about a million years ago the hominids of Africa were represented by only a single species: that great Lower to Middle Pleistocene opportunist, *Homo erectus*, who bestrode the African stage like a colossus, freed from any challenge of competing hominid cousins.

Homo erectus in southern Africa

Only sparse remains from southern Africa are attributable to *Homo erectus*. These are derived from the Swartkrans cave in the Transvaal, where *A. robustus* remains were found from 1948 onwards. On 29 April 1949 J T Robinson, Dr Robert Broom's assistant, brought to light a

Recent Stages in the Earth's History

Era	Period	Epoch	Sub-division of epoch	Years Before Present
Cenozoic (From 65 Myr to the present)	Quaternary	Holocene		0
				10 000
		Pleistocene	Upper	
			— — —	125 000
			Middle	
			— — —	/00 000
			Lower	
				1 800 000
⋮	Tertiary	⋮ Pliocene	⋮ Upper	⋮

The Last Million Years

Homo erectus in the Old World

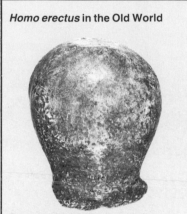

The top of the brain-case of 'Java man', discovered by Eugene Dubois.

By 1,0 Myr BP (before the present) hominids were no longer confined to the African continent. Their remains are to be found in Europe and Asia, and indeed the first specimens of *Homo erectus* came from Asia. In 1891 and 1892 a young Dutch army surgeon, Eugene Dubois, discovered the vault of a cranium, a thigh-bone and a few teeth at Trinil on the Solo River in central Java. He concluded that the fossilized remains belonged to a new species which he named *Pithecanthropus erectus* (literally, upright ape-man).

Today it is recognized that Dubois's *Pithecanthropus* is not an example of an intermediate form between man and the apes, but an early form of man, and the name was subsequently changed to *Homo erectus*. The discovery was largely responsible for the focusing of the scholarly world's attention upon Asia as the probable cradle of humanity, and for a time Darwin's prediction about Africa was forgotten. However, the find revealed a phase of emergent humanity, earlier and more archaic-looking than anything known before, and compelled anthropologists to allow a place in the Hominidae for even such as *Homo erectus*.

lower jaw, which was catalogued as S K 15. Broom and Robinson were satisfied that the mandible belonged to 'what is manifestly a new type of man', whom they proposed to call *Telanthropus capensis*, intermediate between apeman and true man. In 1961, however, Robinson formally proposed that the mandible and several other fragments found subsequently in the same pocket of breccia had their closest affinities with *Homo erectus*. Most investigators now agree that the sample provides good evidence of the presence in South Africa of early *Homo erectus* perhaps older than 1,0 Myr BP. Thus the Swartkrans evidence seems to confirm that obtained from East Africa, namely that *H. erectus* existed in the Lower Pleistocene of sub-Saharan Africa.

As the fossil record in the sub-continent is still very incomplete, it is not yet possible to give earliest and latest dates for *H. erectus* in southern Africa. He seems to have been present in the Transvaal by some time between 1,2 and 0,8 Myr BP, according to the views of J M Harris, T D White and E S Vrba.

What kind of person was *Homo erectus?*

Most of the striking features which distinguished *H. erectus* are evident in the skulls and the teeth. The average capacity of the brain-case was about 940 cubic centimetres (cc), more than double the average of 442 cc for *Australopithecus africanus* and about 46 per cent greater than the average of 645 cc in *Homo habilis*. Clearly there had been a quantum jump in brain size, though the average for *H. erectus* was still only some 70 per cent of the average in modern *Homo sapiens*.

In body size *H. erectus* was bigger than *H. habilis*, and about the size of modern man. The limb-bones and pelvis of *H. erectus*, though similar in most details to those of *H. sapiens*, did show some anatomical departures from today's man, but still bespoke a hominid whose mode of standing and walking could not have been very different from that of modern human beings.

The brain-case of *H. erectus* was low, with sides that tapered upwards, and the bones of the skull-vault were extraordinarily thick. Over the eye-sockets was a strongly jutting ledge of bone, while a markedly thickened shelf of bone adorned the hind end of the cranium. It is a mystery why *H. erectus* developed these strangely specialized characteristics. In most other features, such as the teeth, brain and locomotor system, the bodily structure of *H. erectus* fulfilled what might have been predicted for an intermediate stage between *A. africanus* and *H. habilis* on the one hand, and early *H. sapiens* on the other.

In the opinion of most students of fossil man, *H. erectus* evolved from *H. habilis*, and was the immediate ancestor of *H. sapiens*. There is fair agreement that the transition from *H. habilis* to *H. erectus* occurred at about 1,6-1,5 Myr BP. Estimates as to the second transition, from *H. erectus* to *H. sapiens*, vary between as early as 0,5 Myr BP and as late as 0,1 Myr BP. The reason for this lack of consensus is that there is a group of fossils showing transitional features, and authorities differ in their judgement about the identity of these intermediate specimens.

The emergence of *Homo sapiens*

An array of African, European and Asian specimens suggests that in the Middle Pleistocene (between 0,7 and 0,125 Myr BP) a number of departures from the typical *erectus* structure started appearing in some human populations. These anatomical departures were generally in a *sapiens* direction. The array of *erectus* and *sapiens* characters combined in these populations could be regarded as marking the first emergence of the *sapiens* differentiation from the substrate of a basically *erectus* population.

Apart from these transitional populations, four great subspecies are recognized as early full expressions of *Homo sapiens*: they are *Homo sapiens rhodesiensis* of sub-Saharan Africa, *Homo*

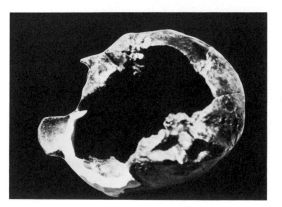

sapiens soloensis of Java, *Homo sapiens neanderthalensis* of Europe, Western Asia and the Mediterranean littoral, and *Homo sapiens afer* of sub-Saharan Africa. The first three subspecies showed features which are considered to have been derived from *Homo erectus*. The average cranial capacities in *rhodesiensis* (over 1 250 cc) and *soloensis* (1 151 cc) are greater than the average for any *erectus* samples, though not as great as that for modern *Homo sapiens*.

Homo sapiens rhodesiensis

The recognition of this distinct form of premodern hominid goes back to 1921, when it was one of the earliest African discoveries of fossil hominids.

The first specimen was discovered in 1921 in the Broken Hill Mine at Kabwe, in the Central Province of Zambia, during the course of mining operations. Later, in 1925, further human bones were found. At least three, and possibly four, different individuals are represented by the cranial and post-cranial remains. The principal cranium, formerly known as the Broken Hill skull or 'Rhodesian Man', is characterized by a heavy supra-orbital torus but thin bones, a cranial capacity of 1 280 cc and a long face with a prominent upper jaw and large palate. Along with the human remains were found stone tools which have been said to be of an early Middle Stone Age aspect, as well as the fossilized remains of mammals, about a quarter of which have become extinct. Recent dating suggests that the site may be about 125 000 years old, close to the junction between the Middle and Upper Pleistocene.

In 1935 and 1938 the fragments of two or three fossil crania were discovered on the north-eastern shore of Lake Eyasi in northern Tanzania. The anatomical structure of the cranial bones suggests that the Eyasi 1 specimen might have represented a female of the *rhodesiensis* group. The latest dating suggests that the specimens date back to 34 000 years BP, thus representing the latest occurrence of the *rhodesiensis* subspecies in the fossil record.

The first human skull fragment to be found in a South African stratified cave deposit in direct association with Acheulian implements was the Cave of Hearths mandibular piece, discovered in September 1947. The Cave of Hearths is an immense cave deposit in the Makapansgat valley, just over a kilometre from the Makapansgat Limeworks where *Australopithecus africanus* fossils have been found. The little jaw, like those of other earlier hominids, has no chin, is thick for its height (partly as a result of its juvenile age) and has several features reminiscent of some north-west African jaws of late *erectus* or *erectus-sapiens* transitional forms. R J Mason, who carried out the major excavation of this cave deposit, has classified the cul-

The Hopefield skull, a thick-boned, heavy-browed brain-case. This skull is very similar to that of Kabwe, and both are considered to represent a primitive subspecies of *Homo sapiens*, ie *rhodesiensis*. It retains *erectus*-like features such as the low, retreating forehead and the prominent eyebrow-ridge.

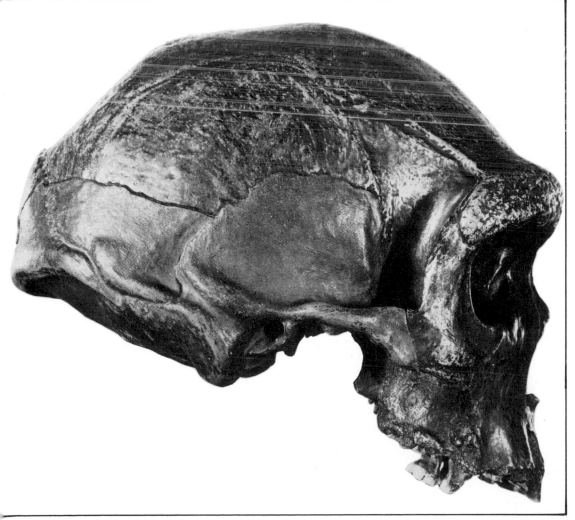

The Kabwe cranium, an early southern African discovery. The skull was at the time the most primitive-looking hominid to have emerged from Africa and some investigators regarded it as representing a new species or even genus of hominid. Today it is considered to have been a member of *Homo sapiens rhodesiensis*.

Carl Linnaeus (1707-1778) was a great Swedish naturalist and the father of the modern system of naming plants and animals by two names, ie the name of the genus (eg *Homo*) followed by the name of the particular species (eg *sapiens*). Apart from placing man firmly within the animal kingdom (when most of his contemporaries saw man as apart from the rest of creation), Linnaeus anticipated several of Darwin's ideas of a century later, such as the Struggle for Existence and the theory of Natural Selection.

The highveld in the vicinity of Makapansgat in northern Transvaal. On the opposite side of the valley can be seen the mouth of the Cave of Hearths, below which is a great mound of debris from its excavation. The deposit in the cave covers well over 100 000 years of intermittent occupation.

Inset: An early human jawbone from the Stone Age part of the Cave of Hearths deposit, discovered by Ben Kitching in September 1947.

tural horizon to which the mandible belongs as Final African Acheulian. The stratum in question is probably of Upper Pleistocene age.

Another specimen assigned to *Homo sapiens rhodesiensis* was recovered in 1953 from an open site on the Elandsfontein farm near the village of Hopefield, 24 km east of Saldanha Bay, Cape Province. The hominid remains comprise 27 pieces that have been fitted together to make a cranial vault, and a piece of lower jaw. The characteristics of the Hopefield skull are very similar to those of the Kabwe remains. There is a rich associated fauna, and 55 per cent of the species of mammals found there are now extinct. It has been concluded that Hopefield was of Middle Pleistocene age and the oldest preserved site of *rhodesiensis*.

Two of the four sites, Kabwe and the Cave of Hearths, are cave deposits, while Eyasi and Hopefield are open localities. The duration of the subspecies in time would, on the presently available samples, be from about 250 000 to roughly 50 000 years BP. In Africa north of the Sahara this time span is overlapped partly by the span of *Homo sapiens neanderthalensis*, remains of which were discovered on the southern Mediterranean littoral, in Cyrenaica and in Morocco. These African neandertal fossils range in time from about 10 000 to 40 000 years BP.

Homo sapiens afer: the phase of modern human emergence

The Swedish biologist Linnaeus subdivided humanity into four varieties in the four quarters of the globe: the red American, the white European, the dark Asian and the black African. This classification has not stood the test of time,

but one of his proposed categories, *Homo sapiens afer*, was revived in the third quarter of the twentieth century as a subspecies in which to accommodate all southern African human remains of the Later Pleistocene age. This subspecies name was applied by L H Wells to embrace populations deemed to be the common ancestor of the Khoisan and Negro populations of present-day sub-Saharan Africa.

A goodly sample of southern African Upper Pleistocene fossils has been allocated to this ancestral African subspecies. They include the fossils of Border Cave at Ingwavuma in northern Natal (Kwazulu), Tuinplaas on the Springbok Flats in Central Transvaal, Fish Hoek, Matjies River and Klasies River Mouth Cave on the southern Cape coast, and Bushman Rock Shelter in the Transvaal. The cranium of Florisbad, near Bloemfontein, might have belonged to the same subspecies, though it retains morphological reminders of *Homo sapiens rhodesiensis*.

Anatomically these specimens of *Homo sapiens afer* are essentially modern in form. Although a number of them are of uncertain stratigraphic placement and dating, claims have recently been made that the specimens of Border Cave and of Klasies River Mouth Cave are over 100 000 years old (early Upper Pleistocene). If further researches prove those claims correct, it would suggest that Africa gave rise to the world's oldest remains of modern-looking *Homo sapiens*, scores of thousands of years before anatomically modern specimens of *Homo sapiens* occur in the European and Asian fossil records. There is no doubt about the structural modernity of the specimens, but there remains some uncertainty about the dating.

Another apparently early form of *Homo sa-*

piens has come from the Kibish formation of the Omo basin in south-western Ethiopia. It is possible that these Kibish fossils may be accommodated within *Homo sapiens afer*, or that they might have represented another, as yet unnamed, subspecies of *Homo sapiens*. For the Kibish remains, too, there is an unconfirmed claim that they are over 100 000 years old, but the dating method still awaits validation.

Palaeo-anthropologists have not yet reached consensus on the claimed early dating of the oldest, anatomically modern African finds. Evidence suggests that anatomically modern man might well have had a longer history in sub-Saharan Africa than elsewhere, yet to date this concept has not been fully assimilated into theories of the emergence of modern *Homo sapiens*. Similarly, the relationship, genetic and phylogenetic, between *Homo sapiens afer* and *Homo sapiens sapiens* remains to the clarified. At least it may be said that the latest African evidence is beginning to provide a possible challenge to the traditional Europe-centred and Mediterranean-centred hypotheses on the origin of modern *Homo sapiens*.

The end of the Pleistocene and through the Holocene

As the record of fossils and archaeological remains approaches the present the stockpile of available evidence becomes richer, additional dating methods such as the carbon-14 technique become more reliably applicable, and the probing back from living descendant populations more helpful. The most important sites in southern Africa yielding skeletal remains from this period are Hora, Fingira and Phwadzi in Malawi, Mumba V, Kalemba, Lochinvar (Gwisho), Chipongwe, Makwe, Maramba and Nachikufu in Zambia, Inyanga in Zimbabwe, Boskop in South Africa, and Otjiseva in South West Africa/Namibia.

By comparing the metrical features of the fossil skulls with those of skulls drawn from modern populations of South African Negroes and San (formerly called Bushmen), H de Villiers and L P Fatti have been led to infer that 'people

Negroid type twins of the Tonga people of Zambia. On the left is the girl, Karinda, and on the right the boy, Timba. (Photo: P V Tobias)

◁▽
A Khoikhoi girl, photographed in the present Botswana in 1959. (Photo: P V Tobias)

▽
A young San girl at puberty. (Photo: P V Tobias)

▷
The Florisbad cranium has in recent years been classified as *Homo sapiens afer,* a subspecies which includes all southern African human remains of the Later Pleistocene epoch. R J Clarke has made a new reconstruction of the cranium. (Photo: R J Clarke)

▷▷
Lateral view of the cranium that was found in the Border Cave in Ingwavuma. Note that the eyebrow-ridge is much smaller and the forehead more vertical than in the more archaic Florisbad skull. The features of this cranium are those of anatomically modern man, though it is more than 100 000 years old.

of undoubted Negro affinities' inhabited north, east and south, but surprisingly not west Africa, well before the advent of the Iron Age. Thus, in North Africa, they have concluded that Negroid populations were established between about 12 000 and 2 000 years BP, and in East Africa between about 7 500 and 4 800 BP. In southern Africa, north of the Zambezi River, they found evidence of people with 'undoubted Negro affinities' from about 8 000 years BP at Kalemba in Zambia and, south of the Zambezi, from 110 000-90 000 years BP, the latter being based on the Border Cave skull and their acceptance of its proposed early dating.

Some of their comparisons show affinities of certain fossils with the modern populations of San, while yet others appear to fall outside the ranges of variation for both modern populations compared. The data do not appear to throw light on the point of departure at which these two major African populations, if they indeed enjoyed a common origin, diverged from each other.

The influence of the study of genetic markers

It is here that studies on the genetic make-up of the living populations have proved especially useful. Populations of living mankind are known to differ among themselves in the frequencies with which they show certain genetic characteristics, such as traits produced by particular mutant versions (or alleles) of specific genes. Some mutant genes, in fact, may serve as 'markers' of genetic affinities among various populations.

Prior to this new approach, many scholars believed that the black peoples of southern Africa constituted a separate racial division of mankind, and many anthropological, biomedical and statistical reports appeared describing the qualities and features of the so-called 'Bantu'.

The findings which resulted from the study of genetic markers reunited the Bantu-speaking black peoples of southern Africa with the peoples of the rest of the sub-Saharan continent. The gene frequencies showed that the variations among the various sub-Saharan Negroid people were relatively minor, compared with the differences which separated them from other divisions of humanity, such as the Caucasoid and Mongoloid groups.

As more genetic markers were discovered and tested for, abundant confirmation came to light on the essential genetic unity of sub-Saharan Africa, including the peoples of West Africa. These genetic tests were applied also to the Khoisan people (previously known as the 'Hottentots' and 'Bushmen'), and it was revealed that they, too, shared the sub-Saharan African genetic affinities, and thus belonged to the same large Negroid division to which other sub-Saharan peoples were attributed.

Subsequent analysis of genetic markers and of morphological traits of simple genetic determination led P V Tobias in 1966 to infer that, although the Khoisan manifestly belong to the same major genetic constellation as other sub-Saharan Africans, the morphological and genetic markers point to a lengthy period in which the two groups developed in relative isolation from each other. The temporary separation of the Khoisans from the rest must have begun a long time ago. Certainly on the palaeoanthropological evidence, it would seem to have been upwards of 6 000 years BP, and it has been suggested that it could even have begun by the onset of the Later Stone Age, about 40 000 years BP.

Once the dichotomy was established, there followed perhaps up to 35 000 years in which the Khoisans lived in reproductive and genetic isolation from the rest of Negro Africa. The Khoisans at this time seem to have gravitated mainly to eastern and southern Africa, while the

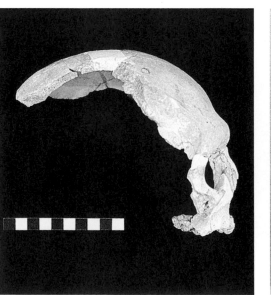

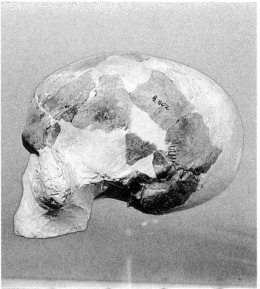

Negroes were living mainly in Tropical and Equatorial Africa. During the period of isolation, certain genetic divergences arose: new alleles (or mutant genes) took root in both populations.

In the southern parts of Africa the San became shorter of stature and of lighter skin pigmentation. A number of other bodily characteristics developed, including the retention of child-like anatomical features in the heads and faces of adult San (a biological process known as paedomorphism). They remained a largely hunting people, pursuing the way of life which had been followed by all mankind practically to the end of the Upper Pleistocene. Further north in Africa, the darker, somewhat taller Negro eventually came to adopt a new way of life, agriculture, and tracts of tropical rain forest were cleared for agricultural purposes. A population explosion ensued and they expanded eastwards, northwards and southwards. Iron-working moved across Africa, certain kinds of pottery appeared in the archaeological annals, and the family of African languages classified as 'Bantu' spread.

Some of the populations moving southwards with the new way of life encountered not only new physical environments, but also their long-lost 'country cousins', the genetically differentiated Khoisan populations. Thus, the numerical and regional expansion of the Negroes broke down the geographical separation which had long isolated them from the Khoisans. This, in turn, led to a remission of genetic isolation. There followed a mingling of marker genes, some of the 'new San alleles' flowed into the genetic constitution of the southern African Negroes, and perhaps a few Negro markers diffused in the reverse direction. New life habits rubbed off on to the San, some of whom, over centuries or even millennia, adopted food-producing pursuits, both agricultural and pastoral.

Recent researches have shown that there was no hard and fast divide between the hunting or 'palaeolithic' way of life and the new approach to survival, by the use of domesticated animals and cultivation. The earlier view was that the living San hunters were the only surviving remnants who had never adopted food production. This has given way to the idea that for centuries, or perhaps even millennia, physical environmental conditions, as well as military and political challenges, have led the recent San to carry on a kind of flirtation with the new ways of life. For a long time, at different periods, they practised both the old hunting and the new pastoral lifestyles. Thus the San who are today seen as 'surviving hunters and gatherers' are simply those populations which, under present conditions, are not running cattle, sheep or goats, but are following the predominantly hunting and gathering lifeways.

These modern populations provide a unique opportunity to study the mechanics and dynamics of the hunting and gathering life. Although it cannot be assumed that Stone Age Man of the Upper Pleistocene, of 50 000 to 25 000 years BP, lived exactly as surviving hunters do today, at least these San hunter-gatherers provide us with living models. Cautious comparison of the lifestyles of different groups of living hunters, from Africa and elsewhere, may reveal common threads running through them. Inferences about prehistoric man are likely to be more valid if they are based not only on what can be learned by digging up the past, but also on what is known about the patterns of life among today's hunters and gatherers.

Suggested Reading List

J Desmond Clark (1959) *The Prehistory of Southern Africa*, Harmondsworth

J Desmond Clark (1970) *The Prehistory of Africa*, London

R R Inskeep (1978) *The Peopling of Southern Africa*, Cape Town

R G Klein (1984) *Southern African Prehistory and Palaeoenvironments*, Rotterdam and Boston

Mary D Leakey (1984) *Disclosing the Past – An Autobiography*, London

R J Mason (1962) *Prehistory of the Transvaal*, Johannesburg

C G Simpson (1974) *The Stone Age Archeology of Southern Africa*, New York

Chapter 3

Hunter-gatherers, Herders and Farmers

The Origin of the Southern African Khoisan Communities

H C Bredekamp

Henry C Bredekamp, senior lecturer-researcher in History at the University of the Western Cape, matriculated at Genadendal in 1962. He obtained his MA degree in 1979, and was awarded a MALS degree at Wesleyan University, Connecticut. He was visiting lecturer at Johns Hopkins University, Washington DC in 1984. His publications include *Van veeverskaffers tot veewagters*, an examination of Khoikhoi-Dutch relations at the Cape prior to 1679.

According to archaeological research, scattered groups of hunter-gatherers formed the sole populace of southern Africa for approximately 8 000 years, from the early Holocene epoch until about 2 000 years ago. Around the time of the birth of Christ the descendants of these hunter-gatherers began to make contact with the Khoikhoi cattle-herders. The Khoikhoi who later migrated to present Namaqualand gave the name 'San' to the indigenous hunter-gatherers. From the reciprocal interaction between the Khoikhoi and the San (and to a lesser extent the Bantu-speaking peoples) a heterogeneous society, about which there is little information available, developed along the Cape coastal region and in the interior.

The rapid advances in socio-scientific investigative techniques during the past three decades have, however, enabled researchers to arrive at new insights into the composition of pre-colonial society at the Cape. The recent use by historians of the terms San ('Bushmen'), Khoikhoi (the name the so-called 'Hottentots' gave themselves, meaning 'men of men' or 'genuine people') and 'Khoisan' for the combined group is partly due to this development. Archaeological, anthropological and linguistic studies have revealed that it is incorrect to make a rigid racial distinction between 'Bushman' and 'Hottentot', since this is at variance with the true structure of pre-colonial society in southern Africa. Since this purely racial distinction is no longer valid, historians are increasingly interpreting the history of the Khoikhoi and San in terms of changes which the heterogenous, indigenous Cape society underwent prior to and during white colonization.

During the last few decades scholars have begun to demonstrate convincingly that the Khoikhoi herders developed from hunter-gatherer societies in southern Africa. In the process they spread, as a less heterogeneous society, from the central interior to the grazing lands of the Cape coastal region in particular. On the basis of studies of linguists and anthropologists, the historian Richard Elphick has established with reasonable certainty that the ancestors of the historic Khoikhoi must, by 500 BC, have been roving about somewhere in the vicinity of northern Botswana as hunter-gatherers of the Late Stone Age. Comparative linguistic studies by Dorothy Bleek, E O J Westphal and L F Maingard have shown that the Tshu-Kwe languages of the San in central Botswana still display surprising similarities to existing Khoikhoi dialects such as Nama and Korana. To the historian this indicates a common southern African derivation. On the other hand, the San of central Botswana find the other San languages from the area between the upper reaches of the Limpopo and south-eastern Angola (including the Kalahari) totally incomprehensible. This linguistic complexity has a dual significance: on the one hand it reinforces the theory that hunter-gatherers for thousands of years had ceased to consider themselves a homogeneous component of the southern African population, and on the other hand the view that the Khoikhoi languages must have developed from a San language. The coining of the term 'Khoisan' by scholars is partly an attempt to indicate the linguistic relationship between the San languages and the Khoikhoi dialects, and to distinguish them from the Bantu languages, which in turn display common characteristics.

The amalgam 'Khoisan' also indicates a complex process of intermingling, intermarriage, acculturation and even assimilation which occurred over centuries between roving San hunter-gatherers and migrating Khoikhoi herders. Twentieth century physical anthropologists have difficulty in distinguishing between

Khoikhoi and San on the basis of race. They have not yet reached unanimity on the reasons for the physical differences between the historic San and Khoikhoi. Some scholars have put forward the theory that larger physique may be attributed to a protein rich diet based on a pastoral economy. Anthropologists prefer to speak of 'Khoisan' in cases where seventeenth to nineteenth century documents omit to indicate the kinship relations of persons from the Late Stone Age.

Scholars are still unable to explain with certainty how the pastoral revolution occurred. It is quite likely that the first Khoikhoi were a community of hunters in the present Botswana who, through robbery or peaceful means, acquired cattle from the first agriculturists who had migrated into the area. These were probably Bantu-speakers, although the possibility of the physical presence of central Sudanic people has been suggested. Population pressure and the need for better grazing then compelled the herders to become migrants.

Theories on the migration routes of the Khoikhoi

There are many differences of opinion about the routes which the ancestors of the Cape Khoikhoi followed from the present northern Botswana. Few, if any, would today suggest that the Khoikhoi originated in Tanzania-Kenya, as put forward by G W Stow in 1905. Stow argued that the Khoikhoi pastoralists migrated from that area across to the Namibian coast, then moved southwards along the coast as far as the south-eastern Cape. They then turned (he maintained) in an easterly direction to the border of the present Transkei, where they were checked by Bantu-speaking agriculturists and stock farmers. Archaeological evidence supports only the last part of this postulated migration.

In 1972 Richard Elphick presented, on the basis of more scientific research, an equally viable theory, though without archaeological evidence to support it. His alternative hypothesis focused on Stow's failure to take into account the lack of good grazing and perennial water sources which made a westward migration unlikely. Elphick maintained that the earliest Khoikhoi herders moved from Botswana in the direction of Matabeleland, through the northern Transvaal and along the Harts River until they came to the Orange River. Here they parted: one group swung westwards towards the mouth of the Orange River, from where the ancestors of the Nama trekked northwards and those of the Namaqua southwards; the other groups (consisting of the ancestors of the Cape Khoikhoi) moved in the direction of the Fish and Sundays rivers. Thereafter the Gona diverged eastwards, while the ancestors of the Attaqua, Hessequa, Cochoqua and Peninsular Khoikhoi moved westwards past the present Mossel Bay until they reached the vicinity of St Helena Bay.

It is quite probable that the herders whom European seafarers encountered along the Cape west coast after 1487 belonged to the westward moving wave of migration of the Cape Khoikhoi. Europeans found the similarities in the so-

'Korah Girls', by Samuel Daniell. (Africana Museum)

'A Korah Hottentot village on the left bank of the Orange River', by the English artist Samuel Daniell, who visited the Cape from 1801 to 1803. The huts in the picture are constructed of a curved wooden frame, covered by woven grass mats. Pots of water or milk hang cooling from a stand, and the youths in the foreground are transporting animals across the river by means of 'swimming logs'. (Africana Museum)

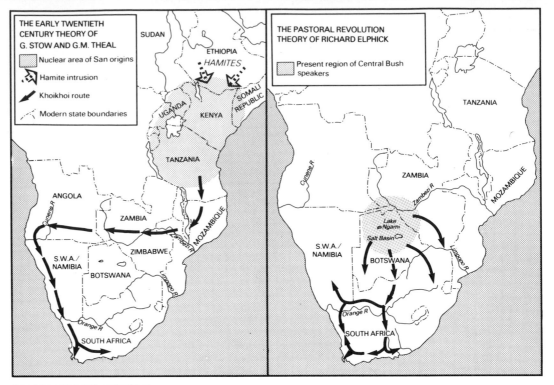

The Migration of the Khoikhoi

▽
'Female Bosjesman', by Samuel Daniell. The text which accompanied the original commented that '. . . few of them (*Bosjesman* women) are so well provided with attire as (the woman) here depicted. . .' (Africana Museum)

▷▷
'A Hottentot', by Samuel Daniell. (Johannesburg Public Library)

cial structures of the separate groups striking. Like the San, they were also hunters and food-gatherers but, more significantly, their existence evolved around a pastoral economy.

The Khoikhoi communities often shared a grazing area until it had been depleted, after which they split up into smaller groups. As semi-nomadic communities they frequently adhered to a fixed migratory pattern according to seasonal changes. In this way some of them moved to the Cape Peninsula in the summer, only to return inland with the onset of the cold and wet winter weather.

Throughout southern Africa their sheep and cattle assured the Khoikhoi of an independent pastoral mode of existence. Livestock were slaughtered in times of emergency and for ritual purposes, and in times of war their long-horned oxen were used for defensive purposes, to shield fighting men. These oxen were also used as pack animals to convey their reed-mat huts and

other worldly possessions. Furthermore the number of cattle possessed by an individual determined his status in the hierarchical Khoikhoi society. The value of livestock as an economic surplus which could increase more quickly than it could be consumed must have made some families richer than others.

Political centralization or unity was, however, frustrated by the pastoral economy of the Khoikhoi, which forced them into a scattered, nomadic existence. Each tribe or horde consisted of a number of sibs or clans (groups made up of blood and other relations) which frequently broke away to form separate clans. This fragile social organization prevented any development of hereditary chieftainship, with the result that the Khoikhoi offered less organized resistance to colonial encroachment than other African societies.

Since the welfare and self-sufficiency of the Khoikhoi were dependent upon the ownership of livestock, disasters such as drought, disease and theft contributed to the impoverishment of communities. When this occurred Khoikhoi herders frequently reverted to the status of hunter-gatherers. In an attempt to build up their depleted herds and flocks again, impoverished individuals or groups sometimes entered the service of more prosperous Khoikhoi as clients and stock herders. This process of possible economic recovery was virtually destroyed when the coming of the Europeans disrupted the geographic isolation of the Khoikhoi.

Rock engraving of an eland with superimposed phosphenes (geometric forms). Scale in centimetres. (Drawing: Department of Archaeology, University of the Witwatersrand)

The San: Life, Belief and Art

J D Lewis-Williams

For at least two million years the inhabitants of southern Africa pursued a hunter gatherer way of life. Their mastery of their environment increased gradually, and two new modes of subsistence were adopted – agriculture and the domestication of animals. Nowadays there are very few communities which still provide examples of a hunter gatherer mode of existence, and the San or 'Bushmen' are numbered among these groups. In former times the San led a nomadic existence throughout southern Africa, but today they are found only in the Kalahari desert. Even these 'surviving' San have in many cases been forced to adopt a pastoral way of life, and it is unfortunate that the twentieth century may see the end of the hunter-gatherer community in southern Africa.

The San today

The Kalahari San are not the descendants of fugitive people driven from the better watered parts of southern Africa; archaeological evidence as well as their very fine adjustment to life in the desert suggest that the San have been living in the Kalahari for thousands of years. Moreover, the languages spoken by these desert dwellers are quite different from those of the now extinct southern groups; most Bush languages are in fact mutually unintelligible. The numerous San groups are today distinguished from one another by their language, not by political groupings; it is therefore incorrect to speak of San or Bushman 'tribes'.

As a result of studies by anthropologists, the San are now one of the best understood hunter-gatherer peoples in the world. Classic hunter-gatherer societies are distinguished by a number of features: they are nomadic, they store hardly any food or other resources, and they have a generally egalitarian social system. The exploitation of various resources is seasonal and carefully planned by the San so that they tend to move around a regular course. Their knowledge of desert foods and waterholes is precise and detailed, and they are able to secure a much easier living than is often thought.

The San as hunter-gatherers

The San are justly famous for their hunting ability. A good tracker can detect the spoor of a wounded antelope among the tracks of a whole herd and follow the wounded animal until it leaves the herd and dies. Hunters can seldom come close enough to an animal to deliver a fatal strike with their puny bows and arrows, and they therefore rely on a poison made from the larvae of the beetle *Diamphidia simplex*, though other groups also used snake venom. The poison is cardio-toxic and does not contaminate the meat; a small piece of flesh around the wound is cut out and discarded, but the rest of the animal can be eaten with impunity.

The arrow which bears the poison is a remarkable piece of technology. It comprises four components: the shaft, a torpedo-shaped 'link', a short reed collar and the point. In earlier times points were made of bone and stone; today fencing wire is often hammered to form a barbed point. The poison is applied just behind the point to avoid blunting it. When the arrow strikes its target the impact causes the link to split the collar and the shaft falls away, leaving the poisoned point embedded in the animal. The short point is less likely to work loose as the animal runs, and it cannot be removed as easily as a long shaft if the animal rubs against a tree.

To counterbalance the uncertainty of securing prey, the San have sharing practices

Professor J D Lewis-Williams is Reader in Cognitive Archaeology in the Department of Archaeology, University of the Witwatersrand. He has conducted extensive research on the rock art of the south-eastern mountains of southern Africa and on nineteenth century San ethnography. His principal publications include *Believing and Seeing* (Academic Press) and *The Rock Art of Southern Africa* (Cambridge).

which ensure that everyone receives an adequate protein supply. The man who owns the arrow which kills an animal is regarded as the 'owner' of the meat and it is his task to distribute the meat according to various kinship ties. Because the San extend their kinship to 'name relationships' each person is assured a portion. In the name relationship, two men whose fathers have the same name regard each other as brothers, and since the San have a restricted range of male and female names, this means that anyone can, when necessary, activate a 'name relationship' and claim his share of the meat.

While the men are engaged in hunting and associated tasks such as preparing arrows, the women gather plant foods. They are extremely skilled at identifying the smallest wisp of tendril as a sign that a large edible root lies beneath the sand. Unlike the products of hunting, plant foods remain a woman's property; she provides for her own family only. This may be because plant foods are more easily obtained, and there is no need for rules of distribution.

A San camp usually consists of a couple of siblings with their children, some of whom may be married, and, perhaps, the parents of the adults. At certain times of the year a few of these camps may amalgamate, while at other times they disperse. Camps are not restricted to a single resource area, because the highly localized southern African rainfall can leave an area drought stricken for extended periods. At such times of stress camps split up and members go to various camps in better endowed areas.

Under such circumstances a centralized political authority is impossible. Although a man may be nominally the 'owner' of a waterhole, he does not have the powers of a chief. Indeed, the southern /Xam language had no word for 'chief'. A man's abilities are respected in certain but not all circumstances, and decisions, such as when to move camp, are communal, both men and women participating in the process.

The supernatural world of the San

Within this egalitarian society there are no specialists, though about half the men and a third of the women become shamans, or medicine people. Their shamanistic work does not relieve them of other daily tasks. The medicine people form a bridge or link between this world and the supernatural world, but they themselves see both worlds as equally 'real'. At a ritual dance the women sit in a close circle around a central fire as they sing and clap the rhythm of medicine songs believed to contain a supernatural potency, or energy, which also resides in the men themselves. Potency is named after various 'strong' things like eland, giraffe, gemsbok, honey and sun. The modern !Kung of the northern Kalahari call this potency *n/um*; the extinct /Xam of the Cape called it *!gi* or *//ken*.

As the dance increases in intensity, potency is said to 'boil' in the men's stomachs and to rise up their spines until it 'explodes' in their heads and they enter the altered state of consciousness we call trance and the !Kung call *!kia*. Though a novice may occasionally use dagga to help him into trance for the first time, trance is normally achieved without the use of hallucinogens; the rhythmic dancing, the music, hyperventilation and intense concentration are sufficient. In trance some men become cataleptic, but those who are more experienced are able to control the level of trance so that they can move among the people, drawing sickness or evil from them by the laying on of hands. All people, even visitors, are 'cured' because they believe it possible for sickness to be in a person without the person knowing it.

For the San 'sickness' can be physical, psychological and social. After the sickness has been drawn into the medicine men's bodies, they expel it with a convulsive shriek, and it is believed to return to the ever threatening spirits from whom it originated. Some men claim their own spirits leave their bodies to do battle with the *//gauwasi*, the evil spirits, or even with God himself. The modern !Kung believe in two gods, a Great God (≠ Gao N!a) who lives in the east and a lesser god (//Gauwa) in the west; neither is entirely good nor entirely evil.

Very similar beliefs were entertained by the extinct southern groups, but instead of believing in two gods, both the /Xam and the San of the Maluti mountains spoke of a single trickster figure, /Kaggen. Dr Bleek translated this name as 'Mantis' and there is a widespread, though erroneous, belief that the San and the Khoikhoi, or Hottentots, worshipped the praying mantis. While it is wrong to suppose the southern San conceived of /Kaggen exclusively as an insect, the praying mantis was one of his many manifestations; for the most part he lived the life of an ordinary San man, though possessing extraordinary powers. Some of the myths in which /Kaggen appears suggest he was a medicine man, perhaps the original medicine man.

The southern San, unlike the modern Kalahari people, recognized four overlapping categories of medicine men: the curers, who re-

---

Shaft   Link   Collar   Point

A link-shaft San arrow. (Diagram: Department of Archaeology, University of the Witwatersrand)

moved sickness; medicine men of the rain, who were said to capture a 'rain animal' before leading it over the parched land and killing it so that its blood and milk could become precipitation; medicine men of the game, who similarly controlled game and led the animals into the hunter's ambush; and, finally, medicine men of sickness, who were believed to shoot mystical 'arrows of sickness' into people.

The rock art of the San

Recent research has shown that much, possibly all, the rock art for which the San are renowned was associated with medicine men. It is true that the art apparently illustrates many mundane aspects of Stone Age life and even contact between the San and black and white farmers, but the contexts of these seemingly narrative scenes demand closer attention than they have hitherto been accorded. To understand what is probably the most striking and exquisitely detailed hunter-gatherer art in the world, the activities and experiences of medicine men must be examined.

As a medicine man dances and the potency begins to boil inside him, his stomach muscles contract into a tight, painful knot and he bends forward until his torso is almost at right angles to his legs. He trembles and sweats profusely. Among the southern people, medicine men often suffered a nasal haemorrhage when they entered trance, though this appears to be less frequent among the modern Kalahari San. They then entered the terrifying supernatural world.

It is in this transcendent experience that the key to the art is to be found, for trance experience is depicted in the art by a series of metaphors and hallucinations to which individual artists contributed their own insights and understandings. These metaphors include

A Kalahari San throws his spear to kill an antelope already near to death from the poison of his arrows. (Photo: Lorna Marshall)

'flight' and 'underwater', but the most pervasive is 'death'. This metaphor is based on an analogy between medicine men who were, and in the Kalahari still are, said to 'die' in trance and the literal, physical death of antelope. When an antelope dies its behaviour is remarkably similar to that of a man entering trance: it lowers its head, trembles, sweats and bleeds from the nose. A dying antelope's hair also stands on end, and hair was thought to come out on the back of a man in trance. In the art trancers are depicted in a distinctive forward bending, head lowered posture. Blood sometimes falls from their noses and they often have hair standing on end over much of their bodies.

A San hunter wearing a cap with antelope ears. He has an arrow set in the bow, another held ready for rapid shooting and three others lodged between his back and his kaross. A quiver is slung over his shoulder. (Photo: J D Lewis-Williams)

Rock painting of a San medicine dance. Unlike the modern Kalahari dances, the clapping women here are depicted sitting to one side while the men, each with two dancing sticks, dance in the centre. The men wear caps with antelope ears which are associated with medicine men who had control of the game. Scale in centimetres. Colour of painting, red. (Drawing: Department of Archaeology, University of the Witwatersrand)

Part of a rock painting showing the relationship between medicine men and eland-power. Like the eland itself, the man apparently holding its tail has hoofs, erect hair and crossed legs. The man to the right dances in a typical bending-forward posture with outstretched arms. Scale in centimetres. Colours, red, black and white. (Drawing: Department of Archaeology, University of the Witwatersrand)

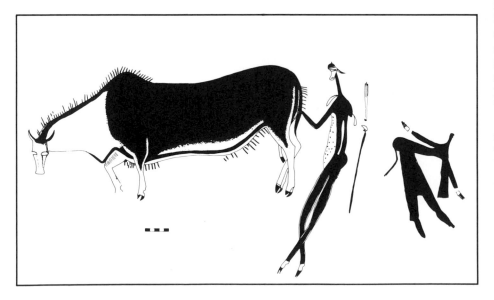

Many of the painted antelope are also in dying postures. Both men and animals exhibit the characteristics of death, and in some paintings the dying antelope is clearly a symbol of a 'dying' medicine man.

The death of an antelope is important in another way as well because a dying eland, the largest and most potent of all antelope, is thought to release its potency at death. In the Kalahari men still like to 'dance eland potency' next to the carcass of a freshly killed eland, believing the place to be redolent with power they can harness for a particularly efficacious curing ritual.

As a man enters trance he experiences at least three stages of hallucination. In the first stage he sees patterns of zigzags, chevrons, spots, spirals and grids. These forms, or phosphenes, are neurologically controlled and, because they are a product of the human nervous system, they are cross-cultural: people from all cultures report seeing such forms in altered states of consciousness. Sufferers from migraine also experience some of these hallucinations. In the next stage the trancer sees emotionally charged objects, which are, of course, culturally controlled. In the third stage the culturally controlled visions blend with one another and the trancer may see himself as part of his own hallucination. He also sees various entities invisible to ordinary people.

All three stages of hallucination are represented in the rock art; the art is, in fact, a comprehensive record of trance experience. The first stage, the geometric forms or phosphenes, are very frequently encountered among rock engravings and among the paintings as well. Sometimes the phosphenes are associated with animals of indeterminate species, as though the animal is being seen through or surrounded by the neurologically controlled forms.

The second stage of hallucination goes further and includes a range of emotionally charged objects. For hunter-gatherers there are few, if any, more powerful things than animals. Chief among all the animals is the eland which is considered to possess more potency than any other creature. In many parts of southern Africa the eland was painted more frequently than any other animal; in other regions, different animals, like the kudu and the giraffe in Zimbabwe, appear to supplant the eland. Much of an eland's potency resides in its fat. Fatness is markedly characteristic of an old bull eland, and many of the rock paintings depict such old eland. They are recognizable by their very large, pendulous dewlaps and, less frequently, by their pale, greyish colour.

In addition to eland, other animals were also associated with medicine men. Among these were felines. Men were believed to go on out-of-body travel in the form of a lion, and the dangerous, violent aspects of trance were symbolized by felines. In the Kalahari today the !Kung use a form of their word for 'pawed creatures' to mean 'to go on out-of-body journeys in the form of a lion'. One medicine man claimed he could, in his feline persona, 'mix with' a pride of lions. Some paintings show felines chasing men. A particularly explicit example shows the men

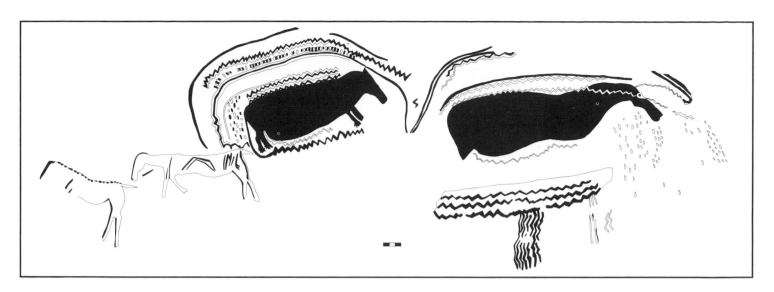

bleeding from the nose and they have antelope heads and hoofs. This painting contrasts the socially beneficial effects of trance performance with its violent, anti-social possibilities. !Kung medicine men told the researcher Richard Katz that some medicine men in leonine form killed people and that they could be seen only by other medicine men, not by ordinary people. Such a painting therefore probably depicts an ancient trance hallucination.

The third stage of trance hallucination is perhaps the most fascinating. In this advanced stage elements merge with one another and various entities, unseen by those in a normal state of consciousness, are visible. The paintings from this stage show many of the features medicine men claim they can see. Some men, for instance, are painted with long lines emanating from the tops of their heads. Because it is from here that a man's spirit departs on extra-corporeal journeys, these lines can be interpreted as representations of the departing spirit. One curious type of painting shows men in the kneeling posture to which trance dancers sometimes fall; they also have their arms extended behind their backs. This very distinctive posture has been explained by a Kalahari medicine man as a position some trance dancers adopt 'when they are asking God for potency'. Frequently streamer-like lines trail back from their arms and from their backs in a manner which suggests they represent either potency entering the spine or, possibly, sickness being expelled from a place in the nape of the neck.

A further feature of these paintings is that the men often have antelope heads and hoofs: in this stage a medicine man feels himself to be fused with his animal power. Another antelope characteristic of many figures is that they are often covered with hair, but the most diagnostic

Two hallucinatory rain-animals surrounded by phosphenes (geometric forms). Medicine men who controlled the rain entered trance to kill such creatures, thereby causing rain to fall. Some of the oldest dated rock art in southern Africa shows similar geometric forms or grids. These are on portable stones excavated by Francis and Anne Thackeray at a site near Kimberley and have been dated by radiometric means to over 5 000 years before the present. (Drawing: Department of Archaeology, University of the Witwatersrand)

A rock painting of men fleeing from a feline. Evil medicine men went on out-of-body travel in feline form. The bleeding noses, hoofs and hair of the men show they are benevolent medicine men. The painting probably depicts a hallucinatory experience. (Drawing: Department of Archaeology, University of the Witwatersrand)

feature of all is that they frequently bleed from the nose as do many trancers in more realistic paintings of dances. The half-man, half-animal figures in fact depict hallucinatory experiences of the medicine men.

It is of great interest that one such therianthropic creature is among the oldest dated examples of rock art in southern Africa. It is painted on a piece of portable stone excavated by Eric Wendt in the south of Namibia. In the painting human hindlegs have been added to what appears to be a feline. The painted stones from this excavation have been dated to 26 000 years before the present, thus giving southern African rock art an astonishing antiquity comparable with some of the Palaeolithic art of western Europe. We do not know if there was an unbroken tradition between the art of such remote antiquity and that which was being painted in the last century. If, as seems very likely, there was such continuity, we are dealing with the longest known artistic tradition in the world.

The paintings are so subtle and complex that one cannot but wonder at the insensitivity of the early white settlers who treated the San as if they were vermin. The earlier black settlers who moved into Africa south of the Limpopo seem to have held a more balanced view. Though there were no doubt skirmishes, particularly in the earlier decades, the San and the black farmers seem to have settled down to a reasonably amicable coexistence. The clicks in some Bantu languages are evidence for a good deal of intermarriage.

This relationship was destroyed when the depredations of the advancing white settlers annihilated the herds of game and reduced the productivity of the veld. The early traveller Sir John Barrow describes the terrible privations of San groups forced to remain in the mountains throughout the cold winters. The only options open to them were to die of starvation or to steal sheep from the white farmers who had taken possession of the milder plains. When they did steal, the whites exacted terrible revenge. Early reports tell of hundreds of San being hunted down and shot. Some farmers tried to establish pacts with the San but found negotiations difficult in the absence of any chiefs or recognized leaders. For their part, San groups did not consider themselves bound by treaties made with other groups. Some, driven to desperation, entered the employment of white farmers as herders and labourers. All too often, hardship, suffering and degradation were the lot of those who took this way out of their dilemma.

Today the condition of many Kalahari San is not much better. Cattle ranching is extending into their hunting grounds, and they are caught up in the conflict between military powers. There seems to be no alternative: the few who still maintain their ancient way of life will also be forced into the modern world with its poverty and disease. Soon their traditions will be lost and all that will remain will be their matchless artistic achievements on the rocks of southern Africa.

▽ A hallucinatory combination of human and animal characteristics. Scale in inches. (Photo: J D Lewis-Williams)

▽▽ An unshaded polychrome eland painted in great detail. It is superimposed on the legs of a large therianthrope. (Photo: J D Lewis-Williams)

'Xhosa village in the Cape Eastern Province', by Samuel Daniell. (Africana Museum)

The Early History of the Black People in Southern Africa

T Maggs

Controversy still surrounds the question of the first arrival of black, Bantu-speaking people at the southern end of the African continent. However, archaeological evidence has now disproved the old historical notion that Bantu-speaking peoples were still in the process of spreading southwards and westwards in the eighteenth century when they first encountered the expansion of white colonists on the Eastern Cape border. Iron Age people had reached this area more than a thousand years earlier and there was no significant westward movement thereafter. Current evidence indicates that the first Iron Age communities were established in Natal and the Transvaal before AD 300.

The period associated with the blacks, broadly identified with what archaeologists call the Iron Age, covers the time dating from their arrival, the evidence being derived from settlements and other material that remains for us to discover on and under the ground. The term Iron Age not only refers to the fact that these people could make metal objects, unlike their Stone Age predecessors, but has several other important connotations for southern African archaeology. For the first time people were able to live a settled village life, unlike the nomadic hunter-gatherers of the Stone Age, for most of them grew crops and kept herds of livestock. They also made pottery and developed other crafts. Although there is no direct evidence of the languages spoken so long ago, the Iron Age spread to precisely those areas known to have been occupied by historic Bantu-speaking peoples, whose way of life was a continuation from the Iron Age. Therefore it is generally agreed that the spread of the Iron Age marked the spread of this language family throughout much of southern Africa.

The Early Iron Age in South Africa

Did these different phenomena – the Negro people, the languages, the settled village way of life, crops, domestic animals, metalworking and pottery – all arrive together as an already developed 'package', or did they reach South Africa at different times from different origins?

Much controversy still surrounds the attempts by various linguists to reconstruct the development and spread of the Bantu family of languages, for this research can only be based on the present forms of the various languages and dialects, since they were not written down until about a hundred years ago. There is, however, broad agreement that the origin of the

Tim Maggs studied for a BA in History and a Ph D in Archaeology at the University of Cape Town. The latter degree, awarded in 1974, was for research on the Iron Age in the Orange Free State. In 1972 he was appointed head of the Archaeology Department of the Natal Museum in Pietermaritzburg. He has done extensive research on the Iron Age in Natal as well as research on rock art and early shipwrecks. He is Chairman of the KwaZulu Monuments Council and Chairman of the Natal Branch of the South African Archaeological Society.

Detail on one of the Lydenburg heads, the only one with an animal snout (AD 500). (Photo: T Maggs)

37

family as a whole was in the Cameroons region of West Africa.

Iron smelting was first discovered in about 1700 BC in the Middle East. It had reached West Africa by about 500 BC and parts of Central Africa by about this time or a few centuries later. Domestic animals – cattle, fat-tailed sheep and goats – were first tamed in Asia but had reached Egypt and the Sahara by about 5000 BC. The earliest securely dated remains of domestic animals in East Africa are from about 2000 BC and it is very likely that it was from here that they spread to southern Africa. Sheep at least, together with a knowledge of pottery making, had reached the south-western Cape Province about 2 000 years ago, a few centuries before our earliest Iron Age sites, the people responsible being nomadic Khoisan pastoralists with a Stone Age technology. Their pottery is not like that of the Iron Age.

Agriculture more than any other factor led to the settled rather than nomadic lifestyle, for crops tie a community down to a particular place during the growing season and because they have to be processed and stored between harvests. The Iron Age crops included grains (sorghum, bulrush millet and finger millet), legumes (cowpeas and the African groundnut) and members of the pumpkin family (bottle-gourd and various melons and squashes). All of these were originally domesticated in tropical Africa but little is known as to precisely where and when.

Virtually all burials excavated from Iron Age sites have proved to be of Negro physical type, whereas the vast majority of Late Stone Age burials are of Khoisan type. This pattern suggests, for South Africa at least, an arrival of a different population coinciding with the spread of the Iron Age, although further north the picture is less clear.

In parts of Central and East Africa typical Early Iron Age sites dated around 2 000 years ago have been found, while a few may be even older at around 400 BC. Iron smelting and village life were already established and, although plant and animal remains are usually not preserved on these sites, crop production and herding of domestic animals were almost certainly present too. Thus it is to Central and East Africa that we look for the origins of the Early Iron Age in southern Africa, although we still do not know how the 'package' first came together in those regions.

One thing seems certain; the 'package' was such a successful way of life that it gave the Early Iron Age communities great advantage over other people in the vast savannah regions of Africa to which it was so well adapted. Avoiding extreme environments like the equatorial forest and the arid north-east, the Early Iron Age swept southwards, reaching South Africa within a few centuries. Controversy still surrounds the reconstruction of this expansion, for not enough archaeological fieldwork has yet been done to fill in all the necessary details. Some historians, as Jeff Peires explains in the section 'The Emergence of Black Political Communities', prefer the concept of gradual segmentation rather than that of migration, implying rapid movement, to explain the dispersion of Bantu-speaking peoples in southern Africa. However, it is accepted that the first route to South Africa was down the eastern coastal belt, reaching the eastern Transvaal lowveld and the Natal coast before AD 300. Sites of this disper-

Almost all Iron Age burials, like this one from Lindley District in the Orange Free State, are of Negro physical type. (Photo: T Maggs)

sion can be readily recognized by the distinctive pottery they contain.

These pioneering villages certainly practised agriculture, but it is possible that at this early stage they did not yet have livestock and therefore depended on wild animals for their meat requirements. However, from about AD 500 there were many Early Iron Age villages in the Transvaal and Natal which had cattle, sheep and goats. It is possible that there was a second dispersion about this time, via Zimbabwe rather than the east coast. The richly decorated pottery with its multiple bands from sites in Natal and the Transvaal resembled contemporary pottery from Zimbabwe.

The Early Iron Age communities were not moving into uninhabited territory for there were Stone Age peoples, the Khoisan hunter-gatherers and, in some areas to the west, herders as well. The newcomers must have had some influence on the earlier inhabitants but it seems that the different peoples found a means of co-existence, for artefacts typical of the Stone Age peoples are frequently found on Early Iron Age sites.

The map shows that the Early Iron Age people did not spread over the whole of southern Africa but confined themselves to savannah (bushveld) areas. They were also limited to areas of more than about 600 mm of mean annual rain within the summer rainfall region. These areas had sufficient rain for their crops, good grazing for stock and timber for fuel and building. It seems that these requirements limited their expansion on to the open highveld and into the drier western regions, for no sites are known from the highveld of the Transvaal and Orange Free State or from west of the Great Fish River in the Eastern Cape. Further west it is too dry for crops without irrigation, a technological concept unknown to these people. These areas remained in the hands of the Khoisan hunters and herders until the spread of white colonists in the eighteenth and nineteenth centuries.

Developments towards AD 1000

During the Early Iron Age, up to about AD 900 in Natal and much of the Transvaal, there seems to have been relatively little cultural difference between areas. Although some changes took place, such as the development of local pottery styles, the basic culture remained essentially as it had been around AD 500. The relative economic independence of each village settlement suggests that each also had a considerable degree of political independence. It is therefore likely that political organization was on a small scale and that for the most part larger political structures and rivalries were absent or poorly developed.

The first signs of a change from this pattern

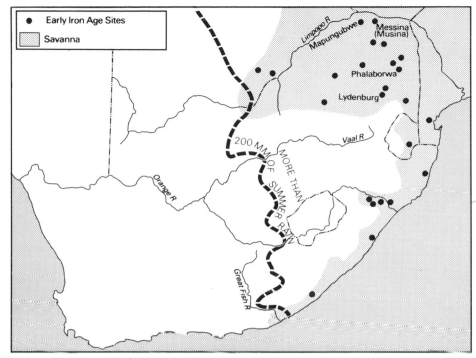

Early Iron Age Sites

towards larger scale political and economic organization comes from about AD 800 in parts of the Limpopo Basin, on sites of the Toutswe ceramic tradition in eastern Botswana and of the related Zhizo tradition in the far northern Transvaal and southern Zimbabwe. Among the Toutswe sites a hierarchy appears, becoming more marked as time goes on. The three very large sites can be regarded as regional centres or even independent capitals. Around each of them and fairly closely concentrated are several second order sites, while numerous third order, small sites are scattered among them and far beyond. The vast accumulations of burnt cattle dung, especially on the largest sites, show the economic importance of livestock. It seems that the accumulation of large herds enabled some individuals or families to obtain political power over much larger areas than had previously been the case. Many of the larger sites were built on naturally defended hilltops, such as Toutswe itself which is surrounded by cliffs with only two easy routes of access. These hilltop locations contrast with the usual Early Iron Age choice of valley bottoms, and suggest a desire for prestige as well as defence.

On the Limpopo in the northern Transvaal sites of the Zhizo tradition, contemporary and related to Toutswe also show signs of political and economic change. Some are large in size and show evidence of large cattle herds, but more important is the evidence of ivory working on some scale, together with numbers of glass beads which were imported, probably from India. They provide the first evidence of long distance trade linking the interior with the Indian Ocean trading system.

Control of such trade would have been a pow-

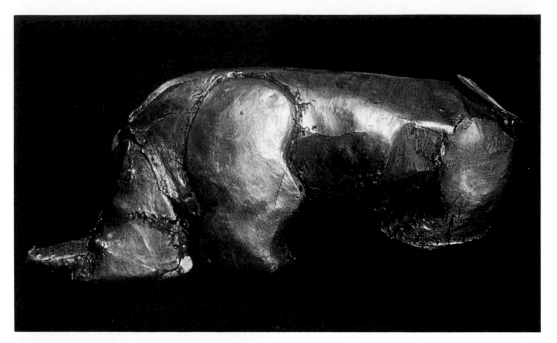

A golden rhinoceros from a grave on Mapungubwe Hill (AD 1200). (Photo: Gold Mine Museum)

A ceramic head, dated to AD 500, found on an Early Iron Age site near Lydenburg, Eastern Transvaal. It is one of seven heads, modelled in clay, fired and decorated, and probably used on ritual occasions, such as initiation ceremonies. These remarkable heads are the oldest surviving Iron Age art south of the equator. The height of this Lydenburg head is 38 cm to the crown, excluding the animal which surmounts it. Fragments from similar sculptures have been found on other Transvaal and Natal Iron Age sites, suggesting that they were a widespread aspect of life in this period. (Photo: SA Museum)

erful economic and political tool. Its effects seem to be visible already in the ninth century Zhizo sites. They become much clearer from about AD 950 at the K2 site, also on the Limpopo, that must have been the political capital of a sizeable state. It is situated in an arid and sometimes tsetse fly infested area, yet was able to support a considerable population, probably of several thousand people. The large numbers of imported glass beads and evidence of extensive ivory working indicate a much larger volume of trade.

In some respects K2 can be seen as a larger scale development from the important Zhizo sites of the same area. In other respects, however, it represents a break from the past, for ceramically it marks the beginning of the Late Iron Age and its pottery styles probably do not derive from Zhizo. The whole question of the transition from the Early to the Late Iron Age is indeed still a controversial one both in terms of what changed and from where the changes originated.

The Great Zimbabwe cultural tradition

Following immediately on from the century of occupation at K2 is the remarkable site of Mapungubwe, a mere kilometre away. Recent work at this site has shown it to be the forerunner of Great Zimbabwe. Modern archaeological and historical research has proved conclusively that the Great Zimbabwe ruins and the cultural tradition found there and on many related sites are an Iron Age tradition associated with Shona people. Archaeological sites of this tradition have been found not only in most parts of Zimbabwe but in neighbouring Botswana and Mozambique as well as the northern Transvaal.

The Great Zimbabwe Tradition can be divided into three periods – the Mapungubwe Phase 1050-1200, Zimbabwe Phase 1250-1450 and Khami Phase 1450 onwards – each phase following on from the previous one. Historical evidence which exists for the later period shows that several Shona dynasties held power at different times and the whole area was not always united under one ruler. Nevertheless the scale of political and economic organization was clearly much greater than during earlier times.

In the northern Transvaal there are several smaller settlements, built partly of stone, which belong to later periods within the Great Zimbabwe Tradition, particularly the Khami Phase. From their size and paucity of remains it seems that these were short-term provincial centres of a state centred north of the Limpopo whose power extended about as far south as the Zoutpansberg range.

The Late Iron Age

Elsewhere in Iron Age South Africa the coming of the Late Iron Age also saw significant changes but apparently most communities remained small in scale with their economies based essentially on subsistence farming. In some areas, such as Natal, there is an abrupt change in pottery style at the same time as a break from the earlier settlement pattern. In other areas, such as the western Transvaal, there may have been more continuity

There is still no generally accepted explanation for this change. Some authors have suggested that there was a major wave of migration. Both northern and southern origins for such a wave have been proposed but both versions have been criticized. At present, therefore, we clearly do not have sufficient information on which to base a convincing explanation. In particular we need to consider possibilities other than migration. For example, the kinds of change noted in the Limpopo basin are likely to have affected neighbouring peoples as well.

One prominent feature of the Late Iron Age is that regional cultural differences became much more prominent than previously. This is true of pottery styles but also architecture, settlement patterns, iron-smelting furnaces, some tools and ornaments. The relatively uniform Early Iron Age pattern of fairly large villages situated in valleys gives way to a variety of regional responses. In many areas there is a move from valley bottoms and riverside situations to the sides of valleys and even to hilltops.

The basic elements of the Iron Age economy, ie the crop plants, domestic animals and metalworking, remain, though changes in organization of the activities connected with them may well have taken place. Indeed a second important feature of this period is that there is increasing evidence of economic specialization, particularly metal production, by some communities. Specialization implies trade, for the producer must exchange his surplus production for other items.

For the last 400 years or so we can build up a richer picture of the Iron Age for, in addition to archaeology, other sources of information are increasingly available. Oral history is most valuable for the later years but has enabled some genealogies to be traced back for several centuries. From 1488, when Bartolomeu Dias rounded the Cape, scraps of information on the local peoples began to be recorded, though this extended to peoples of the interior only during the nineteenth century. Anthropological studies of more recent years provide insight into the lifeways and beliefs of Iron Age communities, but they have the disadvantage of lacking time perspectives and thus tend to see a society as if frozen in one moment of time.

The move to the grasslands

One of the greatest changes that took place during the Late Iron Age was the expansion from the savannah areas – essentially those occupied previously – into many of the open grassland areas of South Africa. The expansion had started by 1300 and by about 1600 vast new areas had been occupied. The grasslands have

Mapungubwe

Mapungubwe is the earliest site to show many of the characteristic features of the Great Zimbabwe Tradition. Like later capitals it has an elite hilltop area and a less rich though still important lower area, the south terrace. Stone walling, though much less prominent than on later sites, performs similar functions in controlling pedestrian movement in the settlement and thereby defining prestige and other areas. Hut structures are more solid than before and some have elaborate verandahs.

The impressive goldwork from graves on the hilltop is unequalled, but the techniques used, including the covering of carved wooden items with gold sheet held in place by gold tacks, continue into later phases. Mapungubwe is indeed the earliest site to produce evidence of goldworking and it seems to be close in time to the beginning of gold mining and exports via the East African coastline. Written records from the Islamic east coast ports indicate that ivory was the most important commodity until the tenth century; thereafter gold from 'the country of Sofala' takes first place. The transition coincides with the change from ivory production at K2 to gold at Mapungubwe, evidence that these centres played an important part in this trade. As imports there are numerous glass beads as well as Chinese ceramics. Mapungubwe can be seen as the capital of a sizeable Shona state whose power was in part derived from control of trade with the Islamic city states of the East African coast. The centralization of power allowed for the establishment of a complex hierarchy within the state which was very different from the simple structure of most Iron Age communities in southern Africa.

Mapungubwe ('Hill of Jackals') is a flat-topped hill west of Messina in the northern Transvaal. It is a natural fortress with almost vertical sides and is approached by a single, narrow cleft. In the 1930s local farmers found dry stone walling, earthenware pots, iron tools, copper wire, glass beads and bangles, gold plating and beaten work, and the skeletal remains of eleven individuals. Recent research has established that it was 200 years older than Great Zimbabwe, but belonged to the same cultural tradition. (Photo: T Maggs)

Circular cattle pen at the centre of an Iron Age homestead of the eighteenth century near Bergville, Natal, as seen from the air. (Photo: D Noli)

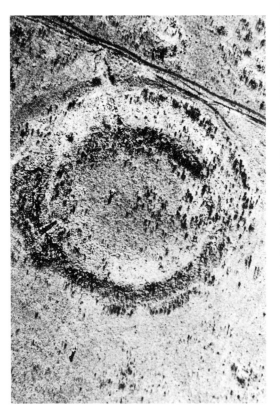

more acid soil and grazing, so modification may have been needed to methods of crop production and herd management. In addition the open, essentially treeless environment necessitated changes to cope with the lack of wood for fuel and building. Stone was commonly adopted as a building material and today thousands of stone-built settlements can still be seen, particularly from the air. Many are so well preserved that they can be mapped in great detail, unlike most savannah settlements which have largely disappeared because they were built of wood and clay. While there is much regional variation in settlement styles, Iron Age villages were made up of the same basic structures – circular pens for livestock and circular huts. There were often additional walls forming courtyards or enclosing the whole homestead.

Largest of all are the settlements of the western Transvaal and north-western Orange Free State. These are veritable towns sometimes several kilometres in extent. Some can be identified as the capitals of Tswana people such as the Rolong and Hurutshe as recently as 1800, while others are much older. They contain features common to the historic Tswana peoples such as rondavel-type huts with verandahs and sometimes even sliding doors.

Related archaeological sites can be traced back to 1300 near Rustenburg in the western Transvaal on the edge of the savannah. It is to this area, the Magaliesberg (named after Mogale, an early ruler of the Kwena people), that many Sotho-Tswana royal lineages trace their origins.

Moving further east on the highveld of the Transvaal and Orange Free State there is a gradual change towards smaller and less concentrated settlements. The separate homesteads of different family groups are easily identifiable. In the Orange Free State the earliest settlements date from about 1400. By 1600 they cover the eastern half of the province and they are so numerous that there must have been quite high population densities. There are changes through time in both settlements and pottery styles, the later sites being linked with historic Sotho peoples such as the Fokeng, Kwena and Taung. The huts are hemispherical in shape and made of reeds and clay or sometimes entirely of stone with corbelled roofs.

Along the escarpment of the eastern Transvaal in the Carolina-Lydenburg area the settlements are remarkable for their extensive terracing. Homesteads are often scattered within terraced areas and linked to one another and the open veld by tracks consisting of two parallel walls. These were evidently built to lead livestock to and from the pastures through the terraces where crops were grown. Many of these sites are in the relatively humid mist belt and as they date to the last few centuries it is possible that the system of terrace agriculture was developed for the American grain, maize, which would be more suited to these conditions than the African grains. Maize was already a staple in the grassland interior of Natal by the eighteenth century, probably as a result of trade contacts at Delagoa Bay. It could also have spread to the eastern Transvaal by this time or a little earlier.

Below the Drakensberg escarpment in Natal, Transkei and the Eastern Cape a similar expansion into grassland areas took place. The earliest evidence of this is from the thirteenth century in Natal when the move may still have been small in scale. By the later centuries, however, a dense population had built up in much of the region between the Drakensberg escarpment and the coast.

From as early as AD 1000 in this region settlements were much smaller than during the Early Iron Age. In the grasslands, apart from a few large defended hilltops, most of the later sites consisted of only a few rather dispersed homesteads. There was less use of stone than on the highveld, the central cattle pen being the only structure commonly built of stone. Around it was a ring of huts placed in the open ground. Apart from the building materials used, there were some differences in settlement patterns between grassland and savannah areas of Natal. For example the grassland stockpens opened uphill and had cobbled entrances while in the savannah they opened downhill and often contained grain storage pits. However, the pattern of relatively dispersed homesteads, each built around a single stockpen, is clearly related to that of the historic Nguni-speaking peoples, a link which is confirmed by ceramic styles and other cultural items.

'Boy blowing the bellows', by E Casalis. The Sotho were extremely skilled craftsmen who mined and smelted iron, copper and tin. Evidence suggests that the ancestors of the Sotho were the chief miners of iron and copper in the Transvaal, and oral tradition credits the founding lineage with the art of smelting. The Rolong have a ritual in which they dance in honour of a hammer and of iron, indicating that iron smelting was a major resource at some stage in the past. The art of smelting was practised at Phalaborwa from the eighth century and at the Melville Koppies on the Witwatersrand from the eleventh century, and there is a close correlation between areas of early Sotho occupation and areas where iron ore was plentiful. (Africana Museum)

Survivors of Portuguese shipwrecks from 1552 onwards described similar settlements near the coast of Natal and Transkei. It is possible from their reports to identify Nguni-speaking peoples in the Transkei and Natal with apparently Tsonga peoples from around Richards Bay to Delagoa Bay where Portuguese ships were already calling regularly to trade. The Nguni-speaking groups were organized in relatively small chiefdoms, some of only a few villages. The shipwreck survivors described well-populated areas rich in livestock and agricultural produce, though some areas, particularly towards the south, were poor and had few inhabitants.

An important interaction between grassland and savannah communities was trade, particularly in metal goods which could not be produced in the grasslands for lack of trees to provide the necessary charcoal fuel. In some of the river valleys of Natal and parts of the Transvaal lowlands, whole communities became economically dependent to a considerable degree on mining and metal production.

High quality steel products included hoes for cultivation, and blades for spears, knives, axes and razors. Softer iron was used mainly for ornaments including bangles and beads. Suitable iron ores are fairly widespread and there is evidence of smelting in many savannah areas. Regional techniques of metalworking developed as reflected in different artefact styles and furnace types, like the sub-triangular furnaces of the north-eastern Transvaal and the double ones of Natal.

As in the Early Iron Age, limits to the expansion into the drier western half of the country were set by rainfall. West of about the 200 mm summer rainfall line, as shown on the map, summer rainfall is too uncertain for communities dependent on crop production.

This provided a natural, ecological boundary between the Iron Age communities to the east and Khoisan hunter-gatherers and herders to the west. There was considerable interaction between the Iron and Stone Age communities across this invisible frontier, until it was finally swept away by the advance of white colonists from the Cape in the late eighteenth and early nineteenth centuries. Iron Age groups made use of the lands to the west for such activities as hunting expeditions and seasonal grazing for their flocks and herds. Individuals and small groups among the Khoisan often served as clients, hunting and herding for a particular Iron Age community in exchange for such things as food, tobacco and iron implements.

It was perhaps this to-and-fro movement across the natural frontier that misled some of the early white observers into thinking that the Bantu-speakers were still in the process of expanding southwards and westwards in the eighteenth century. However, the archaeological evidence has now shown that Iron Age people had reached the eastern Cape Province a thousand years earlier.

A group of Xhosa journeying to a new destination, by Ludwig Alberti. (Africana Museum)

The Emergence of Black Political Communities

J Peires

Jeffrey Brian Peires was born in Cape Town and educated at the University of Cape Town and the University of Wisconsin. His main research interest is the history of the Xhosa people, particularly their oral traditions. His first book on Xhosa history was *The House of Phalo* (Ravan Press, 1981), and his next is entitled *Nongqawuse and the Great Cattle-killing Movement among the Xhosa*. Dr Peires is currently Senior Lecturer in History at Rhodes University, Grahamstown.

It was generally believed for many years that the behaviour of African peoples was governed by the dictates of customs and traditions which had existed since time immemorial, that they had no real history to speak of beyond a meaningless series of faction fights and petty succession disputes, and that their past was so like their present that it could be safely left to the anthropologists. Recently, however, historians have recognized that the African emphasis on custom and tradition was a natural recourse of people who lacked the means to record their political and legal codes on paper. It did not prevent innovation, but changed itself according to changing circumstances.

The archaeological record has demonstrated that the Bantu-speaking peoples of southern Africa did not lead careless, unthinkingly repetitive lives, but fully exploited the possibilities of their natural environments and responded creatively and sensitively to the pressures and opportunities that these provided. Similarly, when the emergence of political communities among the Iron Age peoples is considered, a picture of dynamism and change is presented.

Historical perspective reveals two distinct and contradictory processes which shaped the early history of Iron Age southern Africa, namely segmentation and differentiation.

Segmentation

Segmentation is the name given to the process whereby a group subdivided into two or more groups. It occurred in a domestic unit when the sons of a household grew up and left to establish their own households elsewhere. Scarcity of natural resources led to dispersed settlements, linked by ties of kinship and sentiment to the parent household. Segmentation of this sort was

thus a continuous natural process, a consequence of the eternal human cycle of reproduction and maturation.

The population movements which took place in southern Africa over many hundreds of years were usually described in old-style histories as 'Bantu migrations', and were depicted by thick arrows on maps indicating the alleged lines of march. Migration in the sense of deliberately motivated change of location did of course occur, but it cannot be accepted as a suitable description of the process whereby most of southern Africa became populated by people speaking related Bantu languages. Migration implies rapid movement, whereas archaeological evidence shows that the dispersion of Bantu-speaking peoples within southern Africa occurred over a period of centuries. It also implies nomadism and rootless wandering, which is contrary to the deep attachment felt by Iron Age black peoples for their home places. Finally, migration implies exclusive occupation of a single place by a defined group of people, whereas in southern Africa the dispersion of some peoples did not necessarily imply the ejection of others.

Segmentation, leading to gradual settlement, was a difficult business, which no individual household could undertake on its own. There would be bush to clear, ground to break up and, most probably, enemies to face. The nuclei of most pioneering groups were the age-sets which formed as young men prepared to be initiated in the circumcision lodge. Among the Sotho, Tswana and Xhosa circumcision age-sets grouped around their young chief were the chief agents of segmentation. Among the northern Nguni they were the forerunners of the famous Zulu age-regiments. Both the Sotho and the Nguni use the same word for both 'age-set' and 'age-regiment'.

Segmenting groups did not force other people out. The process of incorporation went hand in hand with segmentation, and although competition for water and pasturage often led to raiding and armed conflict, trade, intermarriage, military alliance and mutual aid during drought and famine occurred more frequently. The possession of desired prestige goods, such as cattle, was often a more effective means of domination than superior weaponry. The anthropologist Monica Wilson has pointed out that incoming lineages, or family groups, who were rich in cattle, could marry more wives than cattle-poor hosts, and might thus come to outnumber them after the passage of a few generations. The Xhosa frequently absorbed weaker groups, such as their Khoi neighbours, and amongst the Sotho-Tswana the weaker group sometimes lost its identity altogether and adopted the name of the stronger.

Differentiation

Differentiation is the name given to the process whereby certain individuals came to secure political, social and economic power over others. At least three distinct social categories can be discerned among southern African peoples: chiefs, commoners and clients. These divisions must have arisen as a result of specific historical processes, but because oral traditions are usually associated with chiefs and rulers, it is often not possible to trace the evolution of social differentiation within a particular society. An examination of the social, religious and economic nature of kinship, however, helps to explain how the different social categories arose.

The basic social and economic unit in almost all southern African societies is that of the homestead. Except in a few exceptional cases, such as advanced senility, the head of the homestead was the eldest male. He enjoyed a position of considerable power, including authority in the spheres of religion, economy and social relations. His authority was derived from his genealogical seniority, and the status of the other males in the homestead likewise depended on their genealogical rank. Women, like children, had rights and obligations, but were regarded as perpetual minors and were excluded from a formal voice in homestead affairs.

The bonds of kinship extended to all other related homesteads, and closely related adult males formed a lineage. Most people lost track of their lineage after the seventh or eighth generation, but they recognized as their relatives anyone who shared a common family name, a common set of praises and (among the Sotho-Tswana) a common totemic animal. A group of people who assumed a common relationship regarded themselves as members of the same clan,

'Fingo village, Fort Beaufort', by Thomas Baines. This early-morning scene at a Mfengu kraal is amusingly described by Baines as follows:
'. . .The majority (of the inmates) came out as they had slept, dragging their sole covering behind them, and arranging it in decent folds as soon as they had room to stand upright. . . a female orator delivered a long and energetic harangue. . . to the individuals of the softer sex, who, on its conclusion, departed to fetch wood and water, while. . . their lords and masters . . . carefully disposed their limbs so as to enjoy with the least possible inconvenience to themselves the luxury of the warm sun and their tobacco pipes. An (aged) female. . . sat at the door of one of the huts with a dish of grease beside her, rubbing a bullock's hide with a large stone to render it sufficiently pliant for an article of dress. . .' (Africana Museum)

'Kaffrarian family travelling', by Samuel Daniell. The travellers depicted are Xhosa, identifiable by the crane feathers worn by the men and the long-shafted throwing spears and oval shields which they carry. Pack-oxen were used to transport passengers, milk-sacks and heavy baggage. (Africana Museum)

lieved in a High God, who created the world and meant men to be happy and live in plenty, men looked to their ancestors for aid and protection against various evil and supernatural forces. The power of the head of the lineage or clan, accepted as the senior son of the senior lineage, and thus the living being most closely related to the semi-mythical founder of the clan, was immeasurably enhanced by his closeness to the ancestors. This conferred on him the right to address them through the medium of sacrificial offerings, and thus the bonds of kinship transcended even death itself.

The economic dominance of the homestead head arose out of his role as a bridge between the dead and living generations. He had inherited, through his father, the accumulated wealth of his forebears, which he, in turn, would bequeath to his sons. He had the right to distribute the labour tasks among the members of his homestead, and to allocate the use of fields and cattle as he saw fit. Thus continuous economic links were established through him across the generations.

The extent of the power in the hands of the lineage and homestead heads was the core of the institution of chieftainship, which dated so far back that it would be futile to speculate when it was introduced. The kinship organization of society clearly contained within it the seeds of hierarchy and domination, and a chief simply replicated the functions of the homestead head on a larger scale. Most southern African peoples explain the exalted position of their chiefs by claiming that they are descended from the first founder of their clan, although the situation is

although they were not all truly related by blood. Refugees, faithful retainers, wives' relatives, in fact any stranger who had settled down amongst them, might be invited to join the host clan, a process in keeping with the tendency of incorporation. Sometimes a clan would recognize a single individual as its head. Among some southern African peoples, clan-headship carried with it the prerogatives of full chiefly power, while among others it was significant only in the sphere of ritual and religion.

Although almost all southern Africans be-

'Tambookies after circumcision', by Thomas Baines. Like the Xhosa and Mpondomise, the Thembu continued to practise circumcision ceremonies after they had been discontinued by the northern Nguni in the late eighteenth century. Baines recorded his meeting with them as follows: '. . . we were met by the whole company. . . six to eight in number and from twelve to sixteen years, dressed in karosses of whitened sheepskin, their eyebrows marked with charcoal and their lips almost red by contrast with the ghastly greyish ash colour imparted to their skins by the thick coating of clay. . .' (Africana Museum)

somewhat more complex owing to the division and amalgamation of groups through segmentation and incorporation. It was most probably a combination of the need for territorial authority with a kinship organization rooted in ancestor veneration which produced the institution of territorial chieftainship common throughout Bantu-speaking southern Africa.

Chieftainship was a system of hereditary devolution of power in which the right to rule was believed to be transmitted through the blood. It divided African society into two classes: chiefs of the blood destined to govern, and commoners, men of ordinary birth, who could not aspire to formal authority whatever their personal qualities. Chiefs were, in general, much richer than commoners. They had the right to levy tributes and could command the labour of their subjects for work on royal buildings and lands. They could demand hospitality for themselves and their entourage from any homestead head, not stopping short of his daughters. Chiefly control of the judicial apparatus enabled them to confiscate the cattle of rich commoners through the manipulation of witchcraft accusations and inheritance laws.

Why did the commoners not revolt against such tyranny? Firstly, people believed that they required a powerful authority figure to adjudicate their lawsuits, invoke the spirits of their ancestors, protect them from their enemies and shoulder the heavy responsibility of providing food in time of famine. They did not expect such men to be friendly, soft-hearted fellows; on the contrary, they liked men with the cunning, magic and majesty to overcome their foes

and bend the universe to their will. The chiefs were careful, on their part, to cultivate the dual image of being mighty and terrible, and yet at the same time the fathers of their people and the defenders of their hearths and herds.

Secondly, chiefly families were no more immune than others to the segmentary pressures of brotherly rivalry. If anything, the pressures were greater because the rewards were greater. Laws of succession were heeded more in the breach than in the observance, and, in succession wars brother chief fought brother chief, while mothers and uncles intrigued on behalf of their candidates. Most conflicts were bloodless, and were amicably resolved by the loser going off to seek his fortune in a new place. Commoners were able to benefit from the segmentation of chiefly families, since before the advent of the firearm the prime determinant of the strength of a chief was the number of his followers. Before 1800 no southern African chief possessed a standing army, and he depended on the voluntary compliance of his subjects to execute his orders. Any chief, whether great or lowly, needed to keep his followers contented. Wise chiefs consulted their people formally, as with the *pitso* (general assembly) among the Sotho-Tswana, or informally, and modified their actions according to the prevailing mood. Commoners could even play off one chief against another and secure the best deal for themselves. However, if the chiefly class could sink its differences and subordinate its private interests to a strong centralized monarchy, the commoners would no longer have any basis for manipulation. This is what happened in Zululand in the time of Shaka.

Clientage was the system whereby a poor man contracted to work for a chief or a rich man in return for payment in kind. It involved varying degrees of labour exploitation, ranging from a voluntary and temporary status to a form of permanent servitude little short of slavery. Clientage in its mildest form was virtually universal in southern Africa. A man in need of cattle would approach a rich man and ask for cattle on loan. As a client, his chief duty was to care for the cattle he was allotted, and in return he could use their milk and could keep some of their calves. A man ceased to be a client as soon as he returned the cattle he had borrowed.

A more onerous form of clientage usually occurred in the wake of mass dispossession or migration. Chiefs welcomed strangers who were rich in cattle, but hesitated when confronted with a large group of empty-handed foreigners. When such mendicant groups practised different customs, clientage relationships often acquired an ethnic tinge. The case of the Mfengu refugees in the Eastern Cape, though taken from the nineteenth century, serves to illustrate this point. They were scattered among the Xhosa as herdsmen, but their Xhosa masters treated them as servants rather than as clients.

Early trade

Reference to Africans as subsistence farmers creates the impression that they had few commercial interests beyond the mealie patch and the cattle kraal. Yet there is abundant evidence of precolonial trade routes spanning the subcontinent. The driving forces were the unequal distribution of minerals in southern Africa and the desire for cattle among the metal-working peoples. A demand for tobacco and dagga amongst the non-agricultural Khoisan also led to a vigorous exchange of goods.

The Hurutshe and Kwena of the Rustenburg-Marico district mined iron and copper, which passed via the 'Briqua' or 'goat-people' (the Tlhaping and Fokeng of the southern highveld) to the Khoi of the Orange River and Great Karoo, and thence to the metal-hungry Xhosa and Thembu of the Eastern Cape. From the northeast the iron and copper miners of Musina (Messina), Venda and Phalaborwa served the eastern Transvaal and trans-Limpopo region. The principal carriers of this trade were the Lemba and Tsonga of Delagoa Bay.

On the Orange River, the exchange rates between metal and cattle were as follows: a heifer was worth eight spears, an axe, an awl, a small bag of tobacco and a small bag of dagga. An ox or a bull was worth only five spears, 'plus all the other things as for a heifer'.

'Bechuana ivory carrier and young girl carrying milk', by Thomas Baines. Ivory was a trade item only, and not a means of subsistence, as were cattle. The depletion of elephant herds therefore did not affect the black communities as directly as the depletion of cattle herds did. (Africana Museum)

47

Nevertheless, the Mfengu were never assigned a subordinate status as an ethnic group. Once established with his own cattle in his own homestead, the Mfengu was fully the equal of any Xhosa homestead head, equal before the law and free to intermarry on an equal basis. In such cases clientship was a transitional stage on the road to full membership of the host society.

The most extreme form of labour exploitation was the *botlhanka* system found among the Tswana. *Botlhanka* clients were usually young children, captured in war, whose parents had failed to pay the required ransom. The status was permanent and hereditary. A *motlhanka* was inherited along with the rest of his master's goods. He was denied political rights or access to the courts, and could not acquire any property of his own. This harsh system may be attributed to the harshness of the Tswana environment, which hindered free movement of peoples and required more male labour than was usually available on a voluntary basis.

Patterns of regional development

Historically minded people tend to be interested in the question of origins. Where did the Bantu-speaking peoples of southern Africa come from? Where exactly did they cross the Limpopo? At which point did the 'Sotho' of the inland plateau branch off from the 'Nguni' of the coastal belt? Such problems fascinated the older generation of historians. G M Theal and G W Stow believed that southern Africa was peopled by successive waves of immigrants coming down from East Africa. Later writers, such as A T Bryant, thought that the earlier migrations of peoples could be deduced by plotting their geographic locations at a later date. Such retrospective reconstructions are no longer acceptable. It is misleading to associate a particular aspect of culture with a particular ethnic group because all people are constantly lending and borrowing ideas, institutions and even linguistic traits. Moreover, the older generation of historians was mistaken in assuming the rapid migrations of distinct ethnic groups, instead of the slow spread of segmenting lineages incorporating and acculturating other lineages.

A cultural map of southern Africa at the beginning of the nineteenth century appears pleasantly simple. The Nguni were settled on the coast and the Sotho-Tswana on the inland plateau. The Venda of the Zoutpansberg arrived later from somewhere north of the Limpopo, and the Tsonga arrived from Delagoa Bay. However, this apparent cultural uniformity disguises complex cultural substrata. Sotho-Tswana domination of the plateau was in fact

'Bechuana huts', by Charles Davison Bell. This painting of a mid-nineteenth century Tswana dwelling depicts a typical rondavel, introduced by the Tswana, Pedi and Venda. (Africana Museum)

'The Bechuana picho', by C J Andersson. The *pitso* or general assembly of the Sotho-Tswana people was usually held in a semi-circular enclosure of timber (the *kgotla*) as depicted in this wood-engraving. (Africana Museum)

preceded by prior Nguni occupation, of which the Transvaal Ndebele were an important remnant. The Shona-related culture of the Venda was not a foreign import from the north, as the archaeological sites at Mapungubwe and Bambandyanalo testify. The later history of the Nguni shows that they were capable of absorbing Sotho ethnic groups, and the Tsonga were influenced by Shona and Sotho cultures long before they left Delagoa Bay. Underlying all these later cultures were the aboriginal inhabitants of southern Africa, some of them Khoisan and others a mysterious Stone Age Negroid people known in oral tradition as the Ngona. In the light of this ethnic diversity, the search for the trail of the 'pure' Sotho and the 'pure' Nguni becomes somewhat ridiculous. A more acceptable way is the adoption of a regional rather than an ethnic focus, moving from area to area rather than from group to group.

The inland plateau

The Sotho-Tswana chiefdoms of the inland plateau were the products of a complex interaction between intrusive segmenting lineages and resident local groups. Oral tradition credits the Ngona and Kheoka, Stone Age Negroid peoples, with the first habitation of the plateau. Another mysterious group is the still extant Kgalagadi, said to be archaic survivors of the very earliest Sotho. Substantial Khoisan populations also lived on the plateau, stretching from the Caledon River valley to modern Botswana. The eastern parts of the plateau were initially settled by Nguni groups which eventually became Sotho-ised, with the exception of the Transvaal Ndebele who clung to their Nguni speech and blended elements of Nguni and Sotho culture.

These earlier populations were eventually absorbed by the greater chiefdoms which were formed as a result of the intrusion of segmenting lineages from the western Transvaal. Most of the ruling Sotho-Tswana lineages originate from this 'greater Magaliesberg' area, which was home to the Fokeng, Hurutshe, Kgatla, Kwena and Rolong clans, who slowly dispersed across the plateau. The Fokeng are regarded by most oral historians as the most senior of the Sotho-speaking peoples. They reached their zenith in the early eighteenth century under Sekete IV, against whom other Sotho chiefs conspired. After his death, the Fokeng scattered over the region, and were succeeded by the Hurutshe, reputedly the ancestral stock of at least five other important chiefly lineages, two of which were the Kgatla and Kwena clans. The Kgatla subdivided into the Tlokwa, the Pedi and the Taung. Some descendants of the Kwena went north to found the Ngwaketse and Ngwato chiefdoms of modern Botswana, and others headed south and subdivided at Ntsuanatsati hill (between the present Frankfort and Vrede in the Orange Free State) around 1500 to produce a number of lineages, including that of Moshoeshoe.

A third major lineage cluster, the Rolong, settled along the Harts River, and their near relations and occasional subordinates, the Tlhaping, settled around Kuruman on the road to the north, where missionaries and travellers made them the best described of all the Tswana peoples. Other Sotho groups include the Phalaborwa, Narene, Thabina, Kxaxa, Birwa and Roka.

Little is known about the specific events which led to the segmentation of the various lineages. Several remember splitting as a result of quarrels over women. Napo, the progenitor of the southern Sotho, left his elder brother because he was 'unwilling to live like a reed overshadowed by a tree'. Nor is much known about the manner in which the original inhabitants were absorbed into the larger chiefdoms, but evidence suggests that as a result of loss of cattle through drought or disease, some groups became willing clients and were eventually swallowed up by the hosts without any fighting.

Settlement patterns among the Sotho-Tswana

The uncertainty of rainfall on the high-veld and the uneven distribution of soils and grasses meant that a community required control over the extensive area to ensure adequate access to natural resources. These environmental factors led to the Sotho-Tswana settlement pattern tending towards large residential towns situated in the midst of communal pasturage, interspersed with individually worked agricultural lands. Some Tswana towns contained as many as 15 000 people, and were not built around a single centre, but consisted of a number of self-contained villages or 'wards'. The Tlhaping capital of Dikathong had as many as thirty wards. A typical Tswana town might consist of a majority of wards headed by the ruling chief and his uncles, brothers and sons, together with wards headed by refugee chiefs and old lineages who had inhabited the country before the arrival of the royals. The history of a Tswana town might almost be read from a list of the origins of its ward heads.

The most important right of a Tswana chief was his power to decide who might live in his territory and where they might be allocated land. He presided over the town courts and collected most of his income from judicial fines. He had the right to call out the age-sets for war or organized cattle raiding. However, the power of the chief was limited by the fact that his control over military and economic manpower was indirect and depended on the co-operation of the ward heads. This was the main reason for the markedly democratic character of Sotho-Tswana politics, exemplified in the *pitso*, or public meeting, of all household heads, which was convened to ratify any major decision affecting the town as a whole.

The Distribution of the Highveld Peoples about 1820

'Inanda Kraal, Natal', by G F Angas. The framework of these beehive-shaped huts of the Natal Nguni consisted of two series of semi-circular arches, intersecting at right angles, a method of construction still used today. The frame was covered by thatching grass secured by thick horizontal grass ropes encircling the hut, crossed by vertical ropes stretching from base to apex and knotted together at intersections. Upright posts inside the hut helped to support the roof. (Africana Museum)

The coastal region

The peoples of the coastal region of southern Africa between the escarpment and the sea are conventionally referred to as the Nguni. The Nguni peoples were not a united political body, but rather a vast number of small-scale communities, each enjoying political and economic autonomy. The rich environmental endowment of the coastal belt contained the sort of combination of natural resources required for mixed pastoralism and agriculture and this permitted a dispersed pattern of settlement. There were no big towns or large villages – even the chief's 'Great Place' rarely comprised more than fifty beehive-shaped dwellings of poles and thatch.

This does not mean that the early Nguni led lonely, isolated lives. The exogamy rule (marriage outside the kinship group) meant that most homestead heads were related to a wide circle of affines (relations by marriage) through their sons and daughters. The Nguni recognized chiefs, and there were few adult males who were not constantly visiting their chiefs on some matter concerned with politics, law, religion or the loaning of cattle. Contacts between chiefs and commoners were, however, limited to specific occasions, and chiefs could not disturb the domestic arrangements of the homestead head without risking the latter's desertion to some rival chief.

How did these autonomous, small-scale communities become the great Zulu, Swazi, Mpondo, Thembu and Xhosa nations of today? These nations did not exist at the dawn of Nguni history, nor are they the products of inherent cultural differences. There was no river or other solid dividing line demarcating the Zulu cultural area from the Xhosa cultural area, and the different local dialects and practices merged imperceptibly into each other, appearing as major cultural differences at only the opposite ends of the Nguni zone.

For reasons which remain unclear, certain southern Nguni clans began to expand their power some time before 1600 and subjected and incorporated neighbouring clans. The best known case is that of Tshawe who founded the Xhosa kingdom by defeating the Cirha and Jwarha clans in battle. After this initial victory had established the royalty of the Tshawe line, his descendants expanded the kingdom further by sending out each succeeding generation of young chiefs to settle new territory and bring new clans under their control. East of the Kei River, the Hala, Nyawuza and Majola clans carved out the Thembu, Mpondo and Mpondomise kingdoms respectively.

Large-scale political units in the southern Nguni area thus predated such units in the northern Nguni area by at least 150 years. However the southern Nguni kingdoms were never able to solve the problem of segmentation. They were the products of the dispersion of their royal clans, but were never able to discipline their junior chiefs or check rivalries within the royal lineage. Thus the southern Nguni kingdoms were extensive but weak, and their kings had no power, prerogatives or control of subject life and labour. It remained for the Shakan state of the nineteenth century to overcome the problem of segmentation and create a truly hierarchical state in which the principle of differentiation would be carried through to its logical conclusion.

The north-east

It was believed until very recently that the Venda nation was Shona in origin, and that it was led by the Singo clan which crossed the Limpopo at the turn of the eighteenth century. Lately, research has shown that the nucleus of a distinctive group possessing specifically Venda characteristics with regard to religion, language and social organization existed long before the Singo invasions, which occurred no earlier than 1730. These early proto-Venda were organized in the state of Thovela, which was made up of a number of ethnic components, including the Stone Age Ngona and various pre-Singo Shona groups. They built in stone, mined gold, copper and tin and hunted for ivory. They traded with the Lemba, scattered descendants of the Muslim traders who ranged between the East African states and the Zimbabwean plateau.

The Singo were a division of the Changamire Rozvi of Zimbabwe, who crossed the Limpopo through the Nzhelele valley, a natural gateway through the Zoutpansberg. Their chief, Thohoya-Ndou (Head of the Elephant), named his capital city Dzata after the ancestral home of the Singo north of the Limpopo. He was the greatest ruler in Venda history, but tradition relates that one day, piqued by the jealousy of his brothers, he simply disappeared, and the Venda state broke up into sections. The segmentary principle had triumphed once again.

Shona influence is also clearly visible among the Sotho-based Lobedu, north of Tzaneen. Their kingdom is said to have been founded by Dzugudini, the daughter of a Shona chief who fled with her illegitimate son to escape the anger of her father. However, there may well have been a Lobedu state in the making even before the arrival of Dzugudini. The curious social structure of the Lobedu derives from the chaos and jealousies which marked the reign of King Mugodo 'the Outcast' and eventually led to him being replaced by his daughter Mujaji (the legendary 'rain-queen'). Ever since, the Lobedu have been ruled by a queen, whose power depended partly on her role in the rain cult, and partly on a complex system of wife-exchanges.

Comparatively little is known about the history of the Tsonga, the most numerous of the peoples in the north-east. They seem to have come from Delagoa Bay and their traditions reveal the familiar theme of diverse origins, including Sotho and Shona influences. The Portuguese recorded the presence of large states among the Rjonga Tsonga in Mozambique as early as the sixteenth century, the most important of which was the kingdom of Tembe. The Tsonga were traders, who sailed their canoes as far as 500 km up the Limpopo and Nkomati rivers, and traded gold, ivory, iron, copper, rhinoceros horn, furs, amber, cloth and beads among the Venda, Phalaborwa, Sotho and Portuguese.

The power of the chiefs increases

From about the middle of the eighteenth century, events in southern Africa developed in such a way as to strengthen the hand of the chiefs. Overpopulation made prime ecological locations harder to find. Competition for resources became sharper, and commoners more willing to subject themselves to those chiefs best able to guarantee their subsistence. Furthermore, the new products traded at Delagoa Bay after 1750 furnished the chiefs with new means of patronage and new incentives to expand their territory.

For various reasons, which will be discussed in Chapter 9, these pressures were particularly acute in what is today northern Natal, leading ultimately to the rise of the Zulu kingdom under Shaka and a period of dispersion known as the *Difaqane* or *Mfecane*.

Suggested Reading List

ORIGIN OF KHOISAN

H C Bredekamp (1982) *Van Veeverskaffers tot Veewagters*, Bellville

R Elphick (1985) *Khoikhoi and the Founding of White South Africa*, Johannesburg

R B Lee (1979) *The !Kung San: Men, Women and Work in Foraging Society*, Cambridge

THE SAN

R B Lee and I De Vore (eds) (1976) *Kalahari Hunter-gatherers*, Cambridge

J D Lewis-Williams (1981) *Believing and Seeing*, London

J D Lewis-Williams (1983) *The Rock Art of Southern Africa*, Cambridge

L Marshall (1976) *The !Kung of Nyae Nyae*, Cambridge, Mass.

P V Tobias (1979) *The Bushmen*, Cape Town

P Vinnicombe (1976) *People of the Eland*, Pietermaritzburg

EARLY HISTORY OF THE BLACK PEOPLE

R R Inskeep (1978) *The Peopling of Southern Africa*, Cape Town

T Maggs (1976) *Iron Age Communities of the Southern Highveld*, Occasional Publications of the Natal Museum, 2

EMERGENCE OF BLACK POLITICAL COMMUNITIES

A T Bryant (1929) *Olden Times in Zululand and Natal*, London

D F Ellenberger and C J Macgregor (1912) *History of the Basutos*, London

J B Peires (1981) *The House of Phalo – A History of the Xhosa People in the Days of Their Independence*, Johannesburg

I Schapera (1953) *The Tswana*, Ethnographic Survey of Africa: Southern Africa, III, London

N J van Warmelo (ed) (1940) *The Copper Miners of Musina and the Early History of the Zoutpansberg*, Pretoria

The copper miners of Musina

The following Sotho text by M F Mamedi was collected by N J Warmelo in the 1930s. It relates the story of how a Tsonga group came to mine copper at Musina.

The Musina people appeared from the east and came to Phalaborwa. . . Then they said, 'Young men, scatter and seek for a place where copper may be found. . .' Then Nkopetsekwa's people found it at Great Musina; they went on and made another mine at Mpedi, after that they made another mine at Small Mpedi, another hill.

The Musina people brought with them hammers and crowbars and bellows. The crowbar was for digging, and was made of a piece of iron inserted into the end of a heavy stick. The bellows were made of a cow hide or the skin of an antelope. They also plaited very long cords of leather which would not break. Then they made a big basket, tied the cords to it, and, getting into it, the sons of Musina went down the shaft. There they mined the copper, by the light of candles made from the leaves of the mokxote tree. . . At that time there was neither girl nor youth nor man nor woman that stayed at home. The girls gathered the leaves of the mephane trees to make the fires with when drawing wire.

When they were mining the copper, they brought the ore to the surface in the skins of impala, buffalo or gnu. They brought the copper out in the form of stones or dust. The stones they then broke up with hammers and put into winnowing baskets. They winnowed this and eliminated the dust, so that only the copper remained, which they put into crucibles and heated up. . .

After the division had been made, each might sell his share. . . but the cattle they did not keep, they slaughtered the animals for the young men who did the hard work and ate meat every day.

51

The arrival of the Dutch East Indiaman
Noordt Nieuwlandt in Table Bay on 21
August 1762. (William Fehr Collection)

Part II

The Cape from 1488 to 1854: The Shaping of a New Society

By the fifteenth century Khoisan and Bantu-speaking people had established settlements in many parts of South Africa. Although these groups were of common origin, thousands of years of separation had led to diverse cultures, languages and modes of subsistence developing. Economic interaction had brought them into contiguity again, and a heterogeneous South African community had been formed. The European thrust, which began at the Cape and progressed into the interior, was destined to alter the shape of South African society drastically over the next 400 years.

The Portuguese circumnavigated the African continent first, but it was the Dutch who inaugurated a European presence at the Cape. The commercial motives and monopolistic nature of the Dutch East India Company decisively influenced all aspects of Cape society until 1795. The introduction of slave labour in the mid-1650s had repercussions for South African labour and race relations long after the abolition of the institution in 1834. Frontier situations introduced further vital formative factors to Cape society. One of the casualties of frontier contacts was Khokhoi society. The breakdown of the fragile Khoikhoi economy by the end of the seventeenth century was accelerated by its inability to cope with the competitive drive of white expansionism.

The transfer of the Cape from Company to British rule was followed by an official autocratic attitude which invoked differing reactions from burghers, Bantu-speaking and Khoisan peoples, and from the immigrant settler community established in the eastern districts. Further new philanthropic legislation towards free persons of colour and an experimental frontier policy led to a significant Boer exodus in the 1830s. The Cape retained the status of an undeveloped crown colony until 1853, when the 'Cape of Good Hope Constitution Ordinance' was ratified and representative government was granted to the colony.

A replica of the *Padrão de São Gregório*, erected on the original site at Kwaaihoek, 8 km west of the mouth of the Bushman's River. *Padrões* were inscribed stone pillars, bearing the Portuguese coat of arms and an inscription stating when and by whom they were raised. Surmounted by crosses, they were assertions of Portuguese sovereignty and symbols of Christianity. (Photo: Rex and Barbara Reynolds)

Chapter 4

The Age of Exploration

Maurice Boucher

From the earliest centuries of recorded history navigators from the lands of the Mediterranean seaboard set out on voyages of discovery along the coasts of Africa. Trade was the spur: the quest for gold, precious stones, ivory, amber, spices and other less exotic commodities which found a ready market in the towns and cities of the ancient world. In the fifteenth century before Christ the Egyptians had sailed down the Red Sea to the mysterious Land of Punt; five centuries later the Israelite King Solomon, with seafarers provided by Hiram of Tyre, found the golden riches of the legendary Land of Ophir along the east coast of Africa, possibly in Somalia. The Phoenicians of Tyre and Sidon founded the city of Carthage on the North African coast, and their sailors braved the Atlantic storms beyond the Pillars of Hercules (now the Strait of Gibraltar), which guarded the western approaches to the Mediterranean. Hanno the Carthaginian led a fleet of sixty triremes as far as the Gulf of Guinea in the fifth century BC. The Greek historian Herodotus recounted, although he himself had doubts about the story, that Phoenician sailors in Egyptian service had already, about the year 600 BC, sailed round the Cape of Good Hope from east to west on a three-year voyage.

Although the east coast continued to be visited by Greek merchants and traders from India and Yemen, so that by the early Christian era it was known as far south as Zanzibar and Dar es Salaam, the west coast route to the south was blocked by Cape Bojador, the point of no return on voyages beyond the Canary Islands. A few daring Genoese and Catalan sailors who ventured past this promontory before the fifteenth century disappeared without trace.

Portuguese explorers

The rise of Islam and its spread across North Africa and into Spain by the early eighth century AD cut Europe off from contact with sub-Saharan Africa. The great clearing-house for the goods brought across the desert by camel caravan was the port of Ceuta in Morocco, and its capture by the Portuguese in 1415 sparked off a drive to the south by the seamen of that nation which would take them round the Cape of Good Hope and into the Indian Ocean before the turn of that century. The architect of this movement was the Infante Dom Henrique (1394-1460), third son of John I of Portugal and the English princess Philippa of Lancaster, or, as he was named by a nineteenth century biographer, 'Prince Henry the Navigator'.

He was present at the capture of Ceuta and set out to solve the riddle of what lay behind the

Maurice Boucher was born in London and was until his retirement in 1984 Professor of History at the University of South Africa. He has written extensively on higher education in South Africa and on aspects of Cape history in the Dutch East India Company period. Professor Boucher received the Hiddingh-Currie award for his study of Huguenot origins, *French Speakers at the Cape* (1981).

Prince Henry the Navigator (1394-1460) who organized voyages of discovery along the West African coast from 1415. He settled at Cape Sagres in 1438, from where he supervised the outfitting of expeditions and the collection of cartographic and navigational information. By the time of his death the most southerly point reached by the Portuguese was only a few degrees south of Cape Verde, slightly more than a third of the way along the sea route to the Cape of Good Hope. (Cape Archives, M1)

The earliest traced depiction of the planting of the *padrão* 'São Filipe' at the Cape, painted by F Benda, a Portuguese. The cross was one of three limestone *padrões* carried by Bartolomeu Dias in his small ships or 'caravels', which are anchored in the bay in the painting. There is no evidence that Dias ever saw Table Bay or the northern face of Table Mountain, as the São Filipe *padrão*, which has remained undiscovered, was erected on 6 June 1488 at the present Cape Maclear, west of Cape Point, on Dias's return journey. (William Fehr Collection)

The Portuguese *padrões*

A *padrão* was a limestone pillar surmounted by a cross and bearing the Portuguese coat of arms and an inscription relating to the voyage. Each was dedicated to a Christian saint. Cão's first, dedicated to St George, was set up on the southern headland of the Congo River; his last, now preserved in almost perfect condition in Berlin, was erected at what is known today as Cape Cross in Namibia.

The first *padrão* to be set up by Dias was dedicated to St Gregory and raised on 12 March 1488 at Kwaaihoek, west of the mouth of the Bushman's River. Fragments of the pillar were discovered there in 1938 by the historian Professor Eric Axelson of Cape Town and the reconstructed *padrão* is housed at the University of the Witwatersrand in Johannesburg. A replica was set up on the original site in 1941. A second *padrão* was raised at the Cape of Good Hope on 6 June 1488 and dedicated to St Philip, but no trace of it has been discovered. Dias erected a third, dedicated to St James, on the Namibian coast in the following month, fragments of which have survived.

Vasco da Gama, as depicted by Charles Gow in 1840. Da Gama sailed from Portugal in July 1497, nine years after Dias, with four ships which were much larger and better equipped than those of Dias. A *roteiro* or log-book of Da Gama's outward voyage, probably written by one Alvaro Velho, still exists. It commences:

'In the year 1497 King Dom Manoel, the first of this name in Portugal, ordered four vessels to go on a voyage of discovery, in search of spices. Vasco da Gama went as commander of the four. . .' (William Fehr Collection)

Muslim lands of North Africa. He hoped to join forces with the legendary Prester John who reputedly ruled the Christians of Ethiopia and thus enclose the enemies of Christendom. A further possible objective was the discovery of a sea route to India. To achieve this, Henry stimulated the perfection of navigational aids and encouraged exploration beyond Cape Bojador. Early attempts to round the promontory failed, but at last in 1434 the seaman Gil Eanes succeeded. The route to the south had been opened and by 1461, Portuguese navigators had sailed along the West African coast. Little more than a decade after Henry's death Portuguese ships crossed the equator.

Henry's nephew, King John II, who ruled Portugal from 1481 until 1495, continued to promote voyages of exploration. In two voyages between 1482 and 1486 the sea-captain Diogo Cão greatly extended knowledge of the west coast by exploring the mouth of the Congo River and the shores of modern Angola and Namibia to within 1 800 km of the Cape of Good Hope. He died off the Namibian coast and the honour of being the first Portuguese captain to round the tip of southern Africa belongs to the now famous navigator, Bartolomeu Dias de Novaes.

Bartolomeu Dias, as he became known, sailed from Lisbon in August 1487 in command of two small caravels and a store-ship. After touching on the Namibian coast in December, he encountered adverse winds and tacked out to sea. The caravels at length took an easterly course, but some days passed and no land was sighted. It was then late January 1488 and the Cape of Good Hope had been rounded. When Dias set a course to the north, land was at last descried, probably near the present Fish Bay to the northeast of the mouth of what was to be known later as the Gourits River. There the Portuguese saw large herds of cattle tended by Khoikhoi herdsmen and they named the spot Bahia dos Vaqueiros, or Bay of the Cowherds. They sailed on in search of water and on 3 February dropped anchor in a bay they named São Bras, later to be called Mossel Bay. The voyage continued as far as the Bahia da Lagoa (Algoa Bay), where the exhausted crews finally demanded that Dias set sail for home. A few extra days were granted to explore and the ships reached their furthest point, either at the mouth of the Great Fish River or at that of the Keiskamma River. On the way back the ships made several calls, including one near Africa's southernmost point, soon to be known as Cape Agulhas, and another in False Bay, named by Dias the Bay between the Mountains. In July 1488 the caravels rejoined the store-ship, which by then had lost most of its crew in attacks by hostile indigenous inhabitants. The stores were transferred to the other vessels and the store-ship destroyed. They reached home in December 1488 after a momentous voyage which had opened up the sea route to the Indies. It was with good reason that Dias named the promontory which guarded the entrance to hitherto uncharted seas the Cabo da Boa Esperança (Cape of Good Hope).

Dias and his predecessor Diogo Cão brought out with them the means to indicate to future voyagers that Portuguese sovereignty had been established along the coasts they explored. These were the famous *padrões*.

Nine years were to elapse before the Portuguese built upon the pioneering discovery by Dias of the sea route into the Indian Ocean. King John was suffering from the kidney disease which was to cause his death in 1495. Moreover, the trade route to India by way of the Cape seemed less profitable when Christopher Columbus told the Portuguese in March 1493 that he had found the Indies by sailing westward across the Atlantic. He was, of course, mistaken, but his achievement, made in the service of Spain, suggested that Portugal might do better to concentrate on the increasingly lucrative West African trade. However, John II's envoy Pedro de Covilhã had visited India by way of Egypt in 1488-1490 and had seen the commercial prospects there, as well as on the African east coast. The Treaty of Tordesilhas of 1494, defining the respective spheres of commercial interest of Spain and Portugal, left the Cape sea route to the Portuguese and John II's successor, Manuel I, prepared another expedition to the East with Vasco da Gama as commander in chief.

Vasco da Gama reaches India

Vasco da Gama sailed on 8 July 1497 from Restelo near Lisbon with four ships. Four months later the expedition reached a bay on the western Cape coast which Da Gama named the Bay of St Helena. Here they met the Khoikhoi, one of whom was taken aboard the commander's ship, the *São Gabriel*, and fed and clothed before being returned to the shore. A misunderstanding arose when a sailor who was on land with the Khoikhoi hailed the ships to be taken back on board. A boat was sent to pick him up and the Khoikhoi, evidently fearing an attack, threw spears, wounding Da Gama and a few companions. The Cape was rounded on 22 November and three days later the expedition entered Mossel Bay. Here Da Gama and his men again encountered Khoikhoi. They could only obtain one ox by barter and it was evident that the Khoikhoi feared the newcomers when they went ashore in strength to seek water. Shots were fired to disperse them and the wooden cross and the stone *padrão* set up by the landing party were overturned by the Khoikhoi as the Portuguese sailed out of the bay.

Adverse winds and currents delayed progress and it was not until 25 December that Da Gama found himself off the Pondoland coast, to which

'Dias erecting his third *padrão* at Angra Pequena', by Charles Davidson Bell. This picture, painted around 1850, was modelled on the earlier painting by F Benda, although it depicts a different event, namely the raising of the *padrão* dedicated to St James on the Namibian coast in July 1488. It has been commented that albatrosses, one of which appears in this painting, are not usually found as far south as Lüderitz Bay. (South African Library)

This depiction of the death of Francisco de Almeida and his men in 1509 has many inaccuracies. The Khoikhoi are shown carrying bows and arrows; the village in the background has an unlikely conical edifice and look-out tower, and the ships in the foreground are Dutch and not Portuguese. The illustration appeared in *Zee- en land-reysen na Oost- en West-Indien* (Leyden 1707) by P van der Aa, and despite its inaccuracy, must be one of the first copperplate engravings to illustrate South African historical events. (Cape Archives, M7)

Francisco de Almeida

He sailed for Portugal on 1 December 1509 after a successful four-year term of office as Viceroy of India. On reaching the anchorage in Table Bay he allowed a party to visit an inland Khoikhoi village to barter for cattle. The party decided to take one of the villagers back to the ships in order to improve relations with the Khoikhoi by clothing him and giving him presents. His comrades, understandably enough, thought he was being abducted and immediately attacked the Portuguese, who fled to their ships. De Almeida thereupon launched an assault on the village, but he and his men were driven back to the beach. Finding that their boats had been moved to another position, they set off to reach them, but were again attacked by the Khoikhoi. De Almeida and over fifty of his companions, including several officers, were killed. The dead were buried in the evening after the Khoikhoi had retreated, De Almeida's body being interred where he had fallen, near the mouth of the Salt River.

A rix dollar note.

Map of Africa by the German cartographer Sebastian Münster, which appeared in *Cosmographia Universalis*, 1544.

he gave the name Natal to commemorate Christmas. In the early months of 1498 the Portuguese voyagers made contact with the Arab civilization of East Africa and the foundations were laid for a long alliance with the sultans of Malindi. From there, with the help of an Arab pilot, the ships sailed for Calicut in India, which they reached on 20 May 1498. The return journey was marred by sickness and death, but the Cape was again rounded on 20 March 1499 and Da Gama reached Lisbon late in August where he was given a hero's welcome.

Portuguese navigators were frequent callers in South African waters during the sixteenth century. One, António de Saldanha, entered Table Bay in 1503 and in order to discover his whereabouts, became the first European to climb Table Mountain. In a skirmish with Khoikhoi over a trade dispute he was slightly wounded. The bay was not then named, but after his visit it became known as Saldanha Bay. It was not until the beginning of the seventeenth century that Table Bay became the usual name, and the name Saldanha Bay was transferred to the anchorage further north.

Quarrels with the Khoikhoi occurred all too often and usually resulted from a breakdown in communication. This was certainly the case

when the returning viceroy of India, Francisco de Almeida, reached Table Bay early in 1510.

The South African coast was never of vital importance to Portugal; her interests in Africa lay elsewhere. It offered no obvious commercial advantages, no expectation of gold deposits, relations with the indigenous peoples were stormy and the treacherous coast caused more than one navigational disaster. The Portuguese left little trace of their century-long dominance of the Cape route. Most of the names they gave to bays and headlands have disappeared from use, and their *padrões* were soon reduced to fragments.

Challengers to the Portuguese monopoly: English, French, Danish and Dutch

Covetous eyes were soon cast on the Portuguese crown monopoly. French pirates operated against Portuguese galleons from early in the sixteenth century, and the English were not far behind. The French were in the Mozambique Channel as early as 1509 and two decades later the brothers Parmentier from Dieppe had reached the Indonesian archipelago. For the English, Francis Drake's voyage around the world in 1577-1580 paved the way for further maritime expansion.

Drake, who was knighted for his exploit by a grateful Queen Elizabeth I in 1581, sailed past the Cape of Good Hope in June 1580 on his return voyage in the *Golden Hind* after a successful campaign against Spanish ships and settlements in the Pacific Ocean. The winter weather was perfect, giving the lie to Portuguese assertions, far from unfounded, of storms and dangers to mariners. 'This Cape,' as the chronicler of Drake's voyage put it, 'is a most stately thing, and the fairest Cape we saw in the whole circumference of the earth.'

The union of the crown of Portugal with that of Spain in 1580, when the Spanish king, Philip II, became ruler of both nations, brought Portuguese commerce under the close scrutiny of Philip's enemy England and the Spanish monarch's Dutch provinces in open revolt against his authority. The English were the first in the field. By 1588 Thomas Cavendish had emulated Drake's feat; three years later, James Lancaster sailed into Table Bay. A voyage round the Cape by Benjamin Wood followed in 1596 and the stage was set for the chartering of the first of the great national commercial companies which were to dominate the eastern trade until towards the end of the eighteenth century.

The English East India Company, or the Company of Merchants of London trading with the East Indies, was chartered in January 1601 by Queen Elizabeth I. Its first fleet was despatched under James Lancaster in the following month, reaching Table Bay in September 1601. Lancaster dosed his men on the *Red Dragon* with lemon juice, thus protecting them

East India House, the headquarters of the Dutch East India Company in Amsterdam. From the initials of the abbreviated Dutch name, *Vereenigde Oost-Indische Compagnie*, the trading company became known as the VOC. (Cape Archives, M64)

from the ravages of scurvy endured by those on the other vessels. The *Red Dragon* returned to England in 1603 and Lancaster was knighted for the treaties he had negotiated with Indonesian princes, although the English later concentrated on the Indian sub-continent, particularly Madras, Bombay and Calcutta.

Before 1580 the Dutch had been active in the Lisbon carrying trade, distributing throughout Europe the wares brought back from the East in Portuguese ships. This commerce was made increasingly difficult under Philip II's rule, and the Dutch therefore decided to challenge Portugal at her sources of supply. In 1592 a group of Amsterdam merchants sent the brothers Cornelis and Frederik de Houtman to Lisbon to find out what they could about the Cape sea route.

Cornelis de Houtman sailed as chief merchant with a fleet despatched by Amsterdam business interests in 1595. Its arrival in Mossel Bay in August, where trade was conducted with the Khoikhoi, was the first contact of the Netherlands with the land that nation was to rule for almost a century and a half. De Houtman returned from Java in August 1597, but fleets were also sent out to the East by other merchants. Table Bay owes its name to the visit of one of them late in 1601 under the command of Joris van Spilsbergen.

Competiton between rival commercial groups was not in the national interest and in 1602 the government of the Dutch republic conferred a charter upon a united company with wide authority which at the same time gave the independent commercial undertakings which had merged in it a measure of autonomy.

The English and the Dutch companies were the main contenders for commercial advantage beyond the Cape of Good Hope in the first half of the seventeenth century, but others also sought a share of the spoils as Portuguese power declined.

The Dutch East India Company

The Dutch East India Company, or *Vereenigde Oost-Indische Compagnie* (VOC) had a federal character, and consisted of six loosely associated chambers, of which that in Amsterdam took pride of place, followed by Zeeland. The other four were in Delft, Rotterdam, Enkhuizen and Hoorn. The supreme direction of the company was vested in a body known as the 'Lords Seventeen' (*Heeren Sewentien*). The States General of the republic excercised a nominal control over the Company and from 1749 the national *Stadtholder* was also chief director. From the start the Company concentrated its activities on the Far East, virtually driving out Portuguese competition and keeping its chief rival, the London company, at bay. In 1609 it set up a permanent administration in Indonesia with headquarters established a decade later at Batavia (Jakarta) on the island of Java. Within sixty years the Dutch East India Company had founded a vast network of settlements and *comptoirs* from the Cape by way of Ceylon (Sri Lanka) to distant Japan.

'Portrait of Jan van Riebeeck', by Jan Pieter Veth, 1898, from an original in the Rijks Museum in Amsterdam. Although there is some doubt as to whether the man depicted here is indeed Van Riebeeck, the reproduction of the Dutch Commander on South African paper currency is still based on this portrait. (William Fehr Collection)

Sir Francis Drake (c1540-1596), who passed the 'Fairest Cape' on his return voyage from the Pacific in 1580.

The post-office stones

The Cape became a meeting place for mariners and also a useful port of call where messages could be left. Inscriptions were chiselled on stones to mark the visits of ships and soon the custom evolved of leaving letters under these stones. A number of them can be seen in the South African Museum in Cape Town. They recorded such information as the names and commanders of ships, their routes and dates of arrival and departure. To this was sometimes added, as by Richard Blyth of the London in 1622, some such instruction as 'Heare under looke for letters'. The correspondence was secured in a bundle and placed in a protective covering, often of tarred cloth. Letters were also occasionally given to a reliable Khoikhoi for transmission to a later arrival.

The Portuguese had earlier used a different method. When Pedro de Ataide reached Mossel Bay from India in 1501, he left a letter in a shoe fastened to a tree. Ships' officers at Saldanha Bay in the next century either placed letters in a bottle tied to a stake or buried them beneath an inscribed wooden marker.

A post office stone recording the dates of arrival and departure of the London, captained by Richard Blyth, in 1622.

A short-lived French East India Company was floated in 1604, and in 1642 Richelieu founded an Eastern Company which concentrated on Madagascar. The exploitation of the Far East began after 1664 by later companies, and ended in a struggle for power with Britain in the eighteenth century in which the French were defeated. French ships were in Table Bay in 1620 and 1622, but the chief interest was in Saldanha Bay as a future refreshment station. The mariner Étienne de Flacourt saw its possibilities when he visited the bay in 1648 and 1655.

A Danish East India Company was chartered in 1616, forerunner of others which made the ships of that nation regular callers at the Cape. The first fleet reached Table Bay in July 1619 under the command of Ove Giedde. Giedde had Ceylon as his objective, but it was Tranquebar on India's Coromandel coast, founded in 1620, which became Denmark's leading commercial centre in the Indies.

Portugal's successors in the East India trade found the Cape of Good Hope a useful half-way house for watering, victualling and the restoration to health of scurvy-ridden crews. Trade forged bonds between the indigenous Khoikhoi and the newcomers although it is clear that the arrival of the Europeans threw a great strain on Khoikhoi society.

Thoughts of settlement at the Cape

It was the English who first thought of permanent settlement at the Cape of Good Hope and in July 1620 the fleet commanders Humphrey Fitzherbert and Andrew Shilling took 'quiet and peaceable possession' of Table Bay in the name of their sovereign. King James I, however, showed no interest in the gift. Twenty-seven years were to pass before an event occurred at the Cape which was to bring the Dutch there as permanent residents.

The *Nieuw-Haerlem*, a Dutch East Indiaman sailing for home from Batavia, was driven ashore in Table Bay by a south-easter in March 1647. Much of the vessel's cargo was saved and the captain, who left on another ship, ordered

the junior merchant Leendert Jansz to remain behind with a party of men. A temporary fort was constructed for defence, and there the men stayed for a year before they were repatriated with the return fleet of 1648. Jansz and a merchant on one of the rescue ships, Matthys Proot, were requested by the Lords Seventeen to report on the Cape as a possible refreshment station for Dutch shipping. The *Remonstrantie* they submitted on 26 July 1649 recommended the construction of a fort on Table Bay and the planting of a garden. A young man who also sailed with the return fleet of 1648 was later asked to comment on the *Remonstrantie*. His name was Jan van Riebeeck.

The Lords Seventeen approved the findings of the *Remonstrantie* on 22 August 1650 and in December 1651 the Amsterdam chamber of the Dutch East India Company appointed Van Riebeeck to lead the expedition which was to add the Cape of Good Hope to its far-flung commercial empire.

Suggested Reading List

E V Axelson (1940) *South-east Africa, 1488-1530*, London

C R Boxer (1965) *The Dutch Seaborne Empire, 1600-1800*, London

W J de Kock (1957) *Portugese Ontdekkers om die Kaap: die Europese Aanraking met Suidelike Afrika, 1415-1600*, Cape Town

H Furber (1976) *Rival Empires of Trade in the Orient, 1600-1800*, Minneapolis and London

R Raven-Hart (1967) *Before Van Riebeeck: Callers at South Africa from 1488 to 1652*, Cape Town

E Strangman (1936) *Early French Callers at the Cape*, Cape Town

Chapter 5

The Cape under the Dutch East India Company

Maurice Boucher

The decision taken by the Lords Seventeen of the Dutch East India Company in 1650 to establish a fortified refreshment station at the Cape of Good Hope opened a new chapter in the history of southern Africa. The arrival of Europeans on what was to be a permanent basis had a profound effect upon indigenous social structures, the political and economic development of the region and upon group relations in an increasingly complex racial situation. These, however, were consequences as yet unseen when Jan van Riebeeck reached Table Bay aboard the *Drommedaris* on 6 April 1652 as Commander of the small contingent of some ninety men, women and children sent out on that ship and her companion vessels the *Goede Hoop*, the *Reijger*, the *Walvis* and the *Oliphant* to garrison the Cape outpost.

There was no suggestion in Dutch East India Company thinking then or subsequently that the Cape of Good Hope was to be regarded as a first foothold for the penetration by Europeans of the southern African hinterland. The settlement had one purpose only: to promote more effectively the profitability of trade between the motherland and the commercial empire of the East Indies. The Cape was to provide for the safety of Company ships and the well-being of

A depiction by Charles Bell of the landing of Van Riebeeck and his men at the Cape, painted in 1850. (South African Library)

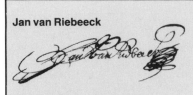
their often fever-wracked and scurvy-ridden crews at a convenient half-way house on long voyages across the oceans. The Commander, permanently elevated to the dignity of Governor in 1691, was a Company employee, as were the members of the Council of Policy who assisted him, and his chief duty was to carry out Company instructions at minimum cost to his employers. The Cape administration had only limited freedom of action, as it was, from the first, subject to the authority of the Lords Seventeen in the Netherlands and, until 1732, to that of the Governor-General and his council in Batavia as well. Only the slow communications of the age allowed for a certain autonomy, but this was further circumscribed by the periodic arrival of senior Company officials, either as designated visiting commissioners or as admirals of the fleet, who took precedence over the Cape's chief executive during their stay.

The Company's priorities with regard to its southern African settlement are clearly indicated in the instructions given to Van Riebeeck. He was to build a fort to house the garrison and to protect it from marauding animals and from attack by land or sea. He was also to devise means to assist incoming vessels to make harbour in Table Bay, to plant a garden and to till the soil for the supply of vegetables, fruit and grain to crews and to foster good relations with the indigenous inhabitants in order to guarantee a brisk barter trade in livestock. Protection of property, adequate victualling and the profits from trade were the mainsprings of Company policy at the Cape and such later developments as additional defence measures, the provision of repair facilities for ships and the sale of surplus commodities were simply extensions of the same pattern of administration.

After the first severe winter and the setbacks it caused, the garden tended by Jan Hendrik Boom began to produce fruit and vegetables and more plants, vines and trees were imported. However, wheat crops were poor, rice did not flourish and the small labour force, often greatly

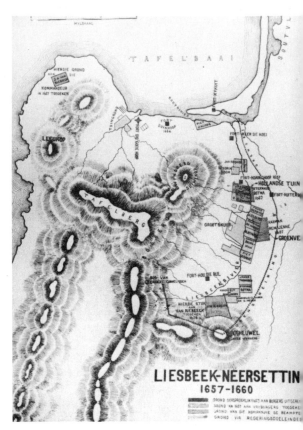

LIESBEEK-NEERSETTIN
1657-1660

reduced through sickness, was reluctant to undertake the duties required of it in the fields. Sailors on passing ships could sometimes be used to help increase productivity, despite official disapproval of manual labour for seamen at a settlement designed to help them regain their lost health. Such men, however, provided no permanent solution to the labour problem. The indigenous pastoralists of the Cape hinterland were at first inexperienced as cultivators, convicts were not available in sufficient numbers and Van Riebeeck's plan of importing Chinese labour evoked no response in Batavia.

Van Riebeeck at length suggested the idea of encouraging the immigration of European burghers to overcome the labour crisis and at the same time to lessen the dependence of the settlement on paid employees of the Company, thus cutting the costs of administration. The Lords Seventeen were not yet prepared to go so far, but the Commander was granted permission to release a handful of his own men, the first nine of whom were allowed to settle as farmers in two groups along the Liesbeek River in February 1657.

These farmers remained subject to Company control; they could be deprived of burgher status for misdemeanours, and they were granted no political rights. They were liable for military service and although they were exempted from land tax for twelve years, they were discouraged from entering into competition with the Company and were required to sell their produce to it at prices determined by the authorities. Restrictions caused the first signs of burgher dis-

Maria de la Queillerie (1629-1664) was married to Jan van Riebeeck at the age of nineteen, bore him eight children, and died of smallpox in Malacca at the age of thirty-five, shortly after miscarrying her ninth child. A Catholic priest, Nicolas Etienne, who stayed at the Cape for ten months, described her as one of the wisest women he had ever met, enjoying the esteem of all people and performing the arduous tasks of Commander's wife with great efficiency. (Cape Archives, M107)

content as early as 1658. Wheat prices scarcely made cultivation profitable and the early farmers gradually turned away from intensive farming to the raising of sheep and cattle on the open veld.

The Commander's small garrison could scarcely cope with the many heavy tasks entrusted to it, including the servicing of visiting ships. The importation of slaves was seen as an obvious solution to the labour problem, both for the Company and the burghers. Slavery was already widely practised throughout the eastern empire of the Dutch East India Company, and in the first years of European occupation of the Cape several officials, including Van Riebeeck himself, owned personal slaves as domestic servants. The Cape's dependence on slave labour was to continue throughout the Company period and beyond it.

Relations between the Dutch and the indigenous pastoral Khoikhoi after 1652 perpetuated and regularized the long-established barter trade with visiting ships, but with two significant differences. The greater demands for livestock by a resident population could not always be met by the Khoikhoi and the conversion of pastures into cultivated land by the newcomers from Europe threatened traditional grazing rights.

The drive for a bigger market in livestock and the lure of precious metals had already taken the Company well into the interior on organized exploratory expeditions, in the course of which Saldanha Bay, the Hottentots Holland mountains and the Land of Waveren (Tulbagh) were reached. After the Khoikhoi-Dutch struggle of 1659-1660, Jan Danckaert penetrated as far as the Olifants River in the north and Pieter Cruijthoff made contact with the Nama.

Jan van Riebeeck's ten years as Commander were marked by both successes and failures. The construction of a jetty at Table Bay made landing there a less hazardous experience, but the defence offered by the mud-walled fort was clearly inadequate. Agricultural production was improved, but the intensive farming which alone could make the Cape self-sufficient was never realized. When he sailed for Batavia in May 1662 he left a white community of some 260 burghers, officials and families. The subsequent history of the Dutch East India Company's southern African outpost is largely concerned with the interaction of its diversity of

◁◁

A map showing the settlement along the Liesbeek River between 1657 and 1660, indicating the land allocated to the free burghers. In 1657 nine free burghers, who divided into two parties, received grants of land. One group, under the leadership of Herman Remajenne, settled at Groeneveld, on the northern bank of the Liesbeek, and a second group, under Stefanus Botma, settled at De Hollandsche Thuyn, directly opposite Devil's Peak. (Cape Archives, L1250)

◁

First part of a document granting land to Jakob Cloete on the northern bank of the Liesbeek River, issued in 1657. The area allotted to Cloete (situated in present-day Rondebosch) is located on the map of the settlement along the Liesbeek River near the Groeneveld area, between the allotments of Frans Gerritse and Martinus de Waght. (Cape Archives, M1171)

The Fort de Goede Hoop

This building was erected on a site on the present Parade near the stream later known as the Liesbeek. It took the form of a square, surrounded by a moat, with four bastions named after the four ships *Drommedaris*, *Walvis*, *Oliphant* and *Reijger*. The walls were constructed of mud, and the first timber buildings within them were soon replaced by a two-storied stone structure. Construction of the fort proceeded under great difficulties. The hard ground, severe winter weather and the exhaustion of the garrison delayed progress. Van Riebeeck noted in his journal on 26 September 1652: '. . . the men are beginning to grumble at the continual and difficult work on the fortifications.' Although by that time the men, women and children had taken up quarters within the fort, it was not until the end of the following year that the work was completed. The mud walls could not stand up to the Cape winter rains, and in 1654 the Walvis bastion collapsed and the fort continued to deteriorate. Van Riebeeck's successor, Zacharias Wagenaer, suggested that a new pentagonal stone structure replace the first fort, and land was allocated for this purpose in 1665.

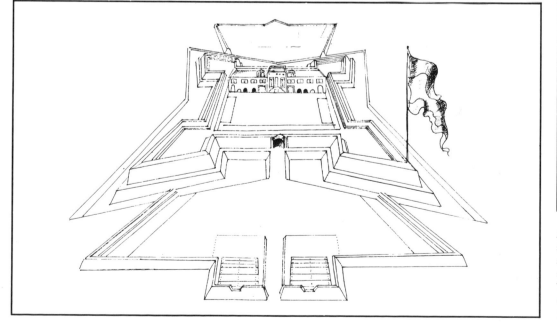

A plan of the Fort de Goede Hoop, showing the four bastions, the moat surrounding the fort, and the two-storied stone structure within the inner square. The hornwork at the back of the fort enclosed the cattle kraal and stables. (Cape Archives, M109)

IJsbrand Goske, Commander and Governor of the Cape from 1672 to 1676. (Cape Archives, E363)

In 1685 Simon van der Stel led an expedition to the Koperberge (Copper Mountains) in Namaqualand. A journal, with sketches presumably made by Hendrik Claudius, was kept. The descriptive text which accompanies this picture reads: 'A plain situated about 3 miles North of the Koperberge in the middle of which was found a flat, horizontal rock, from the pores or holes of which verdigris steadily oozes out.' The discovery of verdigris, a basic copper acetate, indicated the presence of copper for the expedition. (*Simon van der Stel's Journey to Namaqualand in 1685*; Human & Rousseau, Cape Town, 1979)

peoples. To the end of the Company period, however, its major significance on the world scene was as a port of call for ships, both Dutch and foreign, in years of increasing international rivalry for empire in the Far East.

The Company's men

Only five of the chief executives at the Cape after the departure of Jan van Riebeeck held permanent office for longer periods than he. They were Simon van der Stel (1679-1699), Mauritz Pasques de Chavonnes (1714-1724), Hendrik Swellengrebel (1739-1751), Rijk Tulbagh (1751-1771) and Joachim van Plettenberg (1774-1785). The title of Governor, bestowed upon IJsbrand Goske (1672-1676) and his successor Joan Bax (1676-1678), finally superseded that of Commander during Simon van der Stel's term of office. Of all the Cape's commanders and governors only Swellengrebel was born in the colony. Most of the eighteenth century governors also held the rank of Councillor of India and, not surprisingly, a post which carried so much prestige was much sought after.

The senior officials at the Cape and members of the Council of Policy formed an elitist hierarchy around the Governor. Among them were the deputy governor, the heads of the various branches of the administration, the garrison commander and the fiscal who was, after 1690, directly responsible to the Lords Seventeen and not subject to local control. The fiscal's task was to fight corruption at all levels, with particular regard to shipping, but he enjoyed many perquisites of office and was generally resented for his exactions. It was not until 1793, as the Company period drew to a close, that the fiscal's independence was ended.

Many of the senior officials of the Company at the Cape – and others too at lower levels – were men of culture, intelligence and of good social standing. The secretary to the Council of Policy between 1684 and 1694, for example, Johannes Guillelmus de Grevenbroeck, wrote a Latin treatise on the Khoikhoi and compiled a Latin-Khoi vocabulary.

The social and intellectual gulf between the officials and the rank-and-file in the Company's service was enormous. Most of these men were soldiers and sailors, but their numbers also included artisans and agriculturists. As with the officials, they were not exclusively Dutch in origin. The number of foreigners in Company employ included Germans, Scandinavians, Flemings, Swiss and French. The Dutch Reformed Church was the only permitted church until 1780, when Lutherans were given freedom of worship. Before that, they – and the Catholics at all times in the Company period – could only look to the ministrations of chaplains and priests on visiting foreign ships. For the garrison staff, duties were often onerous and promotion prospects poor. Desertion, usually by sea, was not infrequent, but the punishments for those caught attempting it were severe. An avenue of escape from the drudgery of service life was to secure temporary release to work on contract with a farmer as a prelude to a request for discharge from the Company in order to join the ranks of the free burghers. The Cape establishment rose from 120 in 1660 to more than 1 000 in 1745. Fifty years later it was approximately

E. E. den vlachte omtrent 3 miijllen noordwaarts van den Coperbergh gelegen in 't midden van de welcke, en vlacke Horizontale klip men gevonden heeft uijt

twice that figure. Free burghers, however, came to outnumber Company employees before the close of the seventeenth century and by 1795 the proportion was 15:2, although it was not until the 1750s that there were more free adult males than Company men.

The free burghers

When Van Riebeeck left the Cape in 1662 the free burgher population had increased from the original 9 men of 1657 to a total of 130, 37 of them women and children. Settlement was still confined to Table Valley and the banks of the Liesbeeck River, but between March 1677 and the arrival of Simon van der Stel as Governor in October 1679, rights to farmland or pasture had been given to 8 burghers at Hout Bay, Hottentots-Holland, along the Eerste River and east of the Tygerberg. By 1780, when the free population numbered 10 500, the region under Company jurisdiction had advanced to the Orange River to the north and the Great Fish River to the east. The hinterland was sparsely populated by whites and in the entire colony there was only one town of any size, the port settlement in the shadow of Table Mountain, beginning to be known by its modern name, Cape Town, by the middle of the eighteenth century.

Natural increase, together with the regular discharge of men in the Company's service, largely accounted for the growth of the burgher population, for apart from the period 1685-1707 there was no scheme of free passages for intending immigrants. There were also other sources of increase: wives and children joining their menfolk; crew members of foreign ships seeking permanent residence; Company employees returning from the East who found Cape society congenial. The Lords Seventeen sent out a small group of orphan girls from Rotterdam in 1688 to find husbands at the Cape and several men married women who called on passing ships.

Manumission of slaves created another component in the free society of the colony – the so-called 'free blacks'. This group consisted mainly of former slaves of Indian and Indonesian origin, although some had their roots in mainland Africa and Madagascar. To them must be added freed convicts, usually of Eastern origin and including a number of Chinese who had entered Batavia illegally.

There were, in addition, political exiles at the Cape, sent there from the Dutch Indies as security risks or at the behest of relatives to whom they presented a personal or dynastic threat. This small group was kept apart from the Cape community, living in isolation on a government allowance and maintaining retinues of slaves and servants. Finally, there were a few free Asians who decided to make their homes at the Cape. One of them, Abdol Garisch of Amboina, reached Table Bay in a British warship and stayed on to become a valued court interpreter.

It was the immigration scheme of 1685 which brought to the settlement the only sizeable and initially cohesive group to swell the numbers of the colonists. Louis XIV of France had revoked the Edict of Nantes to remove the last guarantee of immunity from the persecuted Calvinists of that country, and the result was to transform the flow of French Protestant refugees to other European countries into a flood, despite all efforts to prevent their flight. Many were destitute and employment was often difficult to find. It is not surprising, therefore, that some were attracted by the Dutch East India Company's offer of a passage to the Cape and the chance to begin a new life there.

Simon van der Stel had introduced a freehold system of land tenure at Stellenbosch in 1679 and this was extended to Drakenstein in 1686. It was here that the French speakers were settled, each receiving an allocation of seed, implements and cattle, the cost of which was to be repaid to the Company.

The system of freehold land tenure, with additional pasture made available on Company land, continued until 1717 and was applied to all new regions opened up for farming in the period, such as the Land of Waveren, where freehold farms were offered by Simon van der Stel's son, Wilhem Adriaen, in 1700. After 1717, however, the Company ceased for more than two decades to allocate freehold land, reverting to the system of loan farms on which an annual quitrent was paid. Governor Swellengrebel's decision in 1743 to permit the conversion of a portion of a loan farm to freehold ownership against the payment of a lump sum was not a great success and largely failed in its purpose of limiting the further expansion of the colony by inducing farmers to retain their existing farms.

The arrival of so many new settlers in the later seventeenth century and the consequent extension of farming activities led to over-production. This, combined with a shortage of cheap labour, high transportation costs and the restrictive policy of the Company regarding marketing and prices led to a depression in arable farming which hit the small producer hard. Only the more efficient, large-scale producers of wheat and wine could keep their heads above water and the wealthy had the additional advantage of being in a position to outbid competitors when the lucrative monopoly leases for the supply of meat, wine and beer were auctioned by the company. These provided the holders with a guaranteed market for their own products. For those harder hit by the economic depression there were other options. Some emigrated and a few joined the Company's service, but more significant in the continuing history of the colony were the movements which took place in two di-

rections: to the port settlement on Table Bay and into the interior.

The port township offered several remunerative avenues of employment. In the course of the eighteenth century a number of well-to-do burghers made their homes there and they needed the amenities of urban life which others could provide. The farmers of the interior could make profitable use of middlemen in the disposal of their produce and the purchase of supplies. Foreign shipping required the services of agents to arrange for the well-being of crews in harbour. The provision of board and lodging for ships' officers was a popular and profitable business and, at a lower level, bars and eating-houses proliferated. The 'free blacks', some of whom had initially farmed with some success in the Cape and Stellenbosch districts, came to concentrate themselves increasingly at the port, where they constituted perhaps as much as twenty per·cent of the population. They were engaged in fishing, were active in retail trades and as artisans, and in all the activities connected with the lodging and entertainment of those who came ashore from passing ships. Whites were also engaged in all these fields and there was at least one business partnership between a 'free black' and a burgher in the mid-eighteenth century in the ownership of a bar. The 'free blacks' and the burghers enjoyed equal status in society, but there was growing discrimination in the second half of the eighteenth century, given a measure of legal sanction.

The trekboer movement

Movement into the interior was closely linked with the change from arable farming to stock farming. The keeping of livestock involved a lower capital outlay in building up herds, was less labour-intensive and did not involve the transportation risks inherent in sending perishables over poor roads. The trekboer movement really got under way when Wilhem Adriaen van der Stel began to issue free grazing permits in 1703 and the small fee charged for them from 1714 did not arrest the movement. The exodus went hand in hand with hunting expeditions into the interior which not only provided the farmers with meat, but also enabled them to learn more about the resources of the hinterland. The increase in herds and the exhaustion of pastures led the cattle farmers even further from the settled areas and government attempts to define boundaries proved ineffective in curbing expansion. The proclamation of new districts to follow the separation of Stellenbosch from the Cape in 1682 did no more than recognize a movement which the Company was unable to control. The district soon to be known as Swellendam in honour of the Governor Hendrik Swellengrebel and his wife Helena Wilhelmina ten Damme, as proclaimed in 1745 and

Baptismal register of the French Huguenots at Drakenstein. (Cape Archives, M973)

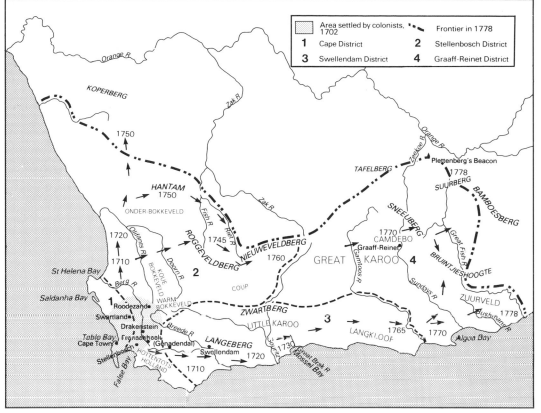

Trekboer Expansion, 1702-1780

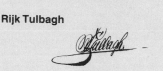
that of Graaff-Reinet, similarly named for the Governor Cornelis Jacob van de Graaff and his wife Hester Cornelia Reinet, was founded in 1786.

By the end of the Company period cattle farmers represented more than two-thirds of all agriculturists in the colony and some idea of the sparseness of the white population of the interior may be gauged from the fact that whereas the average density for the entire region of Dutch settlement was about two persons per square kilometre, that for the pastoral hinterland was at best one per ten square kilometres and arid areas were more than twice as thinly populated.

In so isolated a region the trekboer developed a far greater degree of self-sufficiency than did his fellows in the south-western Cape. The economy was primitive; so too were living conditions. Contact with markets was rare and, for farmers on the distant frontier, almost non-existent. Imported goods were costly and the white settlers learned to be self-reliant in food, clothes and utensils. Life on the periphery of colonial society developed a spirit of independence and an individualistic sense, but a price was paid in social and cultural isolation.

The burghers and the Company

Throughout the entire period of Company rule the burghers had no voice in government decision-making at the highest level and possessed only limited powers in other spheres. Officials held the reins in all subsidiary councils with burgher representation, even after the reconstitution of the Council of Justice in 1783. Moreover, the final selection of burgher members – even of church councils – lay with the Governor and the Council of Policy. Simon van der Stel made a promising start with local rural govern-

A trekboer camp. (Africana Museum)

Hadji Hassan, a Malay priest, at prayers. (Africana Museum)

Nazea, a Malay woman, in her walking costume. (Africana Museum)

ment at Stellenbosch in 1682 by appointing four burghers as *heemraden*, but three years later they were placed under the supervision of a government official as *landdrost*. This became the normal practice in all the rural districts and the *heemraden* were confirmed in office by the Council of Policy. Add to this system an overriding right of veto and it is clear that the Company's administration had in theory full control over the free burghers, even if its writ did not always extend effectively to the more remote corners of the colony.

Nevertheless, from Van Riebeeck's time onwards, burghers were never slow to complain to the authorities when their interests were affected in such matters as land allocation, price fixing, labour, barter trade, taxation, rents and military service. Burgher councillors and *heemraden* came to be regarded as the representatives of the people in these and other cases. On occasion, complainants received short shrift from the authorities. Simon van der Stel and the Council of Policy reprimanded a delegation of French speakers led by their minister Pierre Simond for exhibiting separatist tendencies in daring to ask in 1689 for a separate church congregation. The Lords Seventeen overruled the Governor in this instance, but subsequent requests by this group to preserve language rights were coolly received.

Burgher hostility to privileged officialdom became an open conflict between 1705 and 1707, when in a period of over-production and labour shortage, a group of prominent burghers confronted the Governor, Wilhem Adriaen van der Stel, on the issue of farming activities conducted by himself and other leading officials, and of the manipulation of the market to their own advantage. Victory went to the burghers on this occasion, although the problem of land

ownership by Company employees was not solved until 1716, when renewed burgher complaints were brought to the attention of a visiting commissioner, Abraham Douglas. Economic demands, particularly for free trade, were made by the burghers throughout the eighteenth century, but it was not until 1792 that Cape citizens were allowed to enter the maritime commercial world with their own ships.

The Burgher Protest of 1705-1707 sprang directly from the sale of the meat and wine contracts, and a measure of self-interest is apparent in the fact that one of the leaders of the protest, Henning Hüsing, lost the meat contract to favourites of the Governor, Wilhem Adriaen van der Stel. The Governor's extensive farming operations at Vergelegen in Hottentots-Holland, the irregular manner in which improvements there were carried out and the general highhandedness of Cape officials also caused widespread resentment. Hüsing and his cousin Adam Tas collected testimony from other burghers about official malpractices and it is from the diary kept by Tas that we know a great deal of the tensions of that period. A letter of complaint was drawn up and sent to the Lords Seventeen with the 1706 return fleet but Van der Stel got wind of this move and with the same fleet despatched a testimonial to his own worth, bearing the signatures of 240 persons, although the way in which these were secured left much to be desired.

The Governor went further. Tas was arrested, his desk confiscated and searched and four more ringleaders, among them Hüsing, were apprehended and deported to the Netherlands. One of them died on the voyage. More known opponents of the Governor were thrown into the Castle dungeon or 'Dark Hole'. This induced some of them to recant, to provide Van der Stel with useful 'confessions', but others remained obdurate, including one of the chief protesters, Jacobus van der Heiden. Hüsing and his companions were able to bring the burghers' complaints to the notice of the Lords Seventeen and in April 1707 the decision to recall Van der Stel and other prominent officials reached the Cape. The Governor's farm Vergelegen was to be divided into four portions and the buildings demolished.

On his return to Europe Van der Stel sought to justify himself by publishing a *Korte deductie*, or short statement – of 172 foolscap pages – refuting the charges brought against him of tyrannical behaviour, misuse of labour and economic policies harmful to the colony. His argument lacked conviction, however, and was followed by a reply from his critics in the form of a *Contra-deductie* (1712), supported by telling documentary evidence collected by Van der Heiden and Tas.

In the later eighteenth century the struggle between burghers and the Company assumed new forms and although economic restrictions continued to irritate both the citizens of Cape Town and the farmers of the interior, political considerations coloured attitudes. This wider approach to burgher disabilities was evident in the Cape Patriot movement of 1778, setting in motion a campaign to improve the position of the burghers, who were by now deeply committed to the colony and increasingly hostile to Company administration.

The Cape Patriot protest had its origins in secret meetings held in the Cape Town area in May 1778 and the circulation of a pamphlet endorsing citizens' rights. A burgher delegation of four presented a petition to the Lords Seventeen in October 1779 which called for the lifting of restrictions on private trade, an end to the boards on which they were represented and some say in the deliberations of the Council of Policy, with better representation on the Coun-

cil of Justice. A further petition in April 1782 also recommended a complete division of powers between the legislative and the judiciary bodies. One official in particular, the unpopular independent fiscal, Willem Cornelis Boers, was severely criticized for his extortions and arbitrary acts.

Burgher hostility led to the resignation of Boers in 1783, but the Dutch East India Company made only limited concessions to the petitioners, rejecting free election, but increasing burgher representation on the Council of Justice. Although economic activity by Company officials was again prohibited, the integrity of the administration remained untouched. The Cape burghers then organized a body known as the Commissioned Representatives of the People which elected new delegates to visit the Netherlands and, by-passing the Company, approached the States General directly. Petitions

Vergelegen, the farm of governor Wilhem Adriaan van der Stel. The estate appears prosperous, but hardly as flourishing as that depicted in the *Contra-deductie* of 1712. (Cape Archives, M139)

Vergelegen from a diagram in the *Contra-deductie* drawn up by disgruntled free burghers in 1712. The illustration depicts the free burghers' claims concerning the extensive nature of the estate, with its numerous vineyards, plantations, cattle and sheep kraals and slave quarters. (Cape Archives, M140)

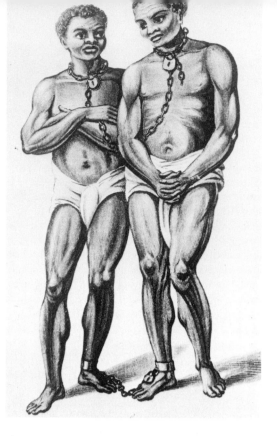

Two slaves, chained at the neck and ankles. (Cape Archives, M375)

Governor Cornelis Jacob van de Graaff and his wife Hester Cornelia Reinet. (Cape Archives, M218 and M219)

were presented to the Dutch Parliament in May 1785 and April 1786, and efforts were made to enlist the support of the public. Little came of this visit to Europe, however, and dissension in the Patriot ranks, coupled with a changed political situation in the motherland after the restoration of Orangist power in 1787, weakened the Cape Patriot movement. Burgher discontent in the south-western Cape intensified, however, as government authority weakened in the last years of Company control and before 1795 voices were raised demanding independence or direct rule by the Dutch state.

The leaders of the Patriot movement were representative of the social elite of the colony and were influenced by currents from abroad, notably the Patriot movement in the Netherlands against the ruling House of Orange, the questioning of social and political structures which stemmed from the Enlightenment and the struggle of the American colonists to gain independence from Britain.

Administrative difficulties multiplied after the arrival of the last Cape Governor, C J van de Graaff, in 1785. His extravagance led the Company to effect drastic economies in 1790 and in the following year Van de Graaff was recalled. From 1792 government devolved upon Commissioners-General. The first of them, Sebastiaan Cornelis Nederburgh and Simon Hendrik Frykenius, gave the burghers free trade, but courted unpopularity by increasing taxes; the last, Abraham Josias Sluysken, who succeeded in 1793, saw out the final two years of Company rule against a background of economic bankruptcy and open rebellion in the frontier districts of Graaff-Reinet and Swellendam. These

problems remained unsolved when the British occupied the Cape in 1795.

The Graaff-Reinet Rebellion was the result of dissatisfaction with Company policy on the frontier with the Xhosa as interpreted by the *landdrost* Honoratus Christiaan David Maynier (1760-1831), who blamed the burghers for deteriorating relations between the two groups. Following a meeting of farmers on 6 February 1795, Maynier was compelled to leave the district. A provisional government, 'The Voice of the People', was set up and in August, Friedrich Carl David Gerotz of Stuttgart was appointed acting *landdrost*. A commission sent by Sluysken to re-establish Company authority failed in its purpose.

The Swellendam Rebellion of June 1795 was a protest against the Company's general economic and Khoikhoi policies. An armed force deposed the *landdrost*, Anthonij Alexander Faure, established a revolutionary National Convention and appointed Hermanus Steyn as 'national' *landdrost*. A month later the National Convention declared a free republic. The terminology used by the rebels of both districts reflects current democratic and French revolutionary ideals.

The slaves

In 1795 the slaves at the Cape numbered some 17 000 by the official estimate, making the slave population larger than that of the burghers. All but three per cent of the slaves were owned by burghers and since arable farming required a larger labour force than pastoral agriculture, more than nine-tenths of all the slaves were to be found in the southern part of the Cape district and the south-central regions of the Stellenbosch district. Male slaves outnumbered the men of the white community at an early stage, and the severity of punishments in cases of slave insubordination and other crimes clearly reflected fears of rebellion.

The Cape slaves came from many parts of India and eastern Asia, as well as from Madagascar and the African mainland, particularly from the region from Delagoa Bay to Zanzibar. The Dutch East India Company equipped a number of slaving voyages to Madagascar and East Africa and both burghers and Company brought slaves from the East. There was also a transit trade by visiting foreign ships. The condition of slaves imported in large groups was often deplorable and even on the relatively short voyage from Madagascar there were frequent deaths, escape bids and some mutinies. Once at the Cape, many slaves made attempts to escape.

The Company's slaves were chiefly employed as general labourers, but a number were skilled artisans, such as carpenters and masons, and others were employed as domestic servants, gardeners and herdsmen. Most of the Company's slaves were housed in the slave lodge at the port settlement. This became the chief brothel in the town, and a large proportion of the children living in the slave lodge were the bastards of white fathers. Slaves could earn rewards while in government hands and the Company took more care over the education and Christian baptism of slave children than was generally the case with the offspring of the burghers' slaves.

The Company also tended to preserve the original names of their slaves, while among the burghers most slaves were renamed. The months of the year were popular names, as were such biblical and classical names as Samson, Benjamin, Adonis and Apollo. In the country districts most were agricultural workers or domestic servants, but in the port township particularly there were many who followed a trade and some who were allowed to earn a little money by their masters. Although the Cape was essentially a society of small slave-owners, ownership conferred a certain distinction, emphasizing the role of a white elite which was above performing menial tasks. Nevertheless, the burghers were not uniformly slave-holders. In 1750 about one half had none, while something approaching sixty per cent of the remainder owned between one and five slaves. Large-scale slave-holding was confined to the richest estate owners and in 1750 only seven wealthy farmers possessed more than fifty slaves.

Slaves were property, but were not entirely devoid of rights. They could, for example, complain of ill-treatment, although owners were permitted to inflict 'reasonable punishment'. Many slaves were clearly well treated in a paternalistic fashion; some, however, were subjected to barbarous cruelty. In 1702, for example, a Drakenstein burgher, Jan Schepping, was accused of maltreating his slave Jan by removing the skin from his back with a curry-comb used to rub down horses. A quarter of a century later Jan Steenkamp of Paarl beat two slaves to death.

Slaves could be freed by their owners, but manumission was subject to Company approval from 1708 and hedged in by an increasing number of stipulations. The death of an owner was a frequent prelude to manumission, either by testamentary bequest or through the action of a surviving spouse. Manumission figures have been analysed for the period 1715-1791 and it has been calculated that the annual rate represented less than one fifth of one per cent of the total slave population in a given year. Corresponding figures for colonial Brazil and Peru suggest a manumission rate there more than five times higher than that at the Cape. Baptism of a slave into the Christian religion was no automatic passport to freedom and, perhaps in part because of this, Islam made significant strides in the Cape Town region among slaves, encouraged by such teachers as Abdullah Kadi Abdu Salaam, an Indonesian prince exiled to the Cape in 1767. The Cape Malays, today an ethnologically mixed group, were originally slaves or political exiles from eastern Asia. Although the languages they spoke died out, their Islamic faith served as a unifying bond, with the mosque and the Koran at the centre of their cultural life.

Khoisan and Xhosa

After the departure of Van Riebeeck, the expansion of the farming frontier and the deeper and more frequent penetration of the interior by expeditions in search of livestock brought the Khoikhoi into closer contact with the Dutch. The growing demand for livestock at the port settlement contributed to the impoverishment of the Khoikhoi and many drifted into the colony to work as herdsmen and shepherds on the farms, or to seek work in the town. This placed them under the laws of the colony. The disintegration of Khoikhoi society in the south-western Cape was completed by the ravages of such diseases as smallpox and scarlet fever, in particular the smallpox epidemics of 1713, 1755 and

The beacon erected by Governor van Plettenberg at present-day Plettenberg Bay. The beacon was inscribed with the VOC monogram and the Governor's personal coat of arms. A similar beacon, marking the north-eastern limits of the colony, was erected near the Zeekoe River in the vicinity of the present town of Colesberg. (Cape Archives, M284)

The interior of the church at Genadendal during a service. (Cape Archives, M246)

Xhosa in the Zuurveld near the Fish River, depicted by F T l'Ons. (William Fehr Collection)

Georg Schmidt

Georg Schmidt, the first Moravian missionary at the Cape.

South Africa's first Moravian missionary, Georg Schmidt, reached the Cape in July 1737. He was given permission to work among the Khoikhoi near one of the Company's posts and he trekked with a group of them to Baviaanskloof (near present-day Caledon), further into the interior. There he preached the gospel and also instructed the Khoikhoi in agriculture. His successes attracted attention and many whites, particularly Lutherans, began to see the need for spiritual action. When Schmidt started to baptize his converts, however, he fell foul of the established Dutch Reformed Church, which would not recognize his right to do so. He therefore left for Europe in March 1744. His memory was preserved by the Khoikhoi and when the Moravians were allowed to return in 1792 to found their mission station Genadendal at Baviaanskloof, they discovered that Georg Schmidt's teachings had not been entirely forgotten.

1767. The 1713 outbreak was caused by a ship's infected linen which had been brought ashore to be washed.

Khoisan resistance to white intrusion continued on the frontier. In 1715 the first purely burgher commando was formed, a service which became compulsory in 1739. Although many of the indigenous peoples settled on trekboer farms, others banded together to fight the frontier farmers. The government left it to the burghers to deal with the problem, and the result was that commando duty became a way of life. Hundreds of Khoisan were killed and their children indentured. On the other hand farms were ravaged and by 1785 the Khoisan controlled large areas of the Roggeveld in the Stellenbosch district and the Sneeubergen of Graaff-Reinet.

In view of the great missionary achievements of the nineteenth century it is surprising that so little was done to bring Christianity to the indigenous races until the last few years of Company rule. The one exception, the Moravian mission of 1737, was wrecked on the shoals of vested church interests.

Contact between colonials and the Bantu-speaking Sotho-Tswana on the northern frontier was slight in the Company period, but the advance of hunters, traders and trekboers to the east brought whites into contact with the Xhosa from as early as 1702.

The Xhosa in the Zuurveld to the west of the Fish River encountered the eastward thrust of the trekboers in the 1770s. Both Xhosa and trekboers were pastoralists and subsistence farmers, but they differed in customs of land tenure. The Xhosa regarded land as a community property, while the whites held it on an individual basis. It was competition for pasture in the Zuurveld which was the first grievance of the trekboers.

The frontier, in the days of the Dutch East India Company, was an area which the historian Hermann Giliomee has called an 'open' frontier. Such a frontier, he explains, is one in which 'two or more ethnic communities co-exist with

conflicting claims to the land, and no authority is recognised as legitimate by all the parties or is able to exercise undisputed control over the area'. This was the position in the Zuurveld, where the whites could look for little help from the Company and the Xhosa lacked a paramount chief.

When Governor van Plettenberg visited the eastern frontier in 1778, crossing the official Gamtoos River boundary of the colony established in 1771, he persuaded some chiefs of the Gwali Xhosa to accept the Fish River as the boundary between the Company's territories and those of the Xhosa. There was, however, as yet no organized local government for the region adequate to keep the peace, nor were the Xhosa as a whole prepared to accept the pledges made by a handful of subordinate chiefs.

Xhosa-trekboer relations speedily deteriorated. A frontier war broke out in 1779, the first clash in a continuing series of skirmishes of which the most intense have been given a numerical sequence by many historians. On this occasion the Xhosa captured many cattle in their turn and commando expeditions were organized in 1779 and 1780 in retaliation. The government, anxious to assert its authority, appointed the farmer Adriaan van Jaarsveld (later to rebel against the British) as Commandant on the eastern border, with instructions to clear the Zuurveld of Xhosa. This he accomplished in 1781 with a mixed force of mounted whites and Khoikhoi, but followed the frontier practice of confiscating cattle.

Company authority was strengthened with the creation of the Graaff-Reinet district in 1786, but the conciliatory policy towards the Xhosa, now back in force in the Zuurveld, enraged the frontier farmers. The German-born *landdrost* of the new district, Moritz Hermann Otto Woeke, was compelled to resign in 1792, and the decision of his successor, Maynier, to come to terms with the Xhosa in November 1793 after a second frontier war between the Xhosa and white settlers was to lead to the rejection of Company rule in the Graaff-Reinet district in 1795.

The frontier was at length to 'close', to the disadvantage of the Xhosa, but in the years of conflict on the 'open' frontier, expediency sometimes dictated the formation of alliances which cut across racial lines, as was the case with some of the Graaff-Reinet colonists who sided with the Rharhabe Xhosa beyond the Fish River since both sought the subjugation of the Xhosa chiefdoms in the Zuurveld.

The Cape sea route

The defence of the Cape sea route was always of paramount importance and the early collapse of Van Riebeeck's mud fort made it imperative that a stronger structure be built. The construction of the Castle still did not provide the Cape with adequate defences. It was, in any case, dominated by Devil's Peak and Signal Hill, occupation of either of which would render it extremely vulnerable. The defences were, however, never put to the test.

The main purpose of the Cape settlement to the Company was to provide adequate facilities for Dutch shipping, together with care for sick sailors. Southern African waters were treacherous, as the number of shipwrecks testified, nor was Table Bay the ideal anchorage, particularly when the strong north-westers blew in the winter months. In June 1722 seven Dutch vessels and three British were wrecked in a storm, with heavy losses of bullion. The Company began construction of a protective mole in 1743 from a promontory on the coast, still known today as Mouille Point. Work continued until September 1747, carried out by slaves and convicts. Heavy seas, however, caused the abandonment of the project, and it was made compulsory for Dutch ships to use False Bay as a winter anchorage. This led to the development of port facilities at what is now Simonstown on False Bay.

Dutch ships were always in the majority at the Cape in every year until 1772, when the Company slid into a rapid decline. Foreign vessels were frequent callers at all times and English shipping dominated in most years from the Anglo-Dutch alliance of 1668 until the middle of the following century. For many years, and particularly from 1735 until 1755, the only

foreign callers at the Cape were British, French and Danish. The Dutch monopoly could not, however, be indefinitely maintained and from 1755 an increasing number of ships from many ports in Europe called at Table Bay and, from 1784, a considerable number from the United States of America as well.

Dutch and foreign vessels brought many distinguished visitors to the colony, among them the French astronomers Guy Tachard, Jean de Fontaney and La Caille, the Swedish naturalists Anders Sparrman and Carl Pehr Thunberg, the French traveller and artist François le Vaillant, and such noted soldiers and sailors as Anson, Robert Clive and James Cook.

For most of the eighteenth century Franco-

Table Bay in 1683, by Aernaut Smit, with the ship *Africa* in the foreground. The detail of the buildings is accurate, and the Castle is depicted with the original entrance or 'sea gate' facing the beach. Simon van der Stel had this entrance closed and erected a land entrance from the parade ground which was completed in 1684. (William Fehr Collection)

Genadendal (Africana Museum)

The heroic deed of Wolraad Woltemade on 1 June 1773. The ship *De Jonge Thomas* was driven aground at Salt River. Woltemade and his horse braved the breakers seven times, and brought fourteen people to safety. The eighth time he and his horse disappeared beneath the waves. Survivors reported his brave deed to the Lords Seventeen, and a substantial award was made to his wife and sons. (Cape Archives, M744)

The Castle

Construction work on the Castle began in January 1666, when Governor Zacharias Wagenaer and other top officials were present at the ceremony of laying the foundations. The design was pentagonal, with a defensive bastion at each angle, and owed much to the fortifications constructed by Louis XIV's master engineer, Vauban. Work proceeded slowly and was only speeded up in times of international conflict. Much of the labour was provided by slaves, convicts and soldiers. By 1674 the garrison was able to move into the building and two years later the bastions were completed and named after the titles of the Prince of Orange: Buuren, Leerdam, Oranje, Nassau and Catzenellenbogen. Governor Bax encouraged the digging of the defensive moat by decreeing that all men passing the site, irrespective of rank, were to carry away twelve baskets of earth and all women, six. In May 1678 the main gateway on the seaward side was completed, but in 1684 Simon van der Stel decided to close it and built the existing gateway and tower between the Buuren and Leerdam bastions. Above the gateway he had the arms of the chambers of the company carved: (from left to right) Hoorn, Delft, Amsterdam, Middelburg, Rotterdam and Enkhuizen. The *'kat'*, a dividing wall across the central courtyard, was built in 1691 and within a few years the new residences for the Governor and his deputy, and a chamber for the Councils of Policy and of Justice were incorporated in the central defensive wall.

The Simon van der Stel gateway, completed in 1684. (Cape Archives, M816)

British rivalry for empire in the East increased, while Dutch power declined. Hostilities between France and Britain brought naval units to the Indian Ocean in force, many of them calling at the Cape. The Netherlands were nominally neutral in the War of the Austrian Succession, but with Britain's entry into the struggle in 1744 and a French threat to the Dutch provinces three years later, the small nation became actively involved. In 1748 the Dutch East India Company took part in a massive operation launched by Britain to deliver a mortal blow to the French east of the Cape.

The Anglo-Dutch Expedition of 1748 assembled in Table Bay under the command of the British Admiral, Edward Boscawen. By far the largest fleet ever seen at the Cape, it consisted of thirteen British naval vessels, fourteen East Indiamen from London and six ships of the Dutch Company. Aboard them was a considerable military contingent, including fifty men from the Cape garrison. The combined fleet sailed on 19 May to wrest Mauritius (Île de France) and Réunion (Bourbon) from the French. The result was a fiasco. Boscawen was reluctant to confront the Mauritius defences, the Dutch sailed off to Batavia and the British turned to their next objective, the Coromandel coast, where Boscawen's efforts were equally unspectacular.

The long Anglo-Dutch alliance began to wear thin after 1750. The republican Patriots of the Netherlands grew in strength and when in 1780 the Dutch refused to fulfil old treaty obligations to help Britain in her conflict with her American colonists, the British declared war on their former allies. This led to a Dutch *entente* with France and a French garrison at the Cape which remained until 1784.

Company control at the Cape of Good Hope was almost at an end. The French Revolution of 1789 unleashed new forces in Europe and in January 1795 Prince William V of Orange fled to England and the Batavian Republic was established in the Netherlands. The Dutch East India Company was taken over by the state in December 1795 to expire a few years later as a

discredited institution. By September 1795, however, the Cape of Good Hope was in new hands.

The conquest of the Cape by the British in 1795 was effected after the arrival of troops brought out by Rear-Admiral George Keith Elphinstone. The first invasion force landed at Simonstown in July under the command of Major-General James Henry Craig and advanced to Muizenberg, where it was joined by another detachment under Major-General Alured Clarke. The Dutch defence was half-hearted. The burgher force distrusted the commanders, there were British sympathizers in the Company ranks and moreover, the British had come not so much as conquerors, but as an occupying force supported by the exiled Prince of Orange. Sluysken, the Commissioner-General, retreated from Wynberg and finally capitulated at Rustenburg on 16 September 1795.

It was the end of an era but not yet, in view of the temporary nature of the occupation, the beginning of a new one. The Dutch East India Company had disappeared at the Cape, but the developments which had taken place under its rule had left a legacy destined to colour the future socio-political history of a sub-continent: in race contacts, in frontier confrontation, in regional variation, and at all levels in the evolving relationship between government and governed.

Suggested Reading List

C Beyers (1981) *Die Kaapse Patriotte Gedurende die Laaste Kwart van die Agtiende Eeu en die Voortlewing van Hul Denkbeelde*, 2nd ed, Pretoria

M Boucher (1981) *French Speakers at the Cape in the First Hundred Years of Dutch East India Company Rule: the European Background*, Pretoria

A J Böeseken (1977) *Slaves and Free Blacks at the Cape, 1658-1700*, Cape Town

G C de Wet (1981) *Die Vryliede en Vryswartes in die Kaapse Nedersetting, 1657-1707*, Cape Town

J S Marais (1962) *Maynier and the First Boer Republic*, reprint, Cape Town

P J van der Merwe (1938) *Die Trekboer in die Geskiedenis van die Kaapkolonie, 1657-1842*, Cape Town

Chapter 6

The Occupations of the Cape, 1795-1854

Basil A le Cordeur

For the inhabitants of the Cape Colony, the coming of British rule in 1795 at first brought few striking changes in the ways of living to which they had long been accustomed. Geography and climate continued to set bounds to the freedom of choice and action of all the people and communities of the region. The vast distances which separated the colony from the centres of world population, the inhospitable coastline, the absence of navigable rivers to penetrate the interior, the irregularity of the rainfall – these, together with the exceptionally sparse population and the absence of cheap labour and advanced agricultural techniques, ensured that the colony's productivity would be limited. Its domestic market was underdeveloped, and until at least one export staple could be produced, ties with the wider world would continue to be all too heavily dependent upon passing ships.

To these environmental constraints upon change was added the profound weight of deep-seated social forces. Contrary to what is traditionally thought, the Cape was one of the most closed and rigid slave societies in the era of European colonization. In 1795 the largest sector of the colonial population was the slaves, of whom there were some 25 000. Next in number came the 20 000 white colonists, followed by 15 000 Khoikhoi and some 1 000 free blacks. During the eighteenth century Cape society had come to be dominated by a privileged white caste, determined to preserve and strengthen the solid legal and customary barriers between free and unfree and between white and black. The habit of differentiation on the basis of race did not originate on the colonial frontier, as has been believed since the classic work of I D MacCrone (*Race Attitudes in South Africa*) in 1937; it was deeply embedded in the society of the original, settled western districts of the col-

Basil A le Cordeur is King George V Professor of History at the University of Cape Town. He is the author of numerous publications on the history of the Eastern Cape and Natal in the nineteenth century, including *The Politics of Eastern Cape Separatism, 1820-1854* (Oxford University Press, 1981). He is a past President of the South African Historical Society, and is currently General Editor of the Brenthurst Series and Editor-in-Chief of the *South African Historical Journal*.

The Heerengracht, renamed Adderley Street in 1850, in the first half of the nineteenth century. The Commercial Exchange, built in 1822, is in the foreground on the left, and the steeple of the Groote Kerk, completed in 1703, is in the background. (Africana Museum)

Lady Anne Lindsay (1750-1825) from a miniature by Richard Cosway. The eldest daughter of James, 5th Earl of Balcarres, she wrote a popular ballad entitled 'Auld Robin Grey' at the age of 21. She acted as hostess to Dr Samuel Johnson in Edinburgh in 1773, and moved in distinguished circles in London, counting among her friends Henry Dundas, Secretary of State for War and the Colonies. At the age of 43 she married Andrew Barnard, who was twelve years her junior. In 1793 he was offered the Colonial Secretaryship at the Cape, and it was from here that Lady Anne Barnard wrote a series of letters to Henry Dundas which are an important source of information about the people, events and social life at the Cape during the first British occupation. (Cape Archives, M280)

Fort Frederick, Algoa Bay. The original wooden blockhouse was erected on the eastern side of the Baakens River in 1799, at the time of the Third Frontier War, and was the first British structure in the Eastern Cape. Later a stone fort was built on the eminence above, and named after Frederick, Duke of York. (Africana Museum)

ony long before a recognizable frontier existed, and continued to evolve there after the frontier had disappeared.

Nor did the Enlightenment thinking of the late eighteenth century have any marked early impact upon the colony. Whatever slogans the activists of Graaff-Reinet and Swellendam might mouth in the 1790s, they were motivated by individual and group self-interest rather than by ideological principles; only in the western districts did Enlightenment ideals reveal any strength among the colonists.

The limited objectives of the British in occupying the Cape in 1795 served to reinforce the maintenance of the status quo. Their primarily strategic aim of preventing the Cape from falling into the hands of the arch imperial rival, France, and their assumption that the occupation would be temporary, resulted in the new British rulers setting their minds to the task of preserving law and order and taking pains to conciliate and to win the loyalty of their new subjects. When the need to make the colony pay for itself was subsequently impressed upon the governors, this merely heightened their awareness of the need to avoid disturbing the delicate social and political equilibrium.

Between 1795 and 1814, while the French revolutionary and Napoleonic wars raged in Europe, the Cape changed hands three times. This transitional period did not end until the Dutch permanently ceded the Cape to Great Britain at the London Convention of 13 August 1814.

The first British occupation, 1795-1803

The British military government which took over the Cape in 1795 was all too conscious of the widespread local opposition to the occupation. While standing firm on matters of fundamental importance to their hold upon the colony, they guaranteed the maintenance of the existing laws and customs of the settlement, including the Roman-Dutch legal system. They promised that no new taxes would be levied, and they guaranteed the property rights as well as the money circulated by the VOC (*Vereenigde Oost-Indische Compagnie* or Dutch East India Company). The Council of Policy was replaced by a Governor, in whose hands all civil and military power was concentrated. On the departure for India of the British fleet under Clarke and Elphinstone, General Craig took over the government, which he administered in a sympathetic and efficient manner. Arrears of land rents were remitted and the commission of the High Court was replaced by a nominated Burgher Senate whose members were appointed by the Governor from lists submitted by the Senate itself, and whose responsibilities were extended.

The new authorities also took full advantage of a social process which had set in from the 1780s, ie the emergence of a colonial gentry and its interpenetration with the class of leading officials. In the latter part of the eighteenth century the *heemraden*, through their control over local resources such as land and labour, were able to assert their pre-eminence in the colonial countryside and to extend this power in part to the central organs of government. Contrary to Afrikaner nationalist tradition, Afrikaner society was not egalitarian, but increasingly stratified. (According to André du Toit and Hermann Giliomee in *Afrikaner Political Thought*, many whites at the Cape by the end of the eighteenth century regarded themselves as being 'rooted in Africa', and this conception found expression in the term 'Afrikaner', which is used in this and in later chapters.)

The local elite of relatively wealthy farmers of the south-western districts, who dominated the hierarchy of *heemraden*, church officials and officers in the militia, established a working alliance with the other major sections of Cape society: the farmers of the other regions, the emerging mercantile elite, and the central government of the colony. From the earliest days of British rule, too, the local Afrikaner notables were courted and wooed, a process in which the

The meeting of Governor Janssens and the Xhosa chief Ngqika at the Kat River in 1803. (Africana Museum)

charming Lady Anne Barnard, whose husband was secretary to the Military Governor of the Cape, Earl Macartney, played an active role. The Governor's wife did not accompany her husband to the Cape, and Lady Anne acted as his official hostess, entertaining the colonial elite at the Castle. Although she endeared herself personally to the colonists by the warmth of her personality and her genuine interest in their way of life, these efforts at conciliation were not conspicuously successful, for the Afrikaner population was sharply divided between those who were prepared to collaborate (the *Anglo-mannen*) and those who rejected the overtures with contempt (the so-called *Jacobijnen*).

The main task confronting the British on their arrival was the restoration of peace on the eastern frontier of the colony, since the naval base, Cape Town, was dependent for its meat supply upon the hinterland, especially upon Graaff-Reinet. By the late eighteenth century, the settlement of the Gqunukhwebe and other peoples in the area between the Fish and the Bushmans rivers in the Zuurveld had begun to be challenged by the whites. Exasperated at the failure of the colonial authorities to protect them against the Xhosa and their refusal even to allow them to defend themselves, the colonists of Graaff-Reinet expelled the unpopular *land-drost*, Maynier, set up a republican government and renounced their allegiance to the VOC in the very week in which the British fleet arrived to occupy the Cape. Swellendam followed suit.

Craig reacted decisively to this threat. He cut off all supplies of goods, including ammunition, to Graaff-Reinet, and when a Batavian fleet which had sailed from Europe to attempt to recover the Cape, was forced to surrender, the Graaff-Reinet farmers submitted to the new regime. Yet in their very submission lay hints of further trouble. They requested permission to be allowed to occupy land beyond the Fish River, which had been the official boundary of the colony since the days of Van Plettenberg. The British, like their Dutch predecessors, lacked the means to embark upon a policy for adequate control of relations between colonists and Xhosa; they therefore fell back upon attempting to maintain a rigid boundary between black and white, and to insist on a policy of non-intercourse. Craig sternly warned against acts of hostility against the Xhosa or against any attempt to dispossess them of their land. 'With what face,' he demanded indignantly, 'can you ask of me to allow you to occupy lands which belong to other people? What right can I have to give you the property of others?. . . Reflect for a moment on what would be your own sensations were you to hear that I was even debating on a proposal. . . to turn you out of your farms, and to give them to others.'

Macartney, too, tried in vain to persuade both black and white to respect the Fish River as the definitive boundary between their respective peoples, but the frontier continued to be a centre of unrest throughout the first British occupation. Fort Frederick was constructed at Algoa Bay, from which troops could be deployed to trouble spots involving either Boers or Xhosa, and Maynier was installed as Resident Commissioner at Graaff-Reinet. However, he lacked anything like the means needed to main-

An early portrait of Earl Macartney, 1737-1806, first British Governor at the Cape of Good Hope. (William Fehr Collection)

Dr J T van der Kemp of the London Missionary Society, who was converted late in life after his wife and child drowned before his eyes in a river in the Netherlands. He established a mission station at Bethelsdorp near Port Elizabeth, married the daughter of a slave woman from Madagascar, and devoted his life to mission work among the Khoikhoi. (Cape Archives, E332)

The frontier wars

Writers of South African history usually refer to the most serious periods of conflict between the whites and black people on the eastern frontier as 'frontier wars'. The following are mentioned in this chapter:
Third Frontier War (1799-1803)
Fourth Frontier War (1811-1812)
Fifth Frontier War (1818-1819)
Sixth Frontier War (1834-1835)
Seventh Frontier War or 'War of the Axe' (1846-1847)
Eighth Frontier War (1850-1853)

Jan Willem Janssens (1762-1838), who accompanied Commissioner De Mist to the Cape as Military Governor in 1803. Although diffident and given to self-doubt, Janssens had much to do with reform in the colony, and held discussions with Ndlambe at the Sundays River and Ngqika at the Kat River in an attempt to restore peace to the frontier. After the resumption of the Napoleonic Wars in Europe, he attempted to strengthen the defences of the colony, but the transfer of his best troops to the Dutch East Indies weakened his force, which was subsequently defeated by the British in 1806. (Cape Archives, M304)

tain peace and order, and antagonised the farmers by forbidding them to use armed parties to recover stolen cattle. Finally, the colonial authorities were obliged to recall him. The frontier remained combustible, and the period from 1799 to 1803 was called, in retrospect, the Third Frontier War. Twice the Khoikhoi went into rebellion in conjunction with the Xhosa, and by 1803 the authorities could do no more than make a peace which merely papered over the cracks. It was in a highly unsettled state that, in terms of the Treaty of Amiens between Britain and France, the Cape was handed over to the new Batavian Republic early in 1803.

The Batavian occupation, 1803-1806

The regime of the Batavians, which succeeded that of the British, is traditionally associated with the spread of the thinking of the Enlightenment, but in fact it was somewhat more conservative than is usually believed. Unlike the British, the Batavians expected to retain the colony permanently, and sent out one of the members of the Council for Asiatic Possessions, Jacob Abraham Uitenhage de Mist, to implement a memorandum which he had submitted in 1802, outlining proposals for extensive reforms in the colony's system of government.

Both De Mist and the Governor, Lieutenant-General Jan Willem Janssens, were intent primarily upon imposing order upon the far-flung and loosely structured colony. Tighter organization led inexorably to an increasing degree of centralization of power and, despite De Mist's strong belief in the sovereignty of law and the rights and freedom of the individual, to a more authoritarian approach. The powers of the Gov-

ernor were extended, and the restored Council of Policy consisted almost entirely of Hollanders, not colonists. The Burgher Council (renamed the *Raad der Gemeente*) remained an appointive body, and attempts were made to reduce its functions further. Central government control was further promoted by the establishment of new *drostdies* at Uitenhage and Tulbagh in 1804. Districts were subdivided into wards, each under a newly created official, the field-cornet, and a weekly post between the *drostdies* was instituted. The most significant judicial change was the creation of a Council of Justice, consisting of six members with legal qualifications. The judicature was to be quite independent of the executive.

The historian G M Theal and those who followed his lead erred in the belief that the ordinances on religion and education shocked the colonists by their radical nature. In fact, the self-supporting church administration which the *Kerkorde* of 1804 inaugurated, received considerable support from church boards and ministers alike. Civil marriage was instituted, but the practice was not very different from what had obtained during the days of the Company. Similarly, the *Schoolorde* of 1805, which was promulgated with the avowed intention of secularizing education in order to train civil servants, was generally welcomed by the colonists because of the advances which it was expected to bring in formal education.

Financial stringency also prevented the Batavians from launching a more positive attack upon the problems of the eastern frontier. De Mist and Janssens had both hoped that their administrative reforms would enable them to establish a firmer grip upon the frontiersmen; but to afford them protection was another matter. Janssens was obliged to continue the policies of his predecessors, merely attempting to keep the peace. Khoikhoi were moved into locations, and Dr J T van der Kemp was granted land for a mission station at Bethelsdorp near Algoa Bay. Other Khoikhoi were persuaded to return from the Zuurveld to labour on white farms in terms of a regulation that employers might hire their labour only on a written contract signed before official witnesses. As for the Xhosa, Janssens found himself without the powers of coercion needed to induce the victorious tribesmen to leave the Zuurveld and continued to pursue a policy of merely maintaining a rigid frontier between black and white.

The Batavians had soon come to realize – like their British predecessors – that they dared not threaten the deeply ingrained habits and prejudices which maintained the stability of the colony's social fabric in the face of severe injustices and inequities. More decisively, the war between Britain and France had been resumed, and now Britain was far more conscious than she had been in 1795 of the value of the Cape in the imperial and commercial struggle against her French rival. After Napoleon's scheme to invade Britain had been checked, a fleet sailed for the Cape. At Blaauwberg, 16 miles (25 km) north of Cape Town, Major-General Baird's troops defeated the Dutch, who capitulated on 10 January 1806. The surrender of Cape Town was signed at Papendorp (Woodstock). Eight days later, Janssens, who had retreated with his men to the Hottentots-Holland Pass, also surrendered.

The second British occupation, 1806-1814

Once again the Cape had become British, and once again it seemed to be merely a temporary occupation. The continuity of social and political processes was marked. An authority on this period had amusingly described how the Burgher Senate reacted to the second British conquest in 1806. 'So complete was the continuity of the Burgher Senate,' he writes, 'that no interruption took place in its sessions. From the arrival of the British fleet on January 4 to January 10, the day Cape Town was occupied, the Burgher Senate sat day after day to support Janssens in his war operations; from January 10 to January 18, the day Janssens capitulated, they held daily sessions to help provide the necessary wagons and horses for the English.'

Until the final cession of the colony was ratified by treaty in 1814, there was no powerful incentive to embark upon administrative or other change. The first Governor, the Earl of Caledon, found that in view of the serious wartime situation, the Colonial Secretary would not consider reform, and he was able to contemplate the introduction of no more than a few of the changes which he had envisaged. The one significant exception to his 'do nothing' policy was a proclamation inaugurating a circuit court system whereby two judges of the High Court were to visit the country districts at regular intervals. They were not merely to hear civil and criminal cases, but also to report fully on all aspects of the situation in each district. In a colony in which there was almost no representation in government, this was a major step in the direction of establishing a direct link between the people of the more distant parts of the colony and the government in Cape Town. Caledon's successor, Sir John Cradock, was unusually popular with the colonists because of the promptitude and the sympathy with which he tackled their problems.

It was from Cradock's governorship that the first revolutionary change in policy on the eastern frontier dated. By the time he assumed office the Zuurveld had lapsed into complete disorder and the loan farms were being abandoned by the whites in rapid succession. In the first two months of 1812, Lieutenant-Colonel John Graham, on instructions from the Governor, led a combined force of regulars and burghers,

which forced 20 000 Xhosa across the Fish River, thus making the whole of the Zuurveld available for settlement by whites and their families. (Fourth Frontier War, 1811-1812.) In order to hold the line of the frontier, 27 military posts were constructed, which were to be fortified by patrols and by the establishment of the garrison towns of Grahamstown (in the Zuurveld) and Cradock. For the first time the colonial government had firmly grasped the nettle on the frontier; Cradock had rightly insisted that unless the hinterland was secure, the retention of the strategic point, the Cape Peninsula, could not be guaranteed. And for the first time the Home Government had accepted that an interventionist, military role was the price that would have to be paid if the frontier – and therefore the colony – was to be permanently retained. In a broader sense 1812 was the turning

Jacob Abraham Uitenhage de Mist (1749-1823), Commissioner-General of the Batavian Republic, who took up residence at the Cape in 1803. A brilliant administrator, he implemented reform of the system of government in the colony, and toured the colony in 1803. Accounts of this expedition were written by Dr Heinrich Lichtenstein and Augusta de Mist. (Cape Archives, M316)

Julie Philippe Augusta de Mist (1783-1832), the tenth child of J A de Mist, who accompanied her father to the Cape in 1802. She kept a travel diary which was privately printed in 1821. She married Baron Otto de Howen in 1809. (Cape Archives, M317)

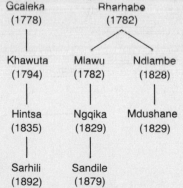

The Xhosa

According to Xhosa tradition, the Xhosa came to be divided between the Gcaleka of the Transkei and the Rharhabe of the Ciskei when, in the second half of the eighteenth century, Phalo was confronted with the task of having to choose a bride. Anxious to avoid offending either the Mpondo king or the Thembu king who had offered their respective daughters in marriage, he followed the advice of a wise man who said, 'What is greater than the head of the chief? And what is stronger than his right hand? Let the one girl be the head wife, and the other the wife of the right hand.' The division of the Xhosa kingdom between the Gcaleka and the Rharhabe was finally sealed by the creation of British Kaffraria in 1847.

(Year of death indicated in brackets)

Phalo
(1775)

Gcaleka (1778) — Rharhabe (1782)

Gcaleka branch:
Khawuta (1794)
Hintsa (1835)
Sarhili (1892)

Rharhabe branch:
Mlawu (1782)
Ngqika (1829)
Sandile (1879)

Ndlambe (1828)
Mdushane (1829)

79

Maqoma at the Battle of Burnshill, April 1846. This battle, in which a colonial force under Colonel John Hare was defeated by a force under Maqoma, half brother of Sandile, heir to the Rharhabe paramountcy, was the first engagement of the Seventh Frontier War. Maqoma and his followers had become embittered by their expulsion in 1829 from the Ceded Territory along the upper reaches of the Kat River, where the Kat River Settlement was subsequently established. Maqoma is portrayed wearing the blue-crane feathers of a warrior who has killed his enemy in battle. (William Fehr Collection)

The battle of the Gwanga, where the Xhosa suffered defeat in June 1846 during the Seventh Frontier War. A large force of Xhosa had made the tactical error of crossing open territory in daylight, and they lost this battle, fought near a tributary of the Keiskamma River. They are shown using firearms as well as spears. (Africana Museum)

point in the history of the frontier; it was then that power tilted decisively towards the whites, since the imperial government had finally thrown its weight into the scales on their side. British power had been indisputably established in the Zuurveld as VOC power never had been; the Zuurveld frontier was now effectively 'closed'.

For many reasons, the transitional period had been characterized by a high degree of continuity in most spheres of colonial life: in social processes, in ideology, in institutions and in matters of social control. Whereas in 1795 the British rulers had observed much disaffection among the Dutch colonists and had justifiably feared rebellion, by 1814 they had succeeded in cementing a firm working alliance with the dominant free burgher class. This had been achieved largely on the basis of an ever closer espousal of the cause of employers and of slave owners and a much clearer identification with the views of frontiersmen on the policies to be adopted towards the Xhosa. On one issue, however, the new rulers were adamant and were to remain so for several further decades: there would be no more popular participation or representation in government than could be avoided. But, as has already become apparent, the pace of change was accelerating each year. Long before 1820 the Home Government had had to recognize that the Cape was a colony, no longer merely a settlement.

Economic change

Among the most important forces of change which worked upon the Cape after 1795 were the economic. During the period of VOC rule the Cape had been part of the Dutch world-wide commercial system; now it was drawn into the orbit of the vastly larger and more dynamic British imperial system, which had far different priorities. Where Dutch rule had been that of a commercial company seeking to maximize profits by enforcing its trading monopolies, British imperial rule was that of the first industrial power of the modern world. It was in the first decades of the nineteenth century that the transition to capitalism at the Cape began. VOC mercantilism came to be replaced by an ideology of free trade, and slavery was abandoned in favour of free, although tightly controlled, labour.

First to go were the rigid monopolies and restrictions on internal trade which had hampered material progress under the Company. It was decreed that 'every man may buy of whom he pleases, and come and go where he chuses by land and water'. The external trade was thrown open to friendly nations, although upon a basis of imperial preference. From as early as the 1780s the Cape economy had been showing meaningful signs of movement towards export-directed production, and this expanded greatly in volume under the stimulus of imperial preference. Imports, too, increased substantially in volume, due in no small measure to the presence of the garrison and of increasing numbers of British officials. In the south-western Cape farming had always been tied to the Cape Town market, but by the late eighteenth century, within two decades of the settlement of the eastern districts by whites, there were clear signs of the beginnings of the commercialization of agriculture in the districts of Graaff-Reinet and Swellendam, and this process was intensified by the coming of the British.

In 1813 the duty on Cape wines entering Britain was reduced to one third of what it had pre-

viously been. By 1822 wine exports exceeded all other Cape exports together; indeed, it was wine exports which saved the colony from total insolvency. Unfortunately, wine-growers did not seize this opportunity to improve the quality of their wine, and when Britain began to withdraw the preferences in 1825 and 1831 the Cape wine trade suffered serious repercussions.

When wine ceased to function as the colony's staple export, the imperial connection again proved invaluable to the colonial economy. By the second quarter of the nineteenth century British textile mills were consuming prodigious quantities of raw wool. From the 1820s the Cape responded by a swift conversion from the indigenous fat-tailed sheep to Spanish merinos and by exporting wool on a vastly increased scale – 20 000 1b (9 000 kg) in 1822, 200 000 1b (90 000 kg) in 1832 and 12 000 000 1b (5 500 000 kg) in 1855. By 1840 wool had become the most important colonial export in value, and was not overtaken by any other product until the advent of diamonds in the 1870s.

These increases in the productivity and the trade of the Cape in the first half of the nineteenth century depended also upon other developments. First, there was the construction of roads and mountain passes, in order to make the country districts accessible: the Tulbagh Pass in 1807, Sir Lowry's Pass in 1830, and between the mid-1840s and mid-1850s, the Montagu Pass, Michell's Pass and Bain's Kloof Pass. Most important for the development of communications was the construction of the hard road across the Cape Flats. Between the 1820s and the 1840s the volume of shipping calling at Cape ports quadrupled, and the Cape was able to take advantage of the services of the finest sailing ships of the time, the East India armed merchantmen.

In 1825 the British Government decided to convert the foreign currencies of annexed colonies to sterling. In view of the considerable depreciation of the rixdollar, (which had fallen from 4s to 1s 6d by 1825), this move caused unprecedented hardship among many Cape creditors in the short term, but in the long run it was a reform of fundamental importance for the economic development of the colony. The greater sophistication of the economy was underlined by the appearance of insurance companies from the 1830s and by the advent in 1837 of the first commercial bank, the Cape of Good Hope Bank.

The small group of active British merchants who settled at the Cape had considerable advantages over the local merchants through their financial and trading connections with London. A small British mercantile elite came to dominate the business life – and, indeed, the public life – of the colony. Private business began to flourish. The number of retail shops in Cape Town grew rapidly, and in 1822 the Commercial Exchange was founded. Productivity and

the development of the export trade were stimulated, too, by reform of the system of land tenure in the colony. The traditional loan farm system of extensive leaseholds had severe disadvantages for the economy of the colony, not least the fact that land could be obtained so easily that there was little or no incentive for farmers to effect permanent improvements.

In 1813 Governor Cradock initiated the reform of the system of landowning. He issued a series of proclamations designed to encourage the voluntary conversion of existing loan places into permanent quitrent tenure and eventual ownership. Despite these measures, between 1813 and 1840, a further 31,5 million acres were alienated for a mere £46 000 and for quitrents of less than £14 000 pa – an annual rent of about one penny for every ten acres.

Economic change had come slowly and in an uneven, haphazard, piecemeal form, but the changes of the first half of the nineteenth century were not without significance; they were not merely quantitative, but also qualitative.

Slaves, Khoikhoi and missionaries

One of the ways in which the British imperial impact upon the Cape was most evident was in the new emphasis upon free labour. In Britain the main role in the campaign against slavery was played by the humanitarians, who were inspired by the Evangelical movement, and who brought considerable pressure to bear in Parliament against the slave trade on moral and religious as well as on economic grounds. By the late eighteenth century a different view of the proper relations between master and servant had evolved against the background of the new industrial world economy. To the emerging business leaders it seemed apparent that the

The attack on Maqoma's stronghold in the 'Kroomie Mountains', north-west of Fort Beaufort, in 1851, during the Eighth Frontier War. (William Fehr Collection)

Original brand of Cape sheep. (Africana Museum)

Improved Cape sheep. (Africana Museum)

The state of Cradock's Pass between George and the Longkloof in the 1840s, showing the difficulties encountered by travellers journeying to the outlying districts. (Cape Archives, M929)

needs of industrialization, unlike those of the previous plantation economy of the empire, would not be best served by chattel slavery, but by a system of free labour, compelled by moral and economic, rather than by legal, forces. The British rulers took steps to reduce the importation of slaves, and in 1808 the British act for the abolition of the slave trade came into force: no slave could legally be landed in any British port after 1 March of that year.

The abolition of the slave trade exacerbated the serious shortage of labour at the Cape. Both colonists and government looked to the Khoikhoi to supply the deficit. By the end of the eighteenth century they had been dispossessed of their land, and subject as they were to the arbitrary exercise of authority by their masters or by colonial officials, their position was in practice inferior to that of the slaves. Governor Caledon's code of 1809 was the first serious attempt to bring the Khoikhoi within the rule of law, but it also made it difficult for them to avoid working for whites. Since the farmers took advantage of the extra controls which they were entitled to enforce and refrained from applying those provisions which were in opposition to their own interests, the practical effect of the code was to throw the weight of the colonial state into the balance on the side of the masters. The further proclamations of 1812 and 1819 on apprenticeship accentuated the immobilization of Khoikhoi labour and left them more than ever at the mercy of the white farmers and officials.

It was as the role of the Khoikhoi in the colonial labour market was being taken into serious consideration by the authorities that there ar-rived at the Cape the representatives of the Christian missionary societies, who were now so popular with the rising middle classes in Britain and the rest of Europe. As agents of cultural change and as men with influential contacts in Britain, they represented the most potent new social force of the period, and the one with the greatest long-term significance.

As a result of the protests to London of Dr J T van der Kemp's colleague, James Read, concerning the ill-treatment of Khoi servants by white farmers, Cradock instructed the new circuit court to investigate the charges. Despite the difficulty of assembling over a thousand witnesses, eight out of the sixty-two whites were convicted of crimes of violence against servants. The 'Black Circuit' of 1812 left a bitter legacy of hatred and misunderstanding. The whites were outraged at the notion that Khoi servants could rightfully claim equality before the law. Three years later a group of whites on the frontier took up arms against the authorities in pursuit of the time honoured right of forcibly making their opposition to objectionable official measures known. The rebellion was suppressed by a government determined that the rule of law should henceforth prevail in the colony, but the ringleaders were regarded by subsequent generations as martyrs.

The repressive codes of Caledon and his successors did little to stabilize Khoi labour. The pressures upon the Khoikhoi increased, but by the 1820s they had acquired a far more important champion – Dr John Philip, Superintendent of the London Missionary Society, who had the ear of influential political figures in London.

Dr Philip believed that the time had come not merely to contest individual cases of injustice, but to reform the entire legal status of the Khoikhoi in the colony. 'I require nothing for them,' he told the Secretary of State, 'but the power of bringing their labour to a fair market.' The Secretary of State agreed to a motion by the leader of the anti-slavery party, Thomas Buxton, that 'directions be given for effectually securing to all the natives of South Africa the same freedom and protection as are enjoyed by other free persons residing at the Cape, whether they be English or Dutch'. The Acting Governor, General Bourke, influenced by a memorandum of the pragmatic and philanthropically minded *landdrost*, Andries Stockenström, published Ordinance 50 in 1828 'for improving the condition of the Hottentots and other free persons of colour at the Cape'.

Ordinance 50 abolished all discriminatory restrictions on the Khoikhoi and placed them on a basis of legal equality with the whites; in particular, they were no longer required to carry passes, and they could legally own land. The ordinance is conventionally hailed as 'the Magna Carta of the Hottentots' and a triumph for Dr Philip. Nowadays many historians inter-

Witnesses who gave evidence before the Select Committee on Aborigines, which sat in London in 1835 and 1836. From left to right: Jan Tzatzoe, Andries Stoffles (seated), James Read (Sr), James Read (Jr), Dr John Philip (seated). (Cape Archives, M262)

Slagter's Nek rebellion (1815)

The Slagter's Nek rebellion was prompted by the refusal of a farmer, Frederik Bezuidenhout of Baviaans River, to obey an order to appear in court to answer charges of cruelty to a Khoikhoi servant. When a white officer and twelve Khoikhoi soldiers were sent to arrest him, he fired upon them and was himself killed in the ensuing exchange. His brother Johannes vowed revenge for his death, invited Ngqika to join in resistance to the colonial government and raised a rebellion on the frontier. The uprising was suppressed at Slagter's Nek, and the leaders were publicly executed in particularly distressing circumstances. A large number of people were ordered to attend the execution, but the rope broke, and the convicted men were hanged only at the second attempt. The rebels were not heroes, and they were not supported at all by the great mass of frontiersmen: they were simply individuals who had taken the law into their own hands as they were accustomed to doing under the VOC.

pret it as at least in part a response by the colonial state to the demands for a more mobile labour force in the expanding labour market of the colony.

Although the ordinance did not unequivocally guarantee the Khoikhoi complete legal equality, it did afford them greater freedom 'in bringing their labour to a fair market'. It rudely disturbed the already unsettled labour market and almost certainly resulted in an increase in vagrancy and crime. To help the landless Khoikhoi to adapt to the new conditions, Stockenström set up the Kat River Settlement on the eastern frontier in 1829, where they could establish themselves as smallholders. The colonists tried to nullify the provisions of Ordinance 50 by passing a Vagrancy Law in 1834, but, largely as a result of representations by the missionaries, the law was disallowed by the Home Government. These were severe blows both to the economic privileges and to the social prestige of the white colonial community.

The labour problem was exacerbated by the emancipation of the slaves, especially in the western districts. After the abolition of the slave trade, the anti-slavery campaigners had hoped that the manumission of all children born to slave parents would open the way towards emancipation, but it was soon clear that this would be a very slow process. Moreover, slave owners at the Cape ignored or evaded regulations aimed at ameliorating the condition of slaves. The colonial state, anxious to retain the political co-operation of the masters, backed them in their efforts to discipline their work force, while often providing no more than nominal additional protection for the latter. A variety of new forms of coercion, often based on currently fashionable ideologies transposed from Britain, was employed, in particular the attempt to reconstruct and control them by 'educational and moral transformation'. However, in the last instance, masters and officials had no hesitation in resorting to violence, and to this the Cape was particularly prone.

Over the decades the anti-slavery movement shifted its objective from amelioration to outright emancipation, and in 1833 Parliament

▽▽
The 'cave' or rocky outcrop from which Frederik Bezuidenhout, his son, and a friend fired on the detachment of soldiers sent to arrest Bezuidenhout. (Cory Library)

▽
The grave of Frederik Bezuidenhout. The site of his house by the 'Karee Boom' can be seen in the background. (Cory Library)

Reverend James Archbell's congregation at Thaba Nchu in 1834. The Wesleyans (Methodists) pioneered mission work among the Barolong in the Maquassi area, and after the Barolong moved to Thaba Nchu, a Wesleyan mission station was established there. Reverend Archbell and Moroko, the Barolong chief, aided the stranded Voortrekkers after the Battle of Vegkop in 1836, and sent oxen to transport them to Thaba Nchu. (Africana Museum)

'The Revd. Mr Moffat preaching to the Bechuana', by C D Bell. Robert Moffat of the London Missionary Society established a well-known mission station at Kuruman. He believed in literacy as a basis of conversion, and organized the translation and printing of the Bible into seTswana. (Africana Museum)

passed an Emancipation Act, which provided for periods of four to six years of apprenticeship for freed slaves and for partial compensation for slave owners. The white masters protested vehemently at the inadequacy of the compensation which they received when their slaves were emancipated – eventually calculated at about a third of the value of the slaves – but a large amount of capital came into circulation in the colony, and individuals were able to invest in sheep farms and embark upon other new business ventures. After the 'freeing' of their Khoi and slave labour, the white colonists were determined to restructure a dependent labour force. In 1841 the Masters and Servants Ordinance was passed, which prescribed criminal sanctions for breach of contract. So effective did the monopoly of white control over land, labour and capital continue to be that an independent peasant class able to produce for subsistence or even

for a market could not evolve. The low level of wages and the cycle of debt continued. Both the colonial state and liberal-minded colonists wanted free but dependent labour working for wages. When the colonists obtained the privilege of representative government, they immediately took steps to extend their domination over their servants. In 1856 a Masters and Servants Ordinance was promulgated, which greatly increased the penalties for servants who broke their contracts, and tightened up control over labour mobility.

The British had thus taken the colony far along the road towards legal equality irrespective of race, but the whites retained effective control over the economic resources, including the land. The Cape Coloured people, descended from Khoikhoi, slaves and whites, became a rural and urban wage-labour force, and it was a long time before a Coloured bourgeoisie emerged. Socially, the habit of deference to whites continued unchanged.

Lord Charles Somerset and the eastern frontier

In April 1814 there arrived at the Cape a new Governor, Lord Charles Somerset, who was not only to make a strong imprint upon the consciousness of the colonists but also to become the subject of a powerful mythology extending down to our own day.

A problem to claim his almost constant attention was that of frontier defence. Cradock's efforts at clearing the Zuurveld by driving 20 000 Xhosa back upon their fellows beyond the Fish River had led to serious overcrowding and tension, the blockhouses had failed to keep black and white apart, and the unrest and cattle-raiding in the Zuurveld had left the area so insecure that burghers could not be prevailed upon to remain there any longer.

In 1817 Lord Charles decided to abandon the

traditional policy of maintaining a rigid line of separation between black and white. He made a treaty with Ngqika, whereby the chiefs were to be rewarded for assisting in the punishment of cattle thieves. In terms of the so-called 'spoor law' colonial farmers were to be allowed to claim compensation from the first Xhosa kraal to which stolen cattle were traced. This arrangement was a failure because Ngqika did not possess the de facto authority of a paramount chief. In the following year (Fifth Frontier War, 1818-1819) Ndlambe's forces routed those of Ngqika on the Amalinde Flats (near King William's Town), but when Somerset's troops restored Ngqika, Ndlambe's war-doctor Makanda (Nxele) led 10 000 Xhosa in an attack upon Grahamstown (April 1819). As in 1812, imperial forces came to the rescue, and Ndlambe's attack was repulsed. Somerset seized the opportunity to declare that the area between the Fish and the Keiskamma rivers was henceforth to be kept free of whites and blacks alike, and this would be enforced by means of military posts and patrols.

Yet, as Somerset was increasingly aware, only the close white settlement of the colonial side of the boundary would act as a truly effective barrier against Xhosa penetration into the colony. In July 1819 the House of Commons voted £50 000 for the implementation of an emigration scheme to the Cape. The scheme was thus devised primarily in order to tackle the problem of frontier insecurity and, at the same time, to alleviate social distress in Britain. It was not a deliberate attempt by Somerset to swamp the Dutch with an influx of English population.

Somerset's policy on the frontier was fraught with the possibilities of trouble. He himself did not regard the area surrendered by the Xhosa as a 'neutral belt'. At the very time of his agreement with Ngqika, he wrote to the Secretary of State about 'the country thus *ceded*', and declared that it was 'as fine a portion of ground as is to be found, and with still unappropriated lands in the Zuurveld it might perhaps be worthy of consideration with a view to systematic colonization'. Penetration of the 'neutral belt' continued from both sides. The whites were granted farms in the area, and traders continued to ply their wares. From their side, the Xhosa were driven into the allegedly unoccupied zone by the severe overcrowding in their own. The congestion had been greatly exacerbated by the forced entry of the Zuurveld Xhosa from the south in 1812 and by the flight of masses of refugees from the *Mfecane* in the north (see Chapter 9). By the early 1820s the range of options open to the Xhosa in seeking escape from their terrible predicament had been severely reduced.

The other principle of Somerset's frontier policy – close settlement – was also a failure. The soil of the Zuurveld was quite unsuitable for the type of intensive farming envisaged, and

'The freed slave', by F T I'Ons. In his right hand he holds a document which is thought to represent the 'General Order' for the abolition of slavery, passed in August 1833. (Africana Museum)

most of the British Settlers moved into the villages as soon as they could. Rather than acting as a barrier to contacts between black and white, as had originally been intended, they became the chief agents for opening the frontier far wider to a considerable two-way traffic in people, goods and ideas.

Freedom of the press

The arrival of the British Settlers was of long-term significance in other ways. Although few of them had enjoyed the vote at home, they came from a society in which issues of public concern were vigorously and openly debated. Moreover, they had friends in Britain through whom they could make their opinions known in influential quarters. Although their direct political influence can easily be exaggerated, they constituted a not unimportant addition to the growing group of critics of the existing colonial system and particularly of the autocracy of the Governor.

The political struggle against Lord Charles' regime was sparked off by the attempts of the colonists to establish a free press. In 1823 to 1834 the Colonial Secretary, Lord Bathurst, against the express wishes of the Governor, authorized the publication of a bilingual monthly periodical *The South African Journal* and *Het Nederduitsch*

Lord Charles Somerset (Cape Archives, M383)

Dr John Philip (1777-1851)

Dr Philip came to the Cape in 1819 with the Rev John Campbell to report on the state of the London Missionary Society missions. In 1820 he was appointed Superintendent of the LMS missions in southern Africa. He was an earnest, largely self-taught man of exceptional ability and forceful personality, but was self-opinionated, autocratic and often arrogant and unscrupulous.

In 1828 he published a two-volume work, *Researches in South Africa*, attacking the discriminatory regulations against Khoikhoi labour. Until 1834 he campaigned for the recognition of the legal equality of the colonial Khoikhoi with the whites. 'Independent of printed statutes,' he declared in *Researches in South Africa*, 'there are certain rights which human beings possess, and of which they cannot be deprived but by manifest injustice. . . The Hottentot has a right to a fair price for his labour; to an exemption to cruelty and oppression; to choose the place of his abode, and to enjoy the society of his children; and no one can deprive him of those rights without violating the laws of nature and of nations. . .'

Dr Philip also gave attention in the 1830s to the eastern and northern frontier regions of the colony. There he cast the missionaries in the role of agents whereby British authority and the 'benefits of Christian and British civilization' could be extended into the interior. On the northern frontier he mediated the signing of treaties with Waterboer, Adam Kok and Moshweshwe, while on the eastern frontier he attempted (unsuccessfully) to induce the British Government to annex the territory of the various chiefs to prevent the land from falling into the hands of the white colonists and to prepare the way for the work of the LMS.

Dr John Philip (Cape Archives, M450)

Zuid-Afrikaansch Tijdschrift by Thomas Pringle, a leader of one of the settler parties, and Abraham Faure, a Dutch Reformed clergyman and educationist. George Greig, a printer, received permission to publish a newspaper, *The South African Commercial Advertiser*, under editorial management of Pringle and his fellow Scot, John Fairbairn.

Within four months the editors of the newspaper had fallen foul of the authorities. An attorney, William Edwards, was prosecuted for libel, arising out of not unjustified allegations of official incompetence and injustice. The government, anxious lest reports on the case in the popular press reflect adversely on the Governor and his administration, insisted that security be deposited by Greig or that the *Commercial Advertiser* be submitted for censorship before publication. Greig ceased publication of the paper in protest, and was expelled from the colony. Pringle, too, was warned against the publication of material which might question the actions of the authorities. Like Greig, he ceased publication, but petitioned the crown to grant the right of establishing a free press in the colony.

Gradually the victims of Somerset's high-handedness gathered in London and in mid-1825 it was announced in Parliament that he was to be given leave of absence, although, as it turned out, this amounted to his recall. When a more sympathetic government took office at Westminster, Fairbairn continued the struggle in London, and in July 1828 he returned triumphantly to the colony with the freedom of the press guaranteed. Public policy could now be freely discussed, subject not to the whims of the executive but only to the general law of libel as interpreted by the courts, and the courts, too, were now to be independent of the will of the executive. At the beginning of 1825 a Council of Advice, consisting of leading officials, was set up, and two years later unofficial nominees were added to its membership, although nearly three

more decades were to pass before really meaningful constitutional changes occurred.

Legal, administrative and cultural change

One of the problems facing Britain in her second empire was that of cultural or ethnic diversity. After the occupation of the Cape, Britain increasingly felt the need to make over her new possession 'in her own image', to adjust the alien laws, customs and institutions to the realities of British rule. This was not merely a nationalistic urge, but also the expression of a desire by the ruling classes of Britain to make the colony prosperous and more easily governable by collaboration and co-operation rather than by coercion.

Anglicization was never the main objective of British policy; the new rulers did not wish unnecessarily to alienate their Afrikaner subjects. Nor – as, for example, in periods of financial stringency – was it always practicable. There were, however, individual officials, both at the Cape and in the Colonial Office, who were bent upon pursuing a policy of aggressive acculturation to its logical conclusion. Although it was in the 1820s that the drive for anglicization at the Cape was at its most intense, the responsibility for the policy did not, as is so often thought, lie with Lord Charles Somerset. His predecessor Sir John Cradock, for example, had been determined from the outset to remake institutions and policies in terms of British forms.

From 1822 Somerset took steps to encourage or compel the use of the English language in most spheres of public life. Incentives were given to teachers to use English in schools, Scottish schoolteachers were imported, and from 1822 free public schools were set up in many of the country towns and districts to give instruction in English. Many Dutch-speaking parents strongly objected to the attempts to destroy their language and refused to allow their children to attend the free schools.

Anglicization was also promoted within the Dutch Reformed Church. It is true that it was only after Somerset's attempts to recruit *dominees* in Holland had failed that he appointed Scots clergy to vacant pulpits in the Church. But the government persisted with the importation of Scottish Calvinist ministers, and by 1837 half of the DRC Synod consisted of Scots. Yet the anglicizing policy in the Church was not systematically pursued; many of the Scots ministers learnt Dutch and some married into Afrikaner families.

Even more determined efforts were made to anglicize the civil service. Long before the 1820s the process of replacing the old officials by appointees from the mother country had begun, and Cradock had required all civil servants to have a knowledge of English. In 1824 English became the language of the government offices to the exclusion of Dutch, and high salaries were offered in order to attract English-speaking appointees into the administrative service.

Legal reforms instituted from the time of the British occupations were aimed at establishing the rule of law and at more effective control over the colony, but in important respects they, too, were designed to transform Dutch institutions and practices into English. Probably the most important reform of the period was the promulgation of the Charter of Justice in 1828. Although Roman-Dutch law itself was retained, the Charter swept away the whole of the existing system of the administration of justice, central and local. A Supreme Court with a Chief Justice and three judges independent of the executive was set up. A professional bench was established; judges were well paid and were henceforth to be trained lawyers. The fiscal was replaced by an attorney-general and the styles and forms of British legal procedures, including trial by jury, were instituted. In local administration the post of *landdrost* was abolished and replaced by English-style Resident Magistrates with limited jurisdiction in civil and criminal cases. The judicial and executive functions in local government were separated, but in practice – and largely for reasons of economy – the new post of Civil Commissioner was usually held in conjuction with that of Resident Magistrate. In 1828 English became the sole language of the courts, a cause of hardship and of resentment among Afrikaner colonists. Of greater concern to them, however, was the loss of even the limited degree of representation in government which they had enjoyed through the courts of *landdrosts* and *heemraden*, the Burgher Senate (which was abolished), and the judicial powers of their friends, the field-cornets, which also disappeared at this date. The courts, modelled on British lines and extended and reinvigorated in powers and effectiveness, came to be one of the major instruments for the extension not only of effective administration but also of social control by the British ruling class during the nineteenth century.

The language policy of Somerset was enforced until the latter part of the century. When, for instance, representative government was inaugurated in 1854, the use of English became obligatory in the new Parliament. In addition the colonists became increasingly aware of the 'informal' anglicization which was occurring – the transposition to the colony of British forms of social organization, education, architecture and leisure activities. Some Afrikaners, including many of the most sophisticated, resisted these developments stoutly. Many others, especially those in the Western Cape, gradually became more closely identified with British ways of life, culture and traditions; it was in this period that the colony acquired its strongly British character in its institutions and ways of thought.

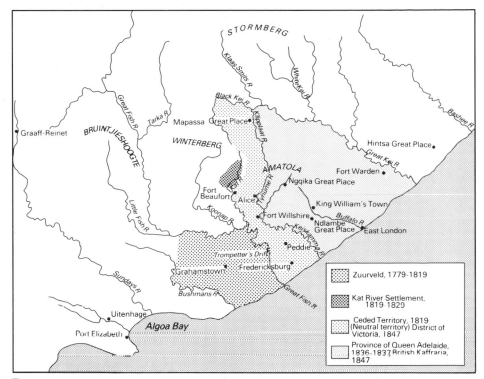

Territorial losses of the Xhosa People, 1779-1848

The treaty system and the Great Trek

With the breakdown of the 'neutral belt' and close settlement on the eastern frontier, the Xhosa continued to lose their land and the colonists were subjected to raids of devastating intensity. Many of the Ngqika, driven almost to desperation by the aggression on all sides, as well as by the recurrent droughts, were resolved, as they put it, not to 'be broke up as the Hottentots were'. The colonial government, instead of introducing a proper police system, continued to rely upon negative and military measures such as patrols, commandos and reprisals.

In London, by contrast, the ministry of Lord Grey was aware of the ineffectiveness of this policy and much more attuned to the reform

Adderley Street in 1851, with 'Old Moses', a well known fruit and vegetable vendor in the foreground. The names on some of the retail shops indicate the presence of a small but active group of British merchants. (Africana Museum)

and philanthropic sentiments of the day. At the end of 1833 the new Governor, Sir Benjamin D'Urban, was given instructions to introduce a more conciliatory policy on the frontier, based on treaties with the chiefs, the payment of financial subsidies and the appointment of white 'Residents' to advise and assist the chiefs in administration. D'Urban was preoccupied with other colonial problems, particularly slave emancipation, and as the military strained every resource to 'drive the last man over the Keiskamma', 12 000 Xhosa under Maqoma and Tyhali swarmed across the entire length of frontier in small raiding parties (Sixth Frontier War, 1834-1835). Scores of refugees poured into Grahamstown; Albany and other districts were almost totally dislocated.

The troops and commandos concentrated upon the destruction of the food supplies of the Xhosa and drove off their cattle in such numbers that this, like the other frontier wars of the period, has often been likened to 'Smithfield cattle driving' (referring to the famous London cattle market) rather than to warfare in the conventional sense. D'Urban's forces compelled Hintsa to make peace, and on 10 May 1835 the Governor proclaimed the establishment of the Province of Queen Adelaide, embracing all the area between the Keiskamma and the Kei rivers. This policy of 'total expulsion' was subsequently abandoned, but before this was reported to the Colonial Secretary, it had provoked howls of protest among the humanitarians in England, where the Parliamentary Select Committee on Aborigines was taking evidence. The new Secretary of State, Lord Glenelg, was aghast at the events on the frontier. In what has come to be regarded as the most celebrated despatch in South African history, he informed D'Urban that he had concluded that the Xhosa had had 'ample justifica-

tion' for invading the colony. He announced the appointment of a Lieutenant-Governor, supported by a new hierarchy of officials both in the colony and in Kaffraria, so that in the future relations between blacks and whites could be based upon a system of treaties rather than upon the practice of reprisals. Andries Stockenström, appointed as Lieutenant-Governor, signed treaties with the Xhosa chiefs, abandoning the Province of Queen Adelaide and allowing the chiefs to return with their people to locations between the Fish and the Keiskamma rivers. Stolen cattle were to be recovered through tribal representatives (*amapakati*) on the frontier, white diplomatic representatives in black territory, and the co-operation of the chiefs.

The much maligned treaty system brought several concrete advantages in the short term. Only a third of the number of depredations occurred during the Stockenström period that had taken place while the D'Urban system was in operation. Stock were recovered and the owners compensated far more expeditiously, and the expansion of the wool industry, so prominent a feature of eastern development after the 1835 war, could only have occurred if there had been a fair degree of security in the frontier districts. Yet by pretending to recognize the independence of the Xhosa peoples the British Government was attempting to evade the responsibility and the expense of administering the frontier; the real problem of establishing stability had merely been postponed, and the periodic outbursts of tension continued. Apart from the Zuurveld, the eastern frontier was not yet 'closed'.

The frontiersmen's insatiable land hunger had much to do with the decision of many of the Afrikaner farmers to abandon the colony permanently and to move northwards into the interior. Many of those who embarked upon the

'A canteen scene during the frontier wars', by W H F L Langschmidt. Members of the Cape Mounted Rifles and Imperial troops survey the lively proceedings. (William Fehr Collection)

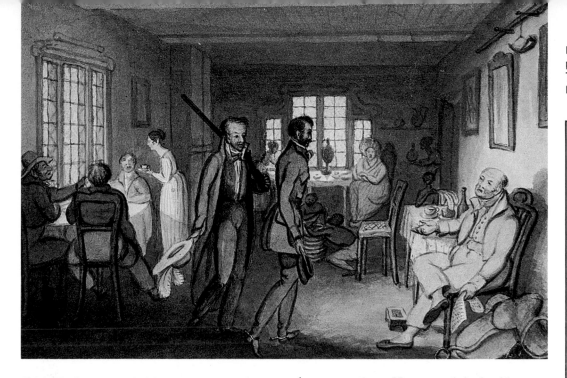

Great Trek were probably Boers who had failed to accumulate sufficient land in the desirable areas in the colony, and who, after the reversal of D'Urban's annexation of the Province of Queen Adelaide, could no longer hope for relief to the east of the colony either.

The Trek owed little if anything to the development of a national consiousness; the impact of the anglicization policy had been less traumatic than is traditionally thought. It was rather a form of revolt against a government which seemed to be dangerously intent on disturbing the 'proper relations between master and servant' by establishing the idea of equality before the law (*gelykstelling*) but which, at the same time, was quite unable to afford them security, physical, economic or psychological.

It should be emphasized, however, that even by 1841 only about one eighth of the total Afrikaner population had left the colony. Some of the remainder continued to live with their English-speaking fellow colonists in the frontier areas, where the weaknesses of Stockenström's treaty system were apparant from the outset. Too much was expected of the chiefs and too little was done by the colonial authorities to police the zone of contact between white and black. Early in March 1846 one of Sandile's relatives stole an axe from a shop in Fort Beaufort, and a mixed force of regulars and colonial volunteers invaded Kaffraria (Seventh Frontier War, or 'War of the Axe', 1846-1847).

The 'War of the Axe' dragged on longer than any previous war on the frontier, and the Treasury was shocked at the expense, due not merely to the costs of materials and transport, but also to the widespread misappropriation of resources, both by officers and by colonists. By the end of 1847 the resistance of the Xhosa had again been broken. The new Governor, Sir Harry Smith, was determined to bring to an end

the treaty system. He annexed the land between the Fish and Keiskamma rivers as the district of Victoria East, and between the Keiskamma and Kei rivers as the crown colony of British Kaffraria. The capital of British Kaffraria was to be King William's Town, whither he summoned the chiefs. At a given signal, a wagon loaded with gunpowder was blown up. 'There go the treaties,' he proclaimed to the chiefs. 'Do you hear? No more treaties.' It was the beginning of a new frontier policy of annexation and direct rule by magistrates. Officially, the frontier had disappeared and with it the enforced separation of black and white.

Smith was convinced that the key to the control of the Trek and thereby of southern Africa lay in the area between the Orange and the Vaal rivers, and he annexed the whole of this territory to the Queen's possessions as the Orange River Sovereignty. This meant that the entire frontier between white and black, from Natal (which had been annexed in 1843) via Basutoland and down to the Eastern Cape frontier, was now in British hands. It was therefore a bitter blow when most of the Natal Trekkers moved instead onto the highveld and founded a series of republics beyond British control (see Chapter 11).

Before anything further could be done to consolidate British power in the sub-continent, Smith's policies both on the eastern frontier and in the Sovereignty collapsed. For all his dramatic threats and his resort to force, *Inkosi Inkulu* ('Great Chief') Smith had failed to impose order on the Xhosa. The chiefs resisted the inroads upon their authority and the tribesmen were deeply resentful of the encroachment upon their land and the attacks upon their tribal customs. They turned to the prophet Mlanjeni with his promises of a return to the familiar ancestral ways. When Sir Harry issued a proclamation

Sandile (Africana Museum)

Suthu, the Great Wife of Ngqika, mother of Sandile. (Africana Museum)

Sandile (1820-1878)

Sandile, who had a withered leg from birth, was about eight years of age when his father, Ngqika, died in 1829. His mother, the much disliked Great Wife, Suthu, was appointed regent until 1840, when Sandile became paramount chief of the Rharhabe. His reign was characterized by his resistance to the growing pressures of white encroachment upon the land of his people, and he became involved in the Seventh, Eighth and Ninth Frontier Wars, as well as in the 'National Suicide' of the Xhosa in 1856-1857. Prior to the Eighth Frontier War (1850-1853) he was temporarily deposed as paramount chief and Charles Brownlee was appointed in his place.

The 'Cape Town Levy' on its way to a frontier engagement. T J Lucas, the artist, described the recruits as 'rascals of all sorts'. (Africana Museum)

deposing Sandile and appointing in his place the Ngqika Commissioner, Charles Brownlee, the whole frontier was ablaze. And for the first time since the beginning of the century, sections of the Coloured people in the Eastern Cape, including a third of those in the Kat River Settlement, went into rebellion in sympathy with the Xhosa and the Thembu.

The Eighth Frontier War, which lasted from 1850 to 1853, was the longest of the frontier wars, and as it dragged on the opposition to colonial responsibilities and their escalating expense swelled. Smith was recalled, and the settlement at the end of the war was devised by his successor, General George Cathcart, and dictated to the chiefs in March 1853. A distinguished soldier with no experience in colonial

administration, he viewed the frontier in largely military terms. He aimed to erect a defensible boundary by establishing a royal reserve in the Amathole, which would serve as a buffer between the Ngqika and the colony, and by locating the loyal tribes in a chain along the east bank of the Keiskamma River. British Kaffraria, the cockpit of frontier strife, was to be maintained as a separate dependency, not absorbed into the colony.

To the north Smith had also failed to consolidate British control. In order to dissuade the Trekkers beyond the Vaal from interfering in the affairs of the Sovereignty, their independence was formally recognized in the Sand River Convention of January 1852. Despite outraged protests by Cape speculators, the British withdrawal from the interior continued, and in February 1854 the Bloemfontein Convention recognized the independence also of the communities between the Orange and the Vaal rivers.

The long road to representative government, 1834-1854

Throughout these decades interested groups of colonists had petitioned for an enlargement of the degree of popular representation in the government of the colony. These requests were all firmly rejected by the Home Government, at first on the grounds that the colonists had not yet attained sufficient political maturity to be able to work a representative system of government, and by the 1830s because the West Indian assemblies had shown how inconvenient colonial representative systems could be in obstructing efforts at the amelioration of the condition of slaves within their societies. In the case of the Cape, the Secretary of State was convinced, too, that the population was too small and too scattered, so that 'power would speedily centre in the hands of those who resided in and near Cape

Town'. It would in addition set English and Afrikaner against each other.

Constitutional advance at the Cape thus depended less upon pressure from the colony itself than upon the momentum towards overall reform in the empire. The great Reform Bill of 1832 found concrete expression in a series of measures at the Cape. slave emancipation, the local government ordinances of 1836 and, not least, the creation of a Legislative Council in 1834 consisting of five officials and five to seven nominated colonists.

In 1841 yet another petition for representative institutions was rejected by the Secretary of State. Lord Stanley, the Secretary of State for the Colonies, argued that at the Cape there would be unusual difficulty in doing justice to the interests of the different groups of the colony's heterogeneous population. He was also apprehensive of the potential dangers of eastern separatism. Since 1823, whenever eastern frustration reached a sufficient pitch, interested groups in the eastern districts (particularly Grahamstown) had raised the cry for 'separation'. This meant a great variety of things. To some few it meant the establishment of a completely separate colony or government from the western districts; to others it signified the removal of the seat of government to the eastern districts where it could be directly influenced by them, and to others it represented the beginning of a federal system within the colony.

Stanley's rejection of the petition for representative government provoked the Cape activists into pressing their demands even more determinedly. By the early 1840s representative government was very much 'in the air'. The Durham Report recommended that the colonists in Upper and Lower Canada be given greater freedom to govern themselves, and the free traders argued that it was unprofitable to govern colonies that could govern and pay for themselves. By the latter part of the decade developments within the Cape itself made Lord Stanley's fears about the colony's immaturity seem less and less valid. Between the start of the Great Trek and 1853 the white population of the colony doubled and wool exports expanded, as did trade and government revenue. In 1836 provision was made for the establishment of municipal councils, and in 1843 road boards, and in these bodies as well as in the school committees and the synods of the Dutch Reformed Church the colonists obtained experience in local government. Public opinion on political issues began to develop, prompted in no small part by the vigorous press of Cape Town, Grahamstown and other towns of the colony. When the Whigs returned to power in Britain in 1846, Earl Grey, the new Secretary of State for the Colonies, instructed the Cape Governor to report on the possibility of further constitutional advance. Various draft constitutions were put forward from the Cape and after prolonged negotiations a constitution was adopted in 1853, a constitution which, with amendments, was to last in the Cape until the Union of 1910. The constitution provided for a two-chamber parliament in which the western districts of the colony received slightly more representation than did the eastern. Both the House of Assembly and the Legislative Council were to be elected by males, irrespective of colour, who earned £50 a year or owned property with a rentable value

Hintsa (Africana Museum)

'Sandile's kraal in the Amathole', by Thomas Baines (1849). The blanket conceals Sandile's withered leg. (William Fehr Collection)

of £25 a year. The Home Government had insisted on the inclusion of a 'colour-blind' franchise, but the actual effect of the introduction of the new constitution was that political power in the colony was effectively transferred to the representatives of the dominant white minority.

Conclusion

By 1854 the Cape Colony was still overwhelmingly a rural society, well over three-quarters of the occupied population being engaged in agriculture. However, it was a much more diversified society than it had been when the British first took possession of the VOC settlement in 1795. The population, which had grown at least eight-fold, came from a greater variety of cultural origins. The British influence had become predominant not only in government, administration and the law, but also in the broadest social and cultural senses; this was especially so in the towns and villages, where the English-speaking population came increasingly to be concentrated. Afrikaners, although reduced in numbers by the Great Trek, continued to constitute a large majority of the white population of the colony, and held sway in the rural areas. The Coloured population consisted of remnants of the Khoikhoi, freed slaves, free blacks and Muslims, and was occupied mainly as farm labourers and fishermen or as artisans in the towns. Numbers of Nguni became recognized as permanent residents of the eastern and midland regions of the colony, starting with the 17 000 Mfengu settled by Sir Benjamin D'Urban in 1835 and the people of the old 'Ceded Territory' annexed by Smith in 1848. In short, although much effort might be devoted to making the Cape a 'fragment' of British society, Cape society came to be distinguished by a growing range of cultural and ethnic diversity.

The colonial economy was still notoriously undeveloped. Between the 1790s and the mid-1830s, it is true, the volume of shipping calling at the Cape had increased eight-fold and the value of the colony's exports had risen to almost £500 000. In addition to being an exporter of wine, the colony had emerged as an exporter of pastoral products, particularly wool, hides, skins and ostrich feathers. But the infrastructure of a colonial economy could not be built upon this relatively insubstantial income, nor could a sound economy remain so heavily dependent upon the military expenditures of the Home Government. In 1848, for example,

The Cape Regiment (or 'Cape Corps') leading an attack against the Xhosa in the Amathole in 1851. This corps, whose troops, known as Pandours, were drawn from the Cape Coloured community, was founded in 1795 by the Dutch East India Company, was redesignated 'The Cape Regiment' by the British in 1806 and served on the eastern frontier during the frontier wars. (William Fehr Collection)

the Treasury had disbursed over £1 million for war purposes in the colony. Until there were more attractive economic opportunities, capital would not be drawn to the colony and domestic capital would continue to accumulate very slowly.

Yet attempts continued to be made to restructure the colonial economy and colonial society. The 'Cape liberal tradition', which provided the mainspring for the direction of policy in the colony from the early decades of the nineteenth century, is usually explained in terms of ideals imposed upon the colony from outside by missionaries inspired by metropolitan humanitarianism. However, the historian Stanley Trapido has emphasized the material base of Cape liberalism and drawn a useful distinction between

the 'great tradition' of liberalism at the Cape, situated mainly in Cape Town and promoted by idealists, newspaper editors, missionaries, parliamentarians and financial and commercial leaders, and a 'small tradition' of those merchants, traders, lawyers and administrators who, in the Eastern Cape particularly, depended for making their livings and their political fortunes upon support from and collaboration with the emergent African independent producers. The principles of Cape liberalism were thus somewhat mixed and even contradictory. Meanwhile the powerful impulses of Cape conservatism continued, despite the low franchise, to entrench and extend the domination of the white minority over all races. Within the colony an ever increasing variety of methods of social control was devised by the ruling classes, and beyond the colonial frontiers similar methods were being used to restructure the productive relations of the adjacent African societies and to draw them under the effective jurisdiction of their now more powerful colonial neighbour. It was the coming of the British which in the first half of the nineteenth century had decisively swung the balance of power between black and white in favour of the latter, not only military, but also in the complex mechanics of control of the natural and human resources of the region.

Suggested Reading List

H Giliomee (1975) *Die Kaap tydens die Eerste Britse Bewind, 1795-1803*, Cape Town

J A Heese (1973) *Slagtersnek en Sy Mense*, Cape Town

B A le Cordeur (1981) *The Politics of Eastern Cape Separatism, 1820-1854*, Cape Town

R Ross (1983) 'The Rise of the Cape Gentry', *Journal of Southern African Studies*, Vol 9, No 2, pp. 193-217

Sarhili ('Kreli') (c 1809-1892)

Sarhili ('Kreli') (William Fehr Collection)

Sarhili succeeded his father, Hintsa, as paramount chief of all the Xhosa and chief of the Gcaleka after Hintsa's death on 12 May 1835. He concluded an agreement with Sir Benjamin D'Urban, ratifying the treaty which his father had made, and in 1844 he made a formal treaty of friendship with the Governor, Sir Peregrine Maitland. However, he and his people were drawn into the frontier wars of 1846-1847, and 1850-1853 (the Seventh and Eighth Frontier Wars), and suffered severely from their participation in the cattle killing in 1856-1857. In 1877 Sarhili's attack on the Mfengu led to war with the Cape Colony. In 1878 his forces, and those of Sandile, were defeated by the whites at Kentani. Sarhili's power was broken, and the last paramount chief of the Gcaleka fled to Bomvanaland where he died. In 1885 Gcalekaland was annexed by the Cape.

'The loyal Fingo', by Thomas Baines. During the Eighth Frontier War (1850-1853) the Mfengu fought on the colonial side against the Xhosa. The soldiers were issued with heavy, front loading muskets. (William Fehr Collection)

Chapter 7

The 1820 Settlers

The Settlers, 1820-1824
MD Nash

M D Nash was born in Grahamstown and holds BA and MA (History) degrees from Rhodes University and a BA Honours degree in English from the University of Port Elizabeth. She is head of the cultural history division of the Albany Museum. Her publications include *Bailie's Party of 1820 Settlers* (A A Balkema, 1982).

In 1819 the British Government advertised and put into operation a scheme to assist approximately a thousand emigrant families to settle at the Cape of Good Hope. They were not the first British emigrants to put down roots at the Cape, but this was the first and last government-sponsored scheme to settle a sizeable community of English-speakers in a particular area of South Africa, and the 1820 Settlers have become a symbol of the British contribution to South African society, tradition and culture. During their own time, and with the encouragement of the influential *Graham's Town Journal* under its settler editor Robert Godlonton, the story of their early struggles and eventual achievements was elevated to the status of a heroic legend that has tended to obscure the historical facts. It is sometimes forgotten that the settlers were a heterogeneous group, with social and political divisions and conflicts, who were motivated – like men at all times and in all places – mainly by self-interest.

The settlement scheme

A dual purpose was served by sponsoring emigration to the Cape in 1819: the relief of unemployment in Britain and the cheap defence of the colony's eastern frontier. Britain was in the grip of post-war depression and unemployment, and the Tory Government, faced with the threat of riots and strikes, was anxious to make a gesture which would placate the parliamentary opposition as well as the disaffected labouring classes. Its 'show of doing something for the people' took the form of a vote of £50 000 to assist emigration to the Cape of Good Hope. Pop-

'Grahamstown in the 1840s from the East', by Reverend Thornley Smith. In the centre is High Street, with St George's Church, the Drostdy Gate, Parade Ground and Military Headquarters. The Military Hospital and Provost are on the left, and Fort Selwyn on the hill beyond. The Wesleyan Mission Premises, consisting of the school, the chapel and the Mission House, are on the left in High Street. (1820 Settlers Museum)

Settler locations

John Bailie (1788-1852) (By courtesy of M D Nash)

ular response to the announcement of the scheme was immediate and overwhelming; contemporary estimates of the number of applicants varied from 10 000 to 90 000, most of the applications coming from the middle and lower-middle classes of society.

The terms of the emigration scheme laid down that no applications from single individuals or families would be admitted. To ensure that land at the Cape was granted only to settlers with the capital and labour to develop it, free sea passages, victuals and land grants were offered only to those emigrants who could afford to engage and maintain at least ten able-bodied men over the age of eighteen, with or without families. The director of a party was required to deposit £10 for each single man or family group, repayable in instalments after the settlers reached the colony, so as to ensure their means

of subsistence until they could become self-supporting. The head of a party would be granted land in the proportion of 100 acres for each adult male settler under his direction, but would acquire full title to his estate only after it had been occupied and cultivated for three years.

Of the sixty-odd emigrant parties that were finally selected by the Colonial Department, only about a dozen in all were made up of masters and their indentured servants. The directors of these 'proprietary' parties were the would-be landed gentry of the new settlement. The majority of the emigrants, in parties ranging in size from ten to one hundred families, consisted of men who had banded together on a joint-stock basis, each paying his own deposit, with one of them selected as the nominal leader to satisfy the Colonial Department's requirements and to conduct negotiations on the party's behalf. These joint-stock parties were made up of men of education and some means, 'persons of a higher class than had originally been intended', as well as artisans and tradesmen. The joint-stock settlers exacerbated the Cape's labour problem by increasing the number of potential employers without introducing a proportionate number of labourers.

The voyage, arrival and journey to the interior

Twenty-one emigrant ships left Britain for the Cape between December 1819 and March 1820, carrying approximately one thousand men and three thousand women and children. The *Chapman* dropped anchor in Algoa Bay on 9 April 1820 after four months at sea, to be followed by the rest of the transports at intervals over the next three months.

Although the colonial authorities had been

The locations for the various settler parties had been hastily measured by the government surveyor; his report drew attention to the scarcity of water in the district. The three largest groups, each comprising nearly one hundred families – the joint-stock parties led by John Bailie, Hezekiah Sephton and Thomas Willson – were allocated land at some distance from one another, with the intention that they should form village settlements which would share their amenities with the smaller parties in their neighbourhood. On the Secretary of State, Earl Bathurst's instructions, the emigrant parties from Ireland and Scotland were not located with the English settlers in Albany. The small group of Scots families led by Thomas Pringle was given land on the Baviaans River, and later granted further land in the valleys of the Mankazana and Koonap rivers. Some 450 Irish settlers were located in the western district of Clanwilliam, but soon rejoined the main body of settlers in Albany.

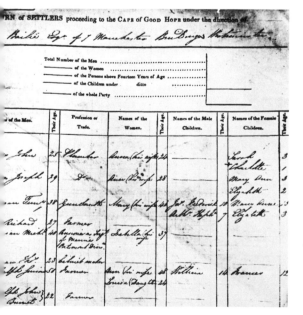

An official return of settlers in John Bailie's party. (Cape Archives)

Left: Sir Rufane Shawe Donkin, Acting Governor of the Cape Colony; *Right:* Captain Henry Somerset (1820 Settlers Museum)

'Landing of the British Settlers in Algoa Bay', by Thomas Baines. (1820 Settlers Museum)

given very short notice of the emigrants' arrival, arrangements for their reception were surprisingly efficient. Soldiers from the garrison at Fort Frederick carried the women and children from the surfboats to the shore; commissariat officials issued rations, stores, tents and tools; and every farm-wagon in the district was commandeered to transport the settlers to their locations. The first arrivals were escorted to their land at the mouth of the Great Fish River by the landdrost of Uitenhage, Colonel J G Cuyler, in person. Although the frontier had appeared settled since the unsuccessful Xhosa attack on Grahamstown in April 1819 and Somerset's subsequent introduction of an unoccupied or buffer zone between the Fish and Keiskamma rivers, Cuyler, an old frontiersman, left them with a grim warning: 'When you go out to plough, never leave your guns at home.'

Lord Charles Somerset had applied for home leave before he learnt that his hopes for large-scale emigration were about to be realized. He sailed for England two months before the first settlers landed, leaving all arrangements for their reception in the hands of the Acting Governor, Major-General Sir Rufane Donkin, who had been invalided to the Cape after the death of his wife in India.

The disintegration of the settler parties

Donkin visited the frontier in person to oversee the location of the emigrants. He founded the village of Bathurst in the centre of the settlement as an administrative and commercial capital, and appointed a provisional magistrate to preserve the peace and settle disputes. Friction had developed in both proprietary and joint-stock parties by the time the emigrants left Britain, and four months on shipboard had aggravated their differences and discontents. In an official attempt to keep the parties together, the colonial pass laws, originally designed to control vagrancy, were applied to the settlement in May 1820. Movement between the locations or to Bathurst or Grahamstown required written permission from the local authorities for all settlers but the heads of parties, and a district pass, subject to the approval of the Acting Governor, was needed by anyone wishing to travel further afield. Within a few weeks of their arrival, professional men and 'ornamental tradesmen' – coach painters, silversmiths and bookbinders – from the joint-stock parties were seeking official permission to leave their locations and move to the towns of the colony, where their skills could be profitably employed.

In September 1820 Albany, hitherto a sub-*drostdy* of Uitenhage, was given the status of an independent magisterial district. Major James Jones, who had served on Donkin's staff in the Peninsula, was gazetted *landdrost* of Albany and commandant of the frontier.

The first settlements

The settlers' first shelters were the tents supplied by the government. These were replaced by thatched cottages of wattle-and-daub or rammed earth, or even simpler dwellings. Some emigrant parties had equipped themselves with implements and tools before leaving Britain. Others purchased agricultural and building tools from the government depot at Algoa Bay, which supplied seed wheat for the first sowing. In most cases the 'Cockney gardeners' ' knowledge of agriculture was as limited as their building skills, and the plough oxen bought from Boer farmers in the neighbourhood proved 'as wild as bucks' in inexperienced hands.

The breakdown of the party system and the settlers' ignorance of agriculture were both factors that contributed to the failure of the government's plans for a close-knit agricultural settlement in Albany. The main cause, however, was the nature of the country itself. The poverty

of the soil and the irregular rainfall made the Albany area altogether unsuitable for intensive agriculture. The Boer stockfarmers knew it, with good reason, as the Zuurveld, but to Somerset on his visit to the district in 1817, as to the settlers on their first arrival, the country had appeared misleadingly verdant and fertile after rain – 'almost like a gentleman's park'.

The settlers' hopes of a good first harvest were dashed at the end of 1820 by the discovery that their promising wheat crop was blighted by rust. It was evident that government rationing would have to continue. Since deposit money was by now exhausted, all further debts incurred for rations were to be converted into mortgages on land, buildings and stock.

Donkin's plans for the settlement

Donkin again visited the eastern frontier in the middle of 1821 and in spite of the failure of the wheat crop he was optimistic about the settlement. Building was progressing rapidly in the village of Bathurst, and there were plans to develop the Kowie River as a harbour for Albany. Of the three largest settler groups, the heterogeneous parties recruited in London by Bailie and Willson were breaking up rapidly, but Sephton's party, bound by a common religious faith, had formed a village settlement which they called Salem, and were 'known for the order with which their affairs were conducted, both spiritual and temporal'.

At the time of Donkin's second visit, the frontier appeared misleadingly stable, and he curtailed Lord Charles Somerset's plans for Fort Willshire, the principle defensive post for the neutral territory, and reduced it to a fortified barrack only. He also granted land in the 'neutral zone' between the Fish and Keiskamma rivers to officers of the recently disbanded Royal African Corps to establish a military village named Fredericksburg. He interpreted the increasingly frequent pilfering of settler cattle by Xhosa raiding parties as a bad habit rather than a danger sign, and planned to hold an annual trade fair at Fort Willshire to encourage the transformation of 'a thieving nation into a commercial one'. The plan was dropped when he left the colony, but was revived by Lord Charles Somerset three years later when it became apparent that if legal trading with the Xhosa were not permitted, illegal trading would continue and be more difficult to control.

In the summer of 1821 the blight of rust again made its appearance in the settlers' wheat, signalling the second failure of their crops. For many joint-stock settlers and proprietary party heads the failure coincided with the expenditure of the last of their limited capital. Many of the settlers in the joint-stock parties had trades to fall back on for a living. Ironically, the failure of the agricultural settlement, due at least in part

to the settlers' ignorance of farming, was, in the long run, of incalculable benefit to the colony in releasing a variety of skilled services to the towns and villages.

On 1 December 1821 Sir Rufane Donkin's two-year rule of the colony came to an abrupt end with the return of Lord Charles Somerset from home leave. Donkin was admittedly ignorant of local conditions, but his good intentions towards the settlers in particular are unquestionable. In the event, however, his term of office, so far from benefitting the colony, generated a bitter feud with destructive effects reaching far beyond the two principal antagonists.

Somerset's return – autocracy inspires conflict

Some weeks before Somerset's return an open and violent quarrel took place in Cape Town between his eldest son, Captain Henry Somerset,

'The 1820 Settlers on shore at Algoa Bay', by C van der Berg. Dutch farmers from the area transported the settlers by ox-wagon from Algoa Bay to their locations in the Zuurveld. The settlers were accommodated in tents on the beach until they could proceed to the frontier. (William Fehr Collection)

'Bathurst in 1840', by Thomas Baines, with St John's Church, which became a place of refuge during the Sixth, Seventh and Eighth Frontier Wars, in the background. (Africana Museum)

97

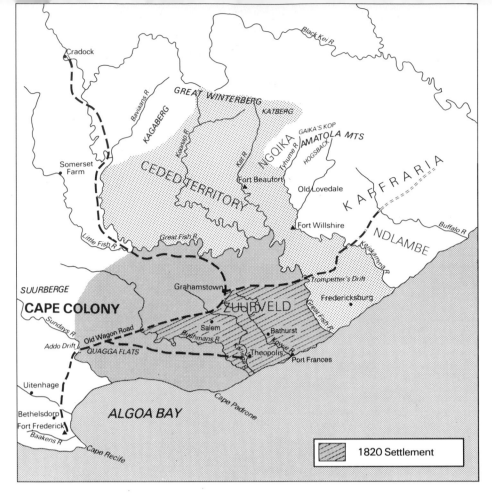

The Eastern Frontier about 1820

Salem village, an engraving from an original by Reverend Thornley Smith, showing the Methodist Church in the centre (built in 1850), and the second chapel, to the right of the church, built in 1832. (Methodist Archives)

and the Acting Governor, which resulted in Captain Somerset's being placed under house arrest. Lord Charles was incensed at this insult; when he landed at Cape Town, he and Donkin refused to meet. For the Albany settlers, the Governor's return heralded three years of conflict. Somerset's antagonism towards Donkin encompassed anyone and everything he had introduced or favoured during his tenure of office, including the whole 'grand innovation' of the Albany settlement. The popular *landdrost*, Major James Jones, was dismissed; Grahamstown was reinstated as the capital of Albany, and the government offices, commissariat and troops were removed from Bathurst, so that the growing prosperity of the new village was abruptly halted. The establishment of Freder-

icksburg in the neutral territory had been a flagrant breach of Somerset's frontier policy, and he refused to support it. By the middle of 1822 it was abandoned and in ruins.

By now it had become clearly evident that Albany was unsuitable for agriculture. The heads of parties saw their only hope of eventual success in pastoral farming, which called for increased grants of land, the replacement of wasted capital in order to purchase stock, and the provision of a more effective system of frontier patrols. As the settlers' herds increased the depredations of Xhosa cattle raiders became more frequent. No extra regular troops were forthcoming: instead an Albany militia force was conscripted, which added to the settlers' grievances.

The new *landdrost* of Albany, Harry Rivers, far from keeping the Governor informed of the full seriousness of the settlers' situation, 'flattered the prejudices that his Lordship had imbibed against the settlers and was the principal cause of the delays with which all measures for their relief were attended'. The aspirant landed gentry of Albany were particularly resentful of the *landdrost's* heavy-handed authority. Two attempts on their part to inform the Governor and then the Secretary of State of their 'insupportable condition' were summarily prevented, and led to Somerset's stigmatizing them all as malcontents and 'Radicals'. The term was unintentionally ironic. The gentleman settlers supported the principle of aristocratic government and would have opposed any movement for popular reform. They had no quarrel with the system of privilege and patronage, only with those officials who denied them its benefits.

In March 1823 they drew up a general petition that would present their case direct to the Home Government. They listed the 'artificial obstacles' that stood in the way of the settlement's progress: inadequate land grants, the lack of markets and a free port, the removal of the seat of magistracy from Bathurst to Grahamstown, and the loss of cattle to Xhosa raiding parties. They complained that the settlers' situation had been misunderstood and misinterpreted since Somerset's return, their safety endangered by his frontier policy, and the right of appeal denied them. They obtained 171 signatures to their petition, and provoked a stormy reaction from those settlers who were loyal to – and in many cases beneficiaries of – the Somerset regime and *Landdrost* Rivers. Two months later the loyalists sent the Secretary of State a counter-petition in support of Somerset, with 164 signatures.

The 'Albany Radicals' were not part of the Cape Town colonists' struggle to modify the autocracy of Somerset's rule, and were more concerned with their personal interests than with the needs of the colony. When the last act of the clash between the Cape colonists and the intransigent Governor was played out in Cape Town,

settler affairs constituted only a minor part. It was recognized in Britain that the whole system of colonial government was ripe for reform, and in July 1822 Parliament appointed a commission of inquiry to investigate the state of the government, laws and administration of justice at the Cape of Good Hope, Mauritius and Ceylon. The arrival of the commissioners in Cape Town the following year heralded major changes for the colony as a whole, among them, the end of Somerset's government.

Settler relief – aid to 'respectable' settlers

By mid-1823 only 438 of the 1 004 men who had made up the parties at the time of landing still remained on their locations to claim title to their land after fulfilling the three-year residence and development stipulation. In October torrential rains caused devastating floods throughout Albany, with the loss of crops, livestock and personal possessions. A charitable society had been formed in Cape Town as early as 1820 to relieve distress among the poorer settlers, and two of the committee members, one of them the redoubtable Dr John Philip, visited Albany in 1823 on a tour of inspection and allied themselves with the 'Albany Radicals'.

The Society for the Relief of Distressed Settlers considered that the wage-earning classes – artisans and labourers – were no longer in need of charity. They had been hardest hit initially by the unforeseen calamities of blight, floods and cattle theft, but they had been the fastest to recover. It was the heads of the proprietary parties and other 'respectable' settlers, the decayed gentry who had expended all their capital and been reduced to near penury, who now needed help. A major fund-raising drive was launched on their behalf in England and India, and raised a considerable sum of money, the distribution of which was in the hands of a sub-committee constituted almost entirely of 'Albany Radicals'. Somerset made a tactical error by proposing that *Landdrost* Rivers should join the sub-committee to bring it under official control. This led to a 'pamphlet war' between Somerset and Dr Philip from which Rivers emerged the loser. Local political feeling was running high when J Bigge and W Colebrooke, commissioners of inquiry, arrived in Grahamstown to a riotous welcome from the 'Radicals' and their supporters. The petition of March 1823 formed the basis of their investigation of the settlers' situation, and the confusion of evidence and conflicting claims to land in particular led them to recommend that a sympathetically disposed special commissioner be appointed to deal with settler affairs.

Lord Charles Somerset paid his first visit to the Albany settlement at the beginning of 1825. His changed attitude reflected the concern that had been shown by the commissioners of inquiry. Fewer that half the settlers remained by now to claim the available land and, on the recommendation of the special commissioner, grants were made on a far more generous scale than the original emigration scheme had laid down. In an expedient reversal of his established policy, Somerset granted additional land to heads of parties and members of joint-stock parties with claims to social superiority. The Albany militia was officially disbanded, *Landdrost* Rivers was transferred to the Western Cape, and the closing of the government-owned Somerset Farm ended its monopoly of supply to the garrison forces and opened a profitable market for the settlers' produce.

The 'respectable' settlers' immediate need for money to put them back on their feet was met by the distribution of the Settlers' Relief Fund, augmented by loans from the government. On the Governor's recommendation, all outstanding ration debts were remitted. Most of the future prosperity of the settlement was to rest, however, on the trans-frontier trade with the black tribes. The profitable illicit trade that had been carried on between settlers and tribesmen was legitimized by the introduction of regular fairs at Fort Willshire, where licenced traders under the eye of the military could barter axes and knives, blankets, cottons and ironmongery, besides the staple currency of glass beads and brass wire and buttons, in exchange for ivory, gum, ostrich feathers, hides, horns and skins.

A new dispensation

The visit of the commissioners of inquiry to the Cape started the process of change whereby the despotically governed colony was to move successively from a Council of Advice in 1825 to a Legislative Council and, in the 1850s, to a Representative Parliament. Somerset's recall to England effectively marked the end of autocratic rule. On the recommendation of the commissioners, a new Charter of Justice was granted to the colony in 1827, which took the laws out of the hands of the Governor and put them under the control of an independent bench. This new dispensation opened opportunities for employment and advancement for educated English-speakers at all levels of colonial government, which the settlers were quick to grasp.

Tharfield, the estate of Miles Bowker, the leader of a party from Wiltshire. The sketch is by Julia Bowker, the wife of Thomas Holden Bowker, and daughter-in-law of Miles Bowker. (1820 Settlers Museum)

Religion

Reverend William Shaw (1798-1872) (1820 Settlers Museum)

The original settlers were composed of members of many diverse religions, but the majority looked to Methodism for religious consolation and support. Its power to inspire mission activities led to young men such as Henry Hare Dugmore, John Ayliff and William Shepstone spreading the gospel beyond the frontier. Their great apostle was the Reverend William Shaw, the minister who accompanied Sephton's party. The remarkable linguistic achievements of these missionaries led to a Xhosa gospel being printed before 1840, and the history of the peoples among whom they worked being recorded.

Ivory and curios on sale in the Grahamstown market-place after the trader David Hume had returned from a trip to the interior in 1850. Painting by Thomas Baines. (1820 Settlers Museum)

The Dispersion and Influence of the 1820 Settlers
Guy Butler

Guy Butler was born in Cradock in 1918. He was educated at Rhodes University and Oxford, and is Research Professor in the English Department at Rhodes University. He has published poems, plays and two volumes of autobiography, and has edited two books on the 1820 Settlers, *When Boys Were Men* (Oxford University Press, 1969) and *The 1820 Settlers: An Illustrated Commentary* (Human & Rousseau, 1974).

The events of the previous four years had resulted in the settlement taking on an entirely different character from that conceived by its architects. Two-thirds of the settlers had left their locations and were scattered throughout the country. Marriages between English settlers and Dutch colonists had taken place, and there is also some evidence of mingling with indigenous Khoikhoi, Xhosa and Zulu. The Albany settlement had attracted significant numbers of new settlers, particularly traders and merchants, once trade became the main activity of Grahamstown.

The settlement in 1824

The most important change in the nature of the settlement was that, far from fulfilling the function of closing the frontier,.as had been originally intended, exactly the opposite effect had been attained. Grahamstown grew from an administrative centre for the settlers and for frontier defence into the second town of the colony and a generating point for many enterprises which affected the entire colony.

This is most apparent in the development of trade by land and sea. The settlement's economic future was dependent upon its having a suitable port, and by October 1820 J B Biddulph had sent a sketch of the Kowie estuary to the Colonial Secretary, in the hope that it could be developed. The growth of Port Elizabeth (named after Sir Rufane Donkin's deceased wife) and Port Frances on the Kowie (named after Lord Charles Somerset's daughter-in-law, Mrs Henry Somerset) was initially inhibited by the regulation whereby all ships importing to or exporting from South Africa had to clear in Cape Town. When this ban was lifted in 1826 exports from the Eastern Cape increased rapidly. By 1830 the overland route between Grahamstown and Port Natal was also in operation.

Among the early alternatives to agriculture chosen by the settlers was trading, first as foot pedlars with back packs and then with settler-built ox-wagons that took them further afield. Grahamstown was their main base, to which they returned with ivory, zoological specimens, hides and fat, besides cartographic, scientific and practical information about the interior.

As the merchants of Grahamstown flourished, they found it necessary to develop systems of credit and banking, and to form joint-stock companies. In 1832 an impressive Commercial Hall was opened in the settler city. If the 1820 settlement failed as an agricultural enterprise, settlers made a major contribution as pastoralists. Many of them, particularly the party leaders, brought with them the advanced ideas in stock farming for which eighteenth century Britain was renowned. Although Western Cape farmers had been reluctant to switch from the fat-tailed local sheep to merinos, the settlers needed little encouragement. Under the initiative of Miles Bowker, George Pigot and others, joint-stock companies were formed to import ewes and rams from Saxony and New South Wales. It is ironic, however, that the preference of the merino for the dry Karoo encouraged settlers to move north to Somerset East, Cradock, Graaff-Reinet and Colesberg, while Albany, where the effective origins of wool farming lay, failed to find a suitable crop.

The role of the settlers in a multiracial society

For the first eight years of the settlement, scarcity of labour remained its greatest problem. Attempts by the settlers to recruit additional labourers in Britain were unproductive, and most

Settlers encamped near the Great Fish River, by F T I'Ons. They are thought to be members of the Bowker family. (William Fehr Collection)

of the local Khoikhoi population who were willing to work were contracted to local Boer farmers. The labour shortage ended in 1828 when the government, with the promulgation of Ordinance 49, permitted tribesmen from beyond the frontiers to enter the colony and look for work.

In the following year Ordinance 50 released the Khoi inhabitants of the colony from the necessity of carrying passes. The undoubted benefits of an increased labour supply were offset by a rapid increase in stock theft and pilfering by wandering Khoikhoi, uncontrolled by any vagrancy law. The effect of available labour on the economy of the settlement was considerable, but it accelerated the unforeseen transformation of the settlers into a white elite. While late into the forties there were still establishments in which every task was performed by whites, the process had begun of differentiation between skilled and menial tasks along racial lines. The children of the settlers would inherit frontiers besides the boundaries of the colony; the far more complex, difficult and dangerous frontiers of class compounded with race.

The effects of the Sixth Frontier War on the settlers

In December 1834 war again erupted on the frontier, shattering the Albany farmers' incipient prosperity. Xhosa warriors drove off an estimated 250 000 head of cattle and sheep, and burned over 450 homesteads. Traders and several farmers in the main path of the invasion were killed, but missionaries were spared. Boer, British and Khoikhoi refugees flooded into Grahamstown. The war led to a further exodus from Albany. Instead of returning to their de-

vastated farms, many large landowners chose to make a fresh start further from the frontier. Speculators bought up extensive tracts of land at very low prices.

The psychological effects of the war were more important, however, than its demographic effects. The Xhosa invasion united the Albany settlers as no other experience had done: it gave them a unity which was reinforced by subsequent frontier policies and polemics. It can be argued that the Sixth Frontier War crystallized a settler identity which already existed in a concentrated fluid state. The traumatic experiences of war, added to their other pioneering trials, baptised the settlers into a frontier tradition which found a voice in the *Graham's Town Journal* – a tradition critical of 'philanthropy' and fine policies devised at a distance, whether in London or Cape Town.

Suggested Reading List

G Butler (ed) (1974) *The 1820 Settlers: An Illustrated Commentary*, Cape Town

W D Hammond-Tooke (ed) (1972) *The Journal of William Shaw*, Cape Town

P Hinchliff (ed) (1971) *The Journal of John Ayliff, 1821-1830*, Cape Town

H E Hockly (1966) *The Story of the British Settlers of 1820 in South Africa*, 2nd ed, Cape Town and Johannesburg

W A Maxwell and R T McGeogh (eds) (1978) *The Reminiscences of Thomas Stubbs*, Cape Town

M D Nash (1982) *Bailie's Party of 1820 Settlers*, Cape Town

E Pringle, E and J A Mark (1957) *Pringles of the Valley, Their History and Genealogy*, Adelaide

Dorothy E Rivett-Carnac (1961) *Thus Came the English in 1820*, Cape Town

Literature and the press

Left: Thomas Pringle (Africana Museum); *Right:* John Fairbairn (Cape Archives, M449)

There were several printers among the settlers, and a printing press in their baggage. The cautious government confiscated the dangerous machine, and the settlement was without a press for a decade. In 1822 Thomas Pringle left his party on the Baviaans River for Cape Town, where, with John Fairbairn and the printer George Greig, he set up the *South African Commercial Advertiser*. Pringle was the main protagonist in the early stages of the press battle with Lord Charles Somerset, but it was fought to its conclusion by Fairbairn and Greig. Pringle was also a creative writer and the publication of a volume of his poems, *Ephemerides*, in 1828 marks the effective beginning of a South African literature in English. His poems express a characteristic tension between feelings of exile from Britain – the old country – and a growing affection for the new country and society to which the settlers were having to adjust.

'Hottentots' removing, depicted nearly a hundred years before the scene by Daniell, in Peter Kolb's *Caput Bonae Spei Hodiernum*, published in Nüremberg in 1719. In both pictures, the use of pack oxen is illustrated. (Africana Museum)

The 'Cabo de Goede Hoop', depicted in 1711 in Abraham Bogaert's *Historische Reizen door d'oostersche Deelen van Asia. . .*, Amsterdam 1711. (Africana Museum)

Chapter 8

The Pre-Colonial and Colonial Khoikhoi

From Fragile Independence to Permanent Subservience, 1488-1713

H C Bredekamp

The geographic isolation in which the traditional Cape society lived for centuries was broken by Dias's circumnavigation of the Cape in 1488. For European seafarers this achievement marked the beginning of a new era of exploration and trade; for the indigenous Khoikhoi and San it was the beginning of a process of colonial subjugation.

Pre-colonial contact with European seafarers

For the Cape Khoikhoi the period 1488 to 1652 was marked by sporadic coastal contact with Portuguese, English and Dutch sailors. Contact with the Portuguese was dominated by violence, which culminated in 1510 when Viceroy de Almeida and fifty soldiers were killed in a skirmish on Table Bay beach.

At the beginning of the seventeenth century Table Valley became a popular point of call for passing seafarers. The English sea captain John Lancaster was successful in establishing friendly relations with the Khoikhoi and in 1601, under his command, no less than a thousand sheep and forty-two head of cattle were bartered within a period of twelve days. Prior to 1610 iron was the principal bartering commodity, but subsequently Khoikhoi began to insist to a greater extent on copper and then brass.

The temporary nature of the Europeans' visits to the Cape coast for a century and a half dispelled any fear that they would settle permanently at the Cape and drive out the indigenous occupants. This led to a sense of false security developing among the Peninsular Khoikhoi. The wreck of the *Haerlem* in March 1647 strengthened this false assumption, but the year-long friendly sojourn of the castaways held far-reaching consequences for the Khoikhoi.

The Dutch East India Company and the disintegration of the Cape Khoikhoi

The slow disintegration of the Khoikhoi's political and economic independence over a period of almost 150 years after the arrival of Van Riebeeck may be attributed to several factors: stock bartering, intertribal disputes, land occupation by whites, military conflicts, contagious diseases and their assimilation as a subordinate labour class into the colonial society. Initially barter was the principal motive for the Dutch East India Company's interest in the Khoikhoi of the Western Cape, but stock bartering never flourished at the fort. The reason for this was growing mutual distrust, exacerbated by the harsh treatment of the Khoikhoi and the murder of a young Dutch herder one Sunday morning in 1653.

In addition the Khoikhoi were not prepared to part on a large scale with their only wealth – livestock. Their entire socio-economic existence depended on their cattle, and they were only prepared to relinquish decrepit, ailing and emaciated surplus livestock to the Europeans. When the directors of the Company refused to grant permission for the seizing of cattle and the enslavement of the Khoikhoi, Van Riebeeck began to send stock-bartering expeditions into the interior.

Though economically unbeneficial, the exploratory expeditions did enable early Company officials to acquire information about the population structure of the indigenous inhabitants of the Cape. The Khoikhoi groups in the seventeenth century appeared to be located in three major geographic areas:

The Peninsular Khoikhoi: The Goringhaicona (Watermans or Strandlopers) were the permanent inhabitants of Table Valley. They were outcasts from the Peninsular Khoikhoi community, and were an example of a former stock-owning Khoikhoi group that had, through internal strife or external disaster, sunk to the level of scraping together a precarious existence as scavengers. Their leader, Autshumao (Harry), in masterly fashion turned the role of intermediary to such personal advantage that by 1658 he owned 227 head of cattle and 260 sheep. He was banished to Robben Island on the advice of two other Peninsular Khoikhoi leaders, Doman and Gogosoa.

Doman and the interpretress Krotoa (Eva) took over Autshumao's role as intermediary in Table Valley. They were both affiliated to the Goringhaiqua of Gogosoa (Dicke Kapiteijn of the Kaapmans), the predominant tribe in the peninsula. They inhabited the mouth of the Salt River, Constantia Valley, Hout Valley, Noordhoek and Bosheuwel, and moved to Table Valley in the dry summer months. The Goringhaiqua and Gorachouqua (known as the 'Tobacco Thieves') constituted the two most important Peninsular Khoikhoi tribes. Their common mo-

'Korah Hottentots preparing to remove', by Samuel Daniell, 1805. (Africana Museum)

tive of wanting to retain the broker's monopoly in the stock-bartering process led to their barring the way of the stock-owning tribes of the interior to the fort.

The Nearby Khoikhoi: The Cochoqua outnumbered all the Peninsular Khoikhoi, and grazed their herds north of Table Bay to the Berg and Olifants Rivers. They consisted of two groups, led by Oedasoa and Gonnema. The latter's headquarters were situated along the Berg River, near Riebeek-Kasteel. Stock bartering with the Cochoqua only began to gain momentum towards the end of Van Riebeeck's administration, partly owing to the struggle the Cochoqua were waging on three fronts against the Peninsular Khoikhoi, the Chainoqua and the Hessequa, and the Grigriqua. The Hessequa lived between the Hessequa-kloof and Attaqua-kloof (from the present Swellendam area up to the Gouritz region). The grazing lands of the Chainoqua extended along the coastal region from the Breede River, over the Hottentots-Holland Mountains, almost as far as the Eerste River.

The Remote Khoikhoi: Along the northern front of the Cochoqua were the Grigriqua, whose grazing lands extended from Saldanha Bay to halfway between Dassen and Robben islands. Former herdsmen of the Cochoqua, they had rebelled and enriched themselves with the livestock of their masters. The Cochoqua launched raids against the Grigriqua, who sought and received protection from the Namaqua, the most widely dispersed Khoikhoi group, who occupied the area from the lower Olifants River to beyond the Garieb (Orange River). To the north-east of the Hessequa lived a number of remote Khoikhoi groups such as the Gouriqua, Attaqua, Inqua, Damasqua, Gonaqua and the Hoengeyqua.

After the 1660s, as the herds and flocks of the

The Khoikhoi intermediaries Coeree and Autshumao ('Harry')

Coeree, a Peninsular stock farmer and probable leader of the Gorachouqua, played an important part in regard to the new selective attitude of the herders when in 1613 he was abducted and taken to England to be trained for the role of intermediary between visiting English seamen and Khoikhoi stock herders. During his stay there, he realized with dismay that the Europeans were offering inferior bartering commodities for precious Khoikhoi livestock. After his return, instead of becoming the official stock barterer, he decided to consolidate his position as an indigenous leader. In a further attempt to encourage stock bartering, the English took Autshumao (Harry), the leader of the so-called Strandlopers, to Bantam in the East in 1631, where he acquired an imperfect knowledge of English. On his return, until 1640, he and some of his followers became postal agents for the English on Robben Island.

Stock-bartering expeditions in the interior

The first official expedition in March and April 1655, to the present Malmesbury-Saldanha Bay area, achieved very little beyond confirming that Harry and the Strandlopers had prevented Khoikhoi who wished to barter cattle from going to the fort. In September another expedition set out for the interior, accompanied by Harry in the capacity of guide and stock barterer. They returned on 5 October without Harry, who reported some two months later at the fort with a mere thirteen head of cattle, and claimed that unknown Khoikhoi had stolen his barter goods. The Commander called a halt to the unprofitable bartering expeditions, but in 1657 Commissioner Rykloff van Goens instructed him to continue his investigations of the possibilities of trade with the interior. In October the same year an expedition under Abraham Gabbema attemped to obtain livestock in the Berg River valley. The river was in flood and they were unable to barter with the Cochoqua, who were reputedly rich in livestock. They obtained a mere seven cows, three calves and forty-one sheep from the uncooperative Gorachouqua and Grigriqua. The next expedition, in 1658, progressed as far as the Tulbagh basin, but the quantity of livestock obtained proved equally small. Four subsequent expeditions were sent by Van Riebeeck in the direction of the Olifants River.

Peninsular and Nearby Khoikhoi began to decline drastically, the colonial government was forced to rely on stock-bartering expeditions to the Hessequa and to some Remote Khoikhoi tribes. For this purpose, Khoikhoi intermediaries were occasionally used. The best known Khoikhoi agent after Autshumao was a Chainoqua chief, Dorhá, or Klaas. By 1686 Simon van der Stel was so convinced of his loyalty that he plied him with trinkets and dressed him in European clothes. But Dorhá realized by 1690 that co-operation with the authorities would not bring him the prosperity he had hoped for, and when the Governor turned against him he tried to form alliances with other Khoikhoi leaders. However, his collaboration with the Dutch had aroused the hatred of his Khoikhoi compatriots to such an extent that they engineered his violent death in 1701.

The short-lived throwing open of the trade in livestock in 1700 and the rapid subsequent expansion of the stock farmers resulted in the herds and flocks of the Company and free burghers increasing dramatically, while those of the Khoikhoi decreased. During the seventeenth and eighteenth centuries the Khoikhoi lost their grazing lands at an even faster rate. As early as 1655 the Peninsular Khoikhoi had informed Van Riebeeck that they regarded the occupied country as their *'eijgen land'*. Van Riebeeck rejected the claim, and ordered the Goringhaiqua in 1657 to regard the area east of the Salt and Liesbeeck rivers as Khoikhoi residential and grazing area. Thus the Peninsular Khoikhoi were deprived of their best grazing lands and traditional water sources. They responded by devastating the farmland of the free burghers and seizing cattle. The result was the First Company-Khoikhoi War (1659-1660), which ended in the military subjugation of the Peninsular Khoikhoi. They continued, however, to dispute the occupation of land by the Dutch, and in 1672, in an attempt to give credibility to their land rights, purchase transactions were drawn up by the Company. These were a mere formality, especially since they were concluded with two Peninsular chiefs who were known for their willingness to be of service to the Company.

The exceptionable way in which the territory from the Hottentots-Holland Mountains up to Saldanha Bay was purchased contributed to the outbreak of the Second Company-Khoikhoi War in 1673. The territory consisted primarily of the grazing and hunting areas of the Cochoqua, yet, as well as paying a ridiculously low price for the land, the Dutch did not consult Gonnema, the Cochoqua chief, an omission which further reinforced his belief that the white authorities held him in contempt. The activities of Dutch prospectors in the Riebeek-Kasteel Mountains from 1670 onwards must also have been a source of concern to Gonnema, hence the attacks on farmhouses that commenced that year. In 1672 the tension mounted when some of Gonnema's followers were brought before a white court and banished to Robben Island. The white authorities thus took upon themselves the right to exercise jurisdiction over recalcitrant Khoikhoi. In 1673, after an attack on a group of hunters, a military force consisting of Company soldiers, free burghers and Khoikhoi adherents set out against Gonnema.

The war lasted until 1677, by which time both sides were ready to conclude a settlement. In terms of the peace treaty, Gonnema had to beg forgiveness for his misdeeds, swear to live in peace with the servants of the Company, punish miscreants among his people according to Dutch law in future, and pay an annual tribute of thirty cattle! The war was the final phase of the Cochoqua resistance and ended in undisputed victory for the Dutch.

The rapid expansion of stock farmers in the eighteenth century led to the sovereignty of the Khoikhoi clans being disregarded, and their traditional grazing lands being taken over for loan farms. Sometimes colonists obtained the permission of a Khoikhoi chief before moving into an area, but more often they simply established themselves without permission as squatter families. The positions soon became reversed and squatting became a stereotype of the Khoikhoi. This phenomenon was primarily the result of the fragility of the social structure of Khoikhoi society, which could not withstand the colonial onslaught.

Contagious diseases, transmitted to the Cape from abroad, had a devastating effect on the Khoikhoi. The worst of these was the smallpox epidemic of 1713, caused by infected linen from a ship, against which the Khoikhoi were defenceless. The remaining independent clans in the south-western Cape virtually disappeared. Some fled to the interior, others returned to a hunter-gatherer existence, and many entered the colonial labour market. They bade farewell to their traditional way of life and became penu-

rious and subservient guides, domestic workers, postmen, stock herders, transport riders and farm labourers.

Yet the Khoisan attacks during the eighteenth century proved that not all of them had meekly accepted their fate, and can be seen as a last form of resistance to the demands made on them by the colonial society.

'After the hunt – a Bushman cave', by Thomas Baines. The picture illustrates the type of existence led by some of the Khoisan who escaped servitude, yet could no longer pursue their former way of life. Baines recorded in his *Journal of Residence*: 'Accompanying hor . . . we found two men of something between the Bushman and Hottentot tribes, one with an old felt hat and sheepskin coat, smoking tobacco out of the shankbone of a sheep, and the other in a red coat, lying outstretched on his back and fast asleep, with an old musket marked G R Tower carefully covered beside him.' (Africana Museum)

'Bushmen driving cattle up a kloof – Boers in pursuit', by C D Bell. This scene was enacted repeatedly during the years of conflict between Khoisan and frontier farmers. The captured cattle are driven back to the mountain fastnesses where the Khoisan have taken refuge, and an ambush awaits the pursuing farmers. In the right foreground, a beast who fails to complete the climb is killed. (Africana Museum)

The Khoisan had access to innumerable natural hiding places in the kloofs. Sometimes they built stone ramparts across the mouths of caves, from behind which they showered their enemies with arrows. (Mendelssohn Collection, Library of Parliament)

Khoisan Resistance to Colonial Expansion, 1700-1828
S Newton-King

Susan Newton-King is head of the Department of History at the University of Bophuthatswana. She was educated at St Cyprian's School in Cape Town and at the University of Cape Town, where she graduated with distinction. Since completing her MA at London University's School of Oriental and African Studies in 1976, she has conducted extensive research on the history of the eighteenth century Cape frontier. She is presently completing a doctoral thesis which deals with the relations between the trekboers and the Khoisan of the Eastern Cape.

Every stage in the long process of European expansion into the hinterland of the Cape met with fierce and bitter resistance from both Khoikhoi and San. As the advancing trekboers gradually dispossessed them of their pastures, plundered their already shrunken herds and hunted down the game on which they greatly depended, significant numbers of Khoikhoi remained on the peripheries of white settlement. There they lived a vulnerable existence as pastoralists, raided alike by white freebooters, San hunters and their Khoi neighbours. Those who were robbed turned to robbery themselves in an attempt to recoup their lost wealth. It was from these disturbed frontier communities that there emerged a sporadic but ferocious resistance to the expansion of the colony.

In the colonial record the resisters were known indiscriminately as *Bosjesmans* or *Bosjesmans Hottentotten*. This term, as it was used in the eighteenth century, referred rather to their lifestyle than to any physical or ethnic differ-

Major Khoikhoi Groupings in the Seventeenth and Eighteenth Centuries

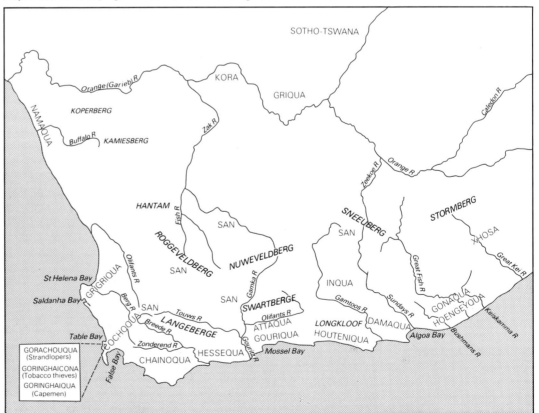

106

ences between them and the 'Hottentots'. *Bosjesmans* was the name given to people who lived in and by the bush, that is, by hunting, gathering and raiding. When Khoikhoi lost their livestock and fell back on the survival strategies of the hunter-gatherer, there was little in the eyes of an untutored and prejudiced *veldkorporaal* to distinguish them from the San. The term *Bosjesman* also came to mean a robber, bandit or 'highwayman', and in 1701 the Company's diarist referred to the Khoisan raiders along the colony's northern border as 'Bushmen or highwaymen, consisting mainly of Grigriquas and Namaquas'. Often, of course, the San *were* involved in the attacks on colonial farms and flocks. The hunter communities living in the mountains and the arid plains of the Karoo and the Roggeveld were doubly threatened, by the relentless spread of the trekboers and by fugitive Khoikhoi.

It is important to reconstruct the story of the bitter struggle between these resisters and the white frontiersmen for two reasons. First, it can be postulated that the so-called 'Bushmen Wars' were in fact a manifestation of continuing resistance by the Khoikhoi as well as by the San to dispossesion and to a life as menials in the colonial domain. Second, it can be argued that it is within the context of this long history of resistance that the peculiar violence of master-servant relations in the South African interior can best be understood.

Khoisan resistance on the northern frontier, 1702-1739

The historian Shula Marks was the first to point to the connection between the *moord- en roofzugtigheid* (lust for murder and robbery) of the *Bosjesmans Hottentotten* and the dispossession of the Khoisan by the advancing frontiersmen. She observed that Khoisan raids frequently followed cattle trading expeditions, which tipped easily over into raiding expeditions when the Khoikhoi were reluctant to barter a sufficient number of cattle on the terms offered.

With the opening of the cattle frontier in 1700, the northern borderlands erupted in violence. *Bosjesmans*, sometimes in parties of several hundred at a time, attacked the cattle posts of the Company, free burghers and loyalist Khoikhoi in the Land of Waveren. They seized hundreds of cattle, but apparently made no attempt to harm the persons of the burghers or their servants. These *Bosjesmans*, identified by the Cochoqua and other loyalist Khoikhoi as mainly Grigriqua and Namaqua, were 'San' only in the sense that their poverty had driven them to robbery.

Despite their attempts to defend themselves, the Khoikhoi along the colony's northern frontier began to decline rapidly in wealth and population. The smallpox epidemic of 1713 spread as far north as the Piketberg, and in 1714 Khoikhoi from this region reported an appalling death rate. After this calamity came two years of drought and seven years of recurrent stock disease. Yet the Remote Khoikhoi were still able to put up resistance against the expansion of the colony. In 1715 and 1716 there were many reports of stock theft along the Berg River and in the Land of Waveren, and it was said that the white stock farmers who occupied these areas were so afraid that 'nearly all slept with their guns in their hands'. They found the Company's protection inadequate and obtained permission to form commandos made up entirely of burgher volunteers, a precedent which became the norm among the trekboers.

By the late 1720s European settlement had spread northwards along the Olifants River as far as its confluence with the Doring River, and there was no longer any mention of independent Khoi villages south of Meerhofskasteel. Yet resistance in the present south-western Cape continued. In 1728 and 1731 bands of *Bosjesman Hottentotten* raided settlers' livestock. In September 1738 a party of some hundred *Bosjesmans* from Little Namaqualand made off with the cattle of Augustus Louwerensz. When captured, and asked why they had stolen the cattle of the Dutch, they replied: 'To chase them out of the country, since they were living in their country; and that this was only a beginning.' The stolen livestock which the raiders could not eat or drive away were killed or so severely wounded that they would be of no use to the colonists. This destruction of livestock was a common practice which seems to have been deliberately intended to weaken the burgher's morale and drive them away.

The following year (1739) there were raids throughout the Koue Bokkeveld and behind the Piketberg; more than 400 cattle and 2 400 sheep were taken, two whites and two slaves were murdered and several farm-houses set alight. According to the historian Nigel Penn the violence seems to have been sparked by an illegal trading expedition. A certain Willem van Wijk had led a party of settlers and their Khoikhoi servants into Little Namaqualand, where they had extorted cattle by force. It transpired that a

Colonel Robert Jacob Gordon, Military Commander at the Cape and explorer and artist, travelled through the Camdeboo in 1777, and came across this grave of a captain of the *Camdeboos hottentotten, Coranas natie genoemt.* 'These people,' he wrote, 'are no longer here except for a few among the Boers.' The grave consisted of a stone cairn, surmounted by the skull and horns of an ox and the captain's quiver and arrows. (Cape Archives, AG7146.95)

A Khoikhoi man riding an ox. (Africana Museum)

'Boers returning from a hunt', by Samuel Daniell. The Khoisan retainer, probably an expert marksman and tracker, carries a firearm. (Africana Museum)

The case of *Onse Liewe Heer*

In 1788 there was a great upheaval among the Khoisan in the vicinity of Swellendam and the Riviersonder-end. Encouraged by their faith in a man they addressed as *Onse Liewe Heer* ('Our Dear Lord'), who was reputedly invulnerable to physical injury, they deserted their masters and prepared to gather at the kraal of a certain Willem Stompje on the Riviersonderend. The emissaries of *Onse Liewe Heer* (whose identity was never discovered but who may have been a certain Cobus Valentijn) had instructed them to burn all their Dutch clothes, build new huts with two doors and slaughter all their white cattle. The burghers of Swellendam were greatly alarmed when a considerable number of newly made arrows and assegais were discovered in one of the kraals and when mysterious fires were lit on the mountain above the *drostdy*.

The conspirators allegedly planned an attack on the burghers which was to coincide with the end of the world (beyond which lay a new world in which the Khoisan would reassert their birthright). But the world endured, and by the end of the year the conspiracy had lost its momentum. The *landdrost* was unable to apprehend *Onse Liewe Heer*, to whom he referred as *'een Doortrapte Vagebont'* (an out-and-out scoundrel). By November 1788 he could report that *'het is tans alles in rust'* (all is now quiet). Clearly this had been a major attempt at resistance, yet its pronounced messianic dimensions suggest that other more practical strategies for loosening the settlers' grip upon the region had by then been exhausted.

number of the Khoikhoi servants, dissatisfied by their meagre share of the booty, had subsequently deserted to the Namaqua and joined in the raids on colonial homesteads. Hence reports that the raiders had guns and could use them.

The involvement of deserters from service was another feature which was to become characteristic of Khoisan resistance during the eighteenth century. Scattered through the records of the Stellenbosch and Graaff-Reinet districts are numerous references to servants who have suddenly and (in the view of their white masters) inexplicably, gone 'vagabonding'. Servants who absconded with horses and guns were particularly feared, for Khoisan shepherds accompanied their masters on commando, and were thus skilled marksmen who knew the ways of their pursuers. Deserters who failed to link up with existing Khoisan bands (or *Bosjesmans*) seldom survived more than a few months in freedom. They were relentlessly pursued and hunted down, for fear that they would attract others to desert or, like the famous Oorlam leader, Jager Afrikaner, become celebrated as a symbol of resistance.

The Roggeveld range and Camdeboo, 1740-1772

After the 'Bushman War' of 1739 white frontiersmen were able to consolidate their hold over the Onder Bokkeveld and to spread out beyond this region in search of fresh pastures.

The settlement reached the Nuweveld range by the 1760s and the Sneeuberge and Cambdeboo by the end of the decade. In the 1750s there were still a number of independent Khoikhoi communities in the Roggeveld, living near the trekboers, but not under their immediate control.

Conflict erupted on the northern frontier in 1754. It was reported that the *Bosjesmans Hottentotten* were 'collecting together' in the Voorste and Agterste Roggeveld and in the Onder Bokkeveld and carrying off whole herds of cattle. Commandos were called out and four encampments were tracked down and attacked. The primary instigator of the raids appeared to be a certain Duijkerpens, who capitulated after a bitter struggle. Together with three other captains, he accepted a copper-headed staff of office and a gift of breeding sheep from the burghers.

The peace brought a lull in the conflict, and the northern frontier remained relatively untroubled for a further fifteen years. The majority of the Khoikhoi in the Roggeveld went into service or lived scattered among the small kraals of 'tame Hottentots' who were not regarded as a threat until the bitter conflicts of the 1770s spread hatred and mistrust across the frontier.

Khoisan resistance and servitude between the Nieuweveld range and Camdeboo, 1772-1795

The primary locus of resistance throughout the eighteenth century remained the escarpment

108

along the northern frontier. In the mid-1770s this resistance reached an unprecedented pitch. The raiders attacked almost daily in large bands, sometimes numbering 200 or more.

The historian P J van der Merwe has argued that this rise in the tempo of violence in the 1770s can be explained by the proximity of the Nuweveld and Sneeuberge to 'the real Bushmanland', which lay north of the Sneeuberge, along the Zeekoe River. It was hunger, he said, which drew the dense San population of this region towards the flocks and herds of the trekboers.

The tactics adopted by the raiders suggest that their motivation was more complex than this. Not only did they plunder vast quantities of livestock, but they also destroyed those animals they could not take with them in their retreat. Houses and farm buildings were often burnt to the ground or besieged and showered with arrows. Khoisan and slave shepherds were brutally murdered, horses were stabbed or wounded and corn was burnt as it ripened in the fields. While it is possible that these aggressive tactics were no more than the inevitable adjunct of armed robbery, they strongly suggest that, like the *Bosjesmans* from Namaqualand in 1738, the purpose of the northern raiders was to drive the settlers from the district altogether.

Professor van der Merwe's assumption that the robber bands on the north-eastern frontier were composed entirely of 'Bushmen' must also be challenged. Apart from the ambiguity of this term in the context of the eighteenth century frontier, travellers' journals, such as those of Robert Jacob Gordon and Anders Sparrman, provide evidence of the presence of cattle-keeping Khoikhoi in the south-west and south-east of the Sneeuberge, and possibly also to the north behind the mountains. However, the Sneeuberge and the country behind *had* long supported a relatively dense San population. These communities were now under intense stress. Squeezed on one side by the expanding Xhosa kingdom and on the other by the advancing trekboers, they were further disturbed by the influx of displaced Khoikhoi from the south-west. Their response was to try and drive the colonists from the country.

The burghers lost no time in hitting back. Since the 'Bushman War' of 1739 all male burghers in the frontier districts had been obliged to serve in the militia. In each district there was a *veldwachtmeester*, appointed by the *landdrost* and *heemraden*, who had the authority to commandeer the services of his neighbours whenever he deemed it necessary. All too often individual farmers went in hot pursuit of stock thieves and only informed the *veldwachtmeester* afterwards. The result was that, in the words of Professor van der Merwe, 'during the last thirty years of the eighteenth century, the farmers were given more or less complete freedom to act against the Bushmen as they saw fit'.

The struggle was unequal. Although the Khoisan population on the frontier was far greater than that of the whites, their technology could not match the combination of gun and horse which was the mainstay of the frontiersmen's defence. The Khoisan did have certain advantages over their pursuers. They knew the terrain with an intimacy which the farmers could not match; they were fast runners and expert trackers, who could melt suddenly into the dense bush, invisible to all but the trained eye. Despite these skills, they were defeated ultimately by the sheer ruthlessness of burgher reprisals.

Despite the decimation of their numbers, Khoisan attacks upon the white frontiersmen did not abate until after the turn of the century. If anything, the savagery of settler reprisals seems to have fuelled their determination to resist. The relentless conflict rendered the recovery of their former lifestyle increasingly difficult for fugitive Khoisan communities north of the Sneeuberge. The co-operative work patterns of the hunting and herding economy were disturbed by the loss of family members and the subsistence strategies of the hunter-gatherers were equally disrupted. Under these conditions, many Khoisan groups must have begun to rely on plunder for their subsistence. They became, indeed, what their enemies supposed them to be – predatory bands, consuming their booty immediately or sending it northwards for safekeeping among more settled people, then returning to rob again.

The effects of the frontier conflict on the Khoisan in the colony

The prolonged and bitter border conflict had equally far-reaching consequences for those Khoisan who lived within the white domain. The majority of colonists regarded their 'Hottentot' servants and their 'Bushman' enemies as one and the same people, which in many senses they were. Thus all Khoisan, whether 'tame' or

A typical Boer frontier family, with Khoisan servants in attendance. Uprooted, given Dutch names, and forced to survive in a strange environment, some 'tame Hottentots' (*mak Hottentotten*) as they were known, were absorbed completely into the small world of the Boer household. They adopted European-style dress, spoke 'Cape Dutch', and became subservient and loyal to their captors. (Africana Museum)

Two 'Hottentot herdsmen', depicted by G F Angas. (Africana Museum)

'Portrait of Juli, a faithful Hottentot', from W J Burchell's *Travels in the Interior of Southern Africa . . .* London, 1822-1824. Juli was a guide who acted as an intermediary between travellers and the black peoples in the interior. (Africana Museum)

'wild', ran the risk of being apprehended as 'vagabonds' and potential stock thieves should they stray from their masters' lands. At best they would be captured and handed over to the *veldwachtmeester* or kept in the service of their captors. At worst they would be beaten or shot on sight. 'Does a colonist at any time get sight of a Boshiesman,' wrote Sparrman, 'he takes fire immediately and spirits up his horse and dogs, in order to hunt him with more ardour and fury than he would a wild beast.'

Even Khoisan who did not stray from their masters were liable to become victims of the general climate of mistrust in frontier districts. Many farm servants were captives, taken by commandos during raids upon *Bosjesman* villages and shared out among commando members. They came, as it were, directly from the ranks of the enemy. Uprooted, given Dutch names and forced to survive in a strange environment, some were absorbed completely into the isolated world of their master's household, becoming subservient and loyal to their captors, but others nurtured the desire to escape. Besides these war captives, or *krijgsgevangenen*, there were many other categories of servants in the frontier districts whose position was that of captives or slaves, and they too sometimes tried to escape.

The farmers' response was to punish desertion swiftly and brutally, usually by whipping, sometimes by a more gruesome combination of punishments. The Hottentot Klijnveld, for example, allegedly had his fingers pulled out of joint with iron tongs, in order that he confess to the theft of a sheep during his absence from his master's place, while an anonymous 'Hottentot girl' who deserted the farmer Coenraad Vermaak from the Lange Kloof was beaten until her back broke.

The 'Black Circuit'

Certain of these cases came to light during the so-called 'Black Circuit' of 1812, where numerous allegations of maltreatment were investigated by the circuit court at Uitenhage, on the basis of testimony collected by James Read and Dr van der Kemp of the London Missionary Society Station at Bethelsdorp. Only eight of the colonists arraigned before the court for assault or murder were convicted in 1812, though other cases were held over for judgement at a later date. It would be a mistake to conclude, however, that where cases were dismissed the crime had not occurred – though such has been the contention of many South African historians since the time of the trials.

Firstly, the court investigated only a small number of the hundred-odd cases reported by the missionaries, namely those assaults alleged to have been committed since the second British occupation of the Cape in 1806. Secondly, many

of the alleged assaults were investigated some years after they had taken place. Thirdly, the nature of frontier society was such that reliable witnesses were difficult to find. The colonists were incensed at the very idea of the trials – they regarded their relations with their servants as a private matter and resented legal interference, except where they requested it themselves. *'Het is ons volk,'* Johannes Schoeman had said of a family which had deserted him six years earlier, *'wij kunnen daarmee leeven zoo als wij willen'.* (They are our people, we can live with them as we wish.) The Khoisan, for their part, had to bear in mind the consequences they might face when they returned to their masters after having testified against them or their relatives in court. Fourthly, and most important, a study of the trials highlights an issue raised by the American historian Eugene Genovese with respect to the American South: cruelty, in relation to an unfree labour force, is difficult to define. Severe corporal punishment was acceptable to colonial society at that time; when and under what circumstances could it be judged as criminal assault?

In the context of the eighteenth century Cape frontier, servitude was bound to be predicated upon the use of force: the Khoisan who became members of the *volk* on frontier farms, for all that they gradually became acculturated as subordinates in colonial society, were drawn nonetheless from the ranks of the very people with whom the farmers were contesting the right to occupation of the Cape interior. They, like the communities beyond the frontier, could remember a time when the land had been theirs and when they had worked for themselves, herding their own animals and hunting according to their own discretion. The rewards of service were scarcely enough to compensate for the loss of this independence.

In these circumstances the very institution of service was called into question, not merely the terms of the arrangement. Khoisan servants in the frontier districts were not so much born to

110

their lot, as forcibly moulded to it. Every trivial conflict over the performance of daily chores raised echoes of the more fundamental conflict over mastery of the land and its people. The master-servant relationship became a battleground upon which the terms of white dominance were at stake. During this period servitude had not yet become a 'natural' condition for the Khoisan in the frontier districts; it was clearly a product of conquest, a political creation, as it were. Thus a revolt against the terms of service could easily overflow into a more generalized rebellion against the very presence of colonists in the area.

This lurking shadow of revolt explains, in part, the ferocity with which the farmers punished their servants. The *sjambok* in frontier society was more than an instrument of domestic discipline; it was, as the settlers themselves acknowledged, a means of 'taming' the indigenous population until such time as they 'improved themselves'. With time, this form of control became redundant. Among the younger Khoisan, who had been born and raised in service, there were many who came to identify with their masters rather than with the 'wild' *Bosjesmans* against whom they served on commando. Loyal servants were frequently sent out by their masters to recapture deserters and were required to be accessories to their punishment.

The Khoisan rebellion of 1799 – the 'servants' revolt'

Despite this inexorable process of acquiescence in the colonial order, the 'servants' revolt' did become a reality. It began in the autumn of 1799 and spread like wildfire, catching the burghers off their guard. By mid-year it was reported that 'the Hottentots had to a man deserted their masters'. Making their base among the Xhosa of the Zuurveld, the rebel Khoisan burnt and plundered farms throughout the southern and central parts of the Graaff-Reinet district. By the end of August 1799, 29 Europeans had been killed and all but a handful had fled the district. The shadow had materialized; the 'tame Hottentots' had turned their guns against them.

Many of the rebels of 1799 had spent their whole lives in service. In that sense they were clearly different from the raiders on the frontiers. They fought almost exclusively with guns, not with bows and arrows, and they could raise a force of 300 horsemen. Their grievances were partly specific to their experience as servants: they wanted compensation for wages withheld and revenge for the punishments they had suffered. However, when asked to define their goals, their spokesman declared, in terms which would not have sounded out of place on the lips of a *Bosjesman*: 'Restore the country of which our forefathers have been despoiled by the Dutch and we have nothing more to ask.'

The rebellion was defeated after nearly four years of simmering tension and intermittent fighting. Afterwards came a period of 'pacification', during which the colonists were resettled and the Khoisan bullied and cajoled into returning to their masters.

The effects of the 'Hottentot Code', 1809, and Ordinance 50, 1828

In 1809 the British authorities introduced the 'Hottentot Code' which, together with subsequent legislation proclaimed in 1812 and 1819, set the seal on the fate of the colonial Khoisan. Though these proclamations had a protective as well as a repressive function, their primary effect was to give legal form to the forced labour practices which had been informally observed on the frontier for so long.

Every 'Hottentot' was to have a 'fixed place of abode', which in practice meant residence with a European. If he was found 'going about the country' without a pass signed by his master or the *landdrost*, he would be regarded as a 'vagabond' and summarily arrested, then returned to his former master or compelled to contract himself to a new one. Thus, while the 'Hottentot Code' upheld the right of individual Khoisan to leave their masters on the expiry of a contract, it condemned them as a group 'to a perpetual state of servitude'.

With the passage of time, the will to resist diminished. Veterans of the 'servants' revolt' who tried to sustain a bandit group in the Winterhoek Mountains, found themselves spurned and finally betrayed by their fellow Khoisan. By the time Ordinance 50 was promulgated in 1828, whereby Khoisan servants were at last freed from forced labour and protected against arbitrary punishment, the era of anti-colonial resistance had passed. They had won their freedom in the eyes of the law, but they had irrevocably lost their land.

Suggested Reading List

R Elphick (1985) *Khoikhoi and the Founding of White South Africa*, Johannesburg

H C Bredekamp (1982) *Van Veeverskaffers tot Veewagters*, Bellville

H Lamar and L Thompson (eds) (1981) *The Frontier in History*, New Haven

S Newton-King and V C Malherbe (1981) *The Khoikhoi Rebellion in the Eastern Cape, 1799-1803*, Cape Town

P J van der Merwe (1937) *Die Noordwaartse Beweging van die Boere Voor die Groot Trek*, The Hague

---

Harsh punishment for deserters

During the Khoisan rebellion or 'servants' revolt' between 1799 and 1803, deserters were especially at risk, for the possibility of their making common cause with the resisters, always latent, was now actual and their frightened masters responded with summary violence. Thus Fredrik Hoffman and Jager Wildschut, who had fled to the Xhosa in 1800, but returned to fetch Hoffman's wife, who was still in service, were captured and summarily shot on the orders of her *baas*, Jan Strijdom. Another servant, Lea Quassarie, was allegedly killed by her master, Carel Bester, while attempting to join her husband, who had deserted to the British at Algoa Bay. Gerrit Windvogel, whose father had been shot in 1799 while trying to leave the place of Zacharias de Beer, alleged that 'the farmers at that time shot all those who they knew had an intention of leaving their master'.

'Portrait of Speelman, a Hottentot', by W J Burchell. (Africana Museum)

The Battle of Vegkop of October 1836, during which approximately forty men, women, children and servants of Hendrik Potgieter's Voortrekker party defended themselves against some 6 000 Ndebele warriors. This depiction by Heinrich Egersdörfer was based on information supplied by the historian G M Theal. The wagons were drawn into laager formation at the foot of the hill Doringkop (subsequently renamed Vegkop) and were bound together with thongs and chains. Whole thorn trees and branches were secured under and between the wagons, forming an effective barricade. (Africana Museum)

Part III

The Transformation of the Hinterland

During the first half of the nineteenth century, the hinterland was transformed by two momentous migratory movements – the *Mfecane* (or *Difaqane*) and the Great Trek.

The social, ecological and economic crisis which originated in Natal Nguni society during the course of the eighteenth century had widespread repercussions which changed the demographic pattern and groupings of the interior. These great movements of black people were larger in scale than the Great Trek, and the resulting devastation and loss of life caused by the *Mfecane/Difaqane* were of major significance for the whole of southern Africa. Even more noteworthy, as the historian John Omer-Cooper has explained, is that the upheaval was 'essentially a process of positive political change'.

The Great Trek was seen by the historian Eric Walker, writing in the 1930s, as 'the central event in the history of European man in southern Africa'. The emphasis may have shifted in the 1980s but the Voortrekker phenomenon remains immensely important. The Great Trek was a migration of a mere 15 000 Afrikaners from the Cape Colony, yet their achievements should not be underestimated. They outflanked the southern Nguni; they defeated the military might of the Matabele and Zulu (despite initial setbacks); and they succeeded in establishing independent republics which were ultimately acknowledged by Britain.

In Part III the interaction between the earlier *Mfecane/Difaqane* and the subsequent Great Trek is stressed, and attempts are made to place these vital developments in perspective. By the 1850s the society of the hinterland had been transformed into a mutually dependent, multi-racial community, characterized by both co-operation and conflict.

Shaka, king of the Zulu, c 1825, based on a sketch made by the trader James King. The depiction is inaccurate in some respects; the spear should be a short stabbing spear, and the shield and plume on the king's head are both too long. However, the picture succeeds in conveying the height and dignity of bearing which impressed those who came into Shaka's royal presence. (Cape Archives, E4291)

Chapter 9

The Mfecane or Difaqane

Ruth Edgecombe

During the second decade of the nineteenth century there occurred among the Bantu-speaking peoples of southern Africa, in the vivid words of De Kiewiet, a 'singular crisis that smashed tribes, scattered others and dashed the fragments into new combinations'. The Nguni-speaking peoples referred to this crisis as the *Mfecane*, meaning 'crushing' in the sense of 'total war'. In its highveld manifestations, the Sotho-speaking peoples called it the *Difaqane* or *Lifaqane*, meaning 'forced migration' or 'hammering'. The geographical scale of the Mfecane was vast, its repercussions being felt over a wide area from the Cape frontier to Central and East Africa. In its dying phases the Mfecane interacted with the Great Trek, and these movements were easily among the major formative factors in the history of southern Africa in the years 1795-1870.

The charting of the causes and course of the Mfecane is a difficult task and perhaps can never be done adequately. Literate sources for this period are few and the writings of white travellers, missionaries and officials in the nineteenth century provide a picture distorted by their own misunderstandings and preconceptions in describing societies that were alien to them. Oral traditions themselves are difficult to use. When a chiefdom is smashed and gone, its traditions go with it; when new formations arise oral traditions are reshaped to suit the new order. The understanding and interpretation of oral traditions become particularly problematic when filtered through the pens of white recorders, such as the missionary A T Bryant and the native affairs official James Stuart. Any synthesis and explanation of the Mfecane must then of necessity be a tentative one, when theories abound and detailed proof frequently escapes confirmation.

Dingiswayo, Zwide and the origins of the Mfecane

The Mfecane had its origins in significant changes among the northern Nguni peoples living north of the Thukela River, and which culminated in the creation of the Zulu kingdom. Towards the end of the eighteenth century there was a tendency for loose confederations to form as chiefs began to expand their followings through the incorporation of weaker neighbours. Previously political formations had been small, warfare was usually resorted to for the settlement of feuds, and was limited in impact and destructiveness. Tensions within these small chiefdoms tended to be resolved by fission – the hiving off of dissident elements into new pastures. With the larger formations, most notably the Ndwandwe under Zwide, the Ngwane under Sobhuza, and the Mthethwa under Dingiswayo, there came changes in political, social and military structures.

Ruth Edgecombe is a graduate of Rhodes and Cambridge universities She has lectured at the University of South Africa and is currently senior lecturer in Economic History at the University of Natal in Pietermaritzburg. Her major research interest is the history of coal mining in South Africa.

The age regiments introduced by Dingiswayo were characterized by individually distinctive dress and shields of different colours. The Ndebele, under Mzilikazi, continued this tradition, and this picture shows the war dress and shields of one of the regiments of *Machaka* or unmarried warriors. (Africana Museum)

115

Mtimuni, nephew of Shaka, by G F Angas. The Nguni-type shield carried by this Zulu warrior was used to deflect flying spears or clubs, and the short stabbing spear was thrust at the enemy in close combat. (Africana Museum)

Towards the end of the eighteenth century, Jobe, chief of the Mthethwa, died. His son Dingiswayo, who had been forced to flee and become a wanderer following an unsuccessful plot to overthrow his father, was then able to return to the triangular area between the sea and the lower reaches of the Mfolozi and Mhlatuze rivers where the Mthethwa lived. Dingiswayo then ousted his brother, who had succeeded his father, and proceeded to effect crucial changes in the organization of his following. The most notable of these was the development of the system of *buthaing* – the drafting of young men of approximately the same age into *amabutho* or regiments.

With this new organization, the Mthethwa became decidedly stronger than their immediate neighbours, most of whom were conquered or brought under submission as Dingiswayo embarked on an expansive course. Generally Dingiswayo spared women and children in his course of conquest, and frequently allowed the local ruling family to remain in power if their loyalty could be secured. While subject chiefdoms tended to remain intact in many respects, their menfolk were conscripted into Dingiswayo's *amabutho*, thereby securing the integration of the chiefdoms into the Mthethwa confederacy.

Further to the north of the Mthethwa, across the Mfolozi, Zwide of the Ndwandwe was building up a similar confederacy, but with one important difference. Unlike Dingiswayo, who incorporated conquered peoples, Zwide was much more ferocious towards those he attacked, stripping them of all their cattle and river gardens and putting whole populations to flight. The historian Philip Bonner has suggested that with the apparent greater degree of permanent military organization and more fully developed notion of kingship among the Ndwandwe, it was Zwide rather than Dingiswayo who was 'the real prototype of Shaka', and it was the Ndwandwe rather than the Mthethwa who served as 'the catalyst of the Mfecane'. For it was Shaka's wars of conquest that unleashed the waves of migrants and wars that constituted the Mfecane.

How can the transition from small to larger political formations among the northern Nguni be explained? Traditionally it has been supposed that the personality of Dingiswayo dominated these changes and that the ideas adopted in restructuring the Mthethwa were derived from Europeans. For instance, Henry Francis Fynn, a white trader who had settled in Natal in 1824, originated the story that when Dingiswayo was wandering about as a refugee from Jobe's wrath, he came across Dr Cowan, a traveller from the Cape. From Cowan, Dingiswayo acquired a horse and a gun and information about the superior ways of white people. Notwithstanding chronological inconsistencies, Fynn's story has been widely accepted, as has Theophilus Shepstone's conjectural account of a supposed visit by Dingiswayo to the Cape Colony, where he learned of the strength of standing armies and the value of discipline and training. Theories of white inspiration are no longer tenable, however, because they cannot explain why similar changes were occurring among other northern Nguni chiefdoms such as the Ndwandwe, the Qwabe and the Ngwane before Dingiswayo's reign, and they do not take into account the fact that long before Dingiswayo the northern Nguni were brought into contact with European ideas and technology through shipwrecked sailors.

A persuasive theory pioneered by Monica Wilson and Alan Smith, and developed fully by David Hedges, seeks to explain northern Nguni transformations in terms of trade centred on Delagoa Bay. In the latter half of the eighteenth century trade in ivory for beads, copper, and cloth flourished as a result of competition among European powers operating there. Tsonga chiefdoms in the vicinity, such as the Tembe and then the Mabudu, built up large trading empires and northern Nguni chiefdoms were increasingly drawn into the trading networks. The chiefs valued this trade because it provided them with commodities such as beads and copper ornaments which could be used for

116

display, exchanged for cattle, and serve as a source of patronage to secure a loyal following. Trade monopolies meant wealth and could be used as a means of consolidating the state. When the Portuguese secured control of the trade at Delagoa Bay in 1799, trade in ivory dwindled with the elimination of competition. Although this was partially offset by demand for foodstuffs and meat by British and American whalers revictualling at Delagoa Bay, contraction of trade intensified competition among chiefs for what was left.

When Dingiswayo became chief of the Mthethwa one of his first actions was to organize a caravan to take ivory and cattle to trade at Delagoa Bay. He entered into an alliance with the Mabudu and made all trade exclusively his prerogative. He sought to cut Zwide and the Ndwandwe off from trade with the Mabudu by surrounding them with a line of chiefdoms subordinate to the Mthethwa. Westward expansion would not only secure this end, it would also enlarge the Mthethwa catchment area for ivory and cattle. For similar reasons the Ndwandwe strove to expand westwards along the southern banks of the Phongolo. This set the scene for conflict between Dingiswayo and Zwide. It is significant that after defeating the Mthethwa and putting Dingiswayo to death, Zwide immediately set about bringing the Mabudu under Ndwandwe control. Trade requirements might also have stimulated the introduction and development of the *amabutho* system. Hunting, for instance, needed to be organized on a more systematic basis as ivory became the object rather than the by-product of hunting expeditions, and indeed increased competition and conflict would of necessity require more effective armies. The *amabutho* system also gave the ruling chief greater control over the labour of his male subjects. While serving in their regiments, men were used increasingly in agricultural production when not fighting battles, and thus the changing circumstances of trade at Delagoa Bay could be met.

While lack of evidence precludes firm conclusions, attempts have also been made to explain northern Nguni transformations in terms of ecological factors – increasing population pressure on scarce and diminishing resources. While there is no hard demographic evidence, oral traditions and accounts of shipwrecked sailors suggest that there was an increase in population in the seventeenth and eighteenth centuries. Dendroclimatology, or the study of climatic patterns through the analysis of tree rings, suggests a period of diminishing rainfall towards the close of the eighteenth century and which culminated in the dreadful drought and famine of 1801-1802. The Madlathule famine, as it was known, affected the entire northern Nguni country. It was a time when, as one of James Stuart's oral informants remembered, people were forced to eat grass and kill and cook dogs to keep hunger at bay. The period of diminishing rainfall and drought had been preceded by one of plentiful rainfall when marginal land was cultivated and the growing of maize was increasingly preferred to the more drought-resistant sorghum. This had stimulated the growth of human and stock populations, which rendered ever more precarious the balance between population and resources, a balance which was shattered by the Madlathule famine. Population pressure restricted the seasonal movement of stock as more and more land came to be occupied by people. This in turn contributed to the deterioration of the environment as pastures became overgrazed and agricultural land exhausted. Moreover tensions built up within chiefdoms as fission, the traditional means for resolving conflicts, became less possible.

Transhumance, or the seasonal moving of livestock from region to region, was essential if

Dingiswayo's introduction of age regiments

Previously among the smaller chiefdoms of the eighteenth century, age groups had been formed primarily for circumcision purposes and were small in scale. It is not known whether it was Dingiswayo himself who abolished circumcision groups in favour of the highly organized *amabutho* or whether he was merely developing changes initiated by his predecessors. What is clear, though, is that the *amabutho* were well established during his reign, and young men under his authority were called up to serve for part of every year. Each age regiment or *ibutho* had its own distinctive dress and shields of a distinctive colour. A kind of 'national' military organization replaced the traditional local organization in which men from each homestead had joined neighbouring homesteads to form fighting groups under local chiefs as and when the ruler required. Fathers and brothers from the same homestead fought in different regiments and owed allegiance primarily to the ruler of the chiefdom rather than to their local chief. Regimental loyalties thus cut across both local and kinship ties.

'Zulu kraal near Umlazi, Natal', by G F Angas. The picture clearly depicts the beehive-shaped huts and reed screens characteristic of the Nguni. (Africana Museum)

Dingane, Shaka's half-brother, who conspired to assassinate Shaka in 1828 and succeeded him as king. He is pictured in his everyday cloak. The artist, Captain Allan Gardiner, a missionary, described Dingane as 'tall, corpulent and fleshy'. (Africana Museum)

Shaka: the stabbing spear and the standing army

Shaka ordered that all Zulu males under the age of forty were to be conscripted into three age regiments, each with its own distinctive shield and headdress. Each regiment was housed in barracks or *amakhanda*, located strategically in the area under his authority, and placed under the control of his officials and one or more of his aged relatives. His own headquarters were at Bulawayo, some 27 km from the present town of Eshowe, where he placed his youngest regiment, the Fasimba. Shaka armed his warriors with short stabbing spears and equipped them with large shields made of hide which afforded protection from the chin to the toes. Once the enemy had discharged the traditional throwing spear, Shaka's men closed in, in hand-to-hand combat with deadly effect. His men were required to go barefoot in order to achieve greater speed and mobility and they were subjected to stringent training and discipline, achieved through keeping them in a permanent state of mobilization. He developed further existing military tactics such as the horned battle formation, which involved a regiment, with one in reserve, fighting at the centre and two others forming horns on either side to envelop the enemy.

---

cattle, the crucial element in Nguni society and economy, were to survive throughout the year. The physical environment of the northern Nguni region was well suited to stock-keeping cultivators. Five major rivers – the Thukela, Mhlatuze, Mfolozi, Mkhuze and the Phongolo – together with their tributaries cut deep valleys in their paths to the sea, leaving high wedges of ground between. This broken topography produced great variations in rainfall and temperature over short distances, and in turn great variations in vegetation. 'Sourveld' on the high ground and coastal areas provided good grazing in the spring and early summer, 'sweetveld' in the river valleys in the winter, and transitional areas of mixed veld kept cattle going for between six and eight months of each year. If full advantage were to be taken of the grazing potential of the region, it was essential that there should be free movement of stock. The location of chiefdoms such as the Mthethwa, the Ndwandwe and the Ngwane appears to have been determined by a particular combination of grazing types and agricultural land, as Webb and Daniel have shown. There also appears to have been a connection between more desirable grazing areas and the direction of expansion of these chiefdoms. While there is no direct evidence, it would not seem illogical to argue that the large social formations emerging by the end of the eighteenth century and increasing rivalry between social groupings in the early years of the nineteenth century, can be explained at least in part by shortage of resources and the need to secure the desired combination of grazing types and agricultural land. This seems to be particularly so when it is remembered that the Madlathule famine occurred at about the same time as Dingiswayo's return from exile.

Not only would larger units be able to provide more manpower for the army and hence be a more effective coercive force in times of insecurity and danger, in seizing cattle and other foodstuffs, and in providing access to a greater range of grazing and arable land, the new military system provided additional advantages. By displacing circumcision as marking the point of transition to manhood, the *amabutho* could be used by the ruling chief as a means of delaying marriage. Men could only get married when the king discharged them from their regiments and gave them permission to do so. In this way control could be exerted over the rate of population growth in a region, for delayed marriages reduced the fertile span of women. While male fertility was less susceptible to the ageing process, later marriages delayed the setting up of new homesteads or productive units, and hence the ruler could exert some control over the intensity with which the environment was exploited.

Although some historians tend to stress one or other of the trade and ecological theories, it seems as though they are complementary in sug-

gesting why political transformations occurred among the northern Nguni.

After Zwide's victory over Dingiswayo, the shattered pieces of the Mthethwa confederacy were picked up by Shaka, who completed the second and final phase of reconstruction among the northern Nguni, during which the Zulu kingdom emerged.

The rise of Shaka and the Zulu kingdom

At the time of Dingiswayo's death, the Mthethwa confederacy had stretched from the Mfolozi in the north to the Thukela River in the south, and extended about 100 to 130 km inland from the coast. Among the small chiefdoms in the Mthethwa confederacy were the Zulu under Senzangakhona. In about 1787 Senzangakhona had fathered an illegitimate son, Shaka, by Nandi, a woman belonging to the Langeni chiefdom. Although Senzangakhona subsequently regularized the union, Nandi was a difficult woman and she and her son were ejected from the Zulu chiefdom. Shaka subsequently spent an unhappy childhood among the Langeni and Qwabe peoples. Although the movements of Dingiswayo in exile remain mysterious and the subject of much speculation, Adrian Koopman, after a careful analysis of oral traditions, has advanced the intriguing theory that he spent at least part of his exile among the Langeni people, where he would have got to know the young Shaka. However this came about, Shaka was conscripted into Dingiswayo's army in about 1809, and rapidly rose to the position of commanding a regiment and then the whole Mthethwa army. With Dingiswayo's support he seized control of the Zulu chiefdom after Senzangakhona's death in 1816, and proceeded to introduce the Mthethwa military system among the Zulu with innovations of his own.

The destructive potential of Shaka's army was awesome. Unlike Dingiswayo, Shaka sought to destroy absolutely the capacity of the enemy to resist by eliminating the ruling family, massacring women and children when necessary, and in the process unleashing hordes of refugees who in their turn would embark on devastating flights. Survivors, if there were any, were incorporated into the Zulu chiefdom and captured cattle distributed among the regiments for the use of their milk. Cattle remained the property of Shaka and cattle wealth became a royal monopoly, ensuring that the ruler had a huge source of patronage with which to reward loyal followers.

While Dingiswayo was alive, Shaka restricted his conquests to his immediate neighbours. After Dingiswayo's death, he regrouped the Mthethwa round the Zulu chiefdom and embarked on a programme of rapid expansion. Shortly after the Mthethwa defeat, the Ndwandwe launched an attack on the Zulu but were beaten off at the Battle of Gqokoli Hill. Subsequently the entire Ndwandwe army was sent to do battle with Shaka but was decisively beaten and Zwide withdrew inland to rebuild his following on the upper Nkomati River. With regard to the trade hypothesis, it is interesting to note that, like Zwide, and departing from his usual policy, Shaka left the Mabudu intact after bringing them under his authority. This might well have been done as a mark of respect to the Mabudu reputation as shrewd traders. It also seems clear that in the early years of his reign Shaka viewed the continued exporting of ivory to Delagoa Bay as important.

The defeat of the Ndwandwe marked a turning point in Zulu history. All serious rivals had been eliminated by 1819 and Shaka controlled an area stretching from the Phongola to the Thukela River, and from the sea to the Mzinyathi (Buffalo) River. Shaka then set about creating a single, unified chiefdom out of many hitherto autonomous chiefdoms, departing from Dingiswayo's idea of a confederacy. By the middle of the 1820s Shaka had created a kingdom that was the most formidable power in south-east Africa.

The repercussions of Shaka's reign of terror

Towards the end of his life Shaka's excesses began to breed mutiny. In 1827 his mother Nandi died and some 7 000 people were believed to have been killed for not displaying enough grief at her passing. He ordered that for a year after her death husbands and wives were not to have sexual intercourse with each other, no crops were to be planted and no cows milked. He sent his armies on one distant expedition after another without rest. In 1828 he sent his warriors south towards Xhosa and Thembu country. Upon their return they were immediately sent northwards to campaign against Soshangane in Mozambique without rest and without baggage carriers. While they were gone Shaka's half-brothers, Dingane and Mahlangane, with the help of Mbopha, who was a principal servant of the king, assassinated him on 24 September 1828. When the army returned after a failed campaign against Soshangane they found Dingane king. They were much relieved because the reward for failure was death.

The death of Shaka brought to an end a most remarkable period in the history of southern Africa. In a mere decade a powerful kingdom had come into being and the outward radiations of this process were felt down to the Cape frontier, across the Drakensberg and the highveld to the fringes of the Kalahari, and deep into Central and East Africa. Hordes of refugees were unleashed in the wake of Shaka's wars and they in turn cut swathes of devastation through south and south-central Africa. In chaos there was

Good relations between Shaka and the English traders at Port Natal

Henry Francis Fynn

In 1824 the first white traders and adventurers came to Shaka's kingdom and settled as a small community at Port Natal. Their main concern was trading in ivory and their presence served to deflect the flow of this commodity away from Delagoa Bay. Perhaps because their numbers were small and some of them, like Henry Francis Fynn, adapted readily to the Nguni way of life, Shaka developed a good working relationship with them. Their status was not unlike that of subordinate chiefs in his kingdom because he allowed them to acquire personal followings. Fynn accompanied a Zulu army sent to deal with the Ndwandwe who had revived under Zwide's son and successor, Sikhunyana. Trader firepower also proved decisive in helping Shaka to subdue a section of the Khumalo people under Beje. An abortive embassy sent to establish contact with the British in the Cape was accompanied by the trader James King.

Dingane's capital, Mgundgundlovu, built in 1829. Like Shaka's capital, Kwa Bulawayo, the town was laid out in a ring of reed fences and huts around an open parade ground. (Africana Museum)

Baquain refugee women and children.
(Africana Museum)

Machaka (unmarried Ndebele warriors) conducting a train of tributary Baquain with supplies for Mzilikazi. (Africana Museum)

also construction as new political formations came into being.

The defeat of Zwide by Shaka in 1819 started a general northward movement of several Nguni chiefdoms. A leader in Zwide's army, Soshangane of the Gaza house of the Ndwandwe, fled into southern Mozambique and settled for a time in the neighbourhood of Delagoa Bay. There he indulged in what appears to have been a highly profitable trade in slaves, so much so that he wanted actually to settle at the bay and have 'a window on the sea'. His following was reinforced by many Ndwandwe refugees after Sikhunyana's defeat by Shaka in 1826. After being attacked by Zulu regiments during Shaka's last campaign in 1828 he moved further north beyond their reach, and created the Gaza kingdom between Delagoa Bay and the lower Zambezi River. The Tsonga inhabitants of this region were absorbed into his kingdom.

At the time of Soshangane's flight Zwangendaba of the Jele chiefdom, which had formed part of the Ndwandwe confederacy, also moved into southern Mozambique. Like Soshangane his following was augmented by further Ndwandwe refugees in 1826. After clashing with Soshangane in 1831, he was driven westwards. In 1835 he moved across the Zambezi and founded the Ngoni kingdom which stretched from the western shores of Lake Nyasa (Lake Malawi) to Lake Tanganyika.

Even before Shaka's accession to power, expansionist movements among the northern Nguni had led to the founding of a new state in a defensible mountainous position north of the Phongolo River in the centre of modern-day Swaziland. The Ngwane-Dlamini had originally been located on the Phongolo near the Ndwandwe, and, because of their close proximity to the Sotho, had conquered and absorbed many of these people. The Ngwane-Dlamini chief, Ndungunya, had successfully held off attacks mounted by both Zwide and Dingiswayo. However, under his son and successor, Sobhuza, who ruled from 1815 to about 1836, the Ngwane-Dlamini clashed with the Ndwandwe over garden lands on the banks of the Phongolo. The Ngwane-Dlamini were defeated and retreated further north into their new home where a large composite state was gradually built up and called Swaziland, after Sobhuza's successor Mswati. Sobhuza followed a programme not unlike that of Dingiswayo and adopted a policy of conciliation towards his more powerful neighbours, first Zwide and then Shaka.

By 1824 the land south of the Zulu kingdom between the Thukela and the Mzimkhulu rivers was devastated. The first impact of the Shakan wars was felt in this area when the northern Thembu under their chief Ngoza were dislodged from their home along the Mzinyathi River and fled southwards across the Thukela

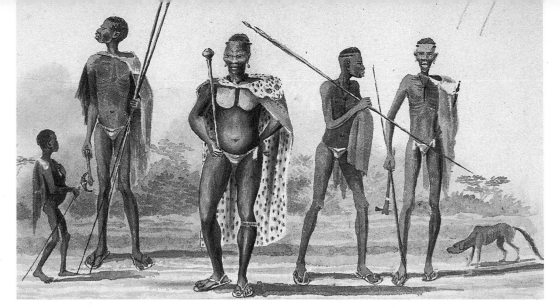

A group of Baquain (Kwena) refugees on the Marico River, pictured in 1835 by C D Bell. The Ndebele under Mzilikazi attacked neighbouring Tswana chiefdoms such as the Kwena, and drove them from the territory north of the Vaal. By 1830, the Ndebele were the undisputed rulers of the area. In the picture, the starving warriors are sharply contrasted with the well-fed chief. (Africana Museum)

and rampaged through Natal. They appeared to settle for a while in northern Mpondo territory under the chief Faku. In about 1822-1823 Faku attacked his troublesome immigrants. Ngoza was killed and Thembu remnants were either absorbed by the Mpondo or returned to their original homes in the Zulu kingdom. The northern Thembu eruption into Natal had in turn set a chain of disruption in motion which involved many chiefdoms. Behind the fugitive waves came annual expeditions of Shaka's warriors. Shaka's motive was to keep his men occupied and to denude Natal to serve as a buffer zone to protect his kingdom. Grain was destroyed and cattle were taken. Those people who were not put to flight were absorbed by the Zulu. By 1824 there was no longer any organized community life in Natal. A few thousand Nguni remained, seeking shelter in the mountains and the bush, living off the land and human flesh, while the protective folds and caves of the Drakensberg Mountains, as for centuries past, gave shelter to bands of San. A major expedition launched by Shaka in 1824 passed right through Natal and launched an attack on Faku and the Mpondo chiefdom. Although many Mpondo cattle were lost to the Zulu, Faku managed to retain most of the fighting strength of his chiefdom by offering his submission to Shaka.

In the vicinity of Mpondo territory overcrowding generated a continuous struggle for existence. New groupings were forged out of refugees, among them the Bhaca chiefdom under Madikane. After Madikane and his successor were killed in battle, the Bhaca were rallied by Ncaphayi who established an independent chiefdom in what is now the Mount Frere district, and from there he constantly raided his neighbours. He was killed in a skirmish with the Mpondo in 1845. Under the wise leadership of Faku, the Mpondo chiefdom managed to remain intact despite a second major cattle raid by Shaka in 1828. This explains perhaps why the southern Nguni chiefdoms were saved from se-

vere disruption by refugees. It is also true that Shaka had no wish to attack chiefdoms adjacent to the Cape frontier for fear of white retaliation. However, many refugees did penetrate into southern Nguni chiefdoms and settled among them. Because they had no cattle or means of sustenance, they became known as the *Mfengu*, from the verb *ukufenguza*, meaning to 'wander about seeking service'.

The Difaqane – the time of troubles on the highveld

The disturbances west of the Zulu kingdom had their origins in an attack on the Ngwane (not the Dlamini-Ngwane), first by Dingiswayo and then by Zwide. The Ngwane lived under their chief Matiwane east of the present Vryheid. Forced to flee, they moved westwards and fell upon the Hlubi, a Nguni chiefdom, living round the sources of the Mzinyathi. The Hlubi were defeated, their chief was killed and they split into several groups. One group fled southwards to become Mfengu among the southern Nguni. A lesser chief, Mpangazitha, led another group across the Drakensberg. The Ngwane under Matiwane were in turn dislodged from the old Hlubi lands when they were attacked by Shaka, and they followed the Hlubi flight path across the mountains. Equipped with the short stabbing spear, the Nguni invaders wrought havoc on the highveld south of the Vaal River. They smashed chiefdoms, took their grain and cattle, killed many people and incorporated survivors.

The first southern Sotho chiefdoms to take the brunt were the Mokotleng Tlokwa and the Sia, living near the passes through the Drakensberg. The Mokotleng Tlokwa were led by a regent, MaNthatisi, in the name of her minor son, Sekonyela, during their time of greatest troubles as a marauding band on the highveld in the aftermath of the initial Hlubi attack. So great a reputation did she acquire that all marauding

121

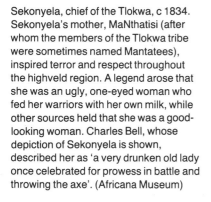

bands were erroneously referred to as 'Manta-tees' and grotesque rumours were generated by her career – that, for instance, a giantess with one eye in the middle of her forehead bestrode the highveld, suckling her warriors at her breast before battle, and sending swarms of bees ahead of them. In contrast to her horrible image among other peoples, to her own following she was affectionately known as Mosadinyana, 'the little woman'.

Between 1821 and 1824 Mpangazitha, Mati-wane and MaNthatisi, leading groups of men, women and children, devastated settlements in the Caledon valley, fought with each other and gained and lost adherents in what seemed like a whirlwind of activity. MaNthatisi went as far as the triangle between the Orange and Vaal rivers and then doubled back again competing with Mpangazitha and Matiwane, who had followed a similar course, for ever diminishing supplies of cattle and grain.

Perhaps because a marauding existence could no longer provide sustenance, MaNthatisi and her following settled on two flat-topped mountains on the north bank of the Caledon River in about 1824. Sekonyela's military skills brought land, cattle and security which served to attract adherents, so that by 1833 the Tlokwa following was estimated at about 24 000.

Moshweshwe and the Sotho

Sekonyela's major rival for predominance in the Caledon River area was Moshweshwe, who, although he never participated directly in a marauding horde, and had remained between the Caledon River and the Maluti Mountains, had used the opportunity of the Difaqane to build up a power base. Moshweshwe had a shrewd sense of the importance of strong defensive positions, choosing finally, in 1824, to occupy a great flat-topped mountain called Thaba Bosiu, which stood isolated amidst a fertile plain in western BaSotholand. People, livestock and provisions could be sustained on the summit in times of siege, while in times of peace the surrounding countryside was capable of supporting a large population. Moshweshwe's most urgent task was to put an end to the lawless activities of bandits and cannibals by gradually winning them back to a more civilized existence. He overcame the horror of his people at having to deal with cannibals by persuading them that these outcasts were living tombs sacred to the spirits of their victims. He provided what broken chiefs needed most, land and cattle, and allowed those who submitted to him to settle in separate villages and follow their own traditions. Moshweshwe had a large herd of cattle which he replenished by raids when necessary. He lent cattle to other chiefs under the *mafisa* system whereby they could use milk in exchange for tending them and giving the offspring to him.

The Hlubi and the Ngwane had also settled down in natural fortresses in 1824. In the following year they clashed in battle, Mpangazitha was killed and the Hlubi dispersed. Some were absorbed by the Ngwane, others sought refuge among the Ndebele and Moshweshwe's BaSotho, while a few returned to their old home below the Drakensberg. For a brief while Matiwane was master of the Caledon area but the lands of Transorangia, ravaged by war and drought, yielded poor sustenance for his large following. The growing herds of the rising chief, Moshweshwe, became increasingly attractive. Moshweshwe, a shrewd tactician and diplomat, paid tribute to Matiwane. He also indicated his allegiance to Shaka by sending him an annual tribute of crane feathers used in Zulu regalia. In 1827 he failed to send his tribute to Shaka. He explained that Ngwane depredations had made it impossible. Although the ensuing conflict between the Zulu and Matiwane ended indecisively, Matiwane decided to withdraw southwards into Thembu country. After a harrowing journey the Ngwane reached Thembu country where they were called *mfecane*, a word having its origins in the Xhosa verb *ukufuca* meaning 'to be weak; emaciated from hunger'. The Ngwane intrusion into southern Nguni country in turn sent refugees into the Cape Colony itself. In August 1828 a group of British soldiers, settlers, Thembu and Xhosa, which had been formed in the face of a threatened expedition from Shaka's Zulu, encountered the Ngwane at Mbholompo on the Mthatha River. Matiwane was driven off and most of his following was dispersed as Mfengu among the Thembu and the Xhosa. Matiwane and a few of his followers returned to the Zulu kingdom where they were put to death by Dingane who had in the meantime succeeded Shaka.

The demise of the two Nguni leaders who had wrought devastation among the southern Sotho, left the way clear for Moshweshwe and Sekonyela to carry on with their work of reconstruction. Thaba Bosiu continued to be a magnet for refugees and growing numbers of people settled in the fertile lands between the Caledon and Orange rivers. After an abortive Ndebele attack on Thaba Bosiu, to which Moshweshwe responded with the diplomatic gift of cattle to feed the retreating warriors, Moshweshwe's main problem, like that of Sekonyela, was dealing with the raids of predatory Korana and Griqua bands. Although small in numbers, their guns and horses made them a considerable nuisance. Moshweshwe responded by capturing their guns and horses in counter-raids. Soon the BaSotho, as Moshweshwe's growing nation came to be called, were adept marksmen and horsemen. Like Sekonyela, Moshweshwe welcomed missionaries in his midst in the early 1830s, and they served as intermediaries in the face of the advancing tides of white settlement. Inevitably both chiefs came into conflict with each other, a conflict that endured for twenty years, and ended only when Moshweshwe totally destroyed Tlokwa independence in 1853.

Even before the emergence of Mzilikazi and his Ndebele kingdom many Sotho refugees created havoc among the Tswana chiefdoms between the Vaal and Limpopo rivers and they in turn became swirling groups of refugees. The Griquas, themselves driven northwards by white expansion in the Cape Colony, added another dimension to the conflict with their horses and their firearms. For instance, when the Tlhaping, based at Kuruman, were threatened by a vast group of raiders estimated by the missionary Robert Moffat at between 40 000 and 50 000 strong, about 100 Griquas and 1 000 Tlhaping warriors succeeded in driving them away at Dithakong on 23 June 1823. Although the Tlhaping and their European missionaries referred to the Difaqane as the 'War of Mantatees', neither MaNthatisi nor the Tlokwa ever appeared to have crossed the Vaal River. Cer-

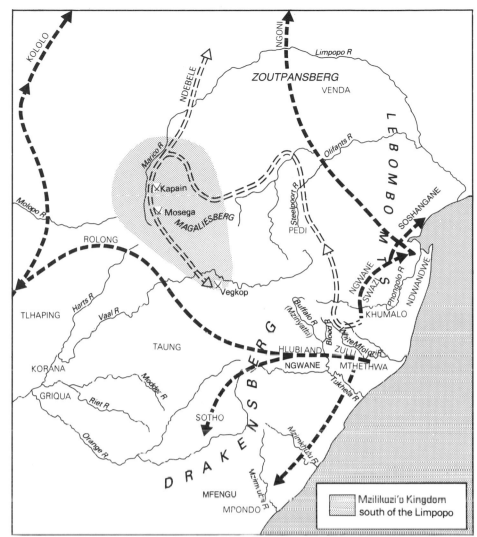

The Mfecane/Difaqane in the 1820s and 1830s

Moshweshwe in tribal dress, in 1833, from Eugene Casalis's book *The Basutos*, London, 1861. (Cape Archives, E3251)

123

A BaSotho warrior, carrying a shield of the type used by the Sotho and Tswana people. (Africana Museum)

Ndebele warriors attacking, by C D Bell. The Ndebele troops carried large, oval, Nguni-type shields and short stabbing spears. (Africana Museum)

tainly they had no part in the attack on Dithakong.

Mzilikazi and the Ndebele

By far the greatest impact in the Transvaal area during the Difaqane was made by Mzilikazi and his Ndebele. During the early years of their migrations they were known as 'Khumalo', 'Zulu', or 'people of Mzilikazi'. It was the Sotho who called them 'Matabele', a name they used for all Nguni strangers from the coast. The Nguni form of this word was 'Ndebele' and so a name was born which Mzilikazi would make famous in the history of southern Africa.

Little is known of Mzilikazi's early life and migrations. Early Ndebele history has to be culled from oral traditions which are difficult to interpret. Mzilikazi was born in about 1795. His father was Mashobane, chief of the northern Khumalo, a small chiefdom among the northern Nguni, located near the Black Mfolozi River almost between the expanding Ndwandwe and Mthethwa confederacies. The Khumalo were inevitably drawn into the conflict between Zwide and Dingiswayo. According to some traditions Zwide had Mashobane killed, thinking that he had aided Dingiswayo, and placed Mzilikazi over the Khumalo as a tributary chief to the Ndwandwe. After Zwide's defeat, Mzilikazi submitted voluntarily to Shaka – an action which kept his chiefdom intact – and rose in the ranks to regimental commander. Mzilikazi then rebelled against Shaka by failing to hand over cattle acquired in a particularly successful raid against the Sotho chief Somnisi. When Shaka sent messengers to remind Mzilikazi of his obligations to the king, he responded by cutting off their plumes, and made ready to flee from the Zulu kingdom.

According to other oral traditions Mzilikazi went over to Shaka when Zwide decided to eliminate him because of his highly effective raids against the Swazi which indicated that he might one day threaten Zwide's position. This was followed by his rebellion against Shaka. The historian Julian Cobbing argues that the sequence of events – Mzilikazi probably left Zwide in about 1819 and by 1821 was fleeing from Shaka – points to a more realistic explanation for Mzilikazi's departure to the highveld: his refusal to submit to Zwide's satisfaction and his subsequent resistance to incorporation under Shaka, as demonstrated by his refusal to give up the captured Sotho cattle. In the ensuing struggle between the Zulu and the Khumalo, many of the latter were killed and the survivors scattered. Mzilikazi regrouped the survivors, an estimated 200 to 300 people, and in about 1822 moved north-west onto the highveld of the northern Drakensberg.

During his sojourn on the highveld Mzilikazi had transformed his fledgling band of fugitives into a powerful kingdom created out of diverse elements. His original Khumalo following was

124

Thaba Bosiu, or 'Mountain of the night', a flat-topped impregnable stronghold where Moshweshwe settled in 1824. (Africana Museum)

augmented over the years by a continuing flow of Nguni refugees from the Zulu kingdom, conquered Sotho elements and Sotho who had joined voluntarily. By 1829 the total Ndebele population was estimated at between 60 000 and 80 000, among whom the Nguni were a minority.

In July 1832 Dingane sent his entire army, led by a renegade *induna* of the Nxa regiment, in search of Ndebele. Although outlying Ndebele homesteads were attacked and over a hundred cattle taken, three Zulu regiments were decimated. More troublesome because of their effective firepower were the constant raidings of the Griqua and the Korana from the south-west. At first Mzilikazi attempted to deal with the problem by declaring that no one should cross the Vaal River without his permission. Then in 1833 he moved in a north-westerly direction and settled between the Marico and Crocodile rivers after driving Tswana chiefdoms out of this area and desolating the surrounding lands. Mzilikazi also sought knowledge of firearms from traders and encouraged missionaries as a means of obtaining weapons, and as mediators with whites.

Many practices adopted by Mzilikazi in his developing kingdom stemmed from those which had arisen among Nguni chiefdoms before 1820, but he added embellishments of his own to suit the context in which he found himself. In Cobbing's words he evolved 'a revolutionary new economy of size and defensive scale to combat the anarchy of the Mfecane' – an anarchy of which he was both the victim and the agent. The raising of *amabutho* continued to be the source and confirmation of the king's power and gave him an advantage over chiefdoms on the highveld but not over the Coloured and white groups equipped with firearms and mounted on horses. Mzilikazi never found an answer to the persistent Griqua and Korana attacks, and it was the superior firepower of the gun-wielding and mounted Voortrekkers that eventually drove him out of the highveld and across the Limpopo.

The significance of the Mfecane/Difaqane

While lack of demographic evidence will forever preclude a precise computation of the full effects of the Mfecane, it seems clear that death, desolation and destruction were widespread consequences of this process. However, the Mfecane was not solely characterized by negative features. New concentrations of people, forcibly united by war or conquest or clustered together for security and defence, replaced the small scattered chiefdoms of the pre-Mfecane period. Initially these composite chiefdoms were not stable entities because the tendency towards fission remained strong, and it is possible that once the crisis had passed they might have dissolved. That this did not happen was probably directly attributable to white expansion into the interior.

In part the Mfecane can be said to have stimulated the Great Trek and facilitated white advance into the interior. The Mfecane had devastated and dislocated the populations of large parts of the southern highveld, the Transvaal and Natal between the Thukela and Mzimkhulu rivers. While these areas were never cleared of people, the tendency of survivors to hide in sheltered places gave the impression of empty lands. Reconnaissance expeditions in 1834 and 1835, before the Great Trek began, told of large tracts of uninhabited land ideally suited to the needs of white pastoralists. What the Trekkers did not realize was that these 'empty' areas were dominated by Dingane and Mzilikazi to safeguard their kingdoms from attacks launched from the south, and that there were many refugees who regarded these areas as their homelands and who had the intention of one day returning when circumstances permitted. The direction of the Trekker advance was determined by the notion of 'empty' lands and Colin Webb has argued that on a socio-economic level the Great Trek was 'an extension of the great demographic revolution that got under way with the Mfecane'.

The Ndebele migration to the highveld

The route taken by the Ndebele into the highveld is a subject of controversy. Some historians maintain that the Ndebele moved in a north-north-westerly direction into Pedi country towards the Olifants River, and crushed the Pedi. In about 1825 the Ndebele then moved in a south-westerly direction to the fertile lands and springs in the Magaliesberg hills. The historian Julian Cobbing, on the other hand, argues that the Ndebele did not make a northern detour via Pedi country and that the Ndebele attack on the Pedi only came in 1826-1827. The historian of the Pedi, Peter Delius, agrees to some extent with Cobbing, but attributes the destruction of the Pedi polity under Thulare to the Ndwandwe under Zwide. Thereafter, in about 1828, Sekwati, a son of Thulare, succeeded in rebuilding the Pedi chiefdom.

While arguments concerning Mzilikazi's initial migratory route cannot be conclusively proved one way or the other, it is clear that by the middle of the 1820s Mzilikazi was established in an area stretching from present-day Pretoria to Rustenburg. From here the Ndebele raided in all directions, subjugating or breaking up chiefdoms, and augmenting Ndebele numbers with new recruits and acquiring vast herds of cattle. Mzilikazi's actions did not stem from destruction for the sake of destruction. Once he had become settled, unlike Moshweshwe and Sekonyela, Mzilikazi did not have a defensive stronghold. A 'scorched earth' policy made tactical strategic sense.

Execution at Mzilikazi's homestead, by C D Bell, 1835. The man standing on the right watching the execution is Mzilikazi, and the executioners are Ncumbati and Calepi. The man was sentenced to be drowned for having connection with a young unmarried girl. Bell commented: 'No other water being procurable within practicable distance, the pool continued to be used by ourselves and Mzilikazi's people as before.' (Africana Museum)

Ndebele-Voortrekker conflict

The arrival of the Voortrekkers in 1836 provided unexpected allies for the people of the Orange and Caledon river valleys against Mzilikazi. Not long before this, in March 1836, a treaty had been concluded between Mzilikazi and the Cape Government from which the Voortrekkers were in flight. The destruction of the Erasmus, Liebenberg and Du Toit parties by the Ndebele initiated a drawn out war between the Ndebele and the Voortrekkers. At the Battle of Vegkop in October 1836 the Voortrekkers in laager succeeded in withstanding the Ndebele attack but lost their livestock. In January 1837 a combined Voortrekker, Griqua and Rolong force defeated the Ndebele at Mosega. A few months later the Zulu army struck again and in November 1837 the Ndebele, while retreating further northwards, were attacked by a Voortrekker-Griqua-Rolong commando, led by Andries Pretorius and Piet Uys. The Voortrekkers had become the dominant power as far as the Zoutpansberg. Rather than submit to their authority, the Ndebele migrated across the Limpopo River and built a new capital in the Matopo hills which they called Bulawayo.

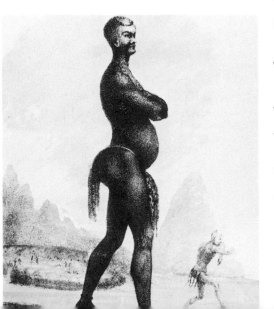

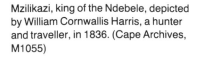
Mzilikazi, king of the Ndebele, depicted by William Cornwallis Harris, a hunter and traveller, in 1836. (Cape Archives, M1055)

The dislocated populations of the 'empty' lands could offer little serious resistance to the advance of the white pastoralists. Indeed the Griqua and Korana bands, who may be regarded as the advance guard of white expansion beyond the Cape frontier, had already demonstrated how effective guns and horses could be as destabilizing elements in the interior. The Trekkers, like the Griquas before them, also tended to be welcomed as allies or potential allies by weaker groups, such as the Rolong, in confrontation with stronger groups like the Ndebele. However, in those areas where concentrations of population had occurred, and 'states' were emerging, resistance strong and effective enough to deflect white advance could be offered. White advance hemmed these states in and threatened their borders, thus continuing the process of consolidation begun during the Mfecane. They preserved themselves as they might not have done if the challenge had been less immediate. Moreover, if lands depopulated during the Mfecane had remained open, this might have encouraged the fissiparous tendencies natural to these societies and promoted disintegration rather than integration.

The Mfecane thus both facilitated the advance of white expansion but also made more difficult the final subjugation of the black populations. The Zulu kingdom created by Shaka survived for some fifty years after his death. His successor Dingane tried to fight the Voortrekkers with disastrous results. He was destroyed by his successor Mpande, who achieved power with Voortrekker help. Thereafter Mpande skilfully ruled his kingdom for 32 years and kept it intact by playing off the British on his southern borders against the Boers on his western borders. Under the rule of his son, Cetshwayo, the Zulu kingdom was defeated by the British in 1879 and torn apart by civil war generated by British 'settlements' imposed in the aftermath of war. The Zulu kingdom was partitioned upon British annexation in 1887 and finally fragmented after take-over by Natal in 1897. In the eastern Transvaal, the Pedi, after severe disruption during the Mfecane, reconsolidated under Sekwati and successfully resisted white pressure until they were overthrown between 1876 and 1879. Further to the east, the Swazi, although enduring many vicissitudes, survived to become an independent state in the 1960s. Further south in the Caledon River area, Moshweshwe's BaSotho kingdom became increasingly truncated as frontier wars with the Orange Free State ate away at its boundaries. British protection in 1868 saved the BaSotho from total incorporation by the Orange Free State and eventually the independent state of Lesotho came into being in 1966. The Mpondo preserved their independence until incorporation by the Cape in 1894. Most of the Tswana chiefdoms on the edge of the Kalahari succumbed to white pressure, except the Ngwato under Kgama who survived to become the independent state of Botswana. Although Mzilikazi and his Ndebele were ejected from the highveld, the kingdom he created north of the Limpopo survived under his successor Lobengula until it was destroyed by the British South Africa Company forces in 1893. The independence of the Xhosa and Thembu peoples adjacent to the Eastern Cape frontier was destroyed with the aid of a 'fifth column' generated by the Mfecane – the Mfengu.

Suggested Reading List

P Delius (1983) *The Land Belongs to Us: The Pedi Polity, the Boers and the British in the Nineteenth Century Transvaal*, Johannesburg

W F Lye and C Murray (1980) *Transformations on the Highveld: The Tswana and Southern Sotho*, Cape Town

J D Omer-Cooper (1966) *The Zulu Aftermath – A Nineteenth Century Revolution in Bantu Africa*, London

J B Peires (1981) *The House of Phalo – A History of the Xhosa People in the Days of Their Independence*, Johannesburg

L Thompson (ed) (1969) *African Societies in Southern Africa*, London

C de B Webb and J B Wright (eds) (1976, 1978 and 1980) *The James Stuart Archives*, Vols 1, 2 and 3, Pietermaritzburg and Durban

Chapter 10

The Great Trek

J T du Bruyn

Between 1834 and 1840 approximately 15 000 Afrikaner frontier dwellers left the eastern frontier area of the Cape Colony and established their own states in the interior. They referred to themselves as 'emigrants' and to their trek as an 'emigration'; the concepts of Voortrekkers and Great Trek only came into vogue after the 1870s.

It is not likely that the Voortrekkers themselves appreciated the significance of their exodus, but to their descendants the Trek was and is an inexhaustible source of inspiration for speeches, historiography, literary works, celebrations and the erection of monuments. Most Afrikaners look upon the Great Trek as an heroic era which produced many of their folk heroes; they see it as an epoch of strife, suffering and sacrifice for the sake of freedom. To Afrikanerdom the Great Trek gave shape to its republican views, ensured the preservation of Afrikaner identity and laid the foundations of race policy.

The Great Trek in perspective

The Great Trek was a resistance movement against British colonialism and oppression, but, ironically enough, it was also an act of colonization. The establishment of independent Voortrekker states in the interior led to the suppression of black communities. To the descendants of the Voortrekkers the Great Trek is a symbol of freedom, but many blacks look upon this event as a period of conquest and loss of freedom. For this reason the Trek has also been described as a short-sighted, disastrous act which aggravated race prejudice and was conducive to disunity and conflict.

South Africans therefore hold divergent views on the Great Trek, but there need be no difference of opinion concerning its outward appearance. The historian C F J Muller described it as an organized physical exodus of thousands of Afrikaans-speaking frontier farmers from the

Johannes T du Bruyn is a senior lecturer in History at Unisa. His main fields of research are the history of the southern Tswana, the Griqua, the Cape northern frontier, the racial attitudes of the Voortrekkers and Transvaal Boers, and European and South African historiography.

A scene by W H Coetzer based on an incident described by Louis Tregardt in his diary. On Tuesday 19 December 1837 Tregardt noted that 'he and Pieta (his son) had brought their wagons down (the mountain) with fair success'. (Africana Museum)

127

Cattle Boer's outspan, Karoo, c 1836, by C D Bell. The trekboer's wife is seated next to the tented wagon, with her feet resting on a brick, while the trekboer surveys his flocks and herds. One servant attends to the horses, while three others sit around a fire cooking food. (Africana Museum)

The fortified farmhouse of Field-Cornet Buckner (Büchner) during the Sixth Frontier War (1834-1835). The farm was situated near the Bushmans River in the Eastern Cape, close to Bathurst. The artist, C C Michell, has depicted the laager inaccurately, as the wagons would have been placed with each shaft fitting under the chassis of the next wagon, instead of side by side. (Africana Museum)

British Cape Colony into the adjoining territories to the north and north-east, who had no intention of ever returning. The idea of migrating did not arise spontaneously; it was carefully fostered and planned.

The Great Trek is frequently described as the key event in South African history and it undoubtedly turned South African history in a new direction. Within less than a generation vast new areas were brought within the orbit of Western Europe. Yet the Great Trek was not the only migration in South African history which had far-reaching consequences. At an early stage migrations and treks had led to the establishment of new frontiers, new ways of life and new groups. In the seventeenth century Khoikhoi groups had in this way already established themselves in the interior in protest against white territorial expansion, and towards the end of the eighteenth century dissatisfied Bastards (who would subsequently come to be known as the Griquas) also emigrated into the interior. There, long before the Voortrekker movement, they established the first independent states at Griquatown and Philippolis. Some of the most important migrations in South African history, however, are without doubt the unprecedented series of population shifts caused by the rise of the Zulu kingdom – the *Mfecane* and the *Difaqane*. In fact, the black migrations far exceeded the Great Trek in numbers and extent. Moreover there was a close interaction between the Great Trek and the *Difaqane*: firstly the black population shifts made the Trek possible by creating living space for the Voortrekkers in the interior and, secondly, uprooted *Difaqane* fugitives streamed into the Cape's eastern frontier area and aggravated the uncertainty and restlessness in this region.

As time wore on the Great Trek came to be seen as an Afrikaner national movement. Most Afrikaners subsequently identified with the Voortrekkers' ideals, but of the Cape Afrikaners only a small section, approximately one tenth, participated actively in the Trek. The "Great" in Great Trek therefore does not denote the scope of this migration and the number of people who participated in it, but rather its significance and its sweeping consequences.

The causes of the Great Trek

It was in the heartland of the eastern frontier of the Cape – from the northern parts of the Albany district as far as Graaff-Reinet and the large Somerset district – that the idea of the Trek took root. To understand why Afrikaner frontier farmers decided to leave the Cape Colony for good, it is worth examining the conditions in this area on the eve of the Great Trek.

Two important themes in the history of the eastern frontier area of the Cape during the first half of the nineteenth century are, on the one hand, the mounting conflicts between the Xhosa and white stock farmers, and on the other the growing political estrangement between frontier colonists and the British Government. When the eastern frontier was still 'open', and sparsely populated, the Cape Government was not able to give the frontier farmers military assistance against the Xhosa; the burghers maintained law and order themselves according to their own perceptions of such matters. As a stronger British Government made its political and military authority felt in the region, the role of the burgher commandos was drastically curtailed. Nevertheless British power in the territory was neither capable of halting, nor strong enough to prevent Xhosa invasions, as the frontier wars of 1819 and 1834-1835 indicated. While the British Government persisted in curtailing the traditional freedom of action and self-defence of the white frontier farmers, it was unable to guarantee their security. The government therefore tried to preserve law and order in the eastern frontier area, but did not have the finances at its disposal to back up its efforts.

This led to general dissatisfaction and a feeling of insecurity among the Afrikaner frontier farmers. The frontier conflicts, and particularly the Sixth Frontier War of 1834-1835, caused the frontier farmers to suffer heavy losses. In February 1838 a Uitenhage farmer made it clear that the damage suffered as a result of wars and cattle theft and lack of confidence in the British Government was a decisive cause of the Great Trek: 'How much have the frontiersmen not had to endure from time to time from the Kaffirs [Xhosa], especially during the last unexpected raid?' After every setback he had managed to get back on his feet again, but then 'the Kaffirs came and robbed me of everything, as was the case in 1819 and again in 1834. . . So what have I got left, after many years of hard work and toil? Literally *nothing*!'

In addition to the heavy losses which the frontier farmers suffered during the Sixth Frontier War, they were required to use their own horses and equipment while engaged in punitive expeditions. They also expected compensation from the government for their losses, but none was forthcoming. On the contrary, in the face of ruin frontier farmers were still expected to pay their normal taxes. As a result of these experiences the conviction began to grow among the Afrikaner frontier farmers that, materially, they were no longer able to subsist in the eastern frontier area.

The turbulence in the eastern frontier territory was also related to a lack of living space and land. Both the Afrikaners and the Xhosa were stock farmers who were dependent for their survival on sufficient grazing. By the 1830s it was becoming clear that the eastern frontier region was overpopulated. In this connection the magistrate of the Albany district (Grahamstown) made a significant statement in March 1836 on the causes of the Trek: 'I have long anticipated a movement of this kind. The early marriages contracted by the people, the consequent rapid increase in population, their disinclination to procure any other mode of subsistence than that which is obtained by the possession of land, the degradation which is attached to servitude (and which prevails in all countries where slavery has been established), these combined causes rendered a movement such as is now contemplated, inevitable, when land could no longer be found within the colony to satisfy the demands of increased population.'

To aggravate matters, land prices rose sharply during the 1820s and 1830s and drought was a serious problem. These conditions threatened the pastoral lifestyle of the frontier farmers, a means of livelihood which had until that stage precluded them from having to offer their services to others as wage workers. There was no land for the younger generation. An alternative was to make a transition to intensive farming methods, but this would be a long, drawn out process, requiring advanced technology and favourable climatic conditions. They did not want to work for other people, because that would mean accepting a lower status. There was, however, a logical alternative. They could migrate and go in search of land and grazing in the interior.

The farming activities of the frontier farmers were further restricted by a lack of labour. They felt that government measures, particularly Ordinance 50 of 1828, prevented them from exercising adequate control over their servants and farm labourers. Many labourers had in fact left the farms and organized themselves into wandering bands. The labour shortage was aggravated with the emancipation of slaves which occured at this time. Although there were far fewer slave-owners in the eastern than in the western districts, important leaders such as Gert

The interior of a trekboer tent in Griqualand, by C D Bell. (Africana Museum)

129

The 'leading' Voortrekkers (1783-1838)

Louis Tregardt and his son Carolus were already in Xhosaland by 1829. In 1833 they leased land from the Xhosa leader, Hintsa. However, when Hintsa clashed with the British authorities in 1835, the Tregardts, with a few other families, trekked northwards across the Orange River. Tregardt subsequently stated that continuous Xhosa attacks, the emancipation of slaves and the introduction of compulsory military service had led to his decision to leave the Cape Colony. Near the Vaal River a party led by 'Lang Hans' van Rensburg joined the Tregardts. At that stage the trek consisted of 9 wagons, approximately 50 whites, 3 000 sheep, 800 head of cattle and a considerable number of horses. Although the two parties remained in contact with one another, relations were not always cordial.

From September 1836 until the end of May 1837 the Tregardt party found itself in the vicinity of the Zoutpansberg, near what was later to become the town of Schoemansdal. They trekked along the Olifants River as far as Strydpoort. While Tregardt remained there, Van Rensburg went on ahead in search of contact with the Portuguese harbours, taking eight families with him. Towards the end of July 1836 the entire Van Rensburg party was killed, probably by the Tsonga.

Tregardt began his epic trek from the Zoutpansberg to Delagoa Bay on 23 August 1837. After a hard journey '46 Christians and 7 servants' reached Lourenço Marques on 13 April 1838. There 24 members of the party, including Tregardt and his wife, died of malaria. In July 1839 the survivors left for Port Natal in the *Mazeppa*.

Louis Tregardt was the only Voortrekker leader who kept a diary during his wanderings. From a linguistic and cultural-historical point of view it is of great importance, and it also contains information on black communities, climatic conditions, and the flora and fauna in the Transvaal in those early days. It is striking to note that Tregardt did not hesitate to use words and expressions which would be termed crude and indecent by modern-day Afrikaans speakers. In his edition of the diary, Gustav Preller decorously translated the unacceptable words and passages into Latin.

Maritz suffered heavy losses as a result of the emancipation of slaves. A well-known Voortrekker, J H Hatting, subsequently had the following to say about the labour situation: 'The Boers were completely deprived of labourers, and, together with their children, had to do all the work and tend to the livestock, so that it was no longer possible to farm in the Cape Colony.' To this problem, too, migration could offer a solution – in the interior a sufficient quantity of cheap labour was available.

The vagrancy of emancipated labourers contributed greatly to a feeling of insecurity among the frontier farmers. This was the first grievance mentioned by the famous Voortrekker leader Piet Retief in his manifesto: 'We despair of saving this country from the potential threat posed by the seditious and dishonest behaviour of vagrants, who have been allowed to spread over all parts of the country; nor do we see any prospects of peace or contentment for our children in a country in which internal dissension is so rife.' To make matters worse, thousands of *Difaqane* fugitives entered the eastern and north-eastern districts of the Cape Colony on the eve of the Great Trek. Many of them eventually found employment with whites, but thousands of others roamed around in the eastern frontier area. This intensified the tension and feeling of insecurity in this region.

Spiritually and psychologically, too, the Afrikaner frontier farmers were offended by the actions of the British Government. They were particularly dissatisfied with the implications of Ordinance 50 and with the lack of self-government accorded to them. The frontier farmers drew a distinction between whites and blacks on the basis of religious convictions, social class differences and physical differences. They were

of the opinion that British policy had terminated the old racial order and undermined white domination. The famous statement by Anna Steenkamp, Piet Retief's niece, testifies to this feeling: '. . . the disgraceful and unjust act of emancipating our slaves, yet it was not so much the emancipation which drove us away as their being placed on an equal footing with Christians, contrary to the laws of God and the natural differentiation of origins and faith. That it was unendurable for every decent Christian to bow down under such a burden was the reason we preferred to leave, so as to be better able to preserve the purity of our faith and doctrine.' Migration was therefore seen as solving this problem as well. In the interior the Trekkers would be free to strive as they saw fit for a 'proper' relationship between whites and blacks.

Another grievance of the Afrikaner farmers was that the British Government had, in the early 1830s, denied them any real say in the administration of the country. They were even deprived of their share in the local government of the frontier districts, to which they had grown accustomed since the time of the Dutch East India Company. In February 1842 the Natal *Volksraad* attributed most of their grievances to the fact that they had had no say in the Cape Government: 'All these iniquities we ascribe to a single cause, namely the lack of a representative government, which was denied us by the executive government of the same people who consider that privilege to be their most sacred civil right and for which every true Briton is prepared to sacrifice his life.'

Naturally not all the frontier farmers migrated for the same reasons. The first Voortrekker, Louis Tregardt, gave another reason, besides the emancipation of the slaves and the unsafe frontier conditions for the Trek. This was that 'the government compelled the Afrikaners to be soldiers'. In addition the individualism and adventurous spirit of some frontier farmers should also be borne in mind. Not all of them were inspired by lofty ideals of freedom. L C de Klerk, who trekked to Natal as a child with his parents, expanded on this reason for the Trek as follows: 'Some people gradually became accustomed to the migratory way of life, to the laagers, so that for years afterwards they were still wandering around from one place to another. And this way of life had its own peculiar attractions. . . it was carefree and for that reason alone attracted many.'

All these grievances indicated that the Afrikaner frontier farmers expected preferential treatment and special protection from the British Government at a stage when the government was in fact striving to improve the lot of all inhabitants of the Cape. The white farmers felt that their existence in the eastern frontier territory had become intolerable and that something drastic had to be done. Armed resistance was

◁◁
After a varied career as farmer, supplier of provisions, general dealer, building contractor, land speculator and Field-Commandant of the Albany burghers, Piet Retief published his famous 'Manifesto' in the *Graham's Town Journal* in February 1837, setting out the reasons why certain farmers in the frontier districts wished to leave the Cape Colony. In April 1837 Retief's party joined the laagers of Potgieter and Maritz beyond the Orange River. (NCHOM)

◁
Angenitha Maritz, widow of Gert Maritz. (NCHOM)

Voortrekker preparations for the Battle of Vegkop

In August 1836, while Andries Potgieter was away on a scouting expedition in the interior, the Ndebele unexpectedly attacked the leading Trekkers who had crossed the Vaal River. The Liebenbergs were almost wiped out, but the other Trek groups succeeded in temporarily beating off the Ndebele attack. When Potgieter and his company returned from the interior towards the end of August he ordered a laager of approximately fifty wagons to be formed at what was later to become known as Vegkop, in the present Heilbron district. Potgieter made his preparations thoroughly. One of his sons subsequently related: 'He walked around and around the laager himself, to ensure that every man was in position, and saw to it that four wagons were drawn together in the middle for the women and small children, and covered over with planks and skins, as protection against falling assegais. To the women there Potgieter said: "Even though you see your menfolk fall, I do not want to hear you utter a single sound!"'

When a scouting patrol reported that a large Ndebele force was approaching, Sarel Cilliers and a group of armed horsemen rode out to confront it. The patrol stopped about 50 m away from the oncoming Ndebele. When Cilliers allegedly wanted to know from the Ndebele, via a Khoikhoi interpreter, what harm the whites had done to them, the warriors merely uttered their war cry of *Mzilikazi!* and charged. The Trekkers fell back upon the laager, firing volley upon volley as they went.

Sarel Cilliers, a respected Voortrekker who fought at Vegkop, and led the people in the swearing of the Covenant before the Battle of Blood River. (Cape Archives, E328)

---

out of the question as previous attempts in this direction had failed. They then decided upon a brilliant and natural solution to their problems – a peaceful mass emigration to the territories to the north and north-east of the Cape Colony. By the time the Cape Government realized what was happening, the Trekkers were already a long way into the interior.

On trek

On the eve of the Great Trek the frontier farmers were already acquainted with conditions in the interior and with the main trek routes. Apart from the information they received from traders, travellers, hunters, missionaries and trekboers, three *kommissie* treks were sent out during the course of 1834 to reconnoitre the interior. Of particular importance was the great *kommissie* trek which the Uitenhage Boer leader, Pieter Lafras Uys, led to Port Natal. Early in 1835 he was able to report that the largely depopulated Natal with its good harbour would be an excellent new fatherland. But it was only in 1836, after the end of the Sixth Frontier War, that preparations for the exodus could be made in all earnest. Families, friends and neighbours organized themselves into various trek parties under recognized, experienced local leaders. They did not leave the Cape Colony simultaneously. The foremost Voortrekkers, Louis Tregardt and Hans van Rensburg, the pioneers of the Transvaal lowveld and Portuguese East Africa, left in 1835. Andries Hendrik Potgieter, the conservative founder of the Transvaal, emigrated towards the end of 1835 or at the beginning of 1836. And Gert Maritz, who would subsequently evolve into a competent administrator of the Trek, left the colony in September 1836.

Initially the British Government hesitated to take any action in regard to the Great Trek. The Governor, Sir Benjamin D'Urban, was of the opinion that the exodus entailed great disadvantages for the colony and he tried to improve frontier conditions and eliminate grievances. Lieutenant-Governor Andries Strockenström simply saw the Trek as a continuation of the trekboer movement and openly declared that no laws could prevent the Voortrekkers from leaving the colony. All that remained was to make the ineffective Cape of Good Hope Punishment Act applicable to the Trekkers as well. This gave British magistrates jurisdiction over British subjects in unoccupied territories in the interior.

Uitdraai on the Riet River, c 1835, by C D Bell. (Africana Museum)

Erasmus Smit (1778-1863), who spent his childhood in an Amsterdam orphanage, and then trained as a missionary. He came to South Africa in 1804, and worked among the Khoikhoi and black people. He married Gert Maritz's sister, who was some twenty years younger than he, and in 1836 they joined Maritz's party on trek. Their son Salomon died tragically in 1837, two months after his 21st birthday. Smit was not accepted as a clergyman by some of the Voortrekkers, and his appointment became a subject of controversy. He recorded his experiences in a diary which has become a valuable source of information for historians. He and his wife ended their days in poverty in Pietermaritzburg. (NCHOM)

The Trekkers' rearguard was therefore safe; for the time being the British authorities would leave them in peace. But across the Orange River new problems awaited them. By 1836 the vanguard of the Potgieter trek had crossed the Vaal River. Mzilikazi, the powerful Ndebele or Matabele leader, regarded with growing suspicion the arrival of so many whites from the same direction as that from which the mounted Griquas and Koranas had threatened him before. He probably realized that such a large group of whites constituted a threat to the survival of the Ndebele.

The Ndebele attacked the Trekkers, but at Vegkop, on 16 October 1836, Potgieter drew up a reinforced laager and successfully beat off an attack. In January 1837 the Trekkers captured Mzilikazi's stronghold, Mosega, and drove the Ndebele far to the north.

In the meantime the Maritz trek had considerably strengthened the Voortrekker community in Transorangia. Gert Maritz had been well known in Graaff-Reinet as a fine wagon maker, an astute businessman and competent administrator. By this time it was clear that the old commando organization was no longer able to meet the needs of the Trekkers and shortly after Maritz's arrival a new, provisional Voortrekker administration was established at Thaba Nchu. A burgher council of seven members was brought into existence with Maritz as 'President' and 'Judge' and Potgieter as 'Laager Commandant', the military chief. These administrative institutions were very primitive and there was no question of separation of governmental powers.

In March 1837 a large group of Trekkers under the direction of Piet Retief was on the move. Even in the Cape Retief had been more than merely the Commandant of the Winterberg Region; in due course he had emerged as the gen-eral spokesman of the farming community in the frontier districts. The Transorangia Trekkers appreciated his qualities of leadership and in April 1837 a popular assembly was convened at which Retief was elected chief leader, with the well-known title of 'Governor'. He was also the supreme military commander. Maritz remained head of the judiciary and was also president of the 'Council of Policy', or chairman of the highest administrative body which would subsequently, in the Republic of Natalia, come to be known as a *volksraad*. Potgieter was not re-elected; his status was merely that of Commandant of his own trekking party.

Retief's election as Governor did not prevent disunity and dissension among the Voortrekkers. As they hailed from different districts, and were furthermore individualistic, conflicts were inevitable. One matter which caused considerable disagreement was the appointment of a Voortrekker minister. The Cape synod had deplored the Trek and no minister of the Dutch Church was prepared to accompany the Trekkers. To make good this deficiency, Retief and other Voortrekkers felt that they should make use of the services of a former missionary of the London Missionary Society, Erasmus Smit. Smit was sickly, sometimes petty, and addicted to liquor; consequently he was unacceptable to many Trekkers. Potgieter and his followers wanted to appoint James Archbell, the Wesleyan missionary at Moroka, as minister.

The destination of the Great Trek also caused dissension. Potgieter was firmly convinced that they should seek the salvation of an independent Voortrekker state in the far north, far away from British influence. There, to the north of latitude 25° south, and therefore out of reach of the Punishment Act, he would seek access to the outside world through the Portuguese east coast harbours. Piet Retief, Gert Maritz and

Piet Uys, who had trekked from Uitenhage in April 1837, in turn preferred the Natal coastal flats, particularly the area between the Thukela and Mzimvubu rivers. For their future state Port Natal, the only safe harbour on a dangerous coast, would offer access to the outside world. It was decided to trek in both directions: the Ndebele had to be finally defeated, and Port Natal reached. In November 1837, after a series of long and hard-fought battles, the Trekkers succeeded in defeating Mzilikazi and the Ndebele were compelled to settle beyond the Limpopo River. In the meantime Retief was making preparations for a settlement in Natal. In October 1837 he trekked to Natal to negotiate with the English at Port Natal and with the Zulu king, Dingane.

On Natal soil

In Port Natal Alexander Biggar and most of the English welcomed Retief as an ally and future neighbour. The negotiations with Dingane too, seemed to go off well. The Zulu king allegedly declared himself prepared to cede the territory between the Thukela, Mzimvubu and the Drakensberg to the Trekkers, provided Retief returned to Dingane the cattle which Sekonyela had stolen from the Zulu, as proof that the Trekkers had not been responsible for the theft. Retief complied with this condition. By 11 January 1838 he had returned with the stolen cattle to the laagers on the Natal side of the mountain. The Boer Governor's actions did not, however, meet with the approval of all his followers. Maritz protested against Retief's actions as undemocratic and, in a letter to Governor D'Urban, Piet Uys criticized Retief's rejection of British authority. In addition Retief was strongly condemned because he intended taking

Dingane, in one of his dancing dresses of beads, skin and ornaments. The picture appeared in Captain A F Gardiner's book *Narrative of a Journey to the Zoolu country. . .*(1836) and was shown to Dingane by Reverend Francis Owen. He recorded that Dingane commented that in his dancing dresses 'Capt Gardiner had just hit him. . .' (Africana Museum)

more men with him on the dangerous journey to Dingane than was deemed necessary. Eventually the Governor left for Mgundgundlovu (Dingane's capital) with seventy whites and thirty coloured attendants. The treaty was duly signed by Dingane on 6 February 1838. As the unarmed Trekkers were taking their leave, however, the Zulu king ordered them killed.

In the early morning of 17 February, Zulu warriors attacked the unsuspecting laagers along the Bloukrans and Bushmans rivers. The loss of human life was appalling. Approximately 500 people, half of whom were servants, were murdered. The Zulu also seized 25 000 head of cattle and thousands of sheep and horses. A counterattack was organized, and on 6 April a Boer commando, in two sections, under Potgieter and Uys, crossed the Thukela in the di-

Charles Bell's depiction of a surprise attack by Zulu warriors on a small party of Voortrekkers encamped near the Bloukrans (Blaauwkrantz) River. Early morning attacks were made on a number of encampments in February 1838, and approximately 500 people, half of whom were servants, were killed. (Africana Museum)

Andries Pretorius was elected Chief Commandant of the Trekkers in Natal on 26 November 1838 at Sooilaer on the banks of the Little Thukela River.

rection of Mgundgundlovu. On the other side of the Buffalo River, at Italeni, they were led into an ambush, however, and both Uys and his son Dirk were killed. An expedition mounted by the Port Natal British, which had come to the aid of the Trekkers, also failed. In this fierce battle approximately one thousand Zulu followers and thirteen whites were killed. The situation was critical.

During the cold winter of 1838 disease struck at the Voortrekkers, who were crowded together into strengthened laagers. This tense period saw old dissensions flare up again with new intensity. After the defeat at Italeni, Potgieter, in the laagers of Retief and Maritz, was openly accused of cowardice. He thereupon withdrew across the Drakensberg, taking with him his invaluable group of horsemen, to endeavour to achieve his old ideal of liberty on the highveld. On 23 September 1838 the Trekkers also lost another leader when Gert Maritz died. Now, of all the principal Natal leaders, only Karel Landman, the Chief Commandant, was left. In their plight the Natal Trekkers turned to Andries Pretorius, a good organizer and gifted soldier.

When Pretorius arrived in Natal on 22 November 1838, he was no stranger to the Trekkers. As a scout he had already been in Transorangia, the Transvaal and Natal. At an early stage he had identified himself with the fortunes of the Trekkers. The Trekkers had so much confidence in him that by 25 November they had already appointed him Commandant-General. Shortly afterwards he began to make preparations for an attack on the Zulu force. By that time it was clear that to attack the Zulu on their own ground with a horse commando was far too dangerous. Consequently Pretorius decided upon a reinforced laager of wagons, supported by horsemen. The great victory which the Voortrekkers won on 16 December 1838 at the famous Battle of Blood River, may be attributed mainly to Pretorius's martial skills, his thorough preparations and his optimism. This overwhelming military victory paved the way for the establishment of the Republic of Natalia.

Natalia: the first Trekker republic

The first republic established by the Voortrekkers was short-lived; it existed only for four years. Nevertheless it represented the efforts of inexperienced stock farmers and agriculturists to establish a democratic state structure according to their own perceptions and their experience in the Cape Colony. It was to eliminate one of their main grievances which they had nurtured against the Cape authorities, namely a lack of representative government. The central government consisted of an elected *Volksraad* of 24 members, with a president or chairman. A Commandant-General was the supreme military commander. As far as local government was concerned, the tried and tested *landdrost* and *heemrade*, the system the Trekkers had known earlier in the Cape frontier districts, were re-established. Furthermore a bond of unity with the Trekkers on the western highveld was reinstated. In 1840 Pretorius reached an agreement with Potgieter to the effect that the entire Trekker territory would be placed under the Natal *Volksraad*; the next year it was decided to establish an adjunct council of twelve members at Potchefstroom, with Potgieter as Chief Commandant.

Now the Trekkers were also able to devote attention to another ideal, that of controlling the relationship between whites and blacks according to their own views. In particular their attitude and conduct towards blacks were characterized by differentiation, servitude, territorial separation and rough treatment. More than anything else it was the system of indenture which drew vehement criticism upon the Trekkers. This system compelled black children to work for the Trekkers in return for food, clothing and accommodation. In some cases, as in the wars against the Zulu, and particularly the infamous campaign against the Bhaca under Ncaphayi, children were captured and violently abducted. Yet the indenturing system was unable to meet all the labour requirements of the Trekkers and in addition, therefore, each was allowed to have five black families living on his farm.

Another Voortrekker goal, contact with the outside world through a harbour of their own, could not be fully realized either. D'Urban's successor, Sir George Napier, had sent Major Samuel Charters to occupy Port Natal in December 1838 and this hampered free harbour traffic. Early in 1842 the Dutch brig *Brazilia* paid a provocative visit to Port Natal, but the Netherlands had no intention of helping the republic actively against Britian. The visit of the American ship *Levant*, too, did not lead to any appreciable trade relations or other contacts with the outside world.

The murder of Retief and his party, by Mrs Elia van Musschenbroek (1906). Dingane, on the right in a cloak, with a shield over his head, pronounces the words *Bulalani abathakathi!* (Kill the wizards). Warriors move in to overpower Retief and his party inside the royal kraal, while outside some thirty servants, tending the Voortrekkers' horses and guns, are already being attacked and killed. In fact, according to the missionary Francis Owen, the Trekkers were killed outside the kraal, on Matiwane, a rocky outcrop of Hlomo Amabutho, or the Hill of Execution. (Africana Museum)

The British Government, through Governor Napier, consistently refused to recognize the independence of the Trekkers. They continued to regard them as British subjects, answerable to the Cape of Good Hope Punishment Act. The resolution of the *Volksraad* in August 1841 to segregate thousands of blacks to the southern frontier of Natal, gave Napier an opportunity to intervene. The Governor was of the opinion that this step constituted a serious threat to the turbulent eastern frontier of the Cape. The Xhosa could be forced across the frontier. This would entail military action and therefore increased British expenditure. Other reasons why Napier decided to occupy Port Natal were the representations by the missionaries that the blacks needed protection against the Trekkers, and the British fear that foreign powers might gain a foothold in Natal. Consequently Napier instructed Captain T C Smith, with 250 men, to march to Port Natal, and in May 1842 the Union Jack was hoisted in the Voortrekker harbour town.

The Natal Trekkers offered military resistance to British interference. Pretorius beat off a night attack by Smith on the Boer camp at Congella on 23 May 1842, with relatively heavy losses to the British forces. While the Trekkers then laid siege to the British camp, Richard (Dick) King and an attendant evaded the Voortrekker forces and in ten days covered the long distance to Grahamstown on horseback to summon help. Late in June a British relief force, under Lieutenant-Colonel A J Cloete, landed at Port Natal. Smith was relieved and the Boer military resistance ended. On 15 July 1842 the *Volksraad* at Pietermaritzburg signed the conditions of submission. In September 1845 Napier's successor, Sir Peregrine Maitland, officially proclaimed Natal to be a separate district of the Cape Colony. This was the end of the Voortrekkers' first republic. Once again they were obliged to trek.

FAC-SIMILE REPRODUCTION

PIETER RETIEF'S TREATY WITH DINGAAN.

Polgieter's Certificate of finding Treaty.

The Covenant

In November 1838 Andries Pretorius planned the punitive expedition against Dingane with great thoroughness. He concentrated on inculcating obedience and alertness in the undisciplined, disheartened men at his command. The idea of a covenant originated with Pretorius and Sarel Cilliers, the aim of which was to strengthen the Trekkers spiritually. The Covenant was made on 9 December at the present Wasbankspruit; subsequently it was repeated every evening. What it amounted to was that if God would grant the Voortrekkers a victory over the Zulu, they would build a church in His honour, and the Trekkers and their descendants would commemorate the day of victory every year.

The treaty between Retief and Dingane, 4 February 1838. This tracing of the original treaty, which disappeared in 1900 during the Anglo-Boer War, also bears the certification by E F Potgieter that it was found in a bag near Retief's remains on 21 December 1838. The Voortrekkers based their claim to Natal on this document. The treaty was drawn up in English, probably some time before it was signed. (Africana Museum)

135

The skirmish at Driekoppen, near Swartkoppies, in May 1845. A line of mounted Dragoon Guards fire at the Boers esconced on the hilltops. (Africana Museum)

The escape of the *Mazeppa* on 10 June 1842. Christopher Joseph Cato, captain of the *Mazeppa*, mobilised his vessel and escaped from Port Natal in order to obtain assistance for the besieged British from ships at Delagoa Bay. The trading schooner had previously brought the survivors of Louis Tregardt's party from Delagoa Bay to Port Natal in 1839. (Africana Museum)

Conditions in Transorangia

The heterogeneous population structure of southern Transorangia gave rise to constant unrest and clashes which soon spurred the British into extending their authority over this region. In the southern part of Transorangia were the Griquas under Adam Kok and in the eastern part the Rolong under Moroka. Eastwards the renowned Sotho leader, Moshweshwe, from his mountain fortress of Thaba Bosigo, expanded his claims to the fertile region west of the Caledon River.

The white population of this region, too, was divided. The loyal trekboers under Michiel Oberholzer were in favour of British protection and dissociated themselves from the republican Voortrekkers who, for the most part, occupied the Winburg region between the Vet and Vaal rivers – the territory which Potgieter had obtained in June 1838 from the Taung leader, Makwana, by barter. The republicans of Winburg retained contact with their compatriots in Potchefstroom and Natal. After it had become apparent, however, that Natal was going to become British, the Potchefstroom-Winburg Voortrekkers severed their federal tie with the Trans-Drakensberg Voortrekkers. In 1843 they set up their own administration and a year later declared their independence. Potgieter and the Burgher Council laid claim to an exercise of authority as far as the Orange River.

In the meantime the British Government made its influence felt to an increasing extent in this territory. When Judge William Menzies heard that Jan Mocke and his Voortrekkers intended to establish a republic north of the Orange, he took it upon himself to declare the land up to latitude 25° south to be British territory. However, the British Government had not yet given authorization for further regions to be annexed and consequently Napier had to declare the proclamation null and void. Nevertheless the Governor attempted to exercise indirect control over the territory; he wanted to protect the northern frontier of the Cape by means of subsidized buffer states without incurring heavy military expenditure. To achieve this Napier concluded treaties with Adam Kok and Moshweshwe in November-December 1843. These treaties provided *inter alia* that the signatories would be trusted friends of the Cape Colony, that they would preserve order in their respective territories, that they would extradite criminals and warn the colony against possible hostilities.

The Trekkers, and even loyal trekboers, were not prepared to subject themselves to the auth-

ority of black leaders. White resistance to Adam Kok increased until British troops intervened and defeated an armed Trekker force at Swartkoppies in May 1845. In June Governor Maitland paid a personal visit to Transorangia, but refused to negotiate with the republican leaders, Mocke and Kock, unless they subjected themselves unconditionally to British authority. He reached an agreement with Adam Kok to the effect that the region south of the Riet River would remain an inalienable and exclusive Griqua reserve. British subjects were able to purchase or lease land in the northern area, but the land would remain under the sovereignty of the Griqua chief. In addition it was decided to establish a British Resident in Griqua territory, and in 1846 Major Henry Warden was appointed in this capacity in Bloemfontein.

Without strong British support it was hardly likely that the Resident would succeed in controlling this vast, remote region effectively. Increasing unrest led to direct British intervention in Transorangia. In February 1848 Sir Harry Smith, who succeeded Sir Henry Pottinger towards the end of 1847, annexed the entire territory between the Orange and Vaal rivers and the Drakensberg as the British Orange River Sovereignty.

Up to this stage Andries Pretorius had wanted to obtain Trekker independence through peaceful negotiations, but this drastic step spurred him into positive action. At the head of the largest commando he had ever led, he marched against Smith in southern Transorangia. On 29 August Pretorius's commando was decisively beaten and British sovereignty over the area was affirmed. As had happened with the annexation of Natal five years earlier, the Great Trek had once again reached a low ebb. Many Voortrekkers had to trek again – this time northwards, towards the Transvaal, the only territory which was still beyond British control.

Tumult in the Transvaal

The Transvaal Voortrekker population was politically divided. The pioneer of the Transvaal area, Andries Potgieter, constantly sought to evade the ambit of the Punishment Act and to seek a new harbour on the Indian Ocean through Portuguese territory. He emigrated further northwards and in the process established two new towns, Andries-Ohrigstad in 1845 and Schoemansdal in 1848. In the meantime Potgieter's powers as 'Governor-in-Chief' were questioned by the new arrivals, who in due course came to be known as the *Volksraad* party. At one stage there were even two simultaneous governments in Ohrigstad, a situation which almost led to bloodshed in 1847.

The political tensions in the Transvaal were aggravated when Andries Pretorius and a number of the last Voortrekkers to leave Natal established themselves in the Magaliesberg in the Potchefstroom area. Pretorius's growing popularity and influence soon led to friction between the *Volksraad* party and Andries Potgieter.

As Commandant-General for Magaliesberg and Mooi River, with effect from January 1851, Pretorius once again had a legal and special status, although in the Transvaal he was only one of four Commandants-General. Nevertheless his prestige was rapidly increasing in the rest of southern Africa. The inhabitants of the Orange River Sovereignty repeatedly requested him to restore order in the territory and to free the republicans from the British yoke. In 1851 Moshweshwe also offered Pretorius an alliance against the British authorities in the sovereignty. Pretorius was more conversant with political developments in southern Africa than any other Trekker leader.

Pretorius was determined to use the precar-

Richard Philip (Dick) King (1813-1871), a British settler who rode some 1 000 km from Port Natal to Grahamstown in ten days to summon help for the British who were besieged in 1842 by the Voortrekkers at Port Natal. (Cape Archives, M486)

The Great Trek, 1834-1838

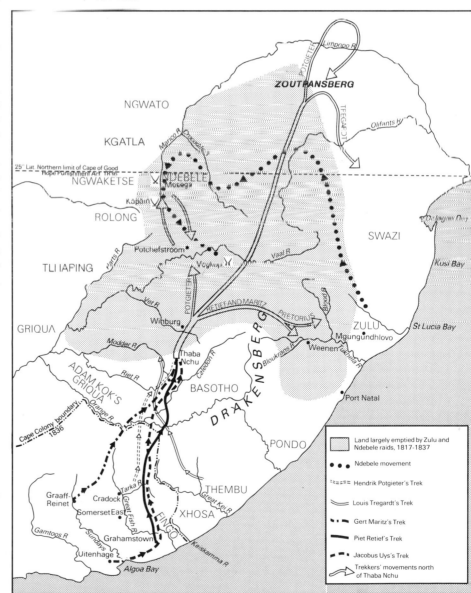

137

Major Henry Douglas Warden (Cape Archives, E 331)

ious position of the British to negotiate on the independence of the Trekkers north of the Orange River. The *Volksraad*, however, continued to curtail his freedom of action. He then decided to act unconstitutionally. After the Lydenburgers had failed to attend a *Volksraad* session in Rustenberg in September 1851, Pretorius and his followers decided to suspend the power of the *Volksraad* provisionally. The administration of the country was entrusted to Pretorius and his military council, and Pretorius was empowered to negotiate with the British authorities on independence.

Independence

In September 1851 Andries Pretorius wrote to Major Warden, advising him that he wished to negotiate on 'a good understanding'. This proposal was immediately seized upon, for at that stage the British Government was experiencing serious problems with its South African possessions. Since 1850 the Cape Colony had been involved in the bloody Eighth Frontier War. In addition Warden, the British Resident in the sovereignty, was unable to maintain the British position, especially against Moshweshwe, without strong military and financial support. Warden's efforts to compel acceptance of his frontier arrangements with a weak force had in fact led to his defeat by the Sotho at Viervoet in June 1851. W S Hogge and C M Owen, the two commissioners who had been sent to investigate conditions in the eastern and north-eastern frontier areas of the Cape Colony, also feared that Andries Pretorius would intervene in Transorangia. Consequently they agreed to meet him at Sand River, in the north of the sovereignty. On 17 January 1852 the Sand River Convention, by means of which Britain officially recognized the independence of the Trekker republic north of the Vaal River, was signed. After eighteen years, one of the main objectives of the Great Trek had at last been realized.

The British authorities did not recognize the independence of the Transvaal Trekkers out of sympathy for their ideal of freedom. It was instead an economizing measure. The Voortrekkers were now to be used as allies to help safeguard the extensive British frontiers in South Africa.

The Trekkers between the Orange and Vaal rivers had not yet received their freedom. In point of fact the British authorities had already decided to vacate the Orange River Sovereignty before the Sand River Convention took place, but at that stage this could not be done without harming the British, and in particular Sir Harry Smith's, prestige. But Smith was recalled in disfavour in January 1851 and his successor, Sir George Cathcart, was in favour of the withdrawal of British authority. In fact it was Mosh-

weshwe who ultimately sealed the fate of the sovereignty. After the Sotho had succeeded in repelling a British attack at Berea Mountain in December 1852, Cathcart proposed to the British authorities that a British commissioner be sent to the sovereignty to establish whether a further Trekker buffer state would not constitute a greater advantage to the British authorities.

The Imperial Government accepted Cathcart's proposal and a special commissioner, Sir George Clerk, began to make arrangements for granting independence to the territory. Despite strong opposition from English traders and other professional men, missionaries and trekboer loyalists, the Bloemfontein Convention was signed on 23 February 1854. In a certain sense this convention was even more remarkable than the Sand River Convention because it was the first time that the British had withdrawn from a Trekker territory that had previously been annexed. In addition British subjects, some of them against their will, were deprived of their British nationality.

After twenty years the Bloemfontein Convention had brought the Great Trek to a logical conclusion. In South Africa there would in future be British colonies and Boer republics.

Significance of the Great Trek

By 1854 the Voortrekkers had realized most of their ideals. The wish expressed by Gert Maritz in 1837, ie the 'wish to be recognized as a free and independent people', had come true. The Trekkers were in fact permitted by their former government to relinquish their British nationality. Through their own labour legislation and regulations, which bordered on slavery, they were assured of a sufficient supply of cheap black labour. There was land, grazing and hunting aplenty.

Yet the Great Trek had failed in some respects. It had not eliminated the uncertainty and insecurity which the Trekkers had felt in the eastern frontier area of the Cape. On the contrary, the Trek created new, insecure frontiers and brought the Voortrekkers into contact with more black communities. During the Trek they had constantly had to fortify themselves in laagers and even after the establishment of the republics they frequently had to evacuate their farms and villages and draw up laagers again. In the Transvaal, in particular, Boers were so preoccupied with their struggle for survival against the surrounding black communities that they were hardly able to pay any attention to building up their own republic.

The Great Trek amounted to the rejection of certain colonial institutions; nevertheless decades went by before the Trekkers came forward with their own substitute organizations. For years they had to do without organized religion,

An imaginary reconstruction of a reconciliation between the two Voortrekker leaders Andries Pretorius and Andries Hendrik Potgieter. (Africana Museum)

education and trade. Although the Trekkers continued to attach great value to their religion and literacy, they were unable to produce ministers and teachers from their own ranks. Then, too, their attempts to acquire their own harbour failed; consequently they were largely dependent on bartering with pedlars. This was conducive to a stagnant, undiversified economy based primarily on extensive stock farming. In a certain sense the Trek also led to intellectual and cultural impoverishment and isolation as the Trekkers formed a 'laager' to keep out new ideas and foreign influences, and even mere strangers.

The Great Trek not only led to the distribution of the small Afrikaner community over a vast area, but it was also conducive to political and social fragmentation and division. Not all the Afrikaners trekked and those who did did not necessarily agree on the destination and meaning of the Trek. In this way a political rift developed between those Afrikaners who trekked and sought their salvation in independent states, and those who remained behind and contributed to the economic development of the Cape Colony. Among the Trekkers themselves bitter, petty disputes occurred which sometimes threatened to obstruct the Trek.

The Great Trek is frequently associated with the subsequent South African race policies of apartheid and segregation. The Trek did in fact lead to the development of republics which were exclusively white, but largely dependent on black labour. This situation was associated with the Trekkers' views that blacks were inferior and should consequently be in servitude to the whites. The principles of the Voortrekkers' race policy continued to exist in the political ideals of their descendants and Boer statements were frequently quoted to justify subsequent race policies. Yet it would be wrong to ascribe race prejudice and apartheid exclusively to the Great Trek. The so-called 'mineral revolution' of the late nineteenth century and the industrial development of the twentieth century will also have to be taken into account.

It was for the Afrikaners in particular that the Great Trek was of exceptional significance. It was in a certain sense crucial to the rise of Afrikanerdom. As C W de Kiewiet put it, the Great Trek linked the future of the entire South Africa inextricably to the Boers. This ascendancy of the Afrikaners has not, however, been accepted unreservedly by other communities in South Africa. And, of course, no ascendancy is of permanent duration. Therefore the significance of this Afrikaner movement cannot yet be finally gauged.

Suggested Reading List

A du Toit and H Giliomee (1983) *Afrikaner Political Thought: Analysis and Documents*, Vol I, Berkeley and Los Angeles

B J Liebenberg (1980) 'Bloedrivier en Gods Hand', *South African Historical Journal*, No 12

C F J Muller (1977) *Die Britse Owerheid en die Groot Trek*, 4th revised ed, Cape Town and Pretoria

C F J Muller (1974) *Die Oorsprong van die Groot Trek*, Cape Town

E A Walker (1956) *The Great Trek*, 5th ed, London

The Kimberley mine which was named after the British Colonial Secretary, the Earl of Kimberley. Within a few months of its opening in 1871, the area was divided into hundreds of small claims, which at first were separated by roadways. These soon became claims themselves, and the 'Big Hole', the largest man-made hole in the world, developed. (National Cultural History and Open-air Museum)

Part IV

Co-operation and Conflict, 1854-1881

By 1854 the British Government had decided to abandon the hinterland in the apparent belief that its interests could be fully served by retaining control of the coastal colonies only. The consequent establishment of two independent Boer republics gave the Voortrekkers territorial power bases and inaugurated a new phase of South African history for all its people.

The Cape Colony, which remained the most prosperous, culturally aware and progressive state of this period, advanced from representative to responsible government, based on a colour-blind franchise. Natal paid mere lip-service to black suffrage, while black and Coloured people were denied any voting rights in the two republics.

The measure of co-operation between black, Coloured and white people in the Cape Colony did not, however, prevent further violence and conflict. The gradual consolidation of white power in the republics was hampered by dissension among the Boers themselves. Black societies in these regions were also unable to present a united front but they were by no means subservient in the face of the increasing alienation of their land. In 1860 indentured labourers from India, many of whom became permanent inhabitants of South Africa, came to Natal.

The discovery of diamonds started the mineral revolution and laid the foundations of a modern South African industrial society. Social, economic and political change was accelerated and although the various races became more interdependent, tension and conflict increased.

In the 1870s renewed imperial interest in the interior resulted in the ill-governed Transvaal losing its independence in 1877 and precipitated a fierce Anglo-Zulu conflict two years later. The war of 1880-1881 ended in the restoration of republican independence in the Transvaal, stimulated Afrikaner nationalism and foreshadowed the far graver Anglo-Boer confrontation at the end of the century.

Burghers encamped outside the Dutch
Reformed Church, Vryheid, on the
occasion of the celebration of *Nagmaal*
(Holy Communion). (National Cultural
History and Open-air Museum
(NCHOM))

Chapter 11

The Boer Republics, 1852-1881

D H Heydenrych

In January 1852 the British commissioners, W S Hogge and C M Owen, met Andries Pretorius, W F Joubert and a delegation of Voortrekkers from the area north of the Vaal River on the farm Sand River in the northern Orange River Sovereignty to sign the Sand River Convention. This was the first British recognition of the independence of a Voortrekker state since the beginning of the Great Trek.

The Cape Governor, Sir Harry Smith, had persuaded the commissioners to retain the Orange River Sovereignty for Britain, but when Smith was replaced by Sir George Cathcart at the beginning of 1852 a fear of uncontrolled expenditure gained the upper hand in British colonial policy. Moreover, there were strong misgivings about the value of colonial possessions: the

famous assessment of Benjamin Disraeli, then Chancellor of the Exchequer in the Conservative government, in 1852, of colonies being 'millstones around our necks' expressed the prevailing feeling in Britain. The Eighth Frontier War (1851-1853), and the unimpressive performance of British forces in June 1851 and December 1852 at Viervoet and Berea Mountain against Moshweshwe's Basotho finally tipped the scales in favour of withdrawal.

The Bloemfontein Convention, which granted independence to the white inhabitants of the Orange River Sovereignty, was signed on 23 February 1854. British withdrawal from the interior was complete and apparently permanent, and the Great Trek had reached its logical culmination.

H Heydenrych is currently Senior Research Assistant at Pretoria University, and is engaged in research on the history of the university since 1960. He obtained his MA in 1965 and his D Phil in 1981, both at Stellenbosch University. His area of specialisation is transport history.

The Orange Free State Republic

In 1848 the British Orange River Sovereignty stretched from the Orange to the Vaal and in the east as far as the Drakensberg escarpment. In 1849 this territory was reduced in size when the Warden Line was drawn more or less along the Caledon River as a frontier between the British territory and that of the Basotho under Moshweshwe. The fertile conquered territory in the Caledon River valley, situated near the Maluti Mountains where the rainfall was higher than in the rest of the Free State, was well suited to the cultivation of grain and was therefore important to the white farmers. To the Basotho it was vital, because the remainder of their country was too mountainous for agriculture.

The inhabitants

Two splinter groups of the Tlhaping – the Baro-

long under Moroko and Lepui's people – had fled to the Transgariep as a result of Mzilikazi's attacks in the early 1830s. The Barolong occupied territory in the eastern Free State, around Thaba Nchu, which had been purchased for them from Moshweshwe by the missionary

Bloemfontein in the 1850s, with the republican flag in the foreground. (Cape Archives, M555)

A Barolong village, from *Les Basoutos* by E Casalis, published in 1859. (Africana Museum)

The encampment of the Griqua chief Adam Kok near the Riet and Modder rivers in 1835, by C D Bell. (Africana Museum)

James Archbell. Good relations based on mutual respect, had existed between the Barolong and the Voortrekkers until the death of Moroko in 1880, and Barolong independence was respected by the Free Staters.

Lepui and his followers, about 3 000 in number, had moved southwards at the same time as Moroko, and had initially settled at Philippolis in the southern Free State. Quarrels with Adam Kok's Griquas caused them to move to Bethulie, where the French missionary J P Pellissier was responsible for territory being demarcated for them. When Lepui sold land to white farmers relations between his people and the Free Staters deteriorated.

The smallest black community in the Free State was the Kholokwe under Witsie who lived at Witsieshoek, south-west of Harrismith. They had also fled from Mzilikazi, and had initially sought refuge with Dingane, but after the Battle of Blood River Witsie and a handful of refugees moved across the Orange River. Following white complaints about cattle thefts or encroachment on their land, Witsie and his people were driven from their territory in mid-1856 by a Free State commando – the first armed clash between whites and black people after the republic had attained its independence.

The Griquas, the largest Coloured group in the area, originally came from the Cape. One group, predominantly of Khoikhoi origin, under Adam Kok, migrated northwards from the vicinity of Piketberg and Van Rhynsdorp around 1771. On the northern frontier of the colony they were joined by more Khoisan, Bastards and white adventurers. After Adam Kok's death in 1795 his son Cornelius (or Cornelis) became leader. Another group which trickled through to the northern frontier was mainly of white origin, and was led by Barend Barends (or Berend Berends). The followers of Kok and of Barends were known as Bastards and also called themselves by that name.

At the beginning of the nineteenth century Cornelius Kok and his people were persuaded by missionaries of the London Missionary Society to abandon their semi-nomadic existence and to establish themselves at a watering place called Klaarwater (later renamed Griquatown). Barends's people also settled there. John Campbell, a director of the London Missionary Society, persuaded the Bastards to adopt the name of Griquas in 1813. This name harked back to the Grigriqua, the original Khoikhoi group from which Adam Kok's people were descended.

The increasing role which missionaries came to play in political as well as in religious matters was not to the liking of the two chiefs, Cornelius Kok and Barend Barends, and the former returned to Namaqualand, leaving his son, Adam Kok II, in his place. Barends also left Griquatown and eventually settled at Danielskuil. In 1820 Adam Kok II resigned as leader, also in protest at missionary interference and joined his family who were already living at Campbell. In

1820 Andries Waterboer was consequently elected chief at Griquatown. John Melvill, the Cape Government agent resident in Griquatown since March 1822, regarded him as paramount chief, although this office was not traditional among the Griquas.

Barends and Kok considered Waterboer's election to be illegal. Waterboer's subsequent growth of prestige further alienated the traditional chiefs. His stature was particularly enhanced in June 1823, when he commanded a Griqua raiding expedition which, with their allies the Tlhaping of Mothibe, defeated a vastly superior force of the Hlakwane at Dithakong, stronghold of the Tlhaping. Andries Waterboer's authority was further increased when Melvill arranged for Adam Kok II, Waterboer's main opponent, to be replaced by Cornelius Kok II as chief at Campbell. Barends later moved to Boetsap near the Harts River, and Adam Kok II, on the invitation of Dr John Philip, moved in 1825 to the mission station of Philippolis. He was succeeded in 1835 by Adam Kok III.

After the 1820s, Dr Philip grew uneasy about white penetration in the Transgariep. His suggestion that Britain should annex Griqua territory to ensure that their property rights were protected did not meet with the approval of the authorities. A treaty was, however, concluded with Andries Waterboer in December 1834, in terms of which, in return for a salary, Waterboer would extradite criminals, warn the colony of pending attacks and protect the Orange River frontier all the way from Kheis to Ramah.

The Great Trek intensified the possibility of land disputes. To consolidate their territorial claims, Waterboer and Kok concluded a treaty in 1838 in which their respective areas of authority were defined. Philanthropic pressure ultimately led to British intervention and the Napier Treaty of 1843 recognized Kok's independence and granted to him the entire territory between the Orange and Modder rivers. White farmers in the area refused to accept Kok's authority. Consequently the Maitland Treaty of 1846 divided Kok's territory into two parts, an inalienable portion from the Orange to the Riet River and its tributary, the Kromellenboog River, in which whites were not allowed to purchase or lease land, and an alienable portion between the Riet and Modder rivers, in which whites could lease but not purchase land. Disputes between farmers who had bought land before 1846 and the Griquas persisted until 1861 when Adam Kok sold his rights north of the Orange River to the Free State and received a new home in Griqualand East.

The lands of the few small Koranna and San tribes who lived to the east of the confluence of the Harts and Vaal rivers had been demarcated by Warden along the Vaal River. None of these groups could resist the temptation to sell some of their land to whites. The last small group within the Free State was Adam Opperman's Bastards at the Berlin Missionary Society mission station. In 1860 Opperman and his followers moved to a farm near Jacobsdal, and his descendants occupy these so-called Opperman Lands to this day.

The Free State society

Free State society remained rural throughout. Of the 12 859 whites in 1856, only 500 lived in

the towns. A significant percentage were English-speaking, and were in fact in the majority in Bloemfontein by 1854. Politically they identified with the Cape Colony with its British institutions, and in due course they came to be called 'reannexationists' because they advocated reannexation of the Free State by the Cape Colony.

The group of Afrikaans-speaking persons who sought amalgamation with the South African Republic were diametrically opposed to these reannexationists. Concentrated mainly in the Winburg district, they became known as 'amalgamationists'. Gradually a third, moderate group developed which attached importance to the independent continued existence of the Orange Free State. After J H Brand became President in 1864 he united this middle group around himself.

By 1880 the main population centre, Bloemfontein, still had only 2 567 inhabitants, of whom 1 688 were whites. The government and town authorities tried to discourage Coloured and black people from moving to the towns. Those who did have work were accommodated in locations away from the white residential area. The locations lacked proper planning, building regulations and sanitation. In the constitution citizenship and the franchise were expressly limited to whites. The freedom of movement of Coloured and black persons was restricted by vagrancy laws which required them to carry passes. Moreover they were not at liberty to settle wherever they wished, since restrictions were placed on the number of blacks allowed on white farms.

Initially there were no laws regulating labour relationships. In 1856 a law was passed which imposed stringent restrictions on the indenturing of black children, but the first proper labour law was only passed in 1873. In principle blacks had a free choice of employer and were not compelled to work, but the law was primarily aimed at protecting the rights of the employer rather than those of the employee. In practice white farmers employed methods outside the law to obtain sufficient labourers. In addition the state also exerted pressure on black people to enter the labour market by means of a hut tax – later replaced by a poll tax.

First hesitant steps

The Bloemfontein Convention was not unanimously and enthusiastically welcomed. Many Free State Afrikaners were dissatisfied because their goal was one Voortrekker republic north of the Orange River, under Andries Pretorius. There was also a significant group of pro-British citizens who held protest meetings in Bloemfontein and Smithfield.

In this negative atmosphere the first elected *Volksraad* began drafting a constitution at the end of March 1854, a task for which it was ill equipped. However, with the aid of a few foreigners, and using the American, French and Dutch constitutions as examples, it succeeded in drawing up a simple but effective republican constitution.

Citizenship was granted to all white inhabitants who had been resident in the country for six months. Men over the age of eighteen were entitled to vote. Legislative authority was vested in the *Volksraad*, which had to meet at least once a year. A State President who was to be elected by the burghers for a. term of five years, was to be the head of the executive authority and was to be responsible for the administration of the state departments. The administration of justice was to be grounded in Roman-Dutch law and would be administered by *land-*

Alluvial or river diggings at Klipdrift on the Vaal River in 1872. (Cape Archives, M654)

drosts. The military system was based on the election of field-cornets in the various districts. In the event of war the field-cornets would choose a Commandant-General from among their number. Commando service was obligatory for all male citizens between the ages of sixteen and sixty. Property rights, personal freedom and freedom of the press were guaranteed. Once the constitution had been accepted, Josias Philippus Hoffman, one of the signatories of the Bloemfontein Convention, was elected as the first State President.

In the small republic's first year political events were dominated by the unstable situation on the border with Basutoland. Realizing their own weakness, the rulers of the republic sought allies. In June 1854 three *Volksraad* members were sent as delegates to the Transvaal *Volksraad* to request that the two states conclude a 'bond of union'. Nothing came of this, however, primarily as a result of unstable conditions and internal discord in the Transvaal. When M W Pretorius visited Bloemfontein in August 1854, the amalgamationists there made vigorous propaganda for their cause, but the decisive actions of a strong group in the *Volksraad* prevented anything coming of these popular cries.

Consolidation under J N Boshof

In February 1855 Hoffman was forced to resign. His successor was J N Boshof, who immediately began to establish the republic's administration on an orderly foundation. He was a firm advocate of Free State independence and opposed any union with the South African Republic. Both the amalgamationists and the reannexationists sought opportunities to further their respective causes during his term of office, but merely succeeded in dividing the white population of the Free State.

In February 1857, in an address to the Free State *Volksraad* M W Pretorius made the outrageous claim that the Free State had been given to his father by the British Queen, and that he had inherited the land. He was compelled by the authorities to leave the Free State, but not before he had threatened to return with an armed force to claim his 'property'.

In May 1857 Pretorius arrived at the Vaal River with a commando and called up his Free State supporters. Approximately 150 men joined him. Boshof rode northwards with a strong commando, but conflict was prevented at the last minute by intermediaries, among whom was Paul Kruger. On 1 June 1857 the Vaal River Treaty was signed in which the two republics guaranteed each other's independence and Pretorius's claims were admitted to be unfounded.

Boshof's greatest test was the impending conflict with the Basotho. The so-called 'Napier Line' of 1843, which had been laid down to protect Basotho rights, had only been in existence for two years when Moshweshwe was asked by Maitland to cede a triangular-shaped piece of territory in the Caledon River valley. Under these circumstances Moshweshwe did not attach great value to the boundary line and turned a blind eye to frontier violations by his people.

On 19 March 1858 Boshof declared war on the Basotho. As a result of uncoordinated and undisciplined conduct the Free Staters did not fare well in the war. The Basotho were formidable opponents, with at least 6 000 mounted tribesmen armed with rifles. Boshof was compelled to seek allies, but Sir George Grey, who became Governor of the Cape Colony in 1854, refused to become involved, and the President was forced to call upon his old enemy, M W Pretorius, who stipulated as condition for rendering assistance that the two republics should amalgamate.

When the *Volksraad* met in June, in Pretorius's presence, Boshof read out a letter from Sir George Grey stating that in the case of amalgamation, the conventions would lapse. Pretorius again returned frustrated across the Vaal River. At the end of September 1858 a treaty was signed with the Basotho through the mediation of Grey, which confirmed Warden's western boundary line, but allocated an additional fifty farms to the Basotho between the Caledon and Orange rivers.

Shortly after becoming Governor of the Cape Colony, Grey had arrived at the conclusion that the fragmentation of South Africa into British colonies and Boer republics was not in the interests of Britain nor of the white inhabitants of South Africa. He wished to create a strong British power bloc from coast to coast as far as the Vaal River and the Drakensberg.

Grey therefore formed ties with the reannexationists in the Free State in the hope that they would prepare the ground for federation with the Cape Colony. On 7 December 1858 the *Volksraad* resolved by a majority of one vote to negotiate with the Cape Colony on federation. When Grey was sounded out by the Colonial Office in London on a possible federation of the Cape Colony, Natal and British Kaffraria he advocated the inclusion of the Free State as well. The Colonial Office, however, dashed this grandiose plan, and in 1860 he was recalled as a disciplinary measure. The amalgamationists accused Boshof of treacherous pro-British inclinations, and he resigned in 1859.

An attempt at amalgamation, and disillusionment

Boshof's resignation gave M W Pretorius, the Transvaal President, an opportunity to involve himself fully in Free State politics. The amalgamationists in the northern Free State openly agitated for Pretorius, and he was elected Presi-

Jacobus Nicolaas Boshof, second President of the Orange Free State Republic. (Central Archives)

Johannes Henricus Brand, fourth President of the Orange Free State Republic, who succeeded M W Pretorius in 1863. (Central Archives)

dent of the Free State by an overwhelming majority at the end of 1859. He immediately took steps to bring the Free State constitution into line with that of the Transvaal, with a view to federation. The Transvaal *Volksraad* feared that the Sand River Convention would lapse if the republics were united, but Pretorius suggested that the Free State *Volksraad* hold a referendum on the question of unification. The people voted overwhelmingly in favour of it, by 1 076 votes to 104.

Armed with this mandate, the *Volksraad* delegated a commission to hold talks with the Transvaalers in July 1860. The executive council in the north was still unwilling to commit the SAR to action, however, it was decided that commissions of the two republics would meet twice a year to discuss matters of common concern. In the meantime, the Transvaal *Volksraad* compelled Pretorius to accept an honourable resignation from his presidency of the northern republic.

Pretorius had not acted as vigorously in domestic Free State issues as his subjects had hoped. Admittedly he did purchase Adam Kok's territory between the Orange and Riet rivers and the Campbell Lands west of the Dawidsgraf-Platberg line for £4 000 in 1861, after Kok's people had received a new homeland in Griqualand East. But he was never really able to resolve the most urgent problem of the Free Staters – the dispute with the Basotho. By January 1862 the situation had deteriorated to such an extent that the farmers of the Smithfield district called up a commando to launch a reprisal attack in reaction to frontier violations. Pretorius prevented this at the eleventh hour, but his indecisiveness was openly criticized. Pretorius's numerous visits to the Transvaal, which prevented him from giving his undivided attention to urgent matters in the Free State, also elicited criticism, and in June 1863 he resigned.

J H Brand: Basotho wars, diamonds and progress

In November 1863 the forty-year-old Cape parliamentarian, Johannes Henricus Brand, was elected President by a convincing majority. He immediately took the initiative and negotiated with Moshweshwe, who objected that the Basotho did not know where the frontier was. Brand asked the Cape Governor, Sir Philip Wodehouse, to demarcate the boundary line between the two states, and in October 1864 Wodehouse reaffirmed the old Warden Line, with a few minor modifications. Brand then persuaded the *Volksraad* to give the Basotho until 31 January to move back to their side of the frontier, after which those remaining would be driven back by force.

The respective positions of the antagonists had undergone a considerable change since the first conflict. The Free State's position was relatively stronger due to more inspired leadership, while the white population had also increased since 1858. Financially, too, the republic was in a better position. Moshweshwe was already approximately 79 years old and losing control over his senior sons and headmen.

The Basotho withdrew but attacks across the border continued nevertheless and tension increased as a result of the undisciplined conduct of the Free State border patrols. Brand mobilized his commandos in June 1865, and this time they were more disciplined. Assistance was also received from a Transvaal commando under Paul Kruger after a number of Transvaal transport riders had been murdered by the Basotho. After two abortive attempts to storm Moshweshwe's stronghold of Thaba Bosiu, during one of which the leader of the southern Free State forces, Commandant Louw Wepener, was killed, the Free Staters changed their tactics. They began to seize Basotho cattle and destroy their crops. After Moshweshwe's son, Molapo, had concluded a separate peace, the king too was compelled to accept the peace of Thaba Bosiu on 11 April 1866, in terms of which Moshweshwe's territory was rolled back to the Caledon River in the west and to the Phutiatsana River in the north, while a large portion of the triangle between the Caledon and Orange rivers was also lost. The northern third of Basutoland was placed under Free State supervision as Molapo's Reserve.

'Evening prayers at Moriah 1834', by C D Bell. 'Moriah' or Morija was the mission station established by Eugene Casalis and Thomas Arbousset of the Paris Evangelical Society in 1833, in response to an invitation from Moshweshwe. (Africana Museum)

The Free State Government was very tardy with the allocation of land in the conquered territory so the Basotho trickled back to the Free State side of the new frontier. Tension grew, and in March 1867 the Free State Government raised an armed force to compel adherence to the agreement. The Basotho in the territory offered little resistance, but this was by no means the end of the tense situation. In June 1867 whites were murdered in the Ladybrand district. When Brand demanded that the murderers be handed over, Moshweshwe replied that he had not agreed to the frontier line of 1866 and that the incidents had therefore not occurred on Free State territory. Free State commandos were again mobilized in July 1867 to wage the third war between the Free State and the Basotho in ten years.

The Free State forces quickly achieved major successes. Moshweshwe pinned his hopes on involving the British Government in the situation, in order to strengthen his case. When he received an unsatisfactory reaction from Sir Philip Wodehouse, he turned to the Lieutenant-Governor of Natal, R W Keate, who forwarded Moshweshwe's request for British intervention to London. Opinion in the Colonial Office had meanwhile swung in favour of intervention and in December 1867 Wodehouse received instructions to negotiate with Moshweshwe for the recognition of his people as British subjects. On 12 March 1868 Basutoland was annexed.

The Free State *Volksraad* was disconcerted at British intervention. A Free State deputation was sent to England to try and have the annexation repealed, but without success. On 12 February 1868 the Second Treaty of Aliwal North was concluded, whereby the frontier line between the Free State and Basutoland was firmly established. Although the Free State had to relinquish much of the conquered territory of 1866, the most fertile part of the Caledon River valley, the western bank, remained in Free State possession. In contrast the Basotho had to reconcile themselves to the permanent loss of much of their traditional homeland. In comparison with the Treaty of Thaba Bosiu they received a large additional piece of arable land in the west, but in comparison with all earlier boundary lines they were worse off. The new dispensation meant, however, that border disputes virtually came to an end.

In the west boundary problems of another kind loomed. The diamond discoveries at Hopetown in 1867 and subsequently in what was later to become Kimberley, involved the Orange Free State in conflicting land claims. Britain had never, since the Bloemfontein Convention of 1854, laid claim to the triangular piece of territory east of the confluence of the Orange and Vaal rivers and moreover M W Pretorius had puchased the land between the Orange and Modder rivers from Adam Kok in 1861. Consequently there was no doubt on the part of the Orange Free State that the diamondiferous territory belonged to that republic.

The attorney David Arnot involved himself in the claims of the Griqua chief Nikolaas Waterboer, whose territory was situated to the west of the confluence of the Orange and Vaal rivers. M W Pretorius, on behalf of the SAR, accepted the arbitration of R W Keate regarding the disputed territories, but Brand refused arbitration. He, unlike Pretorius, perceived that what was involved was power politics, rather than conflicting land claims.

The Basotho issue and the diamond fields dispute had stirred up vehement anti-British feel-

ings among the Free State citizens, and contributed to the fostering of nationalism. Initially this nationalistic sentiment centred mainly around the competent Brand, but by 1877 a growing number of Free Staters believed that he was too inclined to make concessions to the British authorities. His neutral attitude during the Transvaal annexation of April 1877 strengthened these beliefs. Yet the republic made great advances under his leadership.

The economic situation improved and currency recovered after the Free State derived benefits from the transport and food needs of the diamond fields, and a National Bank was established in June 1877. In August 1872 the Free State concluded a Treaty of Friendship, Trade and Extradition of Criminals with the South African Republic.

Great strides were also made in the field of education. Whereas there had been only ten government schools with 348 pupils in the Free State up to 1874, education began to make great progress from this year onwards under the Scot, Dr John Brebner, in spite of a complaint that English was used too extensively as a language medium. In 1875 another newspaper, *De Express*, began to appear with *The Friend of the Free State*, and made a great contribution towards the development of Afrikaner culture and nationalism. The administration of justice was improved when a supreme court was established in 1875, with F W Reitz as chief justice. Under Brand's leadership the young republic built up an efficient public service.

The esteem in which Brand was held as a statesman – which also reflected on his state – may be gauged by the fact that in 1881 he was requested by the British Government to act as mediator to help end the First Anglo-Boer War. Under Brand's leadership the Free State was, by the beginning of the 1880s, in many respects a model republic.

The South African Republic (Zuid-Afrikaansche Republiek)

In September 1853 the name South African Republic was officially adopted for the new state of the 'emigrant Boers North of the Vaal River'. This river was the only boundary mentioned in the Sand River Convention. Several white and black communities lived within this vaguely defined area, where their pattern of settlement and way of life were largely determined by their environment.

Settlement patterns

The southern third of the Transvaal highveld consisted mainly of grasslands and the northern two-thirds of savannah. Both afforded excellent grazing, which suited the white and black stock farmers. The first white farms were established along the rivers and tributaries close to springs. Consequently the banks of the Marico, Mooi and Apies rivers were well-populated at a very early stage.

The Transvaal plateau is broken up by a number of mountain ranges; the Magaliesberg range, the Waterberg, the Zoutpansberg and the Transvaal Drakensberg. When the white people entered the Transvaal the plains were virtually depopulated because most of the black tribes had taken shelter in the mountains owing to attacks during the *Mfecane*.

An important factor which determined the initial settlement pattern was the desire to have access to a harbour to break the economic isolation of the Transvaal. The establishment of Ohrigstad and later Lydenburg were directly related to the endeavour to establish a link with Delagoa Bay, and Schoemansdal was founded in the hope of linking up with Inhambane. Isolation also determined the initial pattern of the economic activities of the whites. Because the nearest available harbour, Durban, was so far away, the high transport costs discouraged the export of agricultural produce, and grain had to be consumed by the producers themselves. The

The Magaliesberg range, pictured in 1864 by A A Anderson. The Voortrekkers named the range after chief Mohale, whose followers inhabited the region. (Africana Museum)

subsistence economy caused many white farmers to hunt during the winter months to obtain a cash income.

The predominantly rural existence resulted in a small, widely dispersed white population pattern. The towns were situated far apart with few inhabitants. The followers of Andries Pretorius concentrated around Potchefstroom and Rustenburg, a group under the leadership of Andries Hendrik Potgieter settled in the Zoutpansberg around Schoemansdal, and in the vicinity of Lydenburg and Ohrigstad there was a concentration under W F Joubert. A fourth small group, living along the Buffels River, adopted the name Utrecht for their community. Although Utrecht was in reality situated outside Transvaal territory, the inhabitants had, by 1852, sought affiliation with Lydenburg.

Other towns were Pretoria, which was laid out in 1855 as a central government centre, and Potgietersrus and Wakkerstroom which were laid out in the 1850s to serve the interests of the established population. Further urban development only occurred with the discovery of alluvial gold and diamonds in 1870 when Bloemhof and Christiana, respectively, were established in the south-western Transvaal and Pilgrims Rest in the eastern Transvaal.

A considerable number of black communities lived in the Transvaal. The Venda lived close to the northern white community in the Zoutpansberg. The Pedi, under their paramount chief Sekwati, lived in the Luluberg between the Olifants and Steelpoort rivers – close to the white settlement of Ohrigstad-Lydenburg. Large numbers of Pedi left the area to seek work in the Cape Colony, particularly in the Port Elizabeth area, and used their earnings to purchase arms and ammunition. The Swazi inhabited the area between the upper reaches of the Vaal River and the Limpopo. They derived their name from Mswati, who was paramount chief from 1839 until 1855. The Lobedo, known for the cult surrounding Mojaji, the rain queen, lived near the Strydpoort Mountains in the vicinity of present Tzaneen. The Langa, under Mapela, lived in the Waterberg and controlled the strategic Makapanspoort, the key passage to the north. In the mountains flanking the Nyl River, Sotho chiefs such as Makapan also gathered together survivors of the *Mfecane*, and between the Venda and the Pedi in the north-east there was a constant influx of Tsonga from the lower Limpopo valley.

Along the Harts River, east of Kuruman, lived the Tlhaping. Further to the north, west of the upper reaches of the Limpopo, were three offshoots of the Sotho-Tswana, the Ngwato, the Kwena and the Ngwaketse. Together these black groups far outnumbered the whites. The fact that they frequently lived in close proximity without any proper boundary lines having been laid down created a tense situation which could very easily result in conflict.

Growing pains of the independent white community

The three geographically isolated white communities had one state institution in common, a *Volksraad*, which exercised the highest political authority, and which met at a different venue every few months. The long distances and the farming interests of the members meant that the sessions were for the most part poorly attended. In December 1852 and July 1853, respectively, two of the leaders, A H Potgieter and Andries Pretorius, died. Potgieter was succeeded by his son, Piet, and after his death two years later the mantle of leadership in the Zoutpansberg fell on Stephanus Schoeman. Andries Pretorius, in turn, was succeeded by his son, Marthinus Wessel. Both M W Pretorius and Stephanus Schoeman were stubborn and ambitious men, and W F Joubert and his Lydenburgers were equally headstrong.

A seat of government was eventually established after a long struggle. Through the efforts of M W Pretorius, two farms were bought along the Apies River in 1853 for the establishment of a central capital, which became known as Pretoria. A *Volksraad* meeting was held in March 1856 in Rustenburg to draft a constitution. The Lydenburg representatives were present but old issues were raked up and the *Volksraad* had to adjourn in disorder without accomplishing anything. In October 1856 matters took a more serious turn when the Lydenburgers declared their independence from the central authority. The first separate Lydenburg *Volksraad* met in December 1856.

Pretorius was elected as President and on 6 January 1857 he was formally inaugurated in Potchefstroom. Stephanus Schoeman was elected Commandant-General but did not attend the inauguration ceremony. After numerous negotiations Schoeman and his followers accepted the constitution. Lydenburg, however, still remained aloof.

The constitution of February 1858 stated that the *Volksraad*, which was to consist of at least twelve members, was to exercise legislative power and to meet at Pretoria. Executive power was to be in the hands of an executive council consisting of the President, as head of state, the Commandant-General and three other members. The President was to be elected for five years by the citizens of the republic, the Commandant-General for an unspecified period and the executive council members for three years. *Volksraad* members, half of whom had to retire annually, were to be elected for a maximum of two years. The Commandant-General was to be in charge of the armed forces with commandants, field-cornets and assistant field-cornets under his command. Judicial authority was to be in the hands of magistrates of whom three would form a supreme court. The *Vierkleur* was accepted as the national flag, and *Eendragt Maakt Magt* (Unity is Strength) the motto.

Utrecht was declared to be a district of the South African Republic in September 1859, and Lydenburg united with the central authority in April 1860. The white communities north of the Vaal River were thus constitutionally united, but it would rapidly become clear that this offered no guarantee of unanimity and co-operation.

Co-existence and conflict between whites and blacks

The peaceful conditions following the flight of Mzilikazi caused the black population in the Transvaal to increase rapidly. By 1852 there were probably approximately 100 000 blacks and 15 000 whites between the Vaal River and the Limpopo; by 1880 their respective numbers were calculated to be 773 000 and 43 260. In such a situation tension could easily arise between whites and blacks over their respective places of abode and grazing and hunting rights.

As in the case of the Free State, franchise rights and citizenship were reserved exclusively for whites. Blacks were also denied the right to own immovable property. Whites expected blacks to work for them, and established residential areas near concentrations of blacks in order to be near sources of labour.

Labour relations were a source of conflict in the republic. There were two kinds of employees: indentured labourers and ordinary workers. Indentured labourers were orphaned black children who were placed in the care of a white person at an early age, usually after campaigns against neighbouring black kraals. The children were indentured to a white person until the age of 25 years and were compelled to work for him. A magistrate or field-cornet had to be satisfied that the child had been obtained in a lawful way. In spite of regulations to obviate abuses, the system of indenturing earned the republic a great deal of censure. It was alleged that it was a refined form of slavery and that black kraals

Two scenes of a Boer farm in the Transvaal around 1860, showing the interior and exterior of the homestead. (NCHOM)

152

were sometimes attacked for the very purpose of obtaining children. After the attack on Setshele's kraals in 1852 the missionary David Livingstone wrote: 'The Boers. . . carried off two hundred of our children into slavery.' The fact of the matter is that it was a system which lent itself to abuse.

Employers could only negotiate with a black chief for ordinary labourers through a field-cornet. In addition there were limitations on the number of black persons per white farm that a farmer could employ to ensure an equitable distribution of farm labourers. In 1864 a general poll tax was levied on blacks. On the one hand it was regarded as a source of revenue and on the other as an incentive to blacks to work. In practice, however, it often proved virtually impossible to collect, and in 1870 a hut tax was substituted for the poll tax. Differential amounts were levied so that blacks who lived and worked on farms and those who were employed elsewhere, paid less than those who were unemployed. Once again the object was to encourage blacks to find employment on farms and elsewhere.

A pass law of 1866 provided that any black person found outside his residential district without a pass from his employer, paramount chief, a missionary, magistrate or field-cornet could be detained by any citizen and handed over for punishment to the nearest field-cornet. The purpose of the law was clearly to exercise control over the movements of black people and compel them to accept a settled way of life. Subsequent legislation differentiated between employed and unemployed blacks. Frequently these arrangements were circumvented or evaded by black people, but in the long run they caused tensions between whites and blacks.

The first white-black confrontation occurred a month after the Sand River Convention. Commandant P E Scholtz summoned the chiefs of the Kwena and Ngwaketse in the west and offered them peace on condition that they paid taxes and provided the farmers with labour. Mosielele, a subordinate chief, refused to accept these conditions and sought the protection of

Setshele, a chief of the Kwena, who refused to surrender him. Scholtz thereupon attacked a number of Setshele's kraals, destroyed crops, took 200 children and women captive and wrecked the house of David Livingstone, the missionary among Setshele's people, at Kolobeng. On the return journey an attack was also made on the kraal of Montshiwa, of the Tshidi-Rolong, who had refused to supply men for the commando.

Further conflict resulted from the fact that the Transvaal Government had never established any western boundary. In 1858 the request of Mahura, a chief of the Tlhaping along the Harts River, to have the boundary between his territory and the republic clarified was ignored by the Transvaal Government. When subjects of Mahura and Gasibone, paramount chief, murdered a number of white people later that year, a commando under Paul Kruger was sent against them. Gasibone was killed and his decapitated head sent to Mahura, who sued for peace. A fine of 8 000 head of cattle was imposed on Mahura and he was at the same time

The first diamond diggings on the Vaal River at Klipdrift, by A A Anderson, 1869. The diggers lived in tents, and took the 'diamond ground' down to the river to wash and sort on tables on the banks. (Africana Museum)

A group of black people journeying to their home, having made their 'fortune' in the colony. The men carry rifles, which were much prized as a means to continuing an independent political existence. (Africana Museum)

Thomas François Burgers, in 1875.
(Transvaal Archives)

elevated to paramount chief, even before the Tlhaping had a chance to appoint a successor themselves.

In the north Makapan and his people in the Waterberg attacked and killed the members of a hunting expedition in 1854. In retaliation a Boer commando trapped a number of his people in a large cave and killed approximately 3 000 of them. Further north in the Zoutpansberg, the Venda were provoked into raiding white settlements by attacks on their kraals instigated by João Albasini, superintendent of the black tribes east of Schoemansdal, and other individuals. White inhabitants evacuated Schoemansdal in 1867 and the Venda chief Makhado laid waste to the town. The unrest spread southwards where Makapan and other chiefs rose in revolt. Virtually the entire Zoutpansberg district between the Olifants and the Limpopo rivers was abandoned by the whites.

In the east there was also a potential for conflict over land. In 1846 the Swazi had already sold the entire eastern Transvaal area between the Olifants River in the west and north, the Lebombo Mountains in the east and the Crocodile River in the south to the Boers, including the territory of the Pedi between the Olifants and Steelpoort rivers. In 1857 an agreement was concluded with Sekwati of the Pedi which defined the Steelpoort River as the eastern boundary line between his people and the Boers, but the provisions of the treaty were ambiguous. Moreover, Sekukuni did not participate in the negotiations of 1857, a situation which led to later conflict.

Efforts to end economic isolation

In 1854 Pretorius made representations to the Natal Government to reduce the import duties on goods destined for the Transvaal. However, this was one of Natal's main sources of revenue and the colonial authorities refused to make any concession. Additionally, a request for a special accommodation in respect of the duties on lead and gunpowder was refused.

These problems could have been greatly alleviated if the republic had had its own harbour. In 1853 and again in 1859 negotiations were held in vain with Mpande in an effort to gain access to St Lucia Bay. Furthermore, when Mpande and Cetshwayo appealed to the Natal authorities, Britain took determined action to prevent the SAR obtaining a foothold on the Zululand coast. Pretorius had to admit defeat.

After another failed attempt in 1865-1866 to obtain concessions from Natal in respect of levies on imports, Pretorius unsuccessfully tried to gain access to the east coast through the mediation of Alexander McCorkindale, a British subject who had started a settlement in the eastern Transvaal. He then took an arbitrary and unilateral step to achieve his goal and at the same time include the area around Tati in the north-west, where Karl Mauch had discovered gold in 1867.

In April 1868 with the approval of the *Volksraad*, Pretorius defined the republic's external boundaries properly. According to his proclamation, a small strip of Transvaal territory ran along the southern bank of the Maputo River down to the coast. In the east the boundary followed the Lebombo Mountains and then stretched northward far into present Zimbabwe, then westward to Lake Ngami and then directly southward to the Orange River and along the course of the Vaal.

Portuguese objections to the coastal boundary, together with British rejection of the proclamation in its entirety, were so vehement, however, that it remained a dead letter. The British reaction was attributable to the Colonial Office's renewed interest in the South African interior: failure to determine the republic's boundaries – and specifically its western boundary – and have these recognized, was soon to cost the country dearly.

Diamonds and British imperialism

After the discovery of alluvial diamonds near the confluence of the Vaal and Harts rivers in 1868, the SAR and the black tribes to the west both laid claim to this area. In addition, Britain was naturally interested in the new mineral wealth and the maintenance of the British 'road to the north' was also in jeopardy. By acting as champion of the rights of the blacks and Griquas, the British Government could further its own interests.

When diamonds were also discovered at Du Toits Pan near the present Kimberley in September 1870, the struggle for the possession of the diamond area intensified. M W Pretorius had a naive belief in the strength of his own case. The arbitration proceedings of October 1871 took a disastrous turn for the SAR, due to the competent handling of the Griqua and black claims by the attorney David Arnot, and Pretorius's inept presentation of the republican case. The western frontier of the SAR was established along the Makwassiespruit, a considerable distance from the Harts River. The Transvaal farmers in the vicinity did benefit from the diamond fields by meeting the needs of the diggers for food and transportation, but the loss of territory outweighed this advantage. The *Volksraad* refused to accept the frontier line, and censured M W Pretorius's handling of their case. This left him no option but to resign, which he did in November 1871.

The way of life of the black people north and west of Kimberley, was profoundly influenced by the discovery of diamonds. Up to 1870 individual Tlhaping sold alluvial diamonds to prospectors and dealers on a relatively large scale. Subsequently they took advantage of the opportunity to provide the approximately 50 000 people who were concentrated on the diamond fields by the end of 1871, with milk, game and sorghum, as well as other essentials such as firewood, reeds, woven mats and thatching grass.

This change from a mainly agrarian subsistence economy to a market-orientated economy was temporarily beneficial to a large number of blacks, but in the long run it undermined their economic freedom. Their game, firewood and thatching grass resources became depleted and the majority of the black population were deprived of their subsistence possibilities. The relative prosperity of some individuals and their resultant increased economic independence undermined the authority of the chiefs. In addition white settlement had been encouraged in the territory since the annexation of Griqualand West as a crown colony by Britain in October 1871, with the result that tribal land became increasingly alienated. The reaction came in 1878 in the form of a Griqua and black uprising which was mercilessly suppressed.

The diamond fields also affected black people

further away from the scene. Between 1871 and 1875 approximately 50 000 black people from the interior entered and left Kimberley annually as labourers. Most of these were Pedi from the north-eastern Transvaal who were drawn to the area by wages which were higher than elsewhere in southern Africa. The income so earned was primarily used for purchasing rifles which were regarded as an essential means to ensure the continued political existence of independent communities. Black groups such as the Pedi were therefore well armed and equipped to defend their independence by the mid-1870s.

The republic under T F Burgers, 1872-1877

After appeals had been made in vain to President Brand of the OFS to make himself available for the Transvaal presidency, the choice fell on a 38-year-old clergyman from Hanover in the Cape Colony, T F Burgers, who was sworn in in Pretoria on 1 July 1872.

A formidable task awaited the new President. The state finances were in a parlous state and

---

Sekhukhuni (circa 1810-1882)

Sekhukhuni I was the son of Sekwati, paramount chief of the Pedi. After his father's death in 1861, he overthrew his half-brother, Mampuru, who had succeeded Sekwati, and became chief. He was dissatisfied with the Steelpoort River as his eastern boundary line, where the Pedi had been living side by side with the white farmers for a considerable time, in a typical 'open frontier' situation.

By 1876, the situation in the area was so tense that white farmers in the Lydenburg district had gone into laager. On 16 May 1876 war was declared on Sekhukhuni. The republic could only muster a force of 2 000 men, and President Burgers himself took command, since no other commander could be found. Initial successes were achieved, but an abortive attack by a force of 150 Lydenburgers, supported by 2 000 Swazi warriors, on the kraal of Johannes Dinkwanyane, Sekhukhuni's half-brother, demoralised Burgers's men. On 2 August, during an attack on Sekhukhuni's stronghold, the majority of the commando cravenly sought shelter, and refused to fight any further. Ultimately the President erected forts manned by paid volunteers, and by this method forced Sekhukhuni to sue for peace, which was concluded in February 1877. Shortly afterwards Sekhukhuni repudiated the peace treaty, and the matter was still unresolved when the republic was annexed by Britain in April 1877.

Captain R A Clarke, who was appointed special commissioner to deal with the Pedi, found his task impossible owing to lack of troops. In November 1879 a major confrontation took place, and Sekhukhuni's warriors were forced to capitulate in the face of a superior force of 8 000 Swazi and a few British regiments commanded by Sir Garnet Wolseley. Sekhukhuni was captured and imprisoned in Pretoria, but was released when Transvaal independence was restored in 1881. He was murdered in his sleep at his kraal in the Luluberg by Mampuru in 1882.

The capture of Sekhukhuni's stronghold, from a sketch in the *Illustrated London News*. The Pedi lived on the plain, while the chief's stronghold was situated high in the mountains. In this picture the British troops under Sir Garnet Wolseley are advancing across the plain, towards the chief's kraal. (Transvaal Archives)

The British troops bringing Sekhukhuni into Pretoria as a prisoner-of-war. He was kept in Pretoria jail and released in 1881. He was murdered in 1882 by his half-brother, Mampuru, who was hanged for this crime. (Africana Museum)

Sir Theophilus Shepstone and his staff after the annexation of the Transvaal in 1877. They are seated outside the tent which served as a temporary office in Pretoria. The members of the group depicted are:
Back row: Lieutenant F Phillips, Melmoth Osborn, Colonel Brooke, Captain James.
Front row: W B Morcom, J Henderson, Sir Theophilus Shepstone, Dr G Lyle, H E Finney. Seated in front of the group is Henry Rider Haggard, then aged 21. (Transvaal Archives)

the paper money in circulation was worth very little; economically the republic was still at the mercy of the British colonies; the dispute with the British High Commissioner over the so-called 'Batlhapinia' in the west was still raging; education was primitive; the republic was virtually unknown and without friends abroad; and from time to time unrest prevailed among the black people in and around the Transvaal. Burgers tackled these problems with great zeal, dedication and optimism. He obtained a loan from the Cape Commercial Bank which made it possible to bolster the currency and to place finances on a firm footing. He was further assisted by the discovery of the Lydenburg goldfields in 1873.

A new Education Act, which was largely Burgers's creation, was passed in 1874. A superintendant of education was appointed who was directly responsible to the *Volksraad* and competent personnel were recruited abroad. A Treaty of Friendship, Trade and Extradition of Criminals was concluded between Burgers and Brand and came into operation in August 1872. Later Burgers established diplomatic relations with the Netherlands, Belgium, Portugal and France, while a policy of good neighbourliness with the Portuguese authorities at Delagoa Bay was pursued.

The relatively primitive press in the state was given an important boost when the first Dutch private newspaper, *De Volksstem*, was established in Pretoria in 1873 through Burgers's efforts.

Burgers took the first steps in establishing an infrastructure for the administration of blacks, consisting of a superintendent of native affairs and native commissioners, a system which was utilized during the British occupation.

He arranged for armaments to be imported from Germany, and a German officer was brought out to the republic to establish an artillery force. Thus an effort was made for the first time to establish a permanent force. Two matters, however, the abortive railway scheme and the campaign against Sekhukhuni, resulted in the termination of Burgers's presidency.

Burgers persuaded the *Volksraad* that the government should initiate the project of building a railway line to Delagoa Bay. The President was delegated to go to Europe to raise a loan for this purpose and obtain permission from the Portuguese Government for the building of a railway line. When intrigues in the British Colonial Office made it impossible for him to obtain the necessary finances in Britain he concentrated his efforts on Amsterdam and wrote home to say that the loan would be fully subscribed. In Belgium he ordered railway material to the value of £63 000.

He was given a hero's welcome in Pretoria, but his triumphant reception turned sour when it appeared that only one third of the loan amount of £300 000 had actually been fully subscribed and his entire railway scheme collapsed.

An even greater setback for Burgers and the republic was the war against Sekhukhuni which dealt the state coffers a serious blow. Even more crucial was the fact that many Transvaalers began to doubt the ability of the government to protect them. Losses suffered by the border farmers, in particular, placed a strain on their loyalty to the state. When the diggers' community of the eastern Transvaal took their grievances to the imperial authorities, Britain got a foot in the door and the independence of the republic became endangered.

Annexation, war and independence, 1877-1881

When Lord Carnarvon became Foreign Secretary in 1874, he wanted to federate the British colonies and the Boer republics under the British flag. Burgers favoured co-operation with the British colonies, but not under the Union Jack. When a conference of southern African states, which Carnarvon held in London in August 1876, proved abortive, he resolved to bring the Transvaal into his envisaged federation by annexing the republic, after which the Orange Free State would be unable to maintain its independent existence.

To implement his plan, Carnarvon sent Sir Theophilus Shepstone of Natal to the Transvaal as special commissioner. On 22 January 1877 Shepstone, accompanied by a few Natal officials and an escort of 25 men of the Natal Mounted Police, arrived in Pretoria on a mission which would culminate about three months later in the annexation of the republic.

Shepstone hammered on two weaknesses in the affairs of the republic, namely the financial position and the government's inability to control the black people. In talks with the government he was initially evasive about the purpose of his mission, but at the end of January he admitted to Burgers what he had been instructed to do. When the *Volksraad* met, Burgers tried in vain to convey the seriousness of the situation to its members, and submitted measures in an attempt to accommodate Shepstone's objections and avert the danger. The *Volksraad*, to his annoyance, initially resolved not to discuss the reforms. The financial crisis was eventually disclosed when a commission found that the public debt already amounted to £192 399, and it soon became apparent that even *Volksraad* members had not paid their taxes.

Shepstone eventually made it clear that annexation was inevitable; reforms would not help at this stage, because the government was inherently weak. He even alleged that he had received more than 3 000 signatures in favour of annexation. Under these circumstances Burgers wrote a letter of protest as a last resort. At the same time the *Volksraad* resolved to send a dele-

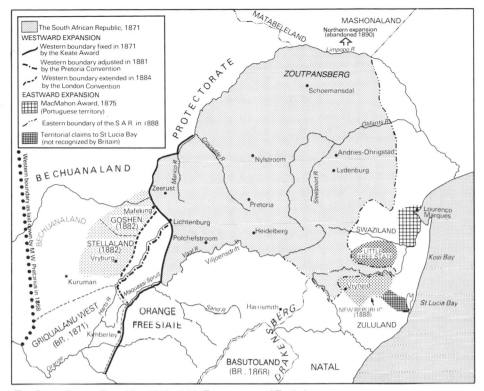

The South African Republic, 1870-1890: Expansion and Encirclement

gation abroad to make the republic's objections to the proposed annexation widely known. An appeal was also made to the citizens to refrain from violence because that would merely prejudice the republic's cause abroad.

The scene was set for a bloodless takeover. At 11h00 on 12 April 1877 the annexation proclamation was read out in Church Square in Pretoria. The South African Republic no longer existed; it was now the British colony of the Transvaal.

Pretoria in 1879, at the time of the British annexation, painted by Lt W J Fowler. (Africana Museum)

157

The Triumvirate of Piet Joubert, Marthinus Wessel Pretorius and Paul Kruger. (Transvaal Archives)

The scene outside O'Neill's farm on the slopes of Majuba after the signing of the peace treaty, 21 March 1881. Sir Evelyn Wood stands in the middle of the front row with his helmet in his hand, and on his right are President J H Brand, S J P Kruger, M W Pretorius and P J Joubert. (Cape Archives, E3095)

Shepstone soon found that the administration of the new colony was infinitely more difficult than the annexation. As Burgers had done, he experienced a great shortage of money and he fell into disfavour with the Colonial Office in London. The building of the railway line to Delagoa Bay had to be postponed provisionally and was ultimately shelved. Native commissioners were appointed to try to improve the administration of black people. Sekhukhuni had failed to pay the fine for which he had accepted liability in the peace treaty with the previous government and Shepstone did not have the necessary troops to compel payment. A year after the annexation the situation in the eastern Transvaal was dangerous. On the south-eastern border Shepstone had as little success with the Zulus and many local farmers had to abandon their farms.

In March 1879 Shepstone was replaced as administrator by Sir Owen Lanyon. In September British authority in the Transvaal, Natal and Zululand was reinforced when Sir Garnet Wol-

seley was appointed High Commissioner for these three territories, and Governor for the Transvaal. An executive council and a legislative assembly were established to give a less autocratic image to the administration; but only less important Boers were willing to serve in this government and the two bodies never had much stature in the eyes of the Boers.

In December 1879, after a campaign lasting twenty months, Wolseley eventually succeeded in subduing Sekhukhuni's people and taking the paramount chief captive. At the same time the Anglo-Zulu War ended in September and put an end to the unrest on the south-eastern frontier. These successes came too late, however, to reconcile the Boers to the British regime. Peaceful protest by the Transvaalers against annexation of their country had in the meantime made rapid progress. As early as May 1877 the first delegation of Paul Kruger, E J P Jorissen and W E Bok, which had been decided upon prior to annexation, had left for Europe. At a mass gathering in Pretoria in January 1878, they had to report that Lord Carnarvon could not be persuaded to admit to the unjustness and unpopularity of the annexation.

The Transvaal burghers held a series of meetings at which the restoration of independence received strong support. But the leaders continued to advocate a peaceful reversal of the annexation. At the beginning of 1879 however, a second delegation returned empty-handed from an interview in London with Carnarvon's successor, Sir Michael Hicks Beach. And when the Cape High Commissioner, Sir Bartle Frere, met the Boer leaders by invitation at Kleinfontein, they too were informed by him that there was no hope of the annexation being rescinded. The impatient Transvaalers were slightly comforted by the success of a mission of Paul Kruger and Piet Joubert to the Cape Colony in 1880. They were lionized by the Cape Afrikaners and the mood in the Cape Colony turned against feder-

ation. Consequently a parliamentary motion by the Cape Prime Minister, Sir Gordon Sprigg, pertaining to the bringing about of a federation, had to be withdrawn.

The joy of this victory was, however, almost immediately clouded by another disappointment. When the Liberal Party under W E Gladstone won the election in Britain in April 1880, a letter was sent to the new Prime Minister asking for the restoration of independence. Gladstone had, after all, as opposition leader, expressed serious misgivings about British policy in the Transvaal. By this time, however, he had come to view matters in a different light and his negative reply ushered in the last phase of resistance.

The support of the Afrikaners south of the Vaal encouraged the Transvaalers. In May 1879 the Free State *Volksraad* for the first time asked unequivocally that Transvaal independence be restored. At the same time Cape Afrikaners, particularly through the Paarl newspaper, *Di Patriot*, gave their northern compatriots tremendous moral support. In October 1880 an editorial in this newspaper stated: 'Passive resistance is now becoming futile resistance.'

When a certain P L Bezuidenhout of Potchefstroom refused to pay charges over and above his tax assessment, his wagon was seized. On 11 November P A Cronje, with 100 men, took the wagon by force from the bailiff and returned it to Bezuidenhout. The national committee which had meanwhile been appointed, perceived the seriousness of the situation, and brought forward the public gathering, which had been convened for 8 January 1881, to 8 December 1880. Between 8 000 and 10 000 men turned up at Paardekraal, near present-day Krugersdorp. Preparations for war were made and field-cornets were appointed. On 12 December the command was placed in the hands of a Triumvirate consisting of Paul Kruger, Piet Joubert and M W Pretorius. The next day the

Triumvirate issued a proclamation announcing the restoration of the republican government. The reconstituted government thereupon left for Heidelberg where the *Vierkleur* was hoisted on 16 December 1880. The Triumvirate demanded that Lanyon hand over the government to them. He refused and took steps to suppress the uprising.

The first shots in the struggle for Transvaal independence were fired on 16 December 1880 at Potchefstroom. Piet Cronje had been sent there with a commando by the Heidelberg government to have its first proclamation printed. While they were there, a patrol of British soldiers from the garrison in the fort outside the town spotted a Boer officer and a few men and shots were exchanged. The result was a fierce struggle between Cronje's commando and the British garrison. The British were beleaguered in the fort and held out courageously for three months before they surrendered. The Heidelberg government had sent troops immediately to seven towns in the Transvaal to lay siege to British garrisons stationed there. This tactic pinned the British troops down within the Transvaal, and enabled Commandant Piet Joubert to make for the Natal border with 800 horsemen on 27 December 1880.

On 20 December, Commandant Frans Joubert made a surprise attack on the 94th Regiment near Bronkhorstspruit while it was on its way from Lydenburg to Pretoria and decimated it. At Laing's Nek, where the road from Natal began to ascend to the escarpment of the Transvaal highveld, Piet Joubert was waiting for the Natal Field Force of 1 146 foot soldiers and 191 cavalrymen, under the command of Major-General Sir George Pomeroy Colley.

Colley first had to get past the Boer positions at Laing's Nek. His first two efforts were unsuccessful. After establishing his base at Mount Prospect, a few kilometres from Laing's Nek, Colley tried on 28 January 1881 to gain a foot-

---

The Battle of Majuba

At approximately 20h00 on the evening of Saturday 26 February Major-General Colley gave the order for 579 men to fall in at Mount Prospect. They were to leave artillery, machine guns and rocket launchers behind, and carry only rifles and side arms. After a tiring march, the first of the men reached the saucer-shaped crest of Majuba at about 03h40 on the morning of Sunday, 27 February.

At daybreak the Boers in the laager directly below Majuba were alarmed when they spotted the British soldiers on the crest. General Piet Joubert rode through the laager asking for volunteers to storm the mountain, and at the same time ordered that the wagons be loaded up and the laager evacuated because a bombardment was expected from Majuba at any moment.

At approximately 06h00, 150 Boer volunteers, under covering fire, began to scale the mountain from various sides. By 11h00 the Boer rifle fire at the soldiers manning the edge of the crest was becoming more and more accurate. Two officers reported this to Colley, but he felt that his position was unassailable and ignored the information. When an officer approached Colley later to report his concern over the approaching Boers he found the general asleep.

At about 12h30 Colley was awakened by heavy rifle fire: contrary to his expectations the first Boers had succeeded in breaking through the line of defenders. Colley could only gaze in stupefaction as his men retreated past him. On the unprotected plateau the British were now forced to defend themselves from behind a rocky outcrop. As more Boers burst over the crest at other points, the British began to lose courage. Some began to flee along the mountain path to Mount Prospect. The panic became contagious and more followed suit. With the last resistance crumbling all around him, Colley received a mortal head wound. Later it was rumoured that the humiliation of utter defeat had led to his suicide on the mountain, but more than one of the burghers subsequently claimed that they had fired the shot which cost him his life.

A contemporary interpretation of the Battle of Majuba, by Otto Landsberg, dated 1881. (Africana Museum)

Major-General Sir George Pomeroy Colley, killed on Majuba 27 February 1881. (Transvaal Archives)

hold on the slopes by occupying a strategic flat-topped kopje a short distance from the road. After an hour he had to beat a retreat, having suffered serious losses. The same fate befell him at Schuinshoogte on 8 February when General Nicolaas Smit ambushed a British patrol.

Determined to prove British superiority over the unsophisticated Boer rebels and to restore his own reputation as a militarist, Colley now had an inspiration: it struck him that the Majuba Mountain dominated Laing's Nek. If he could occupy the crown, he thought, it would give him an unrestricted vantage point overlooking Boer positions and compel them to evacuate the Nek. The road to the Transvaal would then be open.

The British defeat at Majuba was overwhelming. The Boers lost only one man, as against ninety-two killed and at least fifty taken prisoner on the British side. The Boers, of whom Sir Owen Lanyon had said only three months previously: 'I don't believe those cowardly Boers have it in them to fight', had achieved a victory which shook Britain and captured the attention of the world.

This crushing defeat brought independence within the reach of the Boers. Even before the Battle of Majuba attempts, using President Brand of the Free State as an intermediary, were being made by the British to reach a settlement. On 6 March 1881 Piet Joubert and Col-

ley's successor, Sir Evelyn Wood, signed an armistice agreement at Laing's Nek. On 23 March a peace agreement followed.

A Royal Commission began to work on a convention defining the terms of independence. On 3 August 1881 the Pretoria Convention, as it was called, was signed by the Boer leaders, in spite of their misgivings at some of the conditions. Five days later the Triumvirate took over the government of the Transvaal.

Suggested Reading List

S F Malan (1982) *Politieke Strominge onder die Vrystaatse Afrikaners, 1854-1899*, Durban

A N Pelzer (1950) *Geskiedenis van die Suid-Afrikaanse Republiek, I: Wordingsjare*, Cape Town

O Ransford (1967) *The Battle of Majuba Hill: The First Boer War*, London

H J van Aswegen (1971) 'Die Verhouding tussen Blank en Nie-Blank in die Oranje-Vrystaat, 1854-1902', *Argiefjaarboek vir Suid-Afrikaanse Geskiedenis, I*

F A van Jaarsveld (1974) *Vaalrivier. Omstrede Grenslyn*, Johannesburg

F A van Jaarsveld, A P J van Rensburg and W A Stals (eds) (1980) *Die Eerste Vryheidsoorlog, 1880-1881. Van Verset en Geweld tot Skikking deur Onderhandeling, 1877-1884*, Pretoria and Cape Town

F A F Wichmann (1941) 'Die Wordingsgeskiedenis van die Zuid-Afrikaansche Republiek, 1838-1860', *Argiefjaarboek vir Suid-Afrikaanse Geskiedenis, I*

Chapter 12

The British Colonies

The Cape Colony, 1854-1881

J Benyon

In 1854 a representative Parliament consisting of a lower Legislative Assembly and an upper Legislative Council met for the first time, and the new Governor, Sir George Grey, arrived after a successful period of administration in New Zealand. The fact that he was a civilian governor following a long line of soldier-governors at the Cape hinted at changed British attitudes toward rule in South Africa: the new Parliament had to be made to work. The ending of the worst of the eastern frontier wars in 1853 stressed the need for a frontier policy more durable and constructive than the sad succession of failed settlements of the past; and the new semi-diplomatic relationship with the Transvaal and Free State, which was embodied in the Conventions, suggested that Britain's incoming representative should possess both tact and firmness in projecting imperial influence beyond the turbulent north-eastern frontier.

Constitutional and political development

The capacity of the Cape to pay for its new representative legislature of 1854 seemed to portend a fairly short period before the executive departments would be handed from imperial to colonial control under the formula known as responsible government. Yet nearly two decades would elapse before this happened in 1872, and one of the main causes of delay was the issue of race and colour. The low, non-racial franchise was the work of both Downing Street and a group of liberals, both English- and Dutch-speaking, who lived mainly in Cape Town, and took their political cue from the old free press campaigner, John Fairbairn. This 'Cape liberalism' of the colonial metropolis was echoed neither in the Dutch-speaking wine districts of the west nor in the English settler and frontier districts of the east. This polarisation of viewpoints led to Earl Grey, the Secretary of State for Colonies, designing the executive of imperial officials in the new constitution as a counterpoise to the possible irresponsibility on racial issues of a legislature made up of hard-bitten colonists. This was to prove a recipe for deadlock in government.

The inevitable confrontation of legislature and executive was delayed until the 1860s, due partly to the charming personality and master-

John Benyon has been Professor of Historical Studies at the University of Natal (Pietermaritzburg) since 1977. He studied first at Rhodes University in Grahamstown, was Cape Rhodes Scholar to Oxford in 1960, and holds doctorates from Oxford and the University of South Africa. His latest major published work is *Proconsul and Paramountcy in South Africa* (1981).

Port Elizabeth in 1862, by T W Bowler. (Africana Museum)

The opening of the first Cape Parliament by Acting-Governor Sir Charles Henry Darling, in the State Room of Government House on 30 June 1854. The Governor, Sir George Cathcart, had been called away to take a command in the Crimean War. (Cape Archives, M579)

The Cape franchise, 1836-1956

In 1836 a multiracial franchise was introduced in Cape municipalities, creating a precedent for future franchise legislation at the Cape. In 1853, when the ordinance laying down the Cape parliamentary franchise was confirmed, it incorporated a £50 income qualification and a £25 occupation qualification, and was therefore based, in the words of the Colonial Secretary John Montagu (1842-1852), 'on such a moderate qualification as will enable the intelligent and industrious man of colour to share with his fellow colonists of European descent in the privilege of voting for the representatives of the people'.

Despite this initial aim, the Registration Act of 1887, which did not recognize tribal communal tenure as a qualification, excluded the black 'blanket vote' in elections for the two new Transkeian seats. Furthermore, the Franchise and Ballot Act, No 9 of 1892, increased the property qualification from £25 to £75 and laid down a basic literacy test at a time when black and Coloured voters could affect the result in almost a quarter of the Cape constituencies. Nor was possession of a perpetual quitrent allotment under Rhodes's Glen Grey Act of 1894 accepted as a qualification.

In 1909 the National Convention incorporated the multiracial Cape franchise as an entrenched element in the draft Union Bill, but in 1936 General Hertzog's government removed blacks from the common roll, and in 1956 the entrenched franchise rights of Cape Coloureds was ended during the premiership of J G Strijdom. The multiracial franchise had been, for more than a century, a central element in the so-called Cape liberal tradition.

ful governing style of Sir George Grey, and also to economic prosperity and to the continuing squabble over 'separatism' between the white colonists. East/west 'separatism' was always something of a paper tiger – the paper being the *Graham's Town Journal* and the tiger being its editor, 'Moral Bob' Godlonton. Rooted partly in the chronic insecurity of the frontier population, partly in commercial interests with expansive tendencies towards the northern republics and eastern Kaffrarian territories, and partly in Grahamstown's hopes of rivalling Cape Town as a colonial metropolis, the movement made only a spasmodic impact after 1854 – at those times when broad regional issues gave it temporary unity.

One of these issues, involving wool producers, led to the founding of the Separation League in 1860, which for several years combatted the government's proposal for a wool tax. Even the wool growers of Graaff-Reinet, however, could not see eye to eye with Grahamstown's pretensions to being an alternative capital. When Governor Wodehouse held a session of the Cape Parliament in Grahamstown in 1864 in an attempt to break the deadlock between 'colonial' legislature and 'imperial' executive, the experiment cost the taxpayer a third more than the average Cape Town session, and was never repeated.

The easterners felt that they were dominated and discriminated against by the west, yet in fact their allotment of 22 Assembly seats, as against 24 of the west, and their 7 in the Legislative Council, as against the west's 8, was substantial over-representation – and partly explains why English-speakers were preponderant in the Cape Parliament until 1874, when the Seven Circles Act was passed. This Act did

away with the distinct regional representation for the easterners, who then became supporters of a new type of separatism in the form of Lord Carnarvon, the British Colonial Secretary's federalism in the mid-1870s.

Sir George Grey as Governor and High Commissioner

Under his magnetic exterior, Sir George Grey was a stubborn and autocratic proconsul. His shortcomings as an administrator only became clear later, when his dynamic presence was no longer there to carry all before it. But, to begin with, he was able to cajole and conciliate the legislature of colonists and to command full support from the Executive Council of official departmental heads, including the resourceful Cape Colonial Secretary, Rawson W Rawson.

Grey's handling of frontier policy provides the best example of this managerial style of government. From his predecessor, Sir George Cathcart, he inherited a militarized trans-frontier and unstable relations with the Xhosa nation. Though still seemingly truculent, the long-sustained resistance of the Xhosa was beginning to crumble under the steady pressure of white society and the successive major setbacks of the frontier wars. In 1855, when a frontier clash again seemed imminent, Grey saw that he could use it to overturn Cathcart's segregationist 'military' settlement of 1852-1853, and promote the rapid introduction of Western European influences to the black trans-frontier community. In March 1855 he pressed the Cape Parliament to help him fill up British Kaffraria 'with a considerable number of Europeans . . . to increase our strength in that country'. He urged further that unremitting efforts should be made to 'raise' the black people to 'Christianity and civilization, by the establishment among them and beyond our boundary, of missions connected with industrial schools, by employing them on public works'.

The ultimate object behind Grey's frontier policy was to end chronic insecurity and expensive military entanglements. Nevertheless, the policy also encouraged a further alienation of black land resources and a deeper division of the Xhosa into traditionalists and those converted at mission stations to Christianity, Western dress, and participation in the expanding market relations of the colonial economy, either as part of the widening 'peasant' element on the frontier or as labourers among the intruding whites. While Grey's so-called 'assimilationist' policy towards the Xhosa has drawn praise in the past,

The arrival of the Governor, Sir Philip Wodehouse, for the opening of the session of the Cape Parliament in the Shaw Hall, Grahamstown, on 28 April 1864. (Cape Archives, M581A)

Robert ('Moral Bob') Godlonton (1794-1884), editor and owner of the *Graham's Town Journal*. (Cape Archives, E65)

Governors and prominent officials in the Cape Colony 1858-1870. In the centre is Sir George Grey. (Cape Archives, M608)

163

'The witchdoctor', by F T I'Ons. (William Fehr Collection)

King William's Town in 1860, by Thomas Baines. The town was built on the site of the Buffalo mission station, founded by John Brownlee in 1825. It was named in May 1835 after William IV, the reigning British monarch. In 1847 it became the capital of the territory of British Kaffraria, and acquired the status of a borough in 1861, after a visit by Prince Alfred in 1860. (William Fehr Collection)

there are now historians who stress the more negative aspect of the 'underdeveloping' of the Xhosa through the uncompetitive terms upon which the Governor admitted them to a technologically advanced society. Many, however, met the challenge positively, by producing for the colonial market under land tenancy and share-cropping arrangements, but this response might have been less due to Grey's initiative than to a growing perception among the desperate tribesmen that the old Xhosa order had passed.

Instead of victory in war, as in 1847, the old Xhosa order in 1856-1857 aimed at victory through reconciliation with the supernatural, and this resulted in the so-called 'Great Cattle Killing'. The Xhosa believed that on 18 February 1857 the sun would rise and set again in the east, and a whirlwind would sweep all white men and unbelievers into the sea. After months of destroying stock and crops, the great day came without the fulfilment of the prophecy, and the Xhosa nation seemed – in the white man's words – to have committed 'suicide'. How is this catastrophe to be explained?

Superficially, there is the well-known story that a young girl, Nongqawuse, had seen messengers from the land of the dead at a pool where she drew water. These visions or halluci-nations acquired importance when passed on to her uncle, Mhlakaza, a priest-diviner to the senior Gcaleka branch of the Xhosa and, in a more general sense, to the whole Xhosa nation. The prophetic tradition had been well established among the Xhosa by Makanna (Nxele), who had led the Ndlambe combination on Grahams-town in 1819, and by Mlanjeni, who had originally inspired the national resistance of 1850-1853. Hard-pressed by the postwar settlement, by the mounting population in British Kaffraria, by the white settler as a potential claimant of further ancestral land, by the missionary as a breaker of traditional custom, by the pressure of the new labour relations, and by the great lung-sickness epidemic of 1856, the Xhosa resorted to desperate remedies. The evils that now afflicted their world, they believed, could only be eliminated when the nation re-established the bond, through its ancestors, with the supernatural. This involved converting losses already suffered through lung-sickness among the cattle into a great sacrifice. Mhlakaza, interpreting Nongqawuse, set himself to preach its necessity.

Recent studies among anthropologists, particularly in the western Pacific, have shown that this phenomenon of 'millenarianism' or total be-

lief in a supernatural route to the attainment of a better world in the future, is usually associated with the rapid disintegration of traditional societies under severe pressure. Unfortunately for the Xhosa society, there was little perception among white observers of what was happening. Grey chose to interpret the phenomenon as a sinister design to manufacture another frontier conflict, and took steps against the chiefs for their alleged war plot. This confrontational attitude only increased the scale of the disaster – though it is true that the Governor did begin relief work when he began to discern something of the movement's true nature.

Its outcome played right into his hands, for he could immediately extend the magistrate's role as substitute for the chief's administration of justice. Some important chiefs were actually banished, and their starving followers either drafted into the colony to meet the demand for labour or into Grey's public works in British Kaffraria. Others were settled in large, easily controlled, detribalized village communities, where the Governor could push forward earlier experiments in trust and individual land tenure among the Mfengu ('Fingoes') to include the Xhosa as well.

It is estimated that some 30 000 people were lost through starvation, and another 30 000 through migration (only about 30 000 remained). This enabled Grey to introduce three types of immigrant to reinforce the work of returning missionaries and traders. First, there were the footloose soldiery of the disbanded Anglo-German Legion, and later, in 1857, followed the settlement of solid north German peasants. For the latter he risked the displeasure of his London superiors during recruitment through the firm of Godeffroy in Hamburg. Third, the Cape's old black allies, the Mfengu, were allowed to move into the Amatole 'Royal Reserve', which had been cleared of the followers of the western Xhosa paramount chief, Sandile.

Under Grey, the old territorial frontier between black and white was permanently blurred, but a new frontier in labour relations soon became apparent, which was not always to the disadvantage of the black individual. The mission stations which Grey subsidized, such as Lovedale, provided instruction in the skills of carpentry, blacksmithing and wagon making which helped to make their black students more competitive, and the academic education they offered was often first-rate. Indeed, many prominent white colonists were proud to receive their schooling at Lovedale as well.

In the Transkei, Grey began preparing the ground for future annexation by expelling the eastern Xhosa, or Gcaleka, paramount chief Sarhili beyond the Mbashe in 1858. Mfengu peasants moved into this area to create new regional tensions with the displaced Gcaleka and neighbouring Thembu. Further north Grey en-

couraged the location of the hard-pressed East Griqua of Adam Kok in 'Nomansland' in 1861. The annexation of territory to the borders of Natal appeared to be the next logical move in the furthering of Grey's confederation plans of 1858-1859, but here the Governor seriously over reached himself.

Along with his governorship, Grey held the high commissionership, which gave him a certain practical power of intervention beyond Cape borders. The restraint upon it was the 'Convention Policy', which sought to confine British involvement in the interior mainly to diplomatic influence over collaborating Boer republics and, to a lesser extent, over co-operative black chiefdoms. Grey sought to reverse this abstentionist stance with an alternative policy of extending the imperial plan for consolidation of coastal possessions into a full-scale re-incorporation of the Orange Free State as British territory in federal association with the Cape and Natal. Such grandiose undertakings were expensive. The £40 000 granted annually by Downing Street soon dwindled and at no time actually covered the cost of all the High Commissioner's projects in British Kaffraria, let alone in the whole sub-continent. Yet these projects proliferated in the form of the Grey hospi-

'Watching for the return of their dead warriors', by F T l'Ons. This painting, depicting a landscape with rising sun and figures round a burning tree on a hilltop, is thought to represent a scene on 18 February 1857, when the Xhosa waited for the rising sun to herald the fulfilment of the prophecies of Nongqawuse and Mhlakaza. (Africana Museum)

Sir George Grey visits the German military settlers at a camp near East London. Nearly 2 400 troops and officers, 320 women and 182 children emigrated to the Cape in 1858 under the leadership of Baron von Stutterheim, and settled in British Kaffraria. The emigration scheme was financed by the British Government to settle the disbanded members of the Anglo-German Legion who had been enlisted to fight against Russia in the Crimean War. The military settlers were later followed by a larger group of solid, north German immigrants recruited through the firm of Godeffroy in Hamburg. (Cape Archives, E3171)

There were four claimants to the alluvial, or river diggings, around Klipdrift. The South African Republic cited certain treaty arrangements and the fact that the Sand River Convention had not specified a western boundary. The Rolong and Tlhaping chiefdoms argued that they had occupied the territory over a long period; Nikolaas Waterboer (represented by the Coloured lawyer, David Arnot), proposed that his claim of suzerainty over Cornelius Kok had led to the 'Campbell lands' escheating back to himself on Kok's death, and the Free State claimed that it had purchased the land from Adam Kok III.

The valuable dry diggings were claimed by Nikolaas Waterboer and the Orange Free State. Two boundary lines formed the basis of their cases. Northward from Ramah to Platberg ran a line based on a boundary drawn in 1838. David Arnot aimed at establishing the validity of the whole length of this line, so that the four great diamond pipes of future Kimberley would fall within the territory once claimed by Cornelius Kok of Campbell, and later by Waterboer. North of Ramah, this line was intersected by the so-called 'Vetberg line', which Waterboer had accepted in 1855 as the boundary between his territory and the 'Campbell lands' to the north. The Free State claimed that its jurisdiction of the territory north of the 'Vetberg line' dated back to before the Bloemfontein Convention.

In 1871 Lieutenant-Governor R W Keate of Natal was appointed as arbitrator in the dispute. The evidence was limited and badly presented, and Keate ruled fairly enough. The 'Keate Award Line' followed an east-west axis to Platberg (which excluded the Rolong and Tlhaping claims), and a south-north axis up the Makwassie Spruit (which excluded the South African Republic's claims). By implication, the award favoured Waterboer's claim, but did not pronounce definitely on the validity of the entire length of the Ramah-Platberg line.

Waterboer then offered the territory, known as Griqualand West, to the crown, and Sir Henry Barkly accepted. In 1876 Judge Stockenström's Land Court declared Waterboer's claim invalid, and £90 000 was paid to the Free State in 'compensation'.

Nikolaas Waterboer (Cape Archives, E388)

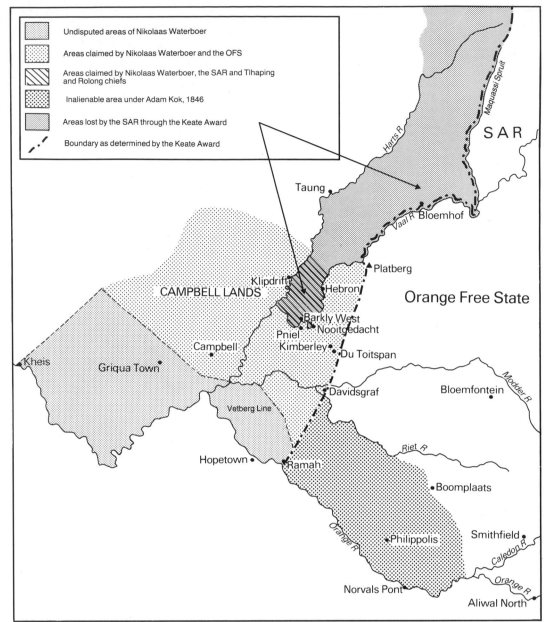

Key:
- Undisputed areas of Nikolaas Waterboer
- Areas claimed by Nikolaas Waterboer and the OFS
- Areas claimed by Nikolaas Waterboer, the SAR and Tlhaping and Rolong chiefs
- Inalienable area under Adam Kok, 1846
- Areas lost by the SAR through the Keate Award
- Boundary as determined by the Keate Award

The Diamond Fields Dispute, 1870-1871

tals in King William's Town and Pietermaritzburg, the Grey College in Bloemfontein, the Grey Institute in Port Elizabeth and the Zonnebloem (chiefs' sons) foundation in Cape Town. The Cape Parliament assisted Grey in finding men and money for some of these schemes, but it, too, was building up a financial deficit by the late 1850s. This laid Grey even more open to recall by the disapproving Secretary of State in London on the grounds that his extravagance and disobedience must stop. This recall was reversed, but Grey returned only for a year during 1860-1861, and was succeeded in 1862 by Sir Philip Wodehouse.

The Wodehouse years

Like Grey, Wodehouse was an autocrat. He was also guarded, austere, and critical of sharing, let alone handing over, his substantial control of black frontier administration under the constitution of 1854. He favoured a conciliar system of imperial dominance, which might have promised a greater protection to threatened black chiefdoms on the frontier than the alternative of responsible government. However, the white colonists of the Cape now challenged Wodehouse's bland assumption that he could govern better than they.

In the Transkei Wodehouse had to call a halt to expansion in 1864. Not only had it emerged that trans-frontier rule through the High Commission was legally questionable, but the cautious Secretary of State and Wodehouse himself were worried over the expenses with which Grey had saddled them. The next step in this rationalization was to attach British Kaffraria, which had been made a crown colony in 1860, to the Cape in 1865. But the colonists were reluctant to accept this further addition to their costs of administration and abused the Governor for forcing it upon them. During the depression of the 1860s the Governor blamed the legislature for keeping him chronically short of funds, and Parliament hit out at Wodehouse and his Executive Council for not allowing the colonists, who paid the expensive piper, to call more of the tune in administration.

As Wodehouse's western colonial opponents led by John Molteno moved unsuccessfully in 1863 and 1867 for responsible government, the Governor counter attacked by mounting the parliamentary session in Grahamstown in 1864, and, in 1867 and 1869, by proposing the abolition of Parliament itself and the establishment of a mixed representative official legislature of under twenty members. Many easterners believed that responsible government would remove the imperial brake on western dominance, and might give the British Government the excuse it sought to recall expensive regiments from the Cape. Around 1870 three major developments combined to end this impasse: the conflict over Basutoland ceased, Gladstone's British ministry decided to couple the issues of troop withdrawal and responsible government, and, hand in hand with the discovery of diamonds, the economy revived.

The credit for solving the Basutoland crisis

The pane of glass on which Reverend Ricards scratched his initials with the Hope diamond in 1867. (Cory Library, Grahamstown)

must go to Wodehouse. Adopting the role of an honest broker, he first intruded his High Commission authority between the Orange Free State and the Basotho, and in March 1868 extended the protection of this authority over them. After Wodehouse's departure, however, Basutoland was annexed to the Cape in 1871, partly because he had used the colony's police and administrators to support his High Commission rule there after 1868 and partly because the British Government had indicated that frontier defence and rule were included in the overall package of Cape responsible government.

The beginning of the mineral revolution: the discovery of diamonds

In 1867 two boys, 'Klonkie' and Erasmus Jacobs, dug a shining stone out of a chalk bank near Hopetown on the Orange River. The stone made its way through the hands of those suspecting its worth first to Colesberg and then to Grahamstown. Here men with some knowledge of diamonds – Atherstone, Macowan, Ricards and Galpin – were able to confirm the possibility that precious stones were to be had near the

De Beers Consolidated establishes a monopoly

Among the early joint-stock flotations of 1874 was the Old De Beers Company of the young Cecil Rhodes, who was at first only a junior associate to his brother, Herbert, the two Rudds and the Cape businessman Tarry. By 1880 the consolidation of claims was giving way to the consolidation of share blocks among the mine companies. Where the uneven deepening of claims in the early '70s had called forth the first small joint operations, now there was a need for one large company to develop a single strategy for mining an entire pipe. For a while Rhodes saw he could prosper by having his New De Beers Company of March 1880 exploit the better parts of his now-substantial holding by opencast methods, but when the competing underground operations in the richer Kimberley pipe came onstream in the late 80s, he would be vulnerable.

Skilfully cementing relationships with the rival *Compagnie Française*, with the share dealer Alfred Beit and, through him, with merchant bankers and capital suppliers of Europe, especially the Rothschilds in London, Rhodes began his great attempt to buy out the Kimberley Central Company. The camp of the enemy supplied a useful ally in the ex-Whitechapel Jew, Barney Barnato, whose support was rewarded with a celebrated membership of the gentile Kimberley Club! Eventually the purchasing power of the Rhodes combination drove the minority of resisting shareholders at Kimberley Central to defeat and a great settlement of over £5 million in 1889. The monopoly of Rhodes's De Beers Consolidated had been duly established over the diamond fields by 1891.

Morning market, Kimberley. (National Cultural History and Open-air Museum (NCHOM))

Black workers at the bottom of the mine, Kimberley. (NCHOM)

confluence of the Orange and Vaal rivers. Further discoveries, like the famous 'Star of South Africa', saw doubters thrust aside and the beginning of the two great rushes, to the alluvial diggings at Pniel and Klipdrift (Barkly West) in 1869 and then to the dry diggings at Du Toitspan and Bultfontein in 1870. By mid-1871 the Kimberley mine ('Big Hole') was being excavated out of the Colesberg Koppie. Its fabulous yield suggested that these great volcanic pipes of diamondiferous gravel would sustain a long-term mineral revolution in South Africa. When they paid over £60 million in their first decade of exploitation, supposition became virtual certainty.

Rough and ready 'diggers' committees' which culminated in a 'Diggers' Republic' under ex-Able Seaman Stafford Parker at Klipdrift in June 1870, marked the pioneering phase of organization on the diamond fields. At different times 40 000 diggers defied President M W Pretorius, paid lip service to Cape and Free State magistrates, and insisted on a colour bar. Imperial annexation in 1871 by Barkly, and a crown colony of Griqualand West in 1872, was followed by a fully fledged administration under Lieutenant-Governor Richard Southey in 1873.

The Cape was now able to draw in external European capital in significant amounts and to generate a complementary quantity of internal revenue and development capital itself. From being chronically debt-ridden the Cape passed suddenly into the unexpected position of being a creditor colony. Railways began to snake inland towards Kimberley from the colonial ports. In spite of the completion of the Suez Canal in 1869 the tonnage of ships calling at the Cape increased steadily during the early 1870s.

Responsible government – inception and early problems

The Cape did not formally annex Griqualand West, as the diamond fields had become known, until 1880, yet the Cape Governor, Sir Henry Barkly, the Cape Colonial Secretary, Sir Richard Southey, and the Cape lawyer David Arnot, had together been responsible for defeating the Free State's claims there. Both this paradox and delay were dependent on the coming of responsible government. The Gladstone ministry of 1868-1874 had decided that the Cape Parliament could no longer dither over accepting responsible government nor the costs of local defence. The imperial garrison was scheduled for recall, and to prompt this move and the substitution of a local defence system, the incoming Governor, Sir Henry Barkly, was briefed to encourage both colonies and states to move towards federation. It was felt that the diamond fields might contain the economic strength to sustain both a federation and a local defence force.

Barkly had had difficulties in setting up the new constitution in 1871-1872 and in finding an Executive Council of representative colonists to replace that of professional administrators in imperial service. Eventually he had to settle for the dour John Molteno, only his fourth choice as premier. Indeed, the latter's intimidating nickname, the 'lion of Beaufort', had been earned as chief opponent to the previous Governor! This prickly colonial was predictably suspicious of what he saw as a busybodying 'imperial factor', which had alienated his Western Cape, Dutch supporters through arbitrarily discounting the claim of their blood relations in the Free State to the diamond fields. After 1872 the British Government had to wait impatiently until the Cape under Molteno came round to the idea of either incorporating or absorbing the diamond fields.

On the eastern frontier and in Basutoland Barkly began integrating what had been an imperial – or 'High Commission' – authority over black administration with that of the newly created Cape Department of Native Affairs under Charles Brownlee. To indicate appreciation of the executive skills which Barkly had put at the disposal of his ministers in frontier administration, Molteno reluctantly agreed to modify the terms of imprisonment of the Natal 'rebel', Langalibalele, on Robben Island, but his attitude should have warned the imperial authorities not to press issues that infringed the constitutional prerogatives conceded to the colonial ministry.

The first great crisis in Cape responsible government arose precisely at the point where frontier issues overlapped with the federal policy which Britain now wanted to promote in South Africa. In 1871 Barkly had appointed a commission to consider this question of federation in relation to the amalgamation of the British possessions and to the possible accommodation of eastern 'separatism' in such a formula for decentralized yet co-ordinated government. He had hoped that the Free State would join this initiative for wider union, but after the Boer republic had dashed these hopes, Barkly left the project in abeyance, since he believed that the initiative for federation should come from the South African states themselves. When the incoming Secretary of State, Lord Carnarvon, attempted to force the pace towards federation in May 1875, Barkly warned him of the dangers attendant on haste.

Neglecting the warning, Carnarvon attempted to impose the policy by browbeating Molteno and by reawakening the 'separatism' issue through the agency of his historian friend, J A Froude. An imperial-colonial confrontation ensued. Though the Cape premier and Carnarvon did eventually half-bury their differences in London in 1876, the latter had already decided to work from a wider territorial base than the Cape Colony. Hence, Shepstone was sent from Natal with authority to annex the Transvaal in 1877. At the same time, Sir Bartle Frere succeeded Barkly as Governor, with the greater additional status of 'High Commissioner for South Africa'.

The legacy of Grey's settlements, drought and the increasing impact of white trade and rule, combined in 1877-1878 to produce rebellion among the Ngqika Xhosa and the last war of resistance among the Gcaleka Xhosa. Frere determined to use this crisis to push forward his major objectives. These were the establishment of a separate black province in the Transkei and Basutoland under British rule, which would serve as an additional unit in confederation, and the introduction of sufficient imperial troops to enable him to effect this settlement quickly. These troops could then be used to reduce the Zulu monarchy to impotence, thereby persuading the Cape that it could safely link up politically with Zululand's neighbours in Natal and the Transvaal. Frere's plans ran contrary to the view which Barkly and the previous British Government had encouraged Molteno to take – namely, that the Cape itself should slowly absorb the Transkei. The question of whether imperial or colonial authorities should give the orders to round off the Ninth Frontier War led to Frere's dismissal of Molteno's ministry in February in 1878. The new ministry, under Sir Gordon Sprigg, was heavily dependent on

Frere, and its paranoia over stricter frontier controls (significantly its members were from Kaffrarian and eastern constituencies) made it fall in too readily with the next step in Frere's search for confederation.

Both Frere and Sprigg believed that disarming the Transkeian chiefdoms and Basotho would make it easier to incorporate them into the planned provincial unit which was to be the 'black' building block of confederation in the south-east. Fearing for the territorial integrity of the 'reserve' that Wodehouse had guaranteed to them in 1868 the Basotho took up new rifles obtained on the diamond fields and prepared to resist disarmament to the death.

The Cape-Basotho 'Gun' War of 1880-1881 was the most successful of South Africa's black rebellions. After military stalemate had developed the British and Cape governments reluctantly agreed on dismantling colonial rule. Ultimately in 1884 the first of the Imperial High Commission Territories was established in Basutoland upon the principle of indirect rule, through chiefs, which the High Commissioner had originally developed there during the interim phase after 1868 and before the Cape annexation of 1871.

The Sprigg Cabinet of 1878. Sir John Gordon Sprigg is seated on the right. (Cory Library, Grahamstown)

Sir John Charles Molteno, first Prime Minister of the Cape Colony. (Cape Archives, J5049)

Paarl, by G F Angas. (Africana Museum)

Reverend Andrew Murray (Cape Archives, E371)

Reverend S J du Toit (Transvaal Archives)

J H ('Onze Jan') Hofmeyr (Transvaal Archives)

From political inertia to action

At the end of the Ninth Frontier War Frere had been quick to regroup his rapidly imported redcoat host and to dispatch it to its second objective, in Zululand in 1879. But here the unexpected disaster of Isandlwana demolished his proconsular reputation and authority. At the same time, the Transvaal Boers looked eagerly around for allies to help them reverse the British annexation of 1877, and were able to make common cause against confederation with Sprigg's and Frere's opponents at the Cape. In April and May of 1880 the Transvaal leaders, Kruger and Joubert, visited the Western Cape, and received a warm public welcome from the *Patriot* newspaper in Paarl. Echoing local sentiment, it demanded that things must now 'come to a head'. The politically sluggish Western Cape had thus wakened from inertia to action, and the complex reasons for this change of attitude included theological controversy and the general character of British rule.

Under the imperial dispensations of 1827 and 1853 the proceedings of colonial courts and Parliament were in English, and marked educational expansion under the able James Rose Innes as Superintendent-General (1839-1859) and as member of the Watermeyer Commission of 1861 had given English a major impact in terms of the Education Act of 1865, especially at the secondary level. For the professionally trained Cape Dutchman of the colonial metropolis this may have been bearable, but for many beyond Cape Town it was simply unacceptable.

The average Dutch- or *Taal-* ('Afrikaans'-) speaker of the countryside lived with the British colonial system, but did not love it. The gloss of English procedures and jury service complicated the familiar Roman-Dutch law, and the 'official' language was largely alien to his ear. After 1865, however, the constitution of divisional councils provided some outlet to rural political talent. For most of the Afrikaner three-quarters of the white population, who were bewildered by the ways of a colonial Parliament dominated by English rules, traditions, language and personnel, another compensation was work in the local church community and farmers' associations (*Boeren Vereenigingen*). By the late 1870s, however, frustrations which had not hitherto been acute blended with developments in Church, the *Vereenigingen* and the wider South African scene to produce the embryo of a nationally based political party at the Cape.

Partly under the impulse of the Scot, Andrew Murray, who was seven times moderator of the Dutch Reformed Church after 1862, the Cape version of the struggle in Europe between liberal reformed clergy and the strict Calvinist evangelicals had been resolved in favour of the latter. To reinforce the revivalism that spread rapidly from Murray's Worcester ministry, the Reverend G W A van der Lingen founded the Paarl Gymnasium in 1858, which in turn fed the recently established theological seminary in Stellenbosch. Shortly afterwards, Arnoldus Pannevis and C P Hoogenhout (both born in Holland) began promoting Afrikaans as a written language, with a view to translating the Bible into Afrikaans. This zeal fused with Calvinist revivalism to provide cultural inspiration to local young men, like the Reverend S J du Toit, whose attitudes were, consequently, 'modern nationalist', rather than 'patriarchal' or 'cosmopolitan'.

The *Genootskap van Regte Afrikaners* that Du Toit began in Paarl in August 1875 first concentrated on popularizing the Afrikaans of the so-called 'First Language Movement'. His propagation of an Afrikaner Bond in June 1879, the support given by the *Patriot* newspaper under the editorship of his brother Daniel (D F du Toit), and the spontaneous widespread sympathy for the Transvaal Boers during the war of 1880-1881 soon portended a pan-Afrikaner political movement across all South Africa. This did not materialize, partly due to the parallel, but not entirely complementary, activity of J H ('Onze Jan') Hofmeyr.

As editor of the *Zuid Afrikaan*, Hofmeyr had been skilfully promoting the cause of Dutch as a parliamentary medium. He was wise enough though to make his work largely supplement that of the Du Toit brothers while he extended his own political base by exploiting western resentment of Sprigg's expensive projects, such as his 'aerial railways' (the Kowie bridge, which collapsed in 1911!), and the disarmament debacles in the Transkei and Basutoland. Hofmeyr was soon establishing farmers' protection associations against the Brandy Excise by which the Sprigg ministry hoped to finance its schemes.

By June 1880 Hofmeyr's group in the Cape Parliament was able to ally with the gathering English-speaking opposition to Sprigg in order to neutralize his proposals for a conference on confederation. This veto led to Frere's immediate recall in August 1880 and the breaking of his career. The support which Kruger and Joubert had received gained momentum with their success in the War of Independence (1880-1881). Du Toit's Afrikaner Bond enjoyed a greater appeal than Hofmeyr's *Vereenigingen* for a while, but peace, and the alliance of the old Molteno group, now under T C Scanlen and John X Merriman, gave Hofmeyr the leverage to secure Dutch as a medium in Parliament in 1882. This led to Hofmeyr's participation in the composite English/Dutch-speaking government under Scanlen of March 1881, which replaced Sprigg's government. At the same time, Hofmeyr began working against the Du Toit brothers by attempting to amalgamate the farmers' movements of the east and west Cape with the Afrikaner Bond. Conferences at Graaff-Reinet, Cradock and Richmond in 1882-1883 brought them all under his influence, if not direct management.

By 1881 a more rigid political grouping in Cape politics was clear. A moderate but strong leader, Hofmeyr, led the Afrikaners. Among English-speakers, by contrast, there was a defensive move to make good the setbacks to the imperial factor in 1880-1881. But, as with the capture of the Afrikaner Bond by the moderate Hofmeyr, the colonial English did not take up an extreme position. Meanwhile the annexation of Griqualand West in 1880 introduced a northward, wealth-generating axis which helped to cancel out the outmoded attitudes of east-west 'separatism'. Embodying this dynamic was the young Cecil John Rhodes, who became Member of Parliament for Barkly West in 1881. As long as both Hofmeyr and men like Merriman and Rhodes remained relatively centrist in attitude, Cape white politics was unlikely to develop the ideological and organizational bipolarity of a rigid party system.

The Cape Colony in 1881

By 1881 the Cape was a very different place to the colony that Grey had taken over in 1854. Its frontier problems had not ended, but these now involved issues of internal regulation rather than external incorporation – indeed, the frontier had been largely 'closed'. For a while the costs of mismanagement in Basutoland induced the cry 'Sprigg, Sprigg, give us back our millions!', but this doubt and introspection soon passed. Instead the 'Native Question' began to turn on how Britains' new black subjects could be accommodated without overbalancing the Cape's 'multiracial' system against the white interest. Many blacks found themselves thrust into new market and political relationships, and their votes soon affected election results in half a dozen eastern constituencies.

The Western Cape Coloured man found his skills as a craftsman, artisan and labourer in greater demand as opportunities developed, particularly on the new railways and elsewhere along their extending tracks. On the debit side, however, the Cape Synod of the Dutch Reformed Church had infringed the colony's multiracial principle in 1857 by starting separate services for Coloureds and blacks 'because of the weakness of some'. It was an ominous portent.

For the colonial English-speaker the environment had also changed. Informative local journals like the *Cape Monthly Magazine* and up to date overseas newspapers and periodicals now supplemented his small town 'daily' or village 'weekly'. From 1872 Sir Donald Currie's Castle Line and its older confederate, the Union Line, provided a weekly travel service 'home' for the growing number who could afford it. Mere 'schools' were growing into more elaborate 'college' foundations, while tertiary education had progressed from Sir George Grey's Board of

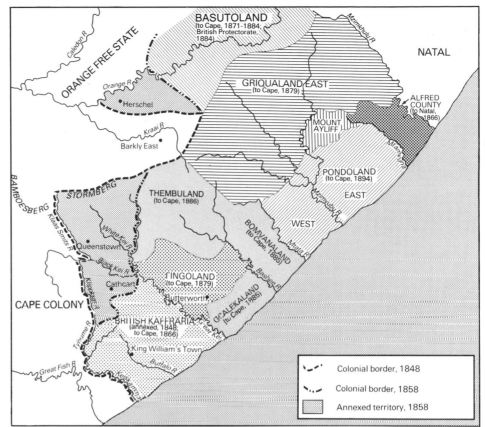

British Annexations on the Eastern Frontier, 1848-1894

Examiners of 1858 to the examining University of the Cape of Good Hope in 1873. Grey's donation of his great library on religious, ethnographic and linguistic subjects provided a further rich store to the growing resources and reputation of the South African Public Library in Cape Town. For the Dutch-speaker there was not only an increased cultural and political awareness, but also a focus for these aspirations in the 'amalgamating' Afrikaner Bond and *Vereenigingen*. Despite several negative features, the Cape was coming of age.

The ceremony of turning the first turf of the railway line from Cape Town to Wellington on 31 March 1857, by the Governor, Sir George Grey. (Cape Archives, M899)

Natal, 1854-1881

Ruth Edgecombe

Although Natal had been formally recognized as British territory in May 1843, it was only on 12 December 1845 that Martin West took the oath of office in Pietermaritzburg as the first Lieutenant-Governor with responsibility for administering the area as a district of the Cape Colony. From an economic point of view the colony was not viewed with much enthusiasm by the British Goverment.

Although coal deposits were known to have existed in the north-western corner of the colony and hopes were entertained about the possibility of cotton cultivation, humanitarian and strategic motives rather than economic reasons determined the move to annex. Proposed Voortrekker policies towards the blacks in Natal, which involved the removal and resettlement of thousands of blacks south of the Mzimkhulu River, threatened to disrupt further the already volatile Cape eastern frontier. The British also wished to deny the Voortrekkers independent access to the sea.

Land policy

Two crucial problems confronted the West administration, namely the chaotic situation arising out of Voortrekker land policies and the settlement of the large black population growing daily with the influx of refugees across the Thukela-Mzinyathi border. Throughout the 1840s large numbers of Voortrekkers left Natal for the interior. Disillusionment with British annexation was compounded by the land policies adopted. The British Government decided to recognize land titles which had been backed up by *bona fide* occupation for twelve months before the British Commissioner Sir Henry Cloete's arrival in Natal. Few Voortrekkers could meet this condition for they had found it difficult to enforce occupation of the land they claimed and had done little farming.

The Voortrekker exodus continued unabated. Some, like the farmers in the triangle between the Thukela and Mzinyathi rivers and the Drakensberg, sought escape from British rule in the declaration of the Klip River Republic in January 1847, under the overlordship of the Zulu king Mpande. Others sent Andries Pretorius to put their grievances to Sir Henry Pottinger, Governor of the Cape Colony and British High Commissioner, in Grahamstown in October 1847. Pottinger refused to see Pretorius. His successor, Sir Harry Smith, intervened by visiting Natal personally in 1848 and declaring that every man could have a farm of 6 000 acres (2 500 ha) to settle and occupy.

Notwithstanding Smith's intervention, the number of Voortrekker families in Natal declined from 400 to 60 during West's period of office. Much of the Voortrekker land passed into the hands of speculators, a process evident as early as 1843. By 1847 13 mercantile firms, most of them based in the Cape, had claim to 62 farms totalling 230 000 acres (93 000 ha), for which they had paid as little as 2d an acre. In matters of land policy, the West administration had made an inauspicious start, particularly when it is borne in mind that the total land area of Natal, after the extension of the southern boundary to the Mtamvuna River in 1866, did not embrace more than twelve million acres (five million ha) and the ruggedness of fifty per cent of Natal seriously limited the amount of land suitable for agriculture.

Policy towards black people

A second key development during the West administration was the question of the settlement of the black population on the land. In 1845 the black population was estimated to be about 100 000 as opposed to a white population of some 2 500. In 1846 West appointed a commission with the objective of carving large areas out of Natal where blacks would be settled and governed apart from whites. The commission proposed that the locations would be headed by powerful magistrates, schools would be built and attempts made to civilize the black inhabitants. However, the British Government insisted that blacks should be governed cheaply and ultimately the locations had merely to be places where blacks could live their own lives.

Initially seven locations were demarcated, of which portions were set aside as mission reserves. Subsequently, further locations and mission reserves were added so that by 1864 there were 42 locations comprising 2 067 057 acres (800 000 ha) and 21 mission reserves comprising 174 862 acres (70 700 ha).

De Kiewiet has argued that 'the history of the colony of Natal, more than that of any other colony, is the history of native policy'. Lying at the heart of 'native policy' was land policy. These two factors shaped the contours of politics, society and the economy of nineteenth-century Natal.

Theophilus Shepstone, the son of a Methodist missionary, had been appointed diplomatic agent to the black tribes in 1845, and he brought to this post his considerable experience in dealing with black affairs on the Cape eastern frontier, as well as a fluency in Xhosa and Zulu. Shepstone was not deaf to the white colonists'

calls for cheap black labour. He remitted the taxes of those who served colonial farmers in 1852 and, in terms of the Refugee Law of 1854, every black immigrant to Natal was made liable for three years' service to farmers at fixed wages. Of greater concern to him, however, was the problem of developing workable machinery for the government of blacks.

Lacking money and manpower, Shepstone was forced to rely on tribal structures for government in the locations. Where hereditary chiefs existed they were recognized, where not, he created them. Central to his policy was the notion of an all powerful 'Supreme Chief'. Such a figure did not exist in tribal society, but Shepstone invented it as a useful device for control. In law these powers were vested in the Lieutenant-Governor, in practice they were exercised by Shepstone himself as Secretary for Native Affairs, as he was designated from 1853.

Shepstone was also the administrator of a separate judicial system necessitated by the Ordinance of 1849 which abrogated Roman-Dutch law and recognized customary law as far as the black population of Natal was concerned. Theoretically customary law constituted a known body of Nguni law and custom, but prior to 1893 such law was not codified and there was no systematic knowledge of what it was before British rule. In effect, it was judge-made common law. In 1863 a black spokesman referred to such law as 'one in which the brains was the only book to which reference was made'. Such a legal system, in which there was one law for blacks and another for whites, cre-

'Mpanda reviewing his troops at Nondwengu', by G F Angas. Mpande, the half-brother of Dingane, joined forces with the Trekkers in 1839. Dingane was defeated at Magongo in February 1840, and fled north to the Lebombo mountains, where he was killed. In 1843, a year after the annexation of Natal, the British recognised Mpande as independent ruler of the territory to the north of the Thukela and east of the Mzinyathi rivers. He reigned for 32 years, becoming the only Zulu king to die peacefully in old age. (Africana Museum)

The Langalibalele 'rebellion'

The Langalibalele 'rebellion' in 1873 was the first serious crisis to threaten the Shepstone system. Langalibalele and his Hlubi followers lived on the slopes of the Drakensberg where they had been settled by Shepstone to act as a buffer against raids from the San. The Hlubi had proved remarkably adept at accommodating themselves to the white economy of Natal. After diamonds had been discovered in Griqualand West in 1869, many of Langalibalele's people found work there and came back with guns. Trouble arose when the chief failed to respond to repeated orders from the magistrate to register guns in the possession of his followers, as required by a largely ignored Natal law. When he ignored an order to report personally to Pietermaritzburg Langalibalele committed an act of rebellion against the Supreme Chief.

Langalibalele had in the meantime withdrawn into Basutoland with his cattle, possibly with the intention of going into real rebellion. The Sotho chief, Molapo, handed him over to the colonial authorities. A skirmish between his followers and the Natal Carbineers in the Bushmans River Pass left three carbineers dead, after which Natal troops moved in, killing 150 Hlubi. Langalibalele was deposed, his chiefdom broken up and Hlubi land and cattle confiscated. The neighbours of the Hlubi, the Ngwe, were similarly dealt with.

Langalibalele was tried by a special court in Pietermaritzburg in January 1874. The court included Benjamin Pine, in his office of Lieutenant-Governor, acting as Supreme Chief under Ordinance 3 of 1849, and Shepstone as Secretary for Native Affairs. Pine had declared Langalibalele an outlaw and had headed the military expedition against him. The court sentenced Langalibalele to banishment for life. Neither the court proceedings nor the sentence could be justified in terms of either British or customary law. Bishop Colenso, almost a lone voice in the colony, did much to highlight the injustice of the proceedings against Langalibalele. Certain reforms were effected by the Native Administration Bill, among them the creation of the Natal Native High Court which removed Shepstone's judicial functions.

ated severe problems of jurisdiction. These problems were resolved by making it virtually impossible for any black man in Natal to attain full British citizenship.

Black Natalians made an important contribution to the revenue of the colony. From 1849 a tax of 7s was levied on every hut. This yielded a considerable income, considering that by 1871 the black population was approaching 300 000 in a colony where the white population was estimated at between 17 000 and 18 000. In 1869 a tax of £5 was imposed on black marriages. Before the Langalibalele rebellion, revenue from blacks was sufficient to cover the costs of civil administration for the country as a whole, and only a small part of this income was devoted to black development. In 1876 the marriage tax was abolished but the hut tax was increased to 14s, in part to augment colonial revenue, and in part to force more blacks out to labour. Not only were direct taxes important. In a colony like Natal a major source of revenue was derived from duties levied on goods imported into the country. Inevitably it was the politically powerless section of the community which bore the main burden, as goods consumed by blacks were the most heavily taxed.

Land policy after 1849

The West administration's inauspicious start with land policy continued under West's successors. The speculators who had acquired the departing Voortrekkers' lands did not seriously consider seeking to make them profitable through commercial farming. Rather they sought to promote Natal as an attractive area for immigration.

Between 1849 and 1852 some 5 000 settlers came to Natal under various immigration schemes, most notably that of J C Byrne. By 1852 the settler population stood at 7 500, most of whom were of English or Scottish extraction. However, inadequate land grants, inexperience, shortage of capital and labour made it difficult for these immigrants to make a go of farming. Many drifted to the urban areas of Durban and Pietermaritzburg, or turned to trading, transport riding, hunting and woodcutting. The lands they left again fell into the hands of speculators. In 1857 Lieutenant-Governor John Scott attempted to encourage immigration through a system of assisted passages. The end result of the scheme was the introduction of fewer than 300 immigrants at the cost of alienating 1 360 000 acres (550 000 ha) of land. The Immigration Board complained in 1864 that immigration was hampered by scarcity of land.

The outbreak of war between the Orange Free State and the Basotho in 1864 precipitated a commercial crisis and depression in Natal. The economy of Natal depended heavily on the 'overberg' trade with Dutch pastoralists, the in-

terruption of which had serious consequences. In the context of the depression land values fell and the market was glutted with cheap land, which became concentrated in the hands of a few speculators. De Kiewiet has estimated that in 1874 only about four million (1 600 000 ha) of Natal's twelve million acres (4 800 000 ha) of land remained in the government's hands and yet the white population was pitifully small, a mere 18 000 or thereabouts. Just how profligate Natal was prepared to be is shown by the attempt to pass bills in 1874 proposing to surrender to the railway construction companies two-and-a-half million acres (one million ha) of the remaining waste land of the colony. In the event, Natal finally resorted to loans and increased taxation of blacks in order to finance railway construction.

An ill-conceived land policy seriously retarded the economic development of Natal. Large landholdings did not bear a reasonable share of taxation, Crown landholdings were insufficient to encourage immigration on a significant scale and a small, scattered white population in the midst of a large black population bred insecurity and a sense of weakness which to some extent explained the harsh and restrictive nature of native policy and the ferocious responses to perceived threats, whether real or imagined, of black insurrection. An estimated five million acres (two million ha) of land in the hands of companies or private individuals were occupied by black squatters who could not be accommodated in the locations. Black farmers had responded well to the challenges of the white economy and in the mid- and late nineteenth century they were the most successful producers of maize and sorghum in the colony, and were able to pay attractive rentals to their landlords. Among the foremost *rentiers*, who after 1876 received rents sometimes as high as £5 per hut, was the Natal Land and Colonisation Company.

The locations, comprising as they did the worst land in the colony, were grossly overcrowded. The situation was better on the mission reserves which had provided a favourable setting for black economic experimentation. Lutheran, Methodist and Anglican missions had purchased extensive farms at a time when land was cheap and so their land resources were sufficient to meet the needs of their converts until about 1879, although in 1880 the black Christian population was small, numbering between 8 000 and 10 000. In the 1860s the missionaries had also actively encouraged blacks to buy land on the open market, but the number who succeeded in doing this was not large. A large proportion of the black population could not be accommodated in the locations or the mission reserves and were accordingly forced to live on land to which they had no legal claim. A potentially dangerous situation could arise when this land was sold for development and the black population ejected.

Constitutional development

In 1856 the Charter of Natal separated Natal from the administrative authority of the Governor of the Cape and gave the colony a limited form of representative government. A new Legislative Council was set up, composed of sixteen members, twelve of whom were elected. The remaining four were officials – the Colonial Secretary, the Colonial Treasurer, the Attorney-General and the Secretary for Native Affairs. All males over the age of 21 who owned immovable property to the value of £50, or rented such property to the yearly value of £10, could qualify for the franchise.

In 1883 the Franchise Amendment Law gave 'lodgers' the vote. In theory there was no colour bar in the constitution but the practical possibility of there being any significant number of black voters was removed by Law 11 of 1865 which disfranchised all blacks who had not been exempted from customary law. Exempted blacks could petition for the franchise if they had been resident in Natal for twelve years and had held a letter of exemption for seven years. Even then, the petition might not be acceded to. Moreover letters of exemption were not readily granted. It is not surprising that by 1905 only three black Natalians had had the vote.

A central problem of the Natal constitution from 1856 through to 1893 was the conflict between the executive and the legislature. The reserved civil list, which included £5 000 reserved for 'native purposes', was not within the control of the Legislative Council. The representatives of the colonists attacked the native reserve fund as a point of principle. Another source of their ire was the locations policy which they believed withheld much needed black labour from them. A bitter point of contention in the first elections held in Natal in February 1857 was the Shepstone policy, and the historian Stanley Trapido has suggested that the Exemption and Native Franchise Laws had been acceded to by Lieutenant-Governor Scott to secure some sort of truce over the native reserve fund and the continued existence of Shepstone's locations.

The only way of resolving the conflict between the executive and the legislature was the granting of responsible government. Responsible government, however, entailed self-defence, which was hardly a feasible proposition given the conditions of Natal. It also entailed full colonial control over black administration, a point the imperial government was reluctant to cede. In 1870 an exploratory demand for responsible government was made and then withdrawn. In 1874 the Natal colonists again asked for responsible government. Instead, in the aftermath of the Langalibalele 'rebellion' and trial, their constitutional liberties were curtailed.

John William Colenso, bishop of Natal. (Cape Archives, M495)

The arrival of the Indians in Natal

In the late 1840s and early 1850s sugar cultivation along the coastlands of Natal was shown to be promising, but sugar demanded regular labour which was in short supply. A solution was found in indentured Indian labour, and the first Indian immigrants arrived in Durban in 1860. By 1866, 6 445 Indians had arrived, of whom two-thirds were men. They were brought to the colony on five-year contracts at agreed low minimum wages. At the end of their contracts they could choose to serve another five years, or obtain their freedom, or return to India. After ten years they would be given a free passage back to India should they so desire. The indentured Indians came mainly from Madras. Eighty per cent of them were Hindu, twelve per cent were Muslim and five per cent Christian. In 1866, with the onset of the depression, Indian immigration ceased for a time, but Indian labour had been largely responsible for the rapid growth of the sugar industry between 1854 and 1866.

When the depression was over Indian labour again came into demand but when the first Indian repatriates arrived in India in 1871 and reported the treatment they had received at the hands of colonial planters, the Indian Government forbade further recruitment. In 1872 special steps were taken to remedy such abuses as flogging and excessive pay deductions for absenteeism and a Protector of Indian Immigrants was appointed. Provision was also made for the introduction of a higher percentage of women, the registration of marriages, land grants for time-served immigrants and the dropping of the pejorative term 'coolie'.

In 1874 the first immigrants under the new conditions arrived in Natal. By 1880 the total Indian population of Natal was 12 823. Indians were subject to the laws of the colony and classed as ordinary citizens, some even qualifying for the franchise. In the late 1870s a new class of 'passenger' Indians had come to Natal, Gujurati-speaking Muslims, whose trading interests competed with those of whites. By 1886 the Indian population of Natal had risen to 29 828.

An Indian family photographed at Umzinto, Natal. (Transvaal Archives)

Sir Garnet Wolseley, sent to Natal as administrator for six months, introduced his 'Jamaica' reform in 1875, which entailed packing the Legislative Council with almost enough nominees to swamp the elected majority. The Natal colonists, with unbuilt railways and a pathological fear of the Zulu across the Thukela-Mzinyathi border, needed British credit and British regiments. Wolseley's changes were not opposed and those advocating responsible government in the elections of 1880 and 1882 were defeated. Natal finally attained responsible government in 1893.

Economic development

The extent of economic development in Natal between 1850 and 1883 can be gauged from the following figures. The general revenue of the colony in 1850 was £29 338; in 1883 it was £962 915. The value of imports by sea increased from £111 015 to £1 751 705 in this period and exports by sea from £17 109 to £831 747. While these figures indicate some degree of development it can hardly be described as spectacular.

A major factor hampering economic development was the lack of an adequate communications network. A good harbour was one of the keys to economic prosperity and 'the dangers of the anchorage and the difficulty of entering the harbour', noted by Sir George Napier in 1842, were not overcome in the nineteenth century. The bay of Natal, on which Durban was situated, was approached by a channel from the Indian Ocean. A sand bar at the entrance to this channel denied access to ships of a large tonnage which had therefore to anchor outside the bay. In 1849 John Milne began the process of conquering the bar but this was only completed in 1904.

For internal transportation the lumbering ox-wagon was relied upon. Its carrying capacity was limited to 2 t. When grazing for the oxen was plentiful in the wet summer season, the roads were quagmires and bridges were needed over the fast-flowing rivers. In the dry winter seasons 'fuelling' oxen was problematic. Epidemics of cattle disease, lung sickness and red-water sickness seriously disrupted the transport system. Because the transit trade and customs duties were such important elements in Natal's revenue, a determined effort was made to substitute steam for the ox.

Although the first ever railway line in South Africa was built to cover the 3 km between the Point and Durban in 1860, it was only in 1880 that a rail link was established between Durban and Pietermaritzburg, a distance of 80 km. The transit trade with the interior was the main objective of railway development. The mineral revolution prompted a sustained

campaign for railway construction to the interior. In order to achieve this, Natal strained her financial resources to the limit in order not to be outdistanced by the stronger Cape Colony. The rail link with Johannesburg was finally achieved in 1895. By 1889 the rail link had reached the coalfields of northern Natal, making the development of a coal industry in Natal possible.

Natal and Zululand

Shepstone, an ardent imperialist, had always been aware that the locations were ultimately inadequate for Natal's black population. This underlay his fervent expansionism in seeking additional land as a safety valve for black people and to extend British influence. In the 1850s he unsuccessfully pursued an attempt to create a 'black kingdom' south of the Mzimkhulu River controlled by him under the British flag. In the 1860s he had designs on Sotho territory and he always observed Zululand as Natal's special preserve. Events in Zululand periodically provided opportunities for his intervention.

In the early 1850s there was intense rivalry among the sons of the Zulu king, Mpande, over the succession. In December 1856, at the Battle of Ndondakusuka, Cetshwayo won a decisive victory over his main rival, Mbuyazi. However, Cetshwayo had not yet achieved the status of manhood which was necessary to become king because his father had not yet given him permission to put on the headring and marry.

His position as heir remained insecure, especially given the fact that his younger brother Mkhungo had escaped to Natal after the battle, giving both Shepstone and Mpande leverage over him. A complicating dimension was added by Boer encroachment on Zulu territory. In the late 1840s and early 1850s Mpande had allowed certain farmers to graze their stock on the upper Mzinyathi River. By the late 1850s they had be-

Cetshwayo, son of Mpande. (Cape Archives, E3248)

come firmly entrenched there, and had even begun to claim land occupied by Zulu to the east of the Ncome River. Worried about Natal's intentions with regard to Mkhungo, fearing a British invasion and sustained by Boer support, Cetshwayo decided to take action against his rivals, in particular his brother Mthonga. Mthonga escaped to the Transvaal via Natal. In March 1861 the Boers surrendered Mthonga to Cetshwayo in exchange for a land agreement, and implicitly recognized Cetshwayo as heir.

In May 1861 Shepstone embarked on his first visit to the Zulu court in order to give British recognition of Cetshwayo as heir. Shepstone had designs on the sparsely settled borderlands of the Zulu kingdom, both as an outlet for Natal's rapidly expanding black population and to serve as a buffer against Boer attempts to reach the sea. Although Shepstone's mission ended

The Battle of Isandlwana

The first serious battle in the Anglo-Zulu War was fought at the eastern base of Isandlwana Mountain, where a temporary camp had been established by the Centre Column.

Just before dawn on 22 January 1879 Colonel Glyn, the leader of the Centre Column, and Lord Chelmsford, the Commander of the British army in Zululand, left the camp with a large force. Unbeknown to them, the main Zulu army of some 20 000 warriors had, on the previous day, taken up position in the valley north of the Nquthu ridge, 5 km away.

Colonel H Pulleine had been left in charge of the camp at Isandlwana, with about 1 774 men. At 08h00 reports were received of large numbers of Zulu approaching the camp from the north-west. At 10h30 Colonel A W Durnford and about 500 men arrived from Rorke's Drift. Shortly afterwards Captain Shepstone was sent with mounted troops to clear the Zulu from the high ground above the camp, and his men accidentally encountered the main Zulu army behind the Nquthu ridge.

This discovery provoked the Zulu forces, deployed in the traditional crescent formation. Shepstone, Durnford and their troops stalled the attack of the Zulu centre with volley fire. The Zulu resumed their attack at 13h00 and organized resistance ended about an hour later. A Zulu combatant subsequently described the scene: 'Some covered their faces with their hands, not wishing to see death. Others ran away. Some entered into the tents. Others were indignant, although badly wounded they died where they stood, at their post.'

A number of men fled and tried to cross the flooded Buffalo River at a point called Fugitives' Drift. About forty men escaped, but among the dead were Lieutenants N Coghill and T Melville who had tried to save the colours of the 24th Regiment. They were subsequently awarded the VC posthumously. On the British side, 52 officers, 806 white troopers and 471 black troopers perished, and Zulu losses exceeded 1 000 men. The battle was a Pyrrhic victory for Cetshwayo, and led to the British and colonial desire for revenge.

The Battle of Isandlwana, by C E Fripp. (National Army Museum, London)

Dinuzulu, son of Cetshwayo. (Transvaal Archives)

Rorke's Drift

When the Centre Column of the British army crossed the Buffalo River into Zululand, troops under Lieutenant John Chard of the Royal Engineers were left to guard the post at Rorke's Drift, which consisted of a Swedish mission church and a house converted into a storehouse and hospital.

At 15h15 on 22 January news of the disaster at Isandlwana reached Rorke's Drift. Even more alarming was the report that a large Zulu force was approaching Rorke's Drift at speed. Lieutenant Chard, with patients in his care, made the only possible decision under the circumstances – the garrison must stand and defend itself. A defensive perimeter of mealie bags, biscuit tins and wagons was constructed round the mission buildings.

Soon after 16h00 a Zulu force of some 3 000 to 4 000 warriors appeared. They had been without proper supplies for several days, and had had to cross the flooded Buffalo River by forming human chains. In the meantime, the Natal Native Contingent, both mounted and infantry, fled, leaving 8 British officers and 131 men, of whom 35 were sick, to try and hold the post. Chard had to reduce the perimeter and began building a line of biscuit boxes across the enclosure. This task was incomplete when the attack began at about 16h30. The Zulu attack was contrary to Cetshwayo's explicit instructions not to invade British territory because he was fighting essentially a defensive war against the British invasion of his kingdom.

One furious Zulu charge after another was launched, often resulting in hand to hand combat across the barricades. The British defenders withdrew from the hospital to behind the incomplete line of biscuit boxes at about 18h00, and then to within a 're-doubt' constructed of mealie bags. The Zulu attack continued until dawn. That terrible late afternoon and night left seventeen British defenders dead and one officer and five men wounded. Zulu losses were estimated at a minimum of 500 dead. Eleven VCs were awarded to the defenders.

The relief troops arriving after the Battle of Rorke's Drift, by M E Newman. (Local History Museum, Durban)

inconclusively, Mpande was pressured into recognizing Cetshwayo as his heir. Mpande continued to play the Transvaal and Natal off against Cetshwayo and sought missionary support to bolster his own position. Cetshwayo in turn allied with white traders from Natal, prominent among whom was John Dunn who became a key adviser in his dealings with the Natal Government and settlers. Through John Dunn, Cetshwayo acquired firearms so that by the early 1870s several hundred of his followers had guns. In 1867 Mpande finally gave Cetshwayo permission to marry and in the following year his son, Dinuzulu, was born.

Using the 1861 agreement as a basis for further land claims, the Boers began beaconing off a boundary in 1864. Cetshwayo appealed to Natal for help and continued to do so on many occasions. By the late 1860s he was willing to cede a buffer strip of land but the British Government prevented Shepstone from taking up the offer. When Mpande died in October 1872, Cetshwayo's position was threatened by five brothers living either in Natal or the Transvaal. Two of these, Mkhungo and Mthonga, who had again escaped to the Transvaal in 1865, were actively plotting against him. Cetshwayo sent a major embassy to Pietermaritzburg seeking assistance. Shepstone responded with alacrity to the opportunity of expanding British influence in the Zulu kingdom, which in turn opened up the vista of British domination of all the independent black-ruled states in south-east Africa. In August-September 1873 Shepstone 'crowned' Cetshwayo as king of the Zulu.

Events leading to war in 1879

By the middle of the 1870s the land dispute with the Transvaal became acute. Cetshwayo continued to appeal to Natal. Shepstone tended to sympathize with the Zulu because Boer encroachments posed a threat to the extension of British influence beyond the northern frontier of Natal. The annexation of the Transvaal in April 1877 abruptly changed Shepstone's perspective. In the words of a colonial official, he 'turned his coat in the most shameless manner'. With the Transvaal as British territory the Zulu now became the aggressors. A conference between Shepstone and a Zulu delegation in October 1877 failed to resolve the issue. From this point onwards war with the Zulu seemed inevitable.

In 1877 Sir Bartle Frere had arrived in South Africa as British High Commissioner with the specific objective of carrying out Carnarvon's confederation policy. In order to prepare the way for the subjugation of the Zulu as a means of furthering that policy, Frere, with Shepstone's assistance, set about depicting Cetshwayo as a bloodthirsty despot and the Zulu nation as a threat to security in the region. The killing of three Christian converts early in 1877 and the departure of missionaries from Zululand in 1878 served as grist to the propaganda mill. Bulwer, the Lieutenant-Governor of Natal, was, on the other hand, anxious to avoid war. In December 1877 he made an offer to Cetshwayo to mediate in the land dispute. A boundary commission was appointed in March 1878 and reported to Bulwer in the following June. Frere received the report in July. Although the main Boer claims were rejected, Frere was not deterred and withheld publication of the report.

Lieutenant-General Thesiger, who later became Lord Chelmsford, was sent to Natal in July 1878 to plan the invasion of Zululand. This was followed by a large build-up of troops in the colony. On 11 December 1878 a meeting of British and Zulu delegations took place on the banks of the lower Thukela. The findings of the boundary commission were made known but the Zulu were only granted title to the land. The Boers were to be left in occupation of the disputed territory. Cetshwayo was presented

with an ultimatum which had to be answered within thirty days. Those guilty of recent border violations had to be handed over to the Natal authorities and fines in cattle paid. Missionaries were to be allowed to resume their work unhindered in Zululand. Open and fair trials had to be conducted. Most important of all, and a condition which Cetshwayo could not accede to because it would destroy the very basis of the power he exercised over his subjects, age-regiments had to be abandoned and his subjects allowed to marry without his permission.

The Anglo-Zulu War, 1879

Zululand was invaded on 11 January 1879. Cetshwayo tried to adopt an essentially defensive strategy, but the humiliating defeat of the British at Isandlwana on 22 January and the battle at Rorke's Drift the following day, which saw Zulu warriors actually treading on Natal soil, ruined his strategy. From the British perspective there could be nothing less than total victory. Late in May 1879 the second and final invasion of Zululand took place. On 28 May Wolseley was appointed Governor of Natal and the Transvaal, High Commissioner in the adjacent territories and Commander-in-Chief of the forces in the field. Cetshwayo was captured and while he was being escorted into exile, the Zulu accepted the terms of peace imposed by the British. Initially there was to be no annexation. While the Zulu retained their independence, the Zulu monarchy was to be suppressed, and a balance of antagonistic forces created in which no one particular segment would be allowed to become dominant. Far from there being peace in Zululand, the country was soon torn asunder by civil war. Cetshwayo was restored in 1883 but under such unfavourable conditions that strife was exacerbated. He died the following year. The British Government finally annexed Zululand in 1887 and ten years later handed the territory over to Natal. By the Zululand Lands Delimitation Commission of 1903-1904, Zululand was carved up into areas for black and white settlement.

Suggested Reading List

THE CAPE

J Benyon (1980) *Proconsul and Paramountcy in South Africa. The High Commission, British Supremacy and the Sub-continent, 1806-1910*, Pietermaritzburg

T R H Davenport (1966) *The Afrikaner Bond. The History of a South African Political Party, 1880-1911*, Cape Town

C W de Kiewiet (1937) *The Imperial Factor in South Africa. A Study in Politics and Economics*, Cambridge

R D Edgecombe (1978) 'The Non-Racial Franchise in Cape Politics, 1853-1910', *Kleio*, Vol 10, June 1978

J L MacCracken (1967) *The Cape Parliament, 1854-1910*, Oxford

S Trapido (1964) 'The Origins of the Cape Franchise Qualifications of 1853', *Journal of African History*, Vol I

NATAL

E H Brookes and C de B Webb (1965) *A History of Natal*, Pietermaritzburg

A Duminy and C Ballard (1981) *The Anglo-Zulu War – New Perspectives*, Pietermaritzburg

R D Edgecombe (ed) (1982) *Bringing Forth Light. Five Tracts on Bishop Colenso and Missions*, Pietermaritzburg

P Welsh (1971) *The Roots of Segregation. Native Policy in Natal, 1845-1910*, Cape Town

J Wright and A Manson (1983) *The Hlubi Chiefdom in Zululand-Natal – A History*, Ladysmith

179

A Boer gun in action at the Siege of
Ladysmith during the Anglo-Boer War of
1899-1902, as depicted by Sylvester
Reisacher. (National Cultural History and
Open-air Museum)

Part V

The Political Restructuring of South Africa, 1881-1910

Less than twenty years after the diamond finds, the world's richest goldfield was discovered along the Witwatersrand on the Transvaal highveld. The consequent enhanced prosperity, large-scale immigration and increased industrialization and urbanisation altered economic and social structures and reshaped political issues. Capitalism became a potent factor in the affairs of the sub-continent.

The discovery of gold transmuted Anglo-Boer relations. The confrontation between Afrikaner republicanism and the new British imperialism – essentially a struggle for political and economic supremacy – dominated the South African scene during the last decade of the nineteenth century.

The outbreak of the Anglo-Boer War in October 1899 inaugurated the closest approximation to total war which South Africa had experienced since the Mfecane/Difaqane. The devastating conflict, which raged for nearly three years, started as a quarrel between white people about exercising power but developed into a truly South African War, which had a profound effect on all the inhabitants of the region. Moreover it had a considerable impact on international relations.

The Boer defeat ended a chapter of republican independence, and the establishment of British supremacy in South Africa became possible, although Afrikaner nationalism had not been crushed. Black, Coloured and Indian expectations of advancement as a corollary to the British victory were not realized. The white rulers of the reconstructed former republics and those of the older British colonies in South Africa consolidated their economic and political interests in a unitary state.

Mining operations at Komatipoort, on
the Transvaal-Mozambique border,
where gold was discovered in 1885.
(Barnett collection, *The Star*)

Chapter 13

Prelude to the Anglo-Boer War, 1881-1899

A M Grundlingh

Although the outcome of the War of Independence (1880-1881) was favourable for the Transvaalers, this certainly did not mean that they were entirely free from British domination. In fact, the next few years were to be characterized by fluctuating yet steadily increasing tension between Britain and the Transvaal. At the same time the discovery of gold on the Witwatersrand in 1886 was to have an important and even decisive effect on this relationship.

The settlement of 1881

On the diplomatic level, relations between the Transvaal and Britain were inaugurated with the Pretoria Convention of 1881. Although the British annexation of the Transvaal was revoked and self-government was granted, the Transvaal was regarded as a British suzerainty and a series of accompanying conditions prevented this state from acting independently in all respects. To the Transvaalers this was an unacceptable state of affairs and in 1883 a delegation consisting of General N J Smit, the Rev. S J du Toit and the newly elected President Paul Kruger left for London to consult with the British Government on possible amendments to the Pretoria Convention. Although the demands of the Transvaal delegation were not all acceded to – for example the Transvaal was not allowed to conclude treaties with any other states except the Orange Free State without British approval, and it was not allowed to expand westwards without hindrance – the signing of the London Convention in 1884 meant that the Transvaal would again in future be known as the South African Republic (SAR) and would for all practical purposes be virtually independent. As the tension between the SAR and Britain mounted during the 1890s, however, the suzerainty issue was reopened. The British Colonial Secretary, Joseph Chamberlain, argued, erroneously, on a technical point that the British suzerainty over the Transvaal had not been fully relinquished. His argument was politically inspired and had no validity in law; in fact, he merely used it as a pretext to intervene in the affairs of the Transvaal both at home and abroad.

In the early 1880s the other states and colo-

Albert Grundlingh is a senior lecturer in the Department of History at the University of South Africa. His publications include a monograph, *Die Hendsoppers en Joiners* (Cape Town, 1979), on the collaborators in Afrikaner society during the Anglo-Boer War of 1899-1902, and a chapter in a social history of the Anglo-Boer War by P Warwick and S B Spies (eds), *The South African War, 1899-1902* (London, 1980).

A public sale on Church Square, Pretoria, in the 1890s. (National Cultural History and Open-air Museum (NCHOM))

An early photograph of Pilgrim's Rest, where gold was discovered in 1873. The creek on the left in the photograph yielded alluvial gold to the value of over R3 million to the diggers. The goldfield was first discovered by Alec ('Wheelbarrow') Patterson, who kept the knowledge of the find to himself. His monopoly was short-lived, as William Trafford came to the area, and registered his claims in September 1873, thus starting the goldrush to South Africa's first payable goldfield. (NCHOM)

The discovery of gold

Gold, the precious metal which captured the imagination of the world, inspired fortune-hunters in the nineteenth century to search tirelessly in three continents for elusive wealth. In the Transvaal, as early as the 1850s, there were already persistent rumours of gold strikes, and in 1853 the Volksraad appointed P J Marais, with experience from the Californian and Australian goldfields, as official prospector. Marais found a little alluvial gold in the Jukskei River, the first discovery of gold in the vicinity of the Witwatersrand.

Gold fever hit the Transvaal in the 1870s, when gold was found on the farm Eersteling near Pietersburg in 1871. This was followed by discoveries in the eastern Transvaal at Lydenburg, Pilgrim's Rest and De Kaap. The War of Independence (1880-1881) brought prospecting to a temporary halt, but after the war S J Minnaar found payable quantities of gold on the farm Kromdraai, approximately 15 km north of Krugersdorp, and in 1885 the farm was declared an open digging. Certain geological features apparent at Kromdraai resulted in other parts of the Witwatersrand coming under observation, especially the area south-east of Kromdraai, where the brothers H W and F P T Struben had begun large-scale prospecting in 1883. In 1884 the Strubens found a promising reef which they named the 'Confidence Reef', but their discovery did not fulfil its initial promise. Nevertheless it attracted hordes of gold-seekers to the Witwatersrand, and before the end of 1886 the epoch-making discovery of the richest goldfields in the world was made.

'Bound for the goldfields', 1894. (Africana Museum)

184

nies in South Africa were also affected by relations between the Transvaal and Britain. The possibility of an overarching and broadly based Afrikaner nationalism, which included Afrikaners in the Transvaal as well as in the Free State and Cape Colony, was mooted for the first time in 1881. The Transvaalers' struggle against British imperialism, as symbolized by the War of Independence, became the focal point of a rapidly burgeoning national consciousness. The Free State Afrikaners identified themselves to a great degree with the resistance movement of the Transvaalers, while Afrikaners in the Cape Colony displayed a similar reaction which found expression in greater support for the Afrikaner Bond. In the predominantly English-speaking Natal the awakening Afrikaner nationalism was regarded with increasing suspicion as a threat to British supremacy and the future of Natal as a British colony. These developments which ensued after the War of Independence were, however, given a completely new dimension by the epoch-making discovery of gold on the Witwatersrand in 1886.

Gold and change

Although gold had been mined since the 1870s, particularly in the eastern Transvaal, it was only on a small scale and in 1885 contributed a mere 0,03 per cent to total world production. After the discovery of the exceptionally rich gold deposits on the Witwatersrand in 1886, the SAR developed into the single biggest gold producer in the world, with a contribution of 27,5 per cent in 1898. From the financial point of view, for the Transvaal Government this find came at an opportune moment. Whereas the republic had eked out a precarious existence prior to 1886, the future now seemed bright. The state revenue grew from approximately £200 000 in 1885-1886 to £1,5 million three years later. In addition, the importance of gold in the international monetary system had increased rapidly

by the end of the nineteenth century and had placed the SAR in an even stronger position. Naturally the surrounding states and colonies also stood to gain economically from the discovery of gold, and the Cape railways and harbours in particular benefited from it. At the same time the Cape Colony relinquished its position as the leading economic state in South Africa and the centre of gravity shifted to the Transvaal. This change meant that a British colony had been surpassed in the economic sphere by a Boer republic and this would contribute to the bitter political struggle which unfolded during the last decade of the nineteenth century.

The Transvaal gold mines were the richest in the world, but also the most difficult to work. The extensive gold-bearing reef lay hundreds of metres deep and the gold content of the ore was exceptionally low. It soon became apparent that individual diggers were not equal to the task of mining it and that the wealth could only be recovered by means of deep-shaft working and by capital-intensive companies having the necessary technical skills. Wealthy businessmen like

Cecil John Rhodes and Barney Barnato, who had already made a fortune on the diamond fields, now made their way to the Witwatersrand where they poured considerable sums of money into the gold-mining industry. At the same time overseas capital, primarily from Britain and America but also to a lesser extent from Germany and France, was invested in the gold mines. The independent digger had a short-lived existence on the Rand; the Gold Law of 1886 not only gave the state political control of the goldfields, but also, from the viewpoint of the capitalist, simplified the process of amalgamation legally and administratively. The amalgamation of smaller mining groups was a common occurrence and by 1895 the scene was dominated by a limited number of large monopolistic companies. These companies were: the Wernher-Beit-Eckstein group, Consolidated Goldfields, the Barnato group, the J B Robinson group, the S Neumann group, the Albu group, the A Goerz group, the Anglo-French group, and the Lewis-Marks group. Of these, Rhodes's Consolidated Goldfields group was the most important.

The nature of the Witwatersrand gold mines, and particularly the low grade of the ore, meant that the cost structure had to be meticulously planned, and that owing to the fixed gold price the industry could only be profitable if production costs could be reduced to a minimum. One important way of economizing was to keep the labour costs as low as possible. The establishment of a cheap, servile labour force was consequently a priority for the mining magnates. To a large extent the foundation for the struggle between capital and labour in South Africa was laid on the Witwatersrand, in conjunction with the labour situation on the diamond fields of Griqualand West. From the mines the demand for labour also spread to other sectors of the economy. Roads and railways lines had to be built, harbours in the coastal colonies had to be

enlarged and new buildings had to be erected. The establishment of new markets in the goldfields also led to increased agricultural production and heavier demand for farm labour. In addition an increasing number of manufacturing industries, related to the mining industry, required labour.

To the black communities in southern Africa these developments meant a considerable disruption of their existing socio-economic structure. Numerous independent black peasant farmers were compelled to become migrant labourers, which in the long run prejudiced the self-sufficiency and political power of these communities.

The social consequences of industrialization which followed upon the discovery of gold also left their mark on the white farming population. Many of them were not fully able to escape the consequences of the new capitalistic order, with its radical transformation of social patterns. Certain impoverished Afrikaners eventually found themselves in Johannesburg, the city of gold, where they formed part of the lower white

Sheba Mine, Barberton. The enormously rich Sheba Reef was discovered by Edwin Bray in 1885, and was said to be 'not gold in rock. . . simply a bit of rock encased in solid gold'. The mining town of Eureka, now in ruins, was built near the Sheba Mine. (Barnett Collection)

'Struben's camp at Wilgespruit', by Edith Mary Struben, the sixteen-year-old daughter of Hendrik Wilhelm Struben, in 1885. (Africana Museum)

The Witwatersrand Main Reef. The shallow trench runs along the outcrop from which the first miners recovered gold. The logs of wood were used to support the vertical walls of the trench, and the openings to an incline shaft can be seen in the foreground. (Transvaal Archives)

An incline shaft at Simmer & Jack Gold-Mining Company, photographed by the Swiss, H F Gros, whose unique pictures have become valuable items of Africana. Gros toured the Transvaal, photographing on site wherever possible, and produced a number of books, of which *Pictorial Description of the Transvaal* is one. (Transvaal Archives)

working class. As the historian C van Onselen has recently indicated, some of the men turned to the manufacture of bricks and all kinds of transport work, and it was not long before girls from some poverty-stricken Afrikaner homes were caught up in the extensive network of prostitution on the Witwatersrand.

To the Kruger government the changes which accompanied the discovery of gold were obviously not an unmixed blessing. From Britain, America, Australia and Eastern Europe, as well as the Cape Colony and Natal, skilled mine workers, businessmen and professional persons flocked to the Rand. The precise number of 'Uitlanders', as these persons were called, is not known since a census of all the republic's inhabitants was never taken. Nevertheless, a strong possibility existed that the male Uitlanders would soon exceed the male Afrikaner population of the Transvaal. Between the Uitlanders from Britain in particular and the rural Boer population there were distinct cultural and political differences. In time these differences would lead to friction that would increase in intensity as Britain displayed a growing interest in the Transvaal.

Both the issue of the franchise for Uitlanders and the administration of the Transvaal aroused a great deal of criticism. The republican machinery of state was primarily geared to meeting the needs of a pastoral-agricultural community and after the discovery of gold the necessary manpower and skill to administer a rapidly growing industrial community effectively was lacking. In addition specific weaknesses in the administration – primarily nepotism through which *'zoonen des lands'* (sons of the land) sometimes obtained positions for which they were ill-equipped, as well as the corruptibility of certain officials – further aggravated the situation. To the mining magnates it was unacceptable that a rich, developing industry should, according to their judgment, be hampered by inefficient administration. What upset them

particularly was that the prices and quality of essential goods for the mining industry were adversely affected by the government's system of concessions, which was in reality a series of state-controlled monopolies. For example, the water supply of Johannesburg, the manufacture and distribution of liquor and dynamite, as well as the construction of railway lines, were all in monopolistic hands. This situation meant *inter alia* that the mining magnates, owing to the lack of competition, were committed to paying fixed prices for goods of a specific quality and that the mining industry could not bargain for items on the open market.

Kruger, on the other hand, regarded the concession system as an important means of strengthening the position of the government. His strategy was to acquire capitalistic allies as a counter-balance to the power of the hostile mining magnates in Johannesburg, allies which were dependent for their welfare on the concession system and on whom the SAR could therefore rely.

The Uitlander leaders' dissatisfaction with the Transvaal Government assumed greater proportions in the 1890s and as early as 1892 it

found expression in the Transvaal National Union (TNU). On behalf of this organization Advocate Charles Leonard, one of the Uitlander leaders, published an extensive series of grievances in 1895 which placed the Kruger government in an extremely negative light. Although the grievances were mostly of an economic nature, political and cultural considerations also played a part as demonstration of the 'total' suppression which the Uitlanders, according to the TNU, had to endure. It is an open question how representative the TNU really was. There were profound differences in the Uitlander community between the capitalists on the one hand and the working classes on the other, and even the interests of the capitalistic group did not always coincide.

The important point, however, is that the Uitlander leaders were able to place the Kruger government under pressure through organizations such as the TNU, and eventually their grievances were expanded into a central political issue between the South African Republic and Great Britain. The discovery of gold, therefore, not only brought about a reorientation of the internal political and socio-economic order, but in the 1890s it would also bring relations with Great Britain to breaking point.

Rhodes, Kruger and Britain up to 1895

Although it may justifiably be argued that conflicting material interests lay at the root of the struggle between Great Britain and the South African Republic, it is undoubtedly also true that these tensions were intensified by the personal differences, fears and ambitions of the leading figures. Cecil John Rhodes and Paul Kruger in particular were poles apart. Rhodes, who was to become premier of the Cape Colony in 1890, had made his millions on the diamond fields and was inspired with an imperial vision for South Africa. Kruger, on the other hand, as

Shaft sinking on the Witwatersrand. The importance of black labour to the diggers is strikingly illustrated in this photograph. (NCHOM)

President of the SAR, was not similarly obsessed with the power of money, and apart from the preservation of republican independence, he cherished no grandiose ideals of Afrikaner domination. In practice these divergent schools of thought manifested themselves in Rhodes's attempt to encircle the SAR with British territory, while Kruger tried to confirm his independence through attempts to obtain a harbour for his republic.

Rhodes was concerned about the possible disturbance of the balance of power between the republics and the British colonies in South Africa if the SAR were to expand. He was convinced that a strong SAR would constitute a threat to British supremacy. In his opinion this would apply particularly if the republic were to obtain access to the sea, since this could arouse the interest of other colonial powers in the South African coast. Here Rhodes had Germany, which had already shown an interest in St Lucia Bay, constantly in mind. A harbour of its own for the SAR could also seriously prejudice the economy of the British colonies, which relied heavily on their import trade with the SAR after the discovery of gold. The encircle-

Cecil John Rhodes (Cape Archives, E2846)

President Paul Kruger (Barnett Collection)

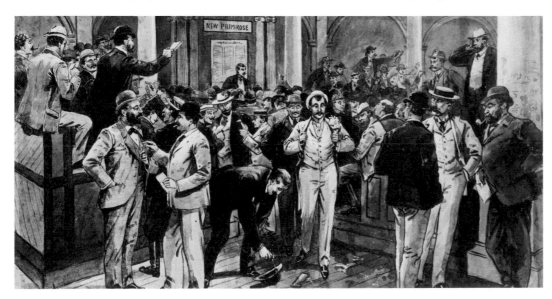

'High Change' at the Johannesburg Stock Exchange in 1895, by Melton Prior, English journalist and war artist of the *Illustrated London News*. (Africana Museum)

Tswana kings Bathoen of the Ngwaketse, Sebele of the Kwena and Khama of the Ngwato travelled to London in 1895, to protest to Chamberlain in person about Rhodes's attempts to incorporate British Bechuanaland into the Cape Colony, and to transfer the Bechuanaland Protectorate to British South Africa Company administration. They toured major British cities, receiving strong public support for their cause and managed to preserve the two areas from incorporation. They were, however, compelled to surrender their eastern frontiers to the imperial government as a railway strip in compensation. (Cory Library, Grahamstown)

ment policy was therefore aimed at reinforcing supreme British authority in South Africa, protecting the political and economic interests of the British colonies and preventing Germany from obtaining a sphere of influence in South Africa.

Rhodes preferred to act independently of the British Government in the implementation of his policy. He wanted to promote the interests of the British Empire from the colonies themselves, without the intervention of London. He was opposed to poorly informed British statesmen, who were frequently in charge of affairs for a certain period only, having to carry out the important task of establishing a united South Africa under the British flag. He was sure that such persons frequently did more harm than good, and therefore wanted the Cape Colony to play the leading role in his plans for the expansion of British authority in South Africa.

Rhodes was undoubtedly in a favourable position to ensure that these grandiose plans did not remain mere dreams. In addition to his tremendous capital power, which stemmed from almost full control over the diamond trade in

and outside South Africa and his interests in the Witwatersrand goldfields, he gradually acquired formal political power as well. In 1881 he became the Member of Parliament for Barkly West. At the same time he gained a measure of control over the press, and his political ideas were proclaimed over a wider front. He also concentrated on canvassing the support of the Cape Afrikaner Bond. He was shrewd enough to realize that the support of this political organization would be of great value in the execution of his plans. This policy indeed bore fruit and in 1890, with the help of the Afrikaner Bond, Rhodes became Prime Minister of the Cape Colony.

At first glance, co-operation between Rhodes and the Afrikaner Bond might appear strange. Rhodes was after all the arch-imperialist who had shown little sympathy for Afrikaner aspirations, while the Bond had originated in the awakening Afrikaner nationalism which followed upon the War of Independence. For J H Hofmeyr, leader of the Afrikaner Bond, however, co-operation with Rhodes was not all that unnatural. Hofmeyr was opposed to political trends which divided the white population and he was of the opinion that interference from the imperial government was in fact conducive to such division – a premise which was in line with Rhodes's feeling that the Cape Colony itself, and not the imperial power, should take the initiative in South Africa. Hofmeyr and Rhodes also shared an aspiration for a united, self-governing South Africa, which for Rhodes, inevitably, and for Hofmeyr, of necessity, would occur under a British flag. Hofmeyr was convinced that political confrontation with Britain would be senseless and even disastrous, and that political realities required a certain measure of co-operation with Britain. In addition, Rhodes's powerful development of the Cape economy, and in particular the promotion of agriculture, met with the approval of the Cape Afrikaners, while Rhodes and the Bond were also able to reach agreement on the raising of voters' qualifications, making it more difficult for blacks to obtain the franchise in the colony. In this way, therefore, Rhodes created a sturdy platform for his more ambitious plans.

Even before Rhodes became premier at the Cape he had already succeeded in resisting republican expansion. In this connection disturbances on the western frontier of the SAR (Bechuanaland) during the period 1882-1884 afforded him an excellent opportunity. A number of white volunteers had participated in the disputes between four black chiefs in the area, and from the lands with which the volunteers were rewarded, the petty republics of Goshen (1882) and Stellaland (1883) arose. The unrest continued, however, and the SAR thought that the solution lay in bringing the pro-Transvaal chiefs, Moshette and Massouw, under republican authority. At the same time it was also hoped to incorporate Stellaland and Goshen and by so doing hold the door open for further westward expansion. Rhodes saw in this the danger of an understanding arising between the Germans in South West Africa and the Boers in the Transvaal. He was also afraid that the trade route to the north would be endangered. With the help of Sir Hercules Robinson, the British High Commissioner, Rhodes succeeded in persuading the imperial government of the desirability of bringing Bechuanaland under British control. In 1884 Sir Charles Warren, with a force of 4 000 men, annexed Stellaland and Goshen and in 1885 the entire area south of the Molopo River was brought under direct British control, while the remainder of Bechuanaland was administered as a protectorate. In this way SAR expansion to the west was blocked.

Any expansionist plans to the north which the SAR might have nurtured were also thwarted when Rhodes's British South Africa Company obtained a charter in October 1889, giving it full financial and administrative responsibility over Matabeleland and Mashonaland. By this step Rhodes's company retained this territory for Britain without any financial contribution by the imperial government. Kruger was prepared to relinquish Transvaal claims to the north voluntarily in exchange for a route to the sea through Swaziland and Amatongaland to Kosi Bay. This was one of Kruger's greatest political blunders because the London Convention (1884) had placed no restriction on Transvaal expansion to the north, while expansion to other territories could take place only with the approval of the British Government.

Britain took similar action when it appeared as though St Lucia Bay in the east might fall into Transvaal or German hands. Rhodes was not directly involved in these developments, but the actions of the British Government nevertheless met with his approval. The SAR could possibly have acquired St Lucia Bay as a harbour through the New Republic (which was established in 1884 from the lands which Boer volunteers received from Dinuzulu after they had helped him to defeat his rival Usibepu). Germany, too, had displayed a sustained and

lively interest in St Lucia Bay. Before the SAR or Germany could take any actual steps, however, Britain forestalled them and annexed this bay in 1885.

Attempts made by the SAR to obtain Kosi Bay through the mediation of Swaziland and Amatongaland were also thwarted. During the late 1880s Swaziland was in turmoil, primarily as a result of the influx of white adventurers. It was clear that either the Transvaal or Britain would have to accept responsibility for law and order in the territory. Under these circumstances Kruger began to negotiate with the British on the expansion of SAR authority over Swaziland. Between 1890 and 1894 three conventions were held before a final decision was reached on the Swaziland issue. Natal interests and the danger of closer relations between the Transvaal and Germany were decisive factors in the British diplomacy which deprived the SAR of its last hope of obtaining its own harbour.

When it seemed possible that the SAR might gain possession of Kosi Bay, the Natal Government protested vehemently. They were afraid that a harbour north of Durban could seriously prejudice their trade with the Witwatersrand. Similarly, the growing friendship between Germany and the Transvaal and the renewed interest of Germany in the South African coast loaded the scales even more heavily against the Transvaal. Although the SAR, at the third convention, acquired the right to extend its jurisdiction over Swaziland, the republic was disillusioned when Britain shortly afterwards (in 1895) annexed the Trans-Pongola area and proclaimed a protectorate over Amatongaland.

By depriving the SAR of expansion possibilities to the east, British encirclement of the republic had been completed, but the policy had not been entirely successful. Rhodes realized that Delagoa Bay afforded the Transvaal an opportunity of acquiring a non-British harbour, and for this reason he made a number of unsuccessful attempts to gain control of Delagoa Bay. In 1894 the railway line between Pretoria and the Portuguese harbour was complete, and the republic had at last acquired its route to the sea. Admittedly Rhodes had denied the Trans-

The Transvaal delegates, P J Joubert and S J P Kruger, at the opening of the Natal-Transvaal railway at Charlestown. Seated between Joubert and Kruger is Sir Charles Mitchell, the Governor of Natal. (Cape Archives, E3139)

Pitsani, in Bechuanaland, from where Dr Jameson launched his raid on the Transvaal in December 1895. (Barnett Collection)

▷▷
Kit inspection for Jameson's men. (Barnett Collection)

▷
Dr Leander Starr Jameson (Cape Archives, J4737)

The failure of the Jameson Raid

The arrangements for the overthrow of the republican government were ill-conceived and the Jameson raid ended in a virtual fiasco. While Jameson waited impatiently on the Transvaal border, the Uitlander leaders on the Rand differed among themselves and with Rhodes on the nature of the government which would be instituted after the envisaged *coup*. Furthermore the run-of-the-mill Uitlanders did not have much enthusiasm for violent action and on the eve of 1896 they were in a mood to celebrate the new year rather than participate in a revolution.

Under these circumstances Rhodes decided to call off the invasion, but Jameson had already crossed the Transvaal border. To the Kruger government the invasion did not come as much of a surprise; Jameson's troops, which on the night of 29 December were supposed to put the telegraph link with Pretoria out of commission, cut the wrong wires, with the result that the SAR Government was already aware of the invasion force the next morning, before Jameson could reach Johannesburg. On 2 January 1896 the republican force was able, without difficulty, to compel Jameson and his men to surrender at Doornkop, near Krugersdorp.

The SAR handed Jameson and his cohorts over to the imperial government, and the Uitlander leaders in Johannesburg were imprisoned and tried. Some of the principal leaders were condemned to death, but these sentences were mitigated to fines of £25 000 each. In Britain a parliamentary commission of inquiry exonerated Chamberlain from complicity in the incident, but there is no doubt that the commission, on which Chamberlain himself served, glossed over the facts.

---

vaal a republican harbour of its own, but he could not succeed in making the SAR fully dependent on the British harbours, thus gradually forcing the republic into the British camp. To place the republic directly under a British sphere of influence and to bring about a British federation, other plans had to be devised.

The Jameson Raid

By 1895 conditions in Britain had become increasingly favourable for more forceful action in South Africa when the Unionist government of Lord Salisbury came into office and Joseph Chamberlain was appointed Colonial Secretary. Chamberlain was an outspoken imperialist and was convinced of the necessity of a South African federation within the British Empire. In respect of imperial policies, Chamberlain allowed himself to be guided by three considerations – the economic development of the empire, the inculcation of the value of the empire in all British subjects and the promotion of political unity within the empire. In Chamberlain, therefore, Rhodes had found a useful ally.

The new spirit which began to prevail in Britain after the change of government was clearly manifested in September and October 1895 at the time of the so-called 'drifts crisis' between the Cape Colony and the Transvaal. With the completion of the Delagoa Bay railway line, the Cape attempted to obtain as much as possible of the Rand's rail traffic by reducing its rates. The Kruger government then increased the rate on the Transvaal section of the Cape railway line in order to protect the 'national railway line', the Delagoa Bay line. The Cape line thereupon conveyed goods as far as the Vaal River by rail and then by ox-wagon to the Rand to eliminate the increased rate on the Transvaal section of the line. Kruger reacted sharply to this step by simply closing the drifts on the Transvaal side of the Vaal River.

The implications of the drifts crisis were of immense importance to Rhodes, and he watched events with considerable interest. He saw in this situation an opportunity to test the attitude of the new British regime. He was not disappointed; the British Government adopted a stern and threatening attitude to Kruger and the latter was compelled to reopen the drifts. To Rhodes it was now clear that to a large extent he could depend on the support of the British Government.

At the same time Rhodes realised that his policy of encirclement of the Transvaal had not been fully successful and that he would now have to exert more direct pressure on Kruger if he wanted to realize his ideal of a British federation and a more acceptable administration in the Transvaal. Consequently it was decided that

the time was ripe for direct intervention in Transvaal affairs. To this end Rhodes planned an Uitlander uprising in Johannesburg, which would coincide with an invasion of the Transvaal from Pitsani in Bechuanaland by Dr L S Jameson, administrator of the British South Africa Company in Southern Rhodesia. By so doing Rhodes hoped to convert the Transvaal into a self-governing British colony which would be willing to join a British South African federation. Chamberlain played a dual role in this conspiracy. Officially he tried to distance himself, but modern researchers have proved convincingly that although he did not play a direct role in the Jameson Raid itself, he was involved in its planning. He advised Rhodes about a suitable date for the proposed Uitlander uprising, and helped him to obtain a departure point in Bechuanaland from which the invasion could proceed.

However important it may have been to Rhodes to draw the Transvaal into a federation under the British flag, it did not necessarily mean that that was his only motive for the invasion. Apart from political goals there was obviously a personal profit motive at stake for Rhodes as well, since his interests on the Witwatersrand goldfields would be advanced by a successful raid. Rhodes had entered the gold-mining industry at a relatively late stage. Whereas the companies which had appeared on the scene first were able to exploit the gold reefs close to the surface and make considerable profits, other companies, such as that of Rhodes, mined the gold reefs that were situated at a far deeper level below the surface. This of course meant heavier operating costs and a shrinking profit margin. It was these companies in particular that were handicapped by Kruger's mining policy, and consequently it would be to Rhodes's advantage to bring about a change of government in the Transvaal.

Reactions to the Jameson Raid

The abortive Jameson Raid had far-reaching consequences. In the Cape Colony Rhodes was forced to resign as premier, because the Afrikaner Bond immediately withdrew the support it had previously shown him and began to move in a new political direction. Whereas Hofmeyr had still sided with Rhodes at the time of the drifts crisis, he now began to identify himself to an increasing extent with the maltreated Transvaal. The Bond, in spite of the fact that as a political organization in a British colony it owed allegiance to the British crown, again became the body pre-eminently representative of exclusive Afrikaner sentiments and aspirations. Furthermore the political dividing lines between Afrikaans- and English-speaking persons in the Cape Colony became more sharply defined than

Joseph Chamberlain, Colonial Secretary. (Transvaal Archives)

Members of the Reform Committee in Pretoria Jail, 1896. (Transvaal Archives)

ever before. While the Bond increasingly came to be identified with a surging national consciousness among the Cape Afrikaners, the South African League, an outspokenly imperialistic organization which sought to affirm British supremacy in South Africa, was established early in 1896. The League gave strong support to the English-speaking Progressive Party in the Cape Colony.

In the 1898 general election the Progressive Party opposed the more moderate South African Party under the leadership of W P Schreiner and John X Merriman, who were unable to associate themselves with the new militant imperialistic trend in South Africa. With the help of the Afrikaner Bond the South African Party narrowly succeeded in coming into office. Convinced pro-imperialist observers interpreted

this victory as a danger sign for Britain sovereign authority and warned that the British position might have to be maintained by force of arms.

In addition to these developments the Free State also moved closer to the Transvaal. In March 1898 the pro-republican leader, M T Steyn, was elected President with an overwhelming majority over his opponent, J G Fraser, who was more inclined towards the British-controlled Cape Colony. The idea of closer co-operation between the two republics gained new momentum, and in March 1897 they concluded the Political Alliance which *inter alia* entailed military co-operation. In this way, on a formal level, the first steps were taken which would subsequently lead to Free State participation in the Anglo-Boer War.

Naturally it was in the Transvaal that the Jameson Raid evoked the most vehement reaction. It was now clearer than ever before that the independence of the republic was being threatened and consequently the Kruger government began to arm its citizens on a larger scale. The Uitlanders were regarded with even greater suspicion and Kruger was more reluctant than ever to grant them any real political power. Kruger's firm action in dealing with the raid had strengthened his position, and he enjoyed increasing support among the Boer population. Some of the citizens who, prior to 1896, had been of the opinion that the Uitlanders should be treated more leniently, were now firmly behind Kruger. In the presidential election of 1898 Kruger won a resounding victory over his more accommodating opponents, Schalk Burger, Piet Joubert and J G Kotze.

The raid also affected relations between Germany and the Transvaal. The German Emperor, Wilhelm II, sent Kruger a telegram (the 'Kaiser's Telegram') of congratulations on the way in which the republic had averted the onslaught. Although the aim of the Kaiser's telegram was to intimidate Britain on a diplomatic level, rather than to give the republic any real support, it nevertheless aroused the false hope in the SAR that in future crises the SAR would be able to rely on Germany as an ally.

However widespread the consequences of the

The swearing in of President Kruger at the Raadzaal, Pretoria, after his electoral victory in 1898. (Barnett Collection)

abortive raid may have been, its importance dims somewhat when the matter is viewed from the perspective of the vast majority of the black inhabitants of the Transvaal. Even if the raid had succeeded the blacks would still, under a new British regime, have found themselves in a subordinate position, treated as a source of cheap labour. As far as the white community was concerned, however, the Jameson Raid was an important milestone along a road that could lead to war.

The tension mounts

After the fiasco of the Jameson Raid it was important for Chamberlain to regain lost prestige. Also it was apparent that if a British federation was to be brought into existence in South Africa, the British Government itself would have to play a more active part in the manipulation of the SAR. This does not mean that Chamberlain was prepared to set a premeditated course for war; he preferred to make use of continuous pressure. Partly as a result of Chamberlain's relentless diplomatic game and, as A Porter indicated in a recent study, his subtle orchestration of public opinion in Britain, relations between Britain and the SAR deteriorated so rapidly, however, that Chamberlain was not in a position to exercise full control over the course of events.

Chamberlain's first diplomatic move was to invite Kruger to London for talks. He saw this as an opportunity, *inter alia*, to obtain concessions from Kruger in respect of the Uitlander franchise, but the republican President was not

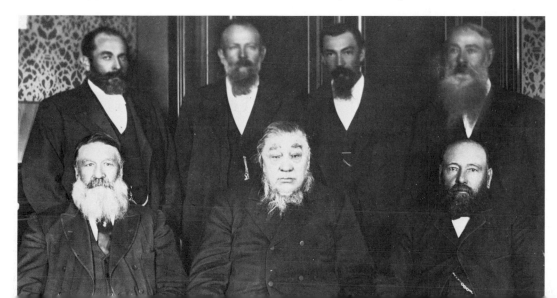

The Executive Council of the South African Republic before the Anglo-Boer War. (Barnett Collection)

prepared to discuss internal Transvaal affairs at an official conference since this would create the impression that the SAR could not determine its affairs of policy independently.

For Chamberlain this was a diplomatic setback, but at this juncture he was not yet considering other alternatives. In the British House of Commons he prophetically declared that a war with the republic would be prolonged, acrimonious and expensive and that the embitterment engendered by a struggle which would take the form of a civil war would continue for generations. He continued along his chosen diplomatic course and resorted next to the London Convention of 1884 in order to intervene directly in Transvaal matters. As previously indicated, Chamberlain had no legal grounds for doing so, but it nevertheless afforded him a political opening to treat the republic like a quasi-crown colony, thus intensifying the pressure on the SAR. In this connection he tried to manipulate the SAR's relations with Portugal and also alleged that republican legislation on the admission of aliens to the SAR was invalid in terms of the convention. Although these efforts on the part of Chamberlain accomplished few tangible results, he nevertheless succeeded in humiliating the republic on a diplomatic level, thereby demonstrating British determination to dictate the course of events in the Transvaal.

To give further effect to this policy he sent Sir Alfred Milner to South Africa as British Commissioner in March 1897. Milner was a brilliant administrator and an outspoken imperialist. In a period during which other industrial countries were vying with Britain in the economic sphere, Milner was convinced of the necessity to stabilize and expand the British position. In his view South Africa was one of the weakest links in the imperial chain. Chamberlain, to a large extent, endorsed this viewpoint, but in contrast to Chamberlain, Milner was more dogmatic and less flexible. In political negotiations Milner almost invariably displayed a haughty inability to understand the standpoints of his opponents. The historian G H L le May is of the opinion that the appointment of Milner virtually ensured the outbreak of the Anglo-Boer War. This is an oversimplified view, but Milner's arrival in a tense South Africa certainly did not make it in any way easier to find a peaceful solution.

Initially Milner was exhorted to exercise patience in the hope that Kruger's position would deteriorate and that the Transvaal Government would then be prepared to carry out important reforms. After Kruger had won the presidential election of 1898 by an overwhelming majority, however, this hope rapidly faded. To Milner this was a demonstration that there could be no possibility of real reform in the Transvaal. In addition he became convinced that Afrikaners in the republics and colonies were making common cause against Britain in order to achieve Afrikaner control in South Africa. In view of

this situation he informed Chamberlain that war appeared to be the only solution. At this stage, however, Chamberlain was of the opinion that circumstances in Britain and the Cape Colony were unfavourable for such a drastic step. He also hoped that the Kruger government would collapse as a result of its suspected internal weaknesses. Milner, on the other hand, was afraid that any further delay might alienate the Uitlanders from Britain.

In the meantime the Transvaal Government tried to avert the threatening crisis by acting in a more conciliatory manner towards the mining magnates. An Industrial Commission of 1897, under the chairmanship of one of Kruger's political opponents, S W Burger, recommended far-reaching economic concessions to the mines and the Uitlanders. The Volksraad eventually watered down the proposals, but within limits the mining industry did benefit from the developments which followed upon the Industrial Commission. The Transvaal also attempted to improve the standards of national administration. The young Jan Christiaan Smuts was appointed as State Attorney and he made a real effort to combat corruption within the police force on the Witwatersrand. But these efforts had little effect on the overall relations between Britain and the SAR. This became apparent from the so-called 'Edgar incident' of 1898, which evoked intense emotions among the Uitlanders.

The Edgar incident occurred while Milner was on leave in England. The acting High Commissioner, Sir William Butler, was of the opinion that there was a group of unreliable mischief-makers among the Uitlanders, who were carelessly stoking the fires of war. According to him, South Africa did not need any surgical operations or blood-letting, but rest and peace and a union of hearts.

This point of view was totally unacceptable to Milner, and on his return from England, he set about forcing a confrontation with the Transvaal. Encouraged by his attitude, the Uitlander leaders drew up a second petition, setting out their grievances and insisting upon British mediation. The petition of 21 000 signatures suited Milner down to the ground. He transmitted it to Chamberlain and insisted on an immediate reaction before the inflamed Uitlanders could cool down and the opportunity to make political gain from the situation was lost. Milner was requested to give added impact to the letter of complaint by reporting on the state of affairs in the Transvaal, which would enable Chamberlain to manipulate public opinion in Britain and strengthen his case before the British Cabinet. Then followed Milner's well-known 'Helot Telegram' of May 1899. The government of the SAR was condemned in strong language as the unrelenting suppressor of thousands of loyal British subjects. The Uitlanders, so Milner alleged, were virtually in the position of 'helots'

though the British spokesmen were from time to time to use other matters as arguments against the republic, such as the sovereignty issue, the treatment of blacks in the Transvaal and the supposed threat of a pan-Afrikaner conspiracy, these matters were not nearly of as much importance as the franchise issue in providing Britain with a *casus belli* and in keeping public opinion in Britain at fever pitch. For those reasons Milner was also mindful of retaining the initiative at all times. Any form of *rapprochement* between the Kruger government and the mining magnates, such as the tentative attempts by Smuts early in 1899 to arrive at an independent settlement with the mine owners, was unacceptable to Milner.

The Bloemfontein conference and subsequent events

In the midst of the mounting tension, Premier Schreiner of the Cape and President Steyn of the Free State attempted to resolve matters by arranging a conference between Kruger and Milner in Bloemfontein. The conference began on 31 May 1899. To Chamberlain, who was not yet fully convinced of the desirability of war as a solution to the South African problem, such a conference seemed to be a possible way out of the impasse. Nevertheless, Chamberlain gave Milner a free hand in the negotiations. Milner went to Bloemfontein with the primary aim of strengthening the case for British intervention and of driving Kruger into a corner. An honest and sincere search for the means by which an acceptable settlement for both parties could be found was therefore not Milner's first priority. Kruger, in turn, approached the conference in a more conciliatory spirit, but he was not prepared to consider proposals which, according to his views, might undermine SAR independence.

The franchise issue was the principal item on the agenda at the conference. Milner demanded

(slaves) and it had become imperative that Britain come to their rescue by persuading the Kruger government to institute acceptable reforms. Chamberlain considered this telegram to be damning, and although he had his misgivings about its long-term implications, it nevertheless afforded him an opportunity to persuade the British Government to accept the Uitlander petition.

With this the franchise issue became the official and, for the British public, the central bone of contention between the SAR and Britain. Al-

The Edgar Demonstration, Johannesburg 1898 – reading the petition to the Queen, in which British intervention in the Transvaal was requested. (Cory Library, Grahamstown)

The Executive Council of the South African Republic, by F Wichgraf. (Transvaal Museum)

that the Uitlanders receive the franchise after a period of five years without any other conditions, while Kruger was prepared to give them the franchise after a period of seven years, subject to specific conditions. With this step Kruger thought that he had made a considerable concession; he had after all reduced the initial period of fourteen years to seven years. Although Milner admitted privately that it was an improvement on the existing situation, he still did not consider it to be adequate. Politely but firmly Kruger's offer was refused.

In Bloemfontein, two worlds had passed each other by: that of the sophisticated, imperialistic Milner who increasingly wanted a confrontation, and that of the unaffected, nationalistic Kruger who preferred peace, but not peace at any price.

It is not inconceivable, however, that Kruger and Milner might have reached agreement on the relatively small difference in their respective demands for the Uitlanders' residence qualifications – if Milner was really prepared to do so. But it was already too late. After Milner's rejection of the seven-year proposals, Kruger passionately accused Britain of expecting him to surrender his land to strangers, while Milner closed the conference with the chilling words that no tangible progress had been made and that there was no obligation on either side arising from it. Chamberlain was perturbed that Milner had terminated the conference so quickly, but Milner dismissed the talks as mere delaying tactics on the part of the Boers.

The failure of the conference in Bloemfontein was an important milestone on the way to war.

It destroyed the SAR's faith in open-hearted and sincere negotiations with Britain and dealt a serious blow to the possibility of a peaceful diplomatic settlement. Unaware of the degree of tension between Milner and Chamberlain, the SAR regarded Milner's arrogant and aggressive attitude as typical of the imperial government. At the same time the number of options open to the British Government also decreased. After Milner's unbending attitude in Bloemfontein the momentum had to be maintained and Britain had to ensure that Milner's demands were carried out – if need be by violent means. The other alternative, to recall Milner as High Commissioner and waive the Uitlander grievances and the idea of British supremacy in South Africa, was at this stage, after the tremendous publicity accompanying the British policy, no longer possible if Britain was not to lose all credibility.

Although British suspicion and inflexibility had seriously damaged relations and reduced the chances of a successful settlement, not all diplomatic channels were closed. Cape men such as W P Schreiner and J H Hofmeyr, as well as the Free Stater Abraham Fischer, still continued to encourage Kruger to seek further compromises in the interests of the SAR. Kruger hereupon amended the seven-year proposal in such a way that, unlike his position during the conference in Bloemfontein, it would be completely retroactive. Uitlanders who had already been resident in the Transvaal for seven years, would therefore be eligible for the franchise immediately. Chamberlain welcomed this step, but Milner considered it to be a bluff and in July 1899 insisted that the franchise provisions be examined by a joint commission of the two governments. To the SAR such a procedure was unacceptable since it would mean that Britain would be elevated into becoming an arbiter of republican legislation, with the further general implication that all internal matters of the republic would be exposed to the dangerous precedent of direct interference by Britain.

Further diplomatic moves followed in August 1899 when Smuts negotiated on a semi-official basis with the British agent in Pretoria, Conyngham Greene, over the possibility of additional concessions on the part of the republic, provided the SAR was told whether these proposals would be accepted by Britain before they were officially made. These proposals, which Smuts was encouraged to make officially, were far-reaching. Milner's demand for a retrospective five-year franchise was complied with, but it was made subject to the British acceptance of express conditions in respect of no further intervention in Transvaal affairs, the arbitration of other unresolved disputes between the Transvaal and Britain and Britain relinquishing its claim of suzerainty over the SAR. The SAR also insisted that the offer should be regarded as a package deal; in other words the conditions could not be separated from the franchise concessions. The coupling of the two aspects involved might have been a step of dubious wisdom since it offered British diplomacy an escape hatch, particularly for Milner who could not afford to lose the franchise as a *casus belli*.

Chamberlain, in replying to these proposals on 28 August, expressed his satisfaction with the five-year franchise, but rejected the accompanying conditions. The republican government thereupon expressed its regret at Britain's negative attitude, and proposed as an alternative that they were not prepared to accept the joint commission of inquiry into the seven-year proposal. To Chamberlain, and in particular to Milner, however, this would have meant a diplomatic defeat; they were not prepared to accept any proposals which in their view had been proved to be inadequate by the republic's own five-year proposal.

The diplomatic negotiations (which in retrospect almost degenerated into a farce because there was no real determination, no discernment of possibilities, especially on the part of Britain, to resolve the position) now drew rapidly to a close. To Smuts it was already clear on 2 September that Milner, with the help of Chamberlain, was bent on either a military conquest of the Transvaal, or reducing the position of the republic through diplomatic channels virtually to that of a British colony. After the failure of a final and despairing attempt by President Steyn to negotiate further with Milner, the Transvaal and its ally, the Free State, had to face up to the unpleasant fact that Britain in reality desired no peaceful solution

and that it would be advantageous to the republics to attack first before the arrival of further British troop reinforcements, which might deprive them of the military initiative as well.

Consequently, on 9 October, the republicans demanded by way of an ultimatum that British troops be withdrawn from their borders, that troop reinforcements at sea be recalled and that all reinforcements of the British army since 1899 be removed from South Africa within a reasonable period of time. The ultimatum would expire on 11 October at 17h00, and if the Transvaal Government had not received a satisfactory reply before that time, the republics would regard it as a formal declaration of war. The British Government itself had already, on 29 September, drawn up a draft ultimatum, but the ultimatum from the Boers suited it perfectly; the republics now appeared the aggressors and it would be possible to incite public opinion in Britain even further. The SAR was notified that there would be no compliance with the requirements, and when the ultimatum expired on 11 October 1899 war between the South African republics and Great Britain became a reality – a war which was to cast a long shadow over twentieth century South Africa and drastically affect the lives of blacks and whites.

Interpretations of the causes of the war

Although a great many imperialistically minded British writers, during and immediately after the war, blamed the Kruger government for the outbreak of hostilities, this was an interpretation which has since been entirely discredited by historians. In order to explain the outbreak of the war, more recent historians have attempted to establish why Britain exerted so much pressure on the South African Republic that the republic eventually proceeded to attack in order to protect its independence.

To some historians, A Keppel-Jones for example, the true cause of the war lay in the fran-

Sir W Conyngham Greene, the British agent in Pretoria. (Transvaal Archives)

The cyanide wheel at Village Main Reef.
(Barnett Collection)

chise issue and the unwillingness of the SAR to comply with British demands in this connection. According to his view the British Government then entered the fray on behalf of the Uitlanders. As has been shown, the franchise issue was indeed the central issue between Britain and the SAR, but it cannot simply be accepted on its face value as the real reason for the outbreak of the war. In important works on the causes of the war, G D Scholtz and J S Marais, among other historians, produced convincing proof that the franchise issue was merely the tip of the iceberg – an ostensible grievance which could conveniently be used to force the SAR into war.

What, then, lay behind the rhetoric of the franchise issue? Various historians (including J S Marais and G H le May) found the general answer to this question in the attempt to establish British supremacy in South Africa. Thus Le May, who attached particular value to the role played by Milner in the implementation of British policy, maintained that Milner persuaded Chamberlain, and Chamberlain in his turn persuaded the British Government that British supremacy in South Africa would be endangered if Britain did not break the power of the Transvaal. By 1895 it was clear that the gold mines were by no means worked out and they would continue to produce unprecedented

wealth for a long time to come. Consequently it was not surprising that the Colonial Office feared that this rapidly growing wealth would place the republic in an unassailable position as the leading state in a possibly united South Africa and that with such a dispensation, British interests would be entirely subordinated. To Marais the heart of the matter lay similarly in British determination to oppose an independently united South Africa; the longer the SAR retained its independence and wealth, the greater was the risk that the British colonies in South Africa would drift away from the empire. Therefore, in these terms the SAR was not only a stumbling-block to British interests, but a real threat.

Since the appearance of these works in the 1960s this interpretation has carried considerable weight and has in the course of time become almost a standard elucidation of the origins of the Anglo-Boer War. Nevertheless during the 1970s, without denying the importance of the issue of British supremacy, critics argued that this interpretation did not do full justice to the complex web of interwoven interests and considerations. Consequently, this issue no longer offered a complete and adequate explanation for the outbreak of the war. Shula Marks and Stanley Trapido, for example, maintain that Le May concentrated too narrowly on Milner's character and personal obsessions, without sufficiently analysing the nature of 'Milnerism' as an expression of late nineteenth century imperialism on an ideological and practical level. In this way the immediate causes of the war were stripped from the structural context in which they were manifested. Concomitantly, according to these authors, the term 'British supremacy' entails a high degree of rhetoric and ought to be examined more thoroughly in order to give it convincing content and meaning.

The role of gold in the international economy ought in particular to receive higher priority in this connection. With increasing American and German competition and the transition of the international monetary system to the gold exchange standard, Britain's central position in the international monetary market was being increasingly jeopardized by the late nineteenth century and it had become essential for Britain to supplement its gold reserves. Although this was of course not the only consideration which led to war, uncertainty over the British gold reserves, according to Marks and Trapido, did play an important role. In the tense 1890s no imperial statesman could run the risk of the future of the South African mining industry being threatened by a regime which, justly or unjustly, was not, according to imperial views, capable in the long run of guaranteeing the interests of the mining industry, and might even make common cause with British competitors.

In addition, since the appearance of J A Hob-

Mine workers in a compound playing an ancient game known as 'wari' or 'hus'.
(Barnett Collection)

Mine workers underground, carrying lighted candles. (Barnett Collection)

son's work in 1902 on the causes of the war, the role of the Rand capitalists has been accorded special attention in the historiography. To Hobson the real cause of the war lay in the influence which the capitalists exerted and the way in which they manipulated the Colonial Office. More recent research has indicated convincingly, however, that this is an over-simplified view and that the capitalists did not display a united front, while the imperial authorities and the mining magnates exercised a far greater reciprocal influence on one another than Hobson had suspected.

Historians basing their views on a historical-materialistic perspective argued in turn that there was too much concentration on the intrigues of individual capitalists, instead of a systematic analysis of capitalism as the underlying structural system. Thus the actual causes of the war should not be sought so much in the role of capitalists as individuals or in vague, general British aims, but in the *form* which capitalism assumed in the Transvaal. Although the Kruger government, according to this interpretation, tried in its own way to create favourable conditions for capitalistic growth, it was unable to succeed in doing this to a sufficient extent. According to C van Onselen, neither Britain nor the mining industry as such was prepared to accumulate capital at the rate dictated by a rural bourgeoisie. Consequently it was essential to replace the republican government with a regime which could offer the optimum conditions for the development of unbridled capitalism. Among other things this meant the effective harnessing of sufficient cheap black labour. Viewed from this perspective, as D Bransky has shown, the position of blacks assumes a new significance. The demands of capitalism resulted in a devasting war being fought in order to ensure that blacks, as subordinates, could fully meet the white community's needs, while their own social structures were subverted in the process. According to Bransky the great struggle between the white communities in South Africa was not the result of the opposing rhetoric of Boer and Briton, but was instead the result of a conflict over the way in which capitalism should be entrenched and how it should develop. And the imperatives of capital dictated that this would take place at the expense of the blacks.

Finally, no comprehensive synthesis has yet appeared which systematically analyses the frequently divergent interpretations of the causes of the war and advances the relative importance of the interwoven factors in a way which demonstrates the niceties and nuances of the situation. Such a synthesis will impose heavy demands. The nature and contents of republicanism and relations between the republican government and the mining industry will have to be assessed anew, and the 'true' rationale behind British policy and the various interest groups which exerted an influence on policy will have to be reconsidered. It will be equally important to place the events which occurred on the surface within the context of the underlying structural capitalist system and to indicate their significance with precision. Only then can we move closer to a total interpretation of the complex events and circumstances which led to the bitter conflict of 1899-1902.

Suggested Reading List

G Blainey (1965) 'Lost Causes of the Jameson Raid', *Economic History Review*, 2nd series, XVIII

G H le May (1965) *British Supremacy in South Africa, 1899-1907*, Oxford

J S Marais (1961) *The Fall of Kruger's Republic*, Oxford

G D Scholtz (1947) *Die Oorsake van die Tweede Vryheidsoorlog, 1899-1902*, Johannesburg

C van Onselen (1982) *Studies in the Social and Economic History of the Witwatersrand, 1886-1914*, London

J van der Poel (1951) *The Jameson Raid*, London

Chapter 14

The Anglo-Boer War, 1899-1902

Thomas Pakenham

Thomas Pakenham, eldest son of the Earl and Countess of Longford, was born in 1933 and educated at Ampleforth and Oxford. Since the late 1960s he has lived for much of the time in Ireland. His publications include *The Year of Liberty: The Story of the Great Irish Rebellion of 1798* (London, 1969) and *The Boer War* (London and Johannesburg, 1979). He is currently involved in research on the topic of British imperialism.

'Kruger and John Bull', a French cartoon by Rouville, 1899. (By courtesy of Thomas Pakenham)

At 17h00 on 9 October 1899, the Transvaal State Secretary, F W Reitz, handed the Transvaal ultimatum to the British agent at Pretoria – 'tipped him the black spot', as Reitz, a reader of *Treasure Island*, cheerfully put it. Forty-eight hours later, on 11 October, the allied republics of the Transvaal and the Free State were formally at war with Great Britain. The first phase of the war seemed at times like a contest in lost opportunities, so difficult did the generals on either side find their tasks.

The outbreak

In the War Office it was as though, in 1899, they were still trying to win the war of 1881. Before a British expeditionary force, raked up from different parts of the empire, could invade the two republics, Natal and the Cape Colony would be vulnerable to a pre-emptive strike by the Boers. In the War Office it was believed that, as in 1881, the Boers' offensive would consist of mere 'raids' across the border by 2 000 or 3 000 men, of whom British regulars would make short work.

With such an assumption, it was natural that the British generals in both London and South Africa should grossly underestimate the reinforcements needed to protect the British colonies from Boer attack. At the beginning of September the number of British troops in the whole of South Africa totalled just over 12 000. For some time Field Marshal Wolseley, Commander-in-Chief at the War Office, had recommended strengthening the garrison in Natal: 10 000 extra men would secure the colony 'as far as Biggarsberg'. On 8 September the British Cabinet reluctantly agreed to send the 10 000 troops, mainly from India. Soon it would be clear that Wolseley had underestimated both

colonies' needs by at least five times. He had also given hardly a thought to co-ordinated defensive planning – or to an offensive strategy. The general hastily sent to take charge of the enlarged garrison in Natal, 67-year-old Lieutenant-General Sir George White, knew nothing of South Africa, and had not been ordered to consult with the acting General Officer Commanding in Natal, Major-General Sir Penn Symons, nor with the man designated to follow him with the main expeditionary force after a few weeks, General Sir Redvers Buller. White landed in Natal in early October to find Symons had been allowed to make a reckless blunder. He had pushed up 4 000 men into the vulnerable northern triangle at Dundee, and put the rest at

200

Ladysmith, a most unsuitable headquarters, itself too far north for safety.

Wolseley's defensive plans for the Cape Colony were equally threadbare. He recognized the threat to the two strategic border towns, Kimberley and Mafeking (now Mafikeng). It was left to locally recruited forces and a half battalion of British regulars to defend Kimberley. At Mafeking the garrison commander, Colonel Robert Baden-Powell, did not even have a half battalion of regulars. His main troops were some 500 men of the Protectorate regiment.

The dispatch of the 10 000 reinforcements recommended by Wolseley finally convinced President Kruger and the Transvaal Executive that war was inevitable, but it took far too long to convince President Steyn that further negotiations were useless. Mobilization was delayed, in the Transvaal until 28 September, in the Free State until 2 October. Almost all the British reinforcements had reached Natal before the ultimatum.

The joint strategic plan then adopted by the two republics was to launch pre-emptive strikes at the two colonies, large in scale, but limited in aims. First they would have to neutralize the main British forces already threatening their borders. Then they must adopt secure defensive positions inside the colonies and try to block the advance of the main British expeditionary force after it began to arrive at the ports some time in late November.

By the outbreak of the war the two republics had managed to mobilize about 32 500 of the 54 000 burghers on the rolls, including several thousand foreign pro-Boer volunteers from the Uitlander community. The Free State army was commanded by General M Prinsloo, the Transvaal army by General P Joubert. The main offensive – with 11 400 Transvaalers and 6 000 Free Staters – was concentrated against Natal. At the same time the republican armies planned to rush the border garrisons, Kimberley and Mafeking, in the Cape. The republics were left with substantial reserves, partly of the men yet to be mobilized, partly of the garrisons deputed to guard the Transvaal's borders with Rhodesia and the Free State's borders with Basutoland. Most of the commandos were well armed with the latest modern rifles, high velocity, smokeless Mauser magazine rifles, and supported by the latest quick-firing Krupp and Creusot field guns, with half a dozen pieces of heavy artillery.

The strength of the combined plan of attack was that its simplicity suited the Boer armies. However, it had a fatal weakness due to the hasty manner in which it had been prepared and there was the same fatal lack of co-ordination between Boer generals as between their British counterparts. Otherwise in October 1899 the Boers might have inflicted, with forces on each

British reinforcements preparing for kit inspection at Cape Town. (Transvaal Archives)

Lieutenant-General Sir George White, Commander-in-Chief of the British forces in Natal. (Transvaal Archives)

General Sir Redvers Henry Buller (Transvaal Archives)

General Piet Joubert (Transvaal Archives)

'The last man of the family to leave', by E J Austen. Burghers between the ages of sixteen and sixty were called up for military duty, but boys of twelve and below and greybeards of well over seventy joined the commandos despite this age limit. (William Fehr Collection)

A group of Boer soldiers in laager.
(Transvaal Archives)

side almost ten times the size, the same crushing humiliation they had inflicted on the redcoats in February 1881.

To many burghers of the two republics the ultimatum brought a sense of relief. At least the months of diplomatic wrangling were over, and there would now be a decision one way or the other. There was heady talk of conquering the two colonies. Jan Smuts, the Transvaal's 29-year-old State Attorney, talked of 'an Afrikaner republic in South Africa stretching from Table Bay to the Zambezi'.

A sense of relief was equally pronounced among the British communities of the Cape and Natal, whose numbers had been increased by British refugees. These Uitlanders, threatened with expulsion from the Transvaal, had been pouring down the railway lines since June. The production of the Rand gold mines slackened, and most shops and offices in Johannesburg had been closed. Thousands of refugees arrived in Durban and Cape Town after several days in open railway trucks, many in a pitiful state. There was a rush to join the irregular units raised in both colonies in October and November.

The group of refugees which suffered most were the thousands of blacks from the two colonies (and Basutoland) who had worked on the Rand mines. Unlike the whites, they were not offered free rail fares home. One courageous of-ficial, J S Marwick, led a group of 7 000 blacks, including 3 000 Zulu, through Joubert's lines and into Natal, but the other colonies offered no official help to black people. Many were left destitute in Johannesburg, or were robbed of their savings when trying to trek back to their homes.

The Boer offensive (October to November 1899)

The first battle of the war, as people expected, took place in northern Natal, 2 km from Dundee. Soon after dawn on 20 October some of the commandos sent by Joubert seized the hill of Talana and began to shell Symons's camp below. For both sides it proved a day of opportunities – and men – cast away. Instead of concentrating his forces, Joubert had diverted General J H M Kock south in the Biggarsberg and chosen only a third of his men, commandos led by Generals Lucas Meyer and D Erasmus, for the combined attack. Erasmus hung back, bewildered by the heavy mist on Mount Impati, and Meyer could only bring into action about 1 500 riflemen with a pair of field guns.

They were soon put to flight by the shrapnel of Symons's 15-pounders, and a bayonet charge from three infantry battalions. However, Symons was mortally wounded when he left the

---

Life on commando during the Anglo-Boer War

All burghers between the ages of sixteen and sixty were liable to be called up for commando duty. Force of circumstance, however, led to older men and youths (penkoppe) also serving in the field. The Boer armies were people's armies committed to the national cause. Religion was important to most Boers on commando. The Bible, particularly the Old Testament, served as a source of inspiration. The Boers identified with the history of Israel and it was fervently believed that their cause was righteous before God.

Lack of discipline was a problem. Absence without leave (verlofpes) was rife because burghers simply went home when they needed to attend to family or farming matters. When the tide of war turned against the republics this tendency was exacerbated. There was a clear correlation between low morale and a high incidence of absenteeism. Virtually from the out-break of hostilities the ponderous wagon laagers accompanying the commandos created difficulties. Measures were taken to obviate matters and during the guerrilla phase there was an improvement, but the problem was never really solved. The burghers did not always comply with orders which they considered would affect their own possessions. Although officers preferred to reprimand offenders, punishment was nevertheless meted out for transgressions such as absence from duty without leave, and insolence. Punishment included fines, double sentry duties or paksaal (where an offender had to carry his saddle together with rifle and bandolier for a certain time around the laager). The burghers were self-reliant, yet they also depended greatly on resolute leaders like Louis Botha, Christiaan de Wet and Koos de la Rey, who won their confidence. Black men served as agterryers, cooks and looked after cattle and horses. In general relations between burghers and their agterryers were paternalistic but cordial.

Commissariat arrangements became increasingly awkward, particularly after September 1900 when Lourenço Marques (Maputo) became unavailable for republican imports. The staple diet consisted of meat (braaied, boiled or in the form of biltong) and mealie porridge (mieliepap). Lack of salt and coffee soon became a problem although 'coffee' made of mealies, sweet potatoes, etc was consumed. Everything was scarce, but nothing ever became absolutely unobtainable. From the winter of 1901 the so-called uitskud of British prisoners of war helped to relieve the alarming shortage of clothing. The capture of enemy convoys augmented supplies of food and also of weapons and ammunition; many burghers came to be armed with British Lee Metford rifles. The Boer was a mounted rifleman and his horse was of cardinal importance to him, but in time horses also came to be in short supply.

Recreation was vital during long periods of military inactivity. Rugby, athletics, cricket, fishing, boxing, musical entertainment, and reading helped to maintain morale. Convivial evenings were spent around the camp fire. Sentry duty was often boring, yet essential, while scouting, though dangerous, introduced an element of adventure. Rain could be irritating but necessary to provide grazing for the horses; more annoying were flies and mosquitoes. In general the burghers succeeded in overcoming the vicissitudes of commando life. Difficulties were met with equanimity and the burghers became resigned to the inevitable boredom and monotony. Nevertheless the longing for home and family was often great. Peace, which brought with it the loss of their independence, struck the bittereinders like a thunderbolt.

F Pretorius

shelter of a wall and strode into the firing line. Earlier, in a reckless attempt to block Meyer's retreat, he had cast away most of his mounted men, who were snapped up by Erasmus. The Boers lost proportionately fewer men killed, wounded or taken prisoner, 155 compared with British losses of 500. Joubert had lost the main chance, though – to capture the Dundee garrison.

Joubert paid the price for dividing his forces. Exploiting the tactical mobility of the railway, Sir George White steamed out from Ladysmith on 21 October and struck at General Kock's two commandos. The battle at Elandslaagte proved a textbook victory for the British, the last for many months. Kock was mortally wounded, and a cavalry charge by Lancers and Dragoons cut up the fleeing Boers.

Talana and Elandslaagte won a breathing space for White and the British. On 24 October, at Rietfontein, they parried Prinsloo and his Free Staters. White now staked everything on

what he called a 'knock down blow' to send the Boers flying. On 30 October ('Mournful Monday') the truth came home to him: man for man the Boers were more effective fighters than the British. Joubert and Prinsloo had finally joined forces and put 7 500 men into the field, supported by thirteen field guns and three heavy guns. The field guns had unusually long fuses and so outranged their British counterparts. After a rash night march to Nicholson's Nek, in an attempt to cut off the Boers, White's force was driven back in confusion to Ladysmith. White lost a total of 1 272 men, killed, wounded or captured. Three days later the railway and telegraph lines to Ladysmith were cut. White's remaining 14 000 men, the field force which was supposed to defend the colony of Natal, were themselves under siege.

On the western and central fronts in the Cape Colony in contrast with Natal there were few British troops to stop the Boers, but the makeshift British garrisons successfully held the at-

◁△
Many refugees were transported in open cattle trucks, and arrived at their destinations in a pitiful state. (By courtesy of Thomas Pakenham)

△
Three thousand black migrant workers were forced to leave Johannesburg in October 1899, as the outbreak of war meant that there was no longer employment for them. The British army recruited many of these unemployed labourers. (Cape Archives, J6139)

◁▽
On 'Mournful Monday', 30 October 1899, the Battle of Ladysmith was fought. White and his troops are seen retreating into Ladysmith, and the four-month-long Siege of Ladysmith commenced. (By courtesy of Thomas Pakenham)

▽
A British gunner smashed by a shell at Ladysmith. (By courtesy of Thomas Pakenham)

Winston Churchill (on the right), the war correspondent of the London *Morning Post*, who was captured on 15 November 1899 by Boers who ambushed an armoured train near Chievely in Natal. He was detained in the State Model School, Pretoria, with other British officers who had been taken prisoner of war. He escaped by climbing over a wall in December 1899, and managed to reach safety at Delagoa Bay. A £25 reward was offered for his recapture, dead or alive. (Transvaal Archives)

Lieutenant-General Lord Methuen, who led the British troops in an unsuccessful attempt to relieve Kimberley. (Cape Archives, J7263)

A field dressing station at Modder River. (Transvaal Archives)

tackers at bay – and kept them from throwing still more weight on Natal. So limited was the Boer offensive on these fronts that no attempt was made to capture the strategic railway bridge at Orange River. By the third week of November it was obvious that the initiative was passing to the British. The first of the 50 000 men in Sir Redvers Buller's expeditionary force had begun to disembark, and were pouring up the railway lines to relieve the three beleaguered garrisons.

Despite the lost opportunities, the Boers had achieved their first strategic aim: to seal off all the garrisons. On all three fronts it was time for the second strategic aim: to dig in and prepare to block the advance of Buller's forces. If they could hold them off, it should be possible to starve the three beleaguered towns into submission.

The first British counter-offensive (November to December 1899)

Sir Redvers Buller, the new Commander-in-Chief in South Africa, landed in Cape Town on 31 October, the day after 'Mournful Monday'. He found Sir Alfred Milner, High Commissioner and Governor at the Cape, 'quaking' at the prospect of the fall of Kimberley and a general Afrikaner uprising in the colony. Panicky telegrams came from Kimberley where Cecil Rhodes had been caught in the siege. White reported from Ladysmith that his supplies could last only sixty days. Reluctantly, Buller decided to discard the original plan of advance along the relatively easy route by way of the railway from Cape Town to Bloemfontein. The Army Corps, a reality only on paper, was split up before even the troop ships docked. Lieutenant-General Lord Methuen was sent to relieve Kimberley with one of the three infantry divisions. Buller himself took another division and part of a third to rescue White's force. Other units, including the cavalry division under Lieutenant-General French and some infantry battalions under Lieutenant-General Gatacre, were pushed up into the threatened north-eastern districts of the Cape Colony where the Free Staters had crossed the Orange.

No one regretted the new makeshifts more than Buller. Despite his brusque manner and bovine appearance, he was one of the few British generals with South African experience. He had not underrated the Boers. He knew he needed weeks to train his men for the novel conditions of war in the veld. He needed to raise mounted men in large enough numbers to

match the Boers in mobility. He needed to organize a proper intelligence. There was no time.

At first Methuen seemed to be making up for lost time. At the battles of Belmont and Graspan (23 and 25 November) he bludgeoned his way through commandos of Free Staters and Transvaalers. At the Modder – or 'Twee Riviere' – (28 November) Methuen's advance faltered. The Transvaalers were now being reinforced by commandos under General Piet Cronjé, detached from the siege of Mafeking. De la Rey pioneered the new tactics by ingeniously digging a concealed defence line along the banks of the Modder River. Tactical co-operation between the commandos, however, eluded the Boers. After a day of heavy losses, 478 in all, Methuen's infantry forced a river passage. At night, Methuen's men could now see the beam of the great signal searchlight of Kimberley reflected on the clouds, but at Magersfontein, Methuen's advance ended in a bloody repulse. Cronjé and De la Rey had set a still more ingenious trap: a trench line set forward from the kopjes and so well disguised as to be invisible to reconnaissance, even by captive balloon. The Highland Brigade marched forward in close column to storm the kopjes just before dawn on 11 December. They were cut down by the concerted rifle fire of thousands of Boers in concealed trenches. Shattered by the loss of 948 men (as opposed to Boer losses of 255 men), Methuen fell back to the Modder to await reinforcements.

An equally humiliating reverse was inflicted on General Gatacre at Stormberg on 10 December. An attempted night march against a small Boer force ended in fiasco: Gatacre lost 135 killed and wounded, and a further 561 taken prisoner.

The culminating reverse was inflicted on Buller at Colenso on 15 December 1899. With the same natural genius for defensive tactics as shown by De la Rey, Louis Botha, who had now replaced Joubert as acting Transvaal commander in Natal, turned the Thukela River into a seemingly impregnable defence line. To relieve Ladysmith, Buller planned to force a crossing at adjoining drifts, one at Colenso itself, the other 7 km upstream, above a loop in the river. Both crossing points proved to be defended by Boers in tier after tier of concealed trenches. Buller called off the attempt before committing more than two brigades but the repulse was costly enough. The Irish Brigade blundered into the loop in the river, losing 523 men. Two field-gun batteries were pushed up so near the enemy by the fire-eating artillery commander, Colonel Charles Long, that ten guns were lost. One of those who died trying to rescue them was Lieutenant Freddy Roberts, son of Field Marshal Lord Roberts. Altogether Buller lost more than 1 100 men at Colenso, while 8 Boers lost their lives and 30 were wounded.

None of these painful reverses lost the British

a metre of useful ground. They did postpone the relief of Ladysmith and Kimberley, but their most important result was the shock they gave to British public opinion. It was finally clear that the war would not be over by Christmas. To be blunt, 60 000 British troops, mostly infantry, were no match for 35 000 Boers, mostly mounted riflemen. Another two infantry divisions – the fifth and sixth – were already on the way. A seventh infantry division was ordered, with nine extra militia battalions and a cavalry brigade. Ten thousand volunteers were to be raised in Great Britain and Ireland, to be called Imperial Yeomanry. Thousands of others were recruited in South Africa, Canada, Australia and New Zealand.

Buller was left in charge of the Natal operations, but was superseded by Lord Roberts as

British soldiers awaiting orders to attack at Colenso on 15 December 1899. Buller's forces were repulsed by Boers under the leadership of Louis Botha. (Transvaal Archives)

◁▽
Louis Botha, acting commander of the Transvaal forces in Natal. (Transvaal Archives)

▽
Lord Frederick Sleigh Roberts (Transvaal Archives)

British dead in the trenches of Spion Kop. Over 300 British soldiers died, and 1 653 were wounded (as against 50 dead and 120 wounded on the Boer side). Recriminations and accusations were exchanged between Sir Charles Warren and Sir Redvers Buller for over two years after the Battle of Spion Kop, which took place on 24 January 1900. (Transvaal Archives)

The Siege of Mafeking (Mafikeng)

The 217-day siege proved no picnic for Baden-Powell's garrison. Six hundred Rhodesians and twelve imperial officers successfully diverted Cronjé and 6 000 Boers to Mafeking during the first crucial two months of the war. They were assisted by a town guard of white civilians and by 300 armed blacks christened the 'Black Watch'. Baden-Powell concealed the weakness of his force by taking what he called 'kicks' at the enemy but suffered casualties as a result. In general the worst hardships in the siege were suffered by the blacks. To spin out the dwindling food supply, Baden-Powell pooled African and European rations. He then decided to force 2 000 blacks – refugees from the Rand and Bechuanaland (Botswana) – to leave the town by refusing them rations. The besiegers would not let them pass, however, and many blacks died of hunger inside Mafeking, while others, including women and children, were shot by the Boers while trying to escape.

A dead Boer sniper at Spion Kop. (Cape Archives, J5262)

Commander-in-Chief in South Africa. To serve as Chief of Staff, Major-General Lord Kichener was brought hurriedly from the Sudan. Within ten days of 'Black Week' Lord Roberts, wearing a black armband, had sailed for Cape Town.

Lord Roberts's advance (January to June 1900)

On the Natal Front, Buller was still outclassed by Botha, as the fate of Ladysmith hung in the balance. At the Battle of Spion Kop (24 January 1900) Buller had entrusted the main force to his second-in-command, General Sir Charles Warren. The plan was for a flank march and a two-pronged attack. Warren forded the Thukela River 32 km west of Colenso, and planned to break through the line somewhere in the Rangeworthy Hills (Tabanyana). Buller himself was to ford the river and break through the hills about 8 km lower down. Then they would advance together to relieve White at Ladysmith. But Warren was so ponderous in his advance that Botha was able to dig in along the crest line and parry the thrust. Warren then sent a column, under Brigadier General Woodgate, to make a night march and storm Spion Kop, the rocky spur that seemed to be the key to the line. The storming party found Spion Kop almost undefended, but they failed to entrench properly on the summit, and when daylight came were raked by converging rifle and artillery fire. Warren failed to support them and Woodgate was mortally wounded. The key became a trap. Though many of the burghers fled back towards Ladysmith, Botha's amazing self-confidence was proved justified. Buller was forced to retreat.

At Vaalkrans Buller found what he called another 'key' to the enemy's line, and it proved equally useless. On 7 February he again withdrew across the Thukela. People began to ridicule him, calling him 'Sir Reverse' and 'the Ferryman'. Botha won nothing but praise for his defensive tactics. Once again the Boers showed their dual genius for rapid changes of position and for digging in. However, the Boers lost nearly 400 men in these battles, men who could not (unlike British casualties) be easily replaced.

Meanwhile Lord Roberts, with the combined objective of relieving Kimberley and invading the republics, had set off and swept all before him. He had by far the largest army yet seen in the war (43 000 men) and a much higher proportion (about a quarter) of mounted men.

With this double advantage he swiftly out-manoeuvred the Boers besieging Kimberley. Cronjé abandoned his great trench line at Magersfontein and fled eastwards up the banks of the Modder River. On 15 February officers of the cavalry division, led by Lieutenant-General French, rode triumphantly up to Kimberley Sanatorium. There they celebrated the relief with champagne given to them by Cecil Rhodes, who took the opportunity to denounce Colonel Kekewich, the long-suffering commander of the British garrison.

Roberts's mounted troops cornered Cronjé, encumbered with a wagon train, in laager at Paardeberg. But Kitchener, acting commander while Roberts was ill, then made one of the costliest blunders of the war, from the British point of view. He threw battalion after battalion at Cronjé's laager, losing more men for less purpose than had Buller at Colenso or Methuen at Magersfontein. Nevertheless the Boers were trapped without prospect of rescue. On 27 February, the nineteenth anniversary of the Battle of Majuba, after days of artillery bombardment, Cronjé surrendered to Roberts with 4 000 men, some women, children and some black servants. Cronjé's surrender at Paardeberg was a tremendous blow to Boer resources and morale. Christiaan de Wet subsequently declared that the effects of the battle 'made themselves apparent to the very end of the war'.

Next day (28 February) on the Natal front, Buller finally hammered his way through and relieved Ladysmith. From 14 to 28 February Buller had slowly squeezed Botha out of his interlocking positions, at last exploiting the full weight of his artillery, and the courage and tenacity of his infantry. Despite severe casualties, Botha's men still kept cool heads – unlike Cronjé's men at Paardeberg. At dusk on 28 February the first British troops – actually two squadrons of Uitlanders in the Imperial Light Horse – plodded into Ladysmith.

Lord Roberts's grand army continued to advance like a steamroller across the level plains of the Free State. Twice the burghers of the two republics tried to make a stand south-west of Bloemfontein, at Poplar Grove (7 March) and at Driefontein (10 March). After a spirited but brief resistance, they fled. Bloemfontein was evacuated with hardly a shot being fired as Roberts's troops tramped into the town on 13 March.

Roberts now made a fatal strategic miscalculation. He believed that, as he reported to Queen Victoria, it would 'not be very long before the war would have been brought to a satisfactory conclusion'. The Free State spirit was broken. When Pretoria was occupied Transvaal resistance, too, would crumble. To encourage the process Roberts proclaimed an amnesty (15 March) for all burghers, except leaders, who took an oath of neutrality and returned quietly to their homes. He made no move to intercept a Boer column of 6 000 burghers, led by General Olivier, apparently trapped close to the Orange River.

At a *krygsraad* in Kroonstad (17 March) both Boer Presidents pledged that the war would be

During the Siege of Mafeking, a court of Summary Jurisdiction sentenced George Malhombe to death for stealing a goat. The document of warrant was signed by Lieutenant-Colonel Baden-Powell and the execution was carried out on 29 March 1900. In the photograph are (from the left) the accused, George Malhombe (bare headed), Melemo the Barolong chief, Lord Edward Cecil (seated with black armband), G H Bell, the resident magistrate (seated), and Heald, the jailer (standing, on the extreme right). (By courtesy of Thomas Pakenham)

◁▽
Cecil Rhodes during the Siege of Kimberley, at the De Beers Mine where 'Siege Soup' at 3d a pint was mixed. Although white civilians at Kimberley could purchase rations of meat and vegetables, blacks were not allowed to buy those foodstuffs, and had to try and survive on a diet of mealies alone. Many deaths from scurvy resulted, particularly in the mine compounds. (Transvaal Archives)

▽
General Piet Cronjé arrives at the British lines on 27 February 1900 to surrender formally to Lord Roberts after the Battle of Paardeberg. (Transvaal Archives)

The Battle of Spion Kop, showing the British troops under Colonel Thorneycroft exposed to withering Boer fire on the plateau of Spion Kop. The painting is by Sylvester Reisacher. (National Cultural History and Open-air Museum (NCHOM))

The Battle and Siege of Paardeberg, by Sylvester Reisacher. For ten days from 17 to 27 February, General Cronjé and over 4 000 men, women and children were pinned down at Paardeberg on the banks of the Modder River by British troop under Generals French, Kitchener and Roberts. The Boers entrenched themselves into the banks of the river, and only 150 casualties were found after the surrender. The suffering of the horses is graphically illustrated in the painting. (NCHOM)

pursued with more vigour than ever. At the suggestion of De Wet and De la Rey, it was planned to make the commandos still more mobile by abandoning the bullock wagons which had been the undoing of Cronjé. Commandos could then raid behind the British lines. Conventional battles would give place to guerrilla warfare. The burghers' spirits, always mercurial, rebounded. As De Wet later recorded: 'There was only one word on every tongue – "Forward".'

De Wet lost no time in showing the advantages of the new guerrilla strategy. On 31 March he ambushed a column, under command of Brigadier-General Broadwood. De Wet had planned to attack the much smaller column defending the main waterworks at Sannah's Post, 32 km east of Bloemfontein. Then Broadwood, whose column had no scouts at its head, blundered into the trap. De Wet's bag was eight field guns and hundreds of prisoners. On 4 April De Wet made a second raid and snapped up half a battalion of the Royal Irish at Reddersburg, before vanishing again northwards. He

had inflicted a total of over a thousand casualties on the British with next to no loss on his own small force.

De Wet's raids postponed but could not prevent Roberts's advance. The second of Roberts's 'tiger-springs' began on 3 May. He had decided to advance in a double column, 43 000 strong, straight along the line of the main railway to Johannesburg and Pretoria. Meanwhile the mobile part of Buller's Natal army, two infantry divisions and two cavalry brigades, would converge on the Transvaal from the south-east. At the same time Roberts sent a small flying column – 1 149 officers and men, mainly Uitlanders from the Rand and colonials from Kimberley, under Colonel Bryan Mahon – to relieve Baden-Powell at Mafeking far to the north-west.

Mahon's column joined hands with a second relief column under Lieutenant-Colonel H Plumer, sent south from Rhodesia months earlier, but too weak to relieve Mafeking unaided. Their march into Mafeking on 17 May was something of an anticlimax. 'Oh yes, I

heard you were knocking about,' said one of the passers-by to the first of the rescuers. There were no hysterical scenes as there were in London when the news of the relief was published a couple of days later – no 'mafficking' (the new English word for this kind of patriotic hysteria) at Mafeking.

In the Free State Roberts's great steamroller rolled on. Roberts's superiority in numbers gave such breadth to his columns that he simply brushed the commandos aside. Blowing up the strategic railway bridges and miles of line had little effect. British engineers, helped by black navvies, built 'deviations' within hours.

On 27 May Roberts splashed across the Vaal drift. The next day the annexation of the Orange Free State was formally proclaimed, and it was renamed the Orange River Colony. The Transvaalers momentarily checked the advance at Doornkop, close to where Dr Jameson had made his last stand in 1896. Then they fled in confusion, abandoning Johannesburg (31 May) and Pretoria (5 June) in turn.

The morale of the Transvaal commandos reached its nadir on 1 June. On that day, at a *krygsraad* in Pretoria, Smuts and Botha drafted a despairing telegram to Kruger, who had fled eastwards down the railway towards Mozambique. In turn, Kruger sent an equally despairing message to President Steyn at his laager near Heilbron. The reply from Steyn came like a slap in the face to the Transvaal leader. The Free State would never surrender. Smuts and Botha and the other Transvaal leaders took heart. It was decided to make a fighting retreat, after all, giving time to the burghers to recover from the shock of abandoning the capital. Despite the apparent confusion a vital breathing space had been won, without which the war could not have continued. The war chest for both republics – £500 000 in gold and gold coin – was safely removed from Pretoria, as were the heavy guns and reserve ammunition. Burghers flocked back to join the commandos. The pendulum swung back towards hope.

The same week the guerrilla strategy developed by Christiaan de Wet brought a new dimension to the war. On 31 May his brother,

Lord Alfred Milner and his staff at Government House, Cape Town. Standing is Violet Cecil, whose husband, Lord Edward Cecil, was besieged in Mafeking. (Transvaal Archives)

The desolate figure of Paul Kruger, standing on the deck of the *Gelderland* in Octobr 1900. His secretary, M Bredell, stands on his right. (Transvaal Archives)

Piet de Wet, surrounded four companies of Irish yeomanry left at Lindley in the eastern Free State, killed 50 men, wounded 80 and captured a further 450. On 7 June Christiaan de Wet himself struck a triple blow at weak garrison posts along the railway line close to the Renoster River and inflicted 486 casualties at virtually no loss to himself. A vast supply dump was looted and burnt. The single line railway linking the Transvaal with the Cape ports was cut for days, throwing Roberts's staff into panic. By the time Roberts's columns had lumbered up, De Wet and Steyn, twin symbols of resistance, had vanished.

The Cape Colony and the war up to June 1900

From the beginning of the war, the position of the Cape Prime Minister, W P Schreiner, proved anomalous. Soon it became impossible. He was the leader of a ministry dominated by Afrikaners and Bondsmen, whose hearts lay with the two republics. He himself was emotionally and politically ambivalent and he found himself trying to keep his strategic colony, in a great imperial war, as near neutral as possible. Schreiner relied on the most solemn assurances he received from Steyn that the Free State would not invade the Cape. To allow the Cape's own forces to be used to invade the Free State might precipitate risings within the colony: an Afrikaner rising in sympathy with the republics, and a black rising, too, in the general confusion.

The Cape Government had dragged its feet in defence preparations and had allowed the Free State to import ammunition by way of the Cape in the weeks before the war broke out. Cape Government forces played no real part in the crucial struggles to defend Kimberley and Mafeking. On the other hand, when it was clear to Schreiner that he had been misled by Steyn's assurances, he allowed himself, step by step, to be led by Milner. As each district was invaded by Free State commandos, it was proclaimed by the Cape to be under martial law, a futile exercise were the Free State to annex the districts, as it soon did. When Buller's and Roberts's forces began to recover these districts south of the Orange, however, they could make their own rules, according to martial law; arrest suspects, requisition supplies and censor letters. The great Afrikaner rising, feared by both Schreiner and Milner, never took place.

Milner claimed that about 3 000 Afrikaners crossed into the Free State before the war, and served with the commandos. A further 10 000 Cape colonials were claimed to have volunteered to join the Free State when the commandos invaded. This had no great military significance. There were only two 'rebellions': at Prieska and in Griqualand West. Both were extinguished without much bloodshed in May and June 1900. Their chief effect was political, as they finally brought down Schreiner's ministry.

Milner, Chamberlain and the British Government wanted the surrendered Cape rebels to be punished severely. Schreiner suggested a compromise: charges of high treason for the leaders, but only five years' disfranchisement for the rank and file. Chamberlain agreed. Then Schreiner was deserted by all except two of his Cabinet. The majority insisted that the 'rebels' should not be treated more harshly than other prisoners of war. They also believed that ordinary civil law should be restored. Schreiner resigned, and back into power came his predecessor, Sir Gordon Sprigg, leader of the Progressives, although he lacked a parliamentary majority. With the help of Schreiner, and a few other of his opponents, Sprigg pushed through an Indemnity Act in October 1900. For the present the Cape rebels were treated leniently enough, although sterner measures were to follow in 1901.

Lord Roberts's command (June to November 1900)

Lord Roberts began his third 'tiger-spring', the advance on Komati Poort, on 21 July. Ahead of him were the bulk of the Transvaal forces still in the field, led by Louis Botha. From Heidelberg to the south-east, Buller prepared to resume his advance and converge on the Delagoa Bay railway. Formal battles, however, now proved of secondary importance compared to the guerrilla strategy being developed by Steyn, De Wet and the Free Staters.

Despite the tempting bait of Roberts's amnesty, De Wet had managed to keep in the field

8 000 burghers in the eastern Free State. Roberts detached five columns, led by Lieutenant-General Sir Archibald Hunter, to round up De Wet. An opportunity of catching Steyn and De Wet eluded him on the night of 15 July when these two, with 2 500 men and a long wagon train, slipped through the cordon and headed north again. Hunter's five columns converged, brushing aside resistance and turning the Brandwater Basin into a trap. Though one of the passes, Golden Gate, remained open, over 4 000 of the burghers under General Marthinus Prinsloo surrendered on 30 July. It was a disaster for the Free State.

Though still burdened by ox-wagons, De Wet's commando yet again slipped through Roberts's column. On 6 August they crossed the Vaal River by one of the main drifts and trundled north in a great cloud of dust. Roberts ordered the passes of the Magaliesberg to be sealed. Behind De Wet were at least 20 000 troops in hot pursuit. Roberts and his column commanders failed to co-ordinate, and De Wet eluded them. The latter's scouts discovered to their astonishment that Olifant's Nek was still open, as General Ian Hamilton, who had been instructed by Roberts to seal it off, had been unable to do so. The wagon train streamed across the undefended nek on 14 August.

Meanwhile, in the eastern Transvaal, Roberts and Buller had joined hands and made a final attempt to win the war in a conventional way. At Belfast (also known as the Battle of Bergendal or Dalmanutha) between 21 and 27 August, Buller attacked Botha's position astride the Delagoa railway. The Johannesburg police fought – and died – with heroism. The burghers scattered, but their morale held. To the south General French cleared the country around Carolina. East of Belfast the prisoner of war camp near Waterval-Onder was reached and the prisoners liberated. On 24 September Lieutenant-General Sir Reginald Pole-Carew's division finally reached the border at Komati Poort. The Boers had fled long before.

On 11 September President Kruger had passed down the railway, on his way to lead a mission to Europe. The Dutch Government sent a cruiser, the *Gelderland*, to take him to Marseilles. The executive power of the Transvaal now rested in the hands of men like Botha, Smuts and De la Rey. Although the commandos were scattered over both republics, the decision remained – to fight to the bitter end.

Lord Roberts was still convinced that the war was 'practically over' and that firm methods were all that was needed. In private he announced that he would 'starve them into submission' by removing the stock and other food supplies from the country. His stated policy towards civilians, expressed in a series of somewhat confusing proclamations, was still a kid-glove policy. Fighting burghers who had already taken the oath of neutrality were still al-

lowed to remain at home. Civilians were promised protection from looting and ill treatment. New proclamations, however, in the Transvaal on 14 August, and in the Orange River Colony on 1 September, warned that burghers who surrendered in future would be treated as prisoners of war.

A new policy of collective punishment had been started earlier. The British Government published in due course a list of Boer farms and other buildings which had been burnt down by the army: 2 in June 1900, 3 in July, 12 in August, 99 in September, 189 in October, 226 in November. The proportions may have been correct, but the scale must have been higher. Eventually the inhumanity of farm burning provoked an outcry in the British House of Commons. In November Roberts issued a new order countermanding, in theory at least, the severities. It was not reason enough to burn a farm simply because its owner was away on commando. There would have to have been some 'act of treachery', as when troops had been fired

A sequence of photographs showing the blowing up of Louis Botha's farmhouse by the British. (Transvaal Archives)

Horatio Herbert Kitchener (Lord Kitchener of Khartoum). (Transvaal Archives)

The Anglo-Boer War, 1899-1902

on, or as punishment for breaking of the railway or telegraph line, or when they had been used as bases of operations. According to the British Government, the result of this new order was that only six houses were burnt in December 1900. Even if this were true, which is highly questionable, the British army continued to strip the veld of all food supplies that could prove useful to the guerrillas. The country continued to be devastated and the plight of the civilians became increasingly desperate.

Before Roberts sailed from Cape Town on 11 December 1900 he repeated, once again, that the war was 'practically over'. Lord Kitchener, the new Commander-in-Chief, had already taken over on 29 November. The size of the army was being reduced month by month. In the last ten months Lord Roberts had made a great change in the map of South Africa. The Union Jack now flew over both Bloemfontein and Pretoria. The two Presidents had fled the capitals – Kruger on a forlorn mission to Europe, Steyn on the run with De Wet and his commandos. The main towns and railway lines of the new colonies were now under British military control.

Roberts was right. The war was practically over: the war of large scale, set-piece battles. But a new war – just as costly in time and money and lives, and far more bitter, because it directly involved citizens – had only just begun.

Kitchener and the guerrilla war (December 1900 to May 1902)

The Boer strategy for the new war had been hammered out by leaders from both republics – De la Rey, Botha, Smuts and Steyn – who met at a farm called Cypherfontein in the southwestern Transvaal in the last few days of October. In the discussions it was the Transvaalers, especially Botha, who apparently felt misgivings about the practicality of guerrilla warfare.

De Wet, though absent, supplied the answer. He had publicly made his point ever since the first ambushes of Roberts's convoys in March, and Roberts, by his counter-measures – burning and looting the farms – now seemed to confirm it. What better way of showing a burgher that his oath of neutrality was null and void than by pointing to his family shivering in the blackened ruins of his farmstead? That was in the short

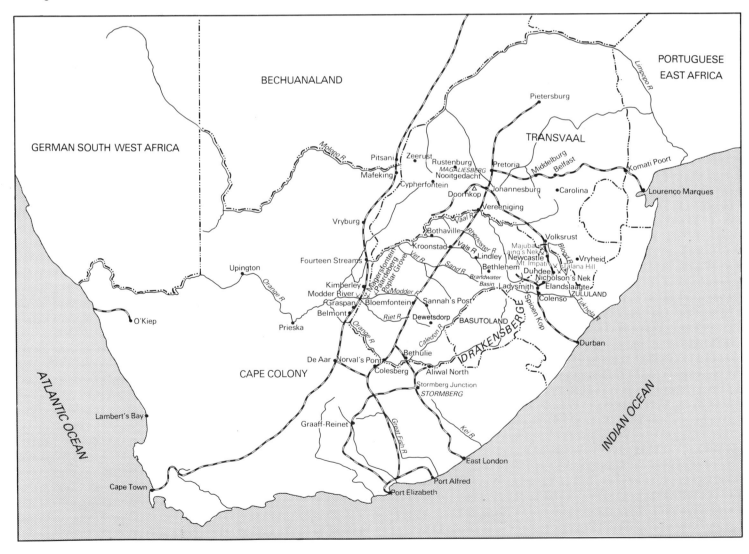

run. In the long run, Roberts's policy of farm burning and crop burning could only work against the commandos. Already some parts of the veld were reverting to desert. The answer from the Cypherfontein discussions was to extend the guerrilla war to the Cape Colony and Natal. Afrikaners would respond readily in the Cape particularly. Both colonies were well supplied with grain and horses and it would be politically impossible in the colonies for the British to resort to farm burning and crop burning.

Had this new policy been carried into effect as a joint offensive it might have changed the whole course of the war, but the divisions between the allies ran too deep. De Wet failed to reach Cypherfontein, as the British began to hustle the guerrillas in the area. The chance of any joint offensive was lost. On 6 November, at Bothaville (Doornkraal) on the Vals River, De Wet and Steyn were for once caught napping by a mounted column of 'khakis'. Only the speed of their own flight, the heroism of their rearguard, and the slowness of the main British column under Major-General Charles Knox saved the Free State leaders from death or capture. By the end of November, however, De Wet was back in his old hunting ground, snapping up convoys in the Free State and burning garrisons with impunity. And on 13 December Smuts and De la Rey found bigger game caught by the horns in the great gorge at Nooitgedacht.

For three months Major-General Clements and his column had been ravaging the 'Moot' – the valley of the Magaliesberg. On 3 December the commandos captured a convoy of ill defended ox-wagons heading for Rustenburg. Clements had chosen a site for his main camp in the gorge at Nooitgedacht, commanded by the mountain ridge, which was itself only lightly guarded. Just before dawn on 13 December General C F Beyers, with 1 500 men, rushed a picket line on the mountain. Commandant C P Badenhorst broke in from the west. General Smuts and De la Rey stormed the camp from the valley below. The attacks were not perfectly

co-ordinated, yet Clements lost heavily: 637 dead, wounded and taken prisoner. However, the survivors cut their way out of the trap and apart from a boost to morale, the victors got nothing but a mountain of stores. To capture the enemy's guns and achieve a complete tactical victory was beyond them. Once again the initiative passed back to the British.

Meanwhile Kitchener's first serious challenge as Commander-in-Chief was the invasion of the Cape Colony by three separate groups of commandos. Understandably Kitchener's priority was to block De Wet and Steyn. On 23 November De Wet captured Dewetsdorp, the town named after his father. He then dodged south, pursued by an increasing number of British columns. He first tried to cross the Orange on 6 December, but the river was in flood, and he was driven back northwards. On 14 December he was nearly trapped at Sprinkaansnek, but managed to cut his way out. Two months later he swooped down a second time and on 10 February succeeded in crossing the Orange at Sanddrif. But once again Kitchener threw such a net of mounted columns around him that De

General 'Koos' de la Rey (Transvaal Archives)

◁◁
Jan Christiaan Smuts, 29-year-old Transvaal State Attorney at the outbreak of war in 1899. (Transvaal Archives)

◁
Gideon Scheepers (Transvaal Archives)

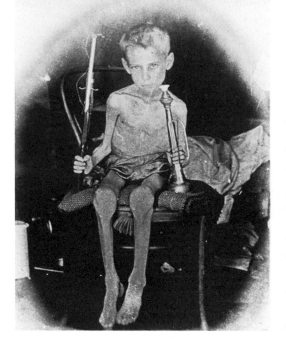

An emaciated Boer child from a concentration camp. One in five children in the camps died. (Transvaal Archives)

The concentration camps

In September 1900 Lord Roberts officially sanctioned the establishment of so-called refugee camps, and three months later Kitchener ordered the removal into camps of all non-combatants in certain areas. By the end of the war there were more than 40 camps, accommodating some 116 000 white people and more than 60 separate camps containing about 115 000 black people.

The majority of the inmates were not really refugees, but people who had been caught up in the British military drives. It was also believed that the presence of Boer families in British camps would induce burghers in the field to surrender. Black people were cleared from the country to prevent commandos obtaining supplies, information and assistance. Subsequently black men were employed as labourers while their families remained in the camps. The concentration camps were devised as a military measure aimed at ending the resistance of fighting Boers.

Kitchener initially ordered that families of surrendered burghers should receive better accommodation and diets than the wives and children of men who were still in the field. Conditions which varied from camp to camp depended largely on the situation of the camp and the personality and ability of individual superintendents. Deliberate ill-treatment, much less extermination, were never sanctioned by the British High Command, nevertheless poor accommodation (mostly in tents), unsuitable diet, insufficient bedding and unhygienic sanitary conditions abounded. These factors, together with the unhealthy state of the environment and extraordinary outbreaks of measles and pneumonia, were aggravated by the concentration of people unused to living in such close proximity.

From the winter of 1901 deaths occurred at an alarming rate in the camps. During the last months of that year conditions started improving but the harm had been done. Altogether 27 927 Boers (of whom 26 251 were women and children) died in the camps while more than 14 000 black people perished in their camps.

S B Spies

Washing day in Bethulie Concentration Camp. (Transvaal Archives)

Wet achieved nothing – except to prove his ability to move faster than his pursuers. Exhausted after 1 000 km of hard marching, he thankfully recrossed the Orange and returned to his old lairs in the Free State.

On 6 December about a thousand burghers under General J B M Hertzog did succeed in fording the Orange River at Sanddrif, while about 700 others under Commandant P H Kritzinger crossed near Burgersdorp. The two groups of commandos rode rapidly south. Hertzog side-stepped every thrust, and by January he turned the Roggeveld passes. Riding hard, his men reached the sea at Lambert's Bay, only to be shelled by a British warship. Kritzinger swooped down into the Zuurberg, brushing aside the enemy. Neither group attracted any useful number of recruits from the local Afrikaners, however, let alone precipitate a general

rising. By the end of February Hertzog had joined hands with De Wet and recrossed the Orange. Kritzinger retreated into the fastnesses of the Zuurberg. As an operation, the Boer invasion of the Cape Colony had failed as completely as the British attempt to catch the invaders.

By 17 January 1901 virtually the whole of the Cape Colony, except the ports and the Transkei, had been proclaimed to be under martial law. At the same time Milner talked Sprigg into recruiting 10 000 loyalists as a militia. With their help, the authorities were able to requisition horses and food supplies in parts of the colony in order to deny them to guerrilla bands trying to live off the country. It needed more subtlety than farm burning, but certainly proved more effective as well as more humane. These new expedients in the Cape – military and legal – continued to be tested until the war's end. By May 1901 parts of the colony were infested by small roving bands of guerrillas, including Kritzinger's. A month earlier special military courts were set up to try colonial rebels caught in arms. As Kitchener's columns gradually hunted them down the toll of the military courts continued to rise. By the end of the war military courts had imposed 700 death sentences on colonial rebels. Of these sentences, 35 were confirmed by Kitchener, and the men shot by firing squad. In addition, sixteen others, Transvaalers, Free Staters and some blacks, were executed. They had been convicted of offences like the murder of blacks or (in the case of several blacks) the rape of white women.

In February Kitchener persuaded Louis Botha to come to the British lines under safe conduct and discuss terms of peace, but the hopes raised by the meeting at Middelburg, Transvaal, on 28 February 1901 proved illu-

Inmates of a concentration camp queuing for rations. (Transvaal Archives)

sory. Kitchener's offer, sanctioned by the British Government, was similar in most respects to the offer that the commandos were to accept when the bitter end was finally reached at Vereeniging in May 1902. Kitchener wished to make one additional concession, ie to let the Cape rebels off with disenfranchisement, but Milner and the British Government blocked this concession. It probably made no difference; the spirit of the fighting burghers wavered but was not yet broken.

Rebuffed by Botha, Kitchener flung himself into the task of flushing out the guerrillas from the veld by extending the concentration camp system and organizing vast military 'drives' to clear the country of people and supplies. At first the number of guerrillas captured in these 'drives' (as opposed to women and children) was frustratingly small.

In March 1901 Kitchener began to devise a new strategy, employing blockhouses, which slowly evolved until it proved decisive. The gigantic grid mesh of tin and stone blockhouses soon straddled the veld, connected to each other by barbed wire fences and linked by telephone lines. By the end of the war there were 8 000 blockhouses: the blockhouse lines covered 6 000 km and were guarded by 50 000 troops and 16 000 blacks employed as scouts and 'watchers'. With the help of the blockhouse lines Kitchener could now ensure that increasingly large areas of the country remained free of the enemy. At the same time the lines could be used to wear down guerrillas. The columns drove the commandos against the lines of the blockhouses. Most guerrillas escaped, but the escapes progressively weakened them. To aid the columns Kitchener added large numbers of blacks as scouts and drivers. Some of these were armed for their own protection as the Boers often shot captured black scouts out of hand. Kitchener also recruited surrendered Boers to join in the drives. In the Transvaal a corps of 'National Scouts' was formed, and in the Free State a corps of 'Orange River Colony Volunteers'.

One other change to the drives was made by Kitchener. He ordered the columns to stop bringing in women and children to the concentration camps. His motive was not humanity, however; he had finally decided that the concentration camp policy was a mistake. The burghers on commando would now be more hampered than helped by the presence of their womenfolk.

By September 1901 the Boer leaders, on their part, were becoming increasingly desperate. Smuts decided that with the two republics being cleared of all supplies, he should invade the Cape Colony to try again to precipitate an Afrikaner uprising. On 3 September he crossed the

Emily Hobhouse (Transvaal Archives)

Black people in the war

In October 1899 there was tacit agreement among both the British and Boer leaderships that the conflict would be a 'white man's war' in which black people would be excluded from serving as armed soldiers. However, it was also recognized that warfare could not be an entirely white pursuit in a society in which black people made up four-fifths of the population. Nor could the British and Boers undertake their campaigns without the assistance of blacks. The British army, especially, needed ancillary services and looked to the African and Coloured populations to provide much of the skilled and unskilled labour that was required. As many as 100 000 black people were employed as transport drivers and leaders, blacksmiths, wheelwrights, farriers and carpenters; as workers engaged in constructing fortifications, portering and communications; as scouts and intelligence gatherers; and as general unskilled labourers and servants in the military camps.

The Boer forces, too, depended on black people to perform ancillary duties. Men were conscripted to drive wagons, dig trenches, gather intelligence, look after horses, collect firewood, and perform a host of other essential tasks. Many burghers were accompanied by one or more farm servants who acted as *agterryers*, attending to their employers' needs while on commando, supervising horses and equipment, and loading rifles when in combat.

As the war progressed black people became much more deeply, and much more controversially, involved in the struggle, especially on the British side. Even during the first weeks of the war some blacks had been armed in the Cape to defend settlements against Boer occupation. Armed blacks were to be found in the trenches of both opposing forces at Mafeking, and Baden-Powell enrolled local Barolong and Coloureds to defend the town. The British employment of armed scouts began at the end of 1900 when, on the grounds that scouts needed to protect themselves, enrolled

men were no longer automatically disarmed. Under Kitchener's command the number of armed blacks with the British army grew as a result of the heavy manpower demands of the anti-guerrilla campaign and the high rate of sickness among British troops. Armed black scouts came to provide much of the British army's intelligence of Boer movements, and black sentries guarded many of the blockhouses and lines of fortification intended to restrict the mobility of the Boer guerrilla groups. Precise statistics were never maintained, but at least 10 000, and probably as many as 30 000 blacks were serving under arms with the British army by the end of the war.

Black people also became actively embroiled in the war on a much less regular basis, especially in the Transvaal, where the republican state collapsed from internal black resistance as well as from external military invasion. From early 1900 onwards large areas of the western, northern and south-eastern Transvaal became inhospitable to Boer families and small groups of Boer fighters because of black hostility. When Smuts travelled through the western Transvaal in mid-1900 he found areas from which all the white inhabitants had fled and where former black tenants had taken over land and farms. Indeed the Kgatla, supported by regiments from across the Botswana frontier, came to control much of the western districts of the Transvaal with the approval of the British army. In the north farms were similarly taken over by blacks and defended against the Boer guerrilla groups.

In the south-eastern Transvaal many Zulu communities conducted a campaign of harassment against local commando units. The relations between the two groups became increasingly embittered, culminating in an assault on the Vryheid commando by a Qulusi *impi* at Holkrans in May 1902 in which 56 burghers perished. Significantly, one of the most important reasons cited by the Boer representatives for accepting peace terms was that many

Kit inspection, Zulu 'Native' Police. (Cape Archives, J567)

blacks were 'armed and taking part in the war against us, and . . . have caused an unbearable condition of affairs in many districts of both republics'.

If the war years were a time of opportunity in which the actions of black people helped to shape the course of the Anglo-Boer struggle, they were also years of disruption and hardship for many others. The suspension of most mining activity at the outbreak of war drove many migrant workers back to the rural areas, where it was difficult to feed all the men normally absent at work. More than anything else it was poverty and the need to earn a wage which drew blacks into British military employment. In the Transvaal and Orange Free State Kitchener's scorched-earth tactics led to the uprooting of black as well as white families, and by the end of the war 115 700 black refugees had been settled in 66 concentration camps. The black camps were used as a source of cheap labour for the British army and prevailing conditions were worse even than in the camps

for white refugees. Over 14 000 blacks died in the overcrowded, insanitary and ill-organized camps, one in ten of the refugee inhabitants.

For those black people who left the concentration camps after the war the future held little hope beyond wage labour. Indeed, for those blacks who had occupied farms and planted new gardens, or rubbed shoulders in a common struggle with British soldiers, or looked forward to a new administration in the conquered Boer states which would be more sympathetic to their interests, hope began to fade even before the ink was dry on the peace agreement. It was clear from the peace terms that a non-racial franchise, similar to that of the Cape, would not be introduced by Britain into her two new South African colonies, as many black people had hoped. Labour regulations were modernized and more effectively administered by the postwar British regime, and among black people disillusionment and a feeling of betrayal crept in.

Peter Warwick

The flogging of blacks occurred in both British and Boer camps. (By courtesy of Thomas Pakenham)

Orange River with about 250 men. They were half starved and unable to get fresh ponies, and failed to precipitate any kind of rising. On the other hand to survive at all was a triumph. Smuts, however, succeeded in cutting his way through to the north-western Cape, and ended the war besieging the British posts at O'Kiep.

Also in September, Louis Botha tried to open a new front by invading Natal. Despite a brilliant stroke at Blood River Poort on 17 September, his 'invasion' fizzled out. He was hunted back into the Transvaal, where he cut up one of Kitchener's best columns, led by Colonel Benson, at Bakenlaagte on 30 October. Kitchener's drives continued, despite isolated Boer successes, to reduce Boer numbers month by month. De Wet scored a brilliant success when storming a camp of 400 Imperial Yeomanry at Tweefontein (Groenkop) on Christmas Day 1901. De la Rey also had some success when he defeated and captured Lord Methuen at Tweebosch on 6 March 1902, but there was no answer to the arithmetic of Kitchener's 'bag': December, 1 579; January, 1 387; February, over 2 000.

The guerrillas were being pushed further and further into the wilderness, beyond the blockhouse lines. At the same time the Transvaal economy began to revive. Black miners were recruited again and by April 39 000 Uitlanders had returned to the Transvaal. A third of the gold mines were working again and already the two new colonies were self-sufficient in revenue. At last the interminable war seemed to be fizzling out.

Assessment

The war had given the British, in Kipling's phrase, an 'imperial lesson'. The British public had expected it to be over by Christmas. It was the longest (almost three years), the costliest (over £200 million), the bloodiest (at least 22 000 British, 34 000 Boer and 15 000 black lives), and the most humiliating war for Britain between 1815 and 1915.

The British estimated that there were over 100 000 casualties of all kinds among the 365 593 imperial and 82 742 colonial soldiers who fought on the British side. Of the British dead, 5 744 were killed in action, and 16 168 died of wounds or of disease. They also recorded that 400 346 horses, mules and donkeys were 'expended' in the war. They did not record the casualties among the 10 000 armed blacks who had been enlisted on the British side, nor among the 40 000-odd unarmed blacks who had served the army as scouts, guides and drivers.

The British estimated that there were 7 000 dead among the 87 365 Boers who had fought in the war, including the 2 120 foreign volunteers

British (above) and Boer (below) prisoners-of-war. (Cape Archives, J548 and Transvaal Archives)

The 'handsuppers' and 'joiners'

Following the fall of Bloemfontein and Pretoria, and the British annexation of the two republics, no less than 10 900 burghers voluntarily laid down their arms and took the British oath of neutrality. The number of Boers who surrendered during the war ('handsuppers') represented about 26 per cent of those who were liable for military service, or 40 per cent of the burghers who were originally mobilized. Some of these subsequently rejoined the commandos. Many burghers conceded defeat because of large-scale demoralization following the capture of the Boer capitals. More specifically, the men who surrendered may be categorized as follows: those who considered the continuation of the struggle as unrealistic and detrimental to the country, those who had become war-weary and who had lost interest in the outcome, and, those who were primarily concerned with their own personal and material well-being. Clearly these reasons were often intertwined. Towards the end of 1900 some of the surrendered Boers, with the encouragement of the British authorities, formed Burgher Peace Committees, by which they vainly endeavoured to persuade the hard-pressed bitter-einders to surrender. These peace emmissaries were regarded as traitors by the Boers in the field and had no credibility as intermediaries. Two of them, M de Kock and J Morgendaal, paid with their lives.

It was particularly during the last six months of the war that some 'handsuppers' fought actively on the British side. By May 1902 these so-called 'joiners' totalled 5 464 men – not an insignificant number, bearing in mind that there were about 17 000 bittereinders in the field when hostilities ceased. The Boers in British ranks served as guides and scouts, attached as individuals to large columns, as well as being organized into small local burgher corps and larger units such as the National Scouts in the Transvaal and the Orange River Colony Volunteers in the Free State. Owing to their intimate knowledge of the terrain they made an invaluable contribution to British military operations.

The Boer leaders in the field, alarmed by these developments, cited the rift in Afrikaner ranks as one of the considerations which induced them to agree to negotiate for peace in May 1902. Indigent bywoners, who had held inferior social and economic status in the pre-war Boer communities, constituted an appreciable proportion of the 'joiners'. As an 'underprivileged' group they fell easy prey to the misleading British promises of untold prosperity; if they fought for the British, they would receive, amongst other inducements, a free farm. Some 'handsuppers' had become 'joiners' because they were frustrated with the depressing monotony of their existence in the concentration camps, where they were placed after their surrender; family considerations probably also played a role, since many 'joiners' were related to each other. Moreover 'joiners' argued that since the republics had already been annexed, the war should be ended for the sake of the women and children in the concentration camps. To many, this was simply a rationalization to justify their own behaviour, yet such considerations may have been important motivations in the cases of leaders such as Piet de Wet (brother of Christiaan de Wet) and Andries Cronjé.

After the war, the defectors were so roundly rejected by the rest of the Boer people, that they even started their own church, but by 1907 most had been re-admitted to Afrikaner spiritual and political ranks. The process of reconciliation was accelerated owing to the attitude of forgiveness adopted by bitter-einder leaders such as Louis Botha and by the British post-war policy of aloofness towards the 'handsuppers' and 'joiners'.

A Grundlingh

The Middelburg conference of 28 February 1901. Botha and Kitchener, seated in the centre, met at Middelburg, Transvaal, to discuss peace terms. The talks achieved little, and were opposed by the Free State Boers and by Milner. The war continued until May 1902, when the Peace Conference of Vereeniging took place. (Transvaal Archives)

and 13 300 Afrikaners from the Cape and Natal.

Some of the military lessons of the war proved valuable to the British in the Great War. The central tactical lesson of the Boer War, however, eluded them. The reason for those humiliating reverses was not the marksmanship of the Boers, nor their better guns or rifles, nor the crass stupidity of the British generals – all myths which British people found it convenient to believe. It was the smokeless, long-range, high velocity, smallbore magazine rifle – plus the trench – that had decisively tilted the balance against attack and in favour of defence. The world learnt this lesson the hard way, in the bloody stalemates of the Dardanelles and Flanders.

The peace talks

The first peace talks began on 11 April, when a special train brought Schalk Burger, Smuts, Botha, De Wet, Steyn and other Boer leaders to the British Army HQ at Pretoria. Kitchener opened negotiations, and Milner did his best to block them. For months the two men had been at loggerheads. Milner had been shocked by Kitchener's policy of ravaging the country, seeing it as both cruel and ineffective. At the same time Milner opposed all peace talks. The war was ending anyway and he felt they should insist on unconditional surrender. This was the only way he could keep his own hands free to remould South Africa after the peace.

The commandos elected sixty national delegates who gathered at Vereeniging by 15 May. After an inconclusive debate about peace, they chose a five-man delegation to negotiate actual terms in Pretoria. The second round of talks began on 19 May. In three respects Kitchener succeeded in making the offer more attractive than that made at Middelburg. There would be an amnesty for most Cape rebels after all (with dis-

enfranchisement) but no amnesty for leaders, nor for Natal rebels. There would be £3 million instead of £1 million to pay for the debts of the two republics. There was a crucial change in the terms of the clause about the possibility of 'the natives' having a vote in the new colonies, which was to have far-reaching consequences.

The second debate at Vereeniging centred, as before, on whether it was practical to fight on. The Free State, led by De Wet (owing to Steyn's illness), said 'yes' while most of the Transvaal delegates said 'no'. The reasons were much the same in each district. They were critically short of horses and of food and those who still remained out on the veld with the commandos could no longer maintain their families. Even in the Cape, Smuts explained, where there had been no farm burning, horses and forage were in such short supply that nothing could be done.

There were two other reasons which inclined the Transvaal to peace. In contrast to the Free State, they feared a 'native' rising. On 6 May a Zulu *impi* had attacked a party of Boers at Holkrans and killed 56 men in reprisal for repeated harassment by commandos. Elsewhere Boer women were at risk. At the same time, the war had cruelly divided the volk. The National Scouts and other 'handsuppers' from the two republics (including De Wet's brother Piet) now numbered 5 400.

A vote was taken in the great tent at Vereeniging. De Wet and the Free State leaders agreed not to split the nation, and voted with the majority. The leaders were rushed back to Pretoria to sign the surrender terms at 23h00 the same night. Schalk Burger, the Vice-President, who had assumed the functions of Kruger, signed first for the Transvaal. De Wet signed as acting President for the Free State. Kitchener and Milner signed last. It was all over in five minutes.

Suggested Reading List

L S Amery (ed) (1900-1909) *The Times History of the War in South Africa, 1899-1902*, 7 vols, London

J H Breytenbach (1969-1977) *Die Geskiedenis van die Tweede Vryheidsoorlog in Suid-Afrika,* 4 vols, Pretoria

A M Grundlingh (1979) *Die Hensoppers en Joiners. Die Rasionaal en Verskynsel van Verraad*, Pretoria

R Kruger (1959) *Good-Bye Dolly Gray. A History of the Boer War*, London

T Pakenham (1979) *The Boer War*, Johannesburg

D Reitz (1929) *Commando. A Boer Journal of the Boer War*, London

S B Spies (1977) *Methods of Barbarism? Roberts and Kitchener and Civilians in the Boer Republics, January 1900 to May 1902*, Cape Town

P Warwick (1983) *Black People and the South African War, 1899-1902*, Cambridge

P Warwick and S B Spies (eds) (1980) *The South African War. The Anglo-Boer War, 1899-1902*, London

Chapter 15

Reconstruction and Unification, 1902-1910

S B Spies

'We are good friends now,' Kitchener told the ten Boer signatories of the peace agreement on 31 May 1902. Crown Colony rule was introduced in the Boer states with supreme authority vested in Lord Milner, High Commissioner for South Africa and Governor of the Transvaal and Orange River colonies. Milner had to operate within the framework of the Vereeniging peace agreement. 'Surely one of the strangest documents in history,' Milner commented. There were certainly unusual features in the peace agreement: no war indemnity levied on the vanquished; the victors would pay £3 000 000 to alleviate the ravages of the conflict; the men who surrendered would retain their property; British sovereignty was proclaimed but self-government was promised.

The significance of Vereeniging

In 1905 Milner declared that his greatest mistake had been to accept Clause 8 of the agreement which postponed a decision on the question of granting the franchise to blacks until after the introduction of self-government, for he had not realized 'the extravagance of the prejudice on the part of almost all the whites – not the Boers only'. However, at Vereeniging in May 1902, according to Boer accounts, Milner had told Smuts and Hertzog, on the question of the franchise for blacks, 'I am at one with you.' Clause 8 did not preclude black political rights being granted, nor did it prevent future British governments putting pressure on white South Africans to legislate in that direction. Nevertheless many Africans were outraged that the Boers who had been the enemies seemed to have been favourably treated, while the blacks were apparently ignored. The necessity to find terms that would induce the *bittereinders* to surrender was

indeed a prime consideration in British military and civil thinking in 1902.

The Boer delegates dispersed to their commandos to arrange for the surrender. Deneys Reitz, in his book *Commando*, has related how in some cases the men 'fired away their ammunition into the air, smashed their rifle butts and sullenly flung their broken weapons down'. The remainder of the 20 000 who had fought to the last, most of them gaunt and sun-blackened, many dressed in rags, gradually made their way back to their homes, or what was left of them.

South African structures 1902-1910: people, power and interests

Although some historians have emphasized Milner's vast authority and his undoubted influence, the revisionist historians Shula Marks and Stanley Trapido have stressed that it is vital to look beyond 'the idiosyncrasies of a single indi-

Burridge Spies, MA PhD (University of the Witwatersrand), is Professor of History at the University of South Africa. His researches have been focused on late nineteenth and early twentieth century South African history. He has written numerous articles, books, and chapters in general histories.

Signing of the peace treaty of 31 May 1902 at Pretoria. (Transvaal Archives)

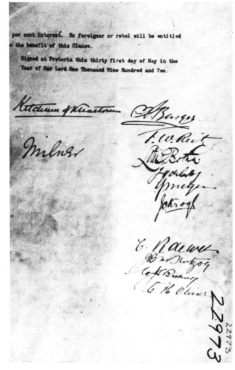

The first and last pages of the peace treaty, with the signatures of Kitchener, Milner, and Transvaal and Free State leaders. (Transvaal Archives)

A romanticized picture of a Boer family returning to their farm after the war. (Africana Museum)

vidual'. Milner's personality and policies should be seen as part of the contexture of complex forces and issues that shaped the post-war years. Politically, British supremacy meant the formation of South African governments sympathetic (or 'loyal') to imperial aspirations and prepared to co-operate (or 'collaborate') in achieving those goals. Moreover it implied the creation of efficient state machinery able to cope with the bureaucratic demands of the time. Economically, it required the development and organization of South African agriculture and industry – more particularly of the vital gold-mining industry – to bolster the monetary and trade resources of the empire and help provide the sinews of war. Strategically it was held to be essential that the Simon's Town naval base, a vital bastion of the long sea route to India, should remain securely and exclusively at the disposal of the Royal Navy.

The issues that concerned the people of the South African states in the period 1902 to 1910 involved group and race as well as class and regional interests. The arguments among whites about imperialism and independence or local autonomy and the question of relations between Boers and South African British continued to be vital considerations. The cessation of hostilities did not end the threat to the Cape Colony's self-governing status. During the Vereeniging negotiations, Milner, supported by some members of the most imperialistically orientated of the local political parties, Jameson's Progressives, revived the attempt to suspend the constitution. His efforts foundered on opposition in London and Cape Town. The accession to power of the Progressives in February 1904 seemed to guarantee the realization of Milner's goal of securing the Cape Colony as a base for further imperial aspirations. In the event, Jameson was forced as Prime Minister to consider Cape as well as imperial interests.

Natal was widely regarded as the 'most loyal' of all the South African colonies despite the fact that only about 2 000 Natalians had volunteered for active service on the British side during the Anglo-Boer War. Natal politicians considered that the war had provided an opportunity to realize their territorial ambitions: the former premier, Harry Escombe, favoured the annexation of the whole of Transvaal by Natal! The British Government, in fact, agreed to the former republican districts of Vryheid, Utrecht and part of Wakkerstroom being transferred to Natal by an Annexation Act passed by the Natal Parliament nineteen days *before* the Vereeniging Agreement (which contained no mention of the annexation) was signed – a procedure of doubtful legality.

The establishment of self-government in the conquered states in 1907 provided the white inhabitants of the Transvaal and Orange River Colony with the institutions to pursue their political goals within a parliamentary framework. The formation of *Het Volk* (January 1905) in the Transvaal and the *Orangia Unie* (May 1906) in the Orange River Colony preceded these grants and meant that Afrikaners in the former republics had party political organizations poised for action the moment the new constitutions were enforced. All the Afrikaner leaders in the Transvaal and the Orange River Colony were men who had remained true to the Boer cause to the end. None of the men who had collaborated with the enemy acquired leadership status. Regarded as a reckless experiment by some British Unionists, the grant of responsible government was in fact a Liberal strategy that had as its goal the maintenance of British supremacy in South Africa by consent and collaboration. If the status of the states was not indefinitely to be frozen into conquest crown colony moulds, there seemed little alternative.

In the Transvaal the *Het Volk* policy of conciliation was motivated by the conviction that it was the best way to heal the wounds of war. It was also, however, shaped by the need to win the votes of English-speakers. Such a policy was not a political necessity for *Orangia Unie* owing to the relatively small number of English-speaking inhabitants in the Orange River Colony, who (led by John George Fraser) formed the Constitutional Party in January 1907. English-speakers in the Transvaal were more divided. The Progressive Party, led by Percy Fitzpatrick and George Farrar, was believed to be associated with the Chamber of Mines, although recent research has modified this generalization. The Responsible Government Association (later

"AS OTHERS SEE THEM."

called the National Association) reflected the interests of economic groups, including elements from the diamond industry, who were opposed to the Chamber of Mines. By 1907 the Nationals had become virtually an ally of *Het Volk*.

An important development was the growth of white trade unionism – particularly the Transvaal Miners' Association. In 1903 Milner declaimed: 'We do not want a white proletariat in this country.' Nevertheless, as the historian Elaine Katz has shown, 'a peculiarly South African white labour movement . . . a trade union aristocracy' came into existence, that was to pose formidable problems to South African capitalists and to the state. Equally important was the influence wielded by the large capitalistic mining and other concerns.

Colour, of course, was a fundamental division cutting across group and class differences. In 1904 only 21,5 per cent of the population of the four British South African colonies were whites. Yet it was a basic Afrikaner and British assumption that South Africa was a 'white man's country'. The Cape was the only South African state where political rights were in some meaningful way shared by people who were not white. But even in that colony in 1909, only ten per cent of the registered voters were Coloureds and less than five per cent were blacks. Although all its members were whites throughout its existence, the Cape Parliament was more attuned to the views and interests of all racial groups than any other such institution in South Africa. Educated blacks such as John Tengo Jabavu believed in becoming involved in the political process dominated by whites.

The African Political (later People's) Organization (APO) founded in September 1902, came to represent the interests of the Coloured people, particularly after Dr Abdullah Abdurahman became president of the organization in April 1905.

Although the Natal constitution did not specifically ban blacks, Indians and Coloureds

John Tengo Jabavu, editor of *Imvo Zabantsundu*, with his son Davidson Don Tengo Jabavu. (Documentation Centre for African Studies, University of South Africa)

J T Jabavu

John Tengo Jabavu was a Mfengu who was educated by Wesleyan missionaries. He abandoned a teaching career to become a journalist and a canvasser for the politician James Rose Innes. He was the first editor of the influential newspaper *Imvo Zabantsundu* (African Opinion) which was started in 1884 with the help of liberal whites. He opposed restrictive legislation against blacks, but at times, in the opinion of certain people, he tended to compromise excessively. His newspaper was closed by the British authorities under martial law regulations during the Anglo-Boer War. He was approached by the Afrikaner Bond to represent it in the 1904 election but he declined.

He played a prominent role in getting Fort Hare College established. His sons, Davidson Don Tengo and Alexander Macaulay Jabavu, were active in black politics until the 1940s. J T Jabavu remains a controversial figure mainly as a result of his gradualism and co-operation with whites. Leonard Ngcongco, who analysed the influence of *Imvo*, considers that Jabavu was the pioneer politician whose work prepared the way for the more spectacular achievements of later African leaders.

A contemporary cartoon depicting various political parties as they may have been seen by their opponents.

Lord Alfred Milner, High Commissioner for South Africa. (Transvaal Archives)

from voting, the law was administered so that 99,1 per cent of the electorate in 1907 were white men. The Natal Native Congress, founded during the war years by Walter Luthuli and others, continued to grow. By 1910 the most influential black leader in Natal was John L Dube, known as *Mafukuzela* ('the one who struggles against obstacles'). Natal Indians and M K Gandhi, an advocate from India, had inaugurated the Natal Indian Congress in 1894 to protect the interests of their people after that colony had received responsible government the previous year. After 1902 Gandhi also concerned himself with the position of Indians in the Transvaal. Even in the Transvaal and the Orange River Colony, where the franchise was stipulated in the constitution as being the exclusive right of white men, black political organizations emerged.

None of the groups, classes or races in South Africa at the beginning of the twentieth century was monolithic. Cross-currents of interests often make neat assessments of attitudes and behaviour impossible. Such interests were influenced, reflected, publicized and orchestrated by a large free press. Probably the most influential were the Argus newspapers. The Argus Company was a subsidiary of the immensely wealthy Wernher-Beit (Corner House) organization which had gold, diamond, coal mining and banking interests, as well as vast land investments. During the years 1902-1910 newspapers under its umbrella usually supported imperialism and capitalism (the Chamber of Mines particularly). Yet the Argus Company did not have an English-language press monopoly. There were influential independent newspapers that represented regional and other interests. Afrikaner interests in the period were probably

Abdullah Abdurahman (1872-1940)

Dr Abdullah Abdurahman (*The Cape Times*)

Abdullah Abdurahman was the grandson of freed slaves. He received his schooling at Marist Brothers College and the South African College in Cape Town and graduated as a medical doctor from Glasgow University. Abdurahman returned to Cape Town with his Scottish wife in 1895. He became a city councillor and a member of the Cape Provincial Council and remained the dominant figure on the APO for 35 years. In his later years Abdurahman was severely criticized by young militant Coloureds who considered him too moderate. His daughter Zainunnissa ('Cissie') Gool also came to play a leading role in political movements that attempted to improve the lot of blacks and Coloureds.

best represented by the Pretoria newspaper *De Volksstem* (The Voice of the People). *Land en Volk* (Pretoria) had originally been started in opposition to *De Volkstem*, but it ceased publication in 1908. The influence of another Dutch newspaper, *Het Westen* (Potchefstroom), extended beyond its own locality.

A number of black newspapers exercised considerable influence. The most prominent of these were *Imvo Zabantsundu* and *Ilanga Lase Natal* (The Natal Sun). As the historian André Odendaal has explained, although the circulation of these black newspapers 'was never high, their impact was wide' as it was the practice for educated Africans to read them to groups of their illiterate fellows. The views and aspirations of the Coloured people were served by the Cape newspaper *APO*, and the cause of South African Indians was advocated by *Indian Opinion*.

Reconstruction and the grand design: May 1902-April 1905

A group of young Oxford graduates who became known as 'the Kindergarten' played prominent roles in Milner's administration of the conquered Boer states. In February 1903 the Legislative Council in the Transvaal was enlarged to consist of fifteen official and fourteen unofficial nominated members. Milner offered Botha, Smuts and De la Rey seats on the Legislative Council, which they declined. The Boers who did accept seats in the Transvaal and Orange River Colony were ineffectual. More influential were English-speaking nominees in the Transvaal such as Percy Fitzpatrick and George Farrar, important members of the Chamber of Mines, the lawyer, H C Hull, and A S Raitt, who represented the trade unions. In March 1903 a South African Customs Union was formed. The establishment of an Inter-Colonial Council in May 1903 further facilitated inter-colonial co-operation.

The Rev John L Dube, founder and principal of the Ohlange High School, Natal, editor of *Ilanga Lase Natal,* author of *The Clash of Colour*, a founder and ex-president of the African National Congress and also a president of the Natal Native Congress. (Documentation Centre for African Studies, Unisa)

By March 1903 the gigantic resettlement of blacks and whites displaced by the war was virtually completed. As Stanley Trapido has pointed out, although political power had been taken from the Boers, traditional agrarian property relations were sustained and underpinned by credit and marketing facilities. Local agricultural societies were formed, together with new agricultural and veterinary departments, wasteful methods were discouraged and irrigation, afforestation and efficient cultivation and stockbreeding were encouraged. Expensive land deals by the state were often to the benefit of the mining companies who were large landowners. Milner's scheme to place considerable numbers of English-speaking immigrants in rural areas was, however, a failure. Another failure of the Milner administration was the so-called Burgher Land Settlement, intended to make poor white farmers *bywoners* (sharecroppers) of the state. The influx to the towns of poor whites, even more ill equipped for urban life than for farming, continued.

Altogether some £16 500 000 was spent by the British Government on repatriation and relief. Louis Botha, J H de la Rey and Christiaan de Wet, who left for Europe at the end of July 1902 to obtain money for their distressed people, raised the disappointingly small sum of £103 819. Their visit to Paul Kruger, in exile on the Continent, had, however, led to control of the remaining republican funds passing to leading Afrikaners in the Transvaal and Orange River Colony. This money was spent on the acquisition of newspapers and on other preparations for the Afrikaner political and cultural revival. Considerable Afrikaner dissatisfaction about the allocation and administration of relief was brought to the attention of Joseph Chamberlain on his visit to South Africa between December 1902 and February 1903. Emily Hobhouse again took up the cudgels for Boer women and children in Britain and South Africa, while the British Quaker community provided further relief.

English was made the medium of instruction in government schools and the curricula had a distinct imperialistic bias. The Colonial Office and Milner agreed that no 'high strung Girton and Newnham girls who might become Emily

Hobhouses' should be appointed as teachers. The educational policy and the new schools, which tended to be modelled on British public school values, strengthened the ties that English-speaking South Africans had with British traditions. Some Afrikaners in the former republics (as had happened earlier at the Cape) succumbed to these anglicizing influences. Milner's cultural imperialism also, however, caused acute resentment and a spirited Afrikaner reaction. The Boers established Christian National Education schools and the Second Language Movement flourished.

Boer wartime hierarchies remained intact after 1902, even to the extent that ex-President Steyn retained the stature he had attained during the conflict, although his health precluded active participation in politics. The agricultural societies sponsored by the Milner regime provided cover for initial organization and grievances against British rule fuelled Boer political activity. After Kruger's death in exile at Clarens, Switzerland, on 14 July 1904, his body was embalmed and sent to South Africa for burial. The funeral in Pretoria on 16 December 1904 further stimulated the Afrikaner political revival.

Milner in 1903 had appointed the South African Native Affairs Commission, consisting largely of English-speaking members under the chairmanship of Sir Godfrey Lagden, the former British Resident in Basutoland, to make

Generals De Wet, Botha and De la Rey and exiled President Kruger attend a church service in Holland in 1902. The generals were trying to raise money in Europe to aid their distressed compatriots. (Transvaal Archives)

President Kruger's coffin, 1904. (Transvaal Archives)

Members of the South African Native Affairs Commission (the Lagden Commission). (Cory Library, Grahamstown)

The Second Afrikaans Language Movement

The movement was heralded by the revival in 1903 by 'Onze Jan' Hofmeyr and other Cape Afrikaners of the *Taalbond*. The *Taalbond* aimed at the recognition and development of the *volkstaal* (people's language) which some of these men regarded as Dutch rather than as Afrikaans. In the north, however, the author and journalist Gustav Preller and the poets Eugène Marais (also an editor), Jan F E Celliers and J D du Toit ('Totius') pressed for the use of Afrikaans. Poems by Marais, Celliers and 'Totius' revealed the expressive range and subtlety of Afrikaans. Two of the most haunting poems, drawing on the folk memory of the sufferings endured during their *Vryheidsoorlog* (War of Freedom) and the Boer predicament after Vereeniging, were Marais's *Winternag* ('Winter Night') and Celliers's *Dis Al* ('That's All'). The austere statements of despair expressed in these poems stirred Afrikaners. It was, however, the work of 'Totius' that had the greatest significance for the development of Afrikaner nationalism.

A cartoon published in *The Star* in 1904 relating to the question of the introduction of Chinese labour on the mines. (South African Library)

recommendations regarding a common 'native' policy for all the states. Its report, produced in 1905, recommended territorial segregation and political separation between blacks and whites and approved the establishment of locations for urban blacks.

The efficient administration of the Witwatersrand mines and the increased production of gold were high priorities to provide the 'overspill' to reactivate the economy of the conquered states. The imperial authorities enabled Milner to raise a loan of £35 000 000 and a *modus vivendi* had been concluded with Mozambique in 1901 for the engagement of workers for Witwatersrand mines in return for arrangements which facilitated the port of Delagoa Bay receiving a substantial share of Transvaal business. The establishment during the war of the Witwatersrand Native Labour Association was designed to ensure an abundance of mine labour. By 1903, however, the mines, which were becoming increasingly committed to the extension of low-grade ore mining, insisted that they had insufficient labour. Africans, it would appear, resisted the wages provided and the new technology and production methods demanded of them. A contemporary maintained that the problems were 'attributable not so much to scarcity of labour as to the abundance of mines starting simultaneously'. Proposals to obtain labourers from other parts of Africa or India came to naught, as did the experiments of mine manager F H P Creswell and other attempts to use white unskilled workers. In March 1903 George Farrar inaugurated a campaign, which won the support of the Chamber of Mines, for the importation of Chinese labour. The scheme was approved by the Transvaal Legislative Council and by the British Government which negotiated a convention with China in May 1904. Between June 1904 and November 1906, 63 695 Chinese labourers, on three-year contracts, were imported to the gold mines. Despite the greater expense involved, Chinese labourers, contracted for longer periods, were actually more profitable than black workers. The value of gold production rose from £16 000 000 (22,6 per cent of the world's output) in 1904 to £27 400 000 (32,32 per cent of the world's output) in 1907. The Chinese labourers were restricted in the work they were allowed to do and as this job reservation was subsequently applied to blacks, the colour bar on the mines was bolstered. The importation of Chinese labourers to the Witwatersrand led to widespread political reaction in Britain and South Africa and to their return to China from 1907.

In 1904 the British Government announced that representative government for the Transvaal would be introduced when Milner left the country in April 1905. Milner believed that he had failed to implement his grand design. Yet members of the 'Kindergarten' and the British Liberal Party came to realize that there were other means – self-government, 'trusting the Boer' and unification – of maintaining supremacy in South Africa.

South Africa without Milner: closer union – problems solved and problems shelved

Milner's successor as High Commissioner was the First Lord of the Admiralty, the Earl of Selborne. Selborne's tenure as Under-Secretary to Chamberlain during the pre-war crisis and the continued presence of the 'Kindergarten' in South Africa provided links with Milner's policies. The most important factor that shaped his high commissionership was, however, the advent of a Liberal government under Sir Henry Campbell-Bannerman in Britain in January 1906. The Liberal electoral victory resulted in the cancellation of the representative government constitution for the Transvaal which had been promulgated in April 1905. The British Cabinet had already decided to grant responsible government to the former republics before Smuts's trip to London in January and February 1906, but that visit strengthened the ties between the conciliatory Boer leaders and the British Liberal establishment. Letters patent promulgating self-government in the Transvaal and Orange River Colony were issued respectively in December 1906 and June 1907. Despite representations from blacks and Coloureds, the franchise was granted exclusively to whites. The elections resulted in *Het Volk* (with Louis Botha as premier) in the Transvaal in February and *Orangia Unie* (with Abraham Fischer as premier) in the Orange River Colony, coming to power in November 1907. In the Cape Colony Afrikaner rebels were re-enfranchised and J X Merriman's South African Party, supported by the Afrikaner Bond, came to power in February 1908.

Campbell-Bannerman was not an advocate of imperial disintegration, nor was he a quixotic idealist who wished to atone for 'methods of barbarism' and other unionist misdeeds by a 'magnanimous gesture' towards the Boers. There may have been an element of miscalculation and some Liberals were disappointed by *Het Volk*'s electoral victory. The grant of self-government was nevertheless grounded in a hard-headed belief that it was the most effectual way in South Africa to further Britain's international, economic and strategic interests.

Louis Botha, in British eyes, was the personification of reconciliation and co-operation. He played an insignificant role at the 1907 imperial

conference in London, but he received more publicity than any other delegate. However, his attitude at the conference and the Transvaal Government's gift of the Cullinan diamond to Edward VII was criticized by some of his own people as being 'too loyal'. Nevertheless in the period after 1907 there was more general goodwill between white South Africans than there had been for a decade, and at the very least a general acceptance of the imperial link. The scene was set for the consolidation of the separate colonies into a single state, as had occurred in Canada in 1867 and in Australia in 1901.

There were urgent economic reasons for the political amalgamation of the South African states. The inland and the coastal colonies had different needs regarding customs tariffs and

Lord Selborne (Central Archives)

A cartoon published in the *Sunday Times* in 1906. The caption reads as follows:

TRANSVAAL GRAND CHALLENGE CUP

From our Rowing Expert
Rosherville Lake, July 15, 1906

The usual struggle for supremacy in this competition will shortly take place, and it is now possible to form some estimate of the chances of the rival boats. The Het Volk crew on the whole pulls well together .... The British four was on the water the other day and appeared all at loggerheads. Solomon, having caught a crab, attempted to save himself by seizing Farrar's oar. With the consequence that Kelty, the cox, considered the water a safer place than his seat. Loveday at two never showed sign of putting his heart into his work, and Whiteside, though he rowed steadily, has neither the power nor the reach to make a good bow.

The betting is 100 to 3 on the Het Volk crew, taken freely.

225

The prelude to the Bambatha Rebellion – the execution of two men who were found guilty of murdering two policemen in the Richmond district of Natal in 1906. The painting is entitled 'Paying the penalty for murder', and the artist is F Dadd. (Africana Museum)

The Bambatha Rebellion

Even before the murder of two white policemen in the Richmond district in February 1906, there had been rumours in Natal that black people were to rebel against the poll tax. It was also said that Dinuzulu, the son of Cetshwayo, had ordered a revolt against the whites. Martial law was proclaimed, and the Natal militia burnt crops and kraals and chiefs were deposed. Some of the participants in the Richmond affair were tried by court martial and shot.

In April 1906 Bambatha, the Zondi chief, supported by other chiefs, started building up his army and engaging in guerrilla activities from a base in the Nkandla forest to which he and his followers had fled. On 10 June 1906 Colonel Duncan Mackenzie defeated the rebels, who suffered heavy losses at Mome Gorge. Bambatha was killed and his head cut off for identification. There were further outbreaks in Mapumulo and the unrest continued during 1907. Dinuzulu was arrested and sentenced to four years imprisonment in 1908 for harbouring rebels. Between 3 500 and 4 000 blacks and about 24 whites were killed during the disturbances. The revolt was a traditional peasant rebellion against the colonial authority and the newly emergent black political associations were not implicated. Nevertheless, as Shula Marks has concluded, it helped engender national unity amongst blacks.

The founder of the Order of Ethiopia, Reverend J M Dwane. (Documentation Centre for African Studies, Unisa)

railway rates. The temporary settlement patched up by the customs union in 1903 was virtually in tatters by 1907. Clashes between labour and capital had occurred and caused concern to the leaders of industry, commerce and to governments. The 1907 gold miners' strike forced Botha to call on imperial troops. A local defence force, as well as legislation to provide for arbitration in industrial disputes, were vital needs.

Widespread white fears about black uprisings were intensified by the growth of the so-called Ethiopian or separatist black churches, which were generally held to be anti-white, and to advocate 'Africa for the Africans'. Zulu unrest, the insurrection of the Herero and other inhabitants in South West Africa from 1904, and the Maji Maji rebellion in Tanganyika, from 1905, added fuel to white apprehensions. The smouldering black discontent in Natal flared up in February 1906, probably as a result of the imposition of poll tax the previous year and two white policemen were killed in the Richmond district. The unrest developed later in the year into the so-called Bambatha Rebellion, which was crushed by the Natal militia and volunteers from all over South Africa, with the imperial authorities merely providing moral support. The rebellion seemed to many people to emphasize the necessity for the establishment of an intercolonial defence force, which, it was believed, could best be accomplished if political unity were forged. The disturbances also focused opinion on the inept Natal Government

(regarded by Churchill as 'the hooligan of the British Empire') and the need for a strong central authority in South Africa.

Indians in the Transvaal constituted another group who protested against discrimination. Gandhi took the lead in organizing non-violent resistance (*satyagraha*) against the restrictions imposed on Indian residential and trading rights and against the immigration law. A tentative and impermanent understanding was reached between Smuts and Gandhi in January 1908.

By 1908 war in Europe between the hostile power blocs (Germany and Austria-Hungary versus France and Russia) seemed to be a distinct possibility. Britain, by that time, had become more committed to the Franco-Russian alliance. South Africa was of vital importance to the British Empire in the threatening big-power conflict because of its strategic position (Cape Town was regarded as one of the 'five strategic keys that lock up the world'), its mineral wealth, its manpower resources, and its proximity to German South West Africa. Selborne, members of the 'Kindergarten', British Cabinet ministers, and leading white South Africans were coming to believe that the critical international situation was another reason why unification was an urgent priority.

A document drafted by Lionel Curtis, subjected to criticism by other members of the 'Kindergarten', and finally approved by Selborne before being published in 1907, set out the reasons why unification was necessary. This 'Selborne Memorandum' was a manifesto rather than a memorandum. It initiated a movement which gained momentum when the intercolonial customs conference resolved in May 1908 that thirty white delegates from the four South African states would meet in a National Convention in Durban in October 1908.

Sir Henry de Villiers, Chief Justice of the Cape Colony, was President of the National Convention. Delegates represented ruling and opposition parties in the four colonies, and Southern Rhodesia sent three observers to Durban. A Cape Town session followed and the Convention concluded its business in Bloemfontein in May 1909. It was remarkable (and an indication of the overriding desire for unification) that the constitution of South Africa was less than a year in the making. Some contentious issues were shelved for future attention and compromise was frequently resorted to to break deadlocks.

The Natal delegates, who were really more interested in settling customs and railways disputes, were in the minority in favouring federation rather than union. The result was the acceptance of a highly centralized Westminster-type union, modified by subservient provincial councils with limited powers. Legislative power in the central government would be vested in a House of Assembly, initially consisting of 121 members (all white) directly elected by the voters of the Union, and a Senate of 40 whites, partly indirectly elected and partly appointed, and laws would have to be approved by a Governor-General, representing and appointed by the Crown. Executive power would be in the hands of the Governor-General and a Cabinet.

The thorny question of who would have the right to vote was resolved (or shelved) by allowing each state to retain the system existing before union. Thus blacks and Coloureds voted together with whites on a qualified franchise in the Cape but did not have the vote in other provinces. Only whites could become members of the House of Assembly or Senate. Rural constituencies came to have fewer voters than urban constituencies owing to the provision that the number of voters in a constituency could be up to fifteen per cent above or below the quota.

An emotive issue was resolved by the unwieldy and expensive device of creating three capitals – Cape Town as the seat of the legislature, Pretoria as the administrative headquarters, while the Appellate Division of the Supreme Court would sit in Bloemfontein.

The constitution could be altered by a simple majority except for the entrenched clauses, Section 35 concerning the franchise in the Cape, and Section 137 concerning English and Dutch as the two official languages of the Union. These two sections could only be amended by a two-thirds majority of both Houses of Parliament in a joint sitting.

Section 151 provided for the admission of additional territories into the Union under certain conditions. A schedule to the bill dealt with the conditions of their administration, if at a future date the High Commission territories of Basutoland, Bechuanaland and Swaziland were transferred to the Union.

In June 1909 the Natal electorate approved the constitution in a referendum and the parliaments of the other three states accepted it. The vast majority of white South Africans were in favour of the draft South Africa Act.

Blacks, Coloureds and Indians were strongly opposed to many provisions of the constitution. As early as December 1907, foreseeing some of the measures that were to become incorporated in the act, black political leaders had organized a conference at Queenstown, which was also attended by Coloureds. It resolved that federation was preferable to unification and that the Cape franchise should be adopted for the whole country. Blacks subsequently sent petitions to the National Convention and a 'South African Native Convention' met at Bloemfontein in March 1909, when the basic details of the new constitution were known. Under the presidency of Walter Rubusana, the 'Native Convention' opposed the colour bar provisions of the draft bill and advocated the unification of the Afri-

cans into 'one great family'. This convention provided the first real example of co-ordinated, nationwide black political action in South Africa. However, the representations made by black and Coloured leaders made no impact on the National Convention.

Eighteen members of the National Convention and 'Onze Jan' Hofmeyr took the draft South Africa Bill to London in mid-1909. A delegation led by the former Cape premier, W P Schreiner, and consisting of Rubusana, Abdurahman, Jabavu and five others, representing black and Coloured interests, also went to Britain, as did Gandhi and other Indians. There were, however, no British party political or public opinion currents in 1909 strong enough to ensure a better deal for blacks in the constitution, although the colour bar restrictions were criticized in the British Parliament and press. On 20 September 1909 the unamended South Africa Act received the royal assent after having been passed by both British Houses of Parliament.

Members of the National Convention sitting in Durban, 12 October 1908. (Documentation Centre for African Studies, Unisa)

Sir Henry de Villiers, Chief Justice of the Cape Colony and the President of the National Convention. (Central Archives)

Suggested Reading List

D J N Denoon (1973) *A Grand Illusion: The Failure of Imperial Policy in the Transvaal during the Period of Reconstruction*, London

N G Garson (1966) '"Het Volk": The Botha-Smuts Party in the Transvaal, 1904-1911', *The Historical Journal*, 9, 1, 1966

S Marks (1970) *Reluctant Rebellion. The 1906-1908 Disturbances in Natal*, Oxford

S Marks and S Trapido (1981) 'Lord Milner and the South African State', in P Bonner (ed) *Working Papers in Southern African Studies*, Vol II, Johannesburg

A Odendaal (1983) *Vukani Bantu. The Beginnings of Black Protest Politics in South Africa*, Cape Town

G B Pyrah (1955) *Imperial Policy and South Africa, 1897-1905*, Oxford

P Richardson (1982) *Chinese Mine Labour in the Transvaal*, London

L M Thompson (1960) *The Unification of South Africa, 1902-1910*, London

The Special Service Battalion, an
armoured regiment of 6 South African
Armoured Division, fording the River Arno
35 km west of Florence during the Italian
Campaign of World War II. The tanks are
Shermans equipped with 75 mm guns.
The artist is Terence McCaw. (South
African Museum of Military History)

Part VI

The Union of South Africa, 1910-1961: White Consolidation and Black Awareness

The 'euphoria' of unification was soon tempered by the harsh realities which faced the inhabitants of the new state in the troubled world of the twentieth century. Class, race, language and cultural divisions had not been bridged and continued to exert powerful pressures on a spectrum of fluctuating political alignments.

During the first dozen years of Union fierce confrontations between capital and labour shook the country. Participation in two world wars exposed wide fissures in the white community, precipitated internal tensions and tested and stimulated the economy.

Economic troughs and peaks, prosperity and poverty were related to international trends. Gold mining continued to generate the greatest share of the national income, although secondary industries multiplied. The tempo of urbanization quickened. Technological advance, in some sectors state-controlled, was an essential component of the modernization process.

The establishment of a republic, for some whites the realization of an ideal and the culmination of the steady march towards full autonomy, also severed a link with Britain which had existed for more than a century and a half.

Race relations remained the prime conundrum of the complex society. Attempted white consolidation and a steady increase in segregatory measures did not halt economic integration, as black awareness and activated protest became more acute.

Striking miners in Rissik Street,
Johannesburg, in 1922. (*Die Burger*)

Chapter 16

Unity and Disunity, 1910-1924

S B Spies

Herbert Gladstone, first Governor-General of the Union of South Africa. (Central Archives)

The first task of the new Governor-General, Herbert Gladstone (a son of W E Gladstone), was to appoint a Prime Minister. The British Government believed that Louis Botha was the politician most suited to be the first premier of the Union of South Africa. The only other serious contender was J X Merriman. Gladstone, after sounding local opinion, endorsed his government's views. Botha commanded the widest support amongst whites, but many blacks and Coloureds, whose views were not canvassed, would have preferred Merriman

Some lines are drawn

Louis Botha rejected L S Jameson's idea of an all party 'best man' government and selected his ministry from the ruling parties in all four states. Merriman refused Botha's offer of a Cabinet appointment. J B M Hertzog was included in the ministry only after the premier's offer to make the Free Stater an Appeal Court judge was turned down. By 31 May 1910 basic executive and judicial structures had been erected on the lines drafted by the makers of the constitution.

The general election on 15 September 1910 was contested between supporters of the government, representatives of two other parties, and a number of independents. The Labour Party (established in January 1910 under the leadership of H W Sampson and F H P Creswell) was an urban party representing the interests of white workers. The Unionist Party (founded appropriately on Empire Day, 1910, and led by L S Jameson) was an amalgam of

John X Merriman (Central Archives)

The Union Cabinet of 1910. From left to right, standing, are J C Smuts, D de V Graaff, H Burton, H C Hull, J B M Hertzog, F S Malan. Seated are D C O'Grady Gubbins, J W Sauer, L Botha, A Fischer, G Leuchars. (Central Archives)

231

M K Gandhi (centre) and the Transvaal Indian leaders in 1912. (S S Singh Collection)

the English-speaking opposition parties from the Transvaal, Cape and Orange River colonies. The South African National Party – soon known simply as the South African Party (SAP) – was only formally constituted in November 1911.

There was no major policy difference between the Unionists and the government. Both agreed on the necessity for a united white South Africa, both staunchly supported the British Empire-Commonwealth, both agreed on keeping the 'native question' outside party politics, both were in favour of white and opposed to Indian immigration. The differences that did exist were created by varying degrees of emphasis placed on these issues, and by the perspectives and prejudices of the two white language groups. The government won the general election with an overall majority of 13 seats.

Approximately 14 000 Coloured and 6 000 blacks in the Cape Province who qualified for the vote could exercise their franchise rights within the white political spectrum. Indians and the overwhelming majority of blacks and Coloureds – about four-fifths of the total population – had no direct roles in the system of parliamentary politics, although they were affected by decisions taken within that system.

It was primarily the initiative of the lawyer, Pixley ka Izaka Seme, that led to the formation in Bloemfontein in January 1912 of the South African Native National Congress (from 1923 to be known as the African National Congress or ANC). One of the hitherto most influential black leaders, J T Jabavu, established his own South African Races Congress in April 1912, to maintain contact with white politicians. Gandhi returned to South Africa at the end of 1910 to find that the strength of the Indian passive resistance movement had declined in his absence. His supporters, however, gave him the use of the Tolstoy farm (dedicated to the ideas of the Russian novelist and philosopher) outside Johannesburg which was to become the centre of the next phase of *satyagraha*.

Troops from the imperial garrison protecting a depot during the 1913 strike. (Institute for the Study of Contemporary History (INCH))

Within the Union, 1910-1914

The announcement by J W Sauer, the Minister
of Railways and Harbours, of the implementation of railway extensions without reference to
the Cabinet, led to the resignation in May 1912
of the Transvaaler, H C Hull, whose department of finance was directly involved. The subsequent Cabinet reshuffle probably left the government weakened.

More serious were the differences between
the policy of conciliation of the Transvaaler,
Louis Botha, and the policy of protection for
the Afrikaner of the Free Stater, J B M
(Barry) Hertzog, who differed widely on such
issues as language, education, relations in general between the two white groups, white immigration and the commonwealth tie.

The final break came after Hertzog's
speeches at Nylstroom in October and at Smithfield and De Wildt (north-west of Pretoria) in
December 1912. He referred to some English-
speaking leaders in South Africa as 'foreign fortune seekers', and advocated two separate
streams for the development of the two white
groups. He also stated 'South Africa was for the
Afrikaner'. Only subsequently did he explain
that he had used the latter term in an unusual
way – to denote those who accepted the Union
as their country. His dictum of 'South Africa
first' incensed the Unionists and some English-
speaking supporters of the government, but it
was difficult for Botha and his followers to deny
that the Union's interests should indeed receive
priority over those of the empire. Natal's indig-
nation at Hertzog's statements was personified
by Colonel G Leuchars's resignation from the
ministry. After attempting in vain to persuade
Hertzog to resign, Botha tendered his own resignation on 14 December 1912. On being asked

by Gladstone to form a new government, he
omitted Hertzog and Leuchars.

Afrikander numerical preponderance among
the white population seemed to be assured. Yet
vast numbers of Afrikaners felt insecure and
dissatisfied and believed that they were being
rejected by what was supposed to be their own
government.

Botha and Smuts, in committing themselves
to co-operation within the commonwealth and
conciliation towards English-speakers in domestic affairs, were probably motivated primarily by the belief that in the prevailing circumstances these were the most expedient means of
serving the interests of the Union and its white
inhabitants (including Afrikaners). Actually
true conciliation should almost certainly have
entailed some sacrifice of the dominance of the
English section in South Africa.

Hertzog's direct championship of Afrikaner
interests was sincere, but often deliberately provocative and in his confidence of obtaining support from his own section he showed scant regard for his party's delicate position *vis-à-vis*
English-speakers. Although no Cabinet minister
and only a handful of MPs sided with Hertzog,
public meetings and party congresses revealed
the strength of his grass-roots support. The National Party of the Free State was established in
July 1914; the Transvaal National Party was
formed the following month and the Natal and
Cape parties in August and September 1915 respectively.

Before the establishment of the National
Party the fiercest parliamentary opposition to
the government came from a handful of Labourites. Outside Parliament the government
was sorely tried by strikes in 1913 and 1914.
The geological reality of deep-lying, low-grade
ore, the financial restraint of a fixed inter-

The 1914 strike

After the government retrenched railway workers at the end of 1913, a
general secretary of their union, H J
Poutsma, announced a strike on 8 January 1914 and six days later, the Federation declared a general strike.
Smuts acted swiftly. Defence force
units (by now properly organized)
were mobilized on 10 January. Martial law was proclaimed. Koos de la
Rey and his commando trained their
guns on the Trades Hall. Strike leaders were forced to surrender. Many
men – including MPs like T Boydell
and F H P Creswell, who were destined to become Cabinet ministers –
were arrested. Some ten days after it
had started, the strike was crushed,
at the cost of only two lives. Smuts
went further – without trial he had
Poutsma and eight other foreign-born
strike leaders put on board the *Um-
geni* and deported to Europe.

national gold price (until the Great War, £4 4s 11½d a fine ounce) together with the South African phenomenon of a white aristocracy of labour, imposed a special pattern on the struggle.

The leadership of the Transvaal Miners' Association (to be renamed the South African Mine Workers' Union after the 1913 strike) and of the umbrella Transvaal Federation of Trade Unions (known as the Federation) was still in the hands of immigrants. An increasing number of South African-born men, particularly Afrikaners (some of whom had been used as strikebreakers in 1907), had, however, been recruited by the mines.

Although statutory recognition of trade unions was delayed until 1924, trade union membership increased and new unions were established. Labour made other gains. In March 1914 the Labour Party gained a majority of one on the Transvaal Provincial Council. During the 1914 parliamentary session, the government introduced Workmen's Compensation and Wages Protection Acts which met some of the demands of white workers.

The white agricultural sector also benefited from legislation during the period. The establishment of the Land Bank of South Africa in October 1912 made special provision for credit for farmers, so strengthening traditional state intervention in agriculture and causing farmers, according to the economist Francis Wilson, 'to look increasingly to the state to solve their problems'.

There were hopes that unification would improve race relations. The election of Walter Rubusana to represent Tembuland in the Cape Provincial Council seemed to suggest that the role of blacks in the new political arena would not necessarily be restricted to that of political pawns manipulated by whites.

Generals Botha and De la Rey in the gardens of the Houses of Parliament in Cape Town during the special session in September 1914. (Transvaal Archives)

'Native policy', however, as in the past, was often determined by white economic demands (particularly those relating to labour and to land), by white fears and prejudices, rather than by black needs. White attitudes were conflations of insecurity and beliefs of black inferiority. Such attitudes were common amongst Europeans concerned with colonial rule in other parts of Africa in the second decade of the twentieth century. It would have been strange if it had been different in South Africa.

The scenario that Louis Botha privately sketched in 1912 bore a resemblance in broad conception to the 'separate development' and 'homelands' programmes of later years. It would be best, he stated, for blacks to obtain political rights – 'naturally under the control of the Union government' – in their own separate areas in the Transkei, Zululand, the Zoutpansberg and the existing High Commission territories of Basutoland and Swaziland. That was a vision for the distant future. The actual statutory regulation of the position of blacks in the Union before 1914 was not on the same comprehensive scale nor as rigid as the laws passed in the 'apartheid era' after 1948. Despite some public demand, no laws were passed forbidding marriage or sex across the colour line. For all that, the Botha administration's 'native policy' was grounded in segregation and discrimination.

Regulations emanating from the Mines and Works Act of 1911 imposed job reservation by restricting skilled work to whites. The Native Labour Regulation Act of 1911 stipulated that blacks involved in industrial accidents would receive less compensation than whites, and, in the tradition of nineteenth century Masters and Servants laws, made blacks criminally liable for breaches of labour contracts and for strikes. The Defence Act of 1912 had declared that men not of European descent were not liable for military training. The pass laws, which restricted their freedom of movement, underpinned the inferior position of blacks in the Union. The Natives Land Act of 1913 provoked the most profound black reaction.

African mineworkers on the Witwatersrand went on strike in July 1913 as did black labourers on the Jagersfontein diamond mine in the Free State after one of their fellows had been killed by a white man in January 1914. The historian Charles van Onselen has represented the crimes of the Ninevite black gangs, which reached a peak in mid-1912, as another form of resistance to a white-dominated state before the politically conscious members of the African elite formed the SANNC.

Peaceful protest, in the form of petitions and delegations, was the reaction of the SANNC led by Dube, before the outbreak of the Great War. Petitions to and discussions with Botha, and also with the British Government in London, did not alter the Land Act or any other disabilities.

External ambitions and links, 1910-1914: neighbours, dominion status and the world crisis

Before 1914, representations by the Union government for the transfer of Swaziland and Bechuanaland were fended off by the imperial authorities. Expansion to the north, the possibility of buying Southern Rhodesia from the British South Africa Company, had been discussed by Botha and other South African leaders before Union. They were informed, however, that their suggested price of £20 million was insufficient. The first years of Union strengthened the existing undercurrent of Rhodesian settler opinion opposed to inclusion in the Union and the Company's charter, due for review in 1914, was renewed for a further ten years.

The Union of South Africa had the same powers and limitations as the other dominions – the self-governing states within the British Empire-Commonwealth, Canada, Australia, New Zealand and Newfoundland. The British Government scrupulously observed the sovereignty of dominion government in the internal affairs of their own countries but in foreign affairs and defence policy the dominions were still clearly subordinate to the United Kingdom. At the 1911 Imperial Conference it was accepted by all delegations that when Britain went to war, all the dominions would automatically be at war too. The Canadian Laurier had, however, insisted on a rider that was not repudiated – the dominion governments were competent to decide the *extent* of their participation.

The South African Government took a vital step towards the assumption of responsibility for its own local defence needs and for providing the wherewithal to make a real contribution to imperial defence when the South African Defence Act was passed in 1912. The formation of the Union Defence Force was one reason for a further reduction in the number of imperial troops stationed in South Africa. The outcry caused by 'the shooting of workers at the behest

of a Boer government', as the events of 1913 were interpreted in some quarters in Britain, was another.

South Africa was the only part of the Empire-Commonwealth with territory contiguous to a German possession, South West Africa. Relations between the Union authorities and their German neighbours were correct, but hardly cordial. After 1910 and particularly after the formation of the Union Defence Force the feeling in British military circles was that South Africa would be able to cope with any German aggression across the Orange. *Offensive* operations against German South West Africa had been discussed by War Office committees, but neither in 1911 (as was subsequently claimed by South African Nationalists) nor at any other stage before the outbreak of the First World War had definite plans been drafted in South Africa, nor in Britain, for such an attack.

On 4 August 1914 the British ultimatum to Germany expired and the Union of South Africa, like the rest of the British Empire, was automatically at war. The South African Government immediately offered to assume responsibility for the duties entrusted to the imperial garrison in the Union. The imperial government enquired whether South African forces could seize Swakopmund and Lüderitzbucht and the radio stations in the interior of German South West Africa; it was stipulated that any territory occupied would have to be at the disposal of Britain for an ultimate settlement after the war. Initially the South African Cabinet was divided on whether their forces should invade German South West Africa. On 10 August 1914 before Parliament had been summoned, the Cabinet agreed and the British Government was so informed. Parliament was summoned to a special session on 9 September. On the following day only Hertzog and his followers voted against the motion in favour of military action against South West Africa which was carried by a majority of 91 votes to 12 and in the Senate the government obtained a majority of 24 votes to 5.

Sol T Plaatje (S A Library)

A permit allowing an Indian man from Durban to reside in Johannesburg. (S S Singh Collection)

Indian women employed on an estate in Umzinto, Natal. (Transvaal Archives)

No. A 2610 **PERMIT** AVAILABLE FOR ASIATICS ONLY.

TO ENTER AND RESIDE IN THE TRANSVAAL AND ORANGE RIVER COLONY.

Name (in full) *Mathurac*

Nationality *British Indian*

Place of Birth *Durban*

Occupation *Waiter*

Last Address *J.H.Burg*

District to which proceeding *Johannesburg*

RE-REGISTERED IN TRANSVAAL.

Place of Issue *J.H.B.*

Date of Issue *5/3/05*

Authority for Issue

This Permit is not transferable, and any person making use of it, other than the original holder, will be liable to prosecution and to the penalties provided... Peace Preservation Ordinances Transvaal and Orange River Colony. See the BACK.

Signature of Holder

Armed protest, rebellion or civil war?

On 9 October 1914, S G ('Manie') Maritz, a Lieutenant-Colonel in the Union Defence Force in charge of the north-western Cape district fringing on South West Africa, crossed the frontier with more than a thousand Citizen Force soldiers (and sixty of his own men as prisoners) to join the enemy. There followed an Afrikaner armed protest or rebellion, which had many of the characteristics of a civil war. These events were sparked by Parliament's decision to attack German South West Africa, but the long fuse of Maritz's treason stretched back to 1902.

Many Afrikaners still hankered after their lost republican independence. Moreover, certain Boer notables claimed that some die-hards in 1902 at Vereeniging had only acquiesced in the peace settlement after it had been agreed that the struggle would be renewed at a future date when Britain was involved in another conflict. In 1912, Maritz, J C G Kemp and other former Boer Generals and Commandants had discussed using their positions in the Defence Force to restore the republics if suitable circumstances should arise.

There were other grievances. Free Staters, particularly, felt neglected, especially after Hertzog's exclusion from office. Severe droughts had affected that province particularly and the rebellion was most strongly supported in the worst afflicted north-eastern Free State and in the poverty-stricken western Transvaal.

But whatever reasons may have prompted the rank-and-file to use physical force, it is unlikely that there would have been an uprising if it had not been for the lead given by certain influential men who commanded the greatest following in those areas where the rebellion blazed the fiercest – C R de Wet in the north-eastern Free State, De la Rey and Kemp in the western Transvaal and Maritz in the north-western Cape. In the final instance, it was the decision to invade South West Africa which blew the clouds of dissension into the storm of revolt.

The first serious signs of discontent which occurred in mid-August 1914 in the western Transvaal were instigated by the highly respected General J H de la Rey, a nominated government senator. De la Rey was much impressed by Niklaas 'Siener' (Seer) van Rensburg of the Lydenburg district, who had seen visions of a fight between a grey bull (Germany) and a red bull (Britain) which was won by the former. He also saw the number 15 on a dark cloud from which blood flowed and then De la Rey without a hat, followed by a carriage covered with flowers – which was interpreted as a coming triumph for De la Rey. Botha and Smuts summoned the old general to Pretoria and the meeting addressed by De la Rey at Treurfontein on 15 August was incident free.

Also in mid-August and thereafter, Maritz, De la Rey, Beyers (who had been informed of the South West African expedition), De Wet and Kemp were in communication with one another. According to the subsequent statements of the participants, a loosely planned coup d'état was sketched, which had as loci the South West African border, the Free State and Potchefstroom. On his return to his headquarters, Maritz contacted the Germans in South West Africa and arranged for Beyers to come to the border to meet Governor Seitz. De la Rey, it was agreed, would address the men in the military camp at Potchefstroom where Kemp was in command. After the special parliamentary session, Beyers, who seemed to have vacillated, decided to resign as Commandant-General and Kemp also relinquished his commission. Seitz came to the border in vain and Maritz seems to have been in the dark about what was happen-

ing in the Transvaal. On the evening of 15 September 1914 De la Rey, who had come to Pretoria, seems to have persuaded Beyers to accompany him to Potchefstroom. On their way, De la Rey was shot dead by police at Langlaagte (Johannesburg) when the car in which he and Beyers were travelling failed to stop at a road block. There is little doubt that the shooting was an accident and that the police mistook De la Rey and Beyers for criminals, the notorious Foster gang.

According to Kemp and other officers who were awaiting De la Rey in the Potchefstroom military camp, his arrival there was to have signalled the start of the rebellion. Kemp heard about De la Rey's death early on the morning of 16 September. In his memoirs he commented: 'At 2 am on 16 September 1914 the whole rebellion came to an end.' Plans in the Free State and western Transvaal were frozen and on the border Maritz and the Germans waited in bewilderment. At De la Rey's funeral feelings ran high. Beyers announced that he had never had rebellion in mind. Protest meetings were held and a resolution was passed condemning the South West Africa expedition. Botha for the first time stressed that only volunteers would be used to invade South West Africa. Hardly had that assurance been given than Maritz was ordered by Smuts to cross the border with his force (which did not consist entirely of volunteers). Smuts and Botha subsequently testified that that order was prompted by a desire to push Maritz (about whom rumours were circulating) into the open. Maritz's offer of resignation was refused and he went into rebellion on 9 October, after being informed that the government troops were on their way to Upington.

The government proclaimed martial law on 11 October 1914 and started commandeering men to suppress the rebellion. Beyers left Pretoria for the Magaliesberg where he was joined

by groups of burghers. Some men who were commandeered refused to obey and by 27 October rebels, inspired by De Wet, had occupied towns and seized and damaged property in the north-eastern Free State. On that date Beyers's commando was dispersed by government forces and skirmishes occurred.

At Sand River on 7 November De Wet was involved in a sharp skirmish and his son was killed. Botha's efforts to use M T Steyn as a mediator failed owing to mistrust on government and rebel sides and increasing bitterness, as violence escalated. De Wet occupied Winburg where his commando behaved, according to the magistrate, as if it were 'a belligerent force occupying an enemy's country'. Botha personally assumed command and defeated De Wet at the farm Mushroom Valley, south-east of Winburg on 11 November, although De Wet and most of his force escaped. Harassed by government troops, De Wet's depleted force was hunted down by motorcars and forced to surrender at the farm Waterbury near Vryburg on 1 December.

A week later Beyers's commando was cornered on the banks of the Vaal River south of Ma-

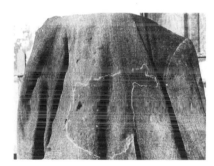

The jacket which General De la Rey was wearing when a ricochetting bullet killed him. (Transvaal Archives)

General Kemp (third from left) and Manie Maritz (third from right) with the Germans at Keetmanshoop. (Transvaal Archives)

Jopie Fourie (Transvaal Archives)

General de Wet and some of the rebels in jail after the 1914 Rebellion. (National Cultural History and Open-air Museum (NCHOM))

quassi. Beyers, attempting to cross the river on horseback, disappeared under the water. His body, when recovered, revealed no bullet wounds and it is believed he died of a heart attack.

Maritz, who had been unsuccessful in fomenting rebellion in the north-western Cape, was wounded in the knee during an attack on Keimoes on 22 October. On 26 November Kemp with some 600 men (including 'Siener' van Rensburg) linked up with Maritz, after an epic march from the Schweizer-Reneke district. On 16 December these two rebel leaders issued a manifesto proclaiming a republic in South Africa and gained a victory at Nous five days later. Repulsed by General Jaap van Deventer on 24 January 1915, they agreed to surrender their forces. Kemp was taken prisoner but Maritz returned to Windhoek and then went to Angola.

The last convulsions of the rebellion in the Transvaal had been fierce. In November and early December 1914 bands led by J J Pienaar (much later to become Administrator of the Transvaal) and Jopie Fourie had proved tenacious and inflicted heavy casualties on government forces at Warmbaths and at Rondefontein, near Hammanskraal. On the farm Nooitgedacht, on 15 December 1914, most of the force, including Jopie Fourie, were captured. Jopie Fourie was court-martialled, as he had gone into rebellion without resigning his commission in the Active Citizen Force. He was found guilty and shot by a firing squad on 20 December. Fourie had, in some quarters, come to be regarded as a martyr of the rebellion. While his execution may have been justifiable in a martial law situation, it was almost certainly a political mistake. Smuts in particular was blamed for his death.

More than 11 400 men rebelled. The government used 32 000 troops to suppress the rebellion. On the rebel side 190 were killed and 132 government supporters lost their lives. Special courts set up to try the rebels sentenced the rank-and-file to short terms of imprisonment and fines. Of the leaders, Kemp received the heaviest sentence of seven years' imprisonment and a fine of £1 000. De Wet got six years and a fine of £2 000. Before the end of 1916, however, all the rebels were out of goal. Maritz only returned to the Union at the beginning of 1924 when he was tried and sentenced to three years imprisonment; a few months later the newly installed Pact government (in which his fellow rebel, Kemp, was a Cabinet minister) released him.

Other impacts of a great war and domestic currents, 1914-1919

Before Maritz's treachery, Union troops had landed at Lüderitzbucht on 18 September 1914 and Brigadier-General H T Lukin's force, which had landed at Port Nolloth already on 1 September, had suffered a setback at Sandfontein. Thereafter operations had to be suspended until the suppression of the rebellion, when a South African force of over 40 000 men invaded German South West Africa. Louis Botha continued in his unique dual role of premier and Commander-in-Chief.

On 6 May 1915 Botha occupied Karibib and six days later he entered Windhoek. The strategic object of nullifying the wireless stations had been realized. Governor Seitz's suggestion that hostilities should be suspended, with the rival military forces retaining the areas that they occupied and that the future of the colony should be decided at the peace conference was, however, rejected. Less than two months later, on 9 July 1915, the continued advance and outflanking movements of the South African columns compelled the German commander Franke to surrender at Korab.

The conquest of German South West Africa was acclaimed a great victory at a time when Allied successes had been minimal. Today it is recognized that the numerical preponderance of the South African army was enormous. There were also unsatisfactory aspects of the conduct of operations: numerous blunders, extravagant expenditure (more than £15 million) and friction between English- and Dutch-speaking members of Botha's force. Yet the subordination of German South West Africa in less than six months, at the cost of less than 300 South Africans killed in action, was a notable military achievement, and the conquest of the German colony was to come to have profound repercussions for South Africa in the latter part of the twentieth century.

Altogether more than 60 000 South Africans

fought alongside Indian, Nigerian, East African and British troops in the protracted East African campaign from February 1916 until the end of the war. They were opposed by an army consisting largely of black Askaris brilliantly led by General Paul von Lettow-Vorbeck. Smuts was Commander-in-Chief from February 1916 to January 1917 and J L van Deventer was in charge of operations from May 1917. More than 1 500 South Africans died in the campaign as a result of military action or disease.

A need for reinforcements arose on the Western Front as the staggering casualty rate mounted in the trenches. From September 1915 a South African contingent consisting entirely of volunteers was recruited to become part of the imperial army. The First South African Infantry Brigade, commanded by Brigadier-General H T Lukin, arrived in Britain in the last quarter of 1915. At the end of the year the Brigade was diverted to Egypt to help subdue the Turkish-Senussi threat to the Suez Canal.

In April 1916 the Brigade went to France and, as part of the Ninth Division became involved in fierce fighting during the Somme offensive in July 1916. The Union's participation reached a climax in the battle of Delville Wood of 15-20 July 1916, when more than 750 South Africans were killed and more than 1 500 wounded.

After being reinforced, the South African Brigade made its most spectacular advance in the Third Battle of Ypres in September 1917. Lukin, with the rank of Major-General, commanded the Ninth Division from December 1916 to February 1918. At Marrières Wood the South African Brigade again suffered heavy casualties in March 1918 and two months later made a great stand at Messines Ridge. In the

last stages of the war, the sadly depleted Brigade was down to a composite battalion.

According to the Official South African War History, over 12 000 South Africans (including over 3 000 blacks and over 700 Coloureds) were killed or died on active service in all theatres during the war. Yet South African casualties, and indeed the Union's commitment to the war effort (in terms of manpower and money provided), were nevertheless less than those of the other dominions.

In one respect – the role played by General J C Smuts – South Africa may be said to have made a unique contribution. No other dominion statesman had such a significant share in the central direction of imperial and allied strategy, as did the Union Minister of Defence. At the

General Louis Botha at Windhoek during the South West Africa campaign in 1915. (NCHOM)

The Battle of Delville Wood, July 1916, showing the trenches and the remains of the wood after the battle. (South African Museum of Military History)

Generals Louis Botha and Jan Smuts during the First World War. (Transvaal Archives)

J C Smuts (seated front row, right) in the Imperial War Cabinet in 1917. (Central Archives)

imperial war conference in March 1917 he opposed renewed efforts to push imperial federation and drafted a resolution affirming the status of dominions as autonomous nations. He declined the offer of the Palestinian command, but stayed in Britain at the insistence of the British premier, David Lloyd George. He became a valuable reinforcement to the exclusive six-man British War Cabinet – constitutionally an anomalous position as he never became a member of the House of Commons. Smuts's sa-

gacity in the wide variety of tasks he performed was widely acclaimed.

In August 1914 there was a resurgence of white fears about a black uprising. Blacks were assured by the government that the war would not affect them. The SANNC decided to stop agitating against the Land Act for the duration of the war. The government declined the offer of black, Indian and Coloured organizations which wished to provide troops for active service from their groups. A small number of Coloureds, who knew the country well, were briefly used as armed scouts in the South West African campaign. A further exception was made when a battalion of Coloureds, the so-called Cape Corps, was armed to fight in East Africa. The Union government, even when the manpower crisis in the trenches was most acute, steadfastly opposed recruitment of blacks as combatant troops. Use had been made of South Africans who were not white in non-combatant capacities (Indians being used as stretcher-bearers) in the African campaigns. The decision to comply with the imperial government's request to send black and Coloured labourers and other auxiliaries to France was taken also with some reluctance and regarded with misgivings by Nationalists, Labourites and even some members of the SAP. The government had some difficulty in recruiting men for the South African Native Labour Contingent (SANLC) although altogether about 21 000 were sent to Europe where they comprised about a quarter of the total labour force employed by the army in France. The members of the SANLC were housed in closed compounds, mainly because it was feared that the experiene of living freely in a country without a colour bar would result in 'social evils or difficulties' on their return to South Africa. The SANLC's industry and efficiency

received high praise. More than any other event of the conflict of 1914-1918, was the loss at sea in the English Channel of 615 members of a contingent of SANLC on *SS Mende* on 21 February 1917 that impinged upon black consciousness of the Great War.

Blacks, Coloureds and Indians hoped that their loyalty would be rewarded after the war. Smuts had believed that white South Africans who had served alongside Indian troops in East Africa might come to regard their Indian fellow citizens in a more favourable light as a result. However, most white South Africans were oblivious of this new dimension. Smuts and others had become concerned about the success achieved by black soldiers, particularly in East Africa, and warned about the future consequences of arming blacks.

After the commission, headed by Sir William Beaumont, to inquire into the allocation of further scheduled land in terms of the 1913 Land Act, issued its report in 1916, a Native Affairs Administration Bill, designed to take territorial segregation further and to reach an overall solution of the 'native problem' was drafted. The bill was subsequently withdrawn, as vested interests made the delimitation of specific additional scheduled areas difficult. Moreover, the courts decided that the bill, which would affect the entrenched franchise rights of certain blacks in the Cape, was inapplicable in that province unless a two-thirds majority of both houses were obtained.

White party politics were stormy during the war years. The influence of the Labour Party, which had been in the ascendant before August 1914, declined steeply. Hertzog, who had been opposed to violence, had nevertheless not been prepared to repudiate the rebellion publicly. National Party criticism of government war policy met with widespread Afrikaner support. The establishment of Nasionale Pers in Cape Town and the appearance of its newspaper *De Burger* in July 1915, with D F Malan as editor, bolstered the Nationalist cause. The Unionists approved of the government's stance on the war issue and its suppression of the rebellion, but at the same time, the SAP's loyal support of Britain had virtually deprived the Unionist Party of its *raison d'être*. The SAP almost certainly lost Afrikaner support after August 1914 (but some of that support had probably been doubtful since the Hertzog-split).

Smuts, who had held the reins while Botha was in German South West, contemplated postponing the general election due to be held before the end of 1915, or even of following the lead of the British Government by not holding a general election while hostilities lasted. However, the Union's second general election was fixed for 20 October 1915. The South African Party, which concluded an agreement with the Unionists to avoid splitting the pro-war vote in certain constituencies, gained a majority of 14 seats over the Unionists and 27 seats more than the Nationalists.

The new government was to be handicapped by Smuts's long absences from the Union on imperial duty. Botha, whose health had deteriorated, tended, without his lieutenant's sanguine support, to lapse into bouts of extreme depression. Union finances, on the outbreak of war, were in a state of confusion. Businessmen and farmers were concerned that banks would call up overdrafts and bonds. Officials of the Union treasury met with bankers, merchants and mining magnates to devise emergency measures. Britain provided financial aid to the Union, as it did to other dominions, but to meet its expenditure needs, the government was forced to introduce income tax for the first time in 1914 and to raise indirect taxation.

Certain industries were hit hard by the war.

Members of the South African Native Labour Contingent (SANLC) in France, with officers. (Cape Archives, AG2101)

Louis Botha and his family at Groote Schuur. (Cape Archives, E2849)

Clements Kadalie (left) and A W G Champion, leaders of the Industrial and Commercial Workers Union (ICU). (S A Library)

Four days after the outbreak of war, the directors of De Beers decided to stop diamond mining at Kimberley, Premier Mine and elsewhere, as it was considered to be unprofitable to continue production. The mines remained closed until July 1916 when operations resumed on a limited scale. The closing of the diamond mines left some 5 000 whites and more than 45 000 blacks without work. De Beers agreed to retain some of the whites in their service on half pay and found work for others.

The arrangements made at the beginning of the war underlined, as the historians Marks and Trapido have pointed out, 'the true significance (for Britain) of having a "friendly" government in power in South Africa'. The Bank of England, it was decided, would take over the entire gold output of the Witwatersrand and local banks were to make advances to the mines – initially the raw gold would not be shipped to London, but would be retained in South Africa until it was considered safe to send the bullion by sea. The gold mines continued operating throughout the war. During the war more Afrikaners became mineworkers to replace men on active service and a limited number of blacks were drafted into doing semiskilled work. The Mine Workers' Union, disturbed at the latter trend, negotiated the so-called Status Quo Agreement with the Chamber of Mines in September 1918, which stipulated that the existing restriction of certain jobs to whites would be maintained. The restriction of imports boosted local manufacturing industries during the war. The establishment of new factories accelerated the process of urbanization – particularly on the Witwatersrand and especially among blacks.

In South Africa, in common with many other countries, the cost of living rose during the war. Blacks, who had suffered most, signalled their dissatisfaction by sporadic strikes on the gold mines in December 1915, January and February 1916 and July 1918, and by boycotting concession stores. African sanitary workers in Johannesburg went on strike for higher wages in June 1918.

The University Acts of 1916, piloted through Parliament by F S Malan, established a federal university, the University of South Africa, consisting of six constituent colleges, and also transformed the Victoria College into the University of Stellenbosch and the South African College into the University of Cape Town. Mainly white students attended these universities and colleges, although people of other races were admitted to the institutions in Cape Town and Johannesburg. In 1916 the 'South African Native College' was opened on the site of Fort Hare near Alice in the Victoria East district.

Louis Botha joined Smuts to represent the Union of South Africa at the Paris Peace Conference. Two other unofficial South African delegations also came to Europe in 1919. The Transvaal Nationalist, Tielman Roos, had conceived an idea that an appeal should be made for the restoration of the independence of the former Boer republics. Hertzog had no great expectations in the matter, but he agreed to lead the deputation to Europe. A four-man SANNC delegation, led by Sol Plaatje, went overseas in 1919 to present a memorial of grievances to the British Government and to plead for a new deal for blacks in South Africa. Neither the Afrikaner nor the black delegations met with any concrete success.

The official South African delegation at Paris was particularly concerned with two matters which became closely linked – the League of Nations and the Disposition of South West Africa. Smuts's paper, 'The League of Nations, a Practical Suggestion', which gave form to inchoate ideas expressed by other statesmen and which incorporated his own suggestions, was a notable contribution to the establishment of the organization.

Before the commencement of the South West African campaign, Smuts told the Governor-General, Buxton, that it would be impossible for the Union to relinquish the territory. Smuts's system of mandates was made applicable to all conquered German colonies: South West Africa became a 'C' class mandate (which

National Members of Parliament and members of the independence deputation in February 1919. (Central Archives)

allowed for the government of the territory by the Union under its laws).

Botha and Smuts both signed the Treaty of Versailles, although Smuts nearly refused to do so, calling it 'an impossible and wrong peace'. The South African premier arrived back in the Union on 24 July 1919. Slightly more than a month later, on 27 August, Louis Botha died of a heart attack. Jan Christiaan Smuts became the second Prime Minister of the Union of South Africa.

Post-war pressures and patterns

The Industrial and Commercial Union (ICU), founded by white trade unionists and a young Nyasalander (Malawian) who had emigrated to the Cape, Clements Kadalie, started attracting large numbers of black and Coloured members by the end of 1919. In March and April 1919 demonstrations on the Witwatersrand against the pass system by black workers was encouraged by the Transvaal branch of the SANNC (although the National President of Congress, S M Makgatho, warned against the use of violence). Over 700 demonstrators were arrested as they sang 'Nkosi Sikelel'i Afrika' (God Bless Africa). In February 1920 black students at Kilnerton near Pretoria went on a hunger strike and at Fort Hare, a few months later, buildings were burnt. A strike started at East Rand Proprietary Mine on 17 February 1920 and lasted until 28 February, by which time about 71 000 black workers on 21 mines had been involved. The strike may be regarded, as Philip Bonner has suggested, 'as part of a broadly based movement of working-class agitation'.

Renewed and sharper antagonism towards Indians in the same period was prompted by increasing numbers of Indians in the Transvaal obtaining property in the names of companies. In 1919 the South African League was formed to agitate for the closing of the legal loopholes by which Indians were acquiring residential and property rights in towns.

The discontent of some Afrikaners at their position in South Africa had grown during the latter part of the war and in June 1918 an organization called *Jong Suid-Afrika* (Young South Africa) was formed. It soon became known as the Afrikaner *Broederbond* with the aim of furthering the interests of the 'Afrikaner nation'.

In the Union's third general election (10 March 1920) the constitutional tie with Britain featured prominently, but the high cost of living and the position of Indians were two other issues on which the opposition parties hammered, while the government was accused of maladministration during the war years. The South African Party suffered a severe setback, winning three less seats than the Nationalists. Smuts could only govern precariously with a parliamentary majority of four, if the Unionist and in-

dependents remained prepared to support the SAP.

Despite its uneasy position, the government passed important legislation during the 1920 parliamentary session to deal with the increasing dissatisfaction of the Union's black inhabitants. The Native Affairs Act of 1920 established the Advisory Native Affairs Commission to consider and to make recommendations regarding 'native' administration and policy and provided for the summoning of 'Native Conferences'. The Act may be seen as an attempt to provide blacks with some outlet of expression. It was, however, also a continuation of the policy of segregation.

Attempts to achieve *hereniging* (reunion) of the National and South African parties culminated in the abortive Bloemfontein Conference in September 1920. Smuts's only real alternative was to approach the Unionists, which resulted in the Unionist Party being absorbed by the South African Party. The general election on 8 February 1921 transformed the political situation. The new SAP, which gained 13 more seats than it and the Unionists together had won in 1920, now had an overall majority of 24 seats. Smuts reconstituted the Cabinet and included three former Unionists, Thomas Smartt, Patrick Duncan and J W Jagger.

Technological developments in aviation and electricity had an impact on South Africa in the early 1920s. On 4 February 1920 two South Africans, Pierre van Ryneveld and Quentin Brand, left London in an attempt to be the first to fly from Britain to South Africa. Forty-five days later, after a loss of two aircraft, they landed at Cape Town. Allister Miller formed the South African Aerial Transport Company in 1919, the forerunner of a state air service. The Electricity Act of 1922, regarded by many municipalities as infringing on their interests, established the Electricity Supply Commission

The Cabinet of 1921. From left to right, standing, are N J de Wet, D Reitz, P Duncan, J W Jagger and H Mentz. Sitting are Sir Thomas Watt, F S Malan, J C Smuts, Sir Thomas Smartt and H Burton. (Central Archives)

243

Blacks leaving Fordsburg during the 1922 strike. (Central Archives)

A bedroom in Sachs's Hotel, Fordsburg, which suffered considerable damage during the strike. (Central Archives)

(ESCOM) as a non-profit making state corporation, with Dr H J van der Byl as its first chairman, to supply and co-ordinate the supply of electrical power in the Union.

In June 1921 Smuts took a memorandum to the London Imperial Conference to define the autonomous constitutional status of the dominions, but did not present it, as the attitudes of the other Commonwealth leaders were unfavourable. Hertzog inherited the memorandum and used it in 1926. Smuts's biographer, W K Hancock, had remarked that the memorandum 'contained by anticipation the Balfour Declaration of 1926 and the entire constitutional achievement from then until the Statute of Westminster of 1931; but Smuts gained no credit from it'. After Smuts's return from London, his correspondence with Churchill formed the basis of the Simon's Town Agreement, which became an important ingredient of South African defence policy before 1939.

The incidence of violence occasioned by hostility between the races and the government's 'native policy' continued to be one of the most alarming features of South African society. On 23 October 1920 the arrest of the local ICU leader, Samuel Masabalala, who had been trying to organize a strike to improve workers' salaries, resulted in crowds carrying sticks thronging around the police station in Port Elizabeth where he was held. Stone throwing was followed by shots being fired by police and white civilian ex-servicemen. One white girl and 23 black men were killed; 1 black woman, 45 black men and 4 white men were injured.

Another serious clash between the South African police and black people occurred at Bulhoek, 40 km from Queenstown, on 24 May 1921. Enoch Mgijima and his followers, known as the Israelites, had squatted illegally at Bulhoek, according to Mgijima, at God's command, to await the end of the world. The South African Government made a number of futile conciliatory efforts to persuade the Israelites to move off the land, which did not belong to them. In May 1921 a force of about 800 heavily armed men under the Commissioner of Police was sent to Bulhoek. Mgijima still refused to move. About 500 Israelites, armed with assegais and home-made weapons, charged the police (it is uncertain whether the police fired first). After twenty minutes of fierce fighting 183 Israelites were killed or subsequently died of wounds, 100 were wounded and 150 were arrested.

In June 1922 the Smuts government again came under severe censure for its expedition against the Bondelzwarts tribe of South West Africa who had become restless as a result of objections to escalating taxes demanded for keeping their hunting dogs, and complaints about white occupation of land. The government force lost 2 men; 115 Bondelzwart men were killed in action and women and children were killed and wounded by bombs.

Hertzog believed that the lack of a definite stand on 'native policy' by the government lay behind the unrest. In 1923 the government turned its attention to blacks in the towns. As T R H Davenport has shown, a comparatively liberal bill, which gave blacks security of tenure in towns, which alleviated the pass laws and which had some black support, was transformed into the Natives (Urban Areas) Act of 1923, which imposed segregation and influx control. The Act was based on the principle that black people's presence in towns could only be justified in so far as they served the needs of whites. Local authorities were given the right to set aside locations for blacks in urban areas, but blacks were not to be granted ownership rights. Registrations of service contracts were entrusted to town councils and unemployed and 'disorderly' blacks could be expelled by town councils. Black opposition to the Act was profound.

In July 1921 white socialists, among whom W H Andrews and S P Bunting were prominent, united their several organizations to form the Communist Party of South Africa. The Communist Party provided a vehicle for multiracial political action in South Africa. Initially, however, the thrust of its efforts were more particularly aimed at improving the lot of the white workers and black discontent was concentrated more on race than class differences. Another, less radical, experiment in multiracial co-operation was launched when two Americans, Thomas Jesse Jones and J E K Aggrey (together with J D Rheinalt Jones), launched Joint Councils on which blacks (including some ANC members) and whites served together to initiate and to encourage greater mutual understanding between the races.

At the 1921 Imperial Conference Smuts rejected the resolution moved by the Indian representative, Srinivasa Sastri, that Indians legally domiciled in other parts of the British Empire were entitled to equal citizenship rights in their new countries. The clash between South Africa's and India's representatives was renewed at the 1923 Imperial Conference. Indians in South Africa, alarmed by white antagonism and by three discriminatory and restrictive ordinances passed by the Natal Provincial Council in 1922 (even though two of these were vetoed by the central government) formed the South African Indian Congress in May 1923. The announcement by the Union government in January 1924 of a Class Areas Bill which was to be introduced, led to fierce protests from Indians in their new country and in their country of origin. The poet and politician, Mrs Sarojini Naidu, who was a member of the Indian National Congress, came to South Africa in February 1924 and became President of the South African Indian Congress three months later.

The end of the Great War had ushered in an economic boom. The gold price rose, low grade mines could continue working and white mine workers received higher wages. In 1921 the Union's own central bank, the South African Reserve Bank, was formed to consolidate the issue of bank notes and the control of currency. An Act of 1919 led to the Pretoria branch of the Royal Mint coming into being in 1923, enabling the Union authorities to mint their own coins. The completion of the Rand Refinery in Germiston in 1921 meant that mining companies would be able to refine their gold in South Africa.

The post-war era of prosperity was short-lived. The agricultural sector was hard hit by the severe drought of 1919. Unfavourable world economic trends which started gathering by the second year of peace, resulted in falling prices for agricultural products. By 1921 there was also a decline in South Africa's coal exports. Inflation in South Africa had been accelerated by the increased gold price and at the same time unemployment figures rose.

A fall in the gold price led to the profitability of many mining companies becoming threatened. The Chamber of Mines desperately started searching for means to reduce the costs of production. In December 1921 the Chamber announced to increasingly militant workers that from February 1922 three changes would be effected to meet the crisis. The wages of the highest paid miners were to be reduced. The status quo agreement would be abolished (which step, it was believed, would lead to the retrenchment of some 2 000 white miners). Underground work would be reorganized so that lower paid blacks would do semi-skilled work previously done by higher paid whites (in 1921 the wage bill for 21 000 white miners was almost double the total salaries paid to 180 000 black miners). The coal miners, who went on strike on 1 January 1922, were the first to react. Nine days later gold miners and power station employees

The declaration of the General Strike on Monday, 6 March 1922. The crowd masses outside the Trades Hall, Rissik Street, in Johannesburg. (*Die Burger*)

also stopped work – more than 20 000 whites and in consequence a large percentage of 180 000 blacks were idle.

'The government', Smuts said on 10 January, 'would draw a ring round both parties, do its best to maintain law and order, and let the two parties fight it out'. It was this statement that led to the erroneous accusation that Smuts had cruelly 'let the situation develop'. In fact the premier had first intervened in November 1921 when he secured a statement from the Chamber that no general attack on white labour was intended; the opening of Parliament was postponed so that ministers could be on hand on the Witwatersrand for negotiation. Smuts worked hard but to no avail to try to get the Chamber and the trade unions to resolve their differences. A conference held from 14 to 27 January 1922 between the two parties under the chairmanship of Judge J S Curlewis ended in deadlock.

National and Labour parties sympathized with the strikers (of whom perhaps as many as 75 per cent, but not the leaders, were Afrikaners) and there was some support for the workers on the *platteland* where some people had ideas of using the situation to establish a republic. By the end of February the 'Augmented Executive', created to represent all trade unions involved in the dispute, had lost control of the strikers. The leadership passed into the hands of a more militant Council of Action, some of whom had Communistic leanings, modified to accommodate their feelings of white superi-

ority. Banners were displayed with the slogan: WORKERS OF THE WORLD FIGHT AND UNITE FOR A WHITE SOUTH AFRICA.

Two further factors led to an escalation of violence: police protection granted to strike-breakers or 'scabs' and the organization of the strikers into semi-military commandos, some of whom were armed. By 17 March resistance had ended and the strike was called off. Accurate casualty figures are difficult to ascertain.

According to official statistics 43 soldiers, 86 policemen and 81 civilians (of whom 39 were revolutionaries and 42 innocent civilians, including a number of blacks) were killed, ie a total of 210. The wounded included 133 soldiers, 86 policemen and 315 civilians, while 5 000 were arrested. One thousand appeared in court, 18 were sentenced to death and 4 (C C Stassen, S A 'Taffy' Long, H K Hull and D Lewis) were hanged.

At the beginning of 1924 the Industrial Conciliation Act was passed to facilitate the peaceful settlement of disputes (although 'pass-bearing' blacks were excluded from its provisions). The government department of mines, aware that mining companies were ignoring the regulations relating to the job colour-bar, instituted a test case in August 1923. The Supreme Court judgment declared the colour-bar regulations emanating from the Mines and Works Act of 1911 to be *ultra vires*. Mining companies thus had been given a blank cheque to break down all colour restrictions relating to job allocations on the mines. About 1 700 fewer white workers

The Witbank Platoon in action during the 1922 strike. (*Die Burger*)

were employed on the gold mines in 1924 than there had been in 1921 and working costs were reduced.

Smuts received blame for the revolt. Linking the events on the Rand in 1922 to other manifestations of violent suppression in Smuts's career, Hertzog said that the Prime Minister's footsteps 'dripped with blood'.

In May and June 1922 South African and Mozambiquan authorities failed to reach a satisfactory agreement on port and railway matters. In October 1922 Smuts's hopes were dashed that Southern Rhodesia would be incorporated to create a larger Union and to strengthen the SAP. White Rhodesians decided by 8 774 votes to 5 989 in favour of responsible government rather than incorporation in the Union of South Africa – a decision which was to have far-reaching consequences for Rhodesia and South Africa.

Hertzog and Creswell had long been on friendly terms and other members of the National and Labour parties had come closer together in their condemnation of the government's handling of the strike. Discussions between the leaders of the two parties culminated in April 1923 in a 'Pact' which was ratified by congresses of the two parties. It was agreed that it was undesirable to split the opposition vote in triangular contests. Already in the 1924 parliamentary session the co-operation between the Pact parties was evident, with Labourites toning down their socialist views and Nationalists steering clear of any hint of supporting secession from the Commonwealth. The unpopularity of the government had been reflected in a series of by-election defeats in the Cape, Natal and the Transvaal since 1921. The defeat of the strong SAP candidate A G Robertson by a little-known National Party candidate, A S Naudé, in the Wakkerstroom by election on 5 April 1924, decided Smuts to resign, although his government's term of office still had two years to run.

The South African Party was defeated by the Pact in the general election, held on 17 June 1924. The Union of South Africa had entered a new phase.

A South African Party election poster, 1924. (United Party Archives, Unisa)

Suggested Reading List

C Bundy (1979) *The Rise and Fall of the South African Peasantry*, London

T R H Davenport (1963) 'The South African Rebellion', *English Historical Review*, 78, 1963

N G Garson (1980) 'South Africa and World War I', in N Hillmer and P Wigley (eds) *The First British Commonwealth: Essays in Honour of Nicholas Mansergh*, London

A M Grundlingh (1986) *Black Men in a White Man's War. South African Blacks and the First World War*, Johannesburg

E N Katz (1976) *A Trade Union Aristocracy: A History of White Workers in the Transvaal and the General Strike of 1913*, Johannesburg

A G Oberholster (1982) *Die Mynwerkerstaking, Witwatersrand, 1922*, Pretoria

G D Scholtz (1942) *Die Rebellie, 1914-1915*, Johannesburg

S B Spies (1969) 'The Outbreak of the First World War and the Botha Government', *South African Historical Journal*, 1, November 1969

Chapter 17

From the Pact to the Advent of Apartheid, 1924-1948

B K Murray and A W Stadler

The first Hertzog Cabinet, the National Party-Labour Party Cabinet of 1924. Front row (left to right) P G W Grobler, F H P Cresswell, J B M Hertzog, the Earl of Athlone (Governor-General), T J de V Roos, D F Malan, T Boydell. Back row (left to right) F W Beyers (second from left), N C Havenga, C W Malan, J C G Kemp. (Institute for the Study of Contemporary History (INCH))

The years 1924 and 1948 marked two significant stages in the rise of Afrikaner nationalism as the dominant political and social force in South Africa, and in the evolution of the country's segregationist race policies.

The National Party under Hertzog which came to power in 1924, with the support of the Labour Party, sought to establish parity for Afrikaners with English-speaking whites within South Africa and to make South Africa constitutionally independent from Britain. Another aim was to create an infrastructure favourable to domestic economic interests. Segregation was to be further elaborated, and entrenched in the industrial arena. Attempts to remove the Cape Africans from the common voters' roll finally reached fruition in 1936, following the split within the Afrikaner nationalist movement and the fusion of Hertzog's National Party with Smuts's South African Party.

By 1948 the contending forces in the Afrikaner nationalist movement had been reunited, and Dr D F Malan's victory in the general election that year prepared the way for National Party dominance in South Africa. The doctrine of apartheid was enunciated and elaborated as the framework for subsequent race policy and industrialization.

The general elections of 1924 and 1948 were novel in that they were the only two elections in the fifty-year history of the Union of South Africa that resulted in a change of government. Both brought Nationalist parties to power.

The period 1924 to 1939

B K Murray

The Pact government formed by Hertzog in June 1924 was dominated by the National Party with the Labour Party very much the junior partner. Generally, however, the Nationalist and Labour ministers managed to act together as a team until 1928. Apart from the creation of a separate Department of Labour, the Labour ministers did not initiate any major items in the Pact government's programme. The overall direction of the government's policies was determined by Hertzog, who alone had any previous experience of government. The major policies pursued by the Pact government may be divided into three broad categories: issues of status, the economy, and race relations. The two last mentioned were often closely linked.

The Pact government, 1924-1929

For the 1924 general election Hertzog's nationalism, notably its republican component, had been muted by the requirements of his alliance with the mainly English-speaking Labour Party. None the less the appeal of his party to the majority of Afrikaners, first made evident in the general election of 1915, was rooted in its nationalist programme, and once in office Hertzog pursued the important aspects of that programme concerning language equality and the sovereign independence of South Africa. In 1925 the meaning of 'Dutch' in the constitution was extended to include Afrikaans, and its equality with English in official use was thereafter insisted upon. D F Malan, as Minister of

Bruce Murray holds a chair in Edwardian British history at the University of the Witwatersrand, Johannesburg. He was educated at King Edward VII School in Johannesburg, Rhodes University in Grahamstown and the University of Kansas, where he obtained his Ph D. Prior to joining the University of the Witwatersrand as a senior lecturer in history in 1970, he lectured in history at the University of Arkansas and Rhodes University. He has written two books: *The People's Budget, 1909-1910: Lloyd George and British Politics* (London, 1980) and *Wits: The Early Years* (Johannesburg, 1982).

General J B M Hertzog and others scrutinizing the new South African flag. (Transvaal Archives)

the Interior, Education, and Public Health, required bilingualism throughout the civil service, thereby opening up the civil service as a major career opportunity for Afrikaners, a development which was to be promoted much more deliberately by the government he formed in 1948.

In 1926, at the Imperial Conference in London, making use of Smuts's memorandum of 1921, Hertzog played a leading role in clearly defining for South Africa and the other dominions equality of status with Britain within the empire and Commonwealth. According to the Balfour Declaration, Britain and the dominions were 'autonomous communities within the British Empire, equal in status, in no way subordinate one to another in any aspect of their domestic or external affairs, though united by a common allegiance to the Crown, and freely associated as members of the British Common-

wealth of Nations'. The assertion of dominion sovereignty led directly to the establishment of a South African Department of External Affairs, with Hertzog at its head. Then in 1928, after prolonged dispute, a new national flag was introduced.

The development of the economy

Hertzog took office at the end of the slump that had bedevilled the Smuts government. The life of his first government coincided almost exactly with a period of economic advance and boom, finally terminated by the Great Depression at the end of the decade. All sectors of the economy shared in the improvement. The gold-mining industry recovered, agricultural prices were generally favourable, the amount of white-owned land under cultivation was considerably

Three of the blast furnaces of the South African Iron and Steel Industrial Corporation (ISCOR) photographed in the 1970s, approximately fifty years after the establishment of the Corporation in 1928. (*Die Burger*)

extended, and the manufacturing industry made significant progress.

The Pact government was the first to adopt a systematic programme for the development of secondary industry in South Africa. The programme took the form of tariff protection, as embodied in the Customs Tariff Act of 1925, and infrastructural development, chiefly the creation of a state-controlled iron and steel industry. Despite two rejections by the Senate, the South African Iron and Steel Industrial Corporation (ISCOR) was established by act of Parliament in 1928 as a public utility. Because of general scepticism regarding the venture's prospects, and suspicion of state control, private enterprise failed to take the shares offered it, and in 1931 the state effectively assumed complete control of the corporation, with all its directors being appointed by the government. In 1934 ISCOR commenced production.

Hertzog's National Party was overwhelmingly a rural party, but it wished to promote the industrial development of South Africa rather than allow the country to remain economically a relatively underdeveloped colony of Britain. Its programme for industrialization derived from the fear that gold mining was a wasting asset, a desire to expand the internal market for the products of South African agriculture, a determination to create employment opportunites for Afrikaners, who were often 'poor whites', moving from rural districts to the towns, and a general concern to make the country more self-sufficient and to check the drain on its reserves. The Labour Party also favoured protection and industrialization so as to promote employment.

The industrial labour policy of the Pact government was that of 'civilized' labour at a 'civilized' rate. It was a policy that went back at least as far as *Het Volk*, and it meant basically that preference should be given to the employment of whites and at higher wages than blacks.

The Mines and Works Amendment Act, or 'Colour Bar' Act of 1926, secured the position of skilled white workers by restoring the validity of colour bar regulations previously invalidated by the Supreme Court. The Wage Act of 1925, for its part, sought to safeguard the earnings of unskilled white workers. To ensure increasing employment opportunities for unskilled whites the Pact government relied both on state enterprises, such as the railways and harbours, which took on a greater proportion of white labourers, and on stipulating that protected industries employ more whites. Tariff protection for an industry was made conditional upon the employment of a 'fair amount' of white labour.

Policy towards Indians and black people

The Pact government's policy towards the Indian community was embodied in D F Malan's Areas Reservation and Immigration and Regis-

Black miners underground, engaged in a drilling operation. The Mines and Works Amendment Act (1926) limited the issue of certificates of competency in certain occupations such as machinists, surveyors and blasters to whites and Coloureds, thus preventing black mine workers from doing these jobs. (*Die Burger*)

tration (Further Provisions) Bill of 1925, which sought to secure the residential and commercial segregation of Indians and reduce the Indian population to an 'irreducible minimum' by facilitating repatriation.

The distinctive feature of Indian opposition to the proposed legislation was no longer passive resistance, but the attempt to gain support from abroad, notably in India itself. At the end of 1925 the South African Indian Council sent a deputation to India to interview the British Viceroy and address a series of public and private meetings. At the same time the Indian Government sent a fact-finding mission to South Africa and, through the intervention of the British Government, a meeting with Hertzog was arranged (see box on right).

As Minister of Native Affairs, Hertzog introduced three 'native' bills in July 1926. The Union Native Council Bill proposed to establish a deliberative council of fifty Africans for the whole of South Africa, thirty-five of them elected. The Representation of Natives in Parliament Bill aimed to remove African voters from the common roll in the Cape and to provide Africans throughout the Union with seven white representatives in the House of Assembly, with power to vote on measures affecting Africans. The Natives Land Act (Amendment) Bill provided for the enlargement of the area allocated to Africans in the 1913 act by releasing certain areas for competitive purchase by blacks and whites.

The round table conferences

A round table conference between the delegates of the Indian and South African governments was arranged for the end of 1926. The conference, held from 17 December 1926 to 12 January 1927, produced the Cape Town Agreement, which provided for combined action to assist voluntary repatriation, and for the appointment of an Agent-General as diplomatic representative of the Indian Government in South Africa. In addition, the South African Government undertook to withdraw the Areas Reservation Bill and to promote the 'upliftment' of those Indians who remained in the country.

For the South African Government the chief component of the Cape Town Agreement was the repatriation scheme, but this proved ineffective in practice. The upshot was a second round table conference early in 1932, which came up with the idea of colonizing Indians in some territory other than India itself. A Colonization Enquiry Commission was established in 1933, which reported in favour of North Borneo, but the colonization scheme never progressed beyond that.

'There is fire here.' The ICU chiefs. A W G Champion is seated in the centre of the front row. (Documentation Centre for African Studies, UNISA)

THERE IS FIRE HERE "I.C.U. Chiefs"

In addition to the 'native' bills, Hertzog also put before Parliament a Coloured Persons Rights Bill which proposed to initiate the process of extending political rights to Coloureds outside the Cape. Hertzog regarded these four bills as integral parts of an overall solution to 'the Native-Coloured question', and stipulated that they would stand or fall together. As they interfered with the entrenched clauses in the constitution, the Representation of Natives in Parliament Bill and the Coloured Persons Rights Bill both required the approval of a two-thirds majority in a joint sitting of the two Houses of Parliament.

In the traditional interpretation, Hertzog's main reason for the proposed legislation was his concern to preserve white political supremacy and European civilization in South Africa by securing uniform political segregation between white and black. Hertzog himself contended that the National Convention had committed a grave political error in permitting Africans in the Cape to remain on the common roll, as they were already a determining factor in twelve constituencies, and he predicted that within fifty years they would outnumber white voters in the Cape. He also feared that the Cape African franchise might serve as the thin edge of the wedge for the Union as a whole. The proposal for making more land available to Africans he regarded as part of the *quid pro quo* for the loss of the Cape franchise.

A recent interpretation by Marian Lacey is that Hertzog's primary aim was to bring Cape Africans under control, and to bring the Cape into line with the patterns of segregation and exploitation already established in the other provinces of the Union. As the Cape franchise was linked to landowning, the Cape, as has been shown, had been excluded from the operation of the 1913 Land Act. In fact all Cape Africans,

and not only voters, were less vulnerable to control and exploitation.

Smuts strongly criticized the bills, including the land proposals, which he considered insufficient and likely to promote rather than diminish the territorial intermingling of the races. In March 1927, after their first readings, the bills were referred to a select committee. In February 1929 Hertzog presented to a joint sitting of the two Houses of Parliament substantially revised versions of the Representation of Natives in Parliament Bill and the Coloured Persons Rights Bill. They were again opposed by the South African Party, and consequently failed to achieve the required two-thirds majority.

Black reactions under the Pact

In 1924 leaders of the major black organizations, notably the African National Congress (ANC) and the Industrial and Commercial Workers Union (ICU), had welcomed the prospect of a Nationalist government. At its conference in May 1924 the ANC, as the SANNC renamed itself, had urged the black electorate to 'vote solidly for a change of government', and Clements Kadalie, the ICU National Secretary, also proffered support to Hertzog. By 1929, however, black leaders were generally disillusioned with Hertzog, and they rejected his 'native' bills. The Native Conference, which had been set up by the Smuts government, rejected by a large majority the proposal to abolish the Cape African franchise.

The leadership of both the ANC and the ICU was drawn overwhelmingly from the small black middle class, and it was precisely this class that felt under attack from the Hertzog 'native' bills. Hertzog was threatening to strip the African elite of their existing rights, and the result was a radicalization of the ANC. Coincidentally the ICU succeeded in mobilizing the greatest mass movement ever witnessed in South Africa. The hitherto cautious, moderate, and even conservative leadership of the ANC embarked temporarily on a new strategy with the election in 1927 of Joseph Gumede as President to turn the ANC into a mass organization. Some ANC leaders even established contacts with the small Communist Party of South Africa (CPSA), which had likewise supported the Nationalist-Labour alliance in the 1924 general election but which had since come to the conclusion that its 'main revolutionary task (was) among the natives'.

The black and Coloured trade union, the ICU, was transformed in the mid-1920s into a mass movement, voicing a broad range of popular grievances and establishing branches throughout the Union and also in the neighbouring territories. In the towns its main success was in organizing workers in the docks, railways, and municipal services, but what gave the ICU its mass base was its penetration of the countryside, notably in Natal and the eastern Transvaal, chiefly by playing on the issues of land, wages, and the pass laws. By 1927, its peak year, the ICU had attracted a membership of some 100 000. Thereafter the movement went into a rapid decline, as a consequence of repression by the state and employers, internal dissension, hopelessly inadequate organization, and disillusionment as to its ability to win material benefits for its members. As one erstwhile supporter complained: 'It all ended up in speeches.'

By 1929 the ICU was already in disarray, but it was against the background of a new assertiveness in black politics that the so-called 'black peril' general election of that year was contested and that Oswald Pirow, Hertzog's new Minister of Justice, launched his campaign against left-wing political activity. The result was a major defeat and retreat for the left. The ANC, abandoning Gumede for the cautious Pixley Seme as President, became distinctly more conservative, and this, together with poor organization, ensured that its political influence in the 1930s would be minimal. The CPSA, for its part, found itself cut off from all popular support. In the assessment of the Comintern, the party was 'practically isolated from the spontaneous movement of the masses'.

The 'black peril' election

In the 'black peril' general election of June 1929, for the first time, the colour question was explicitly made the dominant issue in an election. Herzog's purpose in the election was to rally the country to the support of his 'native' bills. To this end he presented his party as the only reliable champion of the white man in South Africa, and branded Smuts and the South African Party as the advocates of race equality and integration. The charge was preposterous, for though the SAP had opposed the 'native' bills, it too had remained essentially a segregationist party. But the charge stuck, and the outcome of the election was a victory for Hertzog and the Nationalists.

The major exhibit produced to establish the case against the SAP was Smuts's own speech at Ermelo on 17 January 1929, in which he stated that South Africa could not solve 'the Native question' alone, but needed the help of Britain and the co-operation of her northern neighbours. The cardinal object of his policy, he declared, was the creation of 'a British confederation of African states . . . a great African Dominion stretching unbroken throughout Africa'. The response of the Nationalist leaders, contained in the famous 'black manifesto' issued by Hertzog, Tielman Roos, and D F Malan, was to denounce Smuts as 'the apostle of a black Kaffir state . . . extending from the Cape to Egypt'. Despite Smuts's protests that he had been badly misrepresented, one of the main themes of the Nationalist election campaign thereafter was that if Smuts got his way there would be race equality and ultimately black domination. To vote Nationalist was to vote for a white South Africa.

A W G Champion (1893-1975)

A W G Champion (South African Library)

A W G Champion rose to prominence as Clements Kadalie's chief lieutenant and leader of the ICU in Natal. The ICU was more a collection of local branches than a highly centralized organization, and as Natal Secretary Champion's achievement was to build up Durban as its largest and wealthiest branch.

Born in Natal, and educated at the Amanzimtoti Training Institute, Champion's first employment was as a police constable in Johannesburg. From 1920 to 1925 he was a clerk at Crown Mines, becoming President of the Native Mine Clerks' Association. In 1925 he joined the ICU, and was sent to Durban as Natal Secretary. In 1928 he fell out with Kadalie, and declared the Natal branches to be independent as the ICU *yase* Natal. It, too, disintegrated, and Champion's political career from then on was as a member of the ANC. In 1945 he secured the Natal presidency of the ANC, which he retained until his defeat by Albert Lutuli in 1951. He thereupon resigned from the ANC, in which he had been a strong conservative influence.

The African National Congress, Bloemfontein, 1930. First row, seated on ground, left to right: Albert Nzula, John Gomas, next two unidentified, Elliot Tonjeni. Second row: first six unidentified, J T Gumede, Chief Mandlesilo Nkozi, Z R Mahabane, Chief Stephen Mini, next two unidentified, Pixley Seme. Third row: Edwin Mofutsanyana (?), next four unidentified, S M Masabalala, Thomas Mapikela, L T Mvabaza, S M Makgatho, unidentified, Mazingo, unidentified. Back row: P Phatlane, Dave Mark, unidentified, R V Selope Thema, C D Modiakgotla, A W G Champion, Bhulose, Theodore Lujiza, A M Rakaoane (?), T D Mweli Skota, unidentified, Morris Somtunzi, H S Msimang, unidentified. (Documentation Centre for African Studies, UNISA)

A cartoon in *Die Burger*, March 1932. The South African Party urged that South Africa follow Britain in abandoning the gold standard. The cartoon caption reads: 'The SAP's patriotism.' (*Die Burger*)

Tielman Roos (Transvaal Archives)

From Pact to Fusion, 1929-1934

Following the outright victory for the Nationalists in the general election of June 1929, Hertzog sought to continue along the paths he had already mapped out. Although the Nationalists no longer required the support of Labour, and the Labour National Council had broken from the Pact, Hertzog retained two Creswell Labourites in the Cabinet: F H P Creswell himself and H W Sampson. Again, although Hertzog handed over Native Affairs to E G Jansen, the policy of the 'native' bills was persevered with. In 1930 the bills were submitted to another joint sitting, and thereupon referred to a joint select committee of both houses. In the international sphere, Hertzog continued with his quest to secure the full sovereign independence of South Africa, which status was confirmed by the Statute of Westminster in 1931.

Although the 'native' bills did not re-emerge from the select committee until 1935, the African franchise in the Cape was seriously devalued in the meantime by other measures adopted by the Hertzog government. In 1930 the Women's Enfranchisement Act extended the vote to all women of European descent, and in 1931 the Franchise Laws Amendment Act abolished the civilization test for white men in the Cape, thereby adding approximately 10 000 white male voters to the common roll. As a consequence, the weight of the African vote dropped from 7,5 to 2,5 per cent of the Cape electorate, and from 3,5 to only 1,1 per cent of the total Union electorate.

The event that forced the Hertzog government into different paths, and ultimately into coalition and then fusion with the South African Party, was the Great Depression, and more particularly the gold standard crisis of 1931-1932.

The world economic slump known as the Great Depression began with the Wall Street crash in October 1929. From Wall Street the crisis spread to the rest of the American economy, and thence to the rest of the world. In 1931 the depression deepened as a consequence of the 'crisis within the crisis', the European monetary collapse which led to Britain's abandoning the gold standard in September 1931.

By the beginning of 1933, South Africa was off the gold standard, and Tielman Roos, former Minister of Justice, was advocating a national government. In January 1933 Smuts and Roos entered into negotiations for a coalition. These foundered when Roos insisted on the premiership for himself; Smuts was not prepared to stand down for what little Roos had to offer

---

The gold standard crisis of 1931-1932

In 1931, when Britain went off the gold standard, several countries promptly followed. South Africa, however, was not among them. Both Hertzog and his Minister of Finance, N C Havenga, were determined that South Africa should remain on gold. They believed that, as the world's leading producer of gold, South Africa was committed to the preservation of the gold standard, and they were also anxious to demonstrate that South Africa was no longer an economic satellite of Britain. Remaining on gold was an assertion of the country's independence. It also served to intensify the impact of the depression on

South Africa by encouraging the outflow of capital and accentuating the decline of exports, notably diamonds and agricultural commodities. With the South African pound valued at nearly twice the Australian, South African wool growers found it virtually impossible to compete on the already shrunken world markets. The severe drought of 1932, the worst in living memory, heightened the sense of disaster among farmers.

Although the mining industry initially supported the decision to remain on gold as a means of containing costs, the failure to leave the gold standard was soon made a party political issue by Smuts. At an emergency session of Parliament in November 1931 the SAP urged that South Africa follow Britain and aban-

don the gold standard. Otherwise, Smuts warned, 'We are doomed to inevitable and certain destruction.' Throughout 1932 he carried to the country the message that the real interests of South Africa demanded the abandonment of the gold standard. In early December Smuts's *protégé*, J G N Strauss, inflicted a stunning defeat on the Nationalist candidate in a by-election in the hitherto 'safe' constituency of Germiston.

The immediate response to the Germiston by-election was the political intervention of Tielman Roos, Hertzog's former Minister of Justice. Following the general election of 1929 Roos had retired from politics on the grounds of ill health, though he had also been strongly critical of

the continued alliance with the Creswellites. He had been made an Appeal Court judge, but had continued to intrigue against Hertzog. On 16 December 1932, at Haakboslaagte in the western Transvaal, Roos called for the formation of a national government to take the country off the gold standard and end the bitter racial strife among Afrikaans- and English-speaking whites. Six days later he announced his resignation from the Bench. The response to Roos's return to politics was electric. People became convinced that South Africa could no longer remain on the gold standard, and money poured out of the country. On 28 December Havenga announced that South Africa had left the gold standard.

once he had been deprived of the gold standard as his rallying cry. Instead, Smuts turned to the idea of a coalition with Hertzog.

On 30 January Smuts proposed in Parliament a new start for South African politics, and moved 'that the government should tender its resignation forthwith and so afford an opportunity for the formation of a national government'. Rather tactlessly he reminded Hertzog that the government had pledged to maintain the gold standard; it had since gone back on that pledge, and yet still clung shamelessly to office. Hertzog reacted bitterly to Smuts's motion, which he saw more as a motion of no confidence than as a genuine offer of reconciliation. The possibility of coalition seemed hopeless. Behind the scenes, however, J H Hofmeyr, Smuts's lieutenant, continued to work for coalition, and the next day advised Smuts to repeat the offer of a national government. On 1 February Smuts renewed his appeal for national unity. This time the appeal led to direct negotiations.

Hertzog's own Cabinet and caucus were divided on the question of coalition. Despite this division, Hertzog decided to enter into negotiations with Smuts. As he told his party's caucus, they could not hope to win the next election on their own strength, failure to achieve coalition would drive Smuts into the hands of the 'imperialist' wing of the SAP, the country's economic plight demanded a coalition government, and the country-wide desire for unity could not be ignored. The majority in the caucus accepted his diagnosis.

In mid-February negotiations commenced between Hertzog, assisted by Havenga, and Smuts, assisted by Patrick Duncan, and before the month was out agreement had been reached. In March the Coalition government was formed, with Hertzog as Prime Minister and Smuts as Deputy Prime Minister and Minister of Justice. Six Nationalists and six members of the South African Party comprised the new government. D F Malan refused a post in it, and Labour was excluded. The general election which followed in May resulted in an overwhelming victory for the coalition parties.

J B M Hertzog, J C Smuts and N C Havenga after coalition. (INCH)

The formation of the Coalition government constitutes one of the most dramatic chapters in the party political history of South Africa. It brought together two men, very different in personality, style, and outlook, who had been avowed political enemies for two decades. It is sometimes suggested that coalition represented a setback, if not a defeat for Smuts, yet it is not certain that the South African Party would have won the next general election. While there was widespread disenchantment with the government in the country, there was little positive enthusiasm for the SAP. Even had Smuts sensed victory in the next general election, he was not sure that he wanted it. He would rather have seen 'a cessation of the orgy of racial politics which has been the stock-in-trade of our public life'. If the mood of the country was for reunion, Smuts shared it.

For Hertzog coalition certainly made sense, and for reasons other than holding onto office. From his standpoint, the nationalist objectives of his party had already been achieved. The place of Afrikaans and the civil rights of Afri-

Hertzog, Smuts and the Fusion Cabinet of 1933. The Earl of Clarendon, the Governor-General, is seated between Hertzog and Smuts. (Central Archives)

kaners had been established, and the sovereign independence of South Africa secured. The one major item outstanding on his agenda was the Cape African vote, and for that to be settled he required the co-operation of the SAP.

Following the formation of the Coalition government, and its runaway victory in the general election of May 1933, popular pressure, notably in the Transvaal, urged the fusion of the two parties into one. On 5 June 1934 Hertzog published the 'Programme of Principles' he and Smuts had worked out for the combined party, and in December fusion was finally accomplished with the creation of the United Party. Fusion was rejected by D F Malan and his followers among the Nationalists, who formed the *Gesuiwerde* or Purified National Party, and by Colonel C F Stallard and six other English-speaking SAP MPs, who established the Dominion Party.

In the negotiations for fusion, the main obstacle proved to be the question of South Africa's role and rights within the British Commonwealth. For Hertzog South Africa's interests were always paramount, and the Commonwealth merely a convenience; for Smuts the Commonwealth was 'a great cause', and membership of it constituted in fact a paramount interest of South Africa. Malan, in his approach to Hertzog in February 1934 in an attempt to thwart fusion, played on the differences between Hertzog and Smuts over South Africa's rights and obligations in the Commonwealth, including the issues of secession and neutrality in time of war. In the end, Hertzog and Smuts did not resolve their fundamental differences, and instead agreed to differ. What was achieved was the passage of the Status Act, which confirmed South Africa's sovereign status.

The other major question not firmly settled in the fusion negotiations was that of the Cape franchise. The articles of fusion, like those of coalition before them, pledged an 'earnest endeavour' to resolve 'the Native question', and added that members of the new party would be free to vote according to conscience on the question of 'separate representation of Europeans and Natives'.

The Fusion government, 1934-1939

The Fusion government lacked the cohesion of Hertzog's previous governments. This was not only because it brought together disparate elements, unable to agree on certain fundamental issues, but also because of Hertzog's style of leadership. In a real sense, he ceased to lead. He concentrated on two central concerns, his 'native' bills and South Africa's sovereignty. Individual ministers were allowed to go their own way, sometimes in direct conflict with Hertzog's own principles. Hertzog treated foreign policy as his exclusive domain, and even Smuts, his Deputy Prime Minister, was not kept properly informed.

The Fusion government ultimately broke up in September 1939 over the question of South Africa's neutrality or participation in a major war involving Britain. For Hertzog the major achievement had been the enactment of his 'native' bills in 1936; fusion provided him with the two-thirds majority he required. Ironically, it did so at a juncture when economic developments were promoting a greater integration of the races.

A considerable economic upswing followed South Africa's abandonment of the gold standard, and the economic growth continued up to the outbreak of World War II. In all, the national income rose from £234,7 million in 1932-1933 to £394,8 million by 1938-1939, an increase of 68,2 per cent. In the view of D Hobart Houghton, the upsurge in the six years after 1933 marked South Africa's 'take-off' into sustained economic growth.

Gold mining boomed. After the gold standard had been abandoned, the price of gold had jumped immediately from 85s an ounce to 120s, and by 1939 it had reached 154s. The result was a considerable increase in mining activity, with previously sub-marginal deposits coming within the pay limit, and a new goldfield, the West Wits line, was opened. There was significant increased demand for both white and black mine workers, though it was the white workers who benefited most from the boom. Their real wage and employment levels rose faster than did blacks', largely because increased mechanization required the skilled and supervisory functions restricted to white labour.

The gold boom provided a spur for the entire economy. Through the medium of 'surplus profit' taxes, state revenue from gold mining rose dramatically, coming to constitute over 30 per cent of total revenue, as against 5,8 per cent in 1930. The high earnings from gold also provided the foreign exchange to help finance a major expansion in secondary industry. The clothing and textiles, metals and engineering, and stone, clay, and bricks groups of industries, all more than doubled their output. Particularly rapid was the expansion of the metal engineering industries, supplied from 1934 by the now productive iron and steel mills of ISCOR. The explosives and chemical industry in South Africa, dominated by the giant African Explosives and Chemical Industries Limited, throve as a direct consequence of the gold-mining boom. Another major feature of the period was the development of the country's transport network, including railway electrification and the creation in 1935 of the National Road Board, which in the next year launched a comprehensive five year programme for national road construction.

A major consequence of this economic growth, particularly in the industrial sphere, was a rapid increase in the rate of urbanization as both whites and blacks were drawn into the new factories. According to the 1936 census, 31,4 per cent of the total South African population of 9,6 million was urban, including 65 per cent of the 2 million whites. Of the African population of 6,6 million, 45 per cent lived in the reserves, with a high proportion of adult males absent at any given moment as migrant labourers. Of the 55 per cent of the African population living in 'white' areas, 61 per cent were on farms and 39 per cent in urban areas. In the Transvaal, where the main industrial growth was to be found, Africans comprised 53 per cent of the urban population. On the Witwatersrand the white population had increased from 233 000 in 1921 to 410 000 in 1936, and the growth in the black population had been even

Colonel C F Stallard, leader and founder of the Dominion Party. (Central Archives)

Members of the Native Representative Council with the Secretary for Native Affairs.
Back row: Far right, P Mosaka.
Middle row: Second from left, S Tema, A W G Champion, Xiniwe, Z K Matthews, J Moroka.
Front row: Second from left, V Poto.
(Documentary Centre for African Studies, UNISA)

Members of the Native Representative Council (left to right) Dr Moroka, Messrs Sakwe, Mosaka and Mabute during a meeting. (South African Museum for Military History)

▽
The ox-wagons on trek during the Great Trek centenary celebrations in 1938. (*Die Burger*)

▽ ▷
The ox-wagons arrive in Linden, Johannesburg. Crowds follow the flag-bearing women in Voortrekker dress. (*Die Burger*)

more marked, from 304 000 to 620 000. In Johannesburg an entire new township, Orlando, was laid out for African housing. In short, a large black urban population had emerged, and its increase was to be further accelerated during World War II.

Hertzog's 'native' bills

One fundamental accomplishment of fusion was finally to secure the passage in 1936 of Hertzog's 'native' bills. The articles of fusion had provided that the solution to the question of African representation should be sought so far as was possible through agreement, but at the same time 'should be left to the free exercise of the discretion of the individual members representing the party in Parliament'. In the event, a joint sitting of the two houses produced a vote of 168 to 11 in favour of the Natives Representation Bill. The minority included United Party liberals like F S Malan and J H Hofmeyr, as well as the segregationist Colonel S F Stallard of

the Dominion Party. Smuts, who had previously opposed the bill, now voted for the amended version.

Even before fusion it is probable that the majority of the SAP in Parliament had come to accept the principle of removing the Cape Africans from the common roll, and certainly the right wing of the party had shown itself prepared to outstrip Hertzog. In the joint select committee set up in 1930 it was two representatives of the SAP, Heaton Nicholls, MP for Zululand, and Stallard, who took the lead in intensifying the white supremacist character of the proposed legislation. Nicholls, who maintained that the opportunity should be seized to ensure 'the complete and permanent dominance of the European', was responsible for the scheme whereby all African representation in the House of Assembly was to be abolished, with Africans being given instead four representatives in the Senate. Stallard was responsible for the further proposal to establish a Grand Committee of the Senate, consisting of 'all native representatives and at least an equal number of Europeans', to consider legislation and taxation proposals concerning Africans. This would replace the Union Native Council initially envisaged by Hertzog. The committee approved the Nicholls-Stallard proposals in principle, but both were ultimately jettisoned by Hertzog (see box on p 257).

The revival of Afrikaner nationalism

Fusion, and the consequent split between Hertzog and Malan, was of the greatest significance in the history of Afrikaner nationalism. Although, to begin with, Malan's Purified National Party was numericaly exceptionally weak, confined largely to the Cape Province and with only nineteen seats in the House of Assembly, within fifteen years it had established itself as

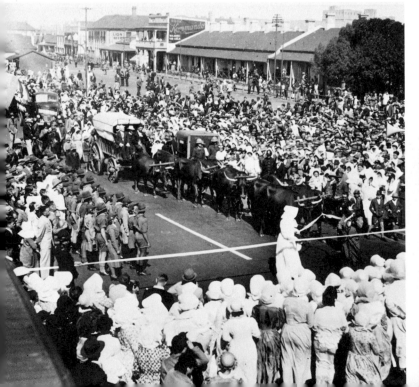

the dominant force in Afrikaner political life and as the new governing party in South Africa. Malan's party was no mere re-creation or 'purification' of Hertzog's old National Party. In its ideology, and in its institutional grounding in Afrikaner life, the party represented a fundamental departure from the Hertzogite traditions of Afrikaner nationalism.

The focus of Hertzog's nationalism was the legal status of Afrikaners. As such his principal objectives had been the securing of language equality for Afrikaners, the civil rights of Afrikaans-speakers, and the constitutional independence of South Africa. His definition of an Afrikaner was not narrowly exclusive, and embraced not only Afrikaans-speakers but also English-speaking whites who were truly loyal to South Africa and accepted language equality. A powerful sense of 'South Africa first' distinguished his nationalism, and this helped to shape his foreign and economic policies. In association with the new party a far more aggressive nationalist ideology was formulated. Strongly republican, and ethnically exclusive, it stressed the distinctiveness of Afrikaner 'culture', and saw as a priority not merely the legal parity of Afrikaners but their social and material predicament. These objectives were given institutional form in a range of political, cultural, and economic agencies with and through which the party worked to articulate Afrikaner aspirations, and to develop and entrench its hold on Afrikaner voters. The key co-ordinating body for these agencies was the Afrikaner *Broederbond*.

Originally founded as a cultural organization, the Afrikaner *Broederbond* became increasingly political in the 1930s. In 1929 the Bond established its first public front organization, the *Federasie van Afrikaanse Kultuurverenigings* (FAK), which thereafter took over much of the cultural work, freeing the Bond to concentrate on other issues, including politics. In the fusion crisis of 1933-1934 the Bond sided decisively with Malan and the Purified Nationalists, and it emerged from the crisis as the vanguard organization of northern Afrikaner nationalism, operating in secret and effectively controlling the Purified National Party in the north. In his famous Smithfield address of November 1935, denouncing the Bond and its activities, Hertzog declared, 'There is no doubt that the secret *Broederbond* is nothing more than the Purified National Party operating secretly underground, and that the Purified National Party is nothing more than the secret Afrikaner *Broederbond* operating in public.'

As seen by the Bond, the survival and advancement of the Afrikaner nation and 'culture' required both Afrikaner unity and Afrikaner dominance in South Africa. Language parity, and even Afrikaner ascendancy in government, were no longer sufficient. Integral to the Bond's attempts in the 1930s to promote both Afrikaner unity (*volkseenheid*) and Afrikaner economic power was the so-called 'economic movement'. For the Bond class cleavages as well as political divisions threatened the prospects of Afrikaner unity, with the most glaring manifestation of class cleavage among Afrikaners being

The foundation stone of the Voortrekker Monument was laid in 1938. The completed monument was inaugurated in 1949 during a ceremony attended by nearly 250 000 people. (*Die Burger*)

The swearing in of Hans van Rensburg as leader of the *Ossewabrandwag* (OB). (INCH)

259

provided by the persistent 'poor white' problem. The purpose of the economic movement was consequently both to mobilize Afrikaner capital and alleviate Afrikaner poverty. At the same time Christian-national trade unions were promoted in opposition to existing unions in order to wean Afrikaans-speaking workers away from organizations based on class, improve their position in the white labour force, and capture their support for nationalism. The *Spoorbond*, a union of railwaymen formed in 1934 by the first chairman of the Bond, Henning Klopper, was the most successful of these new unions. The challenge of the *Afrikanerbond van Mynwerkers* to the existing Mine Workers' Union collapsed when the latter concluded a 'closed shop' agreement with the Chamber of Mines.

Two of the most significant achievements of the Bond, and its front organization the FAK, prior to World War II were the management of the Great Trek centenary celebrations in 1938, and the foundation of the *Reddingsdaadbond* (RDB) the following year. The centenary celebrations, sponsored by the FAK and placed under the control of the Afrikaans Language and Cultural Union of the South African Railways and Harbours, chaired by Henning Klopper, took the form of an ox-wagon trek from Cape Town to Pretoria, and culminated in the laying of the foundation stone of the Voortrekker Monument. The major theme of the speeches that accompanied the trek was the need for Afrikaner unity, and the celebrations did have the desired effect of uniting Afrikaners as Afrikaners. It was to perpetuate this 'ox-wagon spirit' that the *Ossewabrandwag* (OB) was formed, supposedly as a cultural organization. A second theme in the trek speeches was the problem of Afrikaner poverty, and the FAK followed this up by summoning an *Ekonomiese Volkskongres* in Bloemfontein in October 1939. Out of this emerged the *Reddingsdaadbond* to promote the economic advancement of the Afrikaner people by mobilizing Afrikaner capital for investment in Afrikaner business. The head of the *Reddingsdaadbond* was Dr N Diederichs, a future Minister of Finance.

By the time the *Ekonomiese Volkskongres* met, World War II had broken out, Hertzog had been removed from office, and Smuts had taken a divided South Africa into the war, thereby opening a new chapter in the history of Afrikaner nationalism and republicanism.

The period 1939 to 1948
A W Stadler

A W Stadler is Professor and head of the Department of Political Studies at the University of the Witwatersrand. He was educated in Durban and in Johannesburg and attended the University of the Witwatersrand, where he was awarded a doctorate for work on the South African party system. He was an honorary visiting fellow at the University of Sussex.

A cartoon from the *Rand Daily Mail*, 8 September 1939, illustrating how the white electorate became divided over the issue of South Africa's participation or neutrality in the Second World War. (*Rand Daily Mail*)

When the British Prime Minister, Neville Chamberlain, announced on Sunday 3 September 1939 that Britain was at war with Germany, the South African Parliament was sitting in special session to extend the life of the Senate which was due to expire on 5 September. Hertzog used the opportunity to present his colleagues with his decision that South Africa should opt for neutrality, a decision which he had reached in the knowledge that the Purified National Party would support him. The Cabinet was irrevocably split by the decision.

On Monday Parliament met to debate the issue. Hertzog proposed a motion which asserted the country's neutrality, while acknowledging the government's contractual obligations to Britain relating to the Simon's Town naval base and those following from South Africa's membership of the League of Nations. Smuts proposed an amendment that the Union should

DIE PAD VAN SUID AFRIKA

Members of Parliament who supported General Smuts on 4 September 1939. Front row (left to right) P V G van der Byl, F C Sturrock, R Stuttaford, W R Collins, J C Smuts, J H Hofmeyr, C F Steyn, W B Madeley, D Reitz, H G Lawrence, G B van Zyl. (United Party Archives, UNISA)

sever its relations with the Third Reich, and should refuse to adopt a position of neutrality. In the debate that followed, the Prime Minister argued that for South Africa to enter the war with its (white) people divided would be to undo the work of conciliation of the past six years, and intensify the bitterness of political conflict. It was the country's right to remain neutral, and also in its best interests. He cited the decision of the Irish Prime Minister, De Valera, as the appropriate model to follow, and compared Hitler's efforts to achieve German liberty with his own struggles in the cause of Afrikaner freedom. That comparison ended all hope of reconciliation.

Smuts replied that it was impossible to reconcile neutrality with the maintenance of obligations towards Britain and the Commonwealth. Hertzog's motion was defeated. The Governor-General, Sir Patrick Duncan, refused to accede to his request to dissolve Parliament. Hertzog resigned, and Smuts was invited to form a government. On 6 September the new government issued a proclamation to sever relations with Germany.

Hertzog and the National Party

The decision to enter the war precipitated a series of massive conflicts within and among the political parties and in the country. Immediately after resigning from the premiership, Hertzog began negotiations with Malan's party. A rally at Monumentkoppie on 9 October 1939, outside Pretoria, was designed publicly to cement the reconciliation between Hertzog and Malan. But 'hereniging', as the movement towards reconciliation came to be known, proved to be extraordinarily difficult to accomplish.

The issues which impeded the course of reconciliation concerned matters of principle as well as of strategy and organization. Hertzog proclaimed that he was a republican, but he advocated caution in pursuing this objective. In subsequent speeches he refused to break constitutional ties with Britain, or even to accept a republic unless it was brought about on the basis of a broad consensus among whites. Malan, on the other hand, made it clear that he considered that a simple parliamentary majority would provide a sufficient basis for a republic.

Malan was by no means the least compromising member of the political leadership of the National Party. Indeed, he came to assume the role of mediator between Hertzog, Pirow and the 'moderates' on the one hand, and the party's hardliners, J G Strijdom, C R Swart and H F Verwoerd, on the other. The strategic and organizational issues which divided Hertzog and Malan were precipitated by Hertzog's intention to form a new political party, the *Volksparty*, as the instrument for bringing about the political unity of Nationalist Afrikaners. Malan did not want a new party, maintaining that it would threaten the organizational position of the *Gesuiwerde*'s established leadership, but neither

J B M Hertzog (left) and N C Havenga. (*Die Burger*)

Oswald Pirow (INCH)

did he want an irrevocable split with Hertzog. As a compromise it was agreed that the National Party and the *Volksparty* would act as a single party in Parliament under Hertzog's leadership. The National Party was renamed the *Herenigde Nasionale Party of Volksparty*, the Reunited National or People's Party.

Notwithstanding these elaborate devices, the relationship between the Hertzogites and the Malanites became increasingly strained as a result of pressure from republican activists in the HNP to impel the party to pursue the ideal of the republic with greater energy. This pressure

was intensified during the first half of 1940, as British defeat or capitulation in the war became a possibility. A republican campaign was launched during July, which Hertzog strongly opposed.

At the Free State party congress in November 1940, Hertzog's plan which advocated the rights of English-speakers was rejected. Hertzog resigned from the leadership and membership of the party which he had founded a quarter of a century earlier. In a scene so poignant that it moved even his bitterest enemies to rise in silent homage, he walked out of the meeting.

Hertzog's defeat in the Free State on the issue of equal rights for both language groups was followed by his rout in the Transvaal conference in December over his commitment to a republic based on a broad consensus between whites. The Federal Council's programme was amended to make it possible for a republic to be achieved on the basis of a simple parliamentary majority. The party also decided to deny its membership to Jews.

Hertzog still had supporters in the Transvaal party, but they were in a minority. Moreover, even though his support among Nationalist MPs outnumbered Malan's in Parliament and included venerable figures such as N C Havenga and General Kemp, he realized that with his defeat in the Transvaal he had lost control of the party. Hertzog and Havenga resigned their parliamentary seats in December, and in January 1941 they formed the Afrikaner Party. Hertzog's parliamentary support dwindled from 38 to 10, and he died in 1942, embittered by his defeats.

A further issue in opposition ranks was the struggle to determine whether the political leadership of Nationalist Afrikanerdom would lie in

Field Marshal Smuts visiting troops in the desert, North Africa. (United Party Archives, UNISA)

the National Party, essentially an electoral and parliamentary organization, or whether it would be seized by extra-parliamentary movements. The *Ossewabrandwag* was the most threatening of the extra-parliamentary groups to challenge the party's supremacy.

The most important remaining faction opposed to the Malanites in the National Party was Oswald Pirow's 'study group', the New Order, which retained links with Hertzog until his death and, reputedly, with the *Ossewabrandwag*. In 1942 Pirow and his parliamentary supporters ceased attending the National Party caucus and fought the 1943 election as a separate group. They all lost their seats, perhaps not surprisingly, for aside from the hostility of the Nationalists, they declared themselves opposed to such parliamentary institutions as elections.

South Africans in World War II

More than two million South Africans volunteered for service in World War II, including 120 000 blacks. Blacks were constrained to serve in non-combatant roles, but despite being relegated to their traditional function as servants and labourers, many of them performed outstanding feats of courage.

South African troops fought in East Africa, Madagascar, North Africa and Italy. The East African campaign was largely a South African effort. South Africans played a prominent role in the defeat of Italian troops at El Wak in 1940, and in the following year were the most important element in the force which defeated the Duke of Aosta's troops at the Battle of Amba Alagi, decisively breaking the back of Axis power in East Africa. Thousands of Italian prisoners taken during this campaign were sent back to South Africa, and a large number settled in the country after the war.

South African forces were also heavily engaged in the North African theatre. Two divisions, sent to Egypt as part of the British Eighth Army, saw action in the major battles of 1941 and 1942, including Sidi Resegh. There were 10 000 South Africans in the ill-fated force trapped by Rommel at Tobruk. Most of them spent the rest of the war in German prison camps. Many South Africans served under Montgomery at the battle of El Alamein, where the Eighth Army repulsed Rommel's drive to take Egypt. The Sixth South African Armoured Division followed the rest of the Eighth Army to Italy after Parliament had revoked the policy not to send troops outside Africa. The South African Air Force flew many missions over occupied Europe. One memorable mission in which it took part dropped supplies to Warsaw during mid-1944, while the Red Army stood on the east bank of the Vistula, and the Nazis put down the uprising in the city.

War service had an important influence on

the minds and ideas of servicemen. Many returned to South Africa convinced that racism reflected irrational and parochial values. The Springbok Legion, formed after the war, entertained more radical ideas than most white ex-servicemen were able to tolerate, but the Torch Commando, which rallied the struggle to preserve the entrenched clauses of the constitution in 1953, attracted a wide following among ex-servicemen.

Even before the war, the Italian invasion of Ethiopia had brought to the attention of South African blacks the fact that an independent

The 6th South African Armoured transport division in Italy during the war. (*Die Burger*)

British guns in action at El Alamein in October 1942. (South African Museum of Military History)

Black South Africans in North Africa during the war, (left) reading a newspaper specially printed for them in Cairo and (right) being instructed in mine identification. (South African Museum of Military History)

The Cape Corps leaving Egypt. (South African Museum of Military History)

black state existed in Africa, and many Africans aligned themselves with international forces opposed to facism. The war brought home the contradiction between the Africans' lack of political rights and the claims of the cause for which the Allies were fighting. The contradiction was sharpened when Africans who volunteered for service found that they were not to be armed, but would serve as drivers and trench-diggers. The South African authorities even managed to persuade the British Army not to arm blacks recruited in Bechuanaland and Basutoland with weapons any more lethal than kie-

ries and assegais. The African National Congress adopted a conciliatory attitude on this issue, as it had done in the First World War, in order not to thwart the war effort. In 1943, however, the ANC conference discussed the implications of the Atlantic Charter for South African blacks, and demanded full citizenship rights for all in the Union.

Economic development

Economically, the war established the conditions for a full-scale boom which was to last until 1945. The boom coincided with the radical restructuring of the economy which had begun during the depression. A war industry, established to produce a considerable proportion of the Union Defence Force's requirements for artillery, armoured vehicles and munitions, directly stimulated research into a range of war-related activities, for instance metallurgy and communications, and investment in training programmes and labour-saving methods. This industrial expansion in turn stimulated the demand for labour, and accelerated the dissolution of the rural economy and society, already far advanced during the Great Depression of the early thirties. The movement from countryside to cities gathered momentum after 1939, stimulating and aggravating social and political conflicts, especially between blacks and whites exposed to the same process of change, and imposing severe strains on the institutions of government.

Important to the future relations between government and privately owned industry was the establishment in 1940 of the Industrial Development Corporation in order to promote and help finance new industries and industrial undertakings. The Social and Economic Planning Advisory Council, set up in 1942 under the chairmanship of Dr H J van Eck, considered a wide range of social and economic issues, and made proposals for the modernization of the economy and the government which influenced the direction of future relations between the state and the private sector, and set targets for post-war industrial development.

The virtual cessation of the flow of imported manufactured goods from Europe, particularly from Britain, stimulated local manufacturing industry. The market was stimulated by the conditions of high employment which prevailed in most industrial sectors, by the entry of new groups onto the labour market (many white women found jobs in the munitions industry, and many black women entered factories for the first time), and by the transient visits of troops to the seaport cities.

During the decade which ended in 1946, the black urban population of South Africa nearly doubled. This massive urbanization became the single most controversial issue in post-war white politics. It provided the context for the debates between liberals and the advocates of total separation who took power in 1948, and aggravated the fears of Afrikaner workers concerning competition for jobs and for living space in the crowded cities.

During the 1940s Africans migrating to the cities came not only in increased numbers, but as families. The radical deterioration of agriculture in the reserves from the depression onwards had been exacerbated by the measures introduced under the 1936 Native Trust and Land Act. In 1939 the government promulgated regulations designating areas in the reserves as 'betterment' areas. The Native Affairs Department set limits to the amount of land cultivators could plough and on the number of livestock permitted. These measures, as well as widespread failure to pay poll taxes, led to numerous confrontations between police and local peasantry. Cattle culling produced widespread discontent, for cattle constituted the wealth of the reserve tribesmen as well as a source of milk, food and draught power.

The government's programme in the 1930s to reconstruct the agricultural sector enabled white farmers to mechanize production methods, thereby cutting down on the use of black labour. Crippling droughts during the early war years also adversely affected African farm labourers. Maize production fell off in the commercial sector and in the reserves. By the end of the war South Africa was importing maize from the Argentine, and farmers cut the rations of their black labourers. All these developments contributed to the movement of rural people to the cities during the war and early post-war years.

During the war manufacturing and construction industries demanded labour on an unprecedented scale, and from 1943 the government relaxed influx controls and began debating the possibility of revising the pass laws. The wages of workers in secondary industry rose above prewar levels. Despite the demand for labour and the relatively high wages paid to African

Conditions in the squatter camps today do not differ greatly from conditions in the camps in the 1940s. (*Die Burger*)

Migrant labourers on the way home from the mines. (*Die Burger*)

workers, conditions of life in the cities were impoverished, crowded and uncomfortable. Wages did not match the rise in rents, nor in the cost of food and transport. Malnutrition was widespread, especially among children. The great influx of people into the urban areas placed strains on municipal services and the shortage of black housing became acute.

By the end of the war the government was confronted with increasing evidence that the policy established during the 1920s of Africans being 'temporary sojourners' in the urban areas, needed urgent revision. In 1946 Judge Henry Fagan was appointed chairman of a commission of inquiry to consider the revision of the pass laws. By their actions, if not their words, successive post-war governments accepted the *de facto* though not the *de jure* permanency of urban African settlement.

The radicalization of black politics and the government's race policy

The social upheavals of the war intensified the political struggles of Africans on the land and in the cities, both in the form of industrial action and community-based political movements. On the land, resistance to the implementation of the Native Trust and Land Act continued throughout the decade, and attracted the attention of the ANC and the Communist Party. In the cities, tenants' movements and transport boycotts mobilized action against landlords and transport companies. There were food riots in mine compounds and educational institutions. The series of bus boycotts on the Witwatersrand and Pretoria which continued through the war forced the government to investigate the living

conditions and wages of workers. All levels of government were involved in trying to settle the boycott at Alexandra, a township on the outskirts of Johannesburg, late in 1944. The Public Utility Transport Corporation (PUTCO), subsidized by the government in order to keep fares down, was established. Boycotts also forced the ANC to confront the practical problems of the people.

African workers became increasingly militant during and after the war. In reaction against the massive wave of strikes beginning in late 1942, the government introduced War Measure 145, which prohibited strikes by Africans, but the measure was not very effective. The war also witnessed the growth of the African trade union movement. In the late 1930s unions developed rapidly, mainly on the Witwatersrand, but also in the Cape and Natal. African and non-racial unions were often organized by left-wingers with affiliations with the Communist Party, though many were Trotskyists.

The ANC Youth League, which was formed in 1943, took a more radical position than that adopted by the conservative elements which continued to dominate the organization's leadership. In 1944 congress organized an anti-pass campaign, which began with a demonstration in Johannesburg 20 000 strong, but failed to reach the target of a million-signature petition against the pass laws.

The history of the Native Representative Council (NRC) reflected a similar shift. In the first council election held before the war, mainly middle-class Africans of conservative opinion had been elected. The council soon earned the reputation of being a 'talking shop'. In the 1942 elections, however, members with a more radical and aggressive outlook were elected. During the miners' strike of 1946 the council resolved to adjourn in protest. Paul Mosaka, a member of the NRC, described the council as a toy telephone, 'an apparatus which cannot transmit sound'. In 1947 the council rejected an offer by Smuts to enlarge its membership and to extend its powers, as well as recognize African unions, on the grounds that Africans would still not be recognized as citizens of South Africa. In effect the council had collapsed. Its establishment had failed to relieve the three major problems facing the African people: the pass laws, land hunger, and the weakness and limitation on African representation in Parliament.

The government which Smuts formed in 1939 was perhaps the most liberal in South Africa since before Union. J H Hofmeyr, upon whom liberals pinned their hopes of a new policy towards Africans, was Deputy Prime Minister. The Secretary for Native Affairs, Douglas Smit, was a moderate and enlightened official whose work prefigured the Fagan Commission. The Department of Public Health recognized and publicly proclaimed that the health and nutritional problems of the population had social parameters which required action. The South African Institute of Race Relations was a continuous pressure group on government through its friends in Pretoria and in Parliament. Yet even on those issues on which most liberals could agree, little seemed to happen to encourage even the most conservative Africans to believe that any significant improvements would take place in their social and political circumstances.

The government's curtailment of the land rights of Indians in Natal and the Transvaal was a sharp reminder that not all reactionaries were in opposition. Indians had acquired a good deal of land in central Durban during the early war years. After the report of the Broome Commission, Parliament passed the Asiatic Trading and Occupation of Land Restriction (or 'Pegging') Act of 1943, which prevented for three years the further acquisition of land by Indians in the two provinces. In 1946 Parliament passed an act which made the measure permanent. An attempt to placate Indian opinion by offering them representation in Parliament in exchange for the loss of the right to acquire further land, was rejected by Indian leaders. Dr T M Dadoo, Dr G M Naicker and the Reverend Michael Scott were among thousands who offered themselves for arrest in the 1946 campaign of passive resistance. The Indian community also sent a delegation to the United Nations Organization, providing the first of many issues relating to South Africa which would be taken to the international body. The Indian Government broke off relations with South Africa. Racism was clearly not the prerogative of a single party. Indeed the Labour and Dominion parties split over the issue of Indian representation. Though the government enjoyed a comfortable majority in Parliament, broad support both in Parliament and in the country for a liberal colour policy was not in evidence.

The ascent of the National Party, 1943-1948

The Nationalist victory of 1948 was not a foregone conclusion which may be explained by simply extrapolating from the results of the 1943 election. Nor was it the result of a general appeal to Afrikaner sentiment or to colour prejudice. Rather, the party's policy promised solutions to the problems which faced Afrikaner workers and farmers during the last years of the war and the early post-war period which neither the United Party government, nor rival nationalist organizations, were either willing or competent to resolve. Afrikaner nationalist organizations, including cultural associations, were able to take advantage of the weaknesses and divisions in existing working-class organizations, and of the Labour Party's virtual collapse as a workers' party, to mobilize Afrikaner working-class support for the National Party. The party was also able to offer white farmers a policy which would stabilize their labour force. The victory of 1948 was based on the advances the

'Cissie' Gool, the daughter of Dr Abdurahman, addressing a public meeting in the 1940s. (Documentation Centre for African Studies, UNISA)

▷△
J C Smuts and J H Hofmeyr. (Central Archives)

▷
Field Marshal Smuts as a member of the War Cabinet. (Central Archives)

National Party made in the farming districts of the Transvaal, where it had fared poorly in the 1943 election, and in working-class districts along the Witwatersrand and in the lower middle-class areas of Pretoria, where it won many seats for the first time.

Aside from labour problems, farmers were faced with many difficulties following the reconstruction of the industry. The Marketing Act, introduced before the war, was implemented in a way intended to encourage a reduction in the number, and an increase in the efficiency, of farming units, and the act was used to keep food prices down, partly to meet the interests of industry. The mining industry, which supplied rations direct to its labour force, had a special interest in low food prices.

The problems of unskilled and semi-skilled ers in secondary industry complemented those facing farmers. White workers' wages had remained static and in some areas had even declined. Black wages, despite an increase of roughly 50 per cent during the war, still remained lower than those of whites, who still had the old fear of losing their jobs to blacks. Living conditions of white workers varied, but in some areas they were appalling, and there was an acute shortage of housing. While malnutrition among whites was never as severe as among blacks, wartime surveys indicated that about 40 per cent, and in poor areas 50 per cent, of white schoolchildren were malnourished.

The problems of unskilled and semi-skilled white workers were exacerbated by developments in industry, by government labour policy and by the situation in the white unions. The rapid mechanization of industry during the war encouraged the employment of blacks as machine operatives in the manufacturing sector. Many Afrikaners found themselves facing an uncertain future in the labour market, especially in the post-war recession and white workers organized strikes against the employment of blacks as operatives.

The participation of the Labour Party in the coalition gave the government a degree of control over white labour which it could not easily have achieved by simple repression. The leader of the Labour Party, Walter Madeley, was Minister of Labour in Smuts's government. The controller of manpower was a former trade unionist and veteran of the strike of 1914, Ivan Walker.

Afrikaner Nationalist leaders, whose earlier attempts, supported by the *Broederbond* and the FAK, to gain control of the Mine Workers' Union had failed, were able to take over the union by the end of the war. In 1948 the Labour Party did not contest a single seat in a working-class constituency. It had virtually conceded the political leadership of the white working class to the National Party.

The most important left-wing union with a strong Afrikaner membership was the Garment Workers' Union, led by Solly Sachs, a Jewish ex-Communist. The union was effectively organized on non-racial lines in which Afrikaner and Coloured workers were able to act on common interests. This instance of working-class solidarity across the colour line was an exception to the rule which bound most white workers to their racial privileges. But by the end of the war, the pressure of increasing numbers of Coloured workers began undermining the interracial alliance among workers in the industry.

The National Party fought the 1948 election on the basis of its policy of apartheid. The policy, largely undefined, made a strong appeal to those groups of voters, mainly farmers and semi-skilled workers, whose interests were immediately threatened by the liberalization of government policy during the war years.

The Fagan Commission report was published a few months before the election. Its analysis of the urbanization of Africans as an inevitable process, and its recommendation that the pass laws should be revised in order to acknowledge the permanency of an urban African population held little appeal to white workers, or to farmers who found themselves unable to benefit from rationalization in the industry, and were therefore unable to reduce their dependency on poorly paid labour. The Sauer report, prepared for the National Party, shared many of the assumptions of the Fagan Commission, but it underscored the importance of reinforcing influx controls in order to ensure the supply of labour to white farmers.

△
J C Smuts signs the United Nations Organization Charter in San Francisco in 1945. (Central Archives)

◁
J C Smuts with the Royal family during their visit to South Africa in 1947. (Central Archives)

The general election of 1943

The election of 1943 has been viewed by some historians as a triumph for the United Party and the pro-war coalition. Others have seen it as a warning of the Nationalist victory of 1948. There is much to be said in support of both views.

The election provided a clear test of opinion on the war issue, and delivered a decisive mandate to continue the war. The United Party continued to be host to a variety of special and regional interests, and of course the government relied on its coalition with the Labour and Dominion parties to maintain a strong parliamentary majority. Without Hertzog, the party and the Cabinet were able to display greater unity and act with greater decisiveness than before the war. The common commitment to the war helped paper over the fissiparous tendencies which characterized the United Party, and Smuts's own position, in particular, was enhanced.

There were in the election results, however, many signs that the days of United Party rule were numbered. Firstly, by 1943 the HNP had decisively consolidated its control over Afrikaner nationalist politics. For Malan, as for the government, the election was a test of the party's capacity to win support in the country for decisions reached in party conferences and caucuses. Viewed in this light, the election was an almost unqualified success for the Malanites, whose rivals among the opposition groups were eliminated. Above all, the party increased its representation in the House of Assembly from the 27 which the *Gesuiwerdes* had held in 1938 to 43. Not only did the National Party control political Afrikanerdom; it was set in the direction which was to ensure its victory in the election of 1948.

The Cabinet of D F Malan in 1948.
Front row (left to right) C R Swart,
E G Jansen, D F Malan, G B van Zyl,
N C Havenga, J G Strijdom, P O Sauer.
(INCH)

Tactically, the Nationalists softened their stance on the republican issue to the extent of promising to remain within the Commonwealth, and also adopted the Hertzogite principle of equal language rights for English-speakers which they had opposed during the early war years. It is doubtful whether this move gained the party many votes from English-speakers, but it undoubtedly placated many Afrikaners who might otherwise have been alarmed into voting for the United Party. Above all, the appropriation of Hertzogite principles enabled the party to enter the vital electoral alliance with the Afrikaner Party, which posed no threat to Nationalist dominance.

Notwithstanding its declining powers, the *Ossewabrandwag* was still a force to be reckoned with in more than twenty constituencies. Malan firmly refused to allow OB members to stand as candidates for either the National or the Afrikaner Party. Among the aspirant members of Parliament disappointed by this decision was future Prime Minister B J Vorster. Malan also refused to allow Nationalist candidates to accept support from members of the OB. However, those candidates who needed OB support made secret arrangements to secure it.

By contrast, the United Party faced the election in disarray. The common commitment to seeing the war out no longer provided Smuts with the precarious consensus on which he had relied since 1939 to hold his party and its allies together. The government faced manifold problems of adjusting to peacetime shortages of commodities and dislocations, unemployment and strikes, without the benefit of any clear sense of political purpose. Many ex-servicemen found that the heroes' welcome to which they had returned brought with it neither jobs nor housing, and many of them voted against the government. The liberals in the party, led by Hofmeyr, provided a target for Nationalist accusations that the United Party was set on a course which would lead to social integration and the displacement of white workers by blacks. Moreover, Hofmeyr was highly unpopular among conservative elements in the United Party whose preference for a tough colour policy did not differ markedly from the Nationalists'. The party's major political resource was Smuts's charismatic figure and the South African record in the war. Neither was very important to Afrikaner workers and farmers.

The election of 1948 established an epoch of unbroken National Party rule. It has been viewed as a turning point in South African politics. However, the victory was no landslide. The National Party won 70 seats and the Afrikaner Party 9, to the United Party's 65 and Labour's 6. It has been estimated that the Nationalists gained office with the support of less than 40 per cent of the electorate. The coalition with the Afrikaner Party was essential to secure a parliamentary majority for the new government. Although the victory came as a surprise to many observers, it was a result consistent with long-term tendencies in electoral politics. Since 1915 the National Party had demonstrated its remarkable capacity to draw electoral support from Afrikaners. The coalition and fusion of the early 1930s put the party back into opposition, but during the fourteen years which passed before the Malanites came to power they forged a powerful political machine served by cultural and economic associations to mobilize support from among farmers, businessmen and workers.

Suggested Reading List

M Lacey (1981) *Working for Boroko*, Johannesburg
D O'Meara (1983) *Volkskapitalisme: Class, Capital and Ideology in the Development of Afrikaner Nationalism, 1934-1948*, Johannesburg
M Roberts and A E G Trollip (1947) *The South African Opposition, 1939-1945*, London
E Roux (1964) *Time Longer than Rope*, Wesleyan University
N M Stultz (1974) *The Nationalists in Opposition*, Cape Town
C M Tatz (1962) *Shadow and Substance in South Africa. A Study in Land and Franchise Policies Affecting Africans, 1910-1960*, Pietermaritzburg
P L Wickins (1978) *The Industrial and Commercial Workers Union of South Africa*, Cape Town

Chapter 18

The Era of Apartheid, 1948-1961

P W Coetzer

The result of the 1948 election came as a great shock to General Smuts, but to the 74-year-old Dr D F Malan, leader of the *Herenigde* (Re united) National Party (HNP) and to many Afrikaner nationalists, 26 May 1948 represented the crowning achievement of many years of struggle and perseverance.

It was Malan's task to form a Cabinet which could successfully implement the policy of separate development. Choosing the members of this Cabinet did not present any difficulties. N C Havenga, Minister of Finance during the Hertzog era (1924-1939) and leader of the Afrikaner Party, regained his former portfolio. With the practical application of the policy of apartheid imminent, the Native Affairs portfolio was of the utmost importance, and E G Jansen, the former Minister of Native Affairs in the Hertzog Cabinet (1929-1933), was thus appointed. The leader of the HNP in the Transvaal, J G Strijdom, chose Lands and Irrigation, a minor portfolio, in order to devote more atten tion to the building up of the party in the Transvaal, and C R Swart accepted the portfolio of Justice. Only two ministers, Strijdom and B J Schoeman, were Transvaalers, while seven hailed from the Cape. Malan pointed out to his critics, however, that with the coalition in 1934 only one HNP member of the House of Assembly out of a total of nineteen had come from the Transvaal and that the Cape had carried the party for many years.

The growth of the National Party

The way was now open for Malan to implement his policy of separate development; moreover, he would be able to combine the forces of the Afrikaner nationalists and ensure a mandate for future government. For the purpose of consol idation and to ensure the continued growth of the HNP, Malan needed to bring Havenga and his Afrikaner Party into the HNP camp. A prerequisite for permanent political co-operation was consensus between Malan and Havenga on the most important matters of policy. The stumbling block was that Havenga, unlike the HNP, did not wish to curtail the existing political rights of the Coloureds.

In October 1950 it was announced that Malan and Havenga had reached agreement. They declared that the separate exercising of political rights by Coloureds was in the interests of both whites and Coloureds. Legislation to give effect to this decision would be introduced during the 1951 parliamentary session. A year later, on 22 October 1951, Malan's *Herenigde* National Party and Havenga's Afrikaner Party amalgamated under the old name of the National Party.

Pieter Willem Coetzer has been lecturer/researcher at the Institute for the Study of Contemporary History at the University of the Orange Free State since 1974, senior lecturer/researcher since 1978 and deputy director and head of research since 1983. His main publications include *Die Nasionale Party*, Vol 2 and 3 (co-author), *Bibliographies on South African Political History*, 3 vols (co-editor and compiler), *Bibliografie van die Suid-Afrikaanse Sosiologie* (editor) and *South Africa. Progress in Intergroup and Race Relations, 1970-1977* (co-compiler).

D F Malan and N C Havenga. (Central Archives)

The Malan Cabinet of 1953. H F Verwoerd (back row, third from the right) became Minister of Native Affairs. (Central Archives)

Developments in South West Africa also promoted the growth of the National Party. Under the Citizenship Act of 1949 the franchise was extended, *inter alia*, to Germans in South West Africa who had lost the vote during the Second World War. By means of legislation six South West Africans were elected to the South African House of Assembly in the following year. The Germans voted overwhelmingly in favour of Malan, as a result of which, with six additional seats, he was less dependent on the support of the Afrikaner Party.

The issue which dominated the general election of 15 April 1953 was the political rights of Coloureds. The election also afforded voters the opportunity of expressing their opinion of the government's first five-year period of office and the implementation of its apartheid policy. The National Party approached the election with great confidence. The new leader of the United Party, J G N Strauss, who had succeeded

Smuts after his death on 11 September 1950, made a valiant but unsuccessful attempt to avenge the National Party victory of 1948. The National Party increased its number of seats in the House of Assembly from 86 to 94. The NP majority of 13 in the House of Assembly was increased to 29. With the exception of Natal, the National Party improved its position in all the provinces. An interesting feature of this election was that the NP polled more votes (1948: 400 180 votes; 1953: 598 534 votes) and won its resounding victory with a smaller percentage poll than the UP (49,1 as against 49,2).

In October 1954 Malan announced his imminent retirement from politics. His two possible successors were N C Havenga and J G Strijdom, although Malan himself favoured Dr T E Dönges, the Cape leader of the NP. However, Dönges was considered too young, and Malan lent his support to Havenga. He considered Havenga a better choice than Strijdom as he was more moderate, and was the more senior politician. In spite of Malan's work behind the scenes, the fiery republican, Hans Strijdom, emerged as South Africa's fifth Prime Minister. Havenga had withdrawn his candidature, declaring that he was not prepared to wage a nomination struggle against Strijdom.

J G Strijdom as Prime Minister

Strijdom's nomination by the NP caucus was a sign that the political balance had shifted towards the north. Known as the 'Lion of the North' and champion of white hegemony, Strijdom was the NP's answer to the mounting opposition to apartheid at home and abroad. His nomination was also a sign of the intensification of the movement towards a republic. The Strijdom Cabinet included only two new members,

D F Malan and J G Strijdom. (*Die Burger*)

Jan de Klerk, who became senator, and J J Serfontein, the chief whip.

During the Strijdom era the National Party continued to grow steadily. The election of 1958 aroused even greater interest than that of 1953. This can probably be attributed to inspiring leadership on the part of the NP and a fierce onslaught by the opposition United Party. For the third time the policy of apartheid dominated a South African parliamentary election. The government's chances had been greatly improved by the lowering of the age requirement for the franchise to eighteen years. The general expectation was that the younger generation, which was strongly pro-republican, would give the government its enthusiastic support.

The National Party was once again returned to office with a total of 103 seats in the House of Assembly, compared with the 53 of the UP. The 1958 election was remarkable in two respects: with regard to the total number of votes cast, the NP had overtaken the UP for the first time, with 55,28 per cent of the votes polled (642 019 votes) compared with 42,38 per cent for the UP (492 071 votes), while the Labour Party, after 49 years in South African politics, disappeared from the political stage. Sir De Villiers Graaff, UP leader, was defeated in his own constituency of Hottentots-Holland. The results also proved indisputably that the United Party, despite its new leadership, was losing its effectiveness.

J G Strijdom died on 24 August 1958, and was succeeded as Prime Minister by Dr H F Verwoerd.

tration and Development, and also instituted the system of appointing deputy ministers.

South Africa became a republic on 31 May 1961 and Verwoerd immediately announced his first republican ministry. Initially it contained no changes, but in August two deputy ministers were promoted and included in the Cabinet. B J Vorster took over from F C Erasmus as Minister of Justice and P W Botha became Minister of Coloured Affairs, Community Development and Housing.

While South Africans were still adjusting to the establishment of the Republic, Verwoerd announced his decision to bring forward the general election to October 1961. The rationale behind this decision was doubtless to give the voters a chance to express their feelings on the decision to leave the Commonwealth, while Verwoerd would also be able to test his own popularity for the first time.

For the National Party the situation did not change much after this election. The number of seats it held increased from 103 to 105, while the United Party's 53 seats diminished to 49. The reduction in the number of UP seats could be attributed mainly to the fact that twelve members of the party had broken away in November 1959 to establish the Progressive Party under the leadership of Dr Jan Steytler. In South Africa and South West Africa the NP polled 46,28 per cent and the UP 35,68 per cent of the total number of votes. Between 1948 and 1961 the NP increased its representation in the House of Assembly from 49 (together with the Afrikaner Party) to 105.

The era of H F Verwoerd

Verwoerd announced drastic changes in his Cabinet shortly after taking office. He retained the Native Affairs portfolio for a while, but soon appointed M C de W Nel, who took over the portfolio under its new name of Bantu Adminis-

The decline of the United Party

The result of the 1948 election had been unexpected and devastating for the United Party. J H Hofmeyr became the scapegoat for the party's disappointing performance, but Smuts had also become alienated from his political follow-

H F Verwoerd, D F Malan, J G Strijdom, J de Klerk, C R Swart at a *Herenigde* National Party congress in November 1948. (Central Archives)

H F Verwoerd (Central Archives)

Hendrik Frensch Verwoerd was born on 8 September 1901 in Amsterdam and came to South Africa with his parents when he was two years old. An outstanding student and adacemic, he studied at the University of Stellenbosch, and also in Europe. At Stellenbosch he lectured in logic and psychology, as well as sociology and social work. In 1934 he organized the important *Volkskongres* in Kimberley on the poor white problem. He became editor of *Die Transvaler* in 1937.

Verwoerd's political career began to take shape in 1946 when he became vice-chairman of the National Party in the Transvaal. Two years later he became a senator and in 1950 he was elected leader of the Senate. During the same year Malan invited him to become Minister of Native Affairs. After Strijdom's death in 1958 Verwoerd became Prime Minister of South Africa. In September 1966 he was stabbed to death in the House of Assembly by a messenger of Parliament named Dimitrio Tsafendas.

▷
Douglas Mitchell, Natal leader of the United Party. (*Die Burger*)

▷▷
Margaret Ballinger, first parliamentary leader of the Liberal Party. (Central Archives)

ers. Poor administration and preparation for the election on the UP's part also accounted for its electoral defeat.

Within the UP itself there was utter confusion. Harry Lawrence and Arthur Barlow wanted Colin Steyn to take over the party leadership. At a meeting of all the former UP ministers on 31 May E A Conroy demanded Hofmeyr's resignation. Hofmeyr refused on the grounds that Smuts was not present and that their leader still had the right to decide the issue. Smuts subsequently defended Hofmeyr, pointing out that the NP attack on him had been unnecessarily vindictive. Owing to the support given to him by Smuts, confidence in Hofmeyr was to a large extent restored and in November he was re-elected Transvaal leader of the United Party. However, his sudden, tragic death in December 1948 led to significant changes within the party, not least of which was the urgent problem of finding a successor for the now ageing Smuts.

Hofmeyr's death did not mean the end of a liberal element in the UP. Harry Oppenheimer, Morris Kentridge and R J du Toit kept the banner flying, and this liberal tendency led to the resignation of Karel Rood, UP frontbencher from Vereeniging, in 1949. At the subsequent by-election the NP won the seat from the UP by a narrow margin. As a result calls for better organization within the UP echoed throughout the country, while it was increasingly felt that the lack of a definite colour policy, resulting from intense internal dissension, was detrimental to the party. Rood's resignation was followed by that of one of the UP's key senators, J M van H Brink, as well as other leading members of the party such as Major B P Greyling and J du P Basson.

The new leading figure in the United Party was Smuts's confidant and MP for Germiston District, Advocate J G N Strauss. Doubts concerning his leadership ability were an omen of further discord and deterioration in the once powerful UP. After his eightieth birthday, suffering from serious heart problems, Smuts announced his intention in June 1950 of relinquishing the parliamentary leadership of the UP. At Smuts's request Strauss was elected as the party's new parliamentary leader, a decision which left the caucus seriously divided. Smuts remained leader of the UP until his death in September 1950, and in November Strauss was unanimously elected to the position.

Strauss found it no easy task taking over the reins from so skilled a politician and internationally respected statesman as Smuts. His problems were exacerbated by the fact that he took over the leadership of a seriously divided party. By the end of 1950 it was clear that Strauss would encounter great opposition if he tried to improve the United Party's political position by entering into a coalition with Havenga. The young leader was unable to enforce party discipline to the same extent as Smuts. Nor could he, as his predecessor had done, rely on strong support from the English-language press.

The 1953 election was to be the acid test of Strauss's leadership. Eliciting aid from the United South African Trust Fund, established in 1949 with the help of Smuts, UP finances for the election were sounder and election strategy more thoroughly disciplined. The establishment of the Torch Commando, an ex-servicemen's organization, greatly strengthened the United Party. The aims of this organization were to counter the National Party, and to take

action in the constitutional crisis surrounding the Coloured vote.

In May 1951 a vast torchlight procession filed through the streets of Johannesburg and A G 'Sailor' Malan, renowned fighter pilot and hero of the Battle of Britain, was invited to take the salute. Later Malan addressed a mass meeting, playing on the emotions of the ex-soldiers and emphasizing that the decisions of the Act of Union should be complied with in all respects. The Johannesburg protest march was followed by similar demonstrations throughout the country, and culminated in a national congress in June 1951 at which 'Sailor' Malan was elected first national president and leader of the movement. The Torch Commando grew rapidly and membership rose to approximately a quarter of a million.

Strauss supported this group, and at the end of 1951 the United Party, the Torch Commando and the Labourites formed the United Democratic Front, with the specific object of fighting the coming general election on a united basis. Even before the election, however, it was already clear that the UP's chances of defeating the National Party were slim.

The general election of 15 April 1953 was a great disappointment to the UP. Not only did it have to concede defeat to the NP once again, but it saw the number of NP seats grow from 86 to 94, while its own diminished from 65 to 57. The consequences of the election for the UP were far-reaching. Immediately after the election, right-wing and left-wing groups within the party made known their dissatisfaction with the party's policy. Disapproval of the actions of the national chairman of the Torch Commando, L Kane-Berman, and other leaders of this movement led to the resignation of G H Nicholls, as well as several other leading party members, and to the establishment of the Union Federal Party under the leadership of Nicholls in May 1953. The concept of federation, wider powers for the provinces and separation between the two white language groups were central themes of this party's manifesto. The UP did not endorse these radical ideas, and continuing discord often broke out, particularly at congresses. Dissension also became apparent between the *'verligte'* Nicholls and the conservative Douglas Mitchell, Natal leader of the UP.

As early as the 1948 election calls had begun to be heard for the establishment of a Liberal Party, with the liberal UP minister J H Hofmeyr as leader. After the latter's death in 1948 the torch of liberalism was taken up within the UP. The colour policy of the UP, however, was the principal reason for the eventual establishment of the Liberal Party under the parliamentary leadership of Margaret Ballinger in May 1953.

This was the first party since Union to be founded on the principle of multiracialism; it was furthest to the left of all parties in South

J G N Strauss, who succeeded Smuts as leader of the United Party. (United Party Archives, UNISA)

Africa. It called for the elimination of racial discrimination, aimed to place all liberals – regardless of race or colour – on the political platform and to hold out a non-racist democracy to the country, with universal suffrage. The Liberal Party proved short-lived, largely owing to co-operation with the African National Congress, lack of finances, scant support from the press, and, finally, the tactics of its opponents.

After 1953 it became clear that the UP was disintegrating, and that a more dynamic leader was needed. The choice fell on the 42-year-old leader of the party in the Cape, Sir De Villiers Graaff.

The selection in 1956 of De Villiers Graaff as

Alan Paton, a founder and leader of the Liberal Party, and Léopold Senghor, President of Senegal. (INCH)

leader of the United Party was received with enthusiasm both by the party and the English-language press. He was faced with many daunting problems, including those raised by the liberals in UP ranks (Helen Suzman, John Cope, Ray Swart and Colin Eglin were amongst this number), and the fact that rural Afrikaners found it difficult to identify with him.

The founding of the Progressive Party

By 1959 the United Party was once again experiencing serious internal problems. The left wing rebelled against Graaff's leadership, and was also dissatisfied with the conservative Natal leader of the party, Douglas Mitchell. In August of that year a split took place during the central congress of the UP in Bloemfontein.

The principal source of discord was the insistence of the left wing of the party on increased black representation in Parliament and a common voters' roll for all who were entitled to vote. When it became evident that the majority of the UP members were opposed to this principle, a group of twelve caucus members broke away from the congress and established the Progressive Party under the leadership of Jan Steytler. The Progressive Party was in favour of a multiracial government and a multiracial Parliament. The party's constitution was subsequently adjusted and provision was made for a qualified franchise. During the general election of October 1961, only one of the party's twelve members of the House of Assembly, Helen Suzman, retained her seat.

The abolition of the Coloured franchise

In 1948 Malan and Havenga had been unable to reach agreement on the matter of the Coloured franchise, but in 1949 they tried to iron out their differences. Havenga insisted that if Coloureds were placed on a separate voters' roll, they would have to receive the same representation in the House of Assembly as the same number of white voters would have been entitled to. Towards the end of the 1949 session Malan informed the National Party caucus that he would not proceed with legislation on this issue in the coming year.

In 1951 Malan and Havenga reached agreement, and on 8 March 1951 T E Dönges introduced the Separate Representation of Voters Bill in the House of Assembly. This legislation was to herald the beginning of the serious constitutional crisis of the fifties. The United

Sir D P de Villiers Graaff (Central Archives)

Party opposed this contentious bill at its introduction, insisting that the matter be submitted to a joint sitting of the House of Assembly and the Senate, and that it could be agreed to only with a two-thirds majority, which the government did not possess. The Malan government threw out the objection, alleging that the Union Parliament was sovereign and could not allow itself to be bound by the 'dead hand of the past'.

In spite of vehement opposition from the United Party, this legislation was passed in the House of Assembly in May 1951 by 74 votes to 64. The UP decided to contest it in the court, but the Cape Division of the Supreme Court rejected the application of two Coloured voters to have the legislation declared invalid. The UP then decided to take the case to the Appeal Court. In March 1952 the Appeal Court found against the government, whereupon a constitutional crisis arose, the serious aftermath of which would be resolved only four years later.

Malan did not accept the Appeal Court judgment. He had two courses open to him: to dismiss the judges of appeal or find a method by means of which he could comply with the provisions of the constitution in respect of a two-thirds majority. His hands were tied, however, because both courses open to him at this juncture were too drastic. He was afraid of the attitude Havenga and his House of Assembly supporters would take, and he also feared the reaction of the militant Torch Commando.

In the hope of gaining support from the 'conservatives' within the UP, Malan submitted the Separate Representation of Voters Bill to a joint sitting of the two Houses of Parliament in 1953. Support outside the National Party was not forthcoming, and the matter was shelved until Strijdom announced his plans in regard to the Coloured legislation early in 1955. The issue would be dealt with in three successive phases: the composition of the Appeal Court would be amended; the Senate would be enlarged; and the Separate Representation of Voters Bill would be resubmitted to a joint sitting.

Phase one was disposed of by increasing by legislation the number of judges in the Appeal Court from five to eleven and by determining the forum in cases involving the validity of laws of Parliament to be eleven. This was followed by phase two, in which the Senate legislation was taken to the House of Assembly. In spite of vehement opposition from the United Party, the English-language press and the liberal sector, legislation was passed in terms of which the Senate was enlarged from 44 to 89 members. After the Senate election in August, Strijdom was ready to proceed to the third and last phase in the abolishing of the Coloured franchise, namely the passing of the bill to remove Coloureds from the common voters' roll. Early in the 1956 parliamentary session a South Africa Act Amendment Bill was submitted to a joint sitting of the House of Assembly and the Senate, and the required number of votes for a two-thirds majority was obtained.

Once again the UP took the case to court. The Cape Supreme Court ratified the amendment of the South Africa Act in connection with the Coloured vote and the case was taken to the Appeal Court, which also found against the UP with a large majority. The Cape was thereupon divided into four electoral divisions and the Coloureds were given the right to elect one white representative to the House of Assembly in each of these electoral divisions.

In contrast to the other three provinces, Coloureds could be elected Members of the Provincial Council of the Cape until 1956. In this year, however, legislation was passed in terms of which this situation was terminated and in future Coloureds could be represented only by whites in the province. This system of Coloured representation was to continue until the end of the sixties, when it was finally abolished.

The unethical passing of the Separate Representation of Voters Act in 1956 served to alienate even further the Coloureds from the Afrikaners. In addition to the NP's endeavour to implement its policy of apartheid, the party's motivation for the abolition of the Coloured vote was probably the fear that Coloured voters would side with the UP opposition.

A cartoon by Bob Connolly in the *Rand Daily Mail*, 5 January 1956, commenting on the enlargement of the Senate from 44 to 89 members. (*Rand Daily Mail*)

DIFFICULT PROBLEM FINDING OFFICE SPACE FOR NEW NAT. SENATORS IN NEW NAT. SENATE. - CAPETOWN.

'When I ask you to produce proof, I mean your identity card!' A cartoon by David Marais, *Cape Times*, 24 November 1959, showing how the Separate Amenities Act of 1953 and the Population Registration Act of 1950 combined. (*Cape Times*)

Principal apartheid legislation, 1949-1961

Act No 55 of 1949: Prohibition of Mixed Marriages Act

Act No 21 of 1950: Immorality Amendment Act

Act No 30 of 1950: Population Registration Act

Act No 41 of 1950: Group Areas Act

Act No 46 of 1951: Separate Representation of Voters Act

Act No 52 of 1951: Prevention of Illegal Squatting Act

Act No 68 of 1951: Bantu Authorities Act

Act No 67 of 1952: Natives (Abolition of Passes and Co-ordination of Documents) Act

Act No 47 of 1953: Bantu Education Act

Act No 49 of 1953: Reservation of Separate Amenities Act

Act No 19 of 1954: Natives Resettlement Act

Act No 69 of 1955: Group Areas Development Act

Act No 64 of 1956: Natives (Prohibition of Interdicts) Act

Act No 34 of 1959: Bantu Investment Corporation Act

Act No 3 of 1961: Coloured Persons Communal Reserves Act

Act No 31 of 1961: Preservation of Coloured Areas Act

Act No 79 of 1961: Urban Bantu Councils Act

The apartheid policy

The year 1948 was a political watershed for South Africa, since, for the first time, the 'apartheid' tradition was statutorily defined and enforced. The National Party came to power largely as a result of the apartheid slogan, and proceeded to implement the policy in practice by means of legislation.

Even before the 1948 election Malan had explained how apartheid would affect the black people of South Africa. Reserves would be retained, and if possible enlarged. Peasant farmers would receive instruction in scientific farming methods, soil conservation and agriculture in general. Separate residential areas and improved housing schemes would be provided for 'permanent' urban blacks. All temporary labourers would be repatriated to their reserves. On the basis of its intention to convert reserves into homelands with independent systems of government, the Malan government planned to abolish black representation in Parliament and in the Cape Provincial Council. As a temporary measure blacks would continue to have representation in the Senate through white representatives, to serve *inter alia* as their constitutional link with the white government. NP policy in respect of higher education was aimed at creating separate amenities for blacks so that they would no longer be admitted to white universities.

Malan rejected the recommendations of the Fagan Commission, appointed by Smuts in 1946 to investigate the position of blacks in South Africa. The commission had acknowledged a black urban population as an irreversible fact but, in drafting legislation, was not prepared to accept the existence of a permanent urban black population.

During the first two years of the Malan regime, immediate steps were taken to implement the apartheid policy. As a first step the intermingling of races in white areas would be subjected to close scrutiny. Through the Prohibition of Mixed Marriages Act (1949) marriages between whites and people of other colours were prohibited, despite the fact that since 1946, compared with 28 000 white marriages, there had been only 75 mixed marriages. The next year the first amendment of the Immorality Act of 1927 was passed, and it was again amended in 1957 (Act No 23). In terms of the latter act, adultery, attempted adultery or related immoral acts between whites and blacks were prohibited.

During 1950 the Population Registration Act was introduced, by means of which a national register was compiled in which every individual was classified according to his race. A Race Classification Board was also established to take the final decision in dubious cases. The object of the Malan government with this act was probably to prevent Coloured persons being classified as whites.

The Group Areas Act (1950) was the instrument by which the National Party government implemented the process of physical separation between the various races. By this means residential separation, particularly in urban centres, was implemented. Communities, for example the Coloureds in Cape Town and Asians in Durban, were sometimes removed to separate areas. Few whites were affected by this measure. The Prohibition of Mixed Marriages Act and the Group Areas Act were vehemently opposed by the United Party, which considered the laws to be unnecessary and indecent.

The Native Representative Council, which had never come up to the expectations of Hertzog and Smuts, was abolished in 1952, largely owing to the council's continuous demands for greater political say.

One of the most contentious laws was the Separate Amenities Act of 1953, which regulated public amenities on the basis of racial separation, with the intention of eliminating contact and preserving a colour consciousness. The object was to prevent racial mixing and to ensure that the whites continued to maintain their political domination. The act made provision for a colour bar in all public buildings, amenities and public transport by means of 'Europeans Only' or 'Non-Europeans Only' signs.

Amongst the measures which caused greatest dissatisfaction in the black community were the so-called pass laws (Natives Act of 1952). These laws compelled black people to carry identification and other additional documents with them at all times. In this way it was possible to establish precisely where black people worked, while greater control could be exercised over their movements.

The Natives (Prohibition of Interdicts) Act of 1956 provided that black people who were told by officials to leave certain residential areas were in no way able to turn to the courts to have such instructions invalidated. Movement of black people was further restricted by the Urban Areas Act. Clause 10 prohibited them from remaining in a town for longer than 72 hours without the consent of a specific municipal officer.

Economic and industrial apartheid was not neglected either. Under the Native Building Workers Act it became a criminal offence for a black person to perform any skilled work in a town or city other than in an area specifically set aside for black occupation.

The Bantu Investment Corporation Act of 1959 made provision *inter alia* for the financing and co-ordination of financial, commercial and industrial schemes in black areas. With the support of the South African Bantu Trust and individual black investors, a black-orientated investment pattern was created. However, the lack of a rapid development rate, and insufficient financial inputs and stimulation by private enterprise were inhibiting factors in the creation of truly viable and sovereign socio-economic units.

During the 1959 parliamentary session two important measures were introduced relating to tertiary education. The first was the University College of Fort Hare Act, by means of which provision was made for a fully fledged academic institution for the Xhosa. Then came the Universities Amendment Act, in terms of which separate university institutions were created for Asians, blacks and Coloureds.

The Urban Councils Act made provision for the creation of black councils in urban areas on the basis of their national unit. These councils would continue to maintain their ties with the reserves of their particular ethnic groups and their specific authorities, who were mainly tribal. In practice, however, this system did not work very well because the tribal authorities had no say in the functioning of urban black authorities.

In 1950 the Malan government appointed a commission to carry out an investigation into a comprehensive rehabilitation of the black areas in South Africa with a view to the development of their own national structure, based on effective socio-economic planning. It was also an investigation into the ways in which 'homelands' could be developed. The commission came under the direction of Professor F R Tomlinson, and was known as the Tomlinson Commission.

The Bantu Authorities Act (Act No 68 of 1951) abolished the Native Representative Council, thus paving the way for a greater measure of self-government in the homelands. Once a start had been made with tribal authorities, it was possible to proceed to the establishment of

'Vote for him? Not likely! Next thing we'd have Africans living right next door to us!' A cartoon by Jock Leyden in which the situation in many white urban areas in South Africa is graphically portrayed. (*Sunday Tribune*)

◁▽
A cartoon by Jock Leyden commenting on the Separate Amenities Act of 1953. (*Sunday Tribune*)

▽
Comment by cartoonist Abe Berry on the Separate Amenities Act of 1953 which introduced a colour bar in public buildings, amenities and public transport. (*South Africa and How It Works*, Johannesburg, 1900)

Professor F R Tomlinson (Central Archives)

Dr James Moroka (South African Library)

regional authorities. The Transkei was the territory best suited to the establishment of the first territorial authority, a step which the government proceeded to take in May 1957.

Self-government for homelands

In its 1948 election manifesto the National Party had adopted the general principle that the various black people would 'as far as possible' be concentrated in their respective territories, 'where each group could develop into a self-sufficient unit'. Therefore employment opportunities had to be created and economic development had to take place in these territories. E G Jansen, Minister of Native Affairs in the Malan Cabinet until 1950, when he was succeeded by Verwoerd, announced that the government intended to grant the black inhabitants of reserves 'the greatest possible measure of control over their own affairs', but 'with retention of white guardianship'.

In 1951 Verwoerd introduced the Bantu Authorities Act, which provided for the establishment of homelands, regional authorities and territorial authorities. To a large extent the measure enabled inhabitants of such areas to take charge of their own affairs of a local nature. In order to turn chiefs and councillors into 'progressive leaders' a number of training courses were arranged by the Department of Native Affairs. The Bantu Education Act (1953) introduced a state-controlled black education department, which would ensure that the curricula complied with the 'nature and requirements of the black people'.

As an outcome of the Tomlinson Commission report the government decided to support the development of industries in white urban areas on the homeland borders to which black workers could commute daily. It was thought that this would reduce the influx of black labour to large cities and stimulate development of the homelands. However, it was only in the late sixties that some of these border industries were properly established.

After Verwoerd became Prime Minister in 1958, he conceded that his policy could in fact lead to self-governing homelands. In 1959 the Verwoerd government introduced the Promotion of Bantu Self-Government Act (Act No 46 of 1959), in terms of which people in the reserves were afforded the opportunity of eventually governing themselves independently without white intervention or control. This system made provision for the separation or classification of black people into eight different ethnic units, each with its own Commissioner-General, to whom the task of developing the respective territories into self-governing national units was entrusted. Commissioners-general were to form the links between the ethnic units and the white government. In this act provision was also made for the abolition of direct Coloured representation in the Cape Provincial Council. At the same time black representation in the white Parliament was abolished.

During the crisis years of 1957-1962 black political ideology manifested itself in different forms: the movement towards revolutionary violence (the Bambatha ideology), tribal nationalism under government pressure, the inclusive South African nationalism of the African National Congress (ANC) and the exclusive African nationalism of the Pan Africanist Congress (PAC).

Uprisings among the peasant farmers in the

reserves arose as a result of tensions caused *inter alia* by the Bantu Authorities Act, poverty, the deposition of chiefs, restrictions on movement to towns and the requirement that black women carry passes. Unrest broke out in four areas – the Hurutshe Reserve, Sekukuniland, Zululand and East Pondoland. In Zululand the unrest spread to the black township of Cato Manor, leading to police intervention. In East Pondoland the government ordered the restoration of order through the use of tanks and machine guns. Although the unrest died down, dissatisfaction continued to simmer.

The growth of black nationalism – opposition to white politics

When the National Party came into power in 1948 dissatisfaction among blacks already existed, particularly among the trained and professional class, regarding the discriminatory measures of the white government which placed them in a subordinate position. In 1944 an anti-pass campaign was organized, followed by an undertaking by the African National Congress and Transvaal and Natal Asians early in 1947 to campaign for the franchise and social rights. A year prior to the resistance movement against passes the Smuts government had established a Coloured Advisory Committee (CAC) with a view to establishing closer contact with the Coloured community and identifying their needs and aims. However, the National Anti-CAC Committee, which had been established by Coloureds, regarded the CAC as an instrument of apartheid, and sought political co-operation with Asians and blacks in a unified movement against racial discrimination. At the end of 1943 the National Anti-CAC Committee joined forces with the All-African Convention (AAC) to establish the Non-European Unity Movement. Consequently the Coloureds, Asians and blacks united against the whites, their common "oppressor". In their struggle for democratic rights and political change they were supported by the South African Communist Party.

Following 1948, it was the ANC that took the initiative in the black political struggle. At its annual congress in 1949 it accepted a militant Programme of Action, planned by the organization's Youth League. The object was freedom from white domination and the achievement of direct representation in all government bodies by means of strikes, public disobedience, refusal to co-operate and the boycotting of differentiated political organizations.

For the first time since its establishment in 1912, the ANC displayed open resistance. Up to this juncture the ANC had not been a militant organization, but a conservative body with reformist aims, comprised of a black professional elite that advocated power sharing and raising the standard of living of black people. The Youth League of the ANC was, however, a more militant body. Inspired by the success of strikes by the Industrial and Commercial Workers' Union (ICU) and the ideas of the black American Marcus Garvey, who coined the slogan 'Africa for the Africans', the Youth League began to foment a new type of nationalism. Its members were more radical and militant than those of the parent organization, and advocated lawful or unlawful mass action.

In 1949 the ANC acquired a new President-General in Dr James S Moroka. Walter Sisulu of the Youth League was to occupy the key post of Secretary-General.

In March 1950 the ANC's Programme of Action was initiated with the Freedom of Speech Convention in Johannesburg. This convention, opened by Dr Moroka, was the first of the great demonstrations of 1950. It was followed by Freedom Day demonstrations against racial discrimination, sponsored by the Communist Party, in which all race groups participated. Black labourers were urged to stay away from work and half of the black labour force on the Witwatersrand complied. In the accompanying clash between police and strikers eighteen blacks were killed. The last demonstration of 1950 took place on 26 June. The ANC, the Asiatic Congress, the African Peoples Organization (APO) and the Communist Party called for a National Day of Protest and Mourning. In particular the protests were aimed at the Group Areas Bill and the Suppression of Communism Bill, while those black people who had lost their lives during the Freedom Day demonstrations were to be mourned. Although blacks on the

Albert Lutuli addressing a gathering of the African National Congress. (South African Library)

281

Witwatersrand did not stay away from work in great numbers, many were absent in Port Elizabeth and Durban.

In 1950 the South African Communist Party was declared to be an unlawful organization in terms of the Suppression of Communism Act (Act No 44). By this means, Communist activities, as well as those of other organizations propagating the aims of Communism, were completely restrained. On 1 February 1956 the South African Minister of Foreign Affairs, Eric Louw, closed the Russian consulate in Pretoria.

In July 1951 representatives of the ANC, the Indian Congress and the Franchise Action Council organized a resistance campaign against discriminatory legislation. In a letter to Malan, the ANC threatened to hold protest meetings unless all discriminatory legislation was abolished by 29 February 1952. The Prime Minister rejected these demands. The Franchise Action Council had been established by the Coloureds in 1951 to oppose the Separate Representation of Voters Bill. On its initiative strikes were organized in Port Elizabeth and the Cape Peninsula, and these were also supported by blacks and Asians.

At a combined meeting of the African National Congress, the Indian Congress and the Franchise Action Council a Joint Planning Council was appointed to co-ordinate the actions of these organizations. It was agreed that they would join forces against the pass laws, group areas legislation, separate representation and black authorities. During the Van Riebeeck Festival leaders of these three groups addressed meetings on 6 April 1952. On 26 June a resistance campaign commenced, aimed especially at the pass laws and apartheid legislation. Participants in the campaign broke these laws and refused to pay fines, opting to serve terms of imprisonment. The resistance movements were to reach a climax three months later, in October 1952. Violent clashes occurred in the Eastern Cape (New Brighton in Port Elizabeth and in

East London), the Witwatersrand and Kimberley, during which several people were killed.

In terms of countermeasures adopted by the government heavy penalities were imposed upon contraveners of the pass laws and the Suppression of Communism Act. Several black leaders were banned in terms of the Riotous Assemblies Act. Two further laws were passed, the Public Safety Act (Act No 3, 1953), which made provision for the proclamation of a state of emergency, and the Criminal Law Amendment Act (Act No 8, 1953), which was specifically aimed at suppressing public unrest.

This resistance campaign lasted six months and brought with it few advantages for the Joint Planning Council. It allowed the government, through legislation, to clamp down more harshly on resistance movements, various black and Asian leaders were eliminated and not a single piece of apartheid or suppressive legislative was abolished. It did, however, focus international attention on South Africa and aroused world-wide antipathy to the policy of apartheid. At the same time it led to the establishment of two white political parties: the radical, pro-Communist Congress of Democrats and the Liberal Party, a multiracial party under the leadership of Alan Paton. Both parties believed that blacks should have the same rights as whites. During the resistance campaign the membership of the ANC increased to 100 000, the majority of whom were in the Eastern Cape. In December 1952 the 54-year-old Albert Lutuli, a prime mover in the resistance campaign, became President-General of the ANC.

By the mid-fifties black nationalism in South Africa was also being fanned by a growing international front opposed to separate develoment. At the United Nations South Africa came under more frequent attack, a tendency which was also discernible at the Commonwealth Conference in 1956. International criticism reached a climax in 1960 in the charge concerning South West Africa which Ethiopia and Liberia lodged

A group of black people at Evaton, near Vereeniging, listening to a speech by Z M Molete of the Pan Africanist Congress. This large anti-pass gathering was held on 21 March 1960, the same day that the Sharpeville tragedy occurred. (South African Library)

282

against South Africa in the International Court of Justice.

Another black resistance campaign, which was to culminate in the Congress of the People in 1955, gave rise to an even greater measure of interracial co-operation. The success of this campaign was largely counteracted by the failure of two other campaigns staged at approximately the same time. The first, aimed at preventing the implementation of the Bantu Education Act (1953), urged a boycott. Black people were divided on the desirability of a boycott; their choice lay between co-operating or refraining from doing so. The second campaign was aimed at preventing the mass removal of black people from the western area of Johannesburg. The ANC's resistance to the implementation of this territorial segregation was suppressed by the government's vigorous countermeasures.

The Cape leader of the ANC, Professor Z K Matthews, called for a Congress of the People, where demands for change in South Africa could be articulated. This congress, which was held on 26 June 1955 in Kliptown, near Johannesburg, was organized by the ANC, the Indian Congress, the South African Congress of Democrats, the South African Coloured People's Organization and the South African Congress of Trade Unions.

At meetings held throughout the country collective grievances were accumulated and more than 3 000 delegates were appointed. The congress adopted a Freedom Charter which called *inter alia* for equal rights for all ethnic groups, and put foward the claim that South Africa belonged to all its inhabitants. The ideal was not black majority rule but a democratic state, based on the will of the people. Certain socialist principles such as state ownership of minerals, banks and industries were also adopted. The Strijdom government considered the charter to be subversive and reacted by carrying out police raids, banning some congress leaders, and ar-

Robert Sobukwe

Robert Mangaliso Sobukwe was born in Graaff-Reinet in 1924, and was an outstanding student from an early age. He won a bursary to Healdtown, and graduated in 1947. He then enrolled at Fort Hare where he pursued his keen interest in literature. He became a member of the ANC Youth League in 1948, and in 1949 was elected president of the Fort Hare Students' Representative Council, where he proved an able orator.

In 1950 he was appointed to a teaching post at a high school in Standerton, but after speaking publicly in support of the defiance campaign in 1952 he was dismissed but later reinstated. During this period he was divorced from the mainstream of ANC activity, although he was secretary of the ANC Standerton branch. In 1954 he was appointed lecturer in African studies at the University of the Witwatersrand, and moved to Johannesburg, where his outstanding intellect was recognized. He worked mainly behind the scenes, editing *The Africanist*, and in November 1958 he advocated a breakaway from the ANC, and became the unanimously elected president of the newly formed Pan Africanist Congress.

His eloquence on public platforms rallied support for the PAC, and in March 1960, when the PAC launched its anti-pass campaign, he gave himself up for arrest at the Orlando police station hoping to encourage more people to join the movement. He was given an unexpectedly harsh sentence of three years' imprisonment, at the end of which period Parliament enacted a General Law Amendment Act empowering the Minister of Justice *inter alia* to prolong indefinitely the detention of any political prisoner. He was banned to Robben Island, where he remained for six years.

In May 1969 he was released, and allowed to join his family in Kimberley while remaining under twelve-hour house arrest. During his detention he had obtained an honours degree in economics from the University of London and had begun a law degree. In Kimberley he became articled and in 1975 began his own law practice. He was offered numerous posts at American universities but attempts to go abroad were blocked by the government. He died on 27 February 1978.

resting 156 others for high treason. Charges against 65 people were subsequently withdrawn. The trial of the remaining accused commenced in November 1960 and lasted for five years. All charges were eventually withdrawn. The trial brought the leaders of the so-called Congress Alliance closer together, and most of the ANC members continued their activities underground.

To those black nationalists with an African perspective, the Freedom Charter, with its goal of racial co-operation and non-insistence on black majority rule, meant a betrayal of African nationalism. They advocated an exclusive African nationalism, with the emphasis on Africa being ruled by Africans. With this charter the seeds of an ideological rift, which would come to a head in 1958, were sown. In that year, at a provincial congress of the ANC, a group of delegates walked out on the grounds of ideological differences. A few months later, in April 1959, the Pan Africanist Congress was established under the leadership of Robert Sobukwe, then 34 years old.

Shortly before the establishment of the PAC Sobukwe wrote in *The Africanist*: 'We claim Africa for the Africans, the ANC claims South Africa for all.' Like the Youth League of the ANC, the PAC battle cry was also 'Africa for the Africans'. They regarded the Congress Alliance, with Coloured and Asian participation, as an inhibiting factor in their endeavour to achieve the liberation of Africa. It was feared that the Freedom Charter would lead to a domination of Africans by non-Africans. The man who controlled the ANC at this juncture, and who had to accommodate the rift with Sobukwe's PAC, was Nelson Mandela.

Mandela welcomed the 1959 rift within the ANC as a cathartic process and labelled So-

An anti-pass demonstration in the 1960s. (INCH)

283

Nelson Mandela

Nelson Rolihlahla Mandela, a member of the royal Tembu family, was born in Umtata, Transkei, in 1918. He attended Healdtown Mission College, and then enrolled at Fort Hare in 1938, but was suspended in 1940 following his participation in a student protest. He worked as a mine policeman in Johannesburg while completing a BA degree through the University of South Africa, and in 1943 he registered for a law degree at the University of the Witwatersrand. On completion of the degree, he and Oliver Tambo, a fellow graduate, opened a joint legal practice.

In 1944 Mandela joined the ANC and became a founder member of the Youth League, of which he was made national president in 1950. After the 1952 defiance campaign he was given a nine-month suspended sentence and forbidden to leave Johannesburg for six months. He was elected deputy national president of the ANC under Albert Lutuli, but found it difficult to exercise the necessary leadership while restricted by the banning order. In September 1953 a new ban was imposed requiring him to resign from the ANC and prohibiting him from attending gatherings for the movement, but he continued his leadership in secret.

In 1961, after his banning order lapsed, Mandela addressed a conference in Pietermaritzburg and supported the concept of a national convention, calling for a three-day stay-at-home. He then went underground, and spent the next seventeen months as a fugitive. Nicknamed the 'Black Pimpernel', he visited various African countries to obtain support for *Umkonto We Sizwe's* proposed campaign of violence, addressing the Pan-African Freedom Movement in Addis Ababa in January 1962. In July 1962 he returned to South Africa, and was later arrested in Natal. In November he was convicted on charges of incitement and leaving the country illegally, and was sentenced to five years' imprisonment.

When the police raided the Rivonia headquarters of *Umkonto We Sizwe* in July 1963 documents in Mandela's handwriting were found amongst the evidence collected. During the Rivonia trial Mandela was sentenced to life imprisonment.

bukwe's PAC as a break-away faction of the ANC which would show little growth. This was an error of judgment. Within the space of one year the PAC showed more growth than the ANC had done in fifty years. By 1960 the black nationalists had begun to lose patience with peaceful attempts at overthrowing the South African political and social structure, and the methods of the PAC, and even those of the ANC, began to contain a strong revolutionary element. Black resistance was aimed in particular at the hated pass laws, and was based on the resistance movement of 1952. Passes were burnt, and no defence was offered at ensuing court proceedings, while bail was refused and fines were ignored. The 1960 resistance movement differed in two respects from that of 1952: leaders were the first to present themselves for arrest, and only black people were invited to participate. In March 1960 Sobukwe and other PAC leaders gave themselves up at the Orlando police station and were arrested.

Although in most cases the resistance was of a peaceful nature, the two exceptions, Sharpeville and Langa (which are discussed more fully on page 287), resulted in tragic loss of life. A week after Sharpeville, where 69 people were killed and approximately 180 wounded on 21 March 1960, a national day of mourning and one-day strike was held, during which 450 000 black people stayed at home. For a long time Sharpeville and Langa would stir up feelings against South Africa in the outside world. The repercussions in South Africa were felt in many ways.

The Verwoerd government reacted by temporarily relaxing the pass laws, declaring a state of emergency, and banning public meetings. Approximately 11 500 people were detained, of whom 224 were whites. Many blacks fled to adjoining African states. On 8 April 1960 the Unlawful Organizations Act declared the ANC and PAC to be prohibited organizations. Heavy pen-

alties would be imposed upon any person who continued to further their objectives. Consequently the ANC and PAC went underground and began to advocate violent measures to an increasing extent.

The Union becomes a Republic

The year 1948 was a turning point in the political history of South Africa – a republican party was now in power. New developments in the British Commonwealth favoured the republican ideal within the National Party. In 1949 India became a republic within the Commonwealth, which convinced numerous South Africans that the establishment of a republic would not lead to isolation or secession. Hertzog's standpoint that a republic could be established only with a special mandate from the people was reaffirmed by Malan in 1953.

Various steps were taken by the government to emphasize the sovereignty of the Union. The South African Citizen Act was passed (1949), the right of appeal to the British Privy Council was abolished (1950), the supremacy of Parliament was confirmed beyond all doubt (1955), the Union flag was accepted as the only South African flag and 'The Call of South Africa' as the only national anthem (1957). In 1957 the Union also took over the British naval base at Simon's Town. Since 1951 a pro-republican South African, E G Jansen, had been Governor-General. The scene was set for the establishment of a republic. All the most important symbols of a republic had already been introduced by the end of the 1950s – one citizenship, one flag and one national anthem.

In 1955 Prime Minister Strijdom's outspoken comments on a republic led the United Party

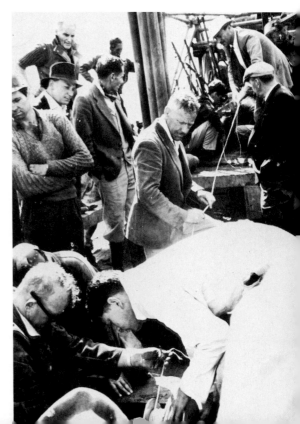

leader, Strauss, to reaffirm in Parliament the importance of the Union's association with the Commonwealth. Strijdom in turn reaffirmed the government's constitutional goal, which was that South Africa's republican objective remained unchanged and that secession from the Commonwealth would be decided by the Union's own interests.

However, it was Verwoerd who was to implement the programme for the attainment of complete independence, not only because of strengthening support for a republic from the white voters, but also because international circumstances were to steer South Africa in this direction. Since the Second World War the former British colonies in Africa and Asia had become independent, and were thus eligible to become members of the Commonwealth. In due course a negative attitude towards South Africa, the country of apartheid and racial discrimination, emerged among members of the Commonwealth. With the growth of Pan-Africanism and the clarion call of *Uhuru* (freedom) resounding through Africa, African member states of the United Nations also united against the Union and waged a purposeful campaign against its policy of separate development.

Verwoerd was convinced that the status of the Union and its relationship with Britain had caused division between English- and Afrikaans-speaking South Africans. He declared unequivocally that only in a republic would there eventually be unity between Afrikaans and English. The result of the general election in April 1958 gave added momentum to republican aspirations and the subject of a republic began to dominate the political scene. The Prime Minister even appealed to pro-republican members of the UP, whereupon the Leader of the Opposition, Sir De Villiers Graaff, declared unequivocally that his party was opposed to a republic.

In 1960 country-wide celebrations were held to commemorate the fiftieth anniversary of the Union of South Africa. On 20 January, during the no-confidence debate in the House of Assembly, Verwoerd took the opportunity of announcing that a referendum on the establishment of a republic would be held. Although the United Party were caught unawares, it immediately declared its opposition to the idea of a republic, while the Progressive Party favoured a multiracial republic.

Before the referendum could be held, several disasters befell South Africa. A day after Verwoerd's announcement it became known that 438 mine workers had been trapped underground at Coalbrook Colliery in the Union's

A Commonwealth Conference held in 1957, while South Africa was still a member. The delegates are as follows: seated (left to right) Dr K Nkrumah (Ghana), J Nehru (India), J Diefenbaker (Canada), H Macmillan (Britain), R Menzies (Australia), S Suhrwardy (Pakistan). Standing (left to right) W H de Silva (Ceylon), T L Macdonald (New Zealand), E H Louw (South Africa), Sir Roy Welensky (Rhodesia). (INCH)

◁◁
Coalbrook Colliery, January 1960. Workers lowering a microphone (attached to the cable) into the rescue shaft to ascertain whether any of the trapped miners have survived. (*Die Burger*)

◁
A team of rescue workers at Coalbrook Colliery returning from underground. (*Die Burger*)

H F Verwoerd and the British Prime Minister, Harold Macmillan, in February 1960. (*Die Burger*)

The 'Winds of Change' speech

Two weeks after Verwoerd's sensational announcement of a pending referendum, the British Prime Minister, Harold Macmillian, who was concluding a tour of Africa, made a speech in the South African Parliament which became known as the 'Winds of Change' speech.

Macmillian stated *inter alia* that since the fall of the Roman Empire, the development of independent nations had been one of the most important features of political life in Europe. Nationalism had also emerged to an increasing extent among African states. He went on to say: 'The most striking of all the impressions I have formed since I left London a month ago is of the strength of this African national consciousness. The wind of change is blowing throughout the continent . . . Whether we like it or not, this growth of national consciousness is a political fact. We must all accept it as a fact. Our national policies must take account of it.

'This means, I would judge, that we must come to terms with it. I sincerely believe that if we cannot do so we may imperil the precarious balance between East and West on which the peace of the world depends.'

Macmillan posed the question what example the Commonwealth could set to win the people of Asia and Africa for the West. To him the answer was to be found in the creation of a society in which individual merit was the only criterion for both political and economic progress. In a country occupied by different races the objective should be to promote partnership among the various groups so that the community could become more of a community. The fact of the matter was, according to Macmillan, that a fundamental difference in viewpoint existed between Britain and South Africa.

Verwoerd's reply to Macmillan was terse: 'There must not only be justice to the black man in Africa but also to the white man . . . This is our only motherland. We have nowhere else to go . . . We see ourselves as a part of the Western world — a true white state in Southern Africa with a possibility of granting a full future to the black man in our midst.'

The 'Winds of Change' speech delivered by Harold Macmillan. (*Die Burger*)

worst ever mine disaster. This was followed by the murder of nine policemen in the black residential area of Cato Manor near Durban.

The 'Winds of Change' speech of the visiting British Prime Minister, Harold Macmillan, in February 1960 (see box on left) was also to have a major effect on South Africa. To many English-speaking people with pro-British feelings it suddenly became clear that their hopes for the future could no longer be pinned on Britain. Some English-speaking people now changed their attitude towards Verwoerd, a change which would swing the scale decisively in his favour during the referendum in October 1960. Wavering Afrikaans-speaking whites, too, were to look with new eyes at a republic, the Commonwealth and the future.

While the echoes of the Macmillan speech were still reverberating through South Africa, and the republican issue remained the topic of the day, the spotlight shifted to another scene of disaster, namely the black residential area of Sharpeville, near Vereeniging (see box on page 287).

A week after Sharpeville, on 8 April, with the support of the United Party, Parliament passed an Unlawful Organizations Act by means of which the PAC and ANC were banned. The government declared a state of emergency and warned that it was prepared to mobilize the army. All public meetings were prohibited and offenders could be detained without trial. Some political parties, welfare and other organizations opposed the government measures and rendered assistance to the families of detainees. These included the Liberal Party, Coloured People's Organization, the Black Sash and the International Red Cross.

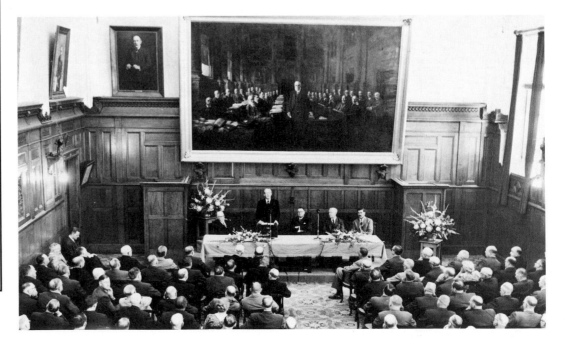

Verwoerd was subjected to a barrage of vehement criticism, not only from the English-language press in South Africa and from overseas but also from clergymen of the English churches in the Union, such as Trevor Huddleston, Archbishop Joost de Blank and Bishop Ambrose Reeves.

On Saturday 9 April 1960 Verwoerd opened the Rand Easter Show in Johannesburg. A wealthy Transvaal farmer, David Pratt, fired two shots at the Prime Minister at close range, striking him in the head. Verwoerd survived the assassination attempt, and resumed his official duties five weeks later.

During 1960 sixteen African states became members of the United Nations. They were soon followed by other states, and this African bloc did everything possible to exert increasing pressure on South Africa to abandon its discriminatory race policy.

On 30 June 1960 the Belgian Congo became independent. A bloody civil war followed which plunged the country into disorder and chaos. Whites fled in large numbers, and many found refuge in South Africa. Some South African whites now began to doubt that an indepenent black government could bring peace, and white public opinion became strongly opposed to liberal ideas. The result was a stimulus for Verwoerd's policy of separate development.

In April Parliament passed the Referendum Act and on 3 August Verwoerd announced that the referendum would be held on 5 October. The run-up to the referendum took place against the background of internal unrest, political disorder in Africa and strong foreign criticism of South Africa. It was an intense and sometimes bitter campaign. On 5 October 90,5 per cent of the white voters cast their votes: 850 458 in favour of a republic and 775 878 against, a majority of 74 580 for the republicans. Natal was the only province in which the

△
The scene at Sharpeville, near Vereeniging, after demonstrators surrounded a police station on 21 March 1960 and were fired upon by police reinforcements. (South African Library)

◁
A reception depot and labour bureau at Langa, after these buildings had been gutted in a fire during disturbances in March 1960. Anti-pass demonstrations led to a clash between police and demonstrators, and two blacks were killed. (South African Library)

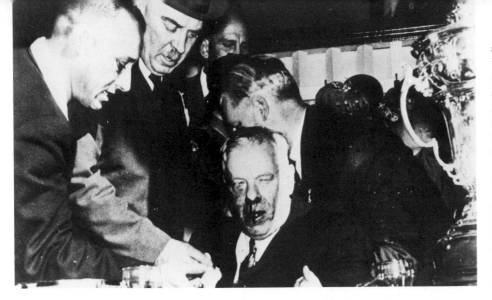

Dr Verwoerd, after he had been shot twice in the head by David Pratt at the opening of the Rand Easter show in Johannesburg on 9 April 1960. (Central Archives)

The Black Sash

The Black Sash was established in May 1955 by six women under the direction of Mrs Ruth Foley. Initially known as the South African Women's Defence of the Constitution League, its protest was aimed primarily at the National Party government's proposed Senate Act. Country-wide protest meetings were organized, marches were arranged and petitions submitted to the Governor-General and to Cabinet members. Members of this organization, wearing black sashes, stood in silent vigil outside official functions attended by Cabinet members, and also at the opening of Parliament. Although not affiliated to a political party, the Black Sash took an active interest in political issues and in urban areas the organization ran advice bureaus for black people who were unsure of their legal position. They also demonstrated for greater educational and social assistance to blacks.

Members of the Black Sash standing silently at vigil in protest against the disfranchisement of Coloured voters. The Prime Minister, J G Strijdom, proceeds to his official vehicle. (INCH)

majority was opposed to the establishment of a republic.

It was obvious that the republican cause had not been won by means of the Afrikaner vote alone, since many Afrikaans-speaking people in fact voted against a republic, merely in order to cast an anti-Nationalist vote. It was also clear after the referendum that many English-speaking people had joined the ranks of the republicans. Verwoerd displayed his goodwill and gratitude to the English-speaking people by including two English-speaking ministers, A E Trollip and F Waring, in his Cabinet.

In March 1961 Verwoerd attended the Commonwealth conference in London. His aim was, as the voters had been promised, to retain South Africa's membership of the Commonwealth. From the outset however, it was clear that the Afro-Asian leaders and the Canadian Prime Minister wanted to ensure South Africa's expulsion from the Commonwealth, in view of the country's race policy. Because of the objections to South Africa's readmission and certain demands which Verwoerd found unacceptable, the Prime Minister decided to withdraw South Africa from the Commonwealth.

The consequences of South Africa's withdraw-

al on 15 March 1961 were less serious than had been expected. It was not necessary to change the pattern of trade and preferential trade agreements in any way, since the British Prime Minister, Harold Macmillian, gave the assurance that these agreements were of a bilateral nature and had been in force since the Ottawa conference of 1932.

Legislation was introduced for the establishment of the Republic of South Africa in January 1961. The most important provision was that the British monarch was replaced by a State President. On 31 May 1961 the Republic of South Africa came into existence. At the same time South Africa's membership of the Commonwealth was terminated. C R Swart was elected as the first State President. South Africa had entered a new era.

Black resistance was inevitable. The banning of the ANC and PAC meant that blacks now had no lawful organizations to serve as their mouthpiece. Local cells were formed and decision-making was centralized as far as possible. Nelson Mandela assumed the leadership of the underground ANC, while his Johannesburg attorney friend and former colleague, Oliver Tambo, was sent abroad to establish a branch of the organization in exile. PAC leaders who had given themselves up to the police, were brought to trial and most of them were sentenced to imprisonment for periods ranging from one to three years. Upon their release, many of them decided to leave South Africa.

The first reaction of the black leaders after the state of emergency was lifted in August 1960 was to reunite their radical forces. Nelson Mandela planned a three-day strike to coincide with the South African decision to leave the British Commonwealth and the acceptance of republican status. Ten days before the strike all public meetings were prohibited and many blacks were detained. Military and citizen force units were called up and the air force was used as a means of control.

Mandela reacted vehemently to the failure of

'Outward bound', a cartoon in *The Argus* on 31 May 1961, when South Africa became a republic outside the Commonwealth. (*The Argus*)

the planned strike. It was felt by the black leaders that if peaceful protests like these were to be put down by mobilization of the army and the police, then the people might be forced to use other methods of struggle. During the month of June the ANC and the banned Communist Party, under the leadership of the advocate Bram Fisher, decided to initiate a campaign of violence. This campaign was to commence on 16 December 1961.

The acts of sabotage which were committed during this campaign were the work of *Umkonto We Sizwe* (Spear of the Nation), a new organization controlled by the ANC and the Communist Party. It was hoped that the sabotage campaign would be sufficient to force the government to rethink South Africa's political future. The main targets were petrol dumps, power lines, government buildings, railway lines and communications.

In the meantime the PAC also remained active. During the second half of 1961 members of the PAC established a new sister organization, *Poqo*, meaning 'pure'. It was apparent that this organization had not received recognition from the top echelons and that it had been established by individual members, particularly those who

had recently served out their terms of imprisonment. Strictly speaking, therefore, *Poqo* was not an underground branch of the PAC, although the nucleus of its supporters were PAC members. The organization had seventeen regional branches and a large number of local branches and cells. While *Umkonto We Sizwe* was a sabotage body, *Poqo* was a terrorist group. *Poqo*'s objectives were to disrupt the country in the industrial sphere and cripple the government.

The planned uprisings never took place, however, because of the effectiveness of the government's measures to combat violence and unrest, and acts of sabotage and terrorism. Nevertheless, various acts of violence did take place for which *Poqo* claimed responsibility.

It was apparent to black and Coloured people by 1961 that the new Republic had given them little cause for rejoicing. They had played no part in its establishment. White African nationalism had been satisfied; black and Coloured African nationalism was left unsatisfied. In the years after 1961 white South Africans would have to take this discontent fully into account.

Suggested Reading List

T D Dunbar Moodie (1975) *The Rise of Afrikanerdom. Power, Apartheid, and the Afrikaner Civil Religion*, Los Angeles

T Lodge (1983) *Black Politics in Southern Africa since 1945*, London

N J Rhoodie and H J Venter (1959) *Apartheid. A Sociohistorical Exposition of the Origin and Development of the Apartheid Idea*, Cape Town

L Thompson and A Prior (1982) *South African Politics*, Yale University

D Worrall (ed) (1975) *South Africa: Government and Politics*, Pretoria

N G S van der Walt (1969) *Die Republikeinse Strewe. Dryfvere en Probleme binne die Suid-Afrikaanse Partypolitiek, 1902-1961*, Potchefstroom

F A van Jaarsveld (1979) *Die Evolusie van Apartheid en Ander Geskiedkundige Opstelle*, Cape Town

F A van Jaarsveld and G D Scholtz (eds) (1966) *Die Republiek van Suid-Afrika. Agtergrond, Ontstaan en Toekoms*, Johannesburg

H F Verwoerd leaving Lancaster House following his decision to withdraw South Africa's membership of the Commonwealth. (INCH)

Johannesburg in 1967. (*Die Burger*)

Part VII

The Republic of South Africa, 1961-1984: Resistance, Challenge and Change

The republican constitution of 1961, which basically replicated the Westminster form of government of the Union, was to last for 22 years. An outflow of capital and the inauguration of a new phase of international isolation were immediate repercussions of South Africa's departure from the Commonwealth, yet economic well-being soon returned. The government continued to command powerful support from the white electorate and pressed ahead with the implementation of its apartheid blueprint. The forces of black resistance were suppressed, driven underground or out of the country.

Governmental pragmatism and appeals for external détente became muted by the mid-1970s as the Republic entered a critical era. The emergence of independent black Marxist states in the sub-continent was followed by the involvement of South African armed forces in military operations and raids beyond the Republic's borders. Internally an escalation in the forced removals of black people from certain areas led to confrontations, and violent racial unrest flared.

A new administration approved a better deal for urban black workers and the abolition of certain discriminatory measures. Influx control, separate group living areas and educational systems were not jettisoned, but the government's new stance and expressed commitment to dismantle apartheid lost it some support from the right. Beyond the borders, a measure of accord was reached, but the external threat was by no means dispelled.

The mining, agricultural and industrial sectors of the economy experienced a boom at the end of the 1970s but by 1984, beset by drought, political uncertainty, disinvestment, a declining gold price and a weakening rand, the country was in the throes of a recession.

The dispensation of 1983 was the most drastic constitutional change since 1910, but it offered nothing to black people. The overriding challenge facing the Republic of South Africa in 1984, in the face of mounting international pressure, remained the need to evolve a system to satisfy the aspirations of the majority of its people.

Soweto in 1975. (*Die Burger*)

Chapter 19

South Africa and Africa, 1961-1984

H J van Aswegen

After the Second World War the wave of African nationalism began to sweep with irresistible force over the continent of Africa. Those European powers with major vested interests in Africa were hastily compelled to adapt their colonial policies to the increasing demands for independence. By 1961 the decolonization process was already in full swing. One African colony after the other shook off the shackles of colonialism and took its place as an independent state in the international community.

The establishment of an African policy

In South Africa the establishment of a republic in 1961 brought about few drastic changes in the internal political situation; nor was South Africa's attitude towards Africa immediately affected by the altered status. However, events in Africa in the years following 1961 were to force the South African Government to reconsider its position on the continent and reassess its relations with the various independent states.

For many years Africa had played an extremely limited role in South Africa's foreign policy. Contact with Africa was maintained primarily through colonial powers such as Britain and France. After the accession to power of the National Party in 1948 the consolidation of power in South Africa was its first priority. It was only during the administration of Prime Minister J G Strijdom (1954-1958), assisted by Eric Louw as Minister of Foreign Affairs, that the first foundations of an African policy were tentatively laid.

The results of this African policy were minimal. The Union of South Africa, as a white African state, remained outside the growing circle of independent African states, from within which criticism of South Africa's apartheid policy became increasingly vehement. South Africa and the other colonial powers, Portugal in particular, were reviled as racists, imperialists and colonialists.

The first cautious attempts on the part of South Africa to achieve closer liaison with independent Africa were made by Dr H F Verwoerd during his term as Prime Minister (1958-1966). These assurances of friendship made little impression, however, the most serious obstacle in the way of normal relations being South Africa's internal policies. To an increasing extent independent African states used their membership of, and influence in, international organizations such as the United Nations Organization to swing world opinion against South Africa.

South Africa's international isolation was taken a step further in 1961 when Verwoerd, under pressure from the Afro-Asian member countries, decided to terminate South Africa's membership of the Commonwealth. South Africa thereby severed formal contact with various African states and influential Commonwealth countries and organizations through which it would have been able to play a role in Africa. After Sharpeville several African states severed their trade ties with South Africa and in 1962 South Africa was expelled from the Commission for Technical Co-operation in Africa

Henning van Aswegen is professor and head of the Department of History at the Rand Afrikaans University. He obtained his MA in History at Stellenbosch University. The thesis for his doctorate at the University of the Orange Free State dealt with "The Relationship between the Whites and Blacks in the Orange Free State, 1854-1902". He is the author of *Die Geskiedenis van Afrika* (Cape Town, 1980) and (with G Verhoef) *Die Geskiedenis van Mosambiek* (Durban, 1982).

H F Verwoerd and Dag Hammarskjöld, Secretary-General of the United Nations Organization. (*Die Burger*)

Eric Louw (Institute for the Study of Contemporary History (INCH))

South of the Sahara. In Africa only Portugal, perilously clinging under mounting world pressure to its African colonies, retained ties of friendship with South Africa.

Pressure from Africa began to assume new proportions in 1963 when the Organization for African Unity (OAU) was established. During the founding conference of the OAU in Addis Ababa the organization expressed itself vehemently opposed to apartheid and race discrimination in South Africa.

During the Verwoerd era South Africa did not establish any formal diplomatic ties with African states. In 1962 Sir Abubakar Tafawa Balewa, Prime Minister of Nigeria, and in 1964 Kenneth Kaunda, the President of Zambia, publicly declared themselves prepared to establish diplomatic ties with South Africa. In both cases these approaches were coldly rebuffed. These were golden opportunities for South Africa to extend a hand of friendship towards black Africa. Invitations to visit the country which South Africa issued to black leaders from time to time were mostly unsuccessful.

With the granting of independence to the three British Protectorates adjoining South Africa, Lesotho and Botswana in 1966 and Swaziland in 1968, South Africa immediately recognized them as fully independent states and pledged to maintain good neighbourly relations. In September 1966 Verwoerd invited the Prime Minister of Lesotho, Chief Leabua Jonathan, to Pretoria for talks. A few days later the South African premier was assassinated and because no complete statement on the talks was issued, the content of the discussions was never fully known. It was nevertheless apparent that Verwoerd and Jonathan laid a foundation for co-operation on the basis of the recognition of the independence and sovereignty of the states, nonintervention in one another's domestic affairs, and peaceful co-existence. Jonathan, however, made no secret of his aversion to apartheid and committed himself to the dismantling thereof by peaceful means.

The talks did not lead to the establishment of diplomatic relations, although Lesotho fa-

voured such a development. South Africa's evasiveness in this area should be seen within the context of Verwoerd's belief in informal and *ad hoc* contact in the form of reciprocal visits by ministers and even telephonic conversations. To Lesotho this was unacceptable, particularly in view of South Africa's establishment of diplomatic ties with Malawi the following year, a move which aroused suspicions regarding South Africa's real intentions.

Other events in southern Africa during the period also had a determining effect on the relations between Africa and South Africa. The first was the unilateral declaration of independence (UDI) by Rhodesia on 11 November 1965. The rejection of British authority by the white minority government of this British colony unleashed strong emotions in black Africa and elsewhere. In South Africa this step was in general received with acclaim and seen as the strengthening of white authority on a continent where whites were rapidly being supplanted.

Dialogue and détente, 1966-1978

In the years following 1966 South Africa's African policy was developed further by Prime Minister B J Vorster, assisted by Hilgard Muller (Minister of Foreign Affairs), Brand Fourie (Secretary for Foreign Affairs) and others. South Africa's outward moving diplomacy and dialogue with various independent African states laid the foundation for a phase of détente politics between South Africa and Africa, and even between South Africa and its Western allies.

One of the main factors which contributed to this dynamic African policy was the increasing international pressure and consequent isolation of South Africa. By 1966 forty African states were already independent and as an influential pressure group acting through the OAU and in the UN they could not be ignored. Cries for South Africa's suspension from the UN and other international bodies on the grounds of the policy of apartheid, which was condemned as a

Mozambique recruits undergoing basic training in the forests of the interior. (*Die Burger*)

'crime against humanity', grew more strident by the day. South Africa became increasingly dependent on the suppport of the USA, Britain and France in the Security Council of the UN and came to the realization that sound relations with Africa had become a condition for acceptance in the international world. In 1968 Muller clearly spelled it out when he said, 'We must simply accept that our relations with the rest of the world are largely dependent on our relations with the African states.'

Closely associated with this realization was the growing consciousness that South Africa had a specific responsibility towards independent Africa. South Africa was in a pre-eminently favourable economic, technological and geographical position to be of assistance to Africa. South Africa could also benefit considerably from its contacts with Africa. New markets could be created for South African commodities, markets which could bring substantial profits to the rapidly developing South African economy. Friendship with Africa in the form of normalized relations and stability would also encourage foreign investment at home.

During the course of the 1960s South Africa also became far more keenly aware of the military-strategic implications of hostile neighbouring states. The calls from the OAU to eliminate 'racism' in South Africa by military force and the beginning of guerrilla warfare in Angola and Mozambique, made the possibility of hostile attack on the Republic from the north a real danger. The danger became even greater in the light of increasing Chinese and Russian activities in Africa. Communist countries supported the liberation movements in Africa and supplied arms to these organizations on an increasing scale. It was realized that good relations with Africa, economic aid, political stability, peace and tranquillity were the best counter-measures to Communist penetration.

The OAU did not succeed in creating unity or unanimity among the African states and fundamental differences between the more radical states (which were mostly under Communist influence) and those with more moderate leanings were soon apparent. South Africa concentrated its focus on the latter group. Initially Lesotho and Malawi received the greatest attention.

In January 1967 Vorster received the Prime Minister of Lesotho, Chief Leabua Jonathan, on an official state visit to South Africa. Matters of mutual importance were discussed, but no formal diplomatic ties were established. Verwoerd had already made contact with Dr Hastings Banda of Malawi through diplomatic channels. In 1964 in the OAU Banda had come out in favour of relations with South Africa. As a pragmatist, he realized that sound trade relations with South Africa were mutually beneficial and that the thousands of Malawian mineworkers in the Republic earned essential foreign exchange for his state.

In 1967 South Africa and Malawi established formal diplomatic ties. This was followed by official visits to Malawi by the Minister of Foreign Affairs, Muller, in 1968 and by Prime Minister Vorster in May 1970. At a state banquet on the latter occasion Banda thanked South Africa for its technical and economic aid, particularly in respect of the construction of Lilongwe, the new capital of Malawi. During Banda's visit to South Africa in August 1971, he was received with full honours and was greeted with acclaim and enthusiasm wherever he went.

South Africa's African diplomacy was not confined to Lesotho and Malawi, however. As early as 1968 Muller announced that South Africa had built up regular contact with several African states and that an average of three delegates from African states per month had visited South Africa during the previous year. Many of these representatives stopped over in this country en route to other destinations and a form of 'airport diplomacy' was developing where inconspicuous meetings and talks were held at airports.

Despite these positive developments the general African attitude during the years of dialogue remained predominantly hostile. Malawi was vehemently criticized at the OAU for its South African ties, particularly by Zambia, and there were calls for Malawi's expulsion from this body. A number of African states, including several former French colonies, were more sympathetically disposed towards Malawi. Africa was divided into two camps over dialogue with South Africa.

During these years the OAU experienced further frustration. Its campaign to bring about the international isolation of South Africa failed, primarily because the major Western powers, the USA, France and Britain, did not allow themselves to be bound by Afro-Asian-inspired UN resolutions on sanctions against South Africa.

An event of cardinal importance in Africa's attitude to South Africa was the acceptance of the Lusaka Manifesto in regard to Southern Africa on 16 April 1969 by fourteen heads of

Black Rhodesians read the news of Rhodesia's Unilateral Declaration of Independence at a news stand in Salisbury on 12 November 1965. The headline reads 'UDI — Rhodesia Goes It Alone'. (*Die Burger*)

B J Vorster and President Banda of Malawi during the South African Prime Minister's visit to Malawi in 1970. (Central Archives)

295

▽
President Julius Nyerere of Tanzania. (INCH)

▷▽
President Kenneth Kaunda of Zambia. (*Die Burger*)

▷▷▽
President Félix Houphouet-Boigny of the Ivory Coast. (INCH)

state from East and Central Africa, under the direction of Presidents Julius Nyerere and Kenneth Kaunda. In the 24-point manifesto the heads of state unequivocally stated their standpoint in respect of the white colonial governments in this region. South Africa was specifically mentioned in certain articles (see box).

Vorster continued his efforts to expand sound relations with South Africa's neighbouring states through contact with African states further north. A few moderate leaders such as President Félix Houphouet-Boigny of the Ivory Coast advocated a more realistic approach to South Africa. In this attitude President Houphouet-Boigny was supported by several other states. From other quarters Houphouet-Boigny was heavily criticized and during the OAU summit conference in 1971 the so-called 'Declaration in respect of Dialogue' was accepted, in terms of which dialogue with South Africa was rejected. By 1971, therefore, it was clear that South Africa's policy of dialogue had achieved limited success. Of the few states which reacted positively to it, most were not prepared to make open contact with the Republic particularly not by means of the establishment of formal diplomatic relations.

South Africa became more closely involved in developments in Rhodesia after UDI. The economic support which South Africa and Portugal gave to Rhodesia helped that state to survive the world pressure and trade embargo which immediately followed UDI. However, it was the danger which an escalating conflict in Rhodesia presented to South Africa which led to further assistance. In August 1967 the Zimbabwe African People's Union (ZAPU) and the banned ANC concluded an agreement of co-operation with a view to an armed struggle against South Africa and Rhodesia. Vorster shortly afterwards reached an agreement with the Rhodesian Government to send members of the South African Police Force to Rhodesia to help in the struggle. South Africa's objective was manifestly to help maintain the white government in Rhodesia so that, with South West Africa and two Portuguese colonies, Angola and Mozambique, a strong buffer could be maintained to the north of South Africa against a hostile black Africa.

The unilateral declaration of independence (UDI) by Rhodesia in 1965 not only emphasized political differences but also and particularly the economic interdependence of the states and colonies of southern Africa. The closing of the border between Rhodesia and Zambia reinforced both countries' dependence on South Africa for their imports and exports. Zambia was strongly opposed to the white 'minority governments' in South Africa and Rhodesia, and Kaunda placed his territory at the disposal of organizations aiming to overthrow the regimes in South West Africa and Mozambique. Despite this ostensibly militant attitude, Kaunda was one of the more moderate leaders of black Africa and his innumerable domestic problems caused him to realize the importance of closer ties with South Africa. Commencing in 1968, he and Vorster became involved in a brief exchange of letters and this was followed by secret talks between representatives of the two countries. The talks did not lead to anything concrete, but they did create goodwill. However, Kaunda's sharp attacks on the internal policies of South Africa, his condemnation of Western arms sales to South Africa, and the presence of South African troops in the Caprivi and Rhodesia angered Vorster. In April 1971 Vorster's public revelation that Zambia, who was so critical of South Africa, had itself made secret contact with the Republic, resulted in relations between the two states becoming strained for a time.

During the years of dialogue relations between South Africa and Lesotho deteriorated considerably. In 1970 Jonathan still endorsed the idea of dialogue and offered Lesotho as a bridge between South Africa and black Africa. South Africa did not accept the offer and concentrated its diplomacy on more 'important' states such as the Ivory Coast. Excluded from the dialogue process, Lesotho's attitude towards South Africa began to harden. Jonathan's criticism of apartheid intensified and he finally pledged his full support to the liberation struggle in southern Africa.

During these years no event had greater impact on inter-state relations in southern Africa than the *coup d'état* in Portugal in April 1974. It ushered in the decolonization of the Portuguese colonial empire in Africa and by the end of 1975 Angola and Mozambique had become independent. These developments had major implications for South Africa. Not only had a friendly Western power, Portugal, been driven from Africa, but the white-controlled buffer strip on the northern borders of South Africa no longer existed and two Marxist-orientated black states had taken Portugal's place.

The South African Government rose immediately to the challenge. In an important policy statement, Vorster made it clear in the Senate on 23 October 1974 that South Africa was committed to peace, prosperity and development in southern Africa and re-emphasized that the principles of sovereignty and non-interference

'Viva Frelimo': Soldiers salute the new independent state of Mozambique. (*Die Burger*)

in the domestic affairs of other states would always be preserved. South Africa was prepared to enter into a non-aggression pact with any African state to demonstrate that it had no militant objectives in Africa.

A day later South Africa's representative at the UN, 'Pik' Botha, also made a significant speech in which he candidly discussed the policy of separate development and admitted that the South African Government had committed errors. Botha made it clear that his government did not approve of discrimination on the grounds of race or colour and that a process of change was already in progress which would have far-reaching consequences for the future.

These policy statements indicated a new phase in Vorster's African policy, namely a peace or détente policy, with the emphasis on peace, stability and co-operation in Africa. In Africa Vorster's words did not pass unnoticed, for on 26 October 1974 Kenneth Kaunda referred to these statements as 'the voice of reason for which Africa and the rest of the world had been waiting'.

Vorster proceeded to convert his détente policy into a practical course of action. In September 1974 he paid a short visit to the Ivory Coast, where he held talks with President Houphouet-Boigny and President Léopold Senghor of Senegal. On his way back he also had talks in Gabon, Botswana and Rhodesia. This was the beginning of a period of intensive contact and dialogue with African leaders which took Vorster, Muller and other South African politicians and officials to various African states. In Septem-

ber 1975 the Minister of Information of the Ivory Coast, L Dona-Fologa, visited South Africa.

Following Mozambican independence on 25 June 1975, Vorster extended the hand of friendship to that country. The initial response was vague but not discouraging. President Samora Machel was a confirmed Marxist and openly supported the revolutionary struggle in southern Africa. Its hard-won freedom after years of bitter struggle would not readily make the state well-disposed to the white South African Government.

For a while Vorster's détente efforts aroused great expectations in South Africa, but among the ranks of the African countries themselves there were deep-seated dissensions and differences. This was clearly apparent during the OAU ministers' meeting in Dar es Salaam in April 1975. Zambia and the Ivory Coast came under heavy criticism by the more radical states for their co-operation with South Africa. The meeting ended with the Dar es Salaam Declaration in which South Africa was once again condemned by all the parties involved for its apartheid policy.

This declaration, accepted by the OAU summit conference in July 1975, together with the Lusaka Manifesto, formed the nucleus of the policy of Africa towards South Africa. In general, with the exception of a few states who were prepared to liaise openly with the Republic, and a few who did so in secret, no reconciliation between Africa and South Africa was possible.

An aggravating factor which contributed

Robert Mugabe (*Die Burger*)

South African troops attacking a SWAPO base inside Angola. (*Die Burger*)

greatly to Africa's opposition to South Africa was the latter's military intervention in Angola in 1975 and 1976. The civil war in Angola, with Cuban support for the pro-Marxist MPLA, constituted a threat to South Africa, Zambia and Zaïre and at the request of the latter two states, and with the initial co-operation of the USA, a South African military force invaded Angola in 1975. A few months later, after several military successes, the force was withdrawn. The invasion had world-wide repercussions. During a special OAU summit conference in Addis Ababa in January 1976 African leaders expressed their deep concern at the violation of Angolan sovereignty and territorial integrity by South Africa. The more radical African states condemned South Africa in acrimonious terms. At the insistence of Kenya the Security Council of the UN met in March 1976 and passed a resolution condemning the South African action.

The riots in Soweto and other black urban residential areas in 1976 further stirred up feelings against South Africa in Africa. The OAU condemned South Africa's suppression of the resistance in the strongest terms and made renewed attacks on the trade ties which the principal Western powers maintained with South Africa. There was world-wide support for the standpoint of the OAU and in November 1977 the Security Council of the UN passed a compulsory arms embargo against South Africa to counteract its oppression of the black population and military aggression against its neighbouring states. International pressure and isolation were steadily mounting.

During the years of détente South Africa's attention was so keenly concentrated on the Rhodesian issue and liaison with certain important African states that relations with its immediate neighbouring states, Botswana, Lesotho and Swaziland, were shifted to the background.

Swaziland, aware of its economic dependence on South Africa, continued to maintain sound relations with its more powerful neighbour and expressed itself clearly opposed to harbouring ANC armed groups, although King Sobhuza II and his government were critical of the internal policies of South Africa.

Botswana was more outspokenly critical of South Africa. As one of the five front-line states, Botswana played an important role in southern Africa and its President, Sir Seretse Khama, was not prepared to co-operate with South Africa merely for the sake of his own advantage. Khama criticized South Africa sharply for its 'oppression' of black people and kept Botswana's doors open to fugitives from South Africa whom he regarded as the 'victims of racism and oppression'. Botswana also promised continued support for SWAPO and criticized South Africa for its military actions across the Angolan and Zambian borders. In 1977 Botswana established diplomatic ties with Cuba.

Relations between South Africa and Lesotho deteriorated considerably during the years of dialogue and détente. After long delays, Vorster and Jonathan met in 1974 to discuss areas of friction between the two states. The discussions did not lead to improved relations and in the years which followed Lesotho expressed open opposition to contact with South Africa.

With the granting of independent status to the Transkei in 1976, several border incidents added to the tension. The following year Lesotho delivered a blistering attack on South Africa and proclaimed that violence was the only solution to the situation in the Republic. Jonathan also revived Lesotho's claim to the so-called 'conquered territory' – a large portion of the eastern Free State. South Africa categorically rejected the claim.

The 'total onslaught' and comprehensive strategies

In the main Vorster's policy of détente was a failure. In addition the Information Scandal towards the end of Vorster's period of office contributed even further to South Africa's already tarnished image abroad. The new Prime Minister, P W Botha, acceded to office in 1978 under difficult circumstances. Supported by the Minister of Foreign Affairs, 'Pik' Botha, and Brand Fourie, Secretary for Foreign Affairs, South Africa's P W Botha took stock of South Africa's position in Africa with a greater measure of realism and pragmatism than his predecessors, and developed his policy accordingly.

Following his advent to power several factors had a determining effect on South Africa's African policy. One of the most important of these was Zimbabwe's independence in 1980. Robert Mugabe, the new Prime Minister, was outspokenly anti-South African and South Africa

A group of South African soldiers seated on crates of ammunition and weapons captured from SWAPO troops. (*Die Burger*)

found itself the only white-controlled state in Africa, bounded on its northern side by several states with Marxist ideologies.

Mugabe's victory also proved to Africa that it was winning the struggle against imperialism, colonialism and racism. The emphasis in the struggle now shifted to South West Africa/Namibia and South Africa. Pressure on the Western countries to impose sanctions on South Africa increased, while Africa openly supported the black resistance movements, the ANC and PAC. This support took the form of provision of arms, bases, training facilities, and free right of passage through most of the neighbouring states of South Africa.

The threat to South Africa was intensified by the increasing aid which its enemies were receiving from the Eastern bloc countries. A formidable Cuban military force was already stationed in Angola while Cuban, East German, Russian and other military and civil personnel were active in Mozambique, Tanzania, Zambia and Zimbabwe.

While the military threat intensified, South Africa received only limited and conditional support from its traditional Western allies. During the Carter administration in the USA relations between the two countries deteriorated considerably. Although the Reagan administration, with its policy of constructive engagement, was more conciliatory, the pressure on South Africa to effect internal reforms and to arrive at a settlement in SWA/Namibia did not abate.

Under pressure from these realities P W Botha began to evolve his African policy. To emphasize that his good intentions were sincere he reconfirmed South Africa's willingness to conclude non-aggression pacts with its neighbouring states. No African state reacted to this offer.

An important condition which Botha proposed for peaceful co-existence was that the neighbouring states should not harbour what South Africa regarded as terrorist organizations, for example the ANC and the PAC. South

Africa repeatedly exhorted its neighbours to refrain from supporting these organizations, warning that the Republic would not hesitate to launch cross-border strikes against them.

A central aspect of Botha's policy was his conviction that the 'total onslaught' on South Africa was orchestrated by the Communists to paralyze the Republic in all spheres and prepare it for a black takeover. In order to counteract this threat the South African Defence Force was allocated a more important part in South Africa's foreign affairs. A further important aspect of the Botha government's African policy was the emphasis on greater regional economic co-operation among the various states of southern Africa.

Deteriorating relations between South Africa and Lesotho as a result of border violations, the theft of livestock, Chief Jonathan's claims to the 'conquered territory' and his establishment of diplomatic relations with the USSR (1980) and China (1983) led to an extremely tense situation. In 1980 P W Botha and Jonathan held talks, concentrating on economic co-operation between the two states. Over the next few years, however, the border situation worsened. In 1983 Pik Botha and E K Sekhonyana, Lesotho's Minister of Foreign Affairs, held talks on subversive activities in their respective countries. An agreement was reached whereby both countries would refuse sanctuary in their territories to any group or organization which planned subversive activities against the other.

South Africa also conducted negotiations with Swaziland on the question of the extension of Swaziland's territory to incorporate the area of Kangwane. They reached agreement in June 1982, but the vehement reaction of KwaZulu and Kangwane to the proposed loss of territory delayed implementation of the agreement.

The low-key diplomacy conducted between South Africa and Mozambique during the 1980's was rewarded when it was decided to appoint four working groups for each country in an effort to normalize relations on the following

---

South Africa and Rhodesia, 1974-1975

One of Vorster's principal objectives was to help find an acceptable and peaceful solution to the Rhodesian conflict. The bush war in Rhodesia had increased in intensity and Africa was strongly opposed to Ian Smith's 'illegal' government. South Africa found itself in a dilemma: in helping to keep the Smith regime in power, the Republic forfeited credibility in the eyes of African leaders. The escalating conflict also constituted a danger to South Africa. Vorster was compelled to reconsider South Africa's support of Rhodesia and certain African leaders, including Kaunda, regarded him as the one influential statesman who could cause Smith to change his views.

Vorster approached the peace initiative in two ways. Firstly he withdrew the South African police force from Rhodesia and secondly he tried to persuade Smith to negotiate with the nationalist leaders. He made it clear, however, that he would not compel Smith to accept black majority rule. His efforts were supported by Zambia, Tanzania, Mozambique and Botswana, the so-called front-line states, who were to invite the black leaders to the conference table. Between September 1974 and August 1975 intensive negotiations were conducted, which culminated in the 'bridge conference' when Ian Smith and a number of black leaders met on 25 August 1975 in a South African railway coach on the bridge across the Zambezi near the Victoria Falls. During the conference Vorster and Kaunda did their utmost to make the talks succeed.

In spite of their efforts the talks failed. Vorster did not consider the failure to be final. When the USA launched new peace initiatives through Henry Kissinger, the US Foreign Secretary, Vorster played an important part in persuading Smith to accept the Kissinger proposals, which in effect amounted to black majority rule. These initiatives also failed, however, and in 1977 and 1978 Vorster continued to play the role of intermediary in the search for a solution which would satisfy all parties. Circumstances beyond his control caused these efforts to founder.

levels through negotiation: economic matters, the security situation, tourism and the Cahora Bassa scheme.

Hostile attacks on SWA/Namibia by SWAPO, operating from Angola and Zambia, and by the ANC and PAC, were on the increase and were resisted by South Africa at every level. In SWA/Namibia the South African Defence Force, supported by the local territorial force, launched major attacks on SWAPO bases in Angola in 1978, 1980, 1982 and 1984. Evidence gathered during the attacks pointed indisputably to Russian support for SWAPO.

South Africa also took military action against ANC groups in other neighbouring states, including Mozambique and Lesotho. In January 1981 and again in May 1983, in retaliation to an ANC bomb blast in the centre of Pretoria, the SADF attacked ANC bases in a series of limited operations. In 1982 ANC bases in Maseru were destroyed after terrorist attacks in Bloemfontein. South Africa let it be known that it would counter similar acts of terror with force of arms.

The ANC and SWAPO attacks and South Africa's counter-actions caused a heightening of tension in southern Africa. While South Africa strongly defended its territorial integrity, simultaneously expressing the wish to live in peace with its neighbours, neighbouring states, with the exception of Malawi and Swaziland, sided with the ANC. To an increasing extent criticism levelled at South Africa's cross-border attacks accused the Republic of deliberately destabilizing southern Africa, politically and economically. South Africa was also accused of supporting certain resistance groups against the legal governments in the neighbouring states. These included Renamo in Mozambique, which operated against Machel and controlled parts of the country, the Lesotho Liberation Army (the military wing of the Basutoland Congress Party), which made various attacks on the Jonathan regime, and UNITA, under Jonas Savimbi, which 'liberated' large parts of Angola from the MPLA regime.

By the end of 1983 South Africa found itself caught between two opposing currents in its African policy. On the one hand a start had been made with the highly sensitive negotiations with African states, particularly with Angola and Mozambique. On the other hand it was deemed necessary to strike out with its powerful military fist at those who threatened it. Accusations of destabilization were hurled back and forth. Beneath the surface of these harsh words a growing realism was already discernible, brought about by the glaring realities of weakening economies, namely that interdependence and co-operation were more essential than, and preferable to, war.

Interdependence in South Africa: regional economic co-operation

Despite the obstacles of political and ideological differences South Africa has traditional economic ties with the states in southern Africa. The dependence of these states on the Republic for their imports is apparent from the fact that Botswana and Swaziland obtain 90 per cent and Lesotho 95 per cent of their total imports from South Africa. In addition a significant percentage of the exports of the states of southern Africa are obsorbed by the Republic.

Ever since the discovery of diamonds and gold, South Africa has been a major provider of employment to black workers from its northern neighbouring states. Although the number of workers from southern Africa has diminished since the late 1970s – primarily as a result of political pressure – South Africa employed approximately 302 000 of such black workers in 1981, 150 422 from Lesotho, 59 391 from Mozambique, 30 602 from Malawi, 29 169 from Botswana and 16 965 from Zimbabwe. The money earned by these workers is an important source of revenue for these states.

South Africa's well-developed transport system also plays a major role in the southern

The Turnhalle delegation at the Union Buildings. Dirk Mudge is seated at the head of the table. (Central Archives)

African region. Several states in this region do not have harbours of their own and the existing rail transportation systems are generally fairly limited. The result is that the black states of southern Africa have to choose between making use of expensive road transportation for their imports and exports, using the Tanzam railway line to Dar es Salaam, or, for the most part, using the South African transport system and harbours. Almost half or more of the imports from all the states (Malawi 60 per cent, Zimbabwe 70 per cent, Botswana and Lesotho 100 per cent) are handled by South Africa. These countries are to a large extent dependent on South Africa's railways and harbours.

Interdependence is discernible in various other spheres. South Africa receives a significant quantity of its power from Cahora Bassa in Mozambique, and this in turn provides Mozambique with essential foreign exchange. Lesotho has water, one of the most important natural resources, and once the Highlands Water Scheme has been completed, South Africa will be able to purchase water for the Pretoria-Witwatersrand-Vereeniging (PWV) area from this neighbouring state.

In spite of economic interdependence few efforts were made in the past to try to co-ordinate regional co-operation in a comprehensive way, though a customs agreement has existed between South Africa and Botswana, Lesotho and Swaziland since 1910 (revised in 1969), while labour and other relations are controlled by various agreements with the individual countries.

In 1979 P W Botha took the initiative of placing economic co-operation in southern Africa on a firm foundation when he proposed the idea of a Constellation of Southern African States (CONSAS). This idea was spelt out and discussed with leading businessmen of the Republic during a conference in Johannesburg on 22 November 1979.

Botha was of the opinion that all states in southern Africa should be members of CONSAS, but at the first summit conference of heads of government in July 1980 it was clear that only the independent national states and the self-governing national states showed any interest in it. Consequently the concept of a constellation was changed to that of a confederation, ie a smaller grouping of states. Since 1980 several meetings have been held and one of the more important consequences of CONSAS has been the establishment of a Development Bank of Southern Africa, which commenced its activities on 1 September 1983.

South Africa's other black neighbours saw CONSAS as a major threat, and some leaders regarded it as an attempt on the part of the Republic to build up a neo-colonial empire. In May 1979 the idea of an opposing organization was raised and in July of that year a Southern African Development Co-ordination Conference (SADCC) was held in Tanzania. On 1

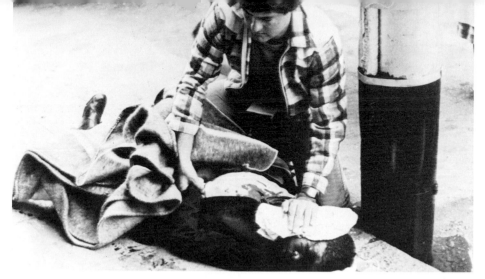

April 1980 the SADCC issued a statement in Lusaka in which nine African states (Angola, Botswana, Lesotho, Malawi, Mozambique, Swaziland, Tanzania, Zambia and Zimbabwe) clearly set out their objective: mutual economic co-operation to the benefit of everyone, with the aim of terminating economic dependence upon South Africa. The aim was not to seek confrontation with South Africa, but gradually to cut themselves loose from the Republic.

A wounded black receives first aid after the bomb blast in Church Street, Pretoria, in May 1983. (*Die Burger*)

Dramatic breakthroughs in 1984

By the end of 1983 it seemed as though the tension between South Africa and certain of its neighbouring states was mounting rapidly. Behind the scenes, however, intensive negotiations on a high level were being conducted and early in 1984 it was already clear that the leaders of southern Africa preferred peace and co-operation to war with its catastrophic consequences.

In December 1983 South Africa announced that it was prepared to maintain a month-long cease-fire in Angola, commencing on 31 January 1984, provided Angola did the same. Angola and SWAPO were initially hesitant, but negotiations continued. In February 1984 the

Damage after the ANC bomb blast in Church Street, Pretoria, in May 1983. (*Die Burger*)

President P W Botha and President Samora Machel inspect the Mozambican troops during the ceremony prior to the signing of the Nkomati Accord on 16 March 1984. (*Die Burger*)

The Accord of Nkomati, 16 March 1984 (extracts)

Preamble: Agreement on non-aggression and good neighbourliness between the governments of Mozambique and the RSA.

Article 1. Agreement to respect each other's sovereignty and independence and to refrain from interfering in the internal affairs of the other.

Article 2. Differences and disputes to be resolved by means of negotiation, enquiry, mediation, conciliation, arbitration or other peaceful means. No force or threat of force to be used against each other.

Article 3. The two states shall not allow their respective territories to be used as a base or thoroughfare by anyone planning to commit acts of violence against the other.

Article 4. The international boundary between the RSA and Mozambique shall be effectively patrolled.

Article 5. Propaganda that incites war or aggression shall be prohibited.

Article 6. There is no conflict between this treaty and other international treaties and obligations of the two states.

Article 7. The agreement shall be interpreted in good faith and periodic contact shall be maintained to ensure the effective application of what has been agreed.

Article 8. The agreement shall not detract from the state's right of self-defence in the event of armed attacks.

Article 9. A Joint Security Commission consisting of high-ranking representatives from each state shall supervise the application of this agreement.

parties concerned met in Lusaka, and the Lusaka Agreement was signed. This agreement provided for a cease-fire, commencing on 1 March 1984, and the gradual disengagement of South African troops from the south of Angola, and a joint South African-Angolan Monitoring Commission to maintain supervision over the implementation of the provisions of the agreement.

In the meantime negotiations between South Africa and Mozambique continued, and in March 1984 it was announced that P W Botha and Samora Machel would sign a peace treaty at Nkomati, on the border between South Africa and Mozambique. On 16 March the Accord of Nkomati was signed by the two leaders. In eleven articles the two countries bound themselves to peaceful co-existence (see box).

The Accord of Nkomati, in spite of reservations as to its real binding force, led to a de-

'Pik' Botha, South African Minister of Foreign Affairs, with a copy of the Nkomati Accord. (*Die Burger*)

crease in tension in southern Africa. Talks between South Africa and Swaziland, as well as Angola, Lesotho and Zambia, to stabilize peace and co-operation were held during the months following 16 March. In Mozambique and in Swaziland the activities of the ANC were substantially curtailed, while South Africa terminated its support for Renamo.

Africa reacted cautiously but positively to these events. President Kenneth Kaunda of Zambia had already begun to pave the way for a summit conference between South Africa and the front-line states. Zambia was prepared to act as host. Kaunda also succeeded in bringing together representatives from SWAPO and the Multi-Party Conference of SWA/Namibia, for talks in Lusaka in May 1984. Although no final solution on the independence of the territory was achieved, a foundation was laid for further negotiations.

An event of cardinal importance was the conference of the front-line states on 29 April 1984 in Arusha, Tanzania. The conference was dominated by Mozambique and President Machel clearly spelt out the realities of conflict as Mozambique had experienced them – an enormous financial loss, famine, disruption and resistance. Statements made during the conference, and the Arusha Declaration issued at its conclusion, indicated a new spirit of *realpolitik* in Africa. The front-line states continued to level criticism at the South Africa's policy of apartheid, however, but the importance of the conference also lay in the act that the front-line states gave their full support to the Accord of Nkomati with Mozambique and to the cease-fire agreement with Angola – a clear commitment to the peaceful solution of the problems of southern Africa. Since the Arusha Agreement, the honouring of terms of the Nkomati Agreement has been critized. Mozambique has repeatedly accused South Africa of not adhering to the agreement and continuing to supply arms to Renamo. Attempts by South Africa to persuade Renamo to negotiate with the Machel government have been unsuccessful. The differences have so far been settled by negotiation, but it is clear that relations between the various southern African states remain tense.

Suggested Reading List

J Barber (1973) *South Africa's Foreign Policy, 1945-1970*, Cape Town

G M Carter and P O'Meara (eds) (1977) *Southern Africa. The Continuing Crisis*, Bloomington

G M Cockram (1970) *Vorster's Foreign Policy*, Cape Town

D Geldenhuys (1984) *The Diplomacy of Isolation: South African Foreign Policy Making*, Johannesburg

A A Mazrui (1977) *Africa's International Relations. The Diplomacy of Dependency and Change*, London

G C Olivier (1977) *Suid-Afrika se Buitelandse Beleid*, Pretoria

Chapter 20

From Referendum to Referendum, 1961-1984

T R H Davenport

Verwoerd's republic, 1961-1966

On 31 May 1961 the Union of South Africa became a republic outside the Commonwealth. The constitution of the Republic of South Africa bore almost no resemblance to any of the other republican constitutions of South Africa's past, and was, in all its main features, a simple reproduction of the Westminster-style South Africa Act of 1909.

Verwoerd's republic, 1961-1966

The manner of the constitutional change had troubled a number of voters, as could be seen by the closeness of the referendum result. There was concern over the exclusion of the Coloured electorate, the inclusion of white South West Africans, and the vagueness of the question asked in the referendum. There were some who felt that if a national convention had been necessary to create the Union of South Africa, then another should have been called to preside over its dissolution.

The Prime Minister, Dr H F Verwoerd, was able to build up a surprising mood of confidence among Afrikaans- and English-speaking whites in South Africa, and – most significantly – among potential friends abroad who were prepared to invest in the country's future even under the shadow of the unrest of 1960. An initial outflow of capital was followed, in the mid-1960s, by a massive growth of investment, both local and foreign, in the country's enterprises, although controls over the export of capital had much to do with this. Economic recovery was accompanied by significant immigration from Europe – a new venture for a Nationalist government which had tended in the past to manifest considerable Uitlander-phobia.

There were also many disconcerting signs which accompanied the birth of the Republic. South Africa's isolation on the continent of Africa was one of these, though here the continued presence of Portuguese regimes in Angola and Mozambique provided a welcome firebreak, while the decision of Ian Smith's government in Rhodesia to declare its independence in 1965 provided evidence of at least one other

Rodney Davenport has held the positions of professor and head of the Department of History at Rhodes University, Grahamstown, since 1965. He has been an honorary visiting fellow at the Universities of Rochester, Sussex, Cambridge, Yale, the Australian National University and University College, Dublin. His major publications include *The Afrikaner Bond, 1880-1900* (Cape Town, 1966), *South Africa. A Modern History* (Johannesburg, new edition 1986) and (with K S Hunt) *The Right to the Land* (Cape Town, 1974).

The first republican Cabinet of 1961 (Cabinet Ministers and Deputy Ministers). Front row (left to right): B J Schoeman, F C Erasmus, E H Louw, H F Verwoerd, C R Swart, P O Sauer, T E Dönges, J J Serfontein. Back row (left to right): B J Vorster, M C Botha, W A Maree, D C H Uys, N Diederichs, P M K le Roux, Jan de Klerk, J J Fouché, M C de Wet Nel, A Hertzog, P W Botha, Marais Viljoen. (Institute for the Study of Contemporary History (INCH))

'Don't worry about the white spots in the black spots – they're purely imaginary. But if you see any black spots in the white spots in the black spots, tell me at once.' The complexities of the homelands policy and the policy of segregation in urban areas are outlined in this cartoon by David Marais from the *Cape Times*. (*Cape Times*)

B J Vorster (Central Archives)

white regime in the sub-continent which seemed to know its own mind and have the courage of its slightly different convictions.

Less easy to calculate was the ability of the black South African opposition movements which had been banned during the 1960 troubles to reorganize as outlawed movements and continue the struggle. But even here developments seemed to favour the calculations of Verwoerd, and of his Minister of Justice, B J Vorster. An ex-OB general, Vorster had experience of paramilitary opposition to an established regime, together with a sense of the pressures of solitary confinement, and an awareness of the difficulties under which a police force had to operate in any campaign against subversion. These insights led him to place on the statute book a succession of tough laws designed both to deter subversion and to facilitate the extraction of information from any who might be thought to have it, whether they had been arrested as suspects or not. Step by step, police officers were empowered to detain suspects in solitary confinement for renewable periods of twelve days (1962), rising through ninety (1963), one hundred and eighty (1965), and for an unlimited period if authorized by a judge (1966), or even if not so authorized (1976). Convictions became easier to obtain when offences additional to high treason and the promotion of Communism – notably 'sabotage' and 'terrorism' – were given sweeping statutory definitions, reinforced by mandatory long terms of imprisonment. Authority to place individuals under house arrest by ministerial fiat, in addition to listing or banning them under the Suppression of Communism Act, was granted by statute in 1962.

Thus armed, the government was able to deal

with the unrest which followed the Sharpeville disturbances in 1960, after a section of the ANC had regrouped as *Umkonto We Sizwe* (the 'Spear of the Nation'), and Cape members of the PAC had regrouped as *Poqo* (the 'purifieds') in 1962. For ideological reasons, as in 1960, these movements failed to work together. The PAC and the Liberal Party withdrew their support from an 'all-in conference' at Pietermaritzburg in March 1961, when it appeared that the ANC was aiming to control the movement with the help of Communist Party funds. *Poqo*, which developed into a populist anti-white movement, did not hesitate to kill informers and chiefs. One of its main targets was Chief Kaiser Matanzima of the Transkei, and it was responsible for an outbreak of violence in Paarl in 1962. The better developed PAC built up a fairly efficient cell system, but police infiltration helped to neutralize its activities within South Africa by mid-1963, aided to some extent by the poor tactical sense of its leader, Potlako Leballo, in exile in Maseru.

Umkonto We Sizwe, under its leader Nelson Mandela, planned a campaign of controlled sabotage which stopped short of the taking of life, so far as Mandela could control his followers, and planned to work up towards the waging of guerrilla war should this prove necessary. It lacked sufficient resources, however, and failed to focus its activities sufficiently sharply on its objectives. When the police broke its cover and arrested the leadership at their headquarters in Rivonia, near Johannesburg, in 1963, it soon became ineffective as a resistance movement inside South Africa.

The African Resistance Movement, a largely white student organization committed to sabotage, operated mainly in Cape Town, Johannesburg and Port Elizabeth, and was broken as a result of its own security lapses in 1964. The security police skilfully infiltrated the Communist Party in the same year. The *Umkonto* leadership was sentenced to life imprisonment, as was Bram Fischer, an advocate and the leader of the Communist Party, who had returned to South Africa after being allowed out on bail to fight an important case before the Privy Council, though he knew he had to stand trial himself on his return. When it became apparent that even the ranks of the Communist Party had been infiltrated, Fischer estreated bail, underwent plastic surgery to escape detection, and attempted to continue the struggle.

Black opposition had been thrown into disarray by the banning of the ANC and the PAC, the Rivonia trial and the trial of the Communist leadership, so that during the late 1960s it was most active from bases in exile. The ANC had some success in winning support from the Russians and from the Organization of African Unity, but managed to send very few trained saboteurs back to the Republic.

By the mid-1960s, therefore, the South African state seemed to have been restored to a condition of orderly prosperity, whatever tumult remained underneath the surface. This was reflected in a 21-seat gain by the National Party in the 1966 general election – the largest since 1953 – even though the party had been in power for eighteen years.

On 6 September 1966, at the height of his triumph, Verwoerd was stabbed to death by a parliamentary messenger, Dimitrio Tsafendas, in the House of Assembly. His assassin was later declared insane, and if there was a political motivation this never became clear.

B J Vorster, 1966-1978: the political economy of Balkanization

B J Vorster was the heir elect to Verwoerd, by virtue of the strong-arm tactics he had used to put down unrest and his ability to project the granite Kruger-like image which Verwoerd himself had tried so hard to promote. Vorster would keep the policy on the road. He would appoint, as Cabinet colleagues, men who possessed the Verwoerdian compulsion for planning, regardless of its effect on the lives of human beings. Vorster himself was not a doctrinaire planner, but he let the planners do their work in their own way without knowing at first that the Tomlinson Commission, on whose report Verwoerd's calculations had been based, had underrated the probable growth of the African population by an enormous margin. The census of 1970 showed that its likely size by the end of the century would be 37 million, not 21, though more recent calculations suggest that this figure may be too high.

For M C Botha, Minister of Bantu Administration and Development, the clearing of the white areas was a challenge both before and after the census figures were known. An instruction issued to magistrates in 1967 listed four categories of Africans who qualified for removal: first, the elderly, the unfit, and those people, mainly women and children, who did not qualify under the Urban Areas Act to live in town; second, redundant people on white-owned farms; third, the inhabitants of 'black spots' in white areas; and fourth, professional people whose skills were needed in the homelands. There was to be provision for various kinds of settlement, ranging from 'Bantu towns' at one end of the scale, with good amenities such as public transport, tarred roads, and water-borne sewerage, examples of which grew up at Mdantsane near East London, KwaMashu outside Durban, and Ga-Rankuwa outside Pretoria. At the other end of the scale, provision was made for rudimentary settlements in the veld where the initial provision was absolutely minimal – prefabricated wooden huts and rations for a short period, and very little else.

Repatriation came to be linked with a new concept of citizenship. Each independent homeland would confer its own citizenship not only on its own inhabitants, but even on blacks living outside its borders if they spoke its language in their homes. The Zulu leadership saw the implications of this policy clearly, and had still not accepted independence by 1984; but two homelands had accepted it by the time of Vorster's resignation in 1978 – Transkei in 1976, and Bophuthatswana in 1977. Venda and Ciskei, though quite unprepared, accepted it under his successor in 1979-1981.

Africans who lost their South African citizenship in this way were to be allowed into the Republic only if work was available, and then only as workers on annual contracts, obliged to return to their homelands at the end of each year. They would thus be required to break the continuity of their stay in the Republic in order to ensure that they could not legally acquire 'Section Ten' rights under the Urban Areas Act by living continuously in the urban area for fifteen years, or working continuously for the same employer for ten.

On 24 July 1964, Frederick John Harris, a teacher and a member of the African Resistance Movement, planted a time bomb in the concourse of the Johannesburg station. It exploded at 16h33, injuring 23 people, one of whom later died. Harris was executed in April 1965. In the photograph, police search for clues at the scene of the explosion. (*Rand Daily Mail*)

◁△
A photograph taken at the time of the Rivonia trial in 1964, showing Bram Fischer (right). Since photographs of Fischer were not allowed to be published, his face was blanked out on this print. (*Die Burger*)

Verwoerd's body is removed from the House of Assembly after he was stabbed by Dimitrio Tsafendas, his assassin. The knife which Tsafendas used is held by the policeman behind Dr G de V Morrison (middle), MP, who supervised the ambulance men. (*Die Burger*)

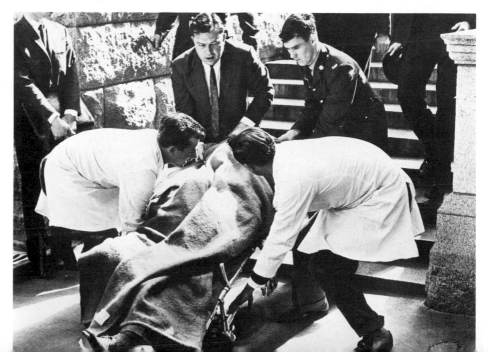

Chief Mangosuthu Buthelezi of KwaZulu.
(*Die Burger*)

The South African Prime Minister,
B J Vorster, and Chief Kaiser Matanzima
sign the Transkei Declaration of
Independence. (Central Archives)

Lucas Mangope of Bophuthatswana.
(INCH)

In 1968 the government took steps to ban the employment of Africans in particular categories of work in the urban areas – behind counters, and as receptionists, typists, telephone operators, clerks or cashiers, or as doctors in urban locations serving their own people – in the expectation that this would encourage them to move to the homelands and apply their skills there. Needless to say, these restrictions proved unenforceable, but an absolute embargo was imposed on the building of houses in the black locations in terms of the theory that single-quarters hostels for migrant workers were all that was required. The same restriction applied to schools, for which government funding was available only in the homelands.

The government also removed the power of existing urban local authorities to control their own black locations, and placed these under the control of Bantu Affairs Administration Boards from 1972. Intended also to promote financial self-sufficiency in the locations, the new system imposed a heavy additional load on the black residents without giving them access to revenue from the central business districts in which many black location-dwellers worked. In Soweto, the relationship between residents and the West Rand Administration Board was often hostile. The system was phased out during the early 1980s, as new legislation transferred their power to black local authorities and redirected the activities of the boards towards development projects.

The industrial strategy of the government's policy was contained in a Physical Planning Act of 1968, to promote the decentralization of industry to the border areas. Industrialists were given incentives to set up border industries through the offer of tax holidays, cheap labour, and other concessions, and disincentives like the power placed in the hands of the government to prohibit increases in the number of black workers they could employ in the existing metropolitan areas.

By and large, the strategy of the Physical Planning Act did not work. New jobs for only 85 554 Africans were found in the border areas and homelands in the years 1960-1972. This figure of under 8 000 jobs a year was well short of the 50 000 jobs a year which the Tomlinson Commission had considered necessary on the basis of its own inadequate figures.

Distress caused by the government's policy was extreme. Only a few of the resettlement areas, like Limehill in Natal, and Sada and Dimbaza in the Ciskei, attracted press publicity, usually as a consequence of investigation by concerned individuals. But the scale of resettlement was nowhere near as great as it would become.

To a small extent the homeland leaders filled the void left by political movements in exile,

Independent and National States in Southern Africa, 1984

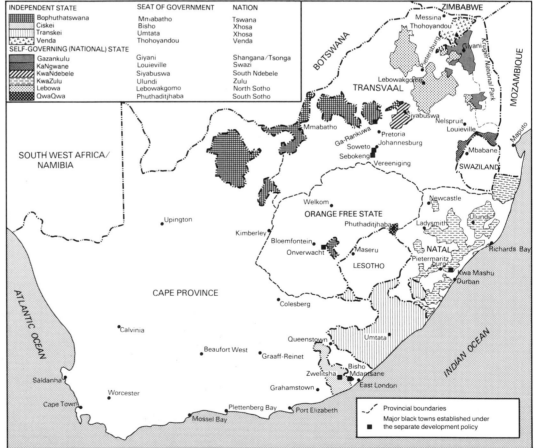

though in general their stance was far too close to official government policy to interest the politically aware. Merely by accepting the system, they had accepted co-optation by the South African Government, and most of them found it necessary to rely on emergency regulations to keep themselves in power. The *Inkatha* movement in Zululand was an important exception, for Chief Mangosuthu Buthelezi revived this cutural association which dated from the 1920s, and gave it a new political motivation. With its backing, he eventually captured control of the KwaZulu Assembly when it acquired self-government in 1977, just as Kaiser Matanzima had secured control of the Transkeian legislature by means of a constitution which enabled him to rule through a majority of chiefs. By 1976 his Transkei National Independence Party had managed, through pressure and patronage, to remove the rival influences of Chiefs Victor Poto and Sabata Dalindyebo, and to fill even the bulk of elective seats with chiefly nominees. Chief Lucas Mangope in Bophuthatswana had no serious rival.

The opposition of the homeland chiefs to the South African Government's version of independent Bantustans came nearest to success in 1973, when a closed summit meeting in Umtata in November discussed the alternative of federation. This gave rise to Buthelezi's proposal at a meeting near East London in December for the setting up of a federal union of autonomous states of southern Africa, which whites might later be invited to join. This also marked the beginning of a period of exploratory co-operation between the Zulu leader and the Progressives, who were themselves moving away from a federalism of checks and balances towards the idea of consociational democracy, which was to provide the basis for their subsequent opposition to the government's proposals for constitutional change.

Confrontation by the outcasts: Soweto and the Coloured Council

In June 1976 trouble arose in Soweto and spread to nearly every black township in South Africa. Described in a *Sunday Times* editorial as 'riots looking for a place to happen', the events were sparked off by a protest against the obligatory use of Afrikaans as a medium of instruction in certain subjects in African schools. This is likely to have been a symbolic reason rather than the only one, for although Afrikaans was sometimes described as the 'language of the oppressor', whereas English had the advantage of being an international language as well, there was no shortage of reasons for the revolt of youth. The administration board system was disliked after the relatively benign control of the Johannesburg City Council. Some have argued that the ANC was active behind the scenes through a revived system of cells; but even if that was the case, the high profile in 1976 was that of the Soweto Students' Representative Council, which seems to have organized the main demonstrations in the form of marches, work stoppages, attacks on shebeens, and a rent strike, and to have carried the older generation along with it.

Steve Biko (*Cape Times*)

A young student carries a critically injured child away from the site of confrontation between police and scholars, Soweto, June 1976. (*The Star*)

Crowds dispersing to avoid tear gas, Soweto, June 1976. (*Die Burger*)

The events were bloody because police opened fire on children throwing stones at them, and the average age of the 700 blacks who died was very low. There was also violence by contract workers against students, for their job insecurity was such that they could not afford to stay away from work. The troubles lasted, with varying intensity, until the banning of the black consciousness organizations by Jimmy Kruger, the Minister of Justice, in October 1977, a

month after Steve Biko's death. Black consciousness, however, showed every sign of being able to survive independent of structural support. The trouble in the schools ended only late in 1980, after the De Lange Commission had been appointed to undertake a searching investigation into the educational system as a whole. The students were highly politicized, and many fled abroad for military training.

The confrontations between the government and the African people were matched by an equivalent crisis in the government's relationship with the Coloured community, which was torn apart by the extension of the school boycott to the Western Cape, both in 1976-1977 and in 1980. These events occurred on the heels of a complete breakdown at the political level between the government and the Coloured Persons' Representative Council.

After the eventual passage of the Separate Representation of Voters' Act in 1956, the Coloured people had had to accept separate representation in the Assembly by four whites. This lasted till 1968, when it looked as if the Coloured seats would be won by members of the Progressive Party. The government blocked this possibility by means of a Prevention of Political Interference Act, and in the same year abolished Coloured representation in Parliament altogether, giving them instead a separate representative council in which there were to be forty elective members and twenty nominated by the government. At first the Federal Party of Tom Swartz, which the government supported, won just enough elective seats to hold power with the support of the governmental nominees; but it lost this control in 1974-1975, when the opposition Labour Party under Sonny Leon used its newly acquired majority to reject the budget. The government was forced to use powers, which it had thoughtfully given itself under the constitution of the CPRC, to dismiss Leon as chairman of the CPRC and put its own nominee, Mrs Alathea Jansen, in office with a mandate to approve the budget and govern.

The Theron Commission report on the Coloured community (see box) proved to be the first step in a process which led to constitutional reform proposals being put forward by the Vorster government in 1977, and to the adoption of substantially the same proposals by a white referendum under the next government in 1983. When the proposed reforms were eventually adopted by the white electorate, this was largely because a subsequent leader of the Labour Party, the Rev Allan Hendrickse, had persuaded his followers to accept the government's *bona fides*.

'Putting their houses in order': the Hertzogites and the Liberals

Even within white politics there was turbulence. There was a rift in the government's

ranks in 1968-1969, when the Prime Minister took the bit between his teeth and dismissed the controversial Dr Albert Hertzog, son of J B M Hertzog. The conflict became identified as one between *verkramptes* (the 'narrow-minded') and *verligtes* (the 'enlightened'). At bottom, personalities apart, it was a dispute between the ideologues who saw apartheid as an all-embracing and self-contained system to be defended in its totality, and the pragmatists who were prepared to abandon 'petty apartheid', the surface irritants like separate queues for different races in post offices and even separate sports teams, for the sake of preserving more easily the grand apartheid of separate residential areas, separate job opportunities and separate electoral systems. The Hertzogites broke away and formed their own *Herstigte* (Refounded) National Party, in an attempt to shed the deviationism of the post-Verwoerd years.

South Africa under Vorster came as near to being a totalitarian state as it had ever been, though the government was prepared to stop just short of outright authoritarian rule. It was still prepared to lose elections to rival parties, and actually fell back by eight seats in the general election of 1970. Though it indulged in exemplary trials, like that of Laurence Gandar, editor of the *Rand Daily Mail*, on a charge of infringing the Prisons Act by publishing sworn statements about conditions in the prisons without obtaining police authority to publish, the government did not have recourse to full-scale censorship.

A battle raged around the activities of the Publications Control Board, which placed on the banned list a very large number of titles – including an Afrikaans novel for the first time in 1974 (André Brink's *Kennis van die Aand*). The number of prosecutions were not large, however. The English-language newspapers were still able to express opinions freely within certain limits, and it was not until the imposition of military censorship at the start of the Angolan war in 1975 that the restraints under which editors were operating became obvious to discerning readers.

Radio controls had operated for rather longer, and could be dated from the introduction of regular daily 'editorial comments' at peak listening times since the Sharpeville unrest. Television itself was introduced in South Africa only in 1976-1977, but the SABC rarely allowed criticism of government policies on sensitive issues, preferring to monitor opinion through its own commentators during election times.

The English-language universities had confronted the government over the exclusion of African, Coloured and Indian students during the Verwoerd era, and lost their fight. Under Vorster, the government's attack moved against liberal organizations like the student forum, NUSAS (once the only student representative body, until the *Afrikaanse Studentebond* broke away in the 1930s, and the African movement, SASO, did the same in the early 1970s). Several NUSAS leaders were banned, as were leaders of the Christian Institute. NUSAS and the Christian Institute were investigated in 1972-1974 by a commission under A L Schlebusch, which also looked into the South African Institute of Race Relations and the University Christian Movement. The last of these dissolved itself, the Institute of Race Relations was humiliated but cleared, and before the Schlebusch Commission had reported NUSAS and the Christian Institute were declared 'affected organizations' under a new act in 1974, which precluded such bodies from receiving foreign funds.

During the 1970s some signs seemed to point towards the 'total onslaught' against South Africa out of which the next government was to be able to make so much political capital, especially with the growth of Soviet involvement in the ex-Portuguese colonies. It was hardly sur-

The Theron Commission

A commission under Professor Erika Theron of Stellenbosch had been appointed in 1973 to look into the position of the Coloured people in general. It was a mixed commission with a small number of Coloured people on it, and its report of June 1976 was noteworthy for the fact that it departed in some respects from a rigid segregationist line. Thus it proposed that Coloured pupils should be allowed to go to white private schools and universities if they were offered places, and it urged the removal of the group areas ban on mixed white and Coloured audiences in theatres, and the inclusion on merit of Coloured people in white sports teams. The commission also criticized the government's record on the provision of constitutional rights for Coloured people, urging that 'the existing Westminster-based system of government would have to be changed to adapt it to the peculiar requirements of the South African plural population structure'.

Professor Erika Theron (*Die Burger*)

A police vehicle used in riot control. (Central Archives)

C P Mulder, Eschel Rhoodie (back ground) and Taiwanese officials. (INCH)

The Information Scandal

Judge A Mostert of Natal, who had been appointed to investigate exchange control malpractices in general, came across details about the Department of Information which troubled him so much that he revealed them to the press. They included the use of public funds for National Party political ends to buy control of English-language newspapers inside and outside South Africa, which had resulted in the founding of a new daily, *The Citizen*.

Immediately on accession to office, P W Botha handled the criticisms of the opposition with considerable pugnacity. He dismissed the Mostert Commission on the argument that the judge had exceeded his authority under the rules governing commissions, and appointed Judge R P B Erasmus of the Free State Bench to investigate the Department of Information, which he had in the meantime closed down.

Erasmus produced his first report in December 1978. It cleared Vorster, while he had been Prime Minister, of conscious connivance in the malpractices, on the ground that they had been concealed from him by C P Mulder, Minister of Information, and by General H J van den Bergh, a close personal friend of Vorster and the head of the Bureau of State Security. It also cleared the new Prime Minister, as Minister of Defence, and the Minister of Finance, Senator Owen Horwood. The latter's worst offence had been to authorize one large irregular payment at Mulder's urgent insistence, without first looking into it carefully. All kinds of irregularities, on the other hand, were laid at the door of the secretary to the department, Dr Eschel Rhoodie, for some of which he was later given a twelve-year prison sentence which was reversed completely on appeal. Mulder was declared to have floated overseas loans without informing the Treasury, and to have lent large sums of public money to a Nationalist supporter to buy opposition newspapers.

Mulder hit back in April 1979 by alleging that Vorster and Horwood had lied in professing ignorance of the newspaper projects, and claiming that Vorster and the previous State President, Dr Diederichs, had met regularly with him to discuss them. Erasmus produced his final report in June, declaring that Vorster had after all known about them. Vorster consequently resigned.

prising that, under such circumstances, the government should have found it necessary to do what it could to counter hostile propaganda outside South Africa's borders and to use whatever resources it could muster to make its countermeasures effective. What the public was not prepared for, though, was the extent to which this could happen without the knowledge of the one body which needed to be able to monitor government activities, namely Parliament.

Vorster's outward policy (see Chapter 19) was matched by the setting up of a Security Services Special Account in 1969, for use by the Prime Minister and subject to audit only at the discretion of the Minister of Finance. In practice the resources of this account came to be transferred to other departments after consultation with the Prime Minister's office. In September 1978 Vorster resigned, partly for health reasons, and was soon afterwards elevated to the office of State President. Before he did so, rumours had already begun to circulate about the misspending of public funds in the Department of Information, under Dr Connie Mulder, who, as leader of the National Party in the Transvaal, was the frontrunner for the succession to the premiership. There can be little doubt that, but for these rumours, Mulder would have been elected by the caucus. In the event, the office of Prime Minister went to the Cape leader, P W Botha, then Minister of Defence, whose department was apparently not suspected of involvement in financial malpractices.

PW Botha, 1978-1984: a search for a new direction

P W Botha soon showed his administrative talents by restructuring the governmental system – not so much by cutting down the numbers of public servants, which he tried to do, as by ensuring that a greater amount of important government business was channelled through the Prime Minister's office, and by seeing that men whose political and administrative talents he valued were moved into key positions.

The tendency to centralization was strong, and well illustrated in the appointment of General Magnus Malan to the post of Minister of Defence to which Botha had clung for a year after becoming Prime Minister. Comments were made from time to time that the State Security Council, in which Malan played a leading role under the Prime Minister, had begun to usurp the powers of the Cabinet itself. The charge was denied by members of the SSC, but, understandably, suspicion was aroused by a committee which, in the name of security, took vital decisions to which only some members of the Cabinet had access.

The new Prime Minister's firm intention of bringing about major reforms in the economic life of the country, in order to meet the mount-

ing social crisis resulting from the population explosion in the black community, led in November 1979 to a meeting with businessmen at the Carlton Hotel, Johannesburg, with the intention of inviting co-operation in his task. For ideological reasons the previous government had allowed the development of black urban townships to stagnate in the hope that the real development would take place in the homelands, and yet had not put enough effort into the development of the homelands. The neglect was particularly serious in that the Vorster government had enjoyed boom conditions at the end of the 1960s, followed by a very steep rise in the gold price during the early 1970s.

Despite some appearances to the contrary, Botha made no real attempt to depart from the broad strategies of the Tomlinson Commission. When the courts came out with judgments favourable to urban blacks on matters which concerned influx control, as they did in the Komani and Rikhoto cases in 1980 and 1981, the former dealing with the right of married women to live with their husbands in town, the latter establishing that a contract worker who had worked for ten years with a single employer had acquired the right to live in the urban area even if he had broken his service to go home on holiday, the government brought in amending legislation to plug the hole in the influx control system.

Meanwhile the government tried, through the Riekert and Wiehahn commissions (see box on p 311) to ease the flow of black labourers into jobs and to give trade union rights to urbanized black workers.

The opening of collective bargaining rights to black workers was a major step, which had been contemplated then dropped by the Smuts government during the Second World War, but consistently rejected by the Nationalists ever since. Africans with urban rights were now empowered to form segregated unions of their own. In 1981, the right was thrown open to contract workers, and racially mixed trade unions, which had been prohibited in 1956, were again legitimized. Because of a tendency among Africans not to register their unions, it was also laid down that even unregistered unions would be obliged to give the registrar of trade unions access to their premises, their books and their membership lists.

Human removals, inflation and drought

The new deal for urban blacks was seen by the government as part of a larger policy for the expansion of industry as a whole, not simply by promoting the decentralization policy of the Vorster era, but by building on existing infrastructures wherever possible, and linking these with existing homeland labour pools, so that the homelands could directly contribute to and receive benefits from their productivity. At first, the main developments were in the Transvaal and in northern Natal. By 1982, however, the government had begun to realize that the most depressed areas were in the Eastern Cape, bordering on the homelands of Transkei and Ciskei, so that there was a switch of emphasis to those areas. The government planned the creation of more 'Sowetos' within the homelands to provide the labour for these new industrial areas. One necessary aspect of this policy was a preparedness to pay very large sums of money to the homelands in the form of taxation diverted from the earnings of blacks who worked within the Republic proper, the canalization of development funds into the various Homeland Development Corporations and banks, and outright financial grants to enable the homelands to remain solvent.

In return for development 'aid' (for so it was officially regarded), the homelands were required to take independence and to receive within their borders large numbers of Africans who lived outside their boundaries but who were considered to be redundant to South Africa's labour needs. The bulk of the 3,5 million

P W Botha (INCH)

people who had been moved since 1960 fell under the heading of the 'repatriation' of black workers as a result of the ending of labour tenancy on the farms. Many other removals resulted from the clearance of 'black spots', that is, pockets of black settlement in the middle of predominantly white areas, often farms for which the original African owners had paid good prices for title before the 1913 Land Act made subsequent purchases unlawful. Much hardship occurred in places like the Mfengu settlement on the Clarkson mission near Humansdorp, whose residents looked back over a continuous occupation since the 1830s, and who deeply resented being made to move to the Keiskamma valley in Ciskei; the Presbyterian settlement at Mgwali in the 'white corridor' between Transkei and Ciskei; and the group of farms around Driefontein in the south-eastern Transvaal, black-owned since 1912.

The most noteworthy aspect of the removals was their scale, linked with the large number of minor confrontations they produced. The removals were comparable to the eighteenth century clearances in Scotland, and the enclosure movement in England from the 1760s, as examples of expropriation by a more powerful interest group, but on a much larger scale. A common characteristic was the use of front-end loaders to clear squatter settlements on the edges of towns, as on the Modderdam Road and at Unibell outside Cape Town in 1977-1978, on the assumption that the residents knew they were breaking the law (which they were, but it was not a law which applied to all people), and had been warned (which they had), and therefore deserved the treatment they received. These organized squatter movements had their nearest parallels in the establishment, by rural immigrants, of some of the shanty towns of Latin America, notably the *barriadas* of Lima, in Peru.

Resettlement pressed so heavily on some regions that the existing agricultural potential of the area was given no chance of coping with the

Washday in a squatter camp. (SA Library)

Forced removals from the Modderdam Road squatter camp near Cape Town. (South African Library)

demand. One such area was the Hewu district of Ciskei, into which over 50 000 people were moved from Herschel and Glen Grey, at their own request, when those districts were incorporated in Transkei. Even though they were moved on to what had been prime farmland on which the previous white owners had been able to produce fine sheep, cattle and crops, within two years the region had been stripped of vegetation as the result of drought and overstocking. The people of Hewu would have died in their thousands but for the provision of government rations on a continuing basis.

Conditions in the Orange Free State were as bad, in the new mushrooming location of Onverwacht, south of Bloemfontein, which soon had a population of well over 100 000 gleaned from the farms of the province, and in the even larger neighbouring rural slum of Thaba Nchu (part of Bophuthatswana), and above all in the homeland of QwaQwa on the edge of the Drakensberg, where upwards of 200 000 people in the early 1980s had to subsist with almost no opportunity to farm, no local industries in the Republic to which they could commute, and only skeleton health and welfare services.

The government was handicapped by a drop in the gold price and by severe drought. Gold had reached an all-time high when its value topped $850 a fine ounce at the beginning of 1980, a year in which it gave the Treasury a record revenue yield of R3,6 billion; but by June 1982 it had dropped back to below $300, and thereafter struggled to reach the $400 mark. This made it extremely difficult for the government to know how much it could afford to spend, especially at a time when the demands on the defence budget were rising steadily on account of the fear of escalating outside pres-

sures on the Republic. On the whole, the Treasury acted with restraint – some said too much restraint during the good years, in view of the magnitude of the problems encountered during the bad ones.

Record-breaking maize and cereal harvests during 1980-1981 were followed in 1982-1984 by the worst drought in living memory, the occurrence of which has to be noted as the background to the rural removals. Ironically, the taxpayer found his pockets drained as effectively after maize surpluses as after harvest failures, on account of a marketing policy which required the state to buy excess produce even when it had no chance to resell it. This left the state in debt to the farmers to the tune of several hundred million rands in 1982. The Land Bank, which lent the farmers funds for investment at premium rates of interest, was so deeply in debt itself to the commercial banks that in 1984 the government had to fund the farmers' debt, though admittedly on a low valuation of their land, in order to prevent a wholesale flow of insolvencies.

When P W Botha held a second meeting with industrialists two years after the Carlton conference, in Cape Town at the end of 1981, there was some dissatisfaction among the businessmen over the lack of progress in relation to the promised reforms. Although the Riekert and Wiehahn commissions had laid the foundation for growth, the harsh features of the policy were still being faithfully carried out. It was to the government's credit that during the lean years from 1982 urban improvement had begun to take place, and industrial development had begun to take off at a few centres in the homelands; but neither had happened on anything like the scale needed.

Consensus by battle: the constitutional debate of 1983-1984

In the middle of 1982 the government had to face a challenge from, and decided to confront, a rebellion on the right led by Dr Andries Treurnicht, MP for Waterberg and Transvaal leader of the National Party. The issue on which the split took place had more to do with semantics than policy, for neither Treurnicht nor the government had any intention of letting power slip out of white hands. Treurnicht would not support a motion of confidence in the Prime Minister in caucus after the latter had come out publicly in favour of an extremely limited dose of 'healthy power-sharing' between whites, Coloured people and Indians during the previous week. Some 22 members of the National Party caucus walked out. They were prevented in their attempt to take over the party by smart manoeuvring by the Transvaal executive, which forced Treurnicht to fight his campaign from the ranks of a new Conservative Party which he founded in 1982. It proved a far bigger split than that between Vorster and the Hertzogites in 1969. In a key by-election early in 1983 the National Party failed to retake Waterberg, and later lost the Zoutpansberg constituency on the resignation of its member, S P Botha. There were also signs, after the Treurnicht breakaway, of the reappearance of paramilitary organizations reminiscent of the *Ossewabrandwag* of the 1940s, also rising up under cover of an Afrikaner cultural movement.

In-fighting between the Afrikaner political parties skewed the reform movement, and led during 1982-1984 to a hectic political battle, instead of what ought properly to have been restrained inter party consultations, over another major aspiration of the Botha government, constitutional reform.

The 1961 constitution followed the 'Westminster' formula, and was deliberately patterned on the South Africa Act of 1909 to reassure the English-speaker who was likely to be asked to abandon his membership of the Commonwealth. It still encouraged confrontation between parties and interest groups in situations where less oratory and more quiet talk might have served the country better. In other respects, a Westminster-style constitution possessed attributes which were admirably suited to South African conditions: a head of state who was not allowed to be a politician, and a two-chamber legislature which may have been expensive, but at least made provision for second thoughts, and a ministry responsible to the electorate. Westminster constitutions may be unitary or federal, rigid or flexible, and they can be made to fit a great variety of electoral systems according to the needs of the society.

Opinion was polarized between black movements like the Azanian People's Organization (AZAPO), a black consciousness element which would attend a national convention only if the ANC, PAC and Black People's Convention (BPC) were allowed to be there and all political prisoners were immediately freed, and at the other extreme the HNP and the CP which would not share power with Africans, Coloured people or Indians under any circumstances other than territorial partition. *Inkatha*, led by Chief Mangosutho Buthelezi, would really have liked a unitary South African state operating under simple majoritarian democracy, which was the desire of most African organizations in view of their obvious numerical advantage. However the KwaZulu legislature, which was dominated by *Inkatha*, had not only endorsed the principle of power-sharing in relation to Zululand and Natal by its adoption of the Buthelezi Commission Report in 1982, but it expressed its willingness to attend a national convention at least to discuss a constitution with built-in protection for minorities.

The Progressive Federal Party under Dr Frederik van Zyl Slabbert was in close contact with Chief Buthelezi, and had probably won the Zulu leader over to the notion of consociational democracy on which its own philosophy was based. This involved three major calculations: first, that communities should be separately represented in a governmental coalition, in which there would be discussion among community leaders before policies were put to their followers; second, that each such group should be represented in the legislature according to its numerical strength, so that even minorities could be sure of representation, and be given a blocking veto to prevent the enactment of thoroughly uncongenial legislation; and third, that each should possess 'segmental autonomy', that is the right to control those affairs which really are its own concern, above all in cultural matters. The Progressives did not see consociational government as a panacea, and realized that unless certain laws which insulted the black communities and stood in the way of their legitimate opportunites were removed from the statute book before a national convention was held, such a convention would stand no chance of getting off the ground.

The New Republican Party, which controlled the Natal Provincial Council, had rejected the Buthelezi Commission report, and was not interested in power-sharing at the provincial level. The National Party, which had driven the Conservatives out over a much milder form of power-sharing, could not allow the Buthelezi initiative to succeed – precisely because it would involve a surrender of the initiative on their own part. The fact that some members of the National Party were drawn to the idea of consociational democracy, among them Dr Denis Worrall, was an argument for the holding of inter-party talks, which could, however, well have preceded a referendum, with advantage to South Africa.

Dr A P Treurnicht (*Die Burger*)

Dr Frederik van Zyl Slabbert (*Die Burger*)

Amichand Rajbansi (*Die Burger*)

313

Members of the Electoral College which unanimously elected P W Botha as South Africa's first executive State President. This was the first time that a multiracial group had sat in the House of Assembly. (*Die Burger*)

The constitution of 1983

The new constitution had made provision for an executive President, chosen indirectly by a college of parliamentarians in which the majority party in the white chamber would have the determining say, and dismissable only if all three legislative chambers agreed. It also provided for three legislative chambers: a House of Assembly for whites, a House of Representatives for Coloured people, and a House of Delegates for Indians, elected on separate voters' rolls, and numerically scaled so that the white Assembly was larger than the other two together. African affairs were to be vested in the State President. There was to be a Cabinet system, straddling separate ministerial councils in each chamber, all members of the Cabinet being chosen by the President, who would not be limited in his choice to Members of Parliament. The Cabinet was to initiate legislation. The President's Council was to remain, most of its members now being chosen by the three chambers on a proportional basis, though a minority were to be chosen by the State President and ten of these on the advice of opposition parties. There were to be joint committees to help resolve deadlocks, and it was understood (though not clearly laid down) that the opposition parties would have some role in these. The judicial structure was to be unaltered, and provincial and local government were to be overhauled in the light of deliberations by committees which had not yet completed their tasks.

On coming to power, P W Botha appointed a parliamentary select committee to review a new constitution which had been drafted by the Vorster government. Its recommendations led to three major constitutional changes during the 1979 session: the abolition of the Senate; the conferment on the State President of the power to appoint twenty members to the House of Assembly, on the recommendation of the party leaders; and the creation of a President's Council, to be selected by the State President from members of the white, Coloured and Indian but not the African communities, with advisory but not legislative powers. The Progressives opposed the last two measures, especially the President's Council, for the reason that it was to contain no Africans. The task of drawing up a constitution then went to a committee of the President's Council, of which Worrall was chairman, in 1982, and that committee produced a report of some quality, which paid a measure of attention to consociational principles.

The fight between P W Botha and A P Treurnicht came into the open over the issue of power-sharing, and Worrall reportedly stated in private that it might be possible, in the long term, for blacks to be included in the new constitutional dispensation. This was to toss a hostage to fortune, where the CP was concerned. Worrall was sent as ambassador to Australia, and a diminished constitutional committee which had now lost two of its three political scientists produced a second report, the tone of which was remarkably different from the first. It bore the clear hallmarks of the speech made by P W Botha at the federal congress of the National Party in Bloemfontein on 30 July 1982. It threw out the notion of a bill of rights, for which the Worrall committee had indicated considerable support, and it expressed such concern over the dangers of deadlock that it proposed the abolition of motions of no confidence from parliamentary procedure (the one controlled, searching bit of confrontation that Westminster does extremely well), and (either in spite of or because of the Information Scandal) it would not allow the unseating of a government on a motion of censure.

The opposition parties stood no chance in the referendum, not least because the form of the question required the Progressives and the Conservatives to vote 'No' for very different reasons, and allowed the government to present its package as a gesture of moderate reform. It was that, in certain respects; but what did not come through clearly during the campaign was that the differences between Botha's constitution bill of 1983 and the draft put forward by Vorster in 1977, which had satisfied the ultra-conservatives, differed not at all save for a few minor changes.

The government won the referendum by a sweeping two-thirds majority on 2 November 1983, after a propaganda campaign of unprecedented intensity in the history of the South African media.

It was subsequently announced that Coloured and Indian opinion would be tested by means of general elections, not by referenda. This enabled the government, which was not confident that its policy had the support of these communities, to avoid a test of opinion on the central issue. Elections were held in due course – for the Coloured community in August 1984, when the Rev Allan Hendrickse's Labour Party was returned by a large majority in a 30 per cent poll; and for the Indians in September 1984, when Amichand Rajbansi's National People's Party was returned by a narrow majority among the 24 per cent of the registered voters who went to the polls. P W Botha was elected in the same month as the first executive State President, and appointed these two leaders to posts without portfolio in the first multiracial Cabinet in South African history.

Suggested Reading List

R T Bell (1973) *Industrial Decentralization in South Africa*, Cape Town

L Platsky and C Walker (1985) *The Surplus People: Forced Removals in South Africa*, Johannesburg

T Lodge (1983) *Black Politics in South Africa since 1945*, London

L Schlemmer and H Giliomee (eds) (1985) *Up Against the Fences: Poverty, Passes and Privilege in South Africa*, Cape Town

B M Schoeman (1974) *Vorster se 1 000 Dae*, Cape Town

D Yudelman (1984) *The Emergence of Modern South Africa*, Cape Town

Select Reading List of General and Biographical and Autobiographical Works

GENERAL WORKS

Bhana, S and Pachai, B, *A Documentary History of Indian South Africans*, Cape Town, etc, 1984

Davenport, T R H, *South Africa. A Modern History*, Johannesburg, 1986

De Kiewiet, C W, *A History of South Africa. Social and Economic*, Oxford, 1941

Elphick, R and Giliomee, H B (eds), *The Shaping of South African Society, 1652-1820*, Cape Town, 1979

Geyser, O, Marais, A H, Le Roux, H J, Coetzer, P W, etc (eds), *Die Nasionale Party*, 3 vols, Bloemfontein, etc, 1975-1982 (further volumes in progress)

Houghton, D H and Dagut, J, *Source Material on the South African Economy, 1860-1970*, 3 vols, Cape Town, etc, 1972-1973

Karis, T and Carter, G M (eds), *From Protest to Challenge. A Documentary History of African Politics in South Africa, 1882-1964*, 3 vols, Stanford, 1972-1977

Kruger, D W, *The Making of a Nation. A History of the Union of South Africa, 1910-1961*, Johannesburg, etc, 1969

Marais, J S, *The Cape Coloured People, 1652-1937*, London, 1939

Marks, S and Atmore, A (eds), *Economy and Society in Pre-Industrial South Africa*, London, 1980

Muller, C F J (ed), *Five Hundred Years. A History of South Africa*, Pretoria, etc, 1981

Muller, C F J, Van Jaarsveld, F A, Van Wijk, T, Boucher, M (eds), *South African History and Historians. A Bibliography*, Pretoria, 1979

Pachai, B (ed), *South Africa's Indians. The Evolution of a Minority*, Washington, 1979

Saunders, C, *Historical Dictionary of South Africa*, Metuchen, 1983

Scholtz, G D, *Die Ontwikkeling van die Politieke Denke van die Afrikaner*, 8 vols, Johannesburg, etc, 1967-1984

Simons, J and Simons, R, *Class and Colour in South Africa, 1850-1950*, London, 1983

Thompson, L M, *African Societies in Southern Africa*, London, 1969

Van Jaarsveld, F A, *From Van Riebeeck to P W Botha: An Introduction to the History of the RSA*, Johannesburg, 1983

Van der Walt, A J H, Wiid, J A, Geyer, A L (eds) (revised by Kruger, D W), *Geskiedenis van Suid-Afrika*, Cape Town, 1965

Walker, E A, *A History of Southern Africa*, London, etc, 1957

Walker, E A, *The Cambridge History of the British Empire.* Vol VIII: *South Africa, Rhodesia and the Protectorates*, Cambridge, 1936

Walshe, P, *The Rise of African Nationalism in South Africa. The African National Congress, 1912-1952*, Berkeley, 1971

Wilson, M and Thompson, L M (eds), *The Oxford History of South Africa*, 2 vols, Oxford, 1969-1971

Yudelman, D, *The Emergence of Modern South Africa. State Capital and the Incorporation of Organized Labour on the South African Gold Fields, 1902-1939*, Cape Town, etc, 1984

BIOGRAPHICAL AND AUTOBIOGRAPHICAL WORKS

a) Collected

De Kock, W J and others (eds), *Dictionary of South African Biography*, 4 vols, Cape Town, etc, 1968-1981 (further volumes in progress)

Karis, T and Carter, G M (eds), *From Protest to Challenge. A Documentary History of African Politics in South Africa.* Vol IV: *Political Profiles, 1882-1964*, Stanford, 1977

Saunders, C (ed), *Black Leaders in Southern African History*, London, etc, 1979

b) Individual

BOTHA, L
Barnard, C J, *Generaal Louis Botha op die Natalse Front, 1899-1900*, Cape Town, 1970
Engelenburg, F V, *General Louis Botha*, Pretoria, 1929

BOTHA, P W
De Villiers, D and De Villiers, J, *P W*, Cape Town, 1984

BRAND, J H
Barlow, T B, *President Brand and His Times*, Cape Town, 1972

BURGERS, T F
Appelgryn, M S, *Thomas François Burgers, Staatspresident 1872-1877*, Pretoria, etc, 1979

BUTHELEZI, M
Temkin, B, *Gatsha Buthelezi: Zulu Statesman*, Cape Town, etc, 1976

CETSHWAYO
Laband, J and Wright, J, *King Cetshwayo KaMpande*, Pietermaritzburg, 1980

DE WET, C R
Kestell, J D, *Christiaan de Wet: 'n Lewensbeskrywing*, Cape Town, etc, 1920

DINGANE
Becker, P, *Rule of Fear. The Life and Times of Dingane, King of the Zulu*, London, 1964

GANDHI, M K
Swan, M, *Gandhi. The South African Experience*, Johannesburg, 1985

GREY, G
Rutherford, J, *Sir George Grey, 1812-1897: A Study in Colonial Government*, London, 1961

HERTZOG, J B M
Spies, F J du T, Krüger, D W, Oberholster, J J (eds), *Die Hertzog-Toesprake*, 6 vols, Pretoria, 1977
Van den Heever, C M, *Generaal J B M Hertzog*, Johannesburg, 1946

HOBHOUSE, E
Van Reenen, R (ed), *Emily Hobhouse, Boer War Letters*, Cape Town, etc, 1984

HOFMEYR, J H
Paton A S, *Hofmeyr*, London, 1964

JABAVU, J T
Jabavu, D D T, *The Life of John Tengo Jabavu, Editor of Imvo Zabantsundu, 1884-1921*, Lovedale, 1922

KADALIE, C
Kadalie, C, *My Life and the ICU: The Autobiography of a Black Trade Unionist in South Africa*, London, 1970

KITCHENER, H H
Magnus, P, *Kitchener: Portrait of an Imperialist*, London, 1958

KRUGER, S J P
Krüger, D W, *Paul Kruger*, 2 vols, Johannesburg, 1961

LUTULI, A
Lutuli, A, *Let My People Go. An Autobiography*, London, 1963

MALAN, D F
Malan, D F, *Afrikaner-Volkseenheid en My Ervarings op die Pad Daarheen*, Cape Town, 1959
Thom, H B, *D F Malan*, Cape Town, 1980

MERRIMAN, J X
Lewsen, P, *John X Merriman. Paradoxical South African Statesman*, Johannesburg, 1982

MILNER, A
Headlam, C (ed), *The Milner Papers*, 2 vols, London, etc, 1931-1933
O'Brien, T H, *Milner. Viscount Milner of St James's and Cape Town, 1854-1925*, London, 1979

MOSHOESHOE
Thompson, L M, *Survival in Two Worlds: Moshoeshoe of Lesotho, 1786-1870*, London, 1975

MZILIKAZI
Rasmussen, R K, *Migrant Kingdom – Mzilikazi's Ndebele in South Africa*, London, 1978

PLAATJE, S
Willan, B, *Sol Plaatje. A Biography*, Johannesburg, 1984

PRETORIUS, A
Liebenberg, B J, *Andries Pretorius in Natal*, Pretoria, etc, 1977

RHODES, C J
Lockhart, J G and Woodhouse, C M, *Rhodes*, London, 1963

ROBERTS, F S
James, D, *Lord Roberts*, London, 1954

SHAKA
Gluckman, M, 'The Individual in a Social Framework: The Rise of King Shaka of Zululand', *Journal of African Studies*, 1, 2, 1974

SLABBERT, F VAN ZYL
Slabbert, F van Zyl, *The Last White Parliament*, Johannesburg, 1985

SMITH, H G W
Harington, A L, *Sir Harry Smith Bungling Hero*, Cape Town, 1980

SMUTS, J C
Hancock, W K, *Smuts*, 2 vols, Cambridge, 1962-1968
Hancock, W K and Van der Poel, J, *Selections from the Smuts Papers*, Cambridge, 1966-1973

SOGA, T
Williams, D, *Umfundisi. A Biography of Tiyo Soga, 1829-1871*, Lovedale, 1978

STEYN, M T
Van der Merwe, N J, *Marthinus Theunis Steyn: 'n Lewensbeskrywing*, 2 vols, Cape Town, etc, 1928

STRIJDOM, J G
Basson, J L, *J G Strijdom: Sy Politieke Loopbaan van 1929 tot 1948*, Pretoria, 1980

VAN DER STEL, S
Boëseken, A J, *Simon van der Stel en Sy Kinders*, Cape Town, etc, 1964

VAN RIEBEECK, J A
Boëseken, A J, *Jan van Riebeeck en Sy Gesin*, Cape Town, 1974

VERWOERD, H F
Scholtz, G D, *Dr Hendrik Frensch Verwoerd, 1901-1966*, 2 vols, Johannesburg, 1974

VORSTER, B J
D'Oliveira, J, *Vorster the Man*, Johannesburg, 1977

317

318

319

320